RUNAWAYS & REVERSALS

CLOAK AND DAGGER: RUNAWAYS AND REVERSALS. Contains material originally published in magazine form as RUN̶̶̶̶̶̶ ̶ ̶R #1, SPIDER-ISLAND: CLOAK AND DAGGER #1-3, AMAZING SPIDER-MAN (2015) #6-8, STRANGE TALES: DARK CORNERS #1, MARVEL K̶ ̶ G SPIDER-MAN (1999) #663 and AMAZING SPIDER-MAN ANNUAL (2016) #1. First printing 2018. ISBN 978-1-302-91058-7. Published by MARVEL WORLDWIDE, INC., a subsidiary o̶ ̶ ̶ LLC. OFFICE OF PUBLICATION: 135 West 50th Street, New York, NY 10020. Copyright © 2018 MARVEL No similarity between any of the names, characters, persons, and/or institutions in this magazine with those of any living or dead person or institution is intended, and any such similarity which may exist is purely coincidental. **Printed in the U.S.A.** DAN BUCKLEY, President, Marvel Entertainment; JOE QUESADA, Chief Creative Officer; TOM BREVOORT, SVP of Publishing; DAVID BOGART, SVP of Business Affairs & Operations, Publishing & Partnership; DAVID GABRIEL, SVP of Sales & Marketing, Publishing; JEFF YOUNGQUIST, VP of Production & Special Projects; DAN CARR, Executive Director of Publishing Technology; ALEX MORALES, Director of Publishing Operations; SUSAN CRESPI, Production Manager; STAN LEE, Chairman Emeritus. For information regarding advertising in Marvel Comics or on Marvel.com, please contact Vit DeBellis, Custom Solutions & Integrated Advertising Manager, at vdebellis@marvel.com. For Marvel subscription inquiries, please call 888-511-5480. **Manufactured between 1/19/2018 and 2/20/2018 by LSC COMMUNICATIONS INC., KENDALLVILLE, IN, USA.**

10 9 8 7 6 5 4 3 2 1

CLOAK AND DAGGER — RUNAWAYS & REVERSALS

STRANGE TALES: DARK CORNERS #1
WRITER: Mike Baron
PENCILER: Alex Maleev
INKER: Chris Ivy
COLORIST: Christie Scheele
LETTERER: Richard Starkings &
Comicraft's Siobhan Hanna
COVER ART: John Estes

MARVEL KNIGHTS DOUBLE-SHOT #3
WRITER & BREAKDOWNS: Peter Gross
FINISHER: Ryan Kelly
COLORIST: Avalon's Jeromy Cox
LETTERER: Richard Starkings
& Comicraft's Jason Levine
COVER ART: Glenn Fabry

RUNAWAYS (2003) #11-12
WRITER: Brian K. Vaughan
PENCILER: Takeshi Miyazawa
INKER: David Newbold
COLORIST: Brian Reber
LETTERER: Virtual Calligraphy's Randy Gentile
COVER ART: Joshua Middleton

RUNAWAYS (2005) #9-12
WRITER: Brian K. Vaughan
PENCILER: Adrian Alphona
INKER: Craig Yeung
COLORIST: Christina Strain
LETTERER: Virtual Calligraphy's Randy Gentile
COVER ART: Jo Chen (#9-10) & James Jean (#11-12)
Special Thanks to C.B. Cebulski

DARK X-MEN: THE BEGINNING #2
WRITER: Paul Cornell
ARTIST: Leonard Kirk
COLORIST: Brian Reber
LETTERER: Rob Steen
COVER ART: Jae Lee & June Chung

CLOAK AND DAGGER (2010) #1
WRITER: Stuart Moore
PENCILER & COVER ART: Mark Brooks
INKER: Walden Wong
COLORIST: Emily Warren
LETTERER: Dave Sharpe

AMAZING SPIDER-MAN (1999) #663
WRITER: Dan Slott
ARTIST: Emma Ríos
COLORISTS: Javier Rodriguez & Edgar Delgado
LETTERER: VC's Joe Caramagna
COVER ART: Humberto Ramos & Edgar Delgado

SPIDER-ISLAND: CLOAK AND DAGGER #1-3
WRITER: Nick Spencer
PENCILER: Emma Ríos
INKERS: Emma Ríos with Álvaro López (#3)
COLORIST: Javier Rodriguez
LETTERER: VC's Joe Caramagna
COVER ART: Mike Choi (#1-2), Emma Ríos
& José Villarrubia (#3)
Dedicated to Bill Mantlo & Ed Hannigan
Special Thanks to Dan Slott

AMAZING SPIDER-MAN (2015) #6-8
WRITER: Dan Slott
ARTIST: Matteo Buffagni
COLORIST: Marte Gracia
LETTERERS: VC's Joe Caramagna (#6-7)
& Cory Petit (#8)
COVER ART: Alex Ross

AMAZING SPIDER-MAN ANNUAL (2016) #1
WRITER: James Asmus
PENCILER: Cory Smith
INKERS: Scott Hanna, Roberto Poggi
& Lorenzo Ruggiero
COLORIST: Rain Beredo
LETTERERS: VC's Travis Lanham & Joe Caramagna
COVER ART: Francisco Herrera & Fernanda Rizo
Neon Dragon designed by Alex Ross

ASSISTANT EDITORS: Dan Hosek, MacKenzie Cadenhead, Nathan Cosby, Daniel Ketchum,
Ellie Pyle, Devin Lewis & Allison Stock
ASSOCIATE EDITORS: Kelly Lamy & Alejandro Arbona
EDITORS: Mark Bernardo, Nanci Dakesian, Stuart Moore, C.B. Cebulski, MacKenzie Cadenhead,
Nick Lowe, Daniel Ketchum, Stephen Wacker & Devin Lewis

COLLECTION EDITOR: MARK D. BEAZLEY | ASSISTANT EDITOR: CAITLIN O'CONNELL | ASSOCIATE MANAGING EDITOR: KATERI WOODY | ASSOCIATE MANAGER, DIGITAL ASSETS: JOE HOCHSTEIN
SENIOR EDITOR, SPECIAL PROJECTS: JENNIFER GRÜNWALD | VP PRODUCTION & SPECIAL PROJECTS: JEFF YOUNGQUIST | RESEARCH & LAYOUT: JEPH YORK
PRODUCTION: SALENA MAHINA | BOOK DESIGNERS: JAY BOWEN | SVP PRINT, SALES & MARKETING: DAVID GABRIEL

EDITOR IN CHIEF: C.B. CEBULSKI | CHIEF CREATIVE OFFICER: JOE QUESADA | PRESIDENT: DAN BUCKLEY | EXECUTIVE PRODUCER: ALAN FINE

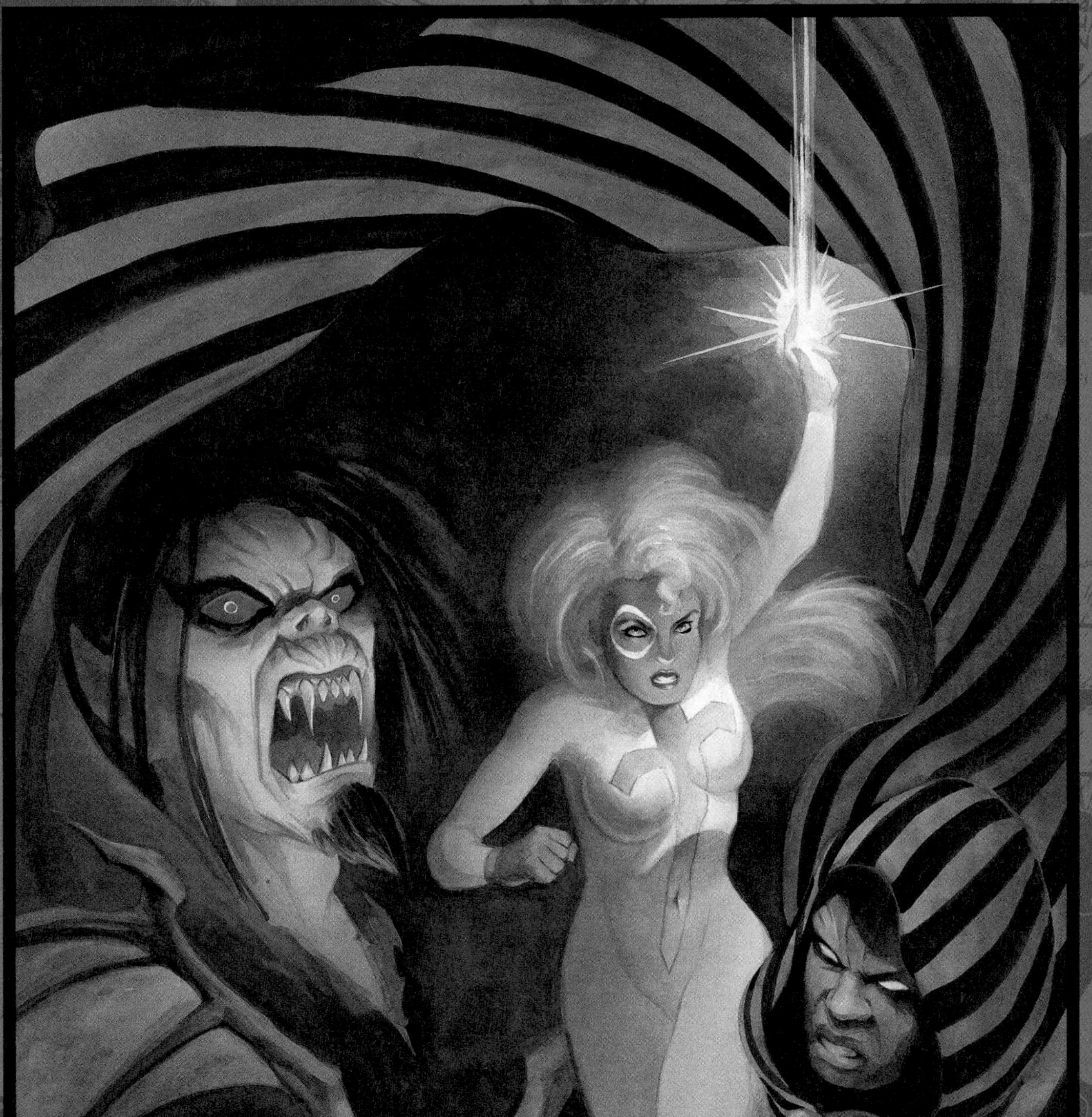

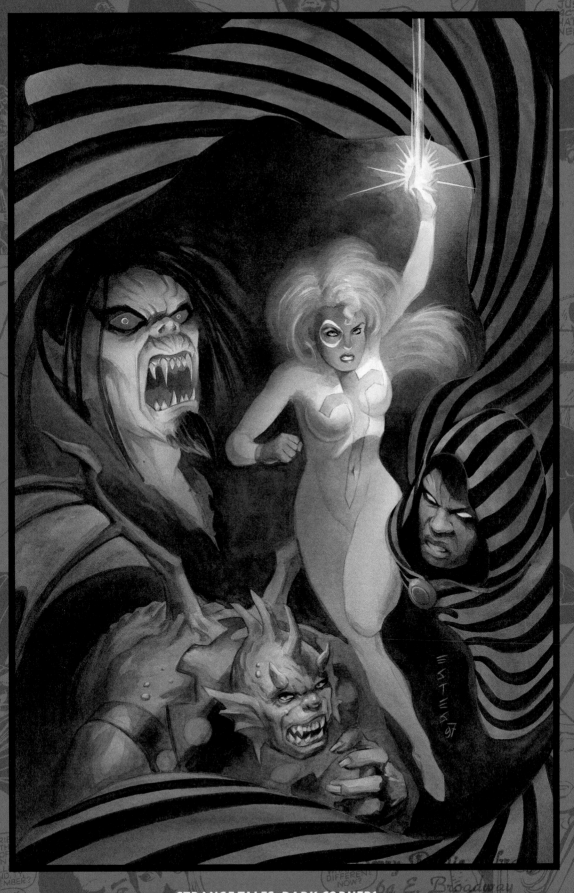

STRANGE TALES: DARK CORNERS #1

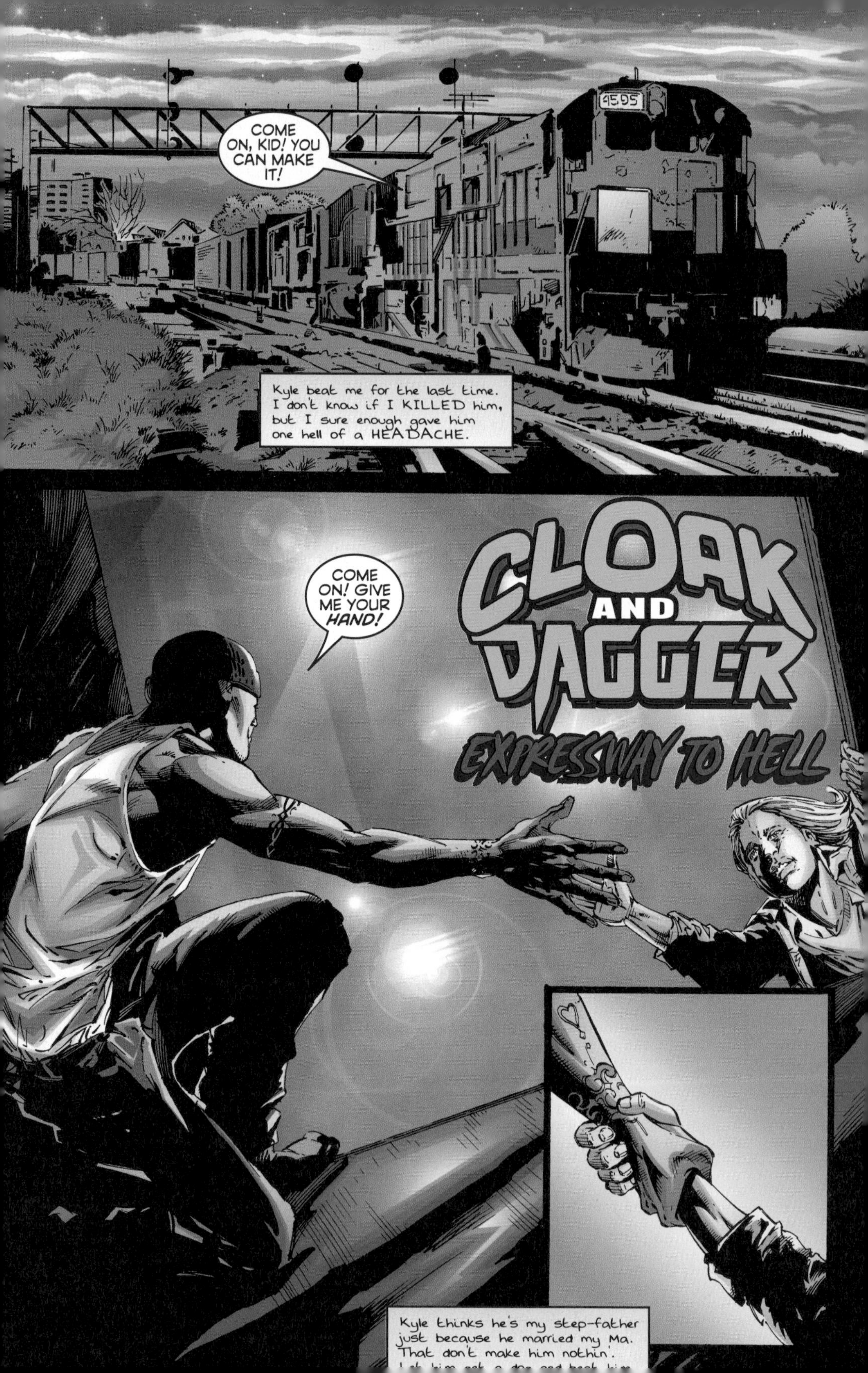
COME ON, KID! YOU CAN MAKE IT!
Kyle beat me for the last time. I don't know if I KILLED him, but I sure enough gave him one hell of a HEADACHE.
COME ON! GIVE ME YOUR *HAND!*
CLOAK AND DAGGER
EXPRESSWAY TO HELL
Kyle thinks he's my step-father just because he married my Ma. That don't make him nothin'.

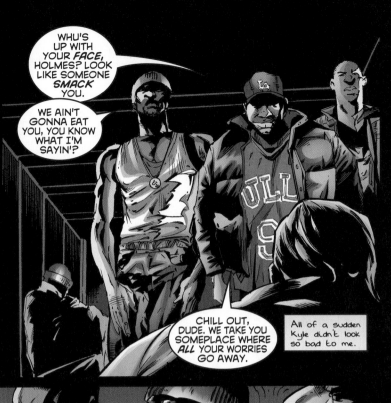

WELCOME ABOARD, HOLMES. WE OFF TO SEE THE WIZARD.

WHU'S UP WITH YOUR *FACE*, HOLMES? LOOK LIKE SOMEONE *SMACK* YOU.

WE AIN'T GONNA EAT YOU, YOU KNOW WHAT I'M SAYIN'?

CHILL OUT, DUDE. WE TAKE YOU SOMEPLACE WHERE *ALL* YOUR WORRIES GO AWAY.

All of a sudden Kyle didn't look so bad to me.

That GIRL didn't look too happy. I wondered what her story was. I guessed I was going to find out.

THANKS, BUT I CAN TAKE CARE OF MYSELF.

YOU WON'T *LAST* BY YOURSELF.

THERE'S *BAD PEOPLE* CRUISIN' THESE RAILS, YOU KNOW WHAT I'M SAYIN'?

YOU GOTS TO HAVE PROTECTION. YOU GOTS TO JOIN A GANG.

I GOT MY *OWN* PROTECTION, THANKS. WHO'RE YOU GUYS?

All I really had was a FILLETING KNIFE. But they didn't know that.

I CAN SEE THAT YOU A DANGEROUS DUDE, HOLMES. WE'RE THE CLEVELAND CAVALIERS.

WE RIDE THE RAILS *HELPIN' OUT* KIDS SUCH AS YOURSELF.

SORT OF A *CHARITY* GROUP, YOU KNOW WHAT I'M SAYIN'?

WHAT'S *HER* STORY?

THAT'S THE ICE PRINCESS. SHE'S *RUNNIN'* AWAY FROM AN ABUSIVE HOME LIFE. AIN'T THAT *RIGHT*, YOUR HIGHNESS?

Just for a second, she didn't look scared. Then she turned her eyes away.

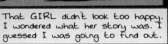

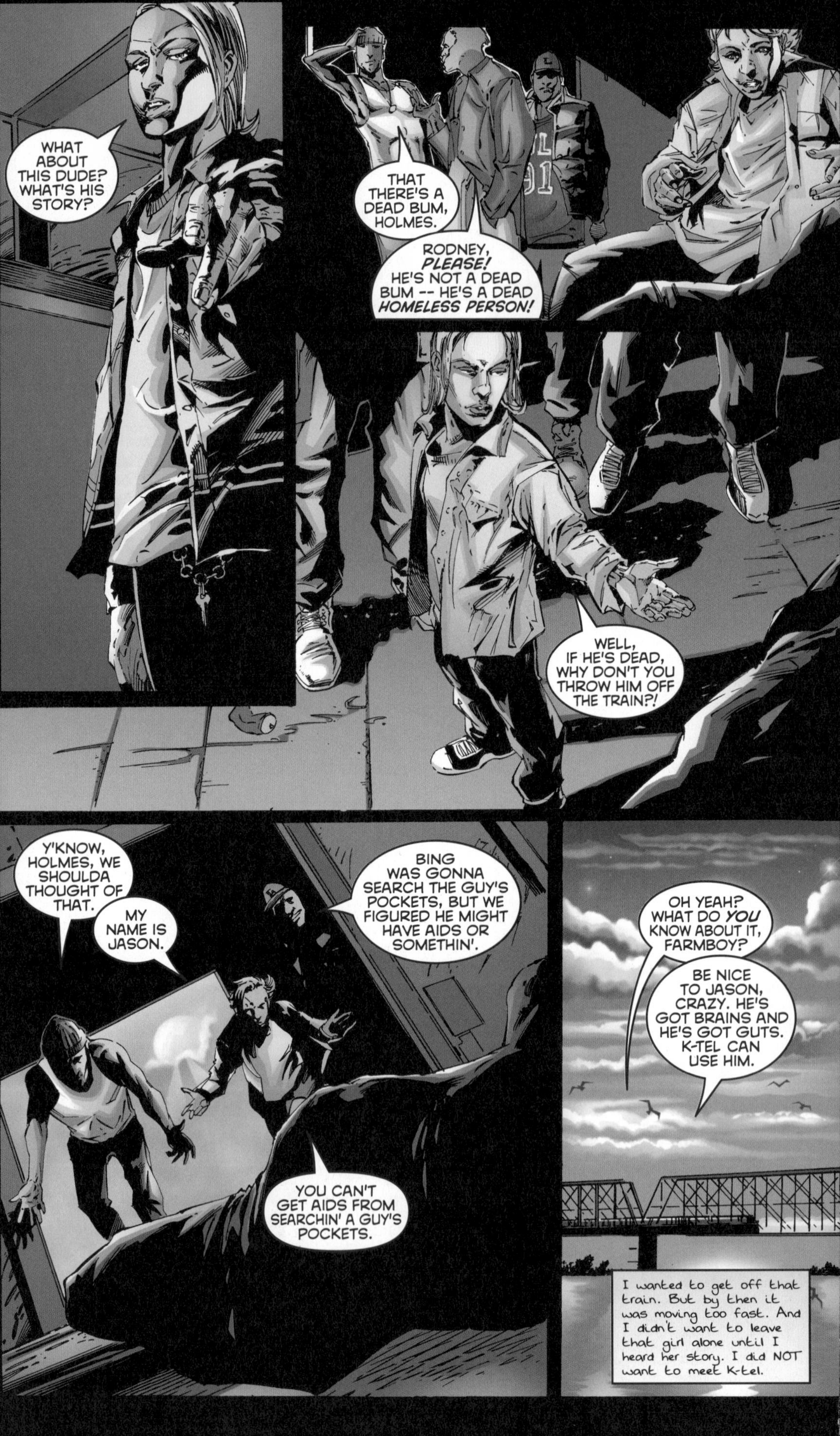

WHAT ABOUT THIS DUDE? WHAT'S HIS STORY?
THAT THERE'S A DEAD BUM, HOLMES.
RODNEY, *PLEASE!* HE'S NOT A DEAD BUM -- HE'S A DEAD *HOMELESS PERSON!*
WELL, IF HE'S DEAD, WHY DON'T YOU THROW HIM OFF THE TRAIN?!
Y'KNOW, HOLMES, WE SHOULDA THOUGHT OF THAT.
MY NAME IS JASON.
BING WAS GONNA SEARCH THE GUY'S POCKETS, BUT WE FIGURED HE MIGHT HAVE AIDS OR SOMETHIN'.
YOU CAN'T GET AIDS FROM SEARCHIN' A GUY'S POCKETS.
OH YEAH? WHAT DO *YOU* KNOW ABOUT IT, FARMBOY?
BE NICE TO JASON, CRAZY. HE'S GOT BRAINS AND HE'S GOT GUTS. K-TEL CAN USE HIM.
I wanted to get off that train. But by then it was moving too fast. And I didn't want to leave that girl alone until I heard her story. I did NOT want to meet K-tel.

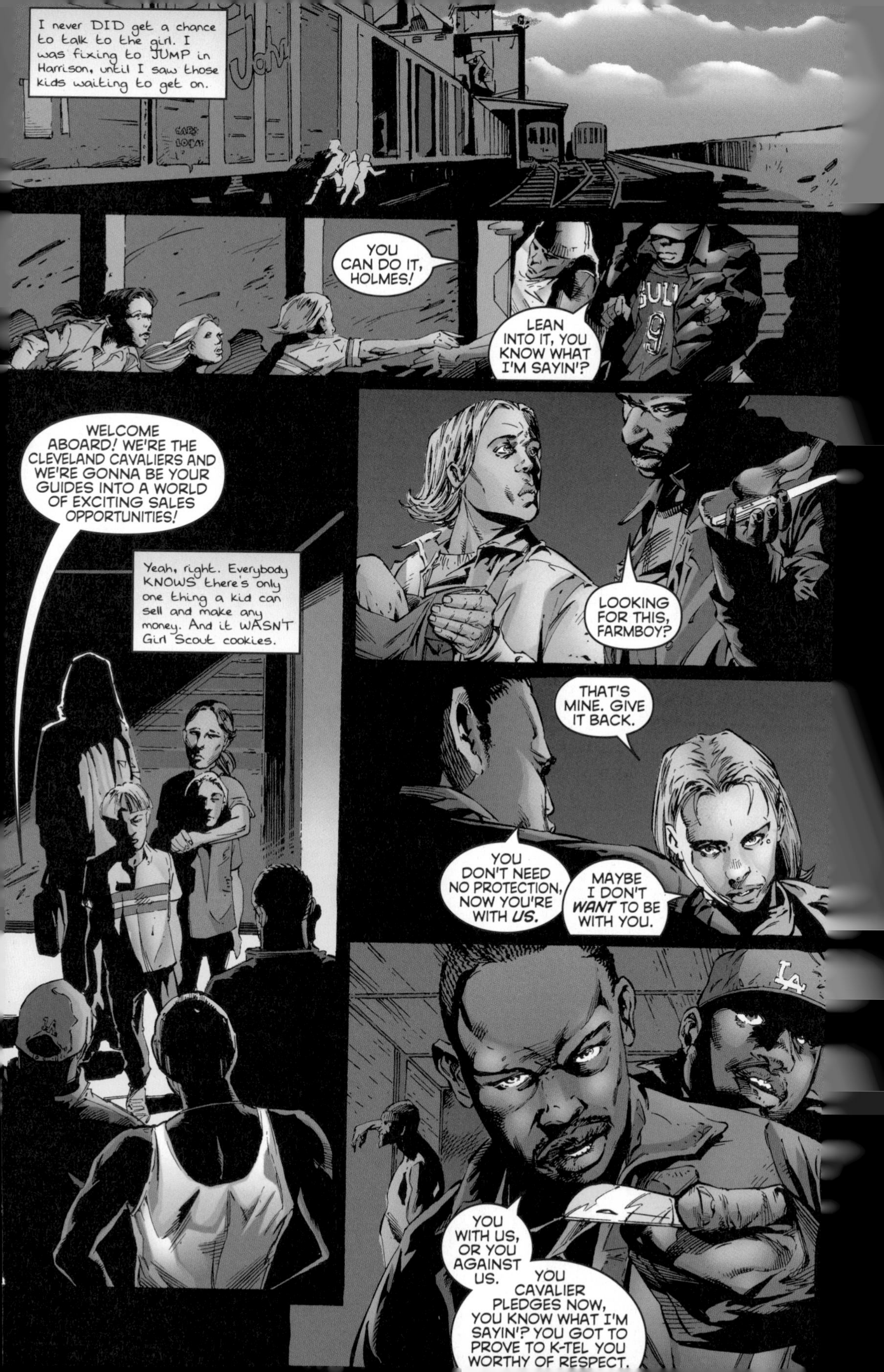
I never DID get a chance to talk to the girl. I was fixing to JUMP in Harrison, until I saw those kids waiting to get on.
YOU CAN DO IT, HOLMES!
LEAN INTO IT, YOU KNOW WHAT I'M SAYIN'?
WELCOME ABOARD! WE'RE THE CLEVELAND CAVALIERS AND WE'RE GONNA BE YOUR GUIDES INTO A WORLD OF EXCITING SALES OPPORTUNITIES!
Yeah, right. Everybody KNOWS there's only one thing a kid can sell and make any money. And it WASN'T Girl Scout cookies.
LOOKING FOR THIS, FARMBOY?
THAT'S MINE. GIVE IT BACK.
YOU DON'T NEED NO PROTECTION, NOW YOU'RE WITH *US.*
MAYBE I DON'T *WANT* TO BE WITH YOU.
YOU WITH US, OR YOU AGAINST US.
YOU CAVALIER PLEDGES NOW, YOU KNOW WHAT I'M SAYIN'? YOU GOT TO PROVE TO K-TEL YOU WORTHY OF RESPECT.

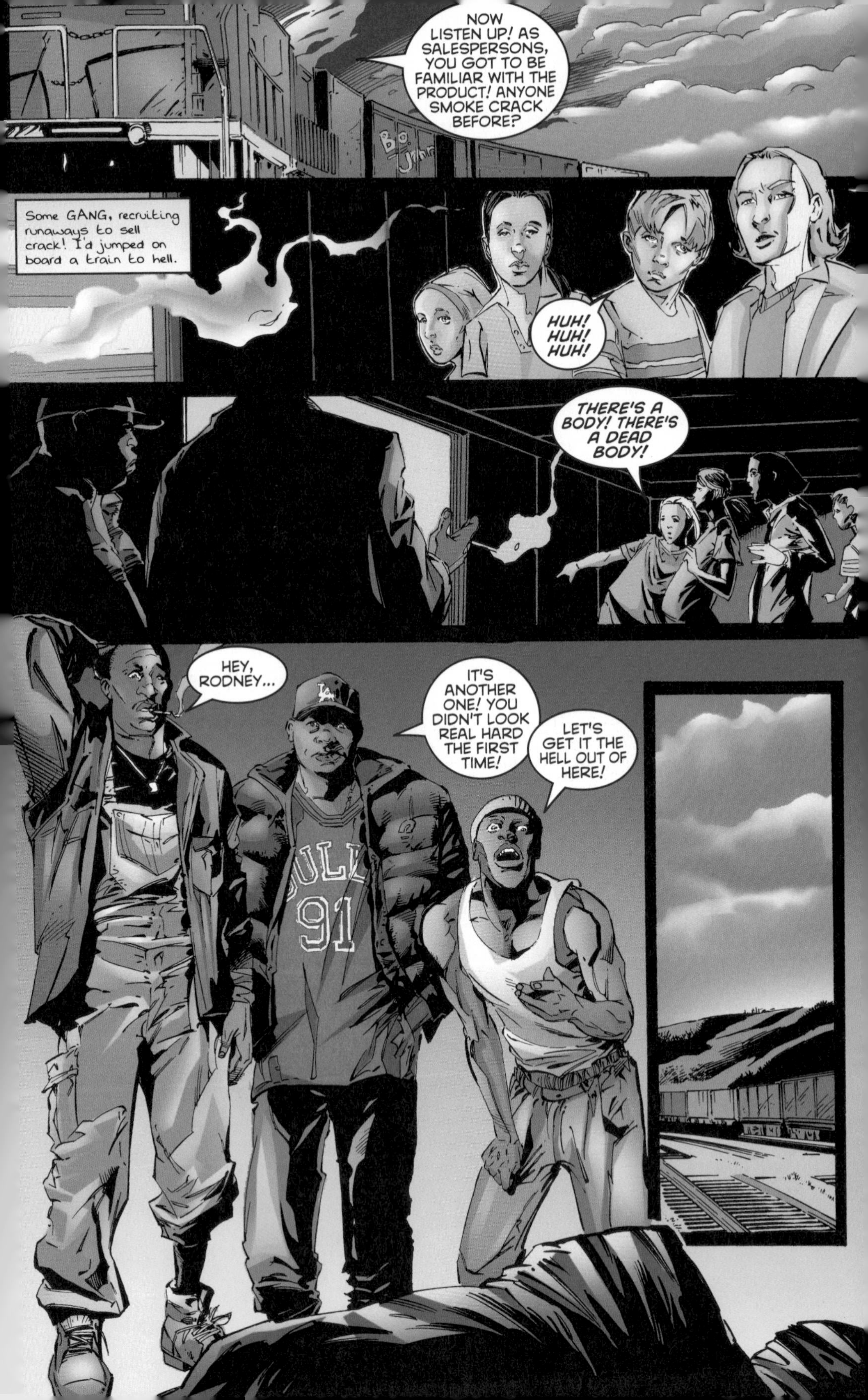
NOW LISTEN UP! AS SALESPERSONS, YOU GOT TO BE FAMILIAR WITH THE PRODUCT! ANYONE SMOKE CRACK BEFORE?
Some GANG, recruiting runaways to sell crack! I'd jumped on board a train to hell.
HUH! HUH! HUH!
THERE'S A BODY! THERE'S A DEAD BODY!
HEY, RODNEY...
IT'S ANOTHER ONE! YOU DIDN'T LOOK REAL HARD THE FIRST TIME!
LET'S GET IT THE HELL OUT OF HERE!

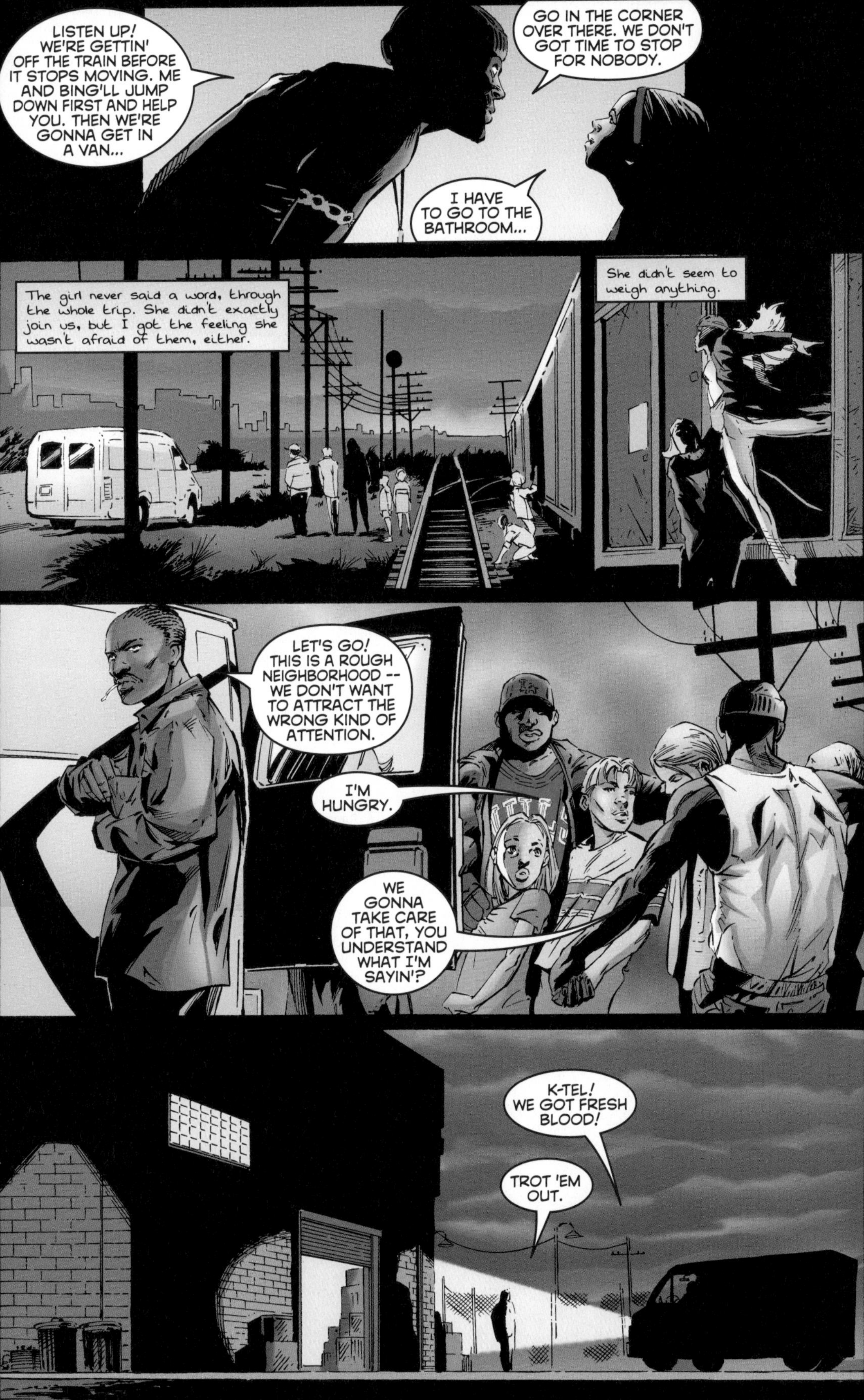
LISTEN UP! WE'RE GETTIN' OFF THE TRAIN BEFORE IT STOPS MOVING. ME AND BING'LL JUMP DOWN FIRST AND HELP YOU. THEN WE'RE GONNA GET IN A VAN...
I HAVE TO GO TO THE BATHROOM...
GO IN THE CORNER OVER THERE. WE DON'T GOT TIME TO STOP FOR NOBODY.
The girl never said a word, through the whole trip. She didn't exactly join us, but I got the feeling she wasn't afraid of them, either.
She didn't seem to weigh anything.
LET'S GO! THIS IS A ROUGH NEIGHBORHOOD -- WE DON'T WANT TO ATTRACT THE WRONG KIND OF ATTENTION.
I'M HUNGRY.
WE GONNA TAKE CARE OF THAT, YOU UNDERSTAND WHAT I'M SAYIN'?
K-TEL! WE GOT FRESH BLOOD!
TROT 'EM OUT.

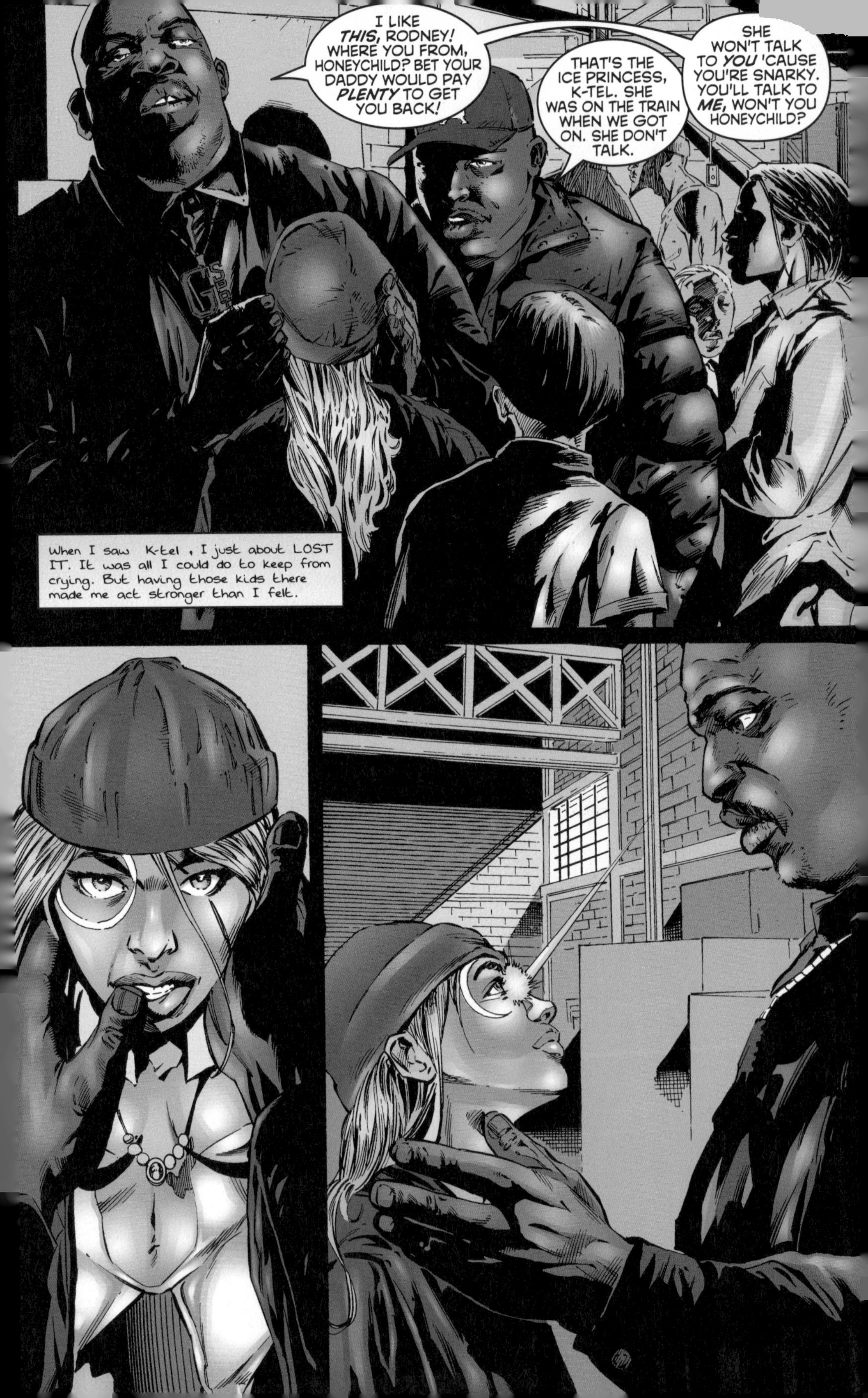
I LIKE *THIS*, RODNEY! WHERE YOU FROM, HONEYCHILD? BET YOUR DADDY WOULD PAY *PLENTY* TO GET YOU BACK!
THAT'S THE ICE PRINCESS, K-TEL. SHE WAS ON THE TRAIN WHEN WE GOT ON. SHE DON'T TALK.
SHE WON'T TALK TO *YOU* 'CAUSE YOU'RE SNARKY. YOU'LL TALK TO *ME*, WON'T YOU HONEYCHILD?
When I saw K-tel, I just about LOST IT. It was all I could do to keep from crying. But having those kids there made me act stronger than I felt.

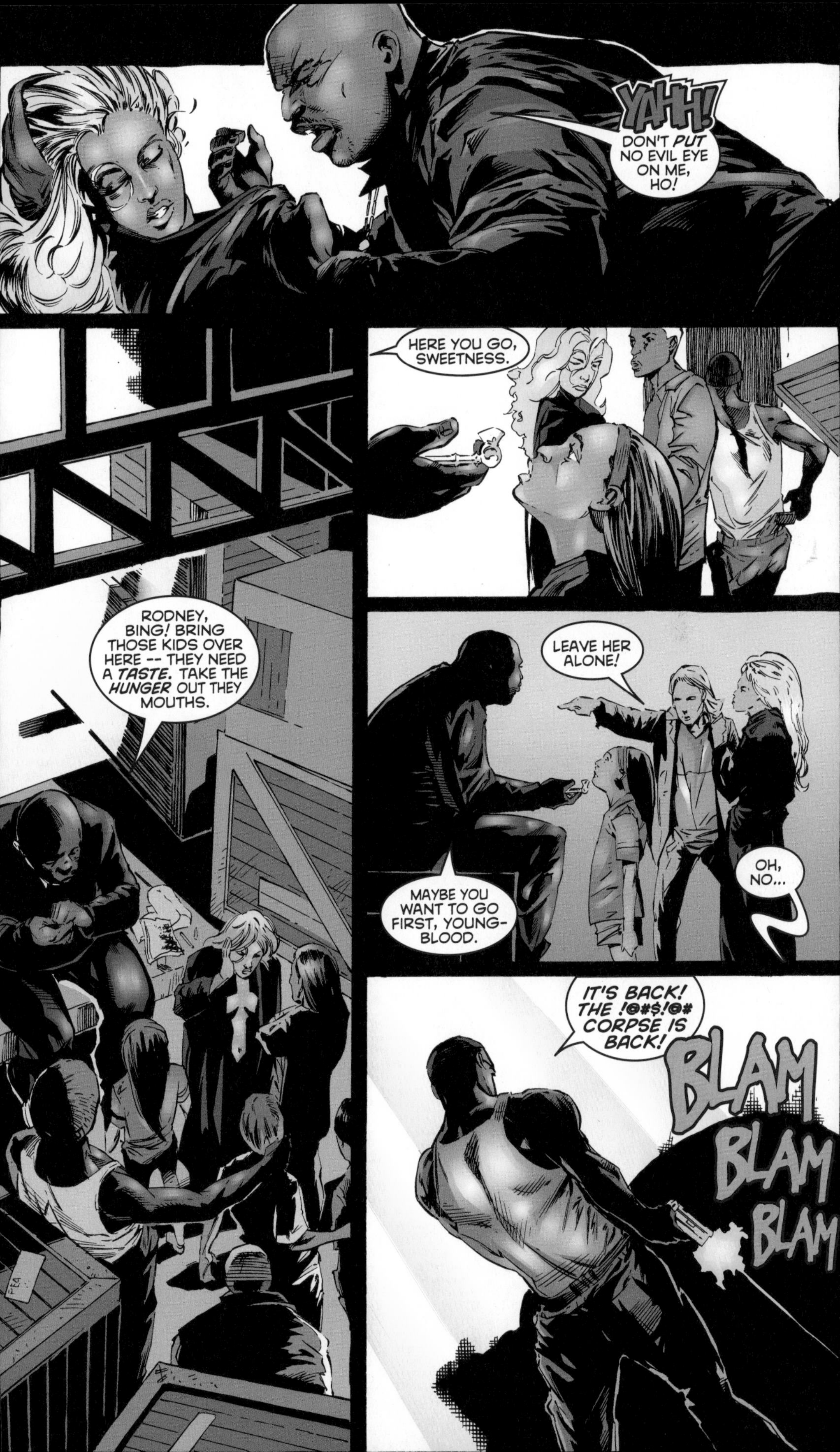
YAHH!
DON'T PUT NO EVIL EYE ON ME, HO!
HERE YOU GO, SWEETNESS.
RODNEY, BING! BRING THOSE KIDS OVER HERE -- THEY NEED A TASTE. TAKE THE HUNGER OUT THEY MOUTHS.
LEAVE HER ALONE!
MAYBE YOU WANT TO GO FIRST, YOUNG-BLOOD.
OH, NO...
IT'S BACK! THE !@#$!@# CORPSE IS BACK!
BLAM
BLAM
BLAM

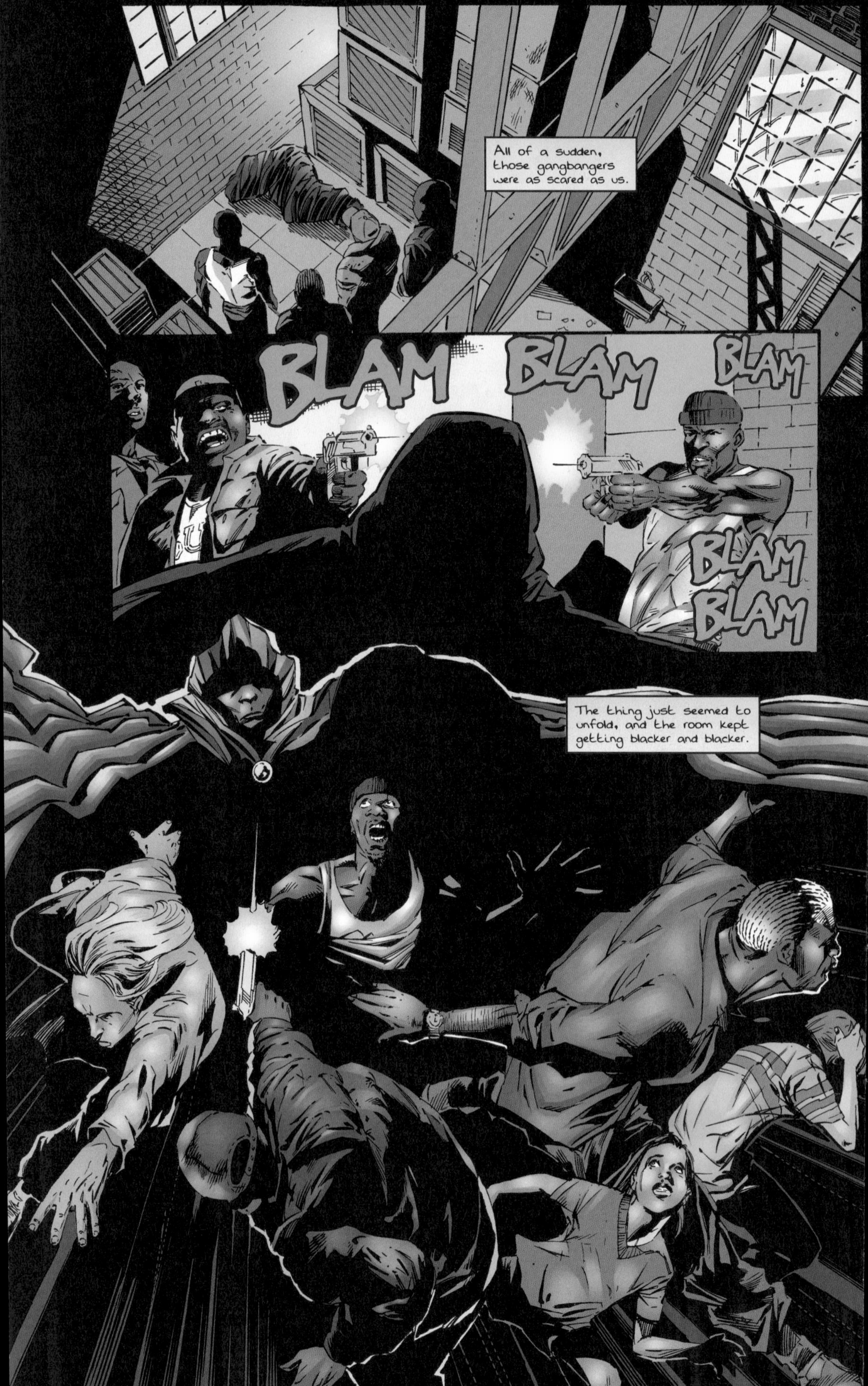
All of a sudden, those gangbangers were as scared as us.
BLAM BLAM BLAM
BLAM BLAM
The thing just seemed to unfold, and the room kept getting blacker and blacker.

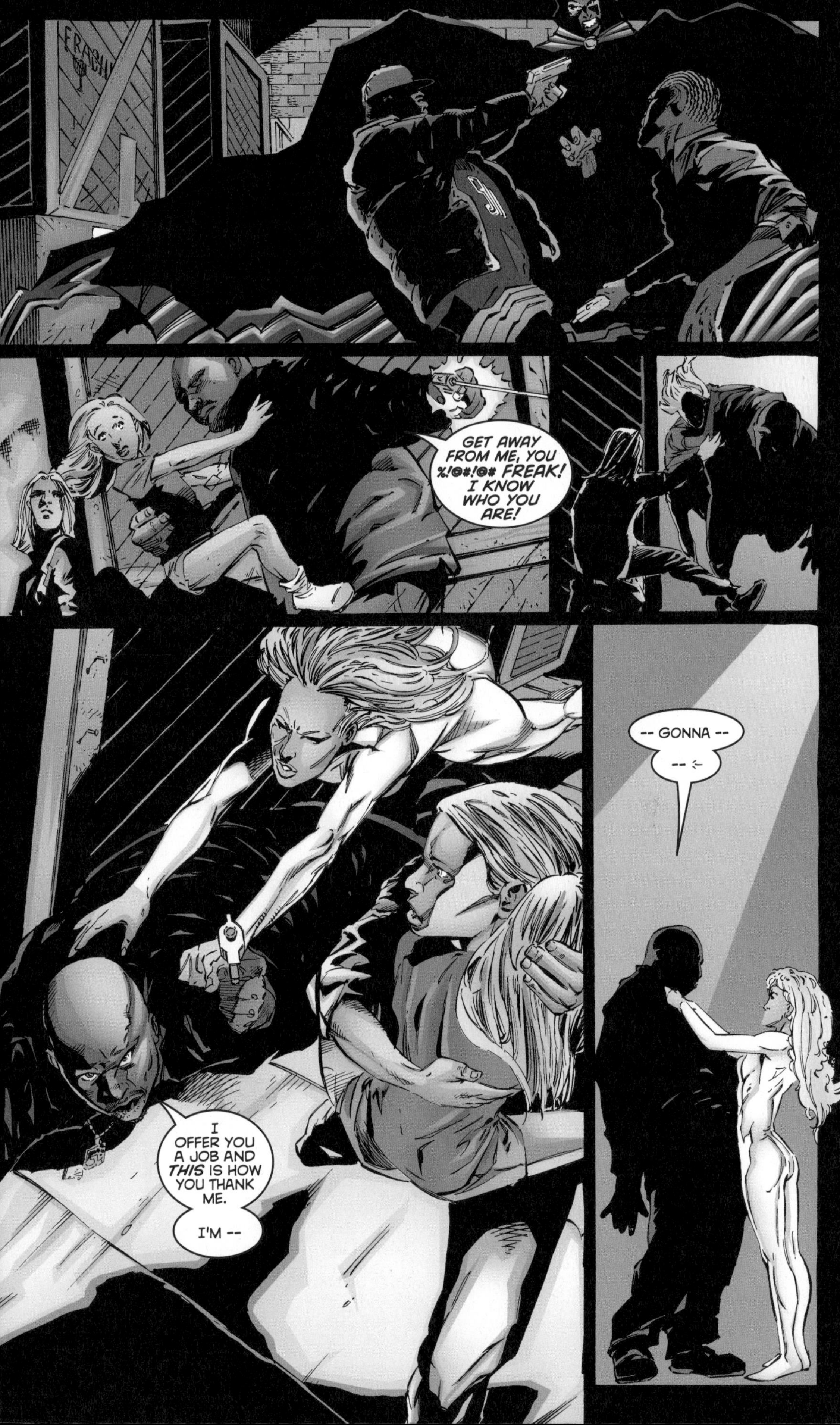
GET AWAY FROM ME, YOU %!@#!@# FREAK! I KNOW WHO YOU ARE!
I OFFER YOU A JOB AND *THIS* IS HOW YOU THANK ME.
I'M --
-- GONNA --

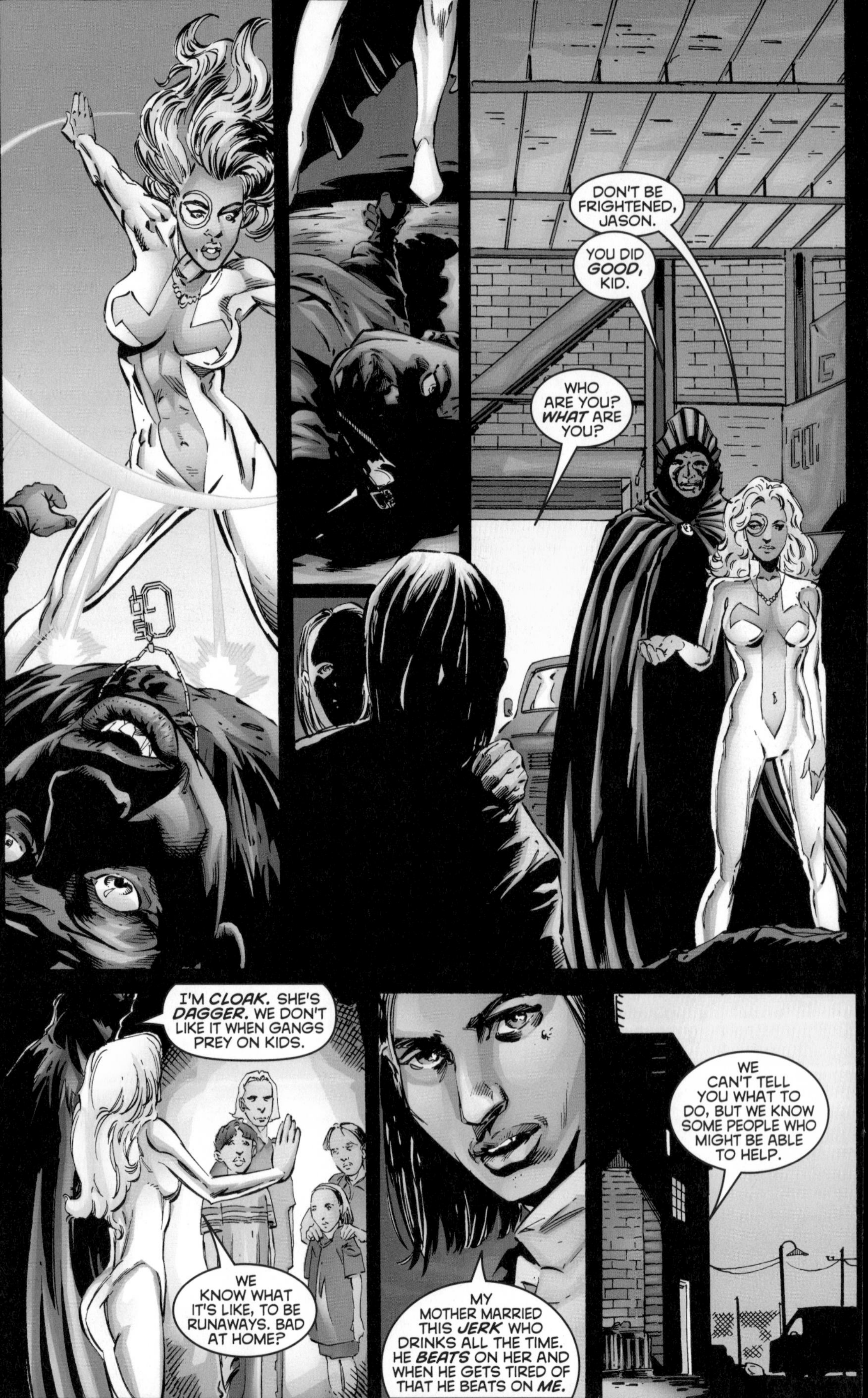
DON'T BE FRIGHTENED, JASON.
YOU DID *GOOD*, KID.
WHO ARE YOU? *WHAT* ARE YOU?
I'M *CLOAK*. SHE'S *DAGGER*. WE DON'T LIKE IT WHEN GANGS PREY ON KIDS.
WE KNOW WHAT IT'S LIKE, TO BE RUNAWAYS. BAD AT HOME?
MY MOTHER MARRIED THIS *JERK* WHO DRINKS ALL THE TIME. HE *BEATS* ON HER AND WHEN HE GETS TIRED OF THAT HE BEATS ON *ME*.
WE CAN'T TELL YOU WHAT TO DO, BUT WE KNOW SOME PEOPLE WHO MIGHT BE ABLE TO HELP.

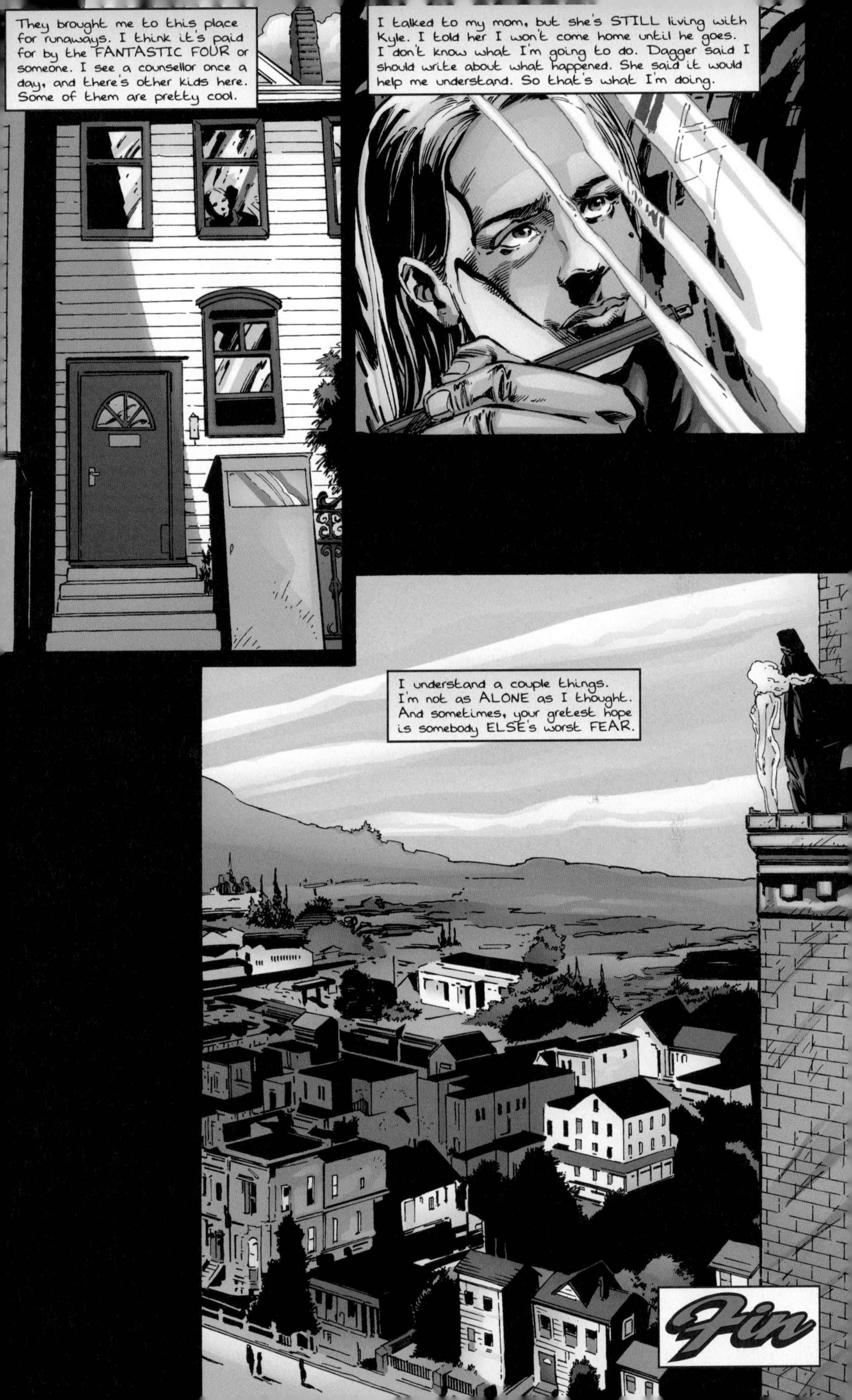
They brought me to this place for runaways. I think it's paid for by the FANTASTIC FOUR or someone. I see a counsellor once a day, and there's other kids here. Some of them are pretty cool.
I talked to my mom, but she's STILL living with Kyle. I told her I won't come home until he goes. I don't know what I'm going to do. Dagger said I should write about what happened. She said it would help me understand. So that's what I'm doing.
I understand a couple things. I'm not as ALONE as I thought. And sometimes, your gretest hope is somebody ELSE's worst FEAR.
Fin

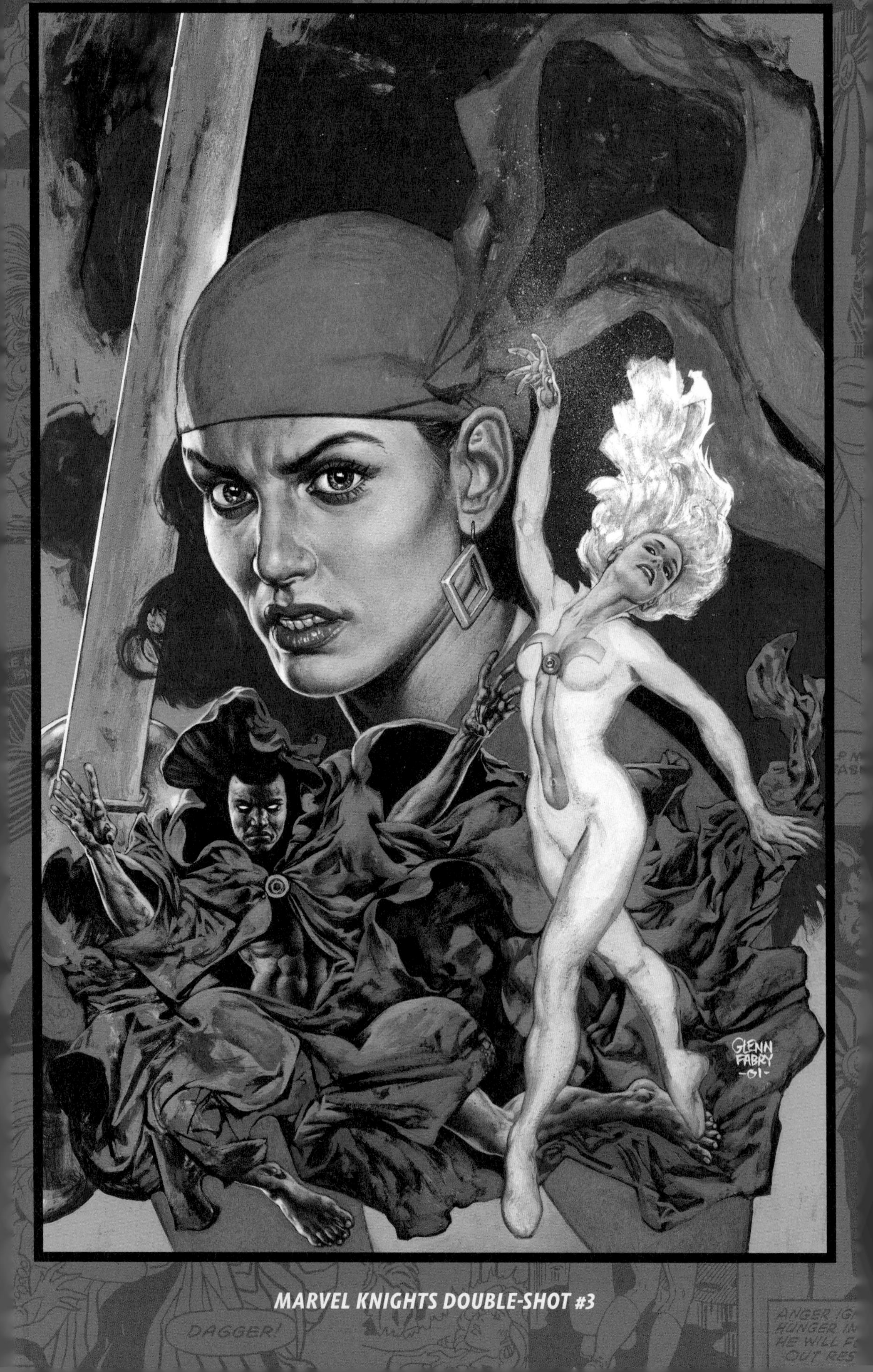
GLENN
FABRY
-01-

MARVEL KNIGHTS DOUBLE-SHOT #3

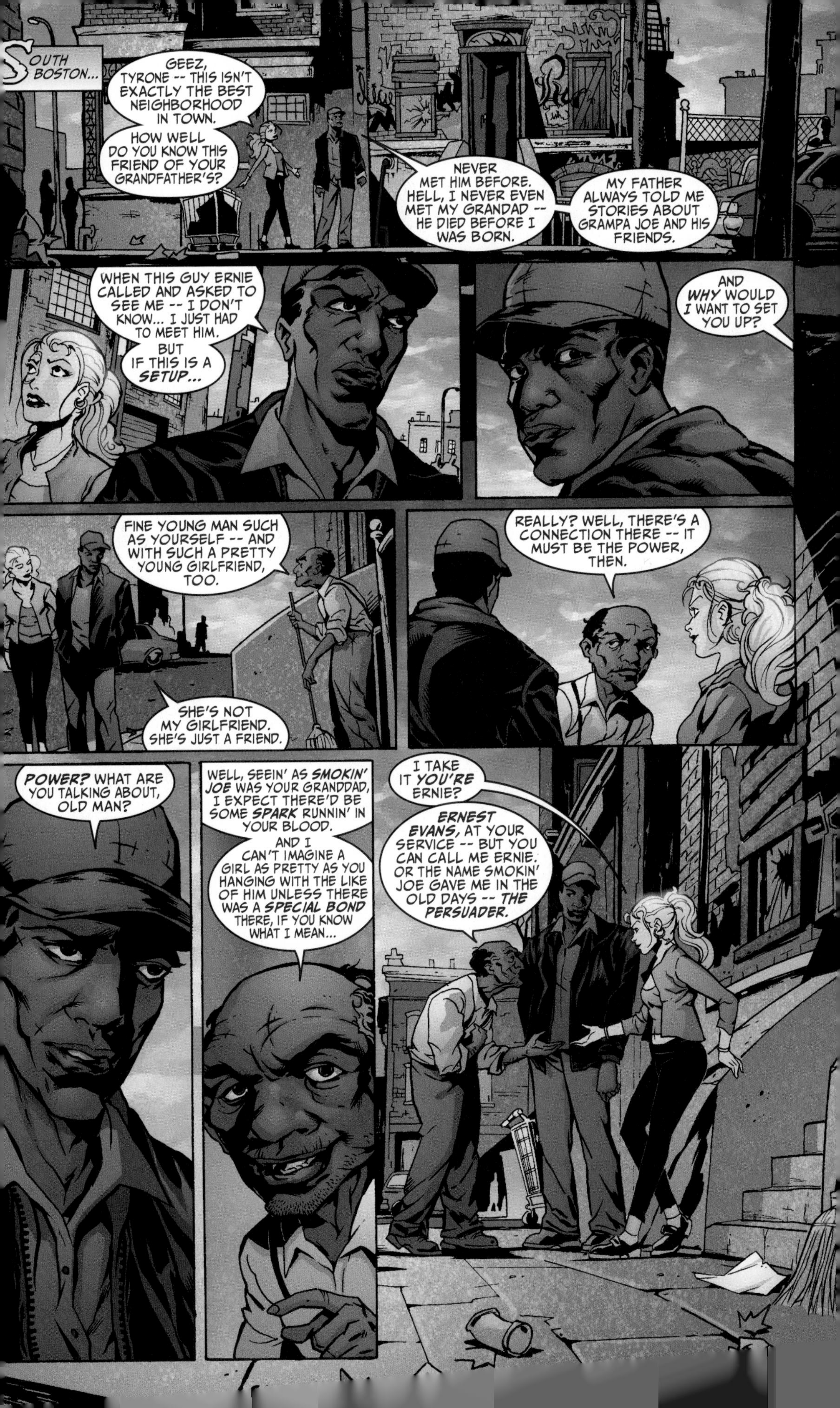
SOUTH BOSTON...
GEEZ, TYRONE -- THIS ISN'T EXACTLY THE BEST NEIGHBORHOOD IN TOWN.
HOW WELL DO YOU KNOW THIS FRIEND OF YOUR GRANDFATHER'S?
NEVER MET HIM BEFORE. HELL, I NEVER EVEN MET MY GRANDAD -- HE DIED BEFORE I WAS BORN.
MY FATHER ALWAYS TOLD ME STORIES ABOUT GRAMPA JOE AND HIS FRIENDS.
WHEN THIS GUY ERNIE CALLED AND ASKED TO SEE ME -- I DON'T KNOW... I JUST HAD TO MEET HIM.
BUT IF THIS IS A SETUP...
AND WHY WOULD I WANT TO SET YOU UP?
FINE YOUNG MAN SUCH AS YOURSELF -- AND WITH SUCH A PRETTY YOUNG GIRLFRIEND, TOO.
SHE'S NOT MY GIRLFRIEND. SHE'S JUST A FRIEND.
REALLY? WELL, THERE'S A CONNECTION THERE -- IT MUST BE THE POWER, THEN.
POWER? WHAT ARE YOU TALKING ABOUT, OLD MAN?
WELL, SEEIN' AS SMOKIN' JOE WAS YOUR GRANDDAD, I EXPECT THERE'D BE SOME SPARK RUNNIN' IN YOUR BLOOD.
AND I CAN'T IMAGINE A GIRL AS PRETTY AS YOU HANGING WITH THE LIKE OF HIM UNLESS THERE WAS A SPECIAL BOND THERE, IF YOU KNOW WHAT I MEAN...
I TAKE IT YOU'RE ERNIE?
ERNEST EVANS, AT YOUR SERVICE -- BUT YOU CAN CALL ME ERNIE. OR THE NAME SMOKIN' JOE GAVE ME IN THE OLD DAYS -- THE PERSUADER.

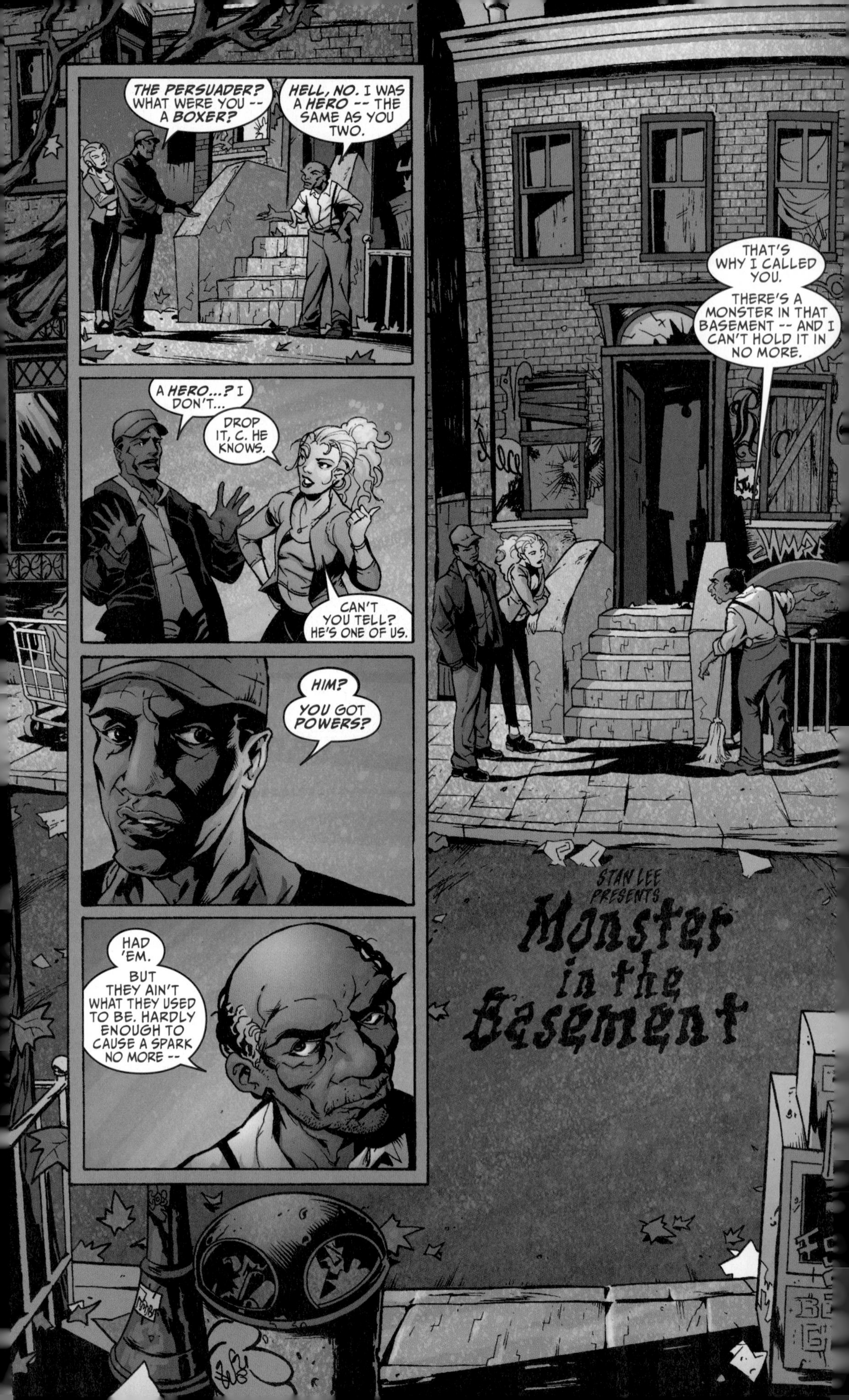
THE PERSUADER? WHAT WERE YOU -- A BOXER?
HELL, NO. I WAS A HERO -- THE SAME AS YOU TWO.
A HERO...? I DON'T...
DROP IT, C. HE KNOWS.
CAN'T YOU TELL? HE'S ONE OF US.
HIM?
YOU GOT POWERS?
HAD 'EM.
BUT THEY AIN'T WHAT THEY USED TO BE. HARDLY ENOUGH TO CAUSE A SPARK NO MORE --
THAT'S WHY I CALLED YOU.
THERE'S A MONSTER IN THAT BASEMENT -- AND I CAN'T HOLD IT IN NO MORE.
STAN LEE PRESENTS
Monster in the Basement

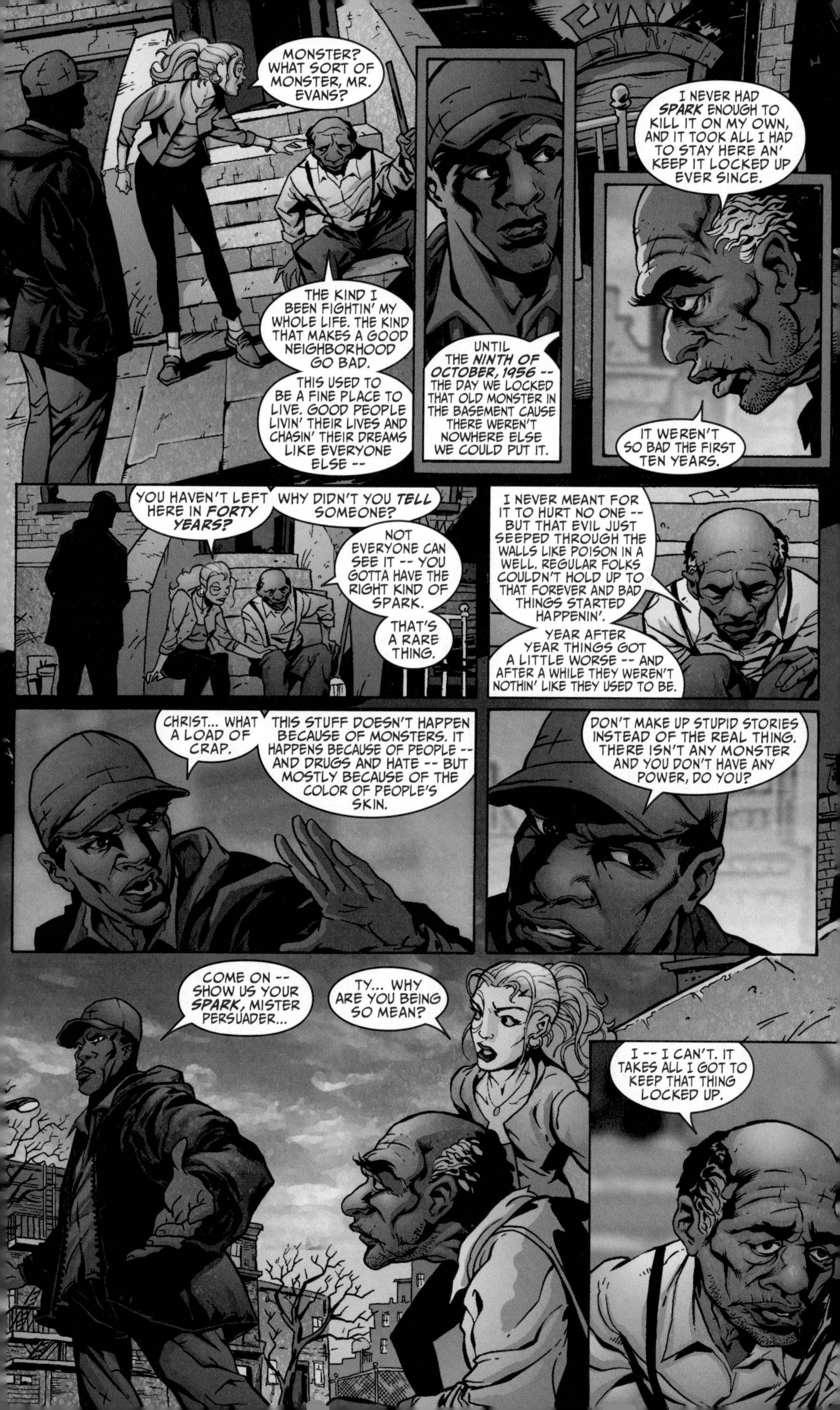
MONSTER? WHAT SORT OF MONSTER, MR. EVANS?
THE KIND I BEEN FIGHTIN' MY WHOLE LIFE. THE KIND THAT MAKES A GOOD NEIGHBORHOOD GO BAD.
THIS USED TO BE A FINE PLACE TO LIVE. GOOD PEOPLE LIVIN' THEIR LIVES AND CHASIN' THEIR DREAMS LIKE EVERYONE ELSE --
UNTIL THE NINTH OF OCTOBER, 1956 -- THE DAY WE LOCKED THAT OLD MONSTER IN THE BASEMENT CAUSE THERE WEREN'T NOWHERE ELSE WE COULD PUT IT.
I NEVER HAD SPARK ENOUGH TO KILL IT ON MY OWN, AND IT TOOK ALL I HAD TO STAY HERE AN' KEEP IT LOCKED UP EVER SINCE.
IT WEREN'T SO BAD THE FIRST TEN YEARS.
YOU HAVEN'T LEFT HERE IN FORTY YEARS?
WHY DIDN'T YOU TELL SOMEONE?
NOT EVERYONE CAN SEE IT -- YOU GOTTA HAVE THE RIGHT KIND OF SPARK.
THAT'S A RARE THING.
I NEVER MEANT FOR IT TO HURT NO ONE -- BUT THAT EVIL JUST SEEPED THROUGH THE WALLS LIKE POISON IN A WELL. REGULAR FOLKS COULDN'T HOLD UP TO THAT FOREVER AND BAD THINGS STARTED HAPPENIN'.
YEAR AFTER YEAR THINGS GOT A LITTLE WORSE -- AND AFTER A WHILE THEY WEREN'T NOTHIN' LIKE THEY USED TO BE.
CHRIST... WHAT A LOAD OF CRAP.
THIS STUFF DOESN'T HAPPEN BECAUSE OF MONSTERS. IT HAPPENS BECAUSE OF PEOPLE -- AND DRUGS AND HATE -- BUT MOSTLY BECAUSE OF THE COLOR OF PEOPLE'S SKIN.
DON'T MAKE UP STUPID STORIES INSTEAD OF THE REAL THING. THERE ISN'T ANY MONSTER AND YOU DON'T HAVE ANY POWER, DO YOU?
COME ON -- SHOW US YOUR SPARK, MISTER PERSUADER...
TY... WHY ARE YOU BEING SO MEAN?
I -- I CAN'T. IT TAKES ALL I GOT TO KEEP THAT THING LOCKED UP.

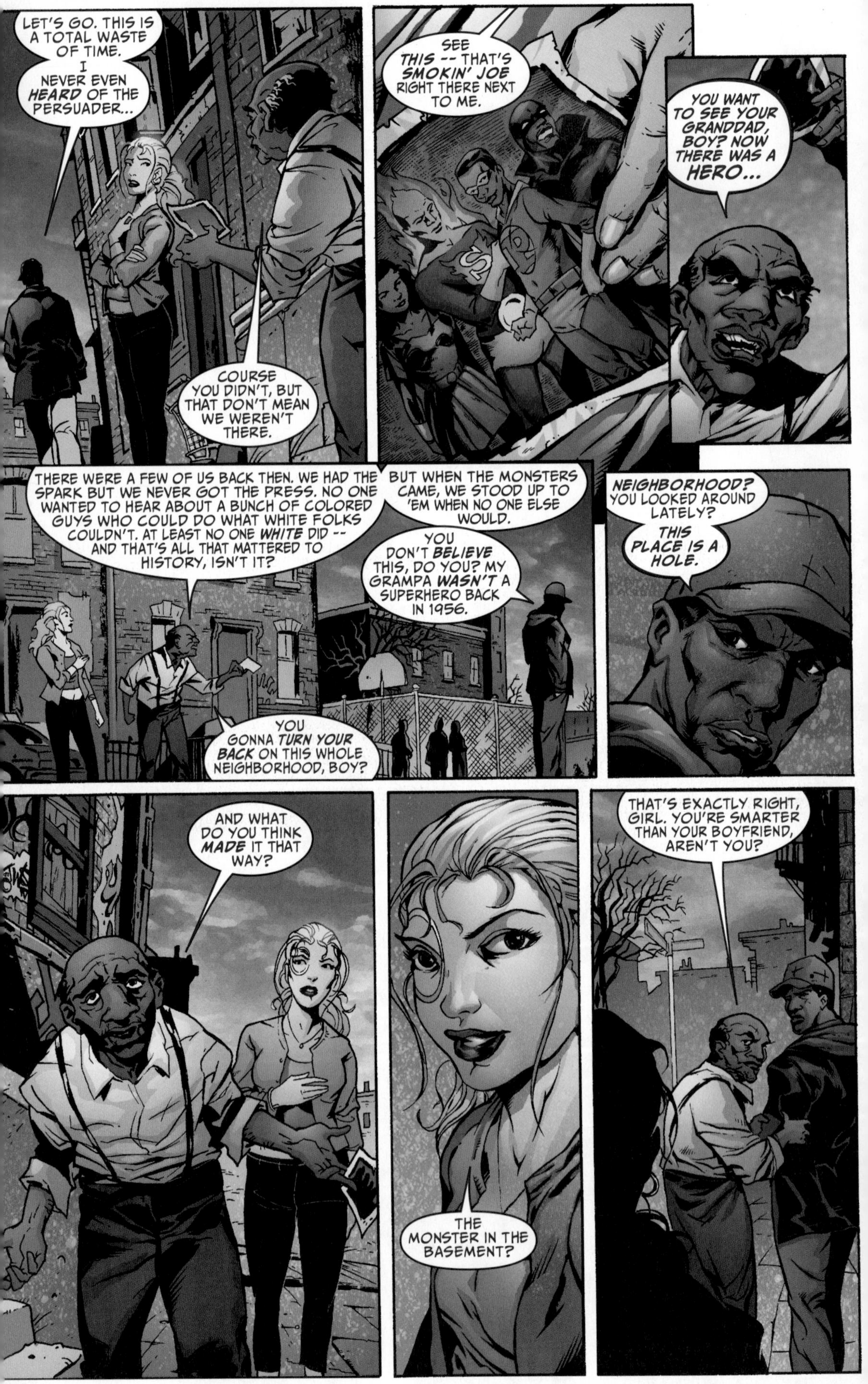
LET'S GO. THIS IS A TOTAL WASTE OF TIME.
I NEVER EVEN HEARD OF THE PERSUADER...
COURSE YOU DIDN'T, BUT THAT DON'T MEAN WE WEREN'T THERE.
SEE THIS -- THAT'S SMOKIN' JOE RIGHT THERE NEXT TO ME.
YOU WANT TO SEE YOUR GRANDDAD, BOY? NOW THERE WAS A HERO...
THERE WERE A FEW OF US BACK THEN. WE HAD THE SPARK BUT WE NEVER GOT THE PRESS. NO ONE WANTED TO HEAR ABOUT A BUNCH OF COLORED GUYS WHO COULD DO WHAT WHITE FOLKS COULDN'T. AT LEAST NO ONE WHITE DID -- AND THAT'S ALL THAT MATTERED TO HISTORY, ISN'T IT?
BUT WHEN THE MONSTERS CAME, WE STOOD UP TO 'EM WHEN NO ONE ELSE WOULD.
YOU GONNA TURN YOUR BACK ON THIS WHOLE NEIGHBORHOOD, BOY?
YOU DON'T BELIEVE THIS, DO YOU? MY GRAMPA WASN'T A SUPERHERO BACK IN 1956.
NEIGHBORHOOD? YOU LOOKED AROUND LATELY?
THIS PLACE IS A HOLE.
AND WHAT DO YOU THINK MADE IT THAT WAY?
THE MONSTER IN THE BASEMENT?
THAT'S EXACTLY RIGHT, GIRL. YOU'RE SMARTER THAN YOUR BOYFRIEND, AREN'T YOU?

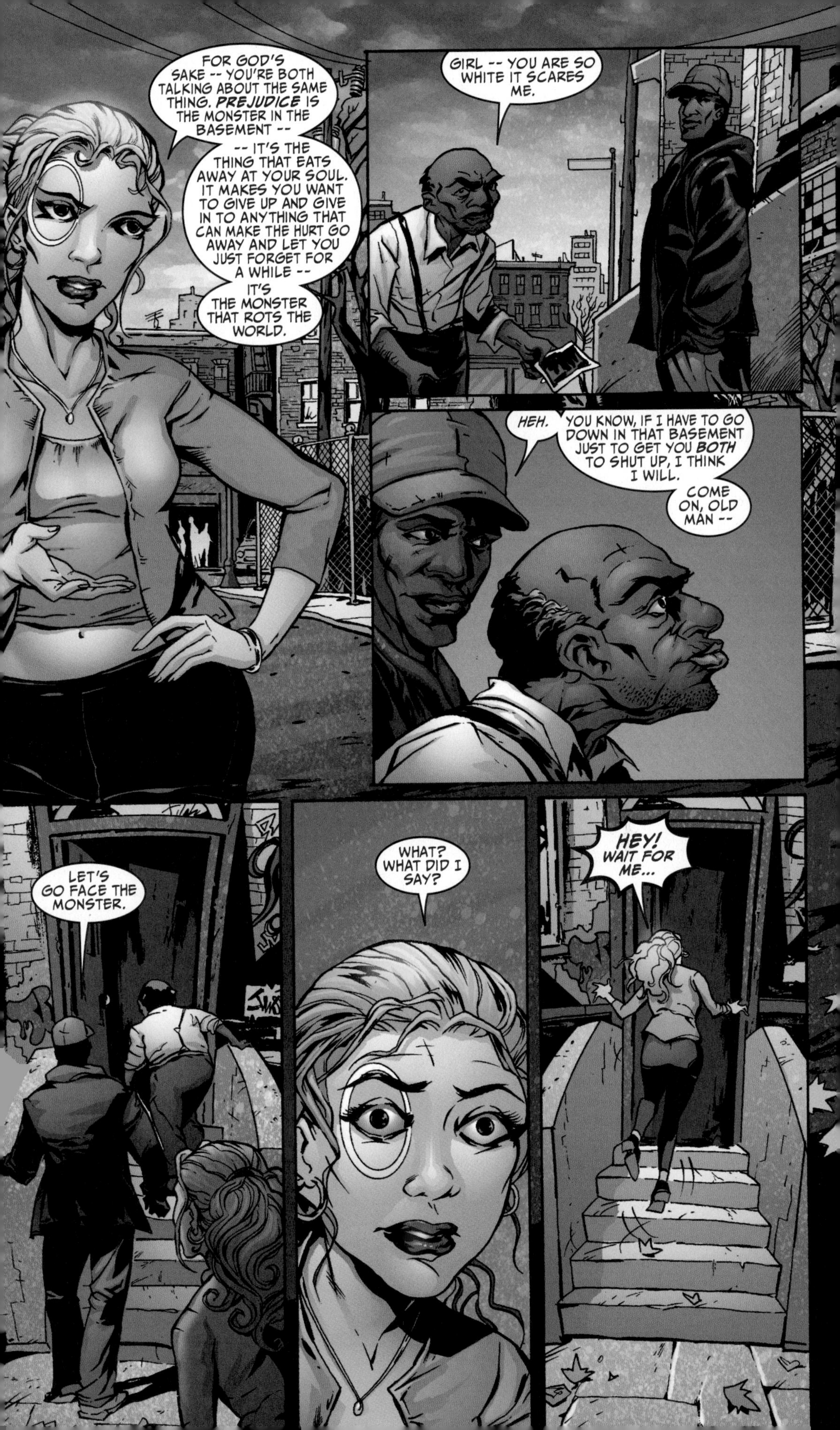
FOR GOD'S SAKE -- YOU'RE BOTH TALKING ABOUT THE SAME THING. PREJUDICE IS THE MONSTER IN THE BASEMENT --
-- IT'S THE THING THAT EATS AWAY AT YOUR SOUL. IT MAKES YOU WANT TO GIVE UP AND GIVE IN TO ANYTHING THAT CAN MAKE THE HURT GO AWAY AND LET YOU JUST FORGET FOR A WHILE --
IT'S THE MONSTER THAT ROTS THE WORLD.
GIRL -- YOU ARE SO WHITE IT SCARES ME.
HEH.
YOU KNOW, IF I HAVE TO GO DOWN IN THAT BASEMENT JUST TO GET YOU BOTH TO SHUT UP, I THINK I WILL.
COME ON, OLD MAN --
LET'S GO FACE THE MONSTER.
WHAT? WHAT DID I SAY?
HEY! WAIT FOR ME...

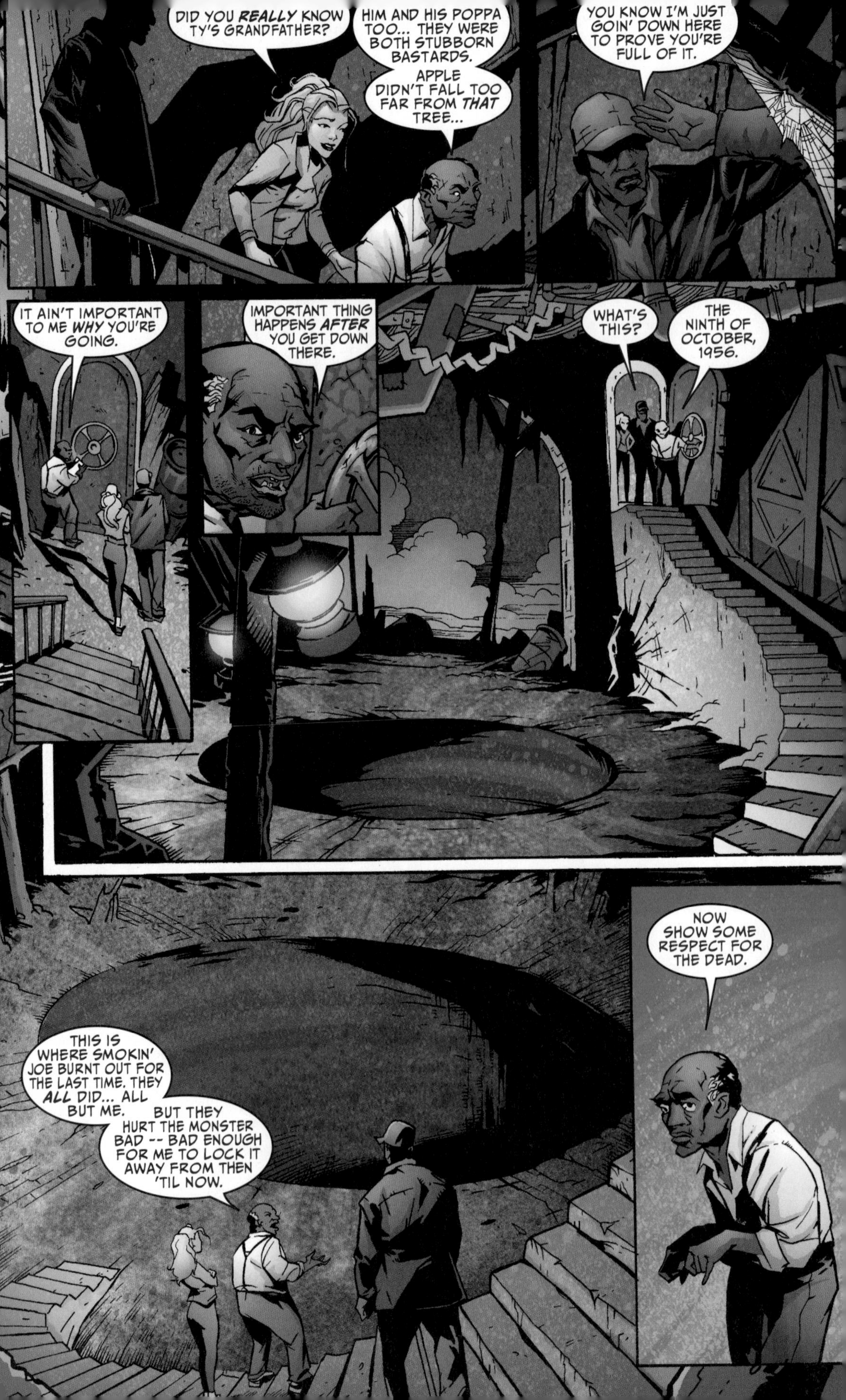
DID YOU REALLY KNOW TY'S GRANDFATHER?
HIM AND HIS POPPA TOO... THEY WERE BOTH STUBBORN BASTARDS.
APPLE DIDN'T FALL TOO FAR FROM THAT TREE...
YOU KNOW I'M JUST GOIN' DOWN HERE TO PROVE YOU'RE FULL OF IT.
IT AIN'T IMPORTANT TO ME WHY YOU'RE GOING.
IMPORTANT THING HAPPENS AFTER YOU GET DOWN THERE.
WHAT'S THIS?
THE NINTH OF OCTOBER, 1956.
THIS IS WHERE SMOKIN' JOE BURNT OUT FOR THE LAST TIME. THEY ALL DID... ALL BUT ME.
BUT THEY HURT THE MONSTER BAD -- BAD ENOUGH FOR ME TO LOCK IT AWAY FROM THEN 'TIL NOW.
NOW SHOW SOME RESPECT FOR THE DEAD.

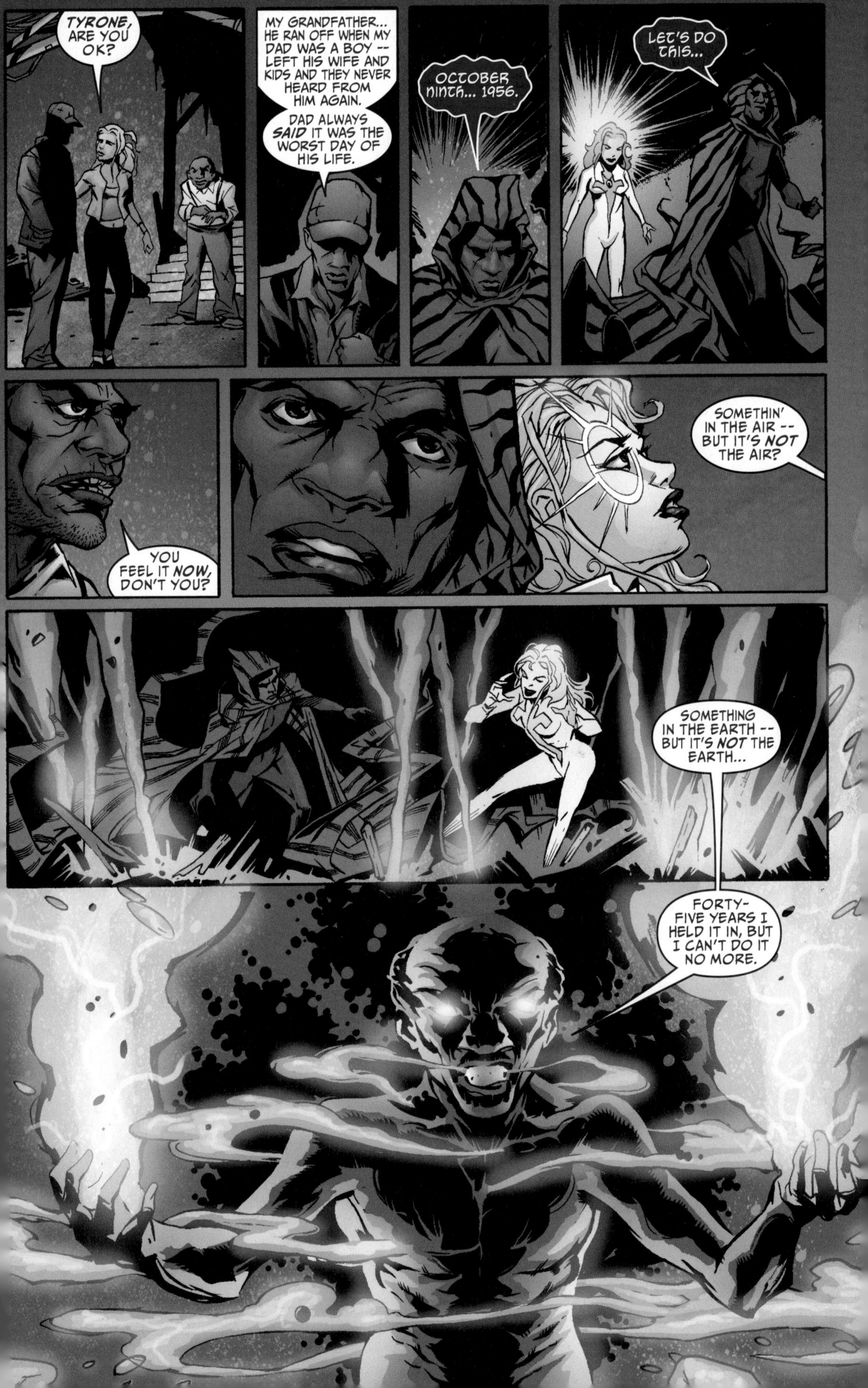
TYRONE, ARE YOU OK?
MY GRANDFATHER... HE RAN OFF WHEN MY DAD WAS A BOY -- LEFT HIS WIFE AND KIDS AND THEY NEVER HEARD FROM HIM AGAIN.
DAD ALWAYS SAID IT WAS THE WORST DAY OF HIS LIFE.
OCTOBER NINTH... 1956.
LET'S DO THIS...
YOU FEEL IT NOW, DON'T YOU?
SOMETHIN' IN THE AIR -- BUT IT'S NOT THE AIR?
SOMETHING IN THE EARTH -- BUT IT'S NOT THE EARTH...
FORTY-FIVE YEARS I HELD IT IN, BUT I CAN'T DO IT NO MORE.

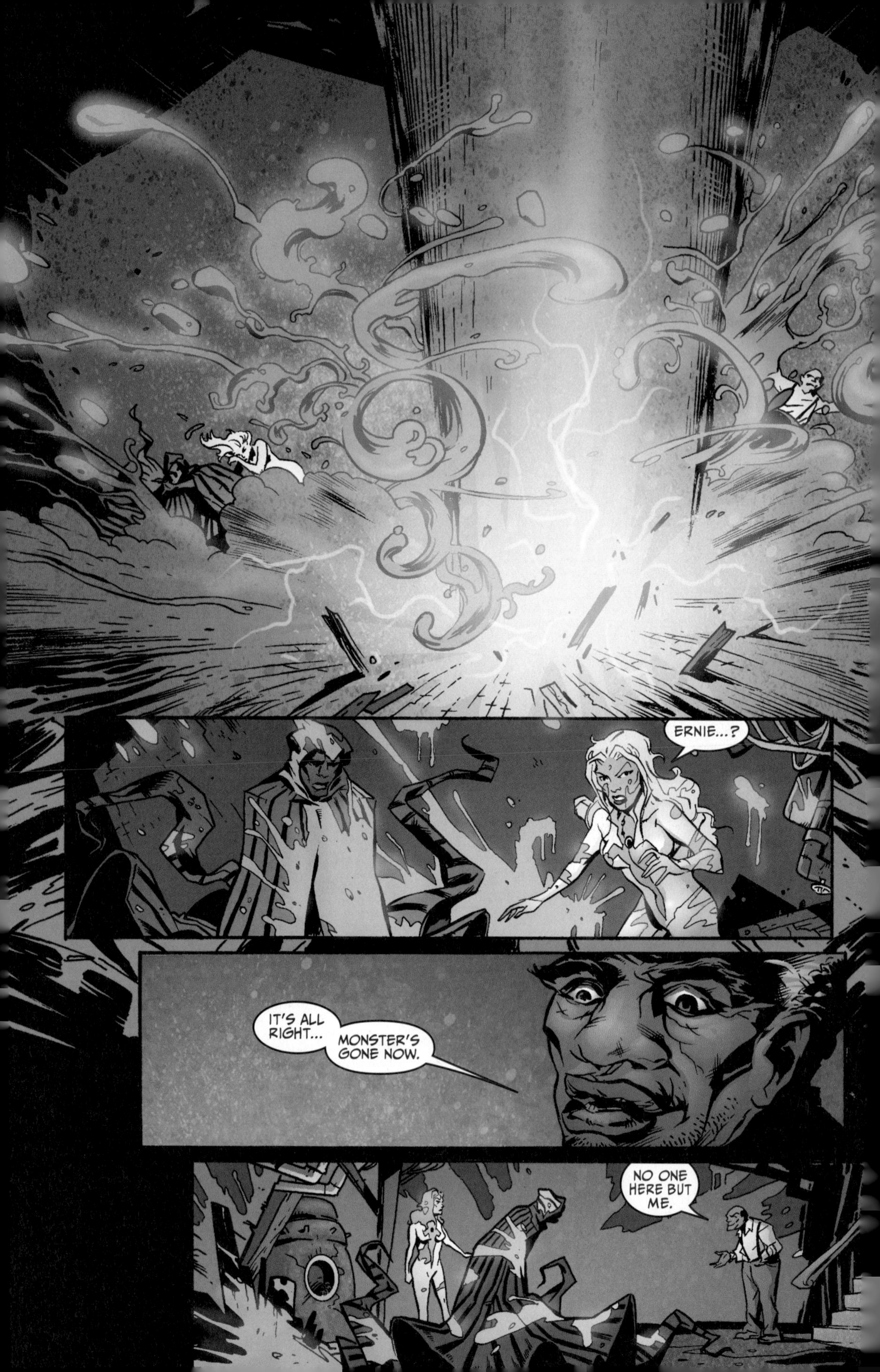
ERNIE...?
IT'S ALL RIGHT...
MONSTER'S GONE NOW.
NO ONE HERE BUT ME.

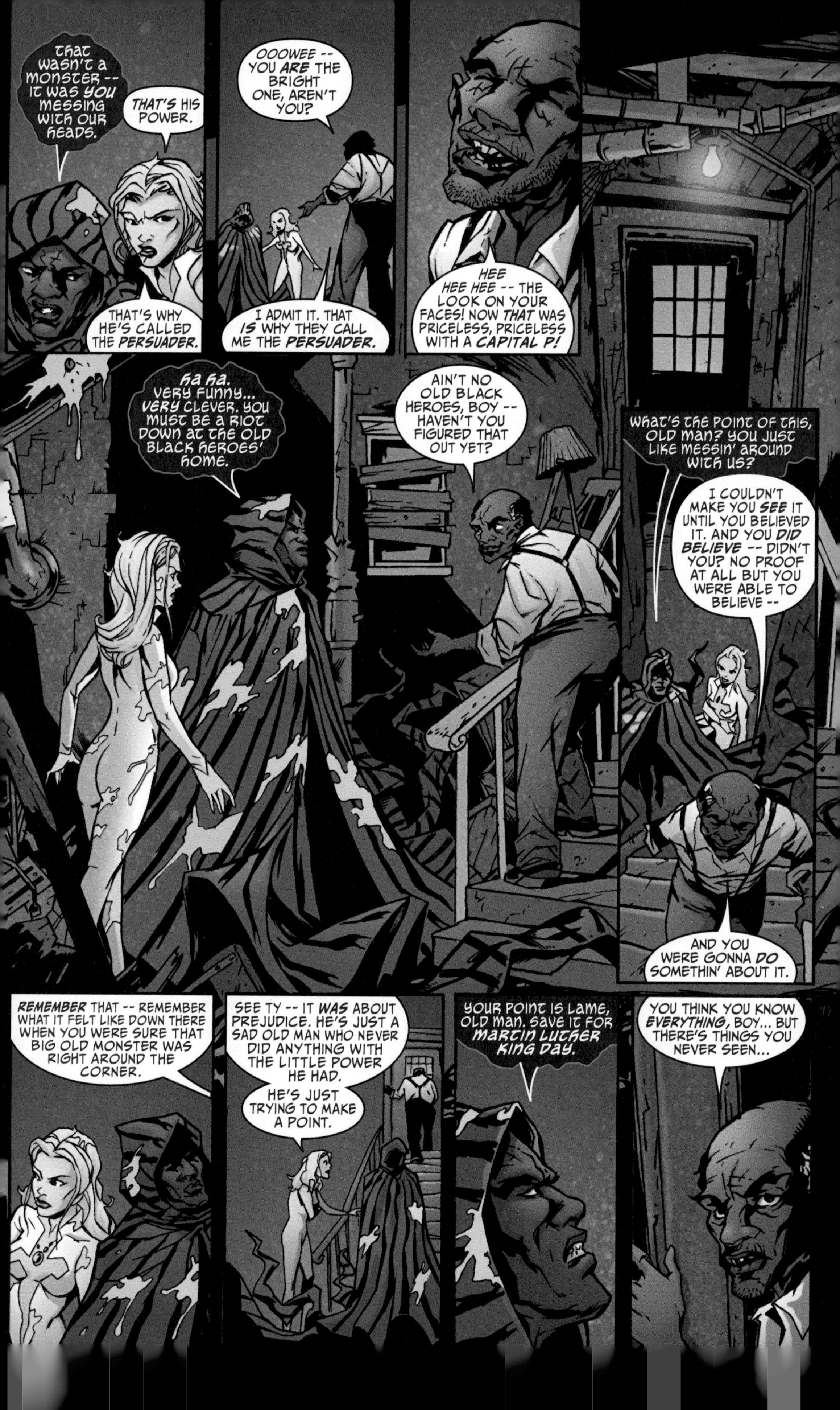

THAT WASN'T A MONSTER -- IT WAS YOU MESSING WITH OUR HEADS.
THAT'S HIS POWER.
THAT'S WHY HE'S CALLED THE PERSUADER.
OOOWEE -- YOU ARE THE BRIGHT ONE, AREN'T YOU?
I ADMIT IT. THAT IS WHY THEY CALL ME THE PERSUADER.
HEE HEE HEE -- THE LOOK ON YOUR FACES! NOW THAT WAS PRICELESS, PRICELESS WITH A CAPITAL P!
HA HA. VERY FUNNY... VERY CLEVER. YOU MUST BE A RIOT DOWN AT THE OLD BLACK HEROES' HOME.
AIN'T NO OLD BLACK HEROES, BOY -- HAVEN'T YOU FIGURED THAT OUT YET?
WHAT'S THE POINT OF THIS, OLD MAN? YOU JUST LIKE MESSIN' AROUND WITH US?
I COULDN'T MAKE YOU SEE IT UNTIL YOU BELIEVED IT. AND YOU DID BELIEVE -- DIDN'T YOU? NO PROOF AT ALL BUT YOU WERE ABLE TO BELIEVE --
AND YOU WERE GONNA DO SOMETHIN' ABOUT IT.
REMEMBER THAT -- REMEMBER WHAT IT FELT LIKE DOWN THERE WHEN YOU WERE SURE THAT BIG OLD MONSTER WAS RIGHT AROUND THE CORNER.
SEE TY -- IT WAS ABOUT PREJUDICE. HE'S JUST A SAD OLD MAN WHO NEVER DID ANYTHING WITH THE LITTLE POWER HE HAD.
HE'S JUST TRYING TO MAKE A POINT.
YOUR POINT IS LAME, OLD MAN. SAVE IT FOR MARTIN LUTHER KING DAY.
YOU THINK YOU KNOW EVERYTHING, BOY... BUT THERE'S THINGS YOU NEVER SEEN...

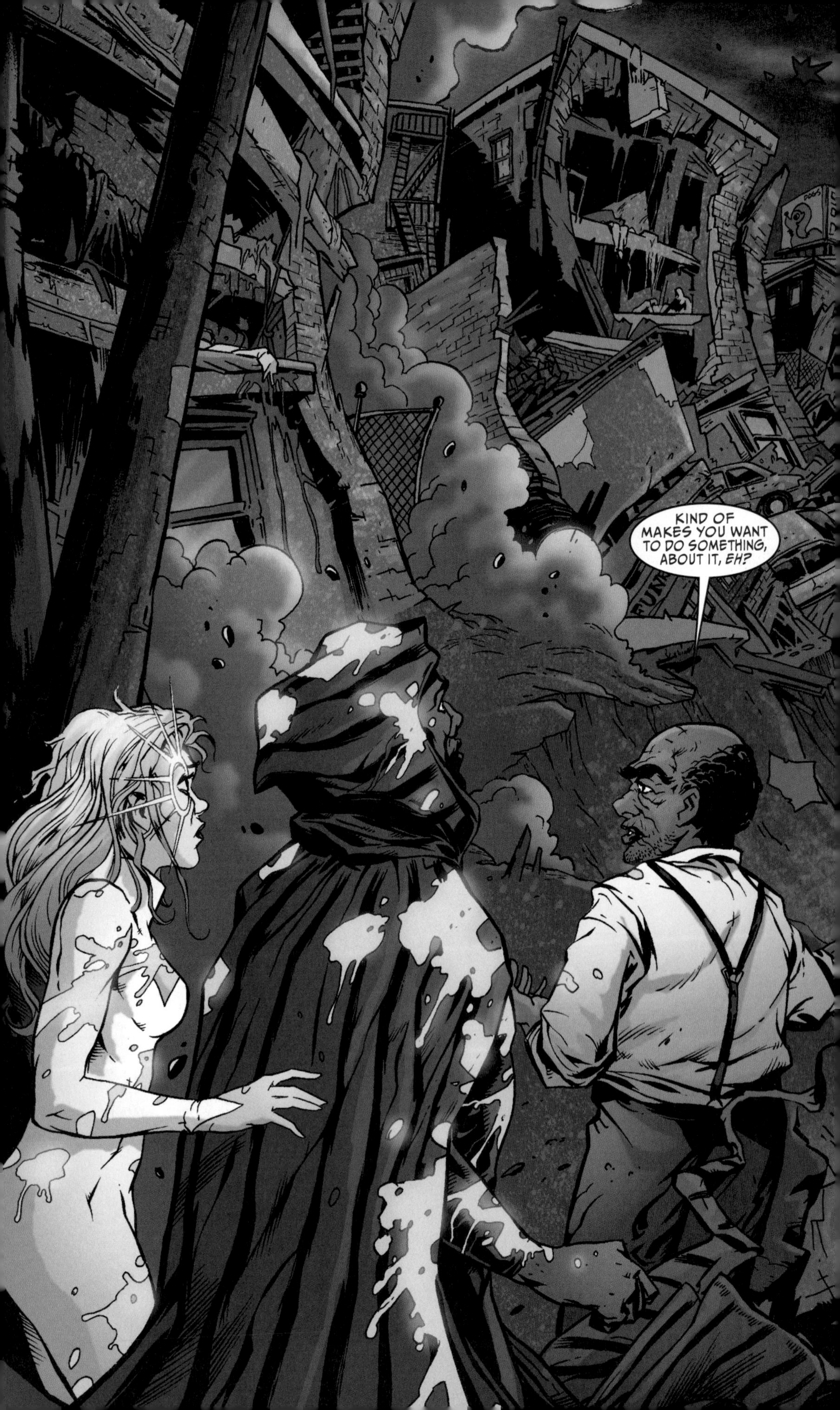
KIND OF MAKES YOU WANT TO DO SOMETHING, ABOUT IT, *EH?*

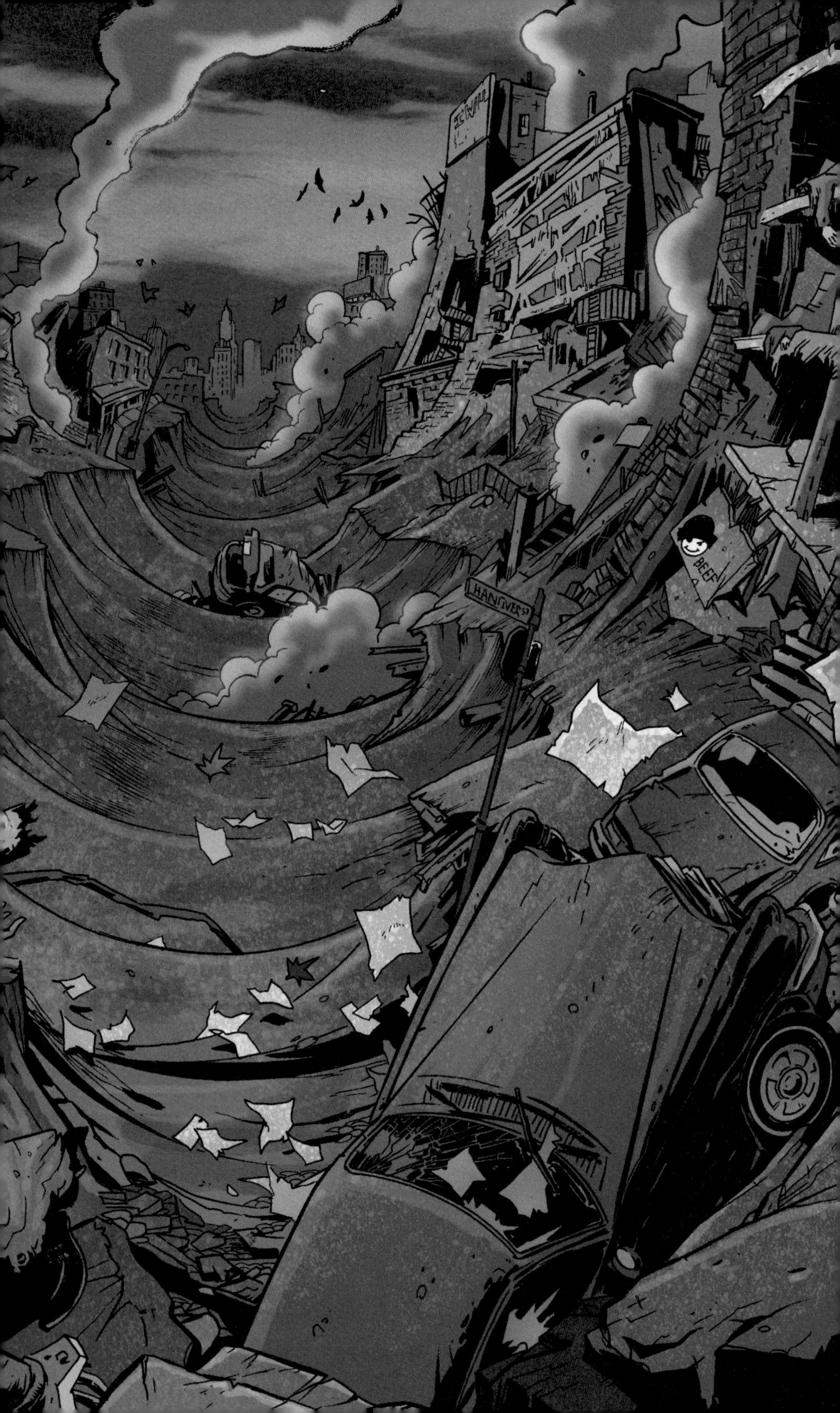
HANOVER ST
BEEF

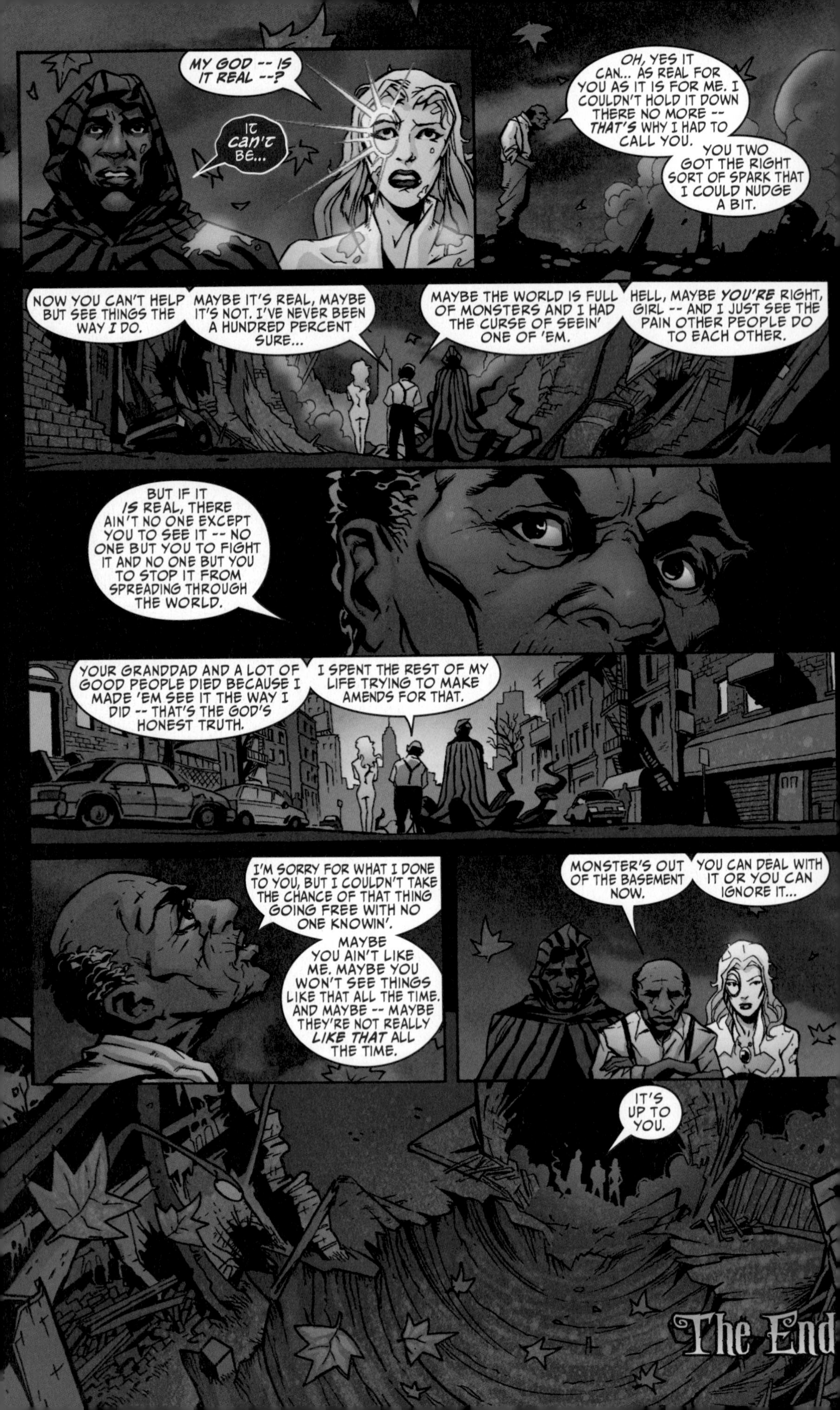
MY GOD -- IS IT REAL --?
IT CAN'T BE...
OH, YES IT CAN... AS REAL FOR YOU AS IT IS FOR ME. I COULDN'T HOLD IT DOWN THERE NO MORE -- THAT'S WHY I HAD TO CALL YOU.
YOU TWO GOT THE RIGHT SORT OF SPARK THAT I COULD NUDGE A BIT.
NOW YOU CAN'T HELP BUT SEE THINGS THE WAY I DO.
MAYBE IT'S REAL, MAYBE IT'S NOT. I'VE NEVER BEEN A HUNDRED PERCENT SURE...
MAYBE THE WORLD IS FULL OF MONSTERS AND I HAD THE CURSE OF SEEIN' ONE OF 'EM.
HELL, MAYBE YOU'RE RIGHT, GIRL -- AND I JUST SEE THE PAIN OTHER PEOPLE DO TO EACH OTHER.
BUT IF IT IS REAL, THERE AIN'T NO ONE EXCEPT YOU TO SEE IT -- NO ONE BUT YOU TO FIGHT IT AND NO ONE BUT YOU TO STOP IT FROM SPREADING THROUGH THE WORLD.
YOUR GRANDDAD AND A LOT OF GOOD PEOPLE DIED BECAUSE I MADE 'EM SEE IT THE WAY I DID -- THAT'S THE GOD'S HONEST TRUTH.
I SPENT THE REST OF MY LIFE TRYING TO MAKE AMENDS FOR THAT.
I'M SORRY FOR WHAT I DONE TO YOU, BUT I COULDN'T TAKE THE CHANCE OF THAT THING GOING FREE WITH NO ONE KNOWIN'.
MAYBE YOU AIN'T LIKE ME. MAYBE YOU WON'T SEE THINGS LIKE THAT ALL THE TIME. AND MAYBE -- MAYBE THEY'RE NOT REALLY LIKE THAT ALL THE TIME.
MONSTER'S OUT OF THE BASEMENT NOW.
YOU CAN DEAL WITH IT OR YOU CAN IGNORE IT...
IT'S UP TO YOU.
The End

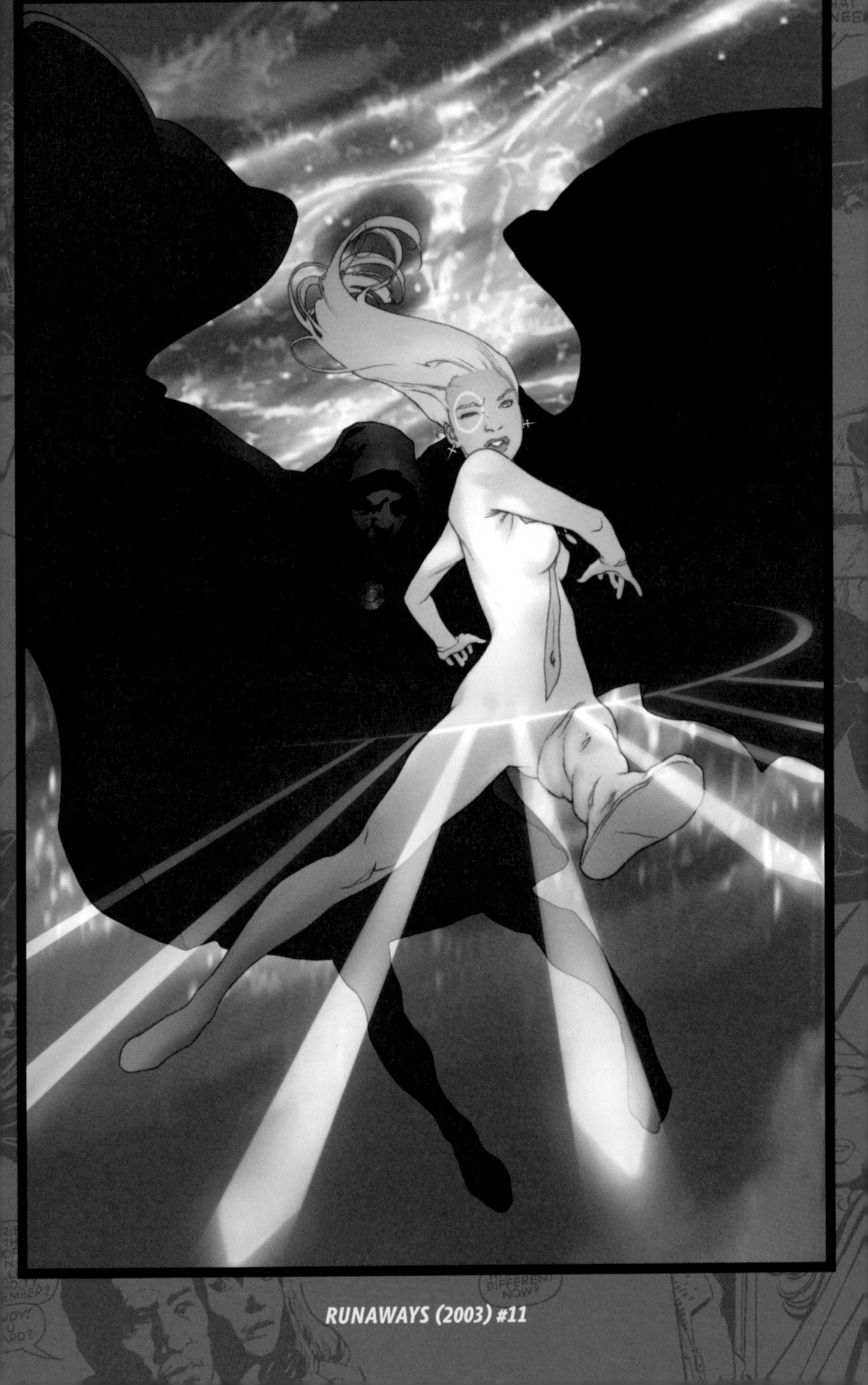

RUNAWAYS (2003) #11

THE PRIDE

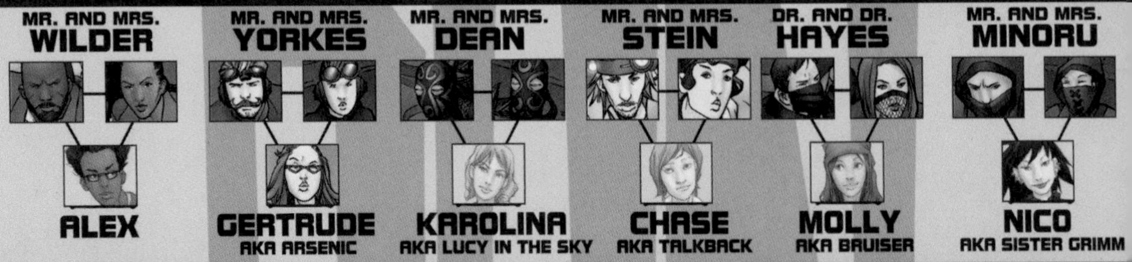
MR. AND MRS. WILDER
MR. AND MRS. YORKES
MR. AND MRS. DEAN
MR. AND MRS. STEIN
DR. AND DR. HAYES
MR. AND MRS. MINORU
ALEX
GERTRUDE
AKA ARSENIC
KAROLINA
AKA LUCY IN THE SKY
CHASE
AKA TALKBACK
MOLLY
AKA BRUISER
NICO
AKA SISTER GRIMM

THE RUNAWAYS

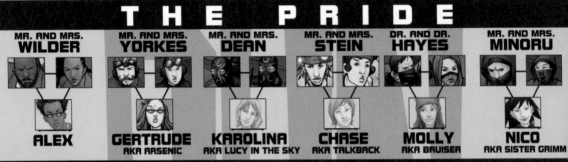

At some point in their lives, all young people think that their parents are evil... but what if they really are?

PREVIOUSLY IN RUNAWAYS:

Teenager Alex Wilder and five other only children always thought that their parents were boring Los Angeles socialites, until the kids witness the adults *murder* a young girl in some kind of dark sacrificial ritual. The teens soon learn that their parents are part of a secret organization called The Pride, a collection of crime bosses, time-traveling despots, alien overlords, mad scientists, evil mutants, and dark wizards.

After stealing weapons and resources from these villainous adults (including a mystical staff, futuristic gauntlets and a psychic velociraptor named Old Lace), the kids run away from home and vow to bring their parents to justice. But with the help of their operatives in the LAPD, The Pride frames their children for the murder *they* committed, and the fugitive Runaways are forced to retreat to a subterranean hideout. Using the diverse powers and skills they inherited, the kids now plan to atone for their parents' crimes by helping those in need.

But the best laid plans of mice and men...

LOST AND FOUND

PART ONE OF TWO

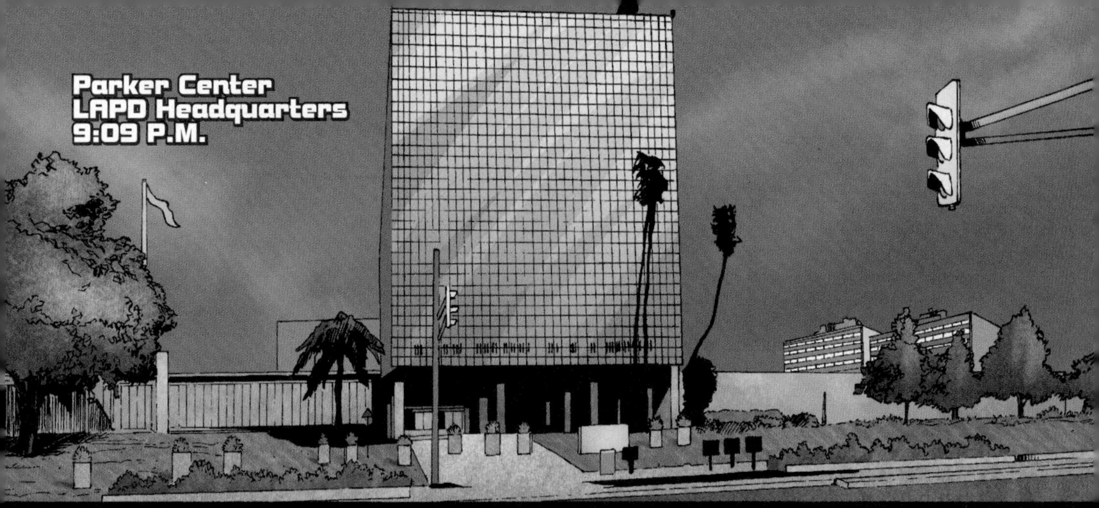
Parker Center
LAPD Headquarters
9:09 P.M.
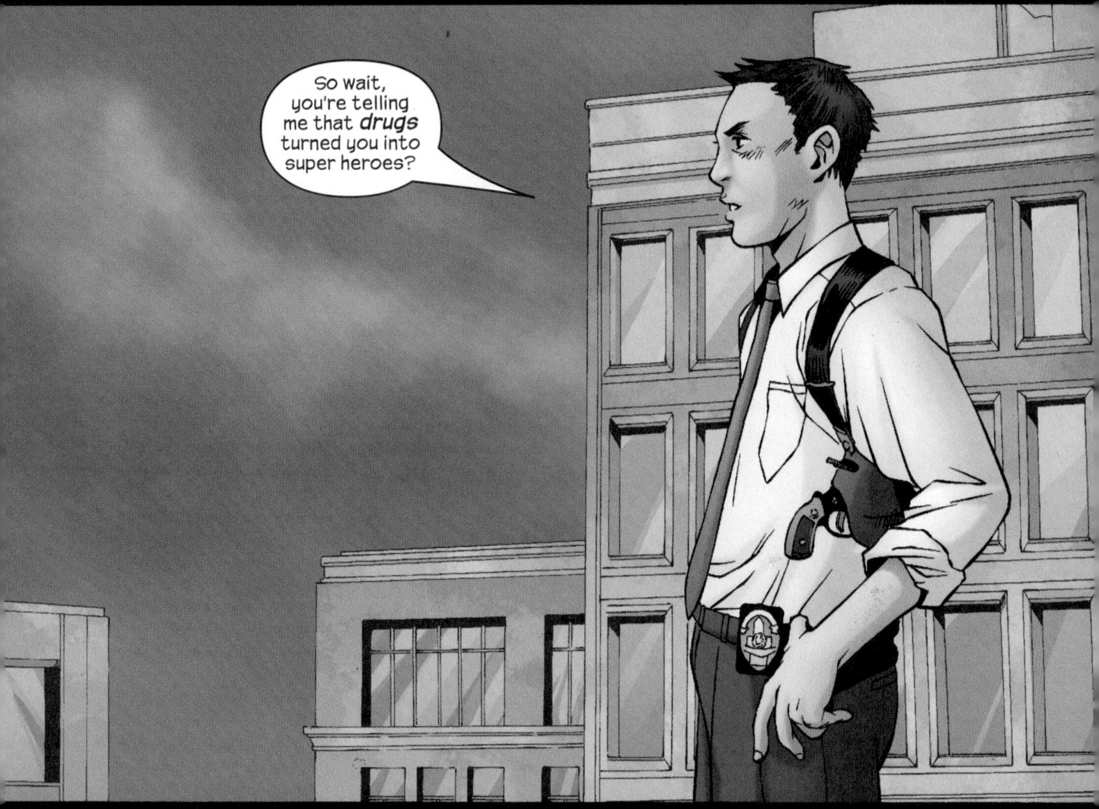
So wait, you're telling me that *drugs* turned you into super heroes?
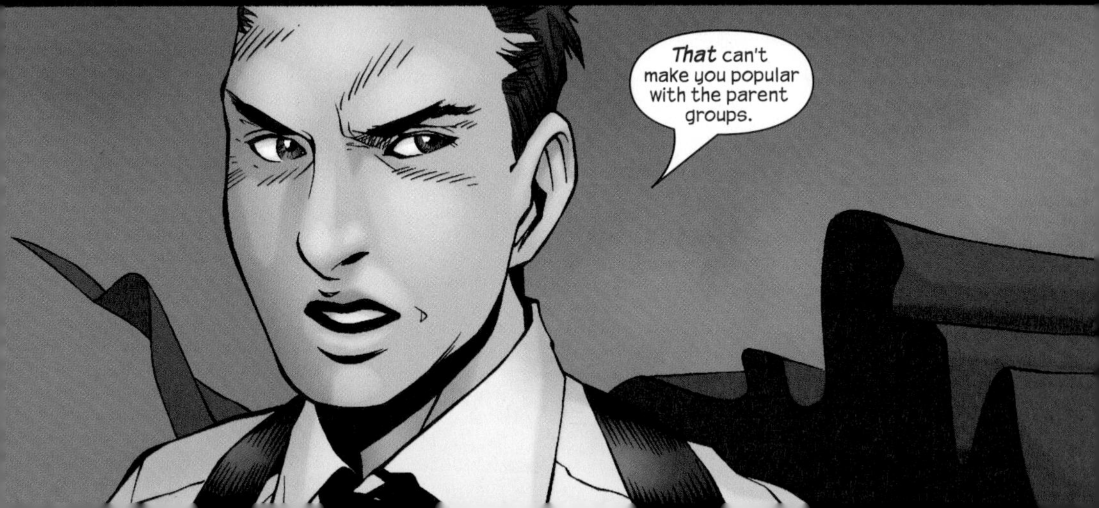
That can't make you popular with the parent groups.

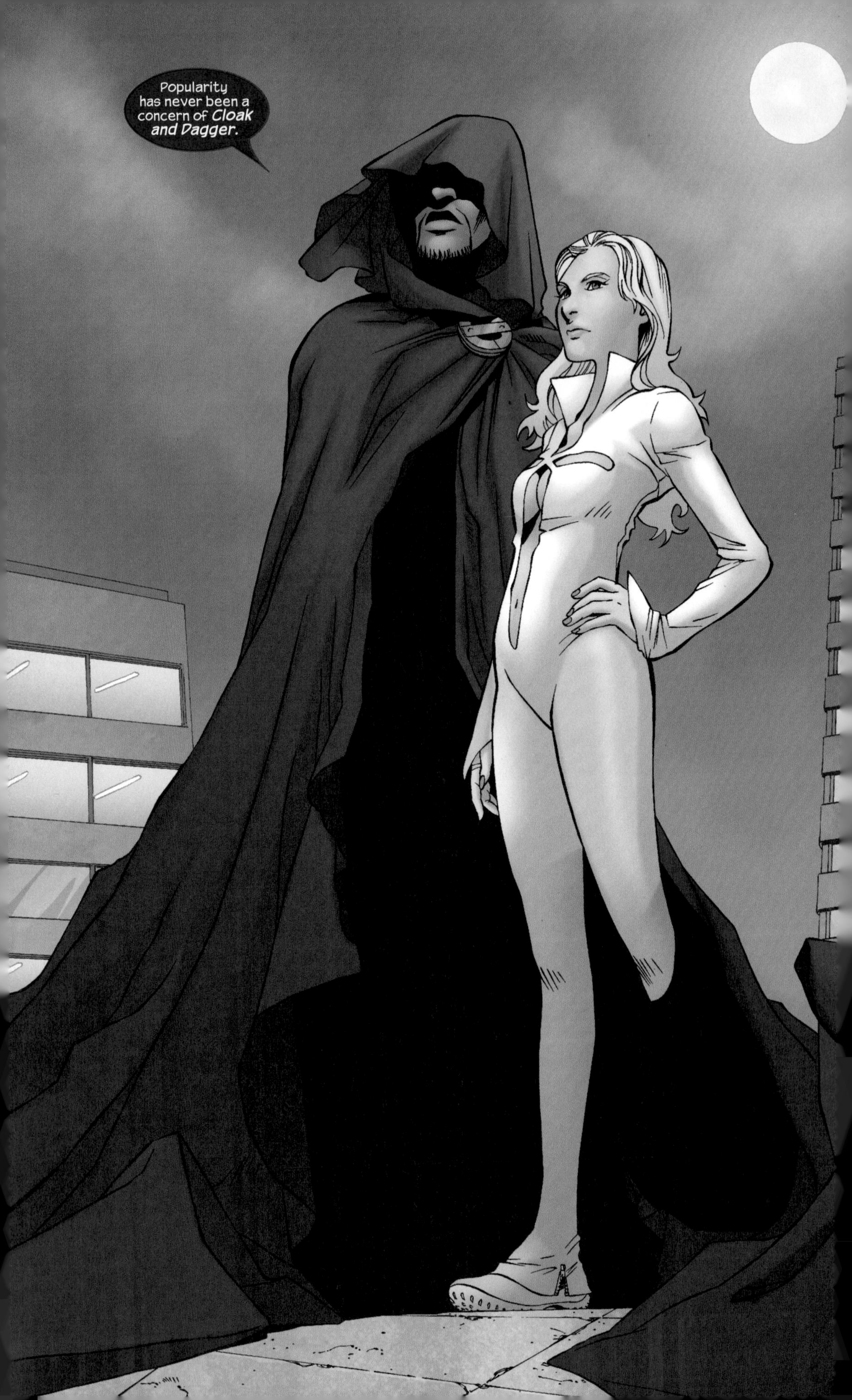
Popularity has never been a concern of *Cloak and Dagger*.

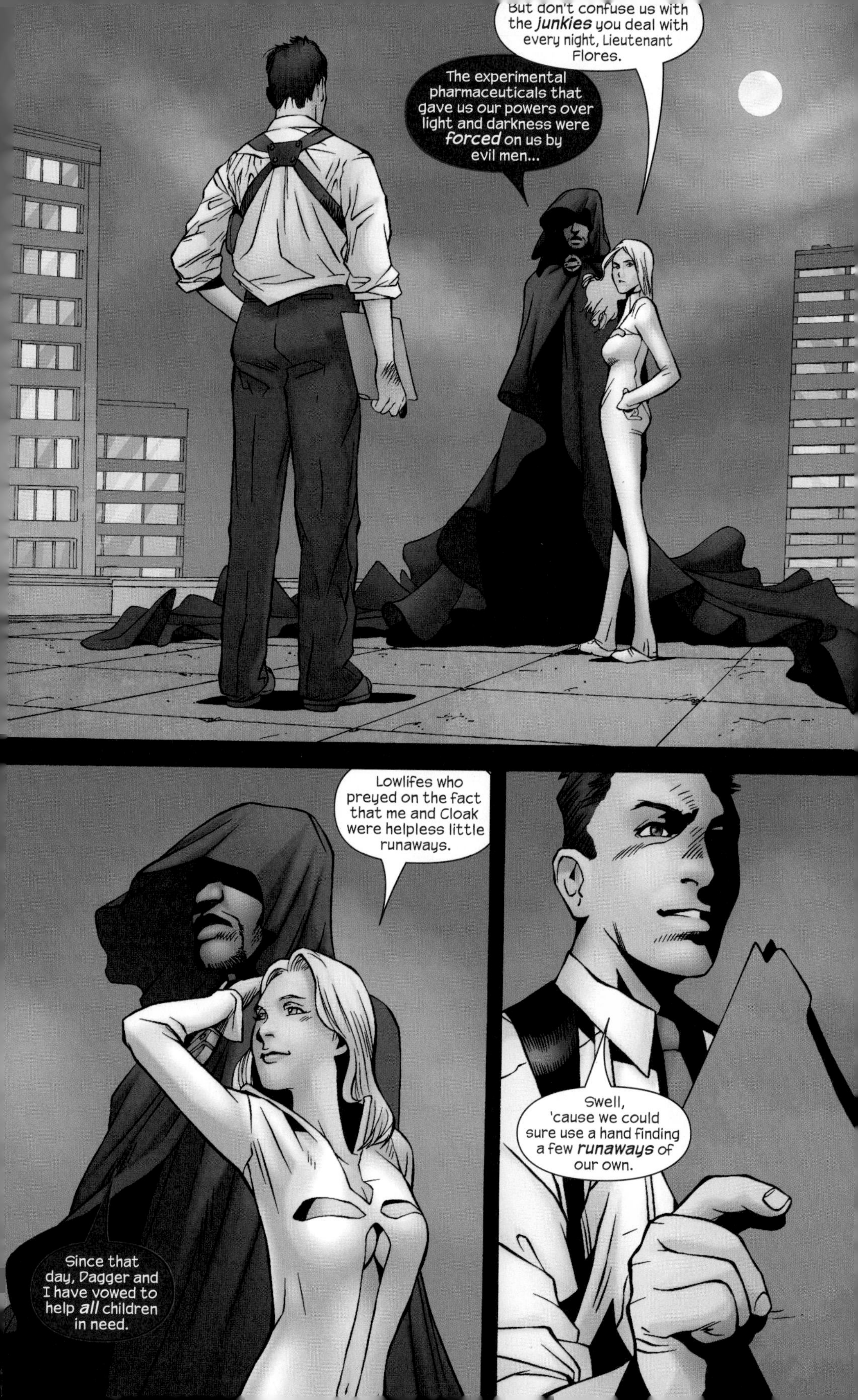
But don't confuse us with the *junkies* you deal with every night, Lieutenant Flores.
The experimental pharmaceuticals that gave us our powers over light and darkness were *forced* on us by evil men...
Lowlifes who preyed on the fact that me and Cloak were helpless little runaways.
Since that day, Dagger and I have vowed to help *all* children in need.
Swell, 'cause we could sure use a hand finding a few *runaways* of our own.

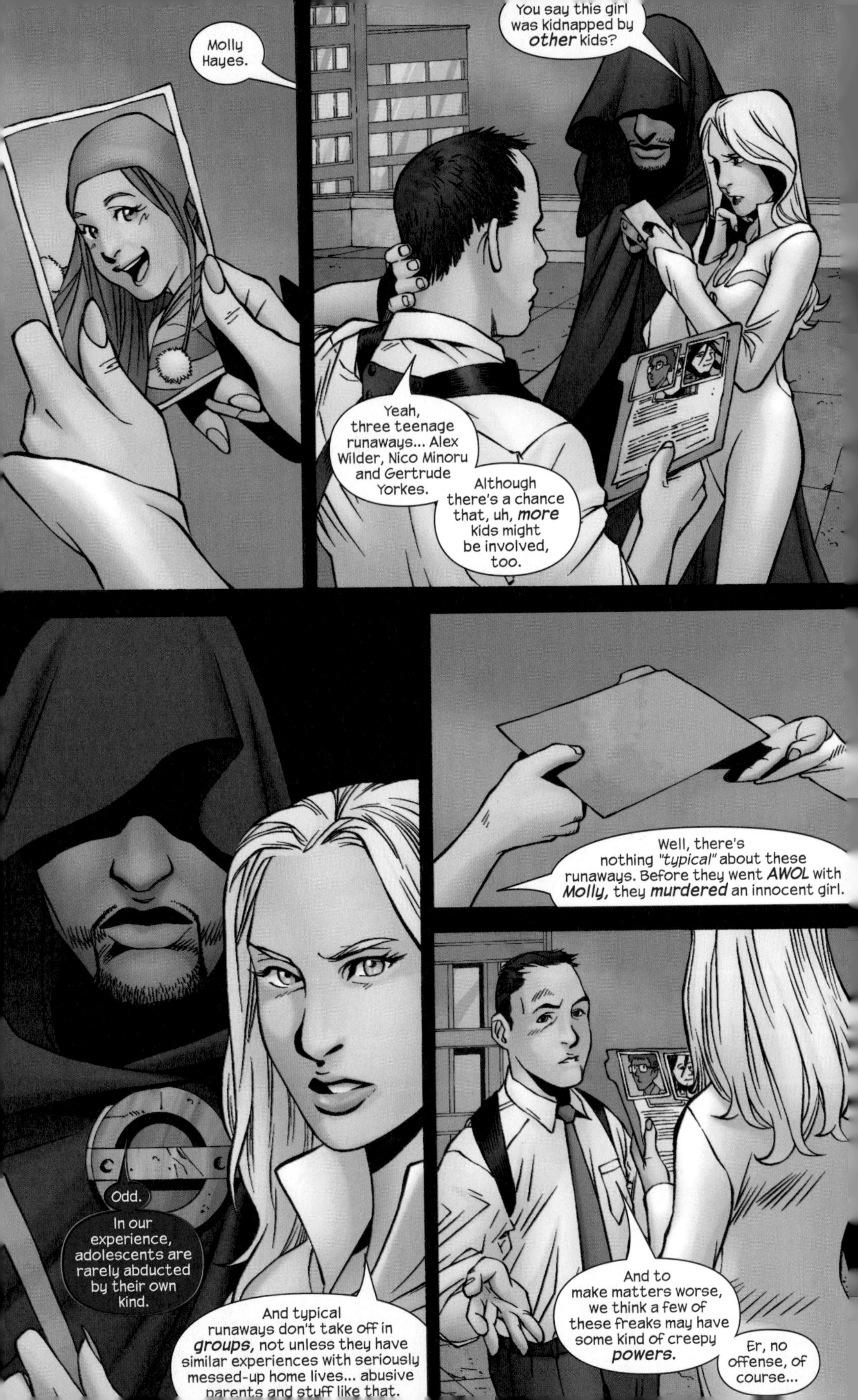
Molly Hayes.
You say this girl was kidnapped by *other* kids?
Yeah, three teenage runaways... Alex Wilder, Nico Minoru and Gertrude Yorkes.
Although there's a chance that, uh, *more* kids might be involved, too.
Odd.
In our experience, adolescents are rarely abducted by their own kind.
And typical runaways don't take off in *groups,* not unless they have similar experiences with seriously messed-up home lives... abusive parents and stuff like that.
Well, there's nothing *"typical"* about these runaways. Before they went *AWOL* with *Molly,* they *murdered* an innocent girl.
And to make matters worse, we think a few of these freaks may have some kind of creepy *powers.*
Er, no offense, of course...

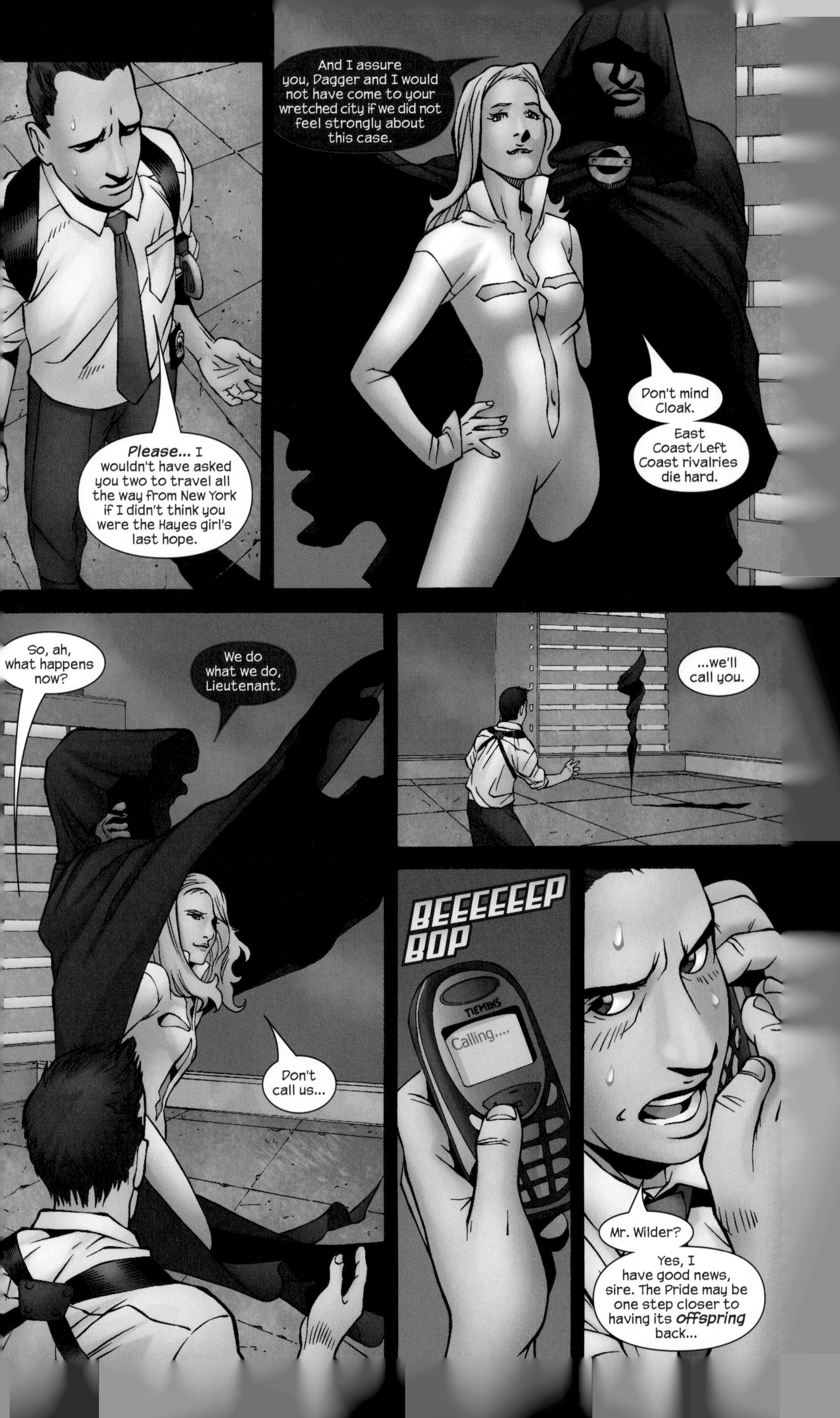
Please... I wouldn't have asked you two to travel all the way from New York if I didn't think you were the Hayes girl's last hope.
And I assure you, Dagger and I would not have come to your wretched city if we did not feel strongly about this case.
Don't mind Cloak.
East Coast/Left Coast rivalries die hard.
So, ah, what happens now?
We do what we do, Lieutenant.
Don't call us...
...we'll call you.
BEEEEEEP BOP
Calling....
Mr. Wilder?
Yes, I have good news, sire. The Pride may be one step closer to having its offspring back...

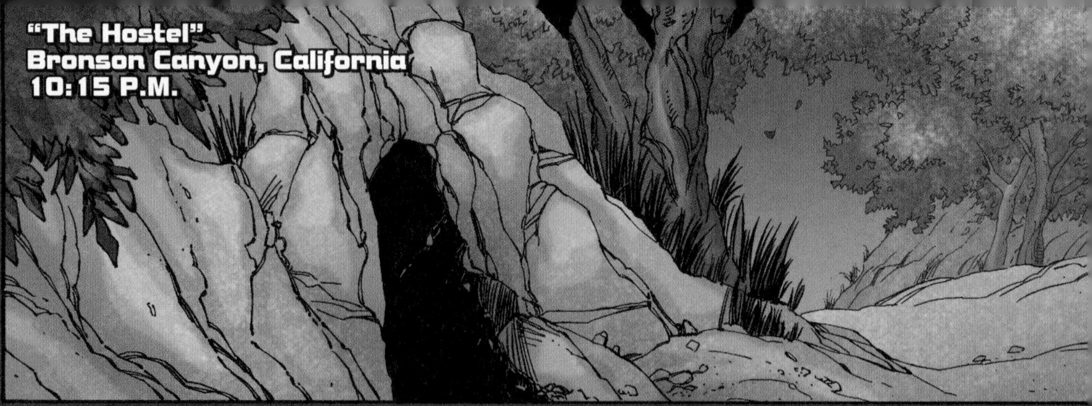
"The Hostel"
Bronson Canyon, California
10:15 P.M.
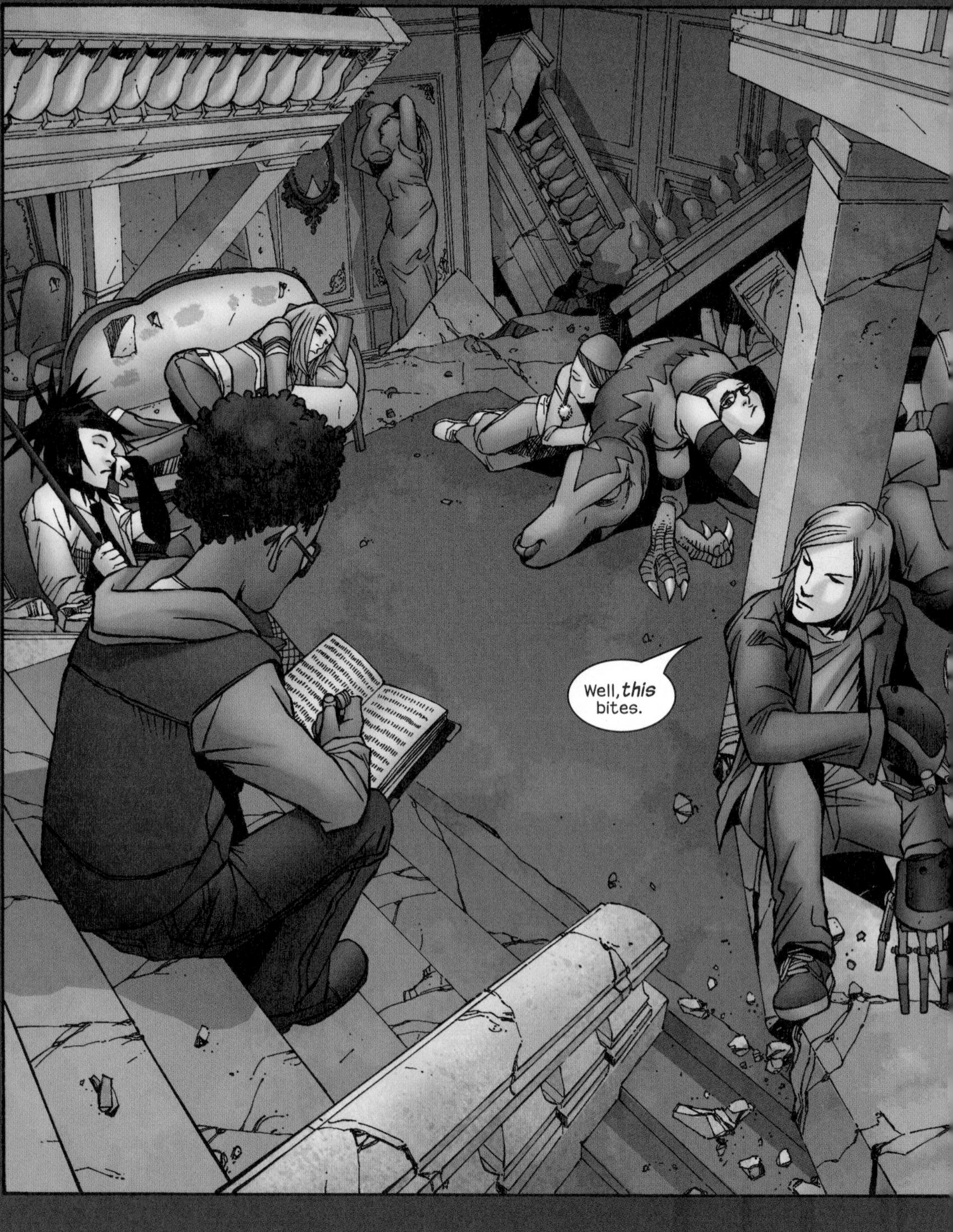
Well, *this* bites.

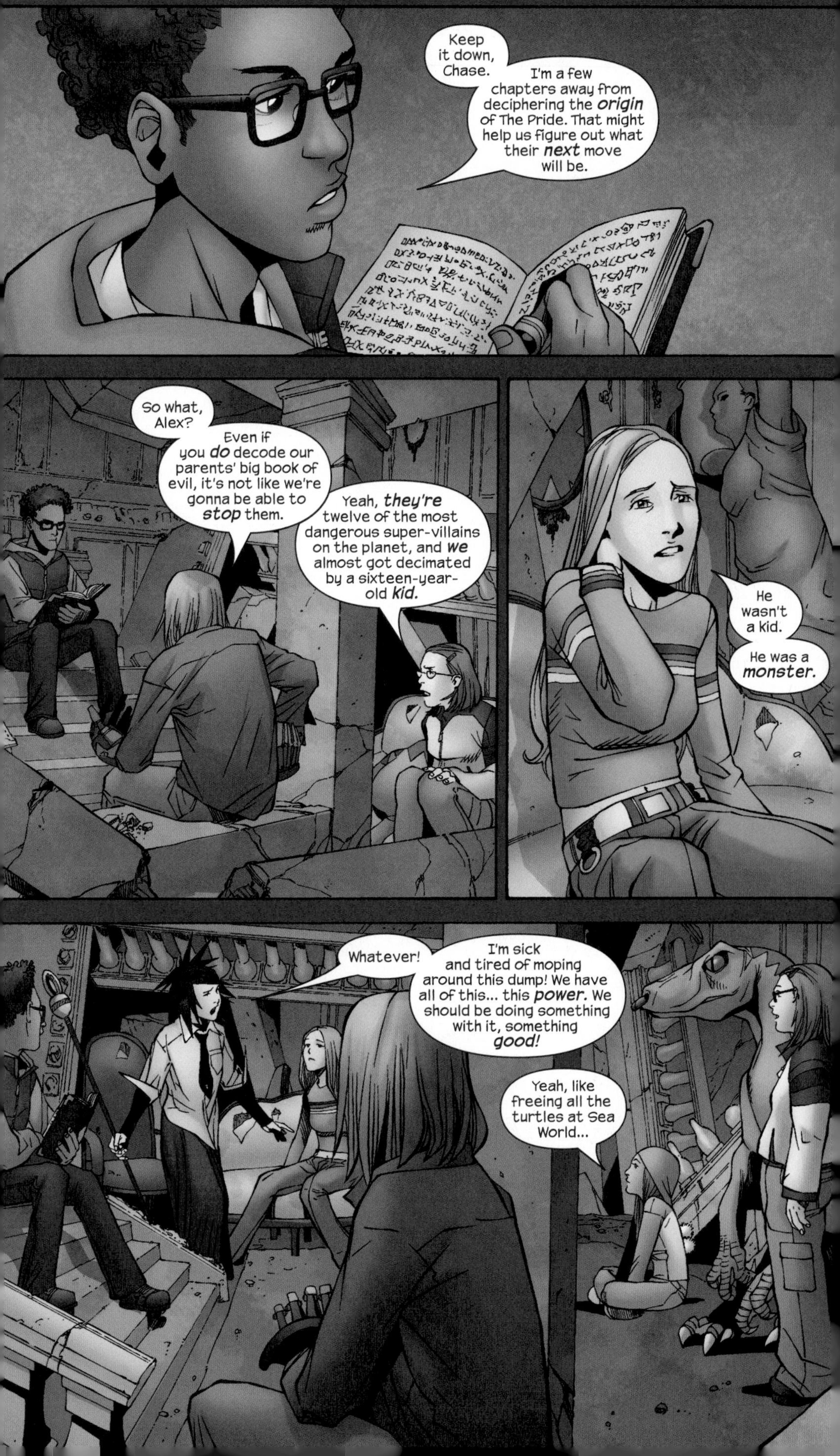
Keep it down, Chase.
I'm a few chapters away from deciphering the origin of The Pride. That might help us figure out what their next move will be.
So what, Alex?
Even if you do decode our parents' big book of evil, it's not like we're gonna be able to stop them.
Yeah, they're twelve of the most dangerous super-villains on the planet, and we almost got decimated by a sixteen-year-old kid.
He wasn't a kid.
He was a monster.
Whatever!
I'm sick and tired of moping around this dump! We have all of this... this power. We should be doing something with it, something good!
Yeah, like freeing all the turtles at Sea World...

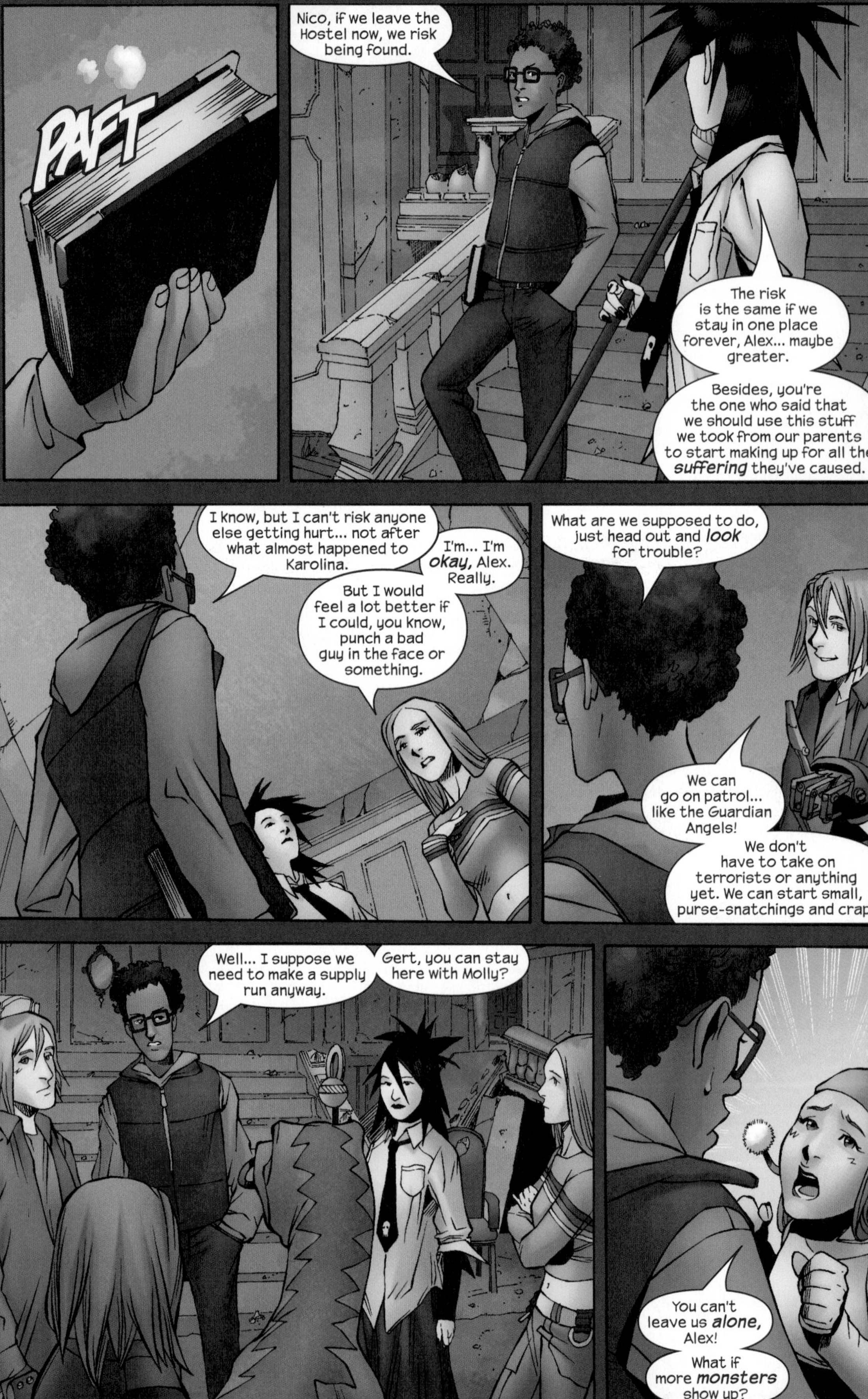
PAFT
Nico, if we leave the Hostel now, we risk being found.
The risk is the same if we stay in one place forever, Alex... maybe greater.
Besides, you're the one who said that we should use this stuff we took from our parents to start making up for all the *suffering* they've caused.
I know, but I can't risk anyone else getting hurt... not after what almost happened to Karolina.
I'm... I'm *okay,* Alex. Really.
But I would feel a lot better if I could, you know, punch a bad guy in the face or something.
What are we supposed to do, just head out and *look* for trouble?
We can go on patrol... like the Guardian Angels!
We don't have to take on terrorists or anything yet. We can start small, purse-snatchings and crap
Well... I suppose we need to make a supply run anyway.
Gert, you can stay here with Molly?
You can't leave us *alone,* Alex!
What if more *monsters* show up?

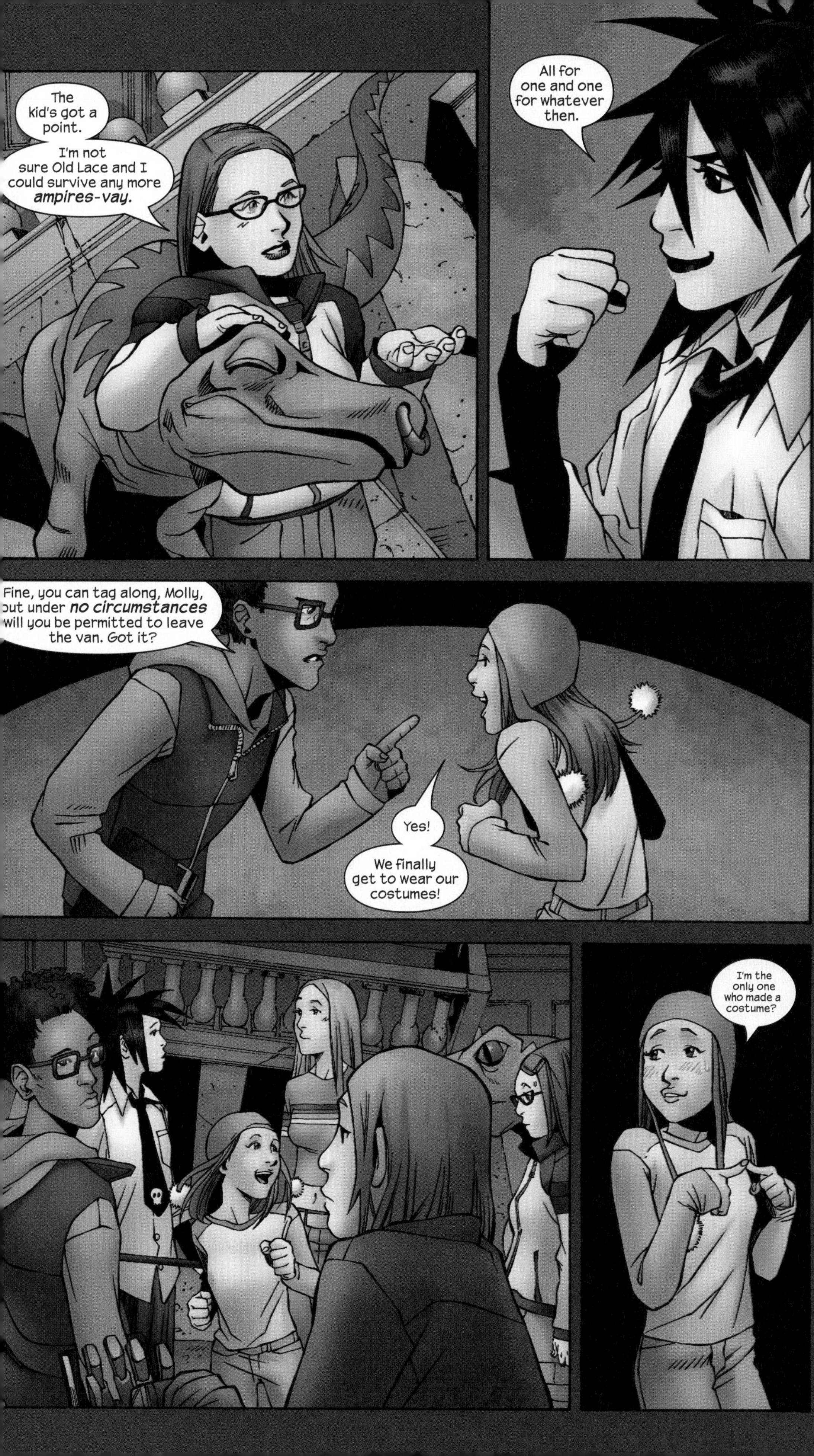
The kid's got a point.
I'm not sure Old Lace and I could survive any more *ampires-vay.*
All for one and one for whatever then.
Fine, you can tag along, Molly, but under *no circumstances* will you be permitted to leave the van. Got it?
Yes!
We finally get to wear our costumes!
I'm the only one who made a costume?

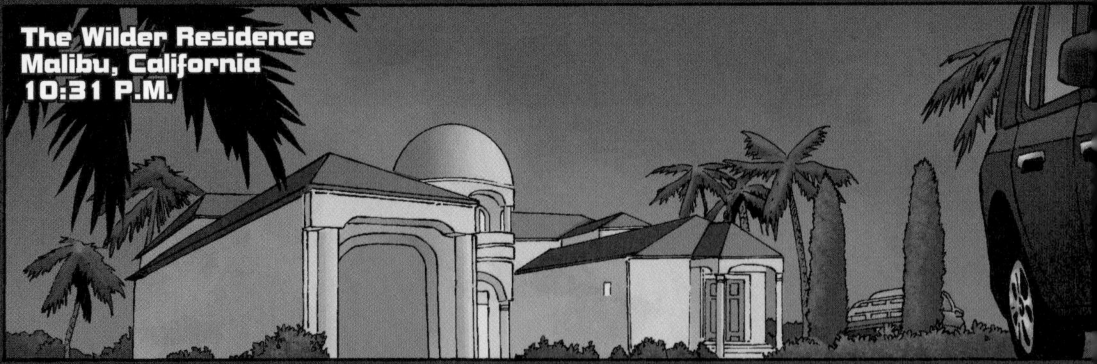
The Wilder Residence
Malibu, California
10:31 P.M.

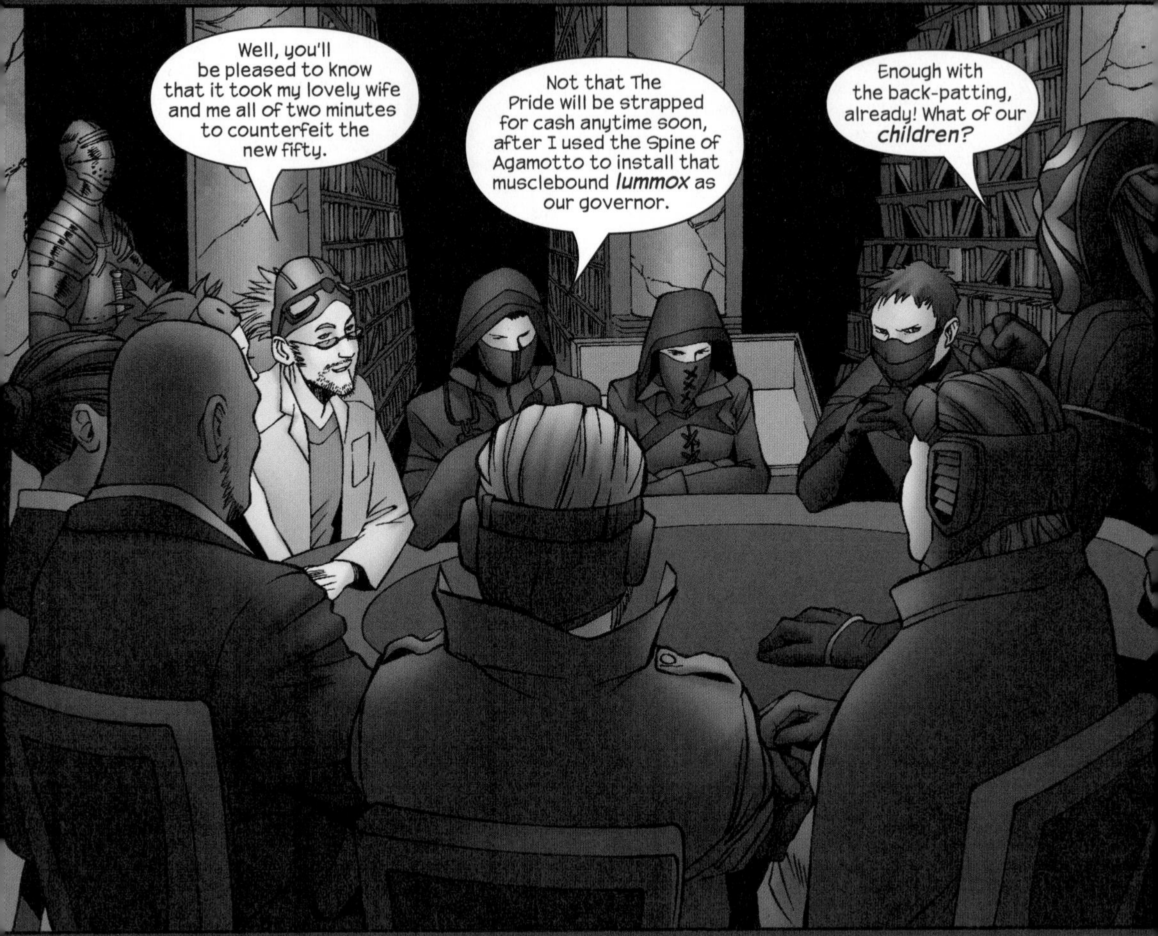
Well, you'll be pleased to know that it took my lovely wife and me all of two minutes to counterfeit the new fifty.
Not that The Pride will be strapped for cash anytime soon, after I used the Spine of Agamotto to install that musclebound *lummox* as our governor.
Enough with the back-patting, already! What of our *children*?

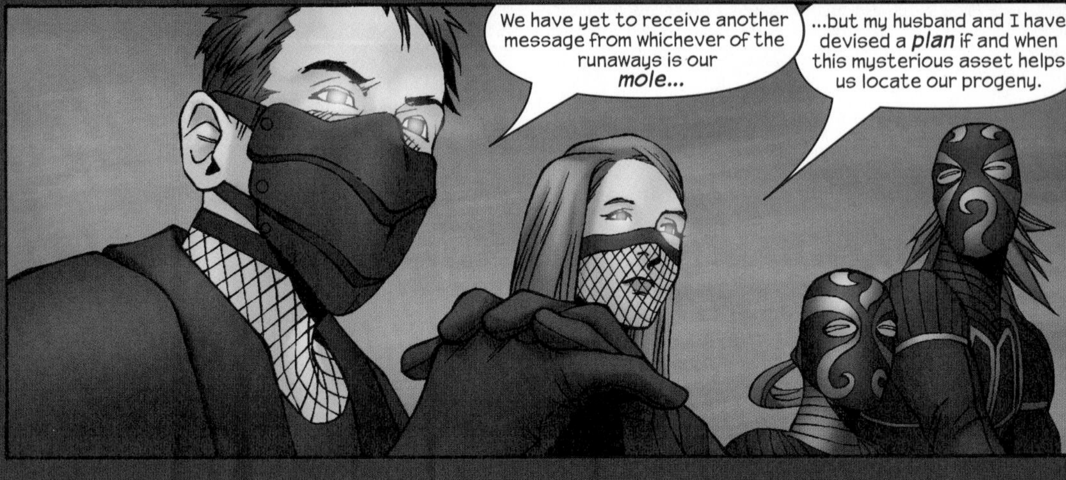
We have yet to receive another message from whichever of the runaways is our *mole*...
...but my husband and I have devised a *plan* if and when this mysterious asset helps us locate our progeny.

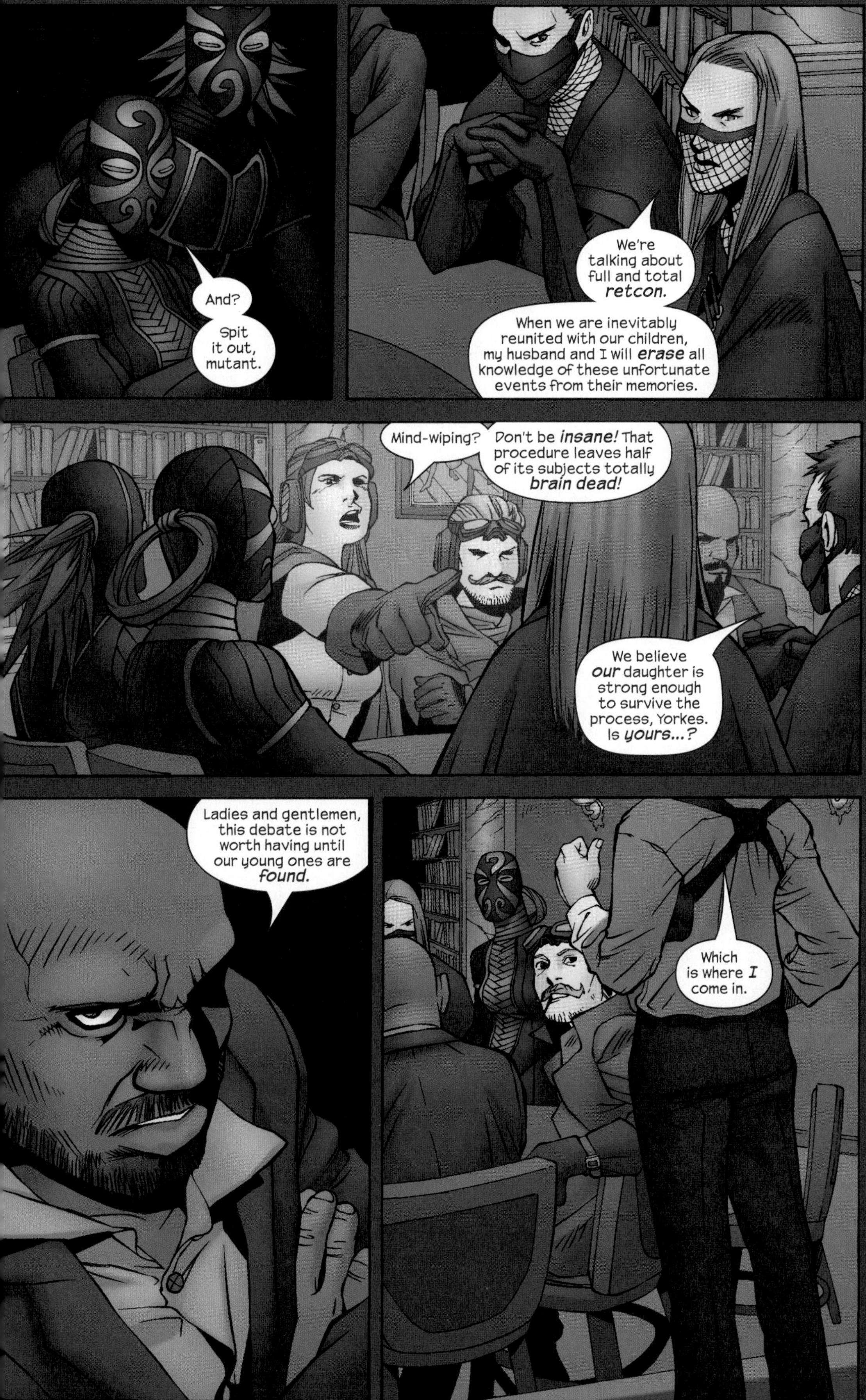
And?
Spit it out, mutant.
We're talking about full and total *retcon.*
When we are inevitably reunited with our children, my husband and I will *erase* all knowledge of these unfortunate events from their memories.
Mind-wiping?
Don't be *insane!* That procedure leaves half of its subjects totally *brain dead!*
We believe *our* daughter is strong enough to survive the process, Yorkes. Is *yours...?*
Ladies and gentlemen, this debate is not worth having until our young ones are *found.*
Which is where *I* come in.

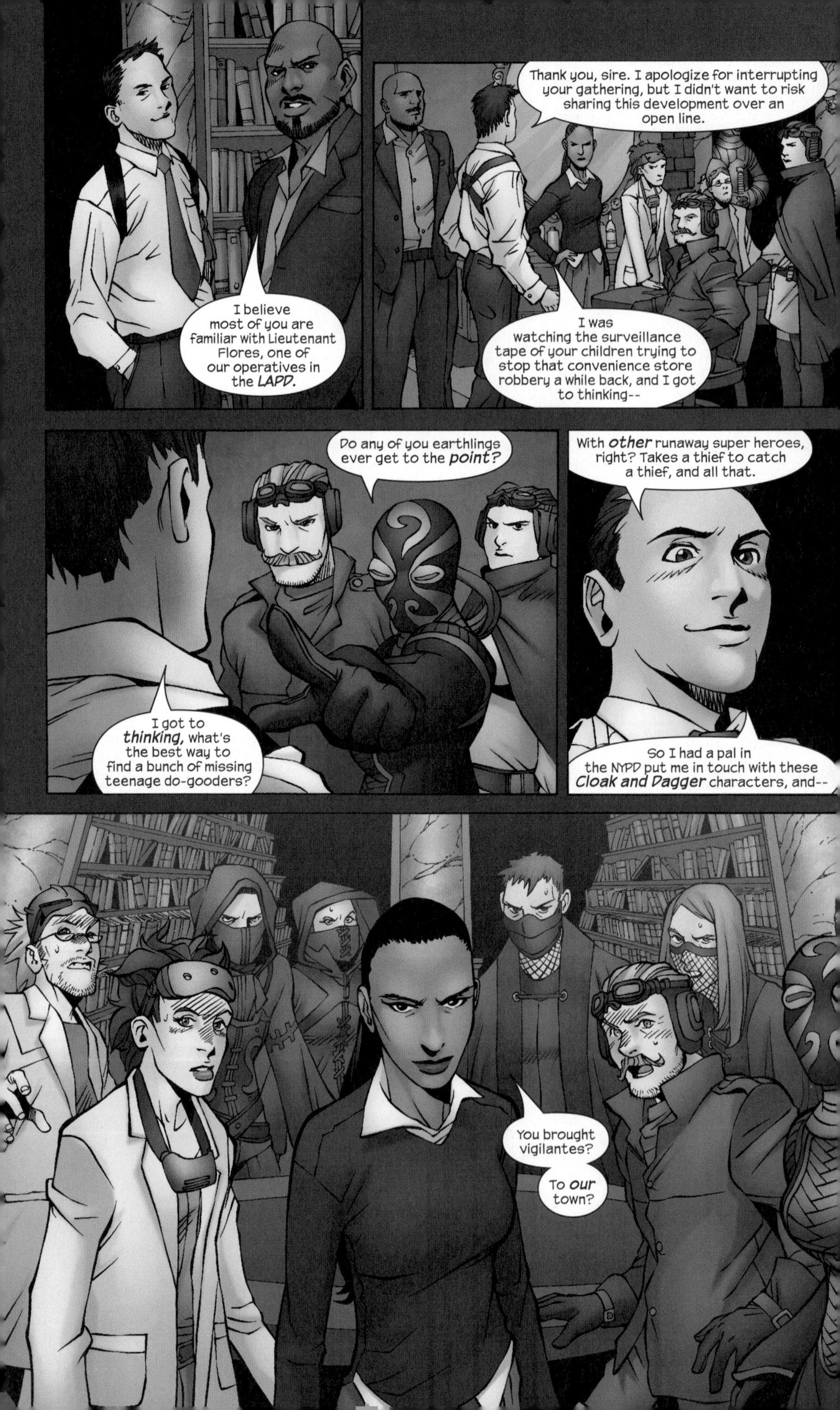
I believe most of you are familiar with Lieutenant Flores, one of our operatives in the LAPD.
Thank you, sire. I apologize for interrupting your gathering, but I didn't want to risk sharing this development over an open line.
I was watching the surveillance tape of your children trying to stop that convenience store robbery a while back, and I got to thinking--
Do any of you earthlings ever get to the point?
I got to thinking, what's the best way to find a bunch of missing teenage do-gooders?
With other runaway super heroes, right? Takes a thief to catch a thief, and all that.
So I had a pal in the NYPD put me in touch with these Cloak and Dagger characters, and--
You brought vigilantes?
To our town?

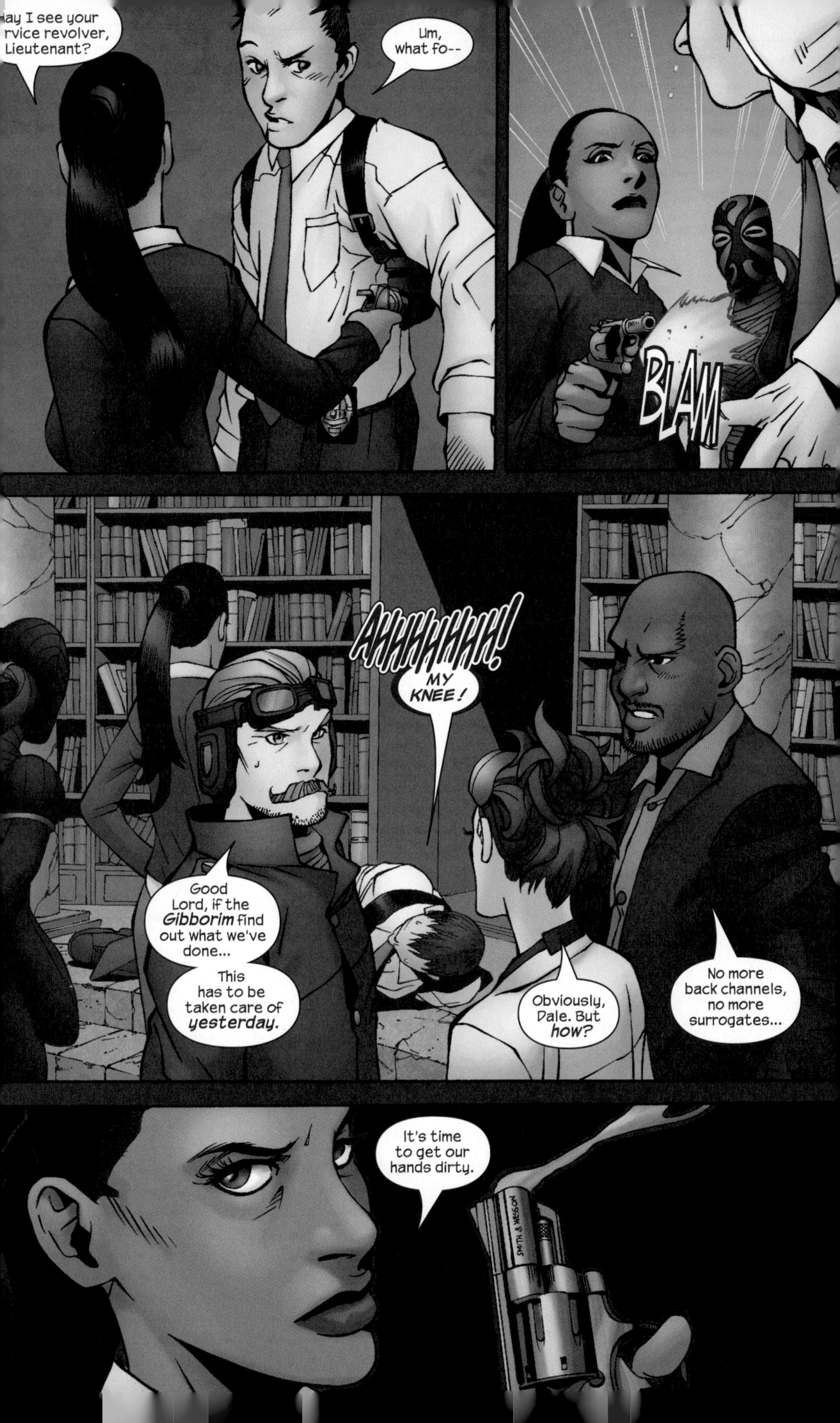
ay I see your
rvice revolver,
Lieutenant?
Um,
what fo--
BLAM
AHHHHHHH!
MY KNEE!
Good Lord, if the Gibborim find out what we've done...
This has to be taken care of yesterday.
Obviously, Dale. But how?
No more back channels, no more surrogates...
It's time to get our hands dirty.
SMITH & WESSON

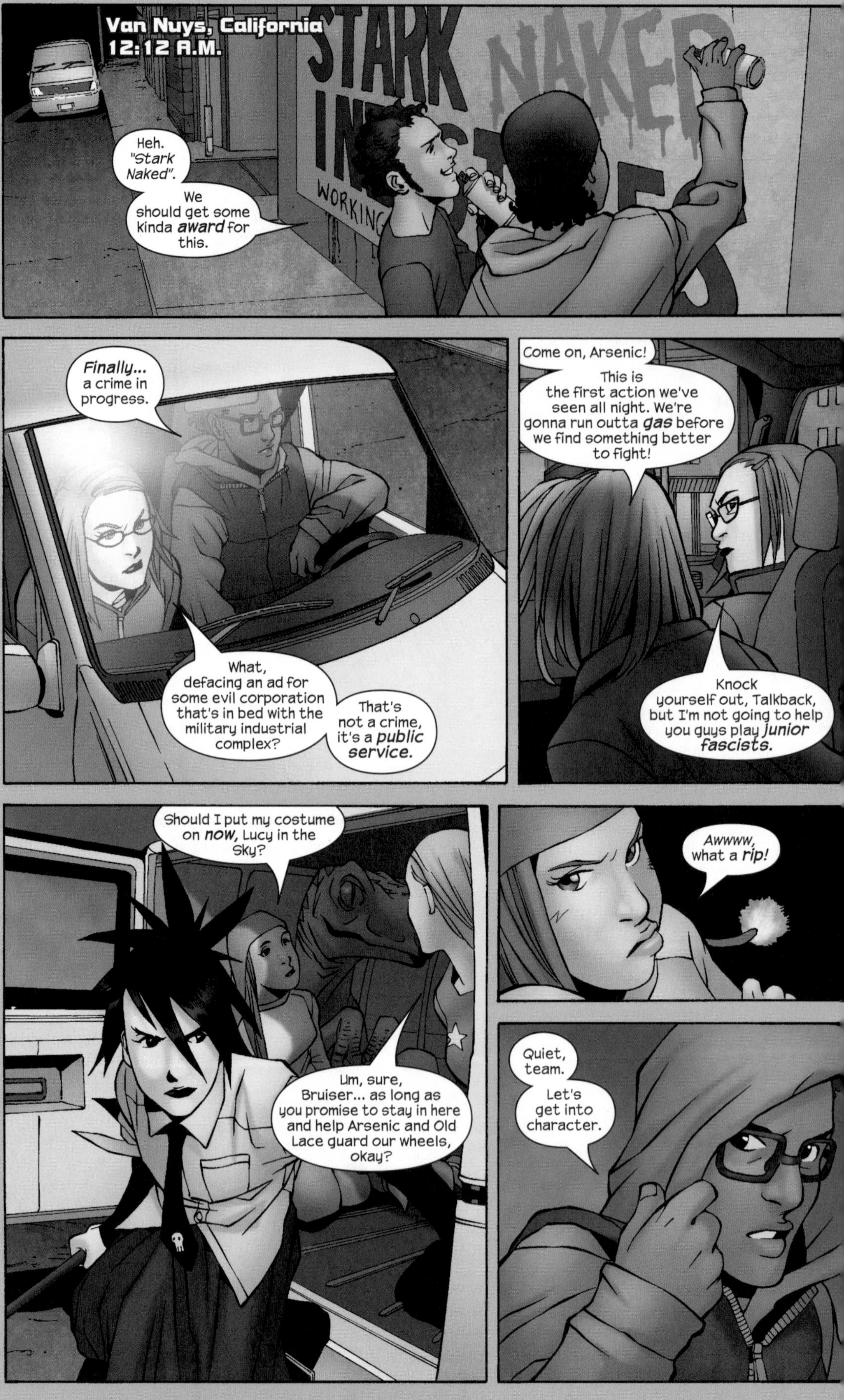
Van Nuys, California
12:12 A.M.
STARK NAKED IN
WORKING
Heh. "Stark Naked".
We should get some kinda *award* for this.
Finally... a crime in progress.
What, defacing an ad for some evil corporation that's in bed with the military industrial complex?
That's not a crime, it's a *public service.*
Come on, Arsenic!
This is the first action we've seen all night. We're gonna run outta *gas* before we find something better to fight!
Knock yourself out, Talkback, but I'm not going to help you guys play *junior fascists.*
Should I put my costume on *now,* Lucy in the Sky?
Um, sure, Bruiser... as long as you promise to stay in here and help Arsenic and Old Lace guard our wheels, okay?
Awwww, what a *rip!*
Quiet, team.
Let's get into character.

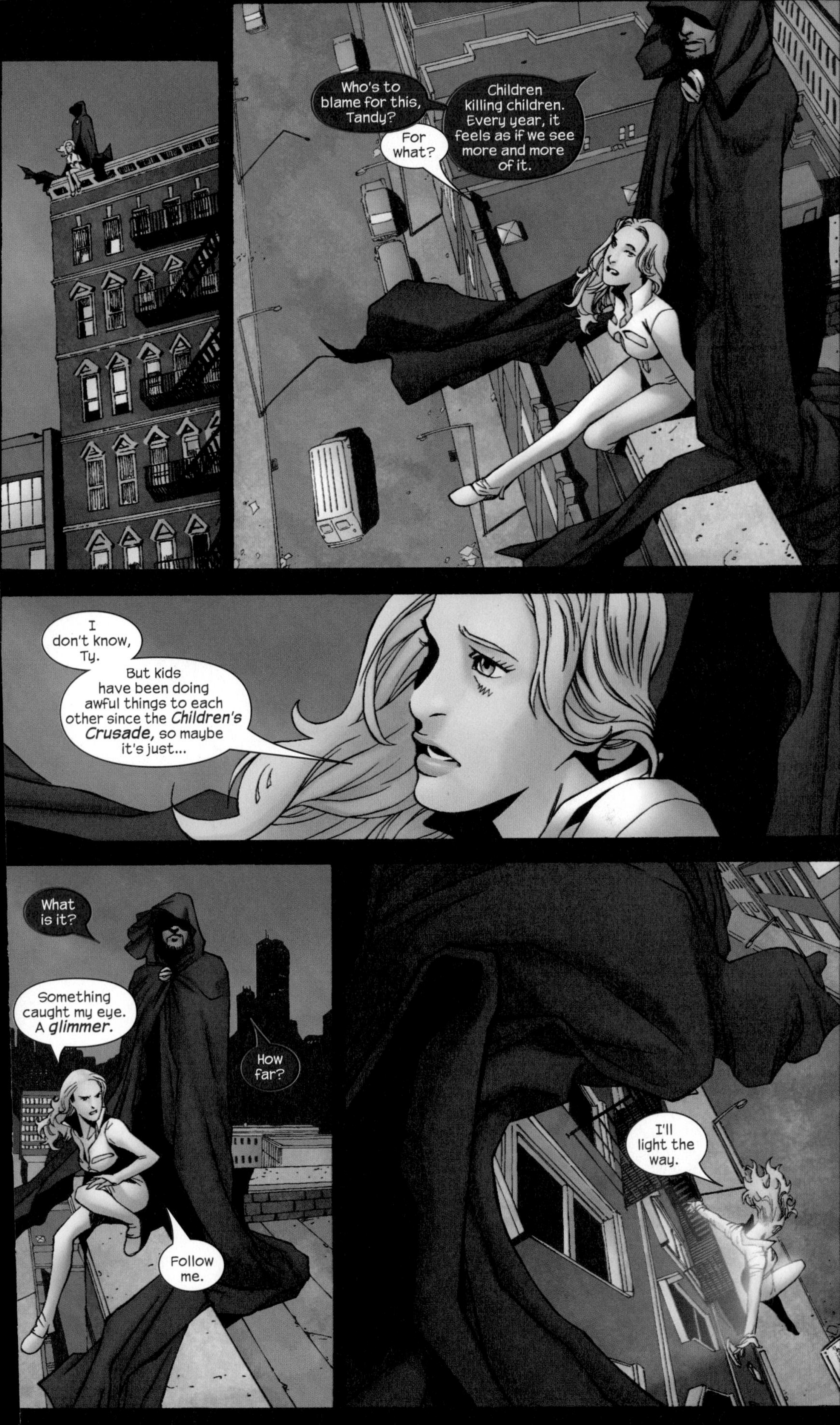
Who's to blame for this, Tandy?
Children killing children. Every year, it feels as if we see more and more of it.
For what?
I don't know, Ty.
But kids have been doing awful things to each other since the *Children's Crusade,* so maybe it's just...
What is it?
Something caught my eye. A *glimmer.*
How far?
Follow me.
I'll light the way.

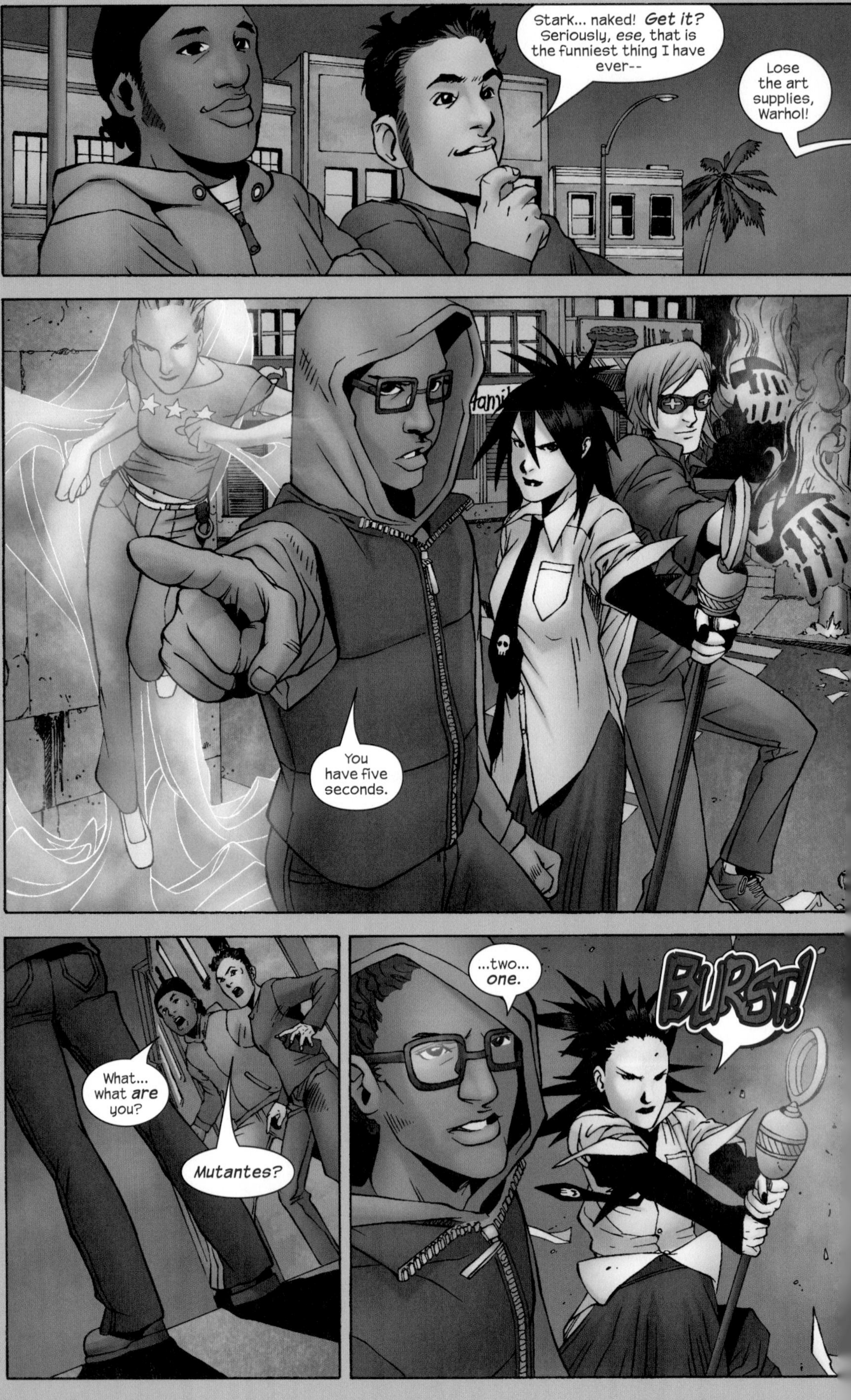
Stark... naked! Get it? Seriously, ese, that is the funniest thing I have ever--
Lose the art supplies, Warhol!
You have five seconds.
What... what are you?
Mutantes?
...two... one.
BURST!

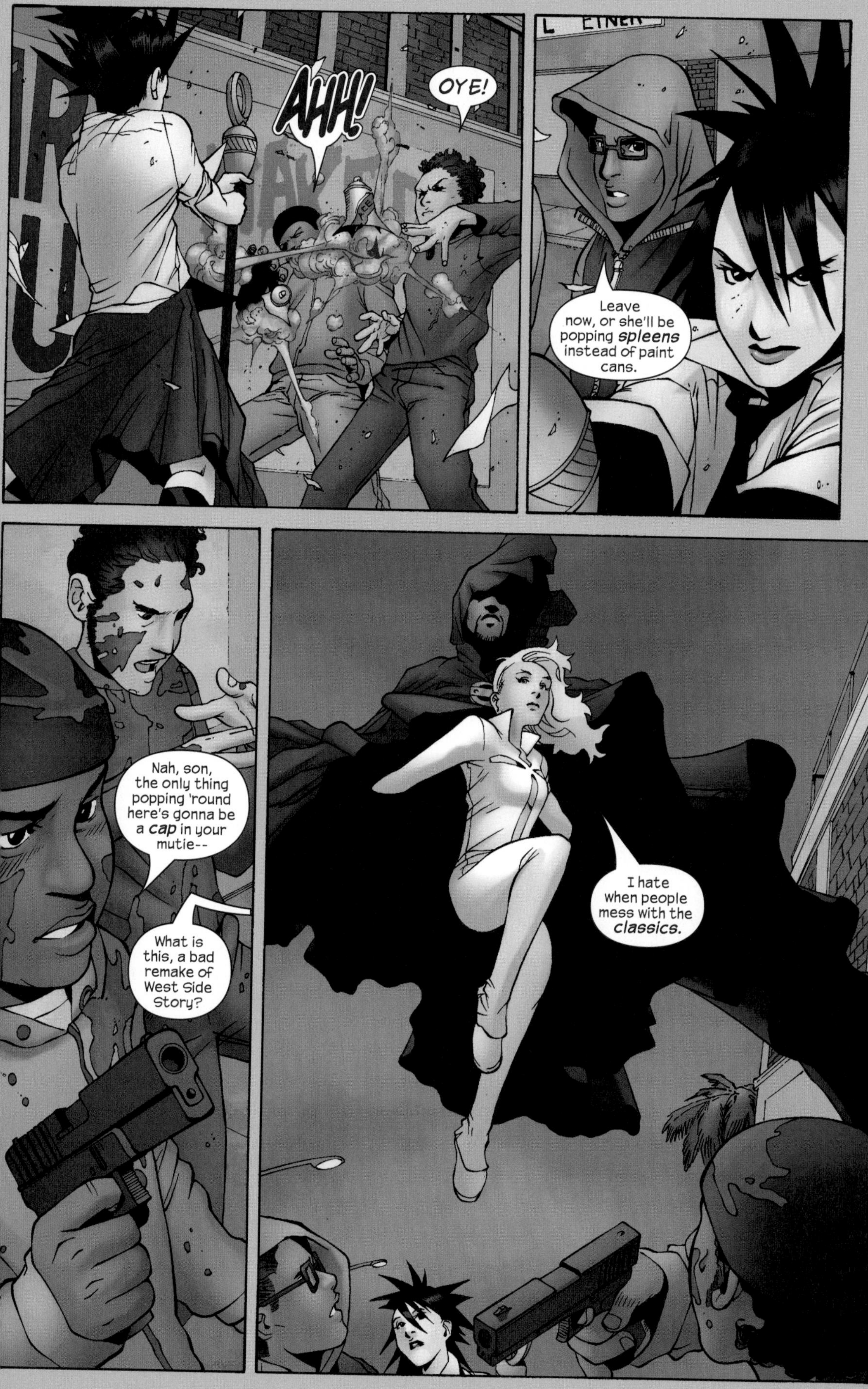
AHH!
OYE!
Leave now, or she'll be popping spleens instead of paint cans.
Nah, son, the only thing popping 'round here's gonna be a cap in your mutie--
What is this, a bad remake of West Side Story?
I hate when people mess with the classics.

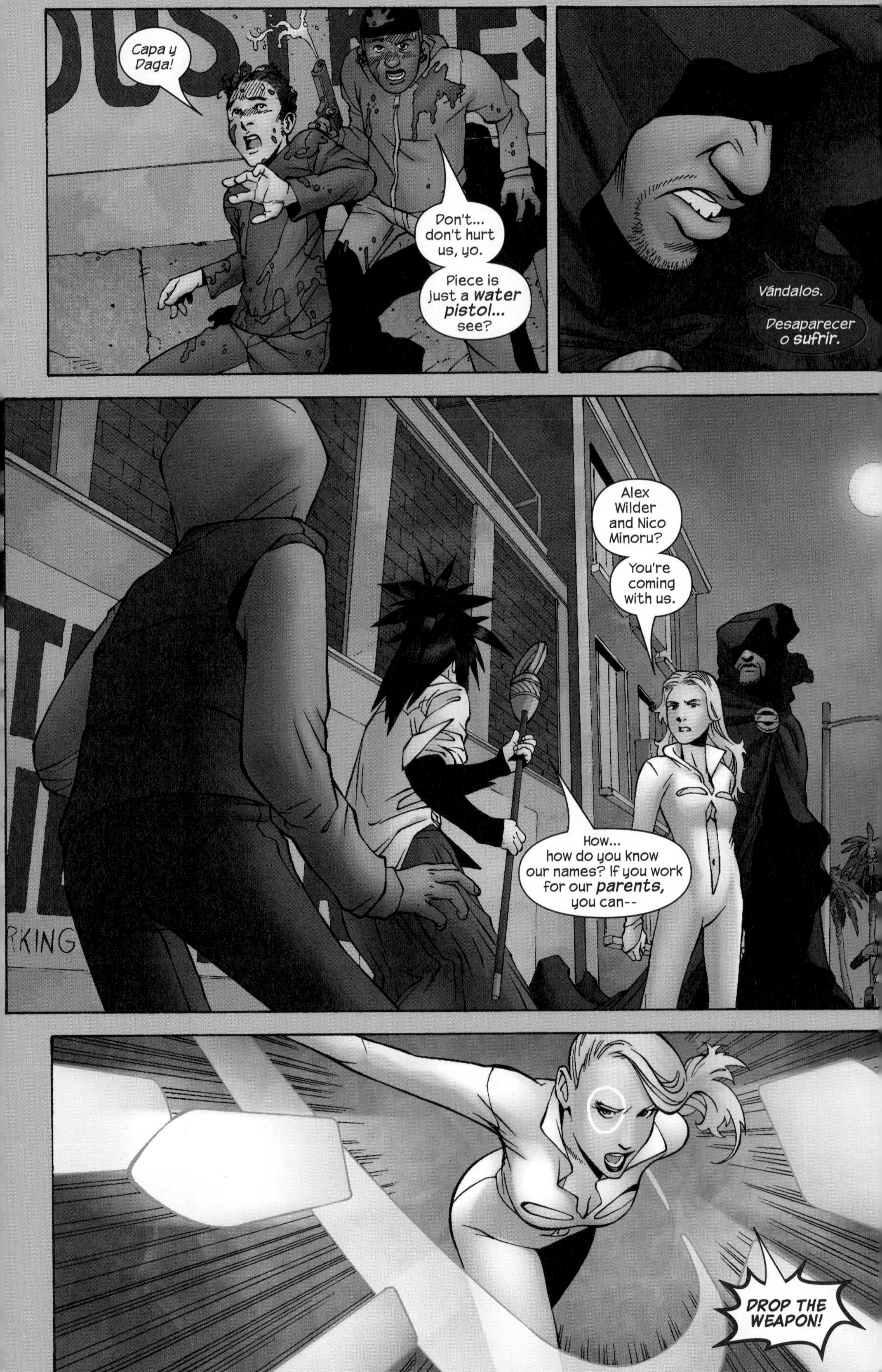
Capa y Daga!
Don't... don't hurt us, yo.
Piece is just a *water pistol...* see?
Vándalos.
Desaparecer o *sufrir.*
Alex Wilder and Nico Minoru?
You're coming with us.
How... how do you know our names? If you work for our *parents,* you can--
RKING
DROP THE WEAPON!

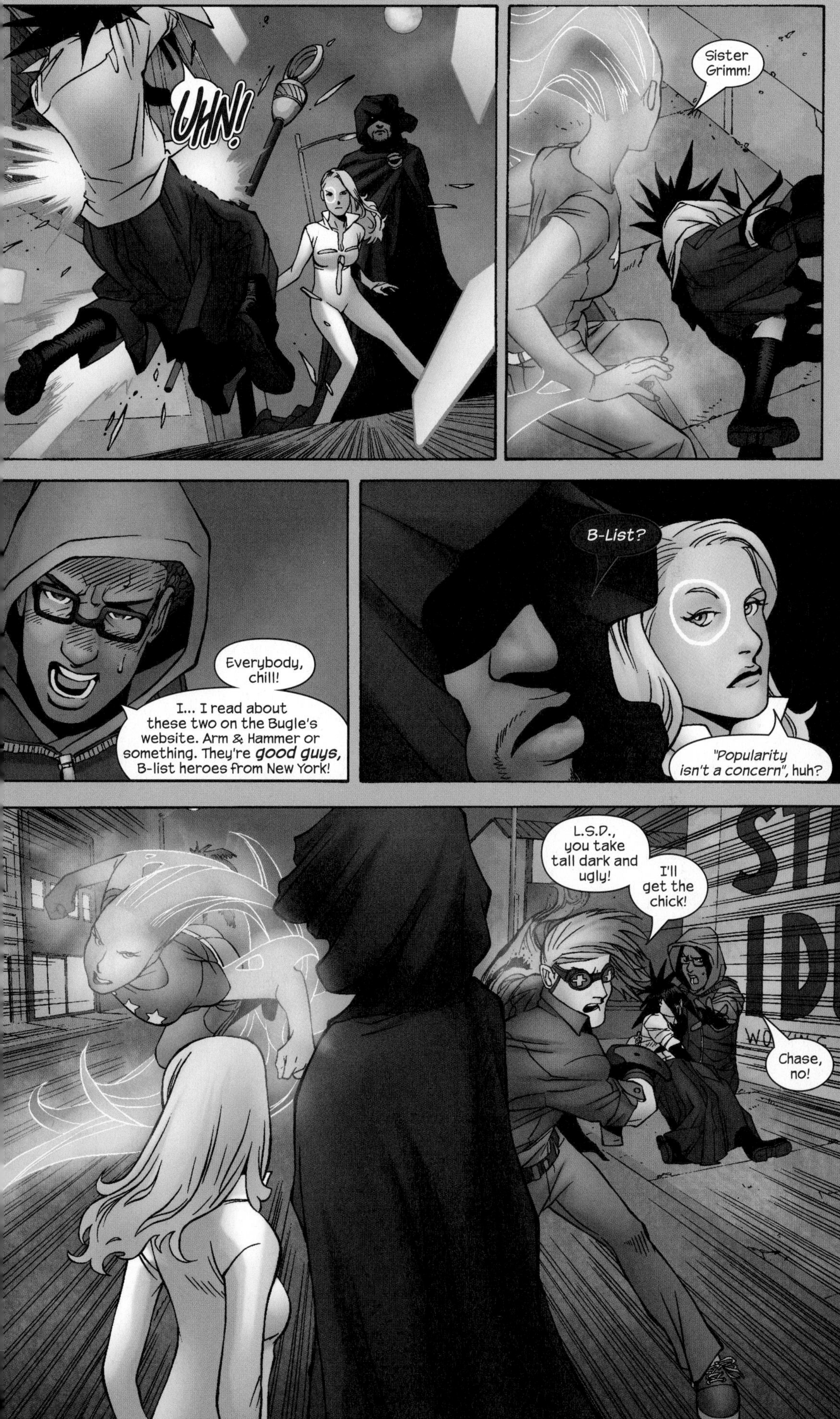
UHN!
Sister Grimm!
Everybody, chill!
I... I read about these two on the Bugle's website. Arm & Hammer or something. They're **good guys**, B-list heroes from New York!
B-List?
"Popularity isn't a concern", huh?
L.S.D., you take tall dark and ugly!
I'll get the chick!
Chase, no!

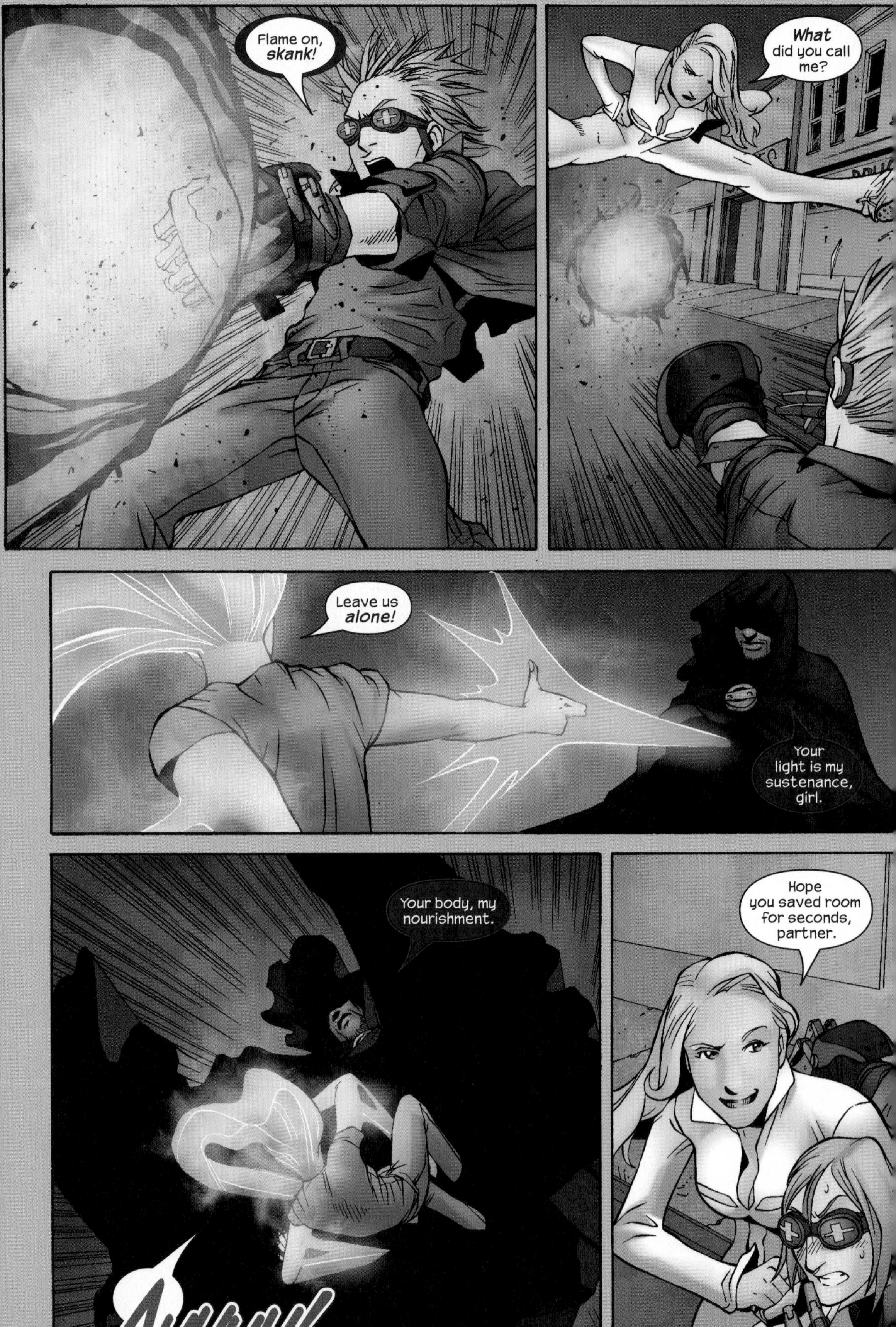

Flame on, **skank!**
What did you call me?
Leave us ***alone!***
Your light is my sustenance, girl.
Your body, my nourishment.
AHHHH!
Hope you saved room for seconds, partner.

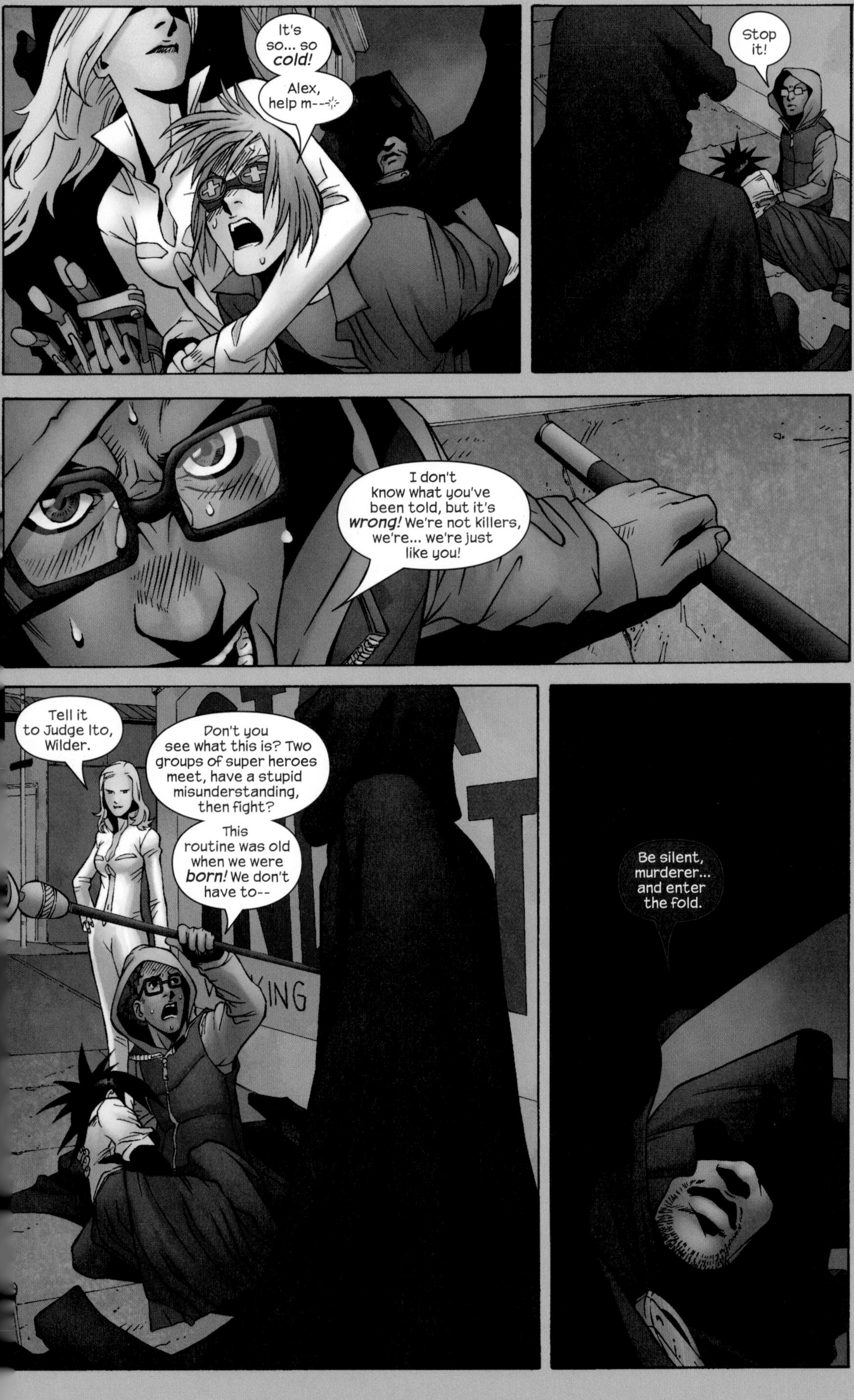
It's so... so *cold!*
Alex, help m--
Stop it!
I don't know what you've been told, but it's *wrong!* We're not killers, we're... we're just like you!
Tell it to Judge Ito, Wilder.
Don't you see what this is? Two groups of super heroes meet, have a stupid misunderstanding, then fight?
This routine was old when we were *born!* We don't have to--
ING
Be silent, murderer... and enter the fold.

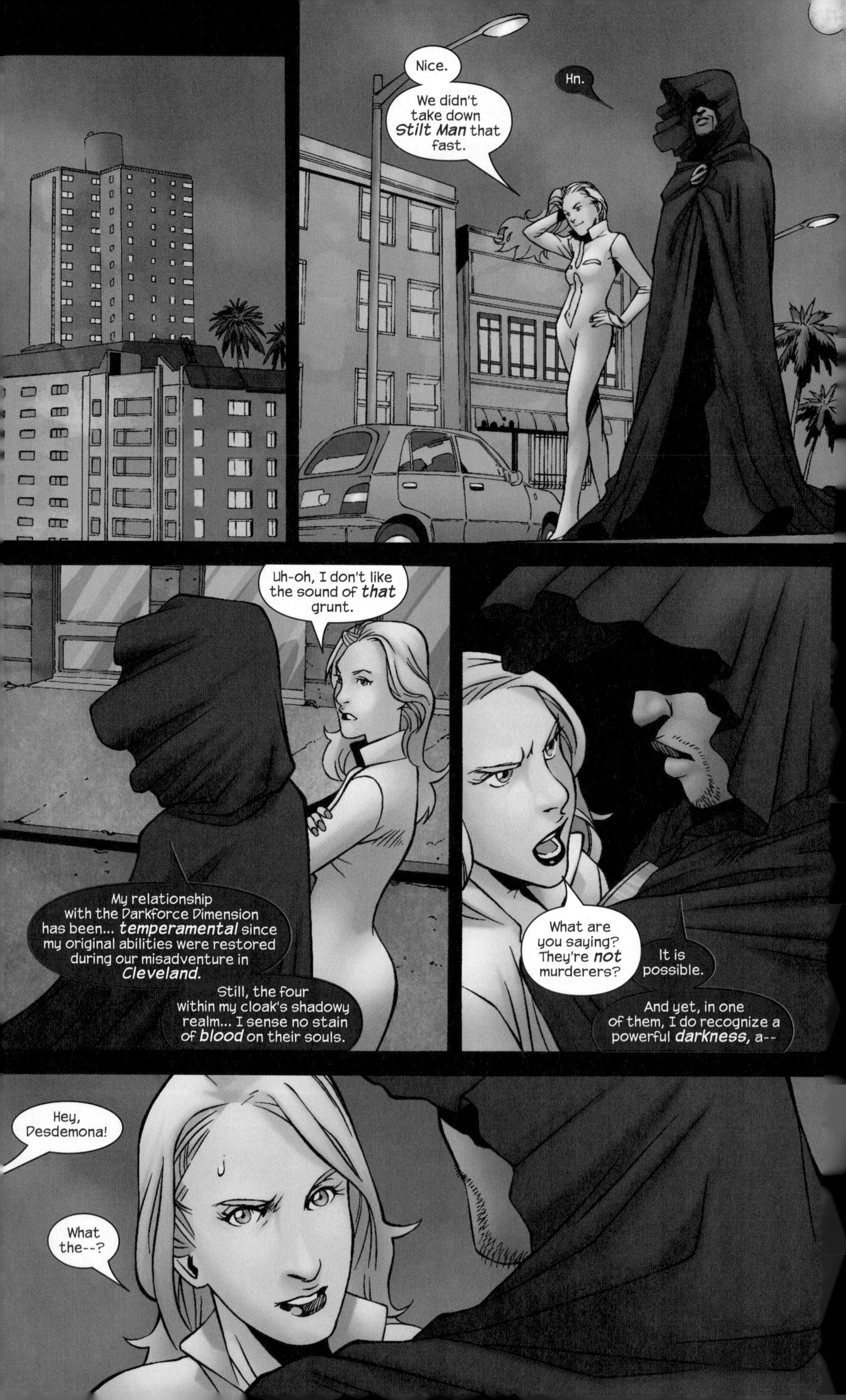
Nice.
We didn't take down Stilt Man that fast.
Hn.
Uh-oh, I don't like the sound of that grunt.
My relationship with the Darkforce Dimension has been... temperamental since my original abilities were restored during our misadventure in Cleveland.
Still, the four within my cloak's shadowy realm... I sense no stain of blood on their souls.
What are you saying? They're not murderers?
It is possible.
And yet, in one of them, I do recognize a powerful darkness, a--
Hey, Desdemona!
What the--?

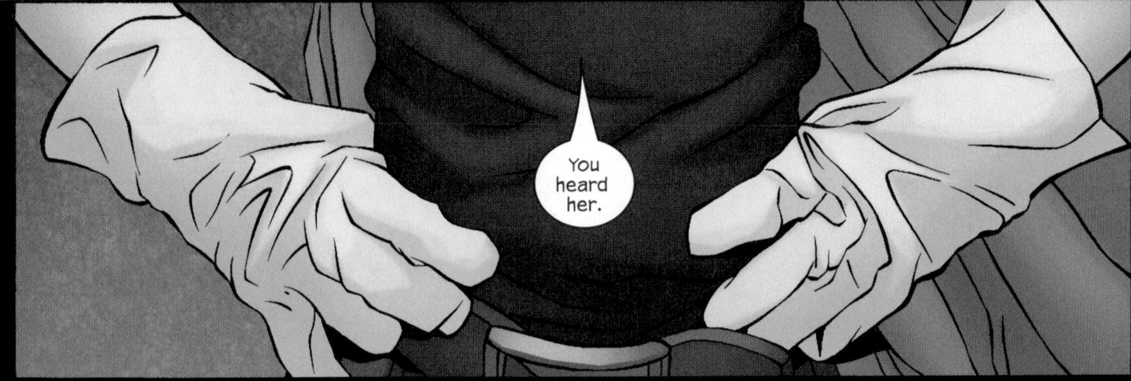
You heard her.

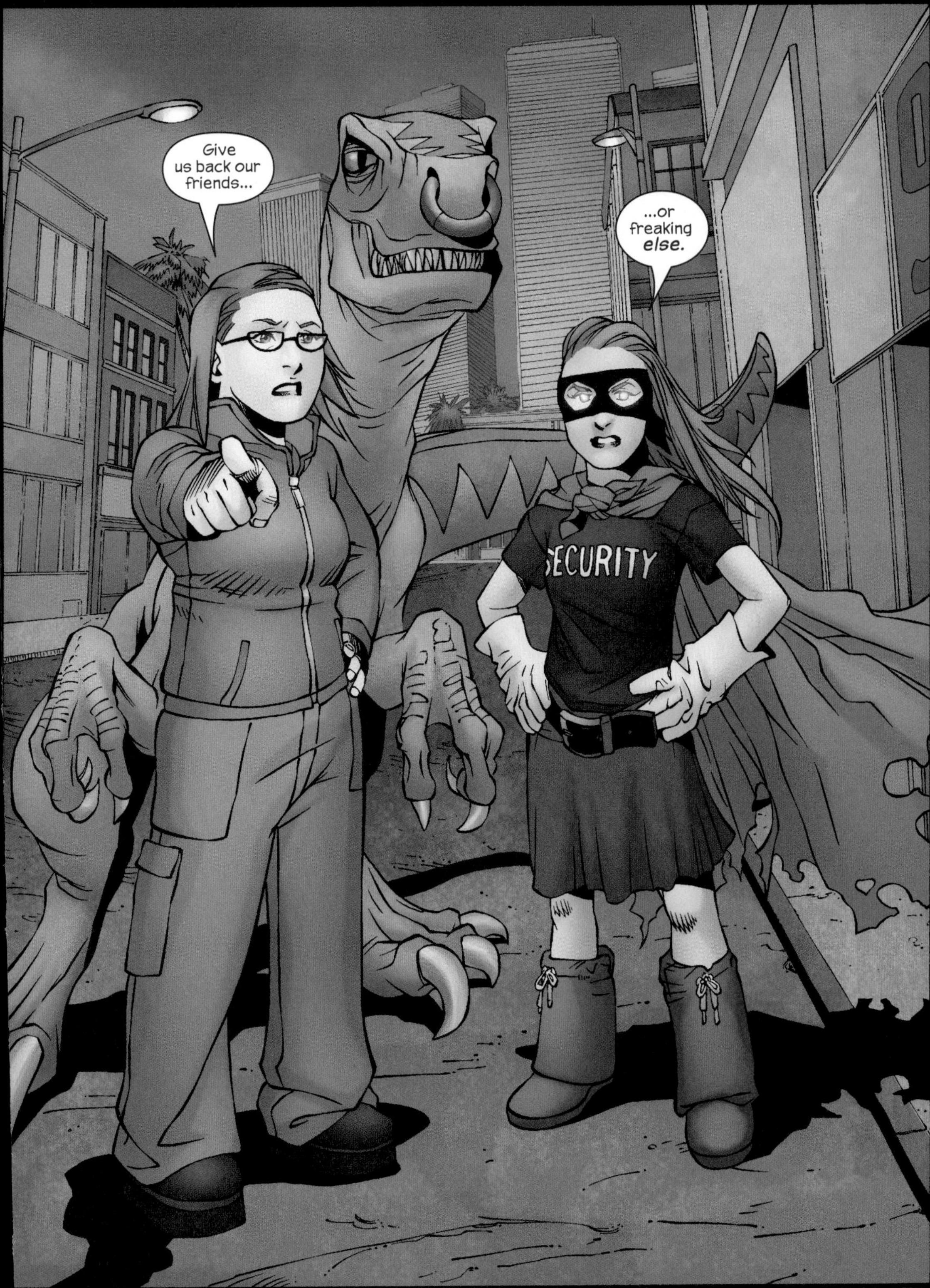
Give us back our friends...
...or freaking *else.*
SECURITY

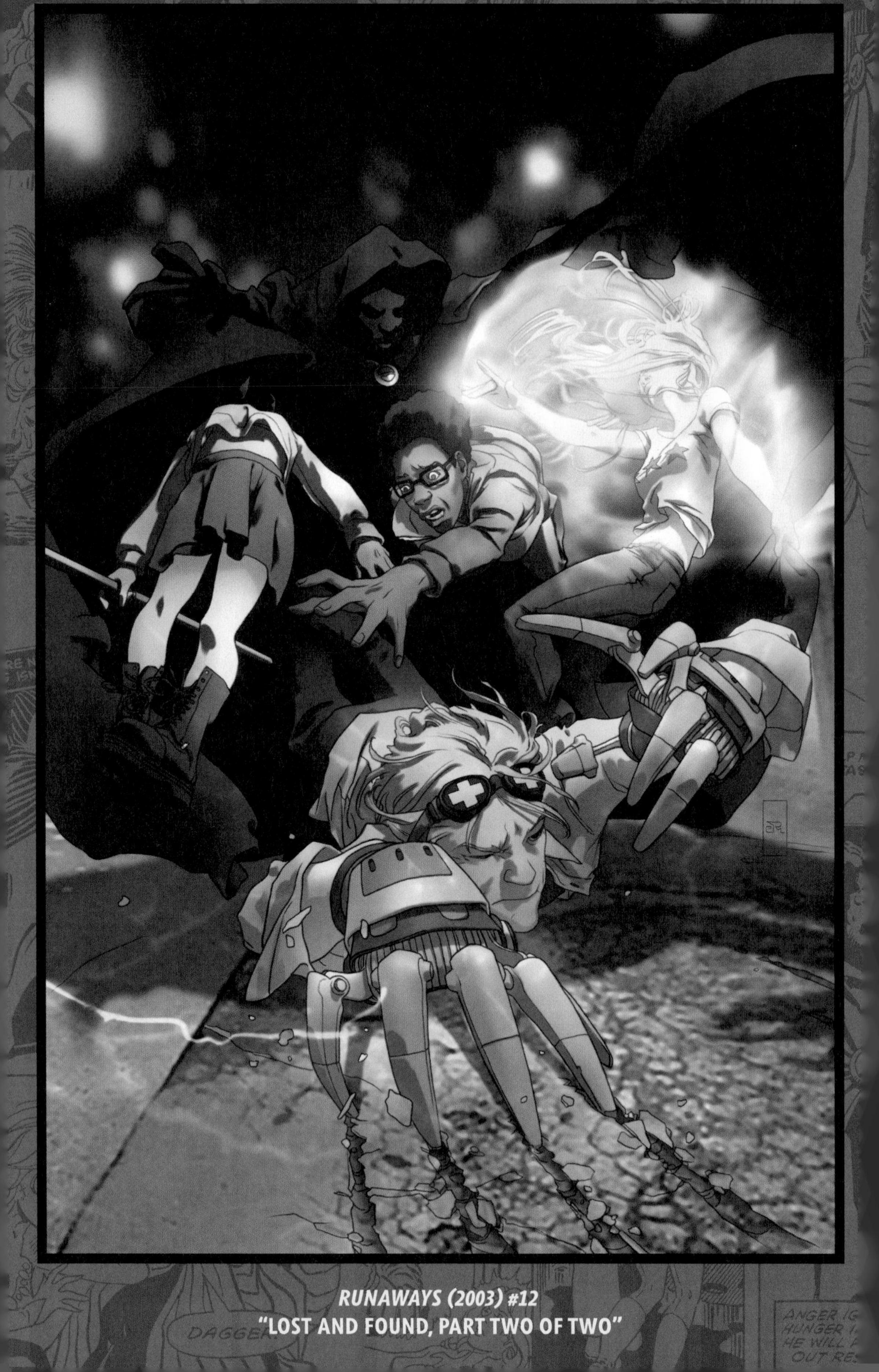

***RUNAWAYS* (2003) #12**
"LOST AND FOUND, PART TWO OF TWO"

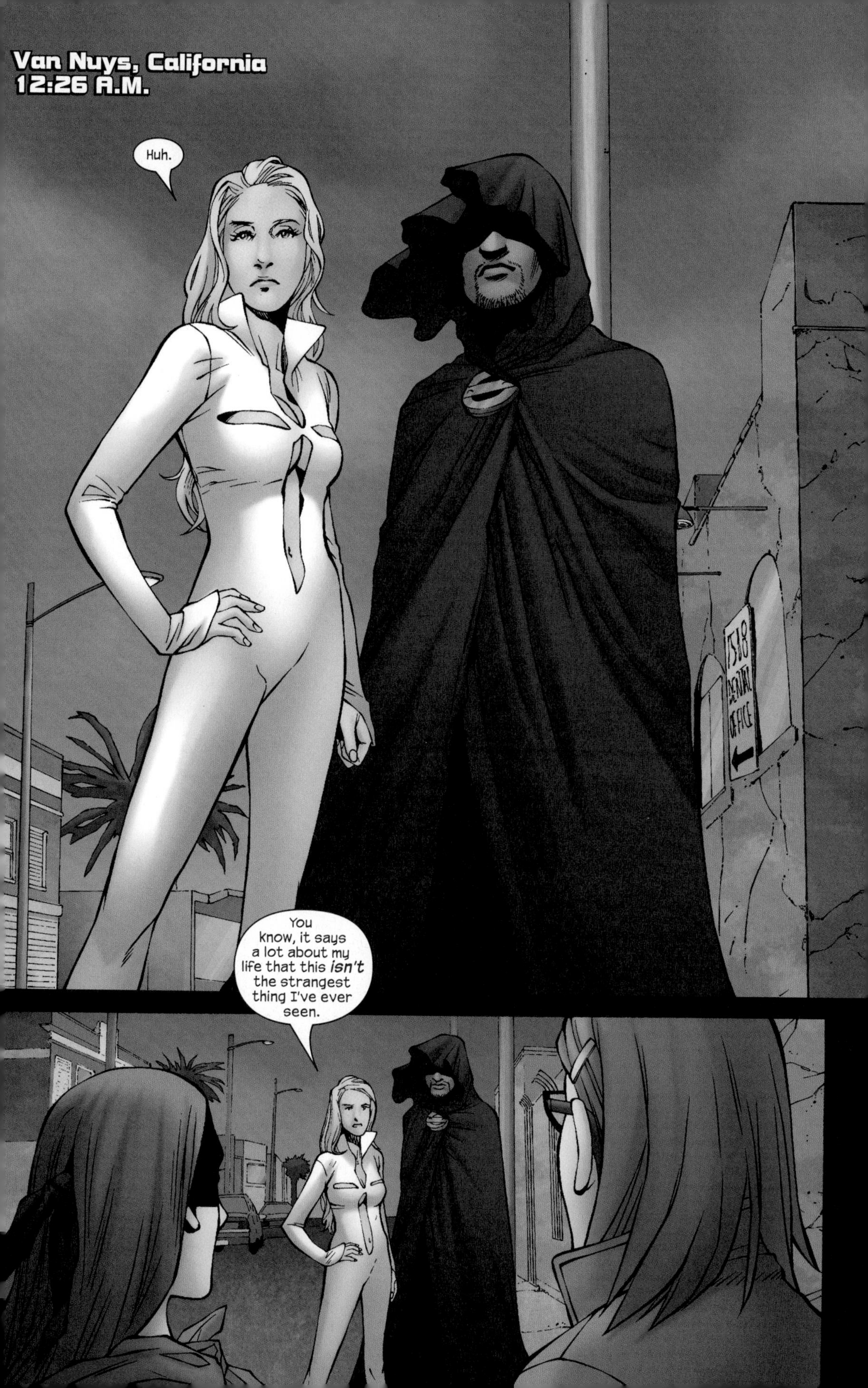
Van Nuys, California
12:26 A.M.
Huh.
You know, it says a lot about my life that this *isn't* the strangest thing I've ever seen.
1518 DENTAL OFFICE

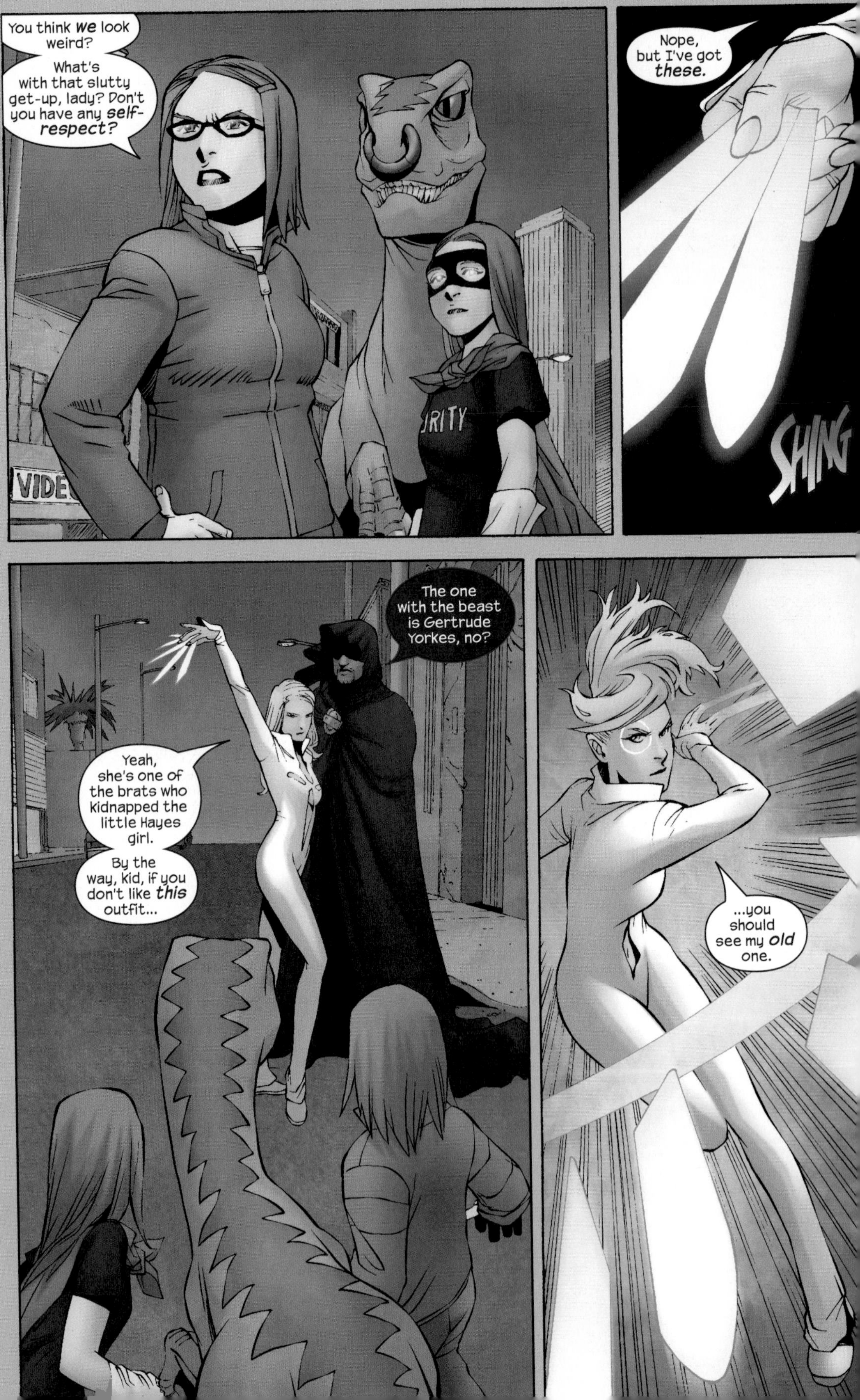
You think *we* look weird?
What's with that slutty get-up, lady? Don't you have any *self-respect?*
VIDE
RITY
Nope, but I've got *these.*
SHING
The one with the beast is Gertrude Yorkes, no?
Yeah, she's one of the brats who kidnapped the little Hayes girl.
By the way, kid, if you don't like *this* outfit...
...you should see my *old* one.

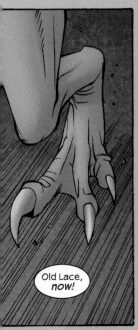

Old Lace, *now!*

RAAARR

Thanks for the cover, O.L.

Is... is she *okay?*

Yeah, just *hungry.*

Um, *problem.*

My powers, they don't have any effect on animals or--

THWIP

Dagger!

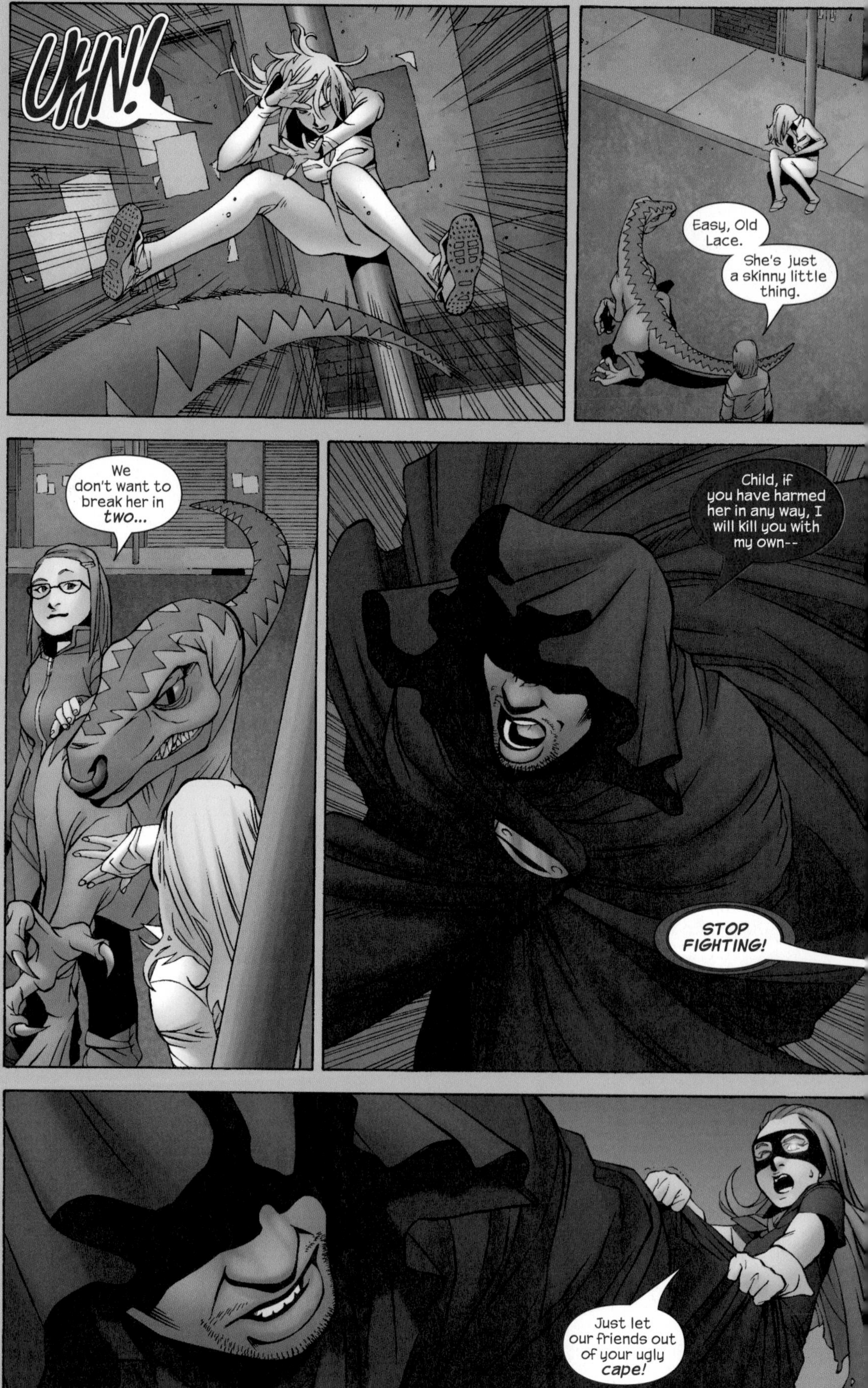
UHN!
Easy, Old Lace.
She's just a skinny little thing.
We don't want to break her in *two*...
Child, if you have harmed her in any way, I will kill you with my own--
STOP FIGHTING!
Just let our friends out of your ugly *cape!*

Come on, I don't wanna have to rip up your bed sheets!

This is not a "sheet", girl. It is a *cloak*, a gateway to another realm permanently bonded to my very being.

Not even a *god* has the strength to rend it from my--

UNPH!

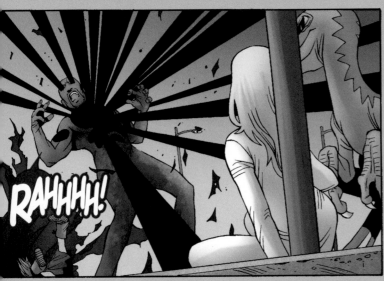

RAHHHH!

TY!

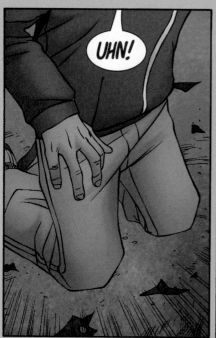

UHN!

Puh-puh-**please.**

Guh-guh-give it buh-buh-**back** to me.

I'm sorry! I thought you were another **monster.**

I didn't know you were a **stutterer.**

You made me ruh-ruh-**revert** to who I was when I fuh-fuh-**first** donned my cloak.

My mommy is a speech therapist. Maybe **she** can help you!

Bruiser, your parents are psychotic **super-villains.**

Oh, yeah.

I keep forgetting...

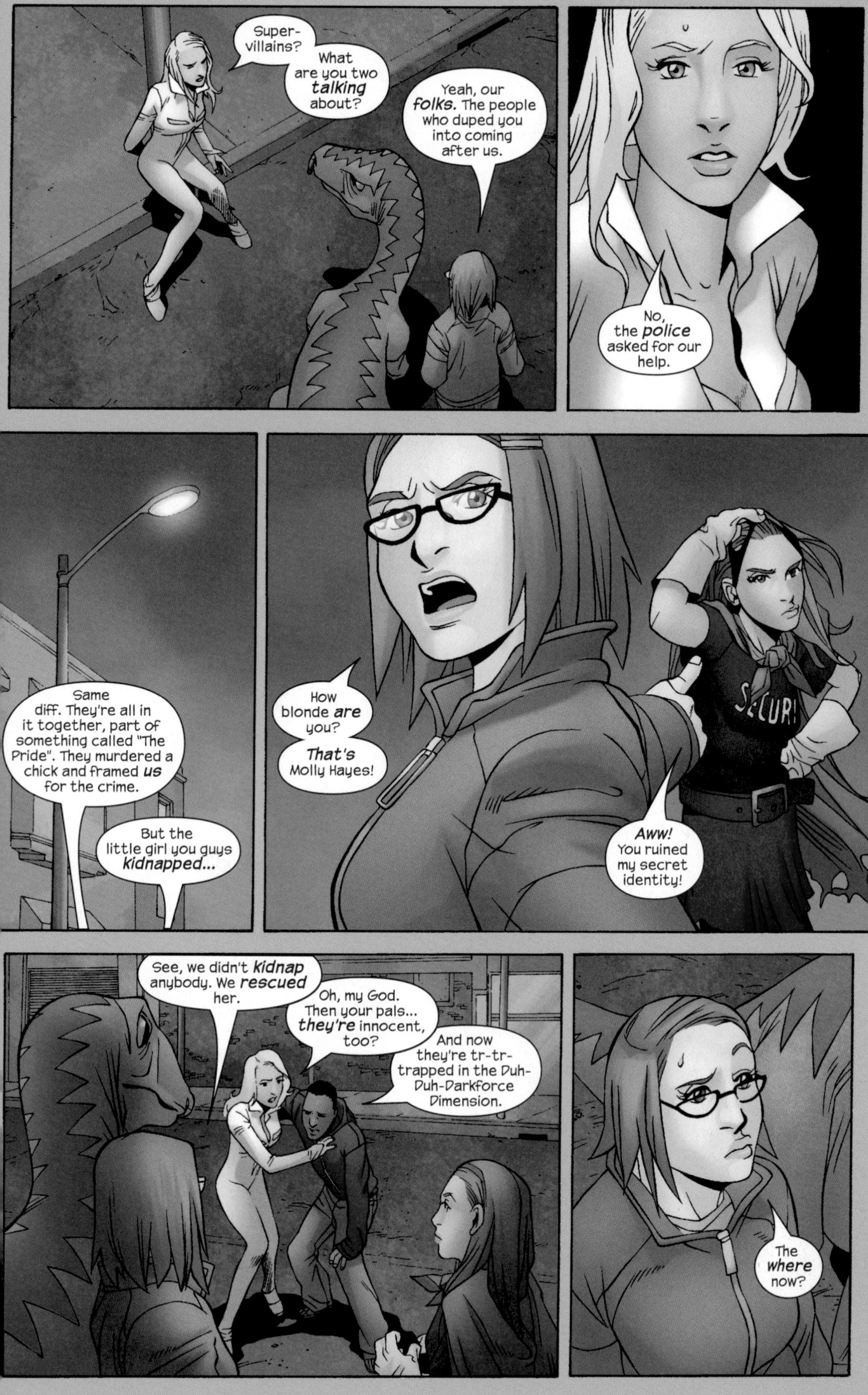

Super-villains?
What are you two *talking* about?
Yeah, our *folks.* The people who duped you into coming after us.
No, the *police* asked for our help.
Same diff. They're all in it together, part of something called "The Pride". They murdered a chick and framed *us* for the crime.
But the little girl you guys *kidnapped...*
How blonde *are* you?
That's Molly Hayes!
Aww! You ruined my secret identity!
SECURI
See, we didn't *kidnap* anybody. We *rescued* her.
Oh, my God. Then your pals... *they're* innocent, too?
And now they're tr-tr-trapped in the Duh-Duh-Darkforce Dimension.
The *where* now?

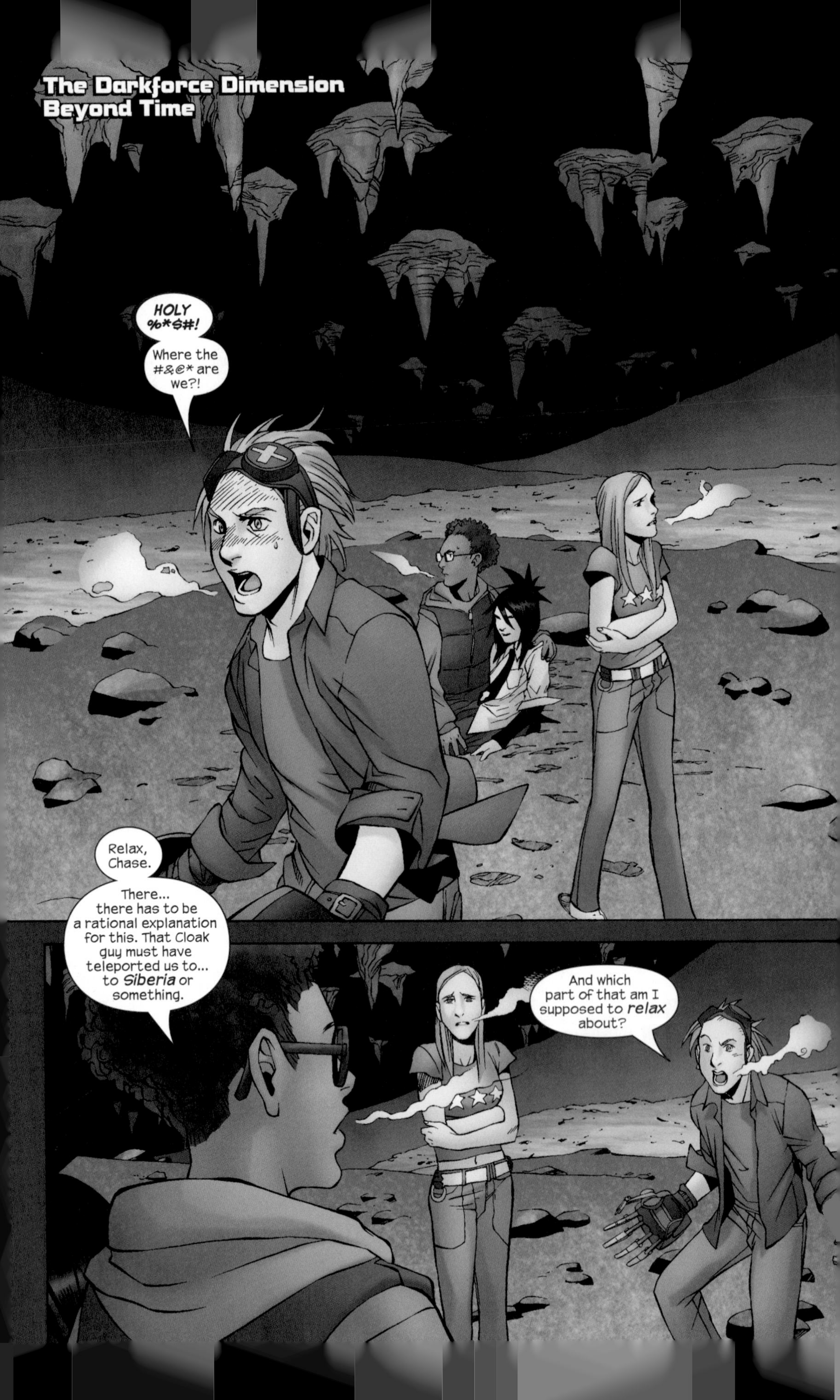
The Darkforce Dimension Beyond Time
HOLY %*$#!
Where the #&@* are we?!
Relax, Chase.
There... there has to be a rational explanation for this. That Cloak guy must have teleported us to... to *Siberia* or something.
And which part of that am I supposed to *relax* about?

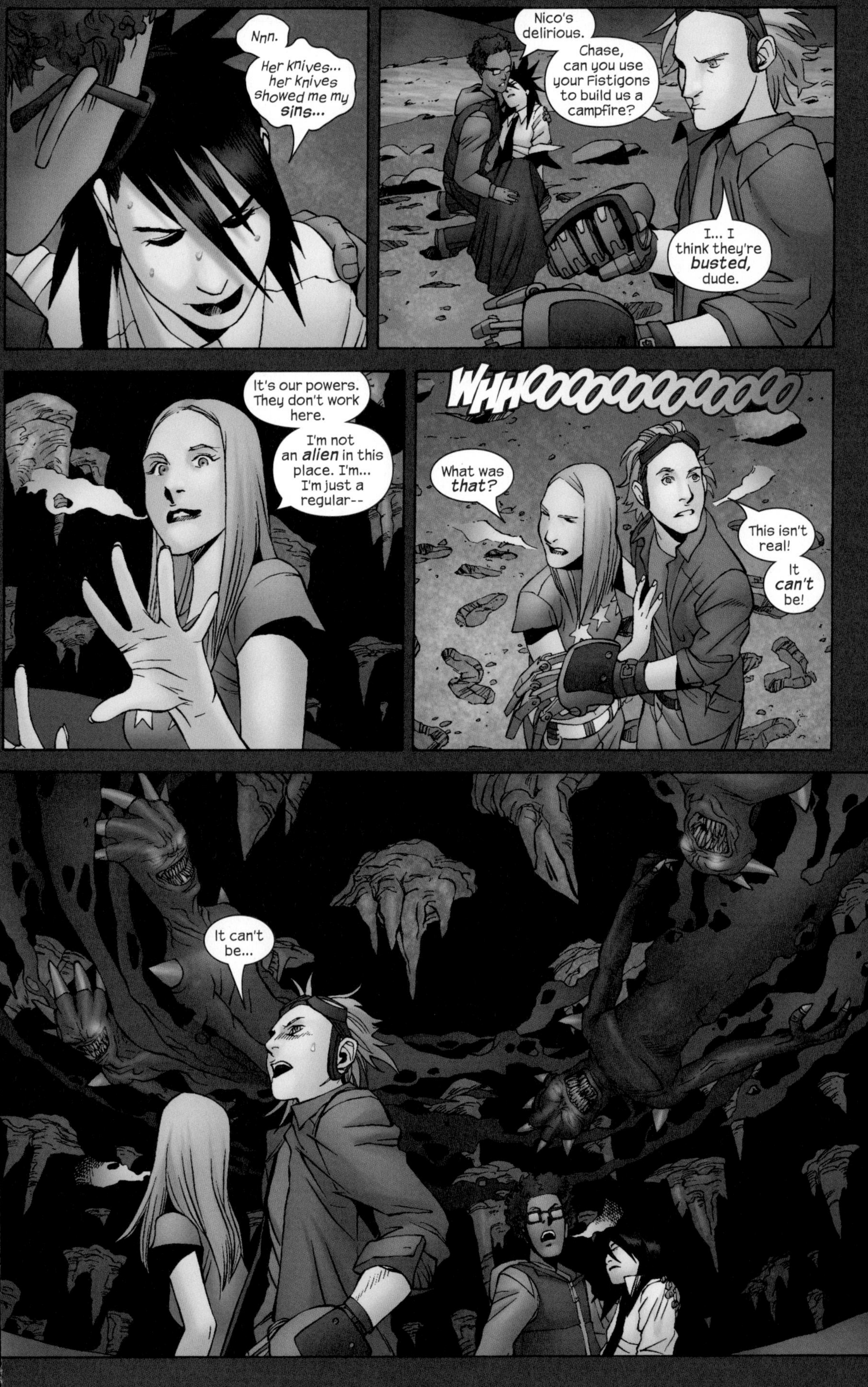
Nnn.
Her knives... her knives showed me my sins...
Nico's delirious.
Chase, can you use your Fistigons to build us a campfire?
I... I think they're busted, dude.
It's our powers. They don't work here.
I'm not an alien in this place. I'm... I'm just a regular--
WHHOOOOOOOOOOOOO
What was that?
This isn't real!
It can't be!
It can't be...

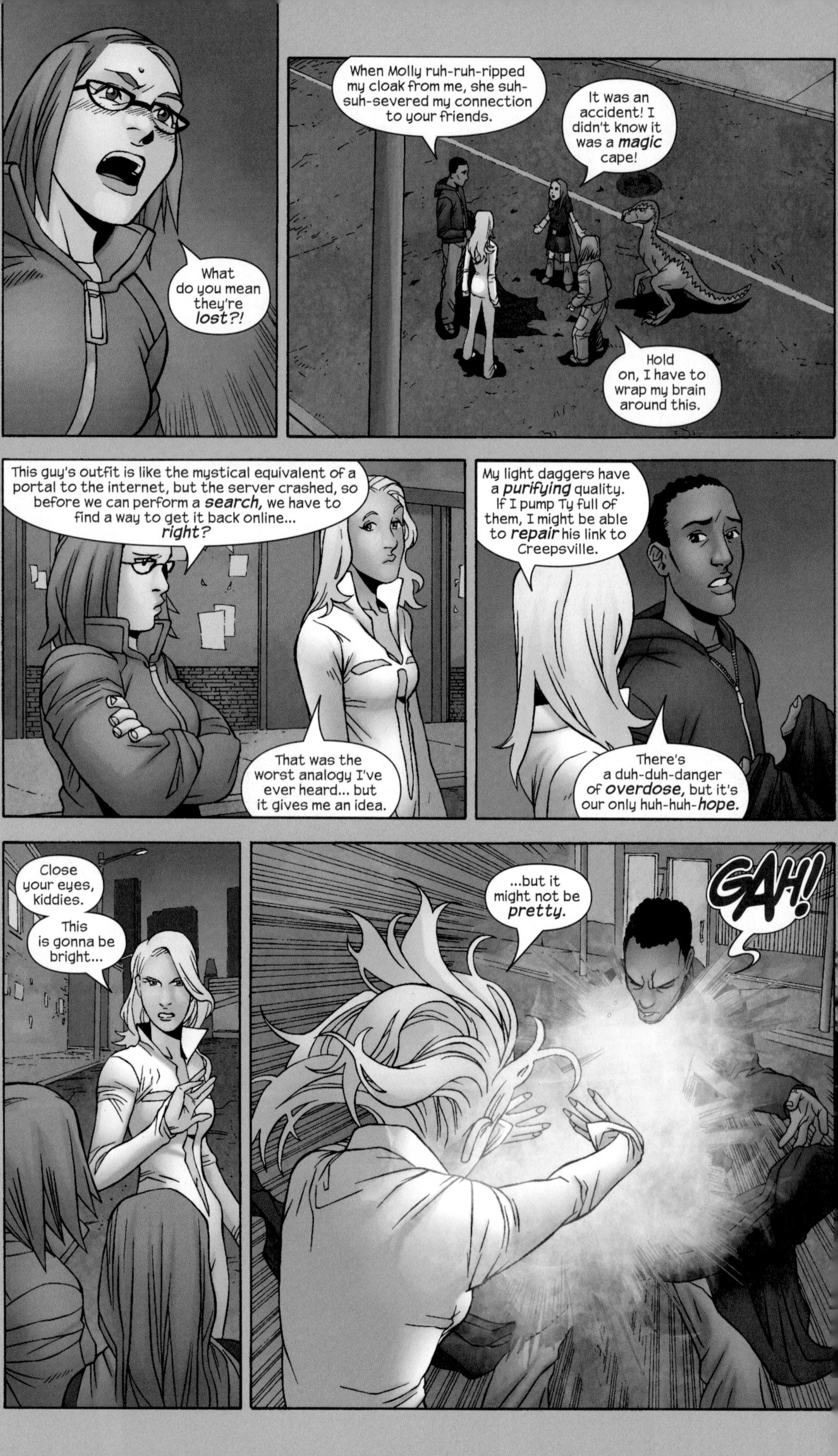
What do you mean they're *lost?!*
When Molly ruh-ruh-ripped my cloak from me, she suh-suh-severed my connection to your friends.
It was an accident! I didn't know it was a *magic* cape!
Hold on, I have to wrap my brain around this.
This guy's outfit is like the mystical equivalent of a portal to the internet, but the server crashed, so before we can perform a *search,* we have to find a way to get it back online... *right?*
That was the worst analogy I've ever heard... but it gives me an idea.
My light daggers have a *purifying* quality. If I pump Ty full of them, I might be able to *repair* his link to Creepsville.
There's a duh-duh-danger of *overdose,* but it's our only huh-huh-*hope.*
Close your eyes, kiddies.
This is gonna be bright...
...but it might not be *pretty.*
GAH!

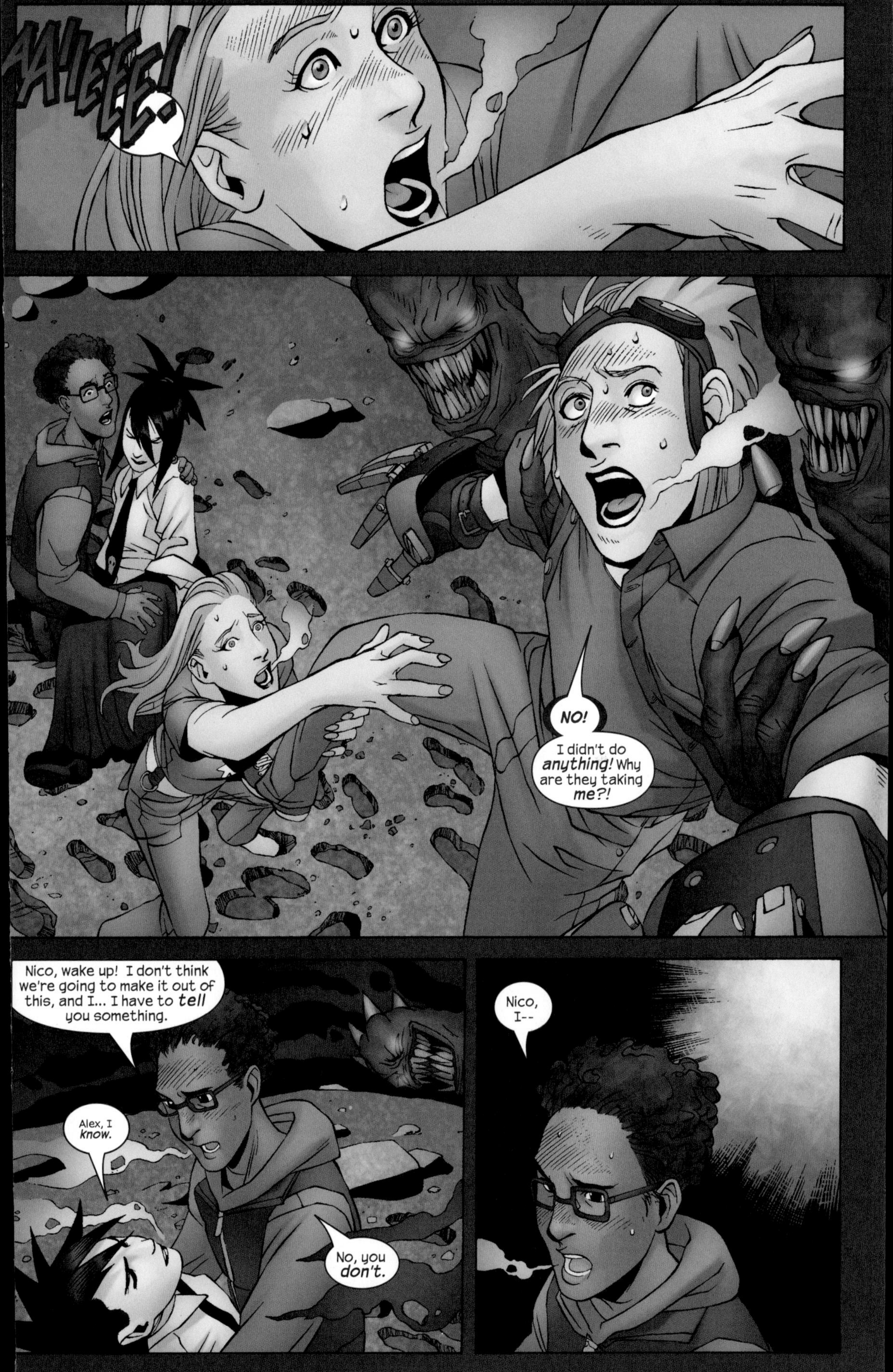
AAIIEEEE!
NO!
I didn't do *anything!* Why are they taking *me?!*
Nico, wake up! I don't think we're going to make it out of this, and I... I have to *tell* you something.
Alex, I *know.*
No, you *don't.*
Nico, I--

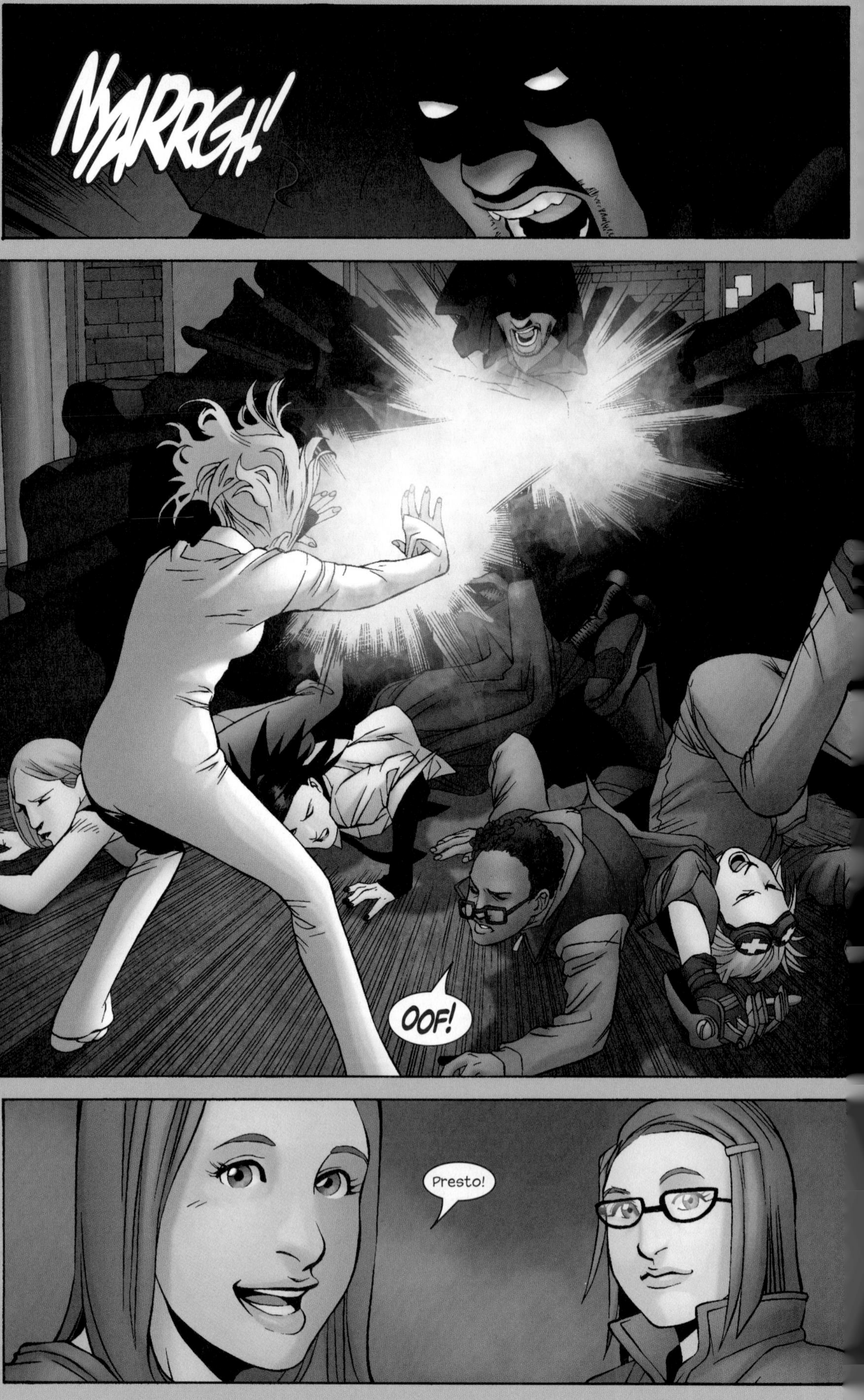
NYARRGH!
OOF!
Presto!

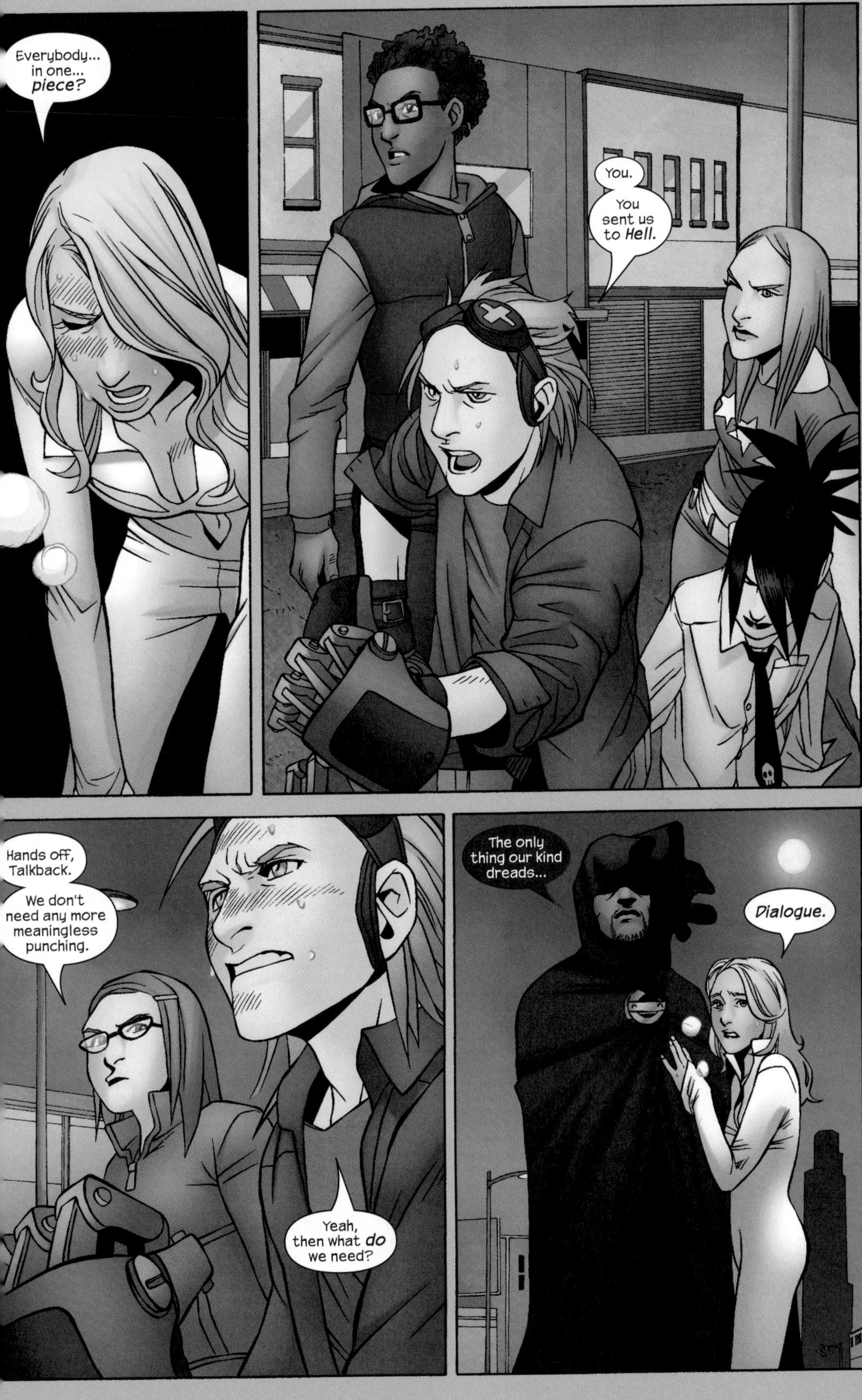
Everybody... in one... *piece?*
You.
You sent us to *Hell.*
Hands off, Talkback.
We don't need any more meaningless punching.
Yeah, then what *do* we need?
The only thing our kind dreads...
Dialogue.

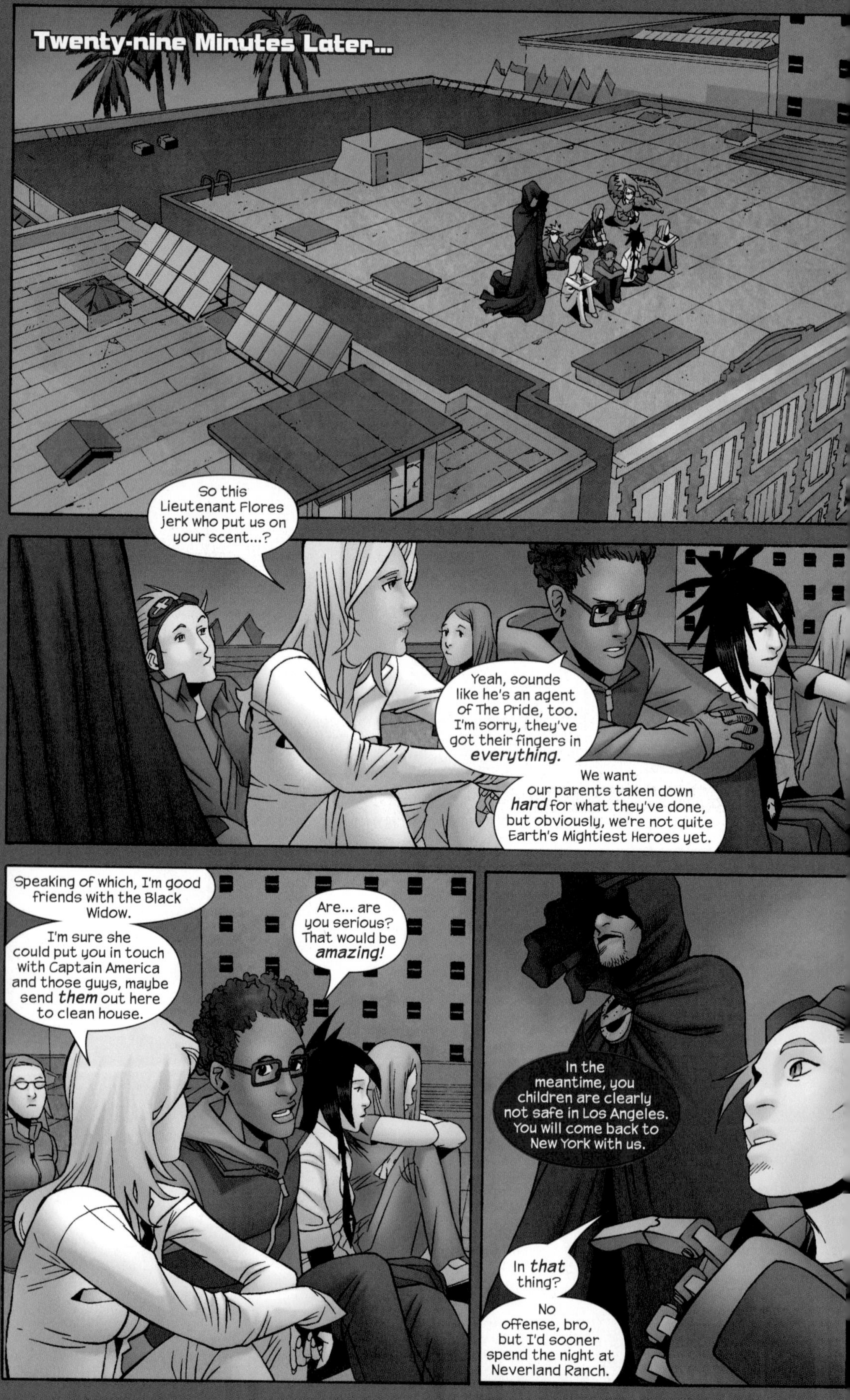

Twenty-nine Minutes Later...
So this Lieutenant Flores jerk who put us on your scent...?
Yeah, sounds like he's an agent of The Pride, too. I'm sorry, they've got their fingers in *everything.*
We want our parents taken down *hard* for what they've done, but obviously, we're not quite Earth's Mightiest Heroes yet.
Speaking of which, I'm good friends with the Black Widow.
I'm sure she could put you in touch with Captain America and those guys, maybe send *them* out here to clean house.
Are... are you serious? That would be *amazing!*
In the meantime, you children are clearly not safe in Los Angeles. You will come back to New York with us.
In *that* thing?
No offense, bro, but I'd sooner spend the night at Neverland Ranch.

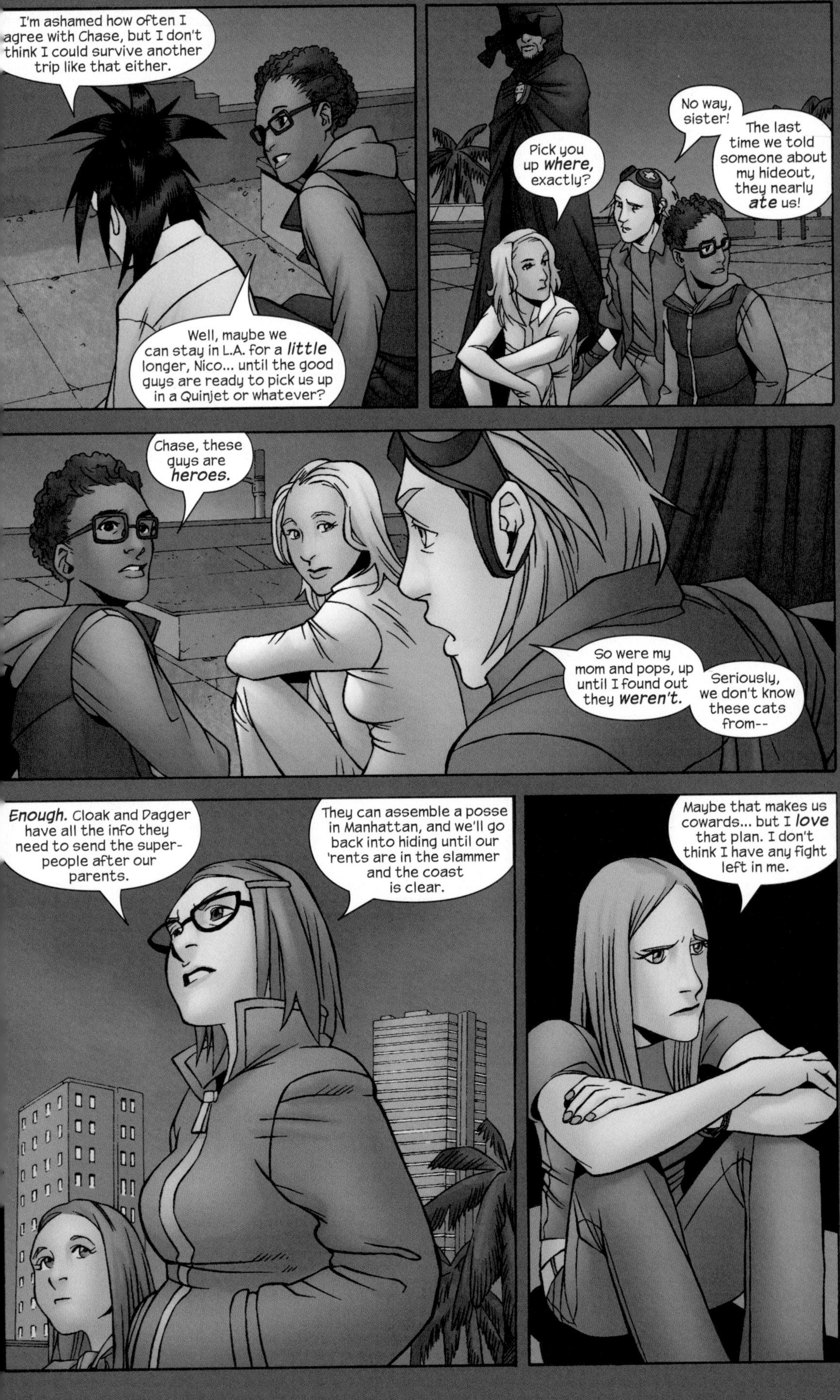
I'm ashamed how often I agree with Chase, but I don't think I could survive another trip like that either.
Well, maybe we can stay in L.A. for a *little* longer, Nico... until the good guys are ready to pick us up in a Quinjet or whatever?
Pick you up *where,* exactly?
No way, sister!
The last time we told someone about my hideout, they nearly *ate* us!
Chase, these guys are *heroes.*
So were my mom and pops, up until I found out they *weren't.*
Seriously, we don't know these cats from--
Enough. Cloak and Dagger have all the info they need to send the super-people after our parents.
They can assemble a posse in Manhattan, and we'll go back into hiding until our 'rents are in the slammer and the coast is clear.
Maybe that makes us cowards... but I *love* that plan. I don't think I have any fight left in me.

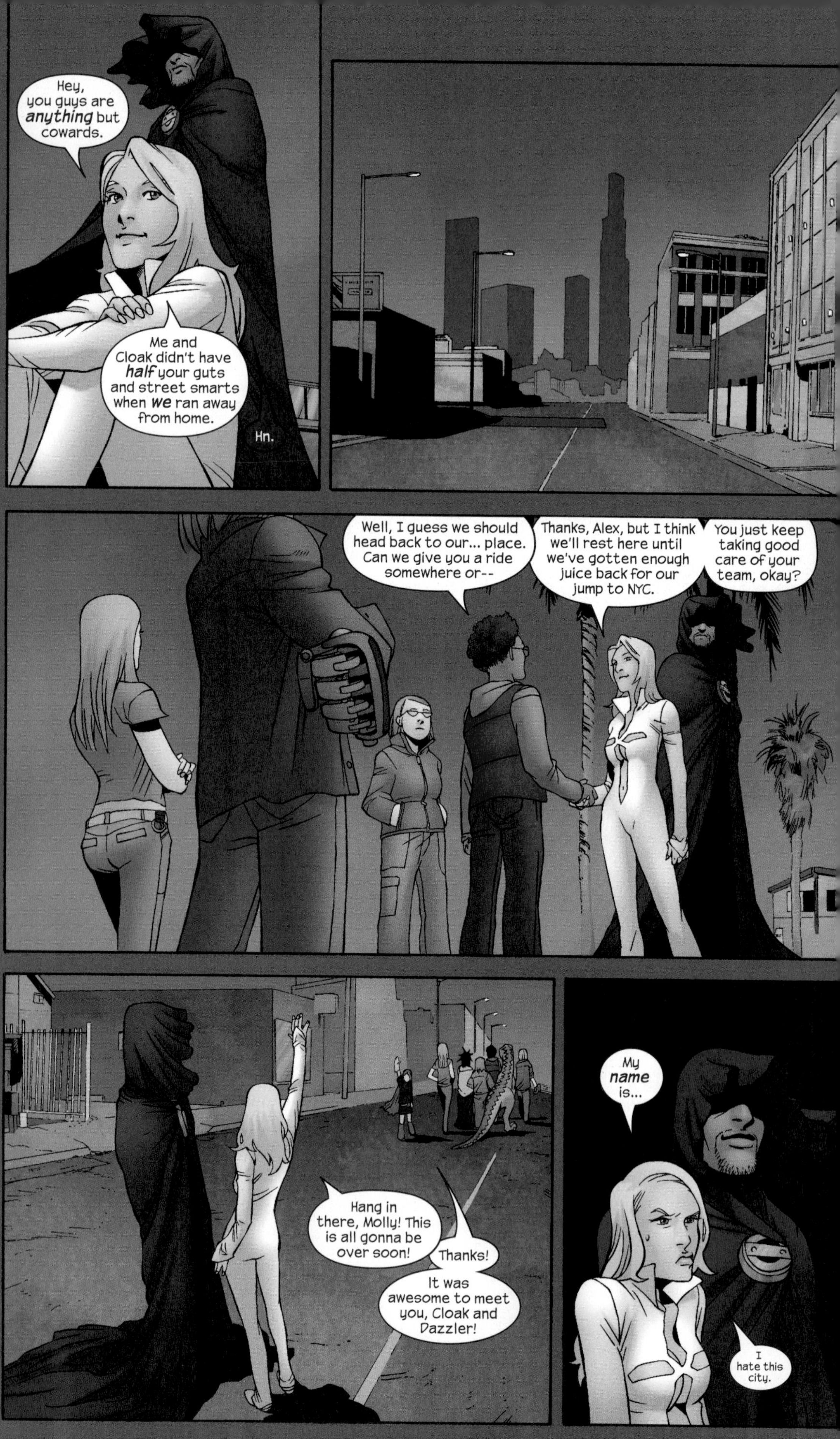
Hey, you guys are *anything* but cowards.
Me and Cloak didn't have *half* your guts and street smarts when *we* ran away from home.
Hn.
Well, I guess we should head back to our... place. Can we give you a ride somewhere or--
Thanks, Alex, but I think we'll rest here until we've gotten enough juice back for our jump to NYC.
You just keep taking good care of your team, okay?
Hang in there, Molly! This is all gonna be over soon!
Thanks!
It was awesome to meet you, Cloak and Dazzler!
My *name* is...
I hate this city.

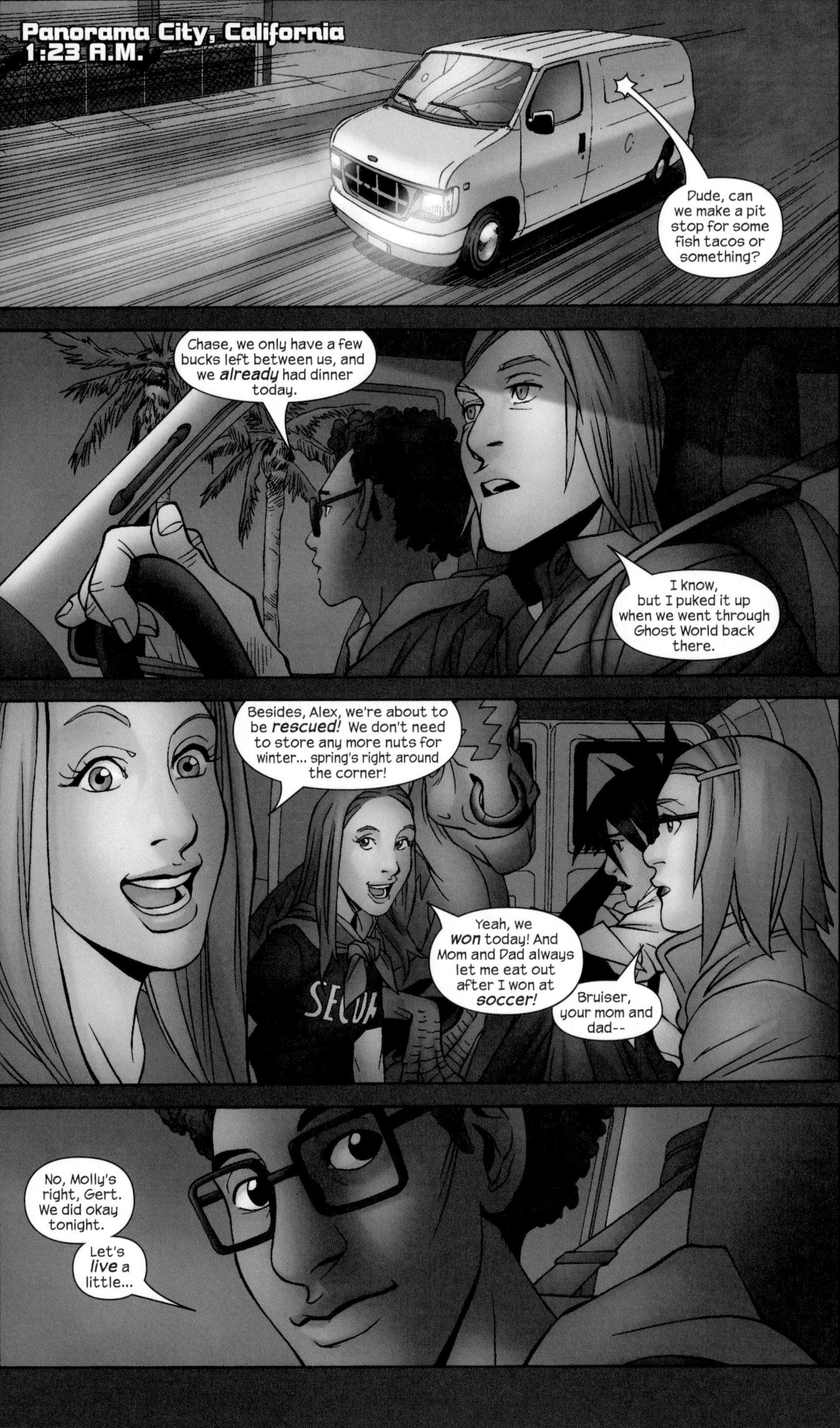
Panorama City, California
1:23 A.M.
Dude, can we make a pit stop for some fish tacos or something?
Chase, we only have a few bucks left between us, and we *already* had dinner today.
I know, but I puked it up when we went through Ghost World back there.
Besides, Alex, we're about to be *rescued!* We don't need to store any more nuts for winter... spring's right around the corner!
Yeah, we *won* today! And Mom and Dad always let me eat out after I won at *soccer!*
Bruiser, your mom and dad--
No, Molly's right, Gert. We did okay tonight.
Let's *live* a little...

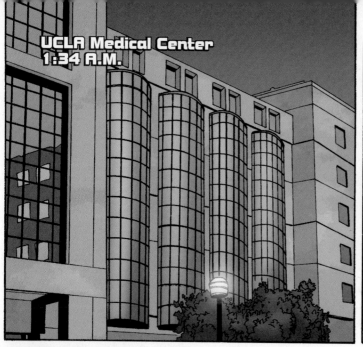

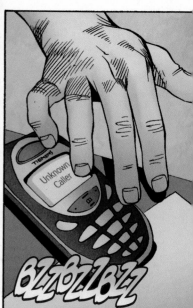

UCLA Medical Center
1:34 A.M.
TIEMENS
Unknown Caller
BZZBZZBZZ
What?
Lieutenant Flores?
Speak up, kid. You're mumbling. I can barely understand--
You're the dork who sent Cloak and Dagger after us, right? I'm surprised our parents haven't *killed* you yet.
Who... who *is* this?

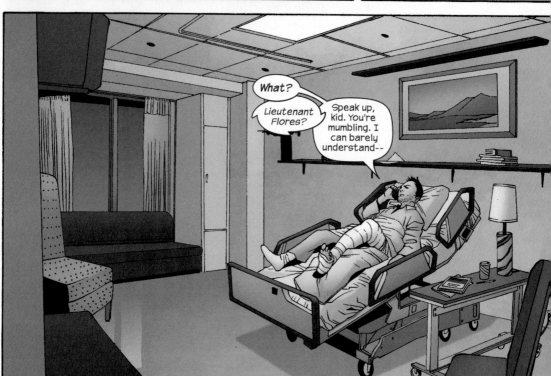

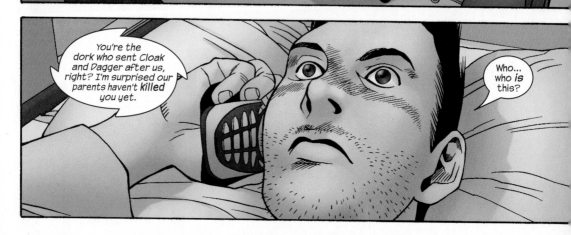

Right now, I'm the only friend you've got.

You're one of their **children**, aren't you?

The Pride told me they might have a **mole** in your gang, but I didn't believe--

Quiet. I don't have long. I'm at a payphone outside some taco shack, and the others think I'm in the bathroom.

What do you--

Listen, Cloak and Dagger are on a rooftop in Van Nuys, but I'm not sure how much longer they'll be there.

Lieutenant, they **know** about The Pride.

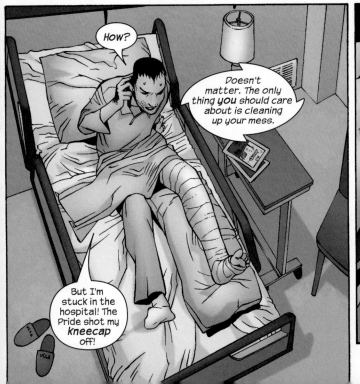

HOW?

Doesn't matter. The only thing **you** should care about is cleaning up your mess.

But I'm stuck in the hospital! The Pride shot my **kneecap** off!

Do **something**... or the next bullet will probably be to your **brain**.

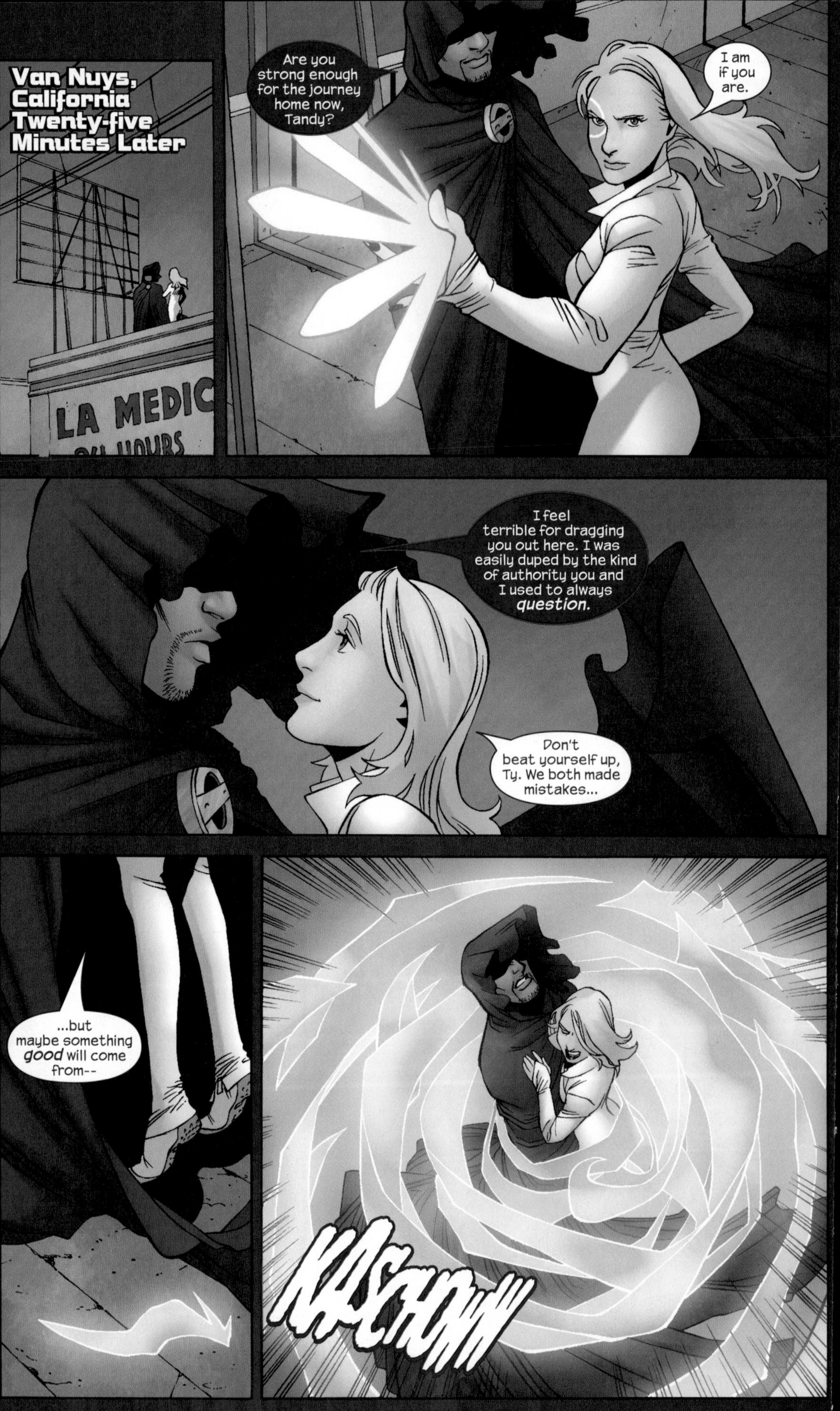
Van Nuys, California Twenty-five Minutes Later
LA MEDIC
Are you strong enough for the journey home now, Tandy?
I am if you are.
I feel terrible for dragging you out here. I was easily duped by the kind of authority you and I used to always *question.*
Don't beat yourself up, Ty. We both made mistakes...
...but maybe something *good* will come from--
KASCHOWW

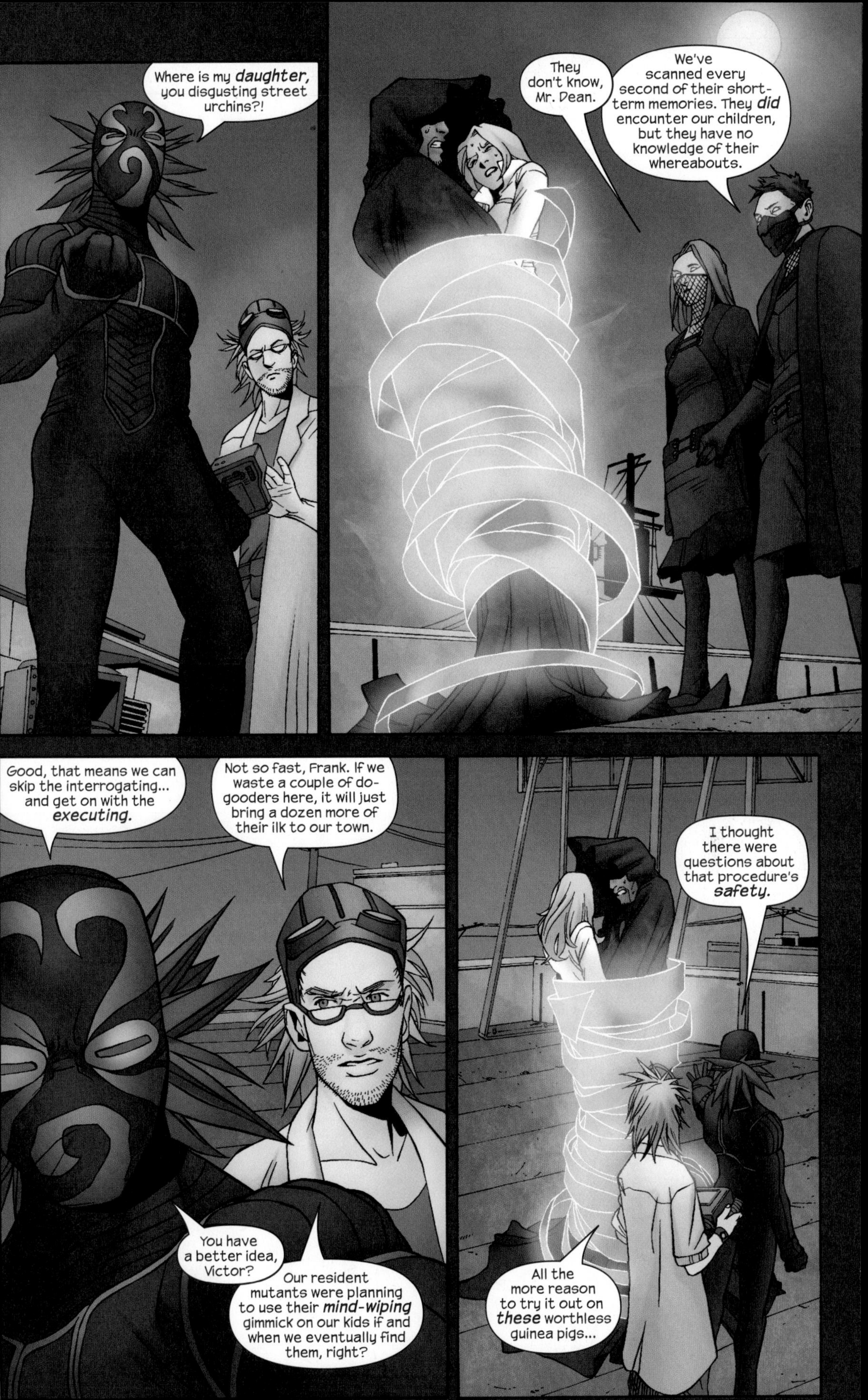
Where is my *daughter,* you disgusting street urchins?!
They don't know, Mr. Dean.
We've scanned every second of their short-term memories. They *did* encounter our children, but they have no knowledge of their whereabouts.
Good, that means we can skip the interrogating... and get on with the *executing.*
Not so fast, Frank. If we waste a couple of do-gooders here, it will just bring a dozen more of their ilk to our town.
You have a better idea, Victor?
Our resident mutants were planning to use their *mind-wiping* gimmick on our kids if and when we eventually find them, right?
I thought there were questions about that procedure's *safety.*
All the more reason to try it out on *these* worthless guinea pigs...

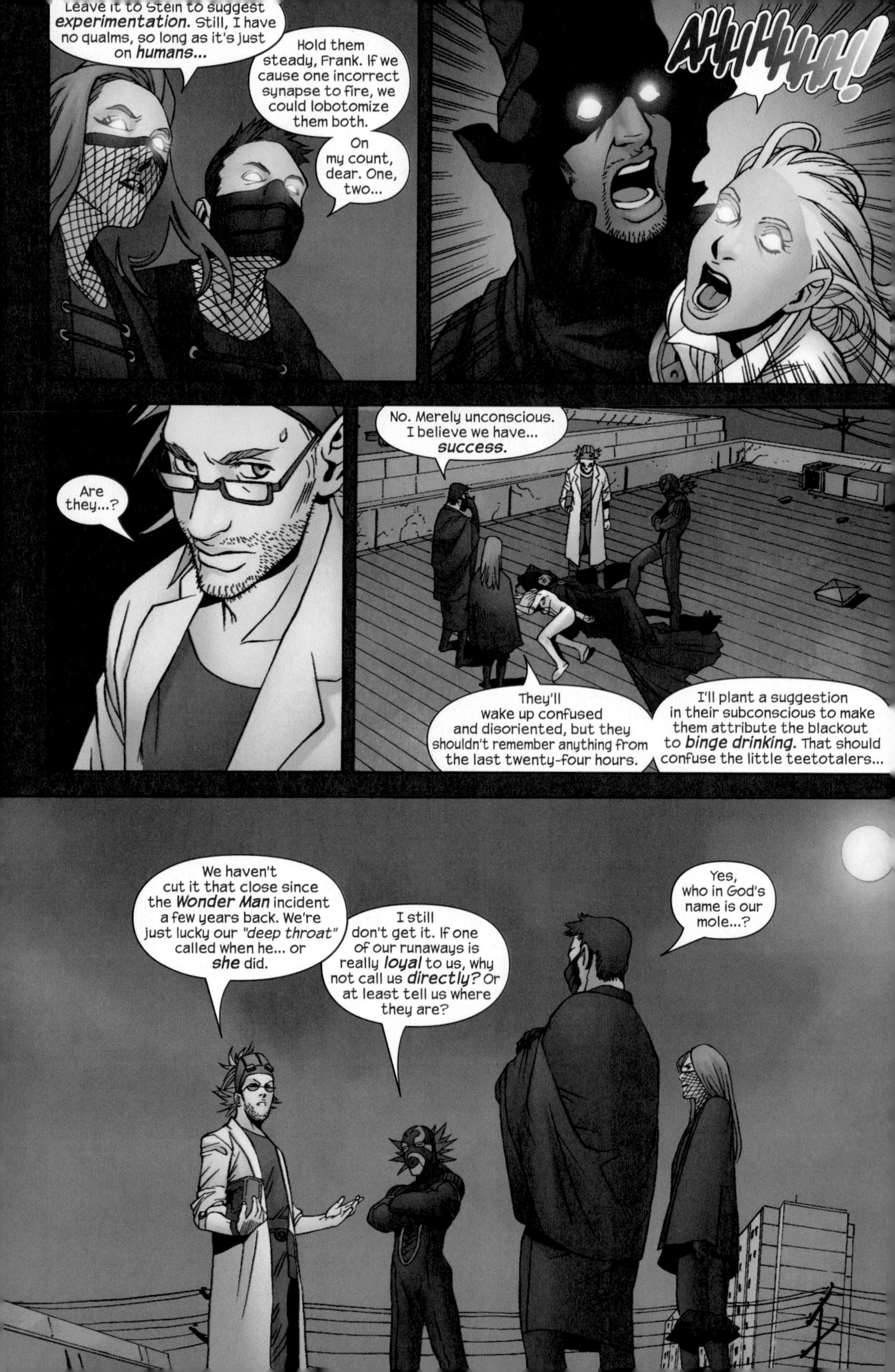
Leave it to Stein to suggest experimentation. Still, I have no qualms, so long as it's just on humans...
Hold them steady, Frank. If we cause one incorrect synapse to fire, we could lobotomize them both.
On my count, dear. One, two...
AHHHHHH!
Are they...?
No. Merely unconscious. I believe we have... success.
They'll wake up confused and disoriented, but they shouldn't remember anything from the last twenty-four hours.
I'll plant a suggestion in their subconscious to make them attribute the blackout to binge drinking. That should confuse the little teetotalers...
We haven't cut it that close since the Wonder Man incident a few years back. We're just lucky our "deep throat" called when he... or she did.
I still don't get it. If one of our runaways is really loyal to us, why not call us directly? Or at least tell us where they are?
Yes, who in God's name is our mole...?

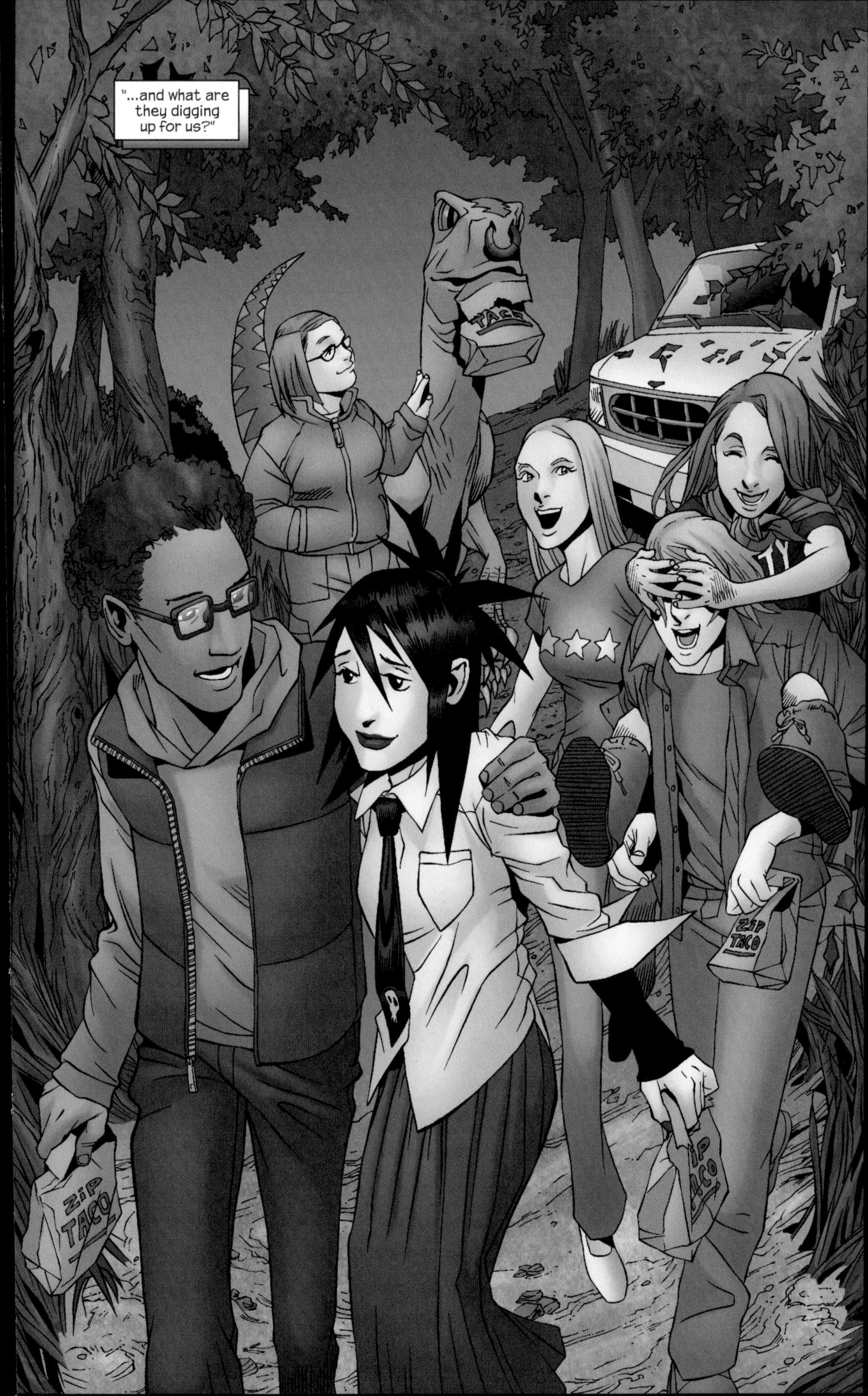
"...and what are they digging up for us?"
TACO
ZIP TACO
ZIP TACO

THE RUNAWAYS SOON CONFRONTED THEIR EVIL PARENTS, THE PRIDE. ALEX WAS REVEALED AS THE VILLAINS' MOLE, AND BOTH HE AND THE PRIDE WERE ULTIMATELY KILLED BY THE GODLIKE GIBBORIM. THE REMAINING RUNAWAYS DEDICATED THEMSELVES TO TAKING ON NEW THREATS TRYING TO FILL THE PRIDE'S VOID — AND ALTHOUGH KAROLINA RECENTLY LEFT EARTH TO DEAL WITH HER ALIEN PARENTS' MACHINATIONS, THE TEAM GAINED A NEW MEMBER: VICTOR MANCHA, THE ROBOTIC "SON" OF ULTRON...

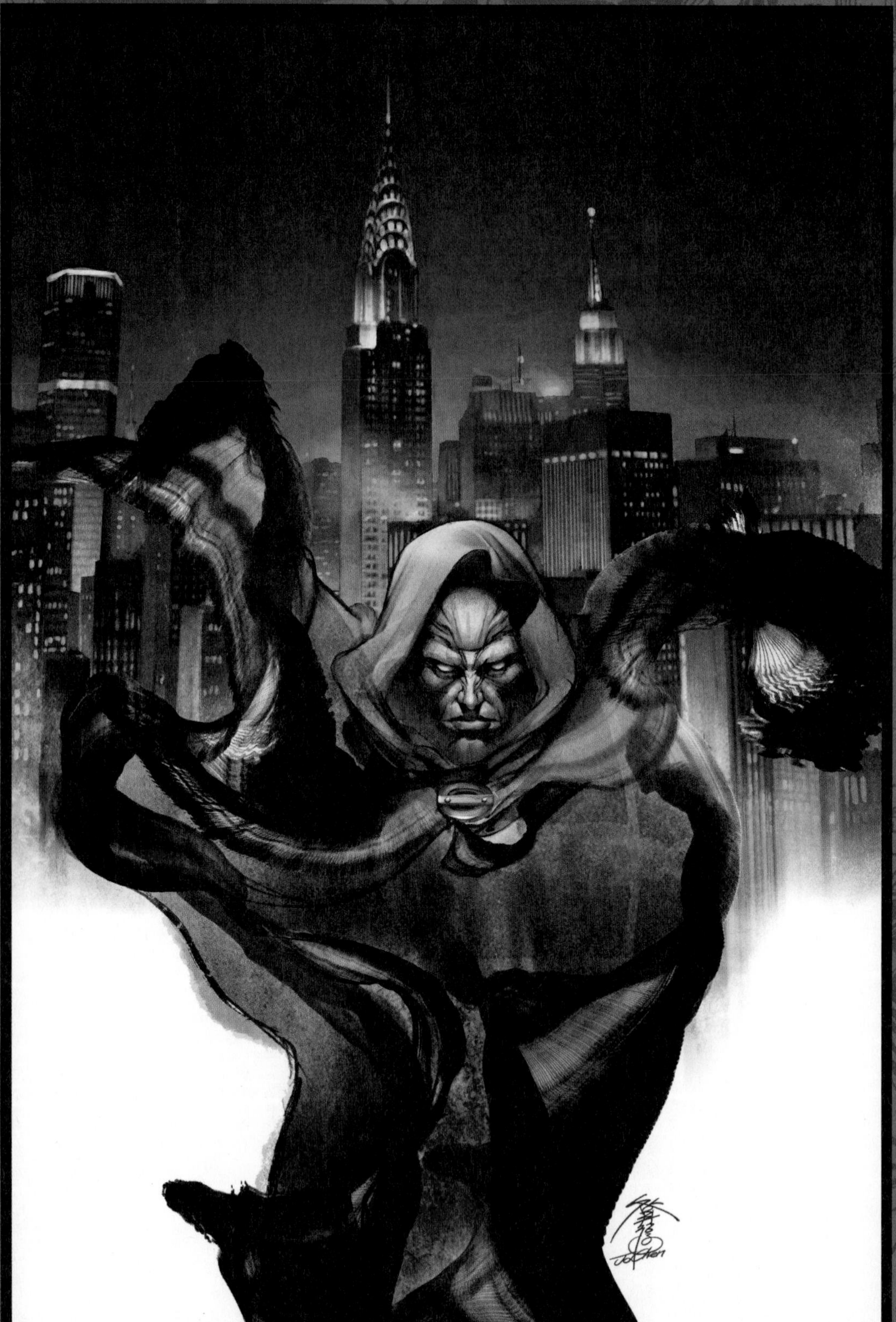

RUNAWAYS (2005) #9
"EAST COAST/WEST COAST, PART 1"

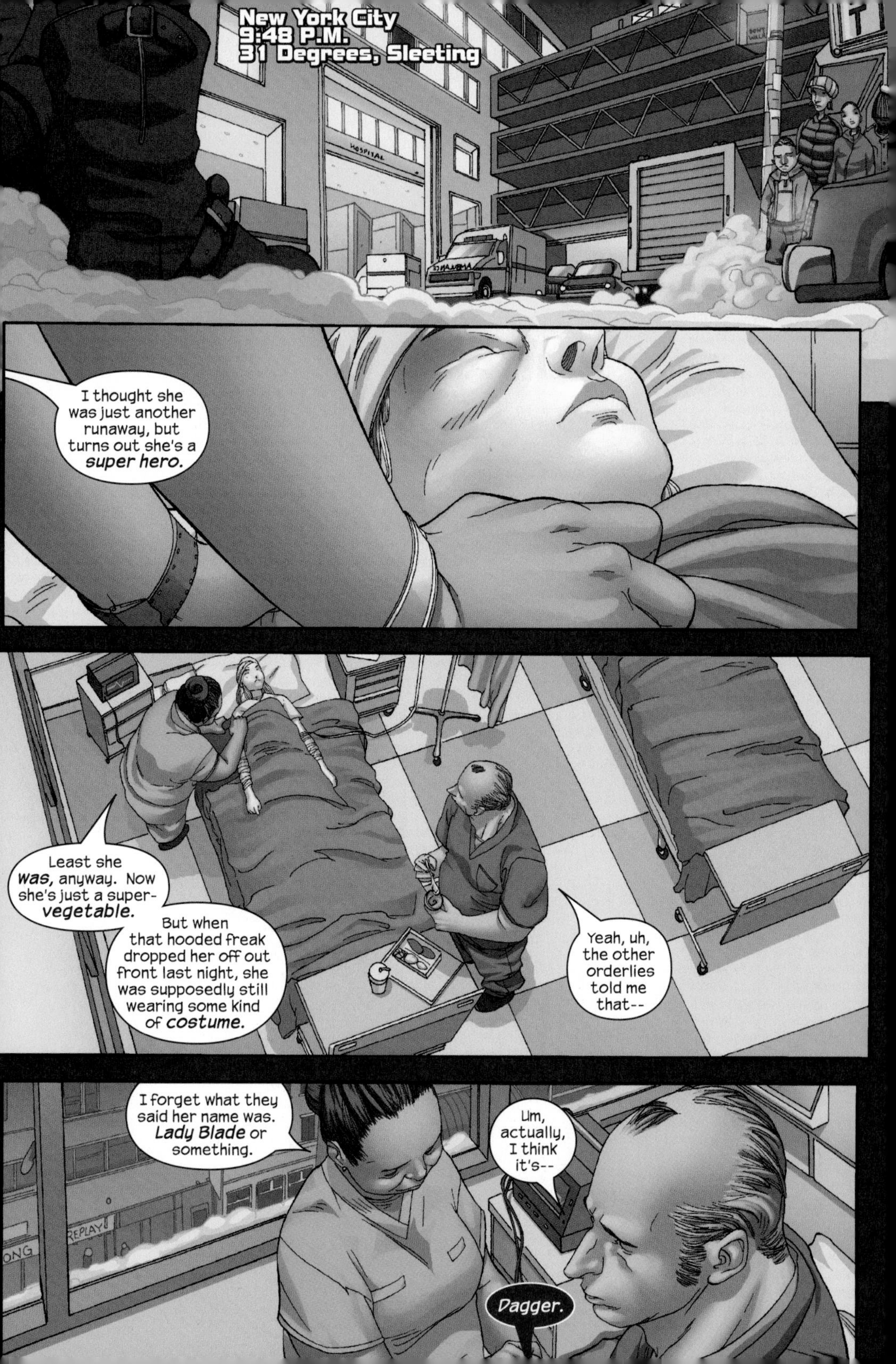
New York City
9:48 P.M.
31 Degrees, Sleeting
HOSPITAL
I thought she was just another runaway, but turns out she's a super hero.
Least she was, anyway. Now she's just a super-vegetable.
But when that hooded freak dropped her off out front last night, she was supposedly still wearing some kind of costume.
Yeah, uh, the other orderlies told me that--
I forget what they said her name was. Lady Blade or something.
Um, actually, I think it's--
Dagger.
REPLAY

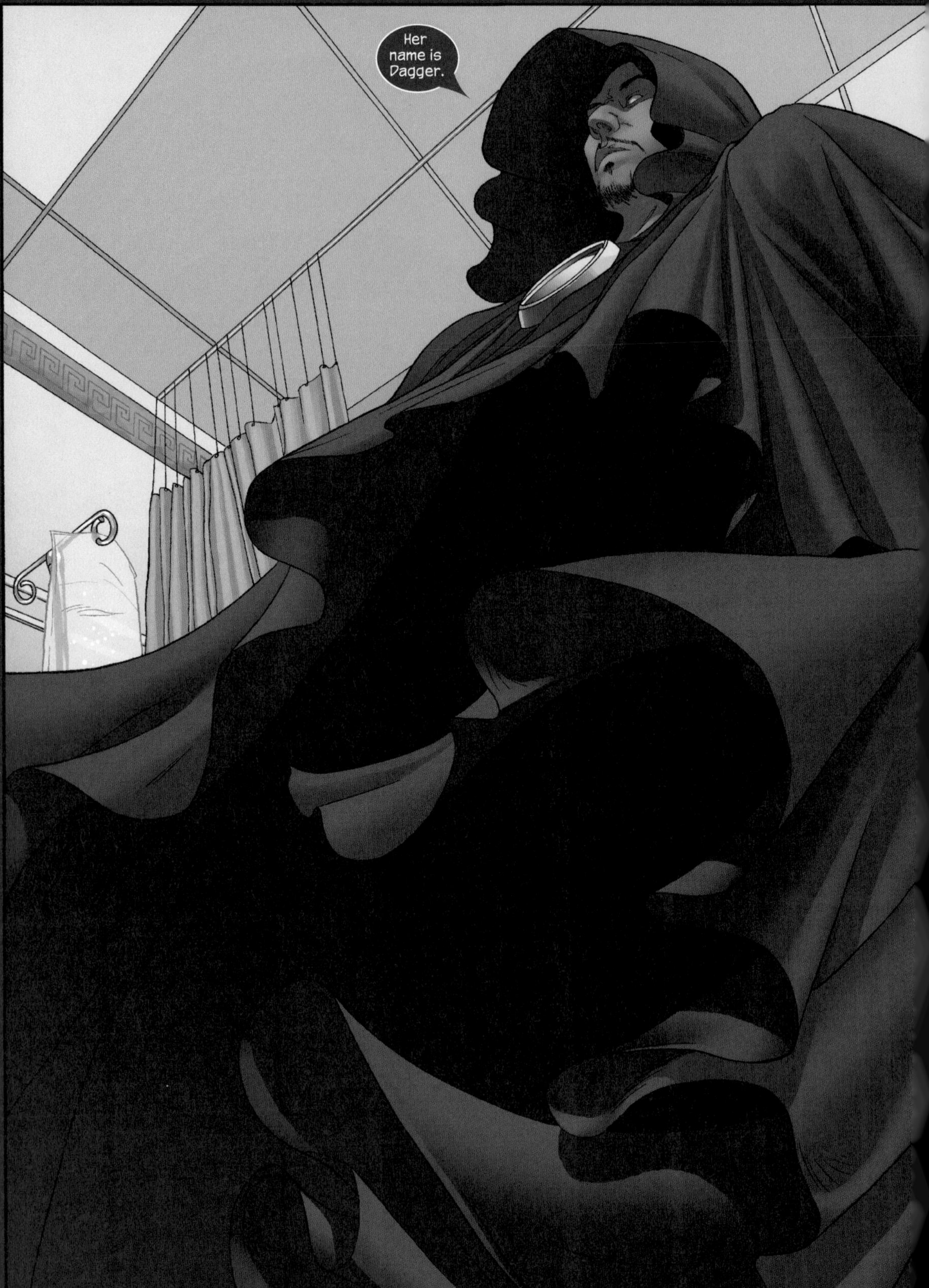
Her name is Dagger.

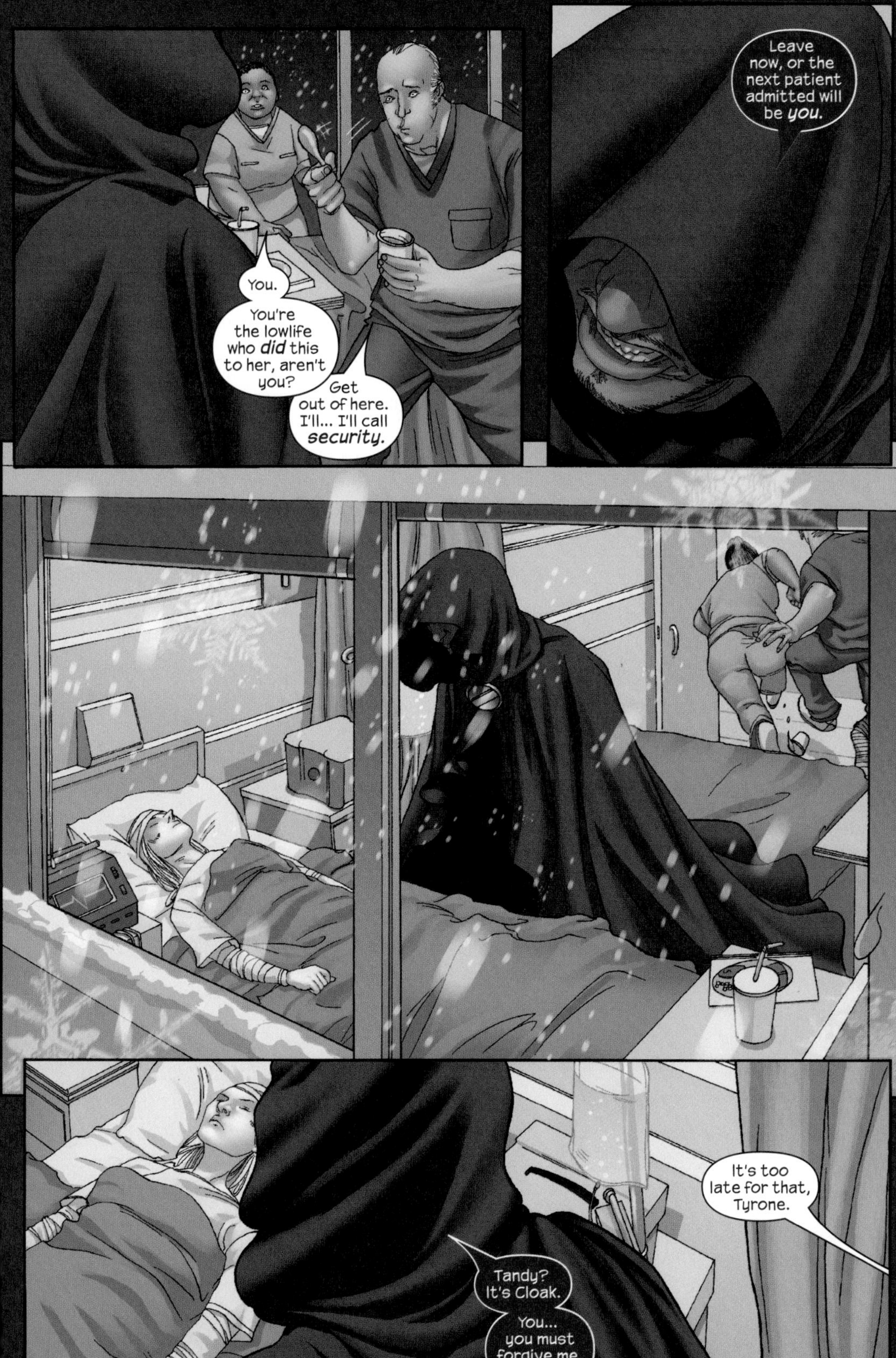
You.
You're the lowlife who *did* this to her, aren't you?
Get out of here. I'll... I'll call *security.*
Leave now, or the next patient admitted will be *you.*
Tandy? It's Cloak.
You... you must forgive me, my love.
It's too late for that, Tyrone.

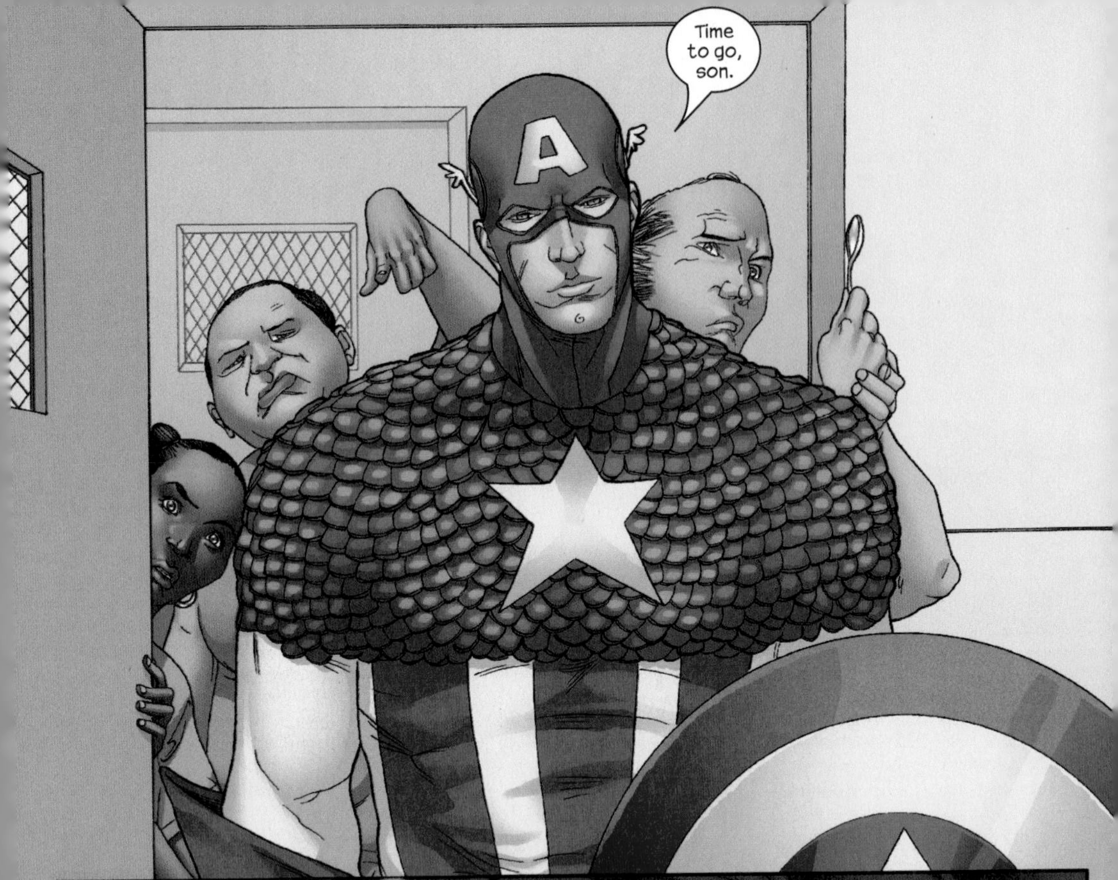
Time to go, son.
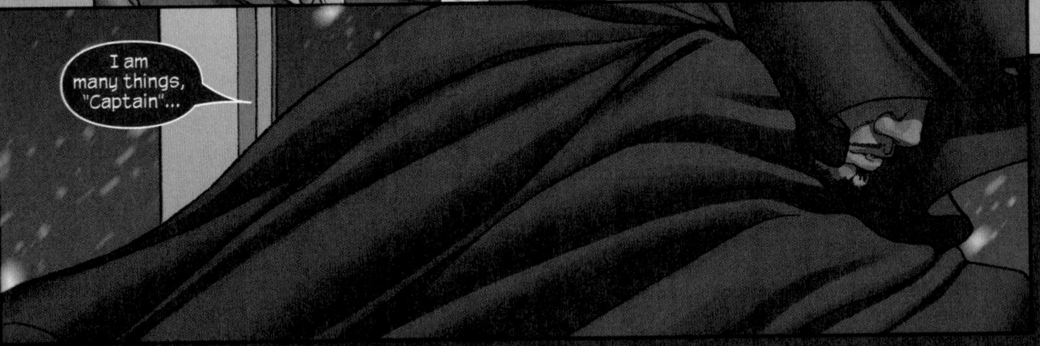
I am many things, "Captain"...
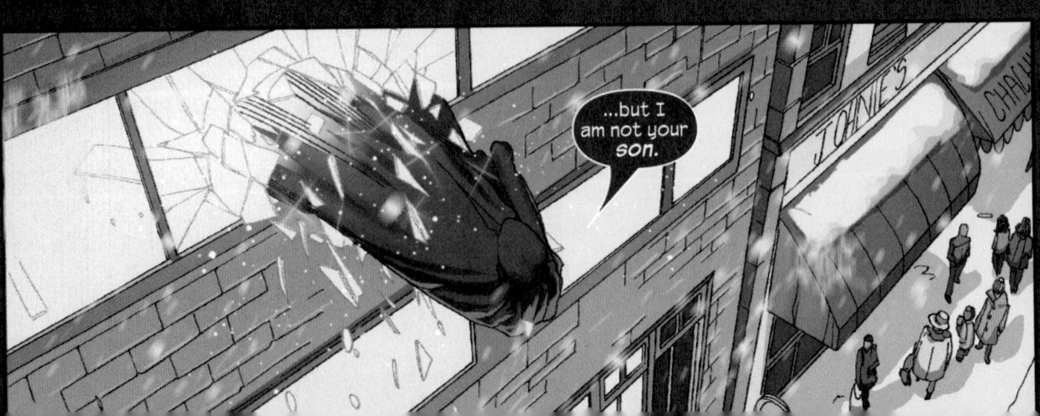
...but I am not your *son*.
JOHNIE'S

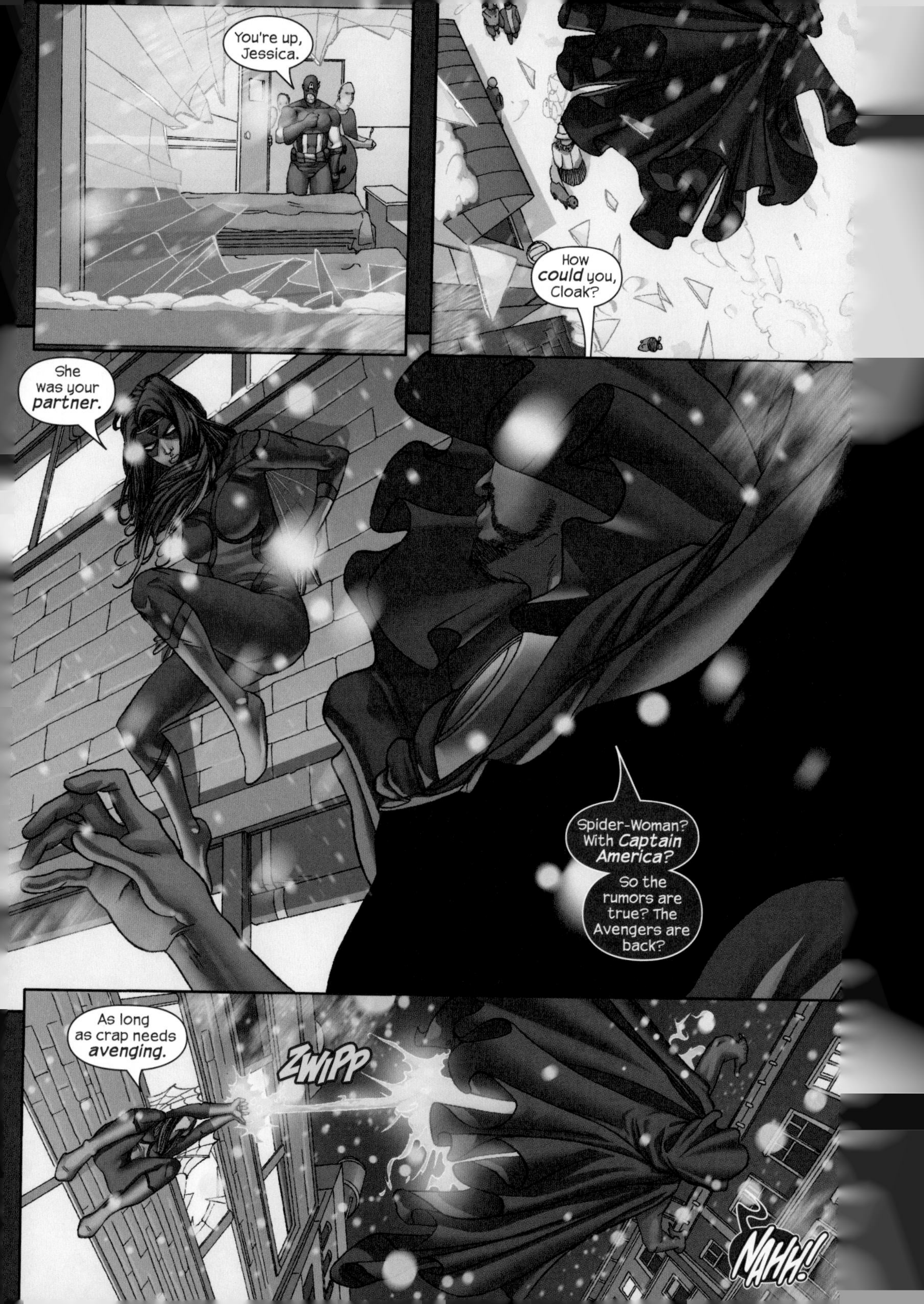
You're up, Jessica.
How could you, Cloak?
She was your partner.
Spider-Woman? With Captain America?
So the rumors are true? The Avengers are back?
As long as crap needs avenging.
ZWIPP
NAHH!

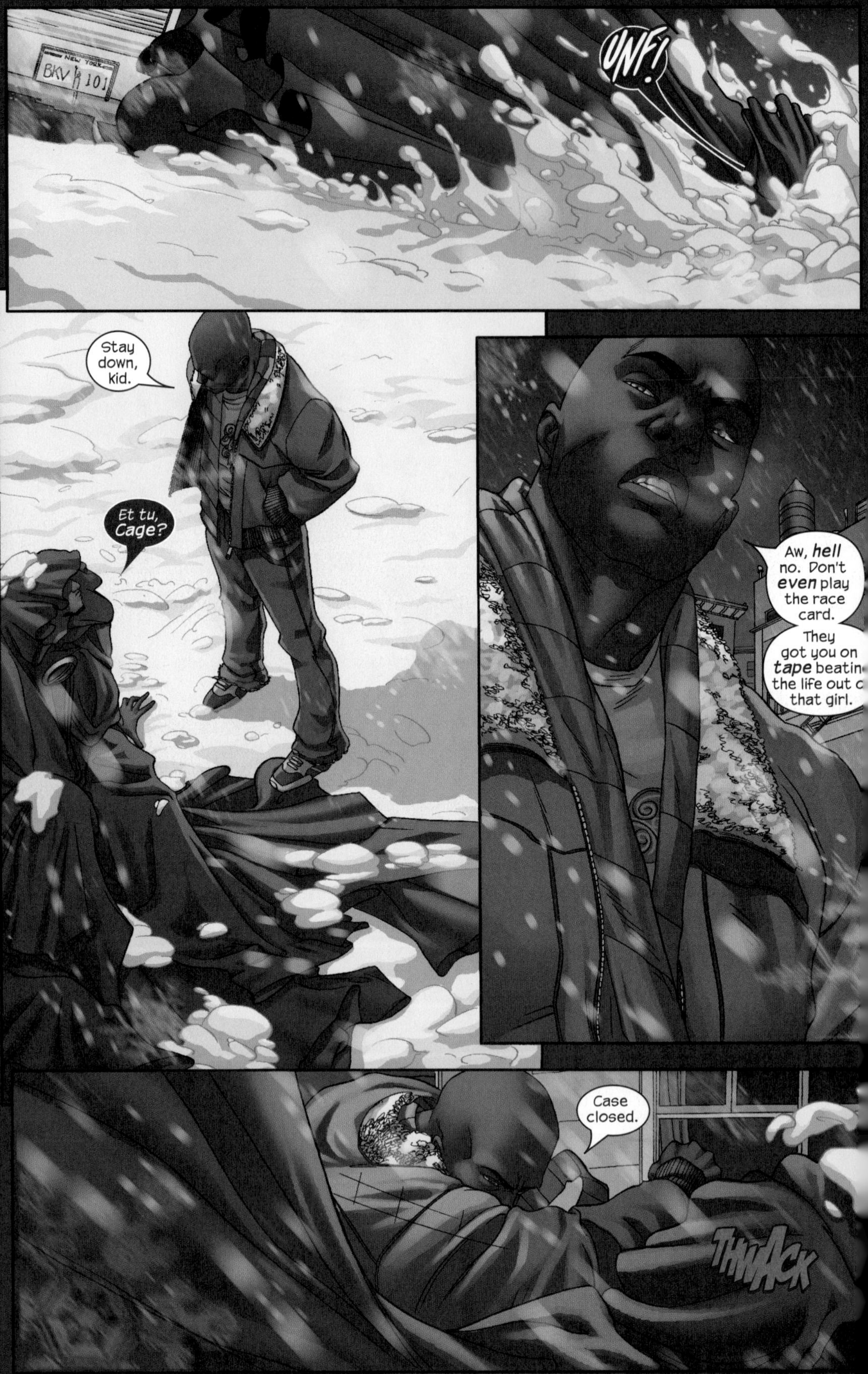
NEW YORK
BKV 101
UNF!
Stay down, kid.
Et tu, Cage?
Aw, *hell* no. Don't *even* play the race card.
They got you on *tape* beating the life out of that girl.
Case closed.
THWACK

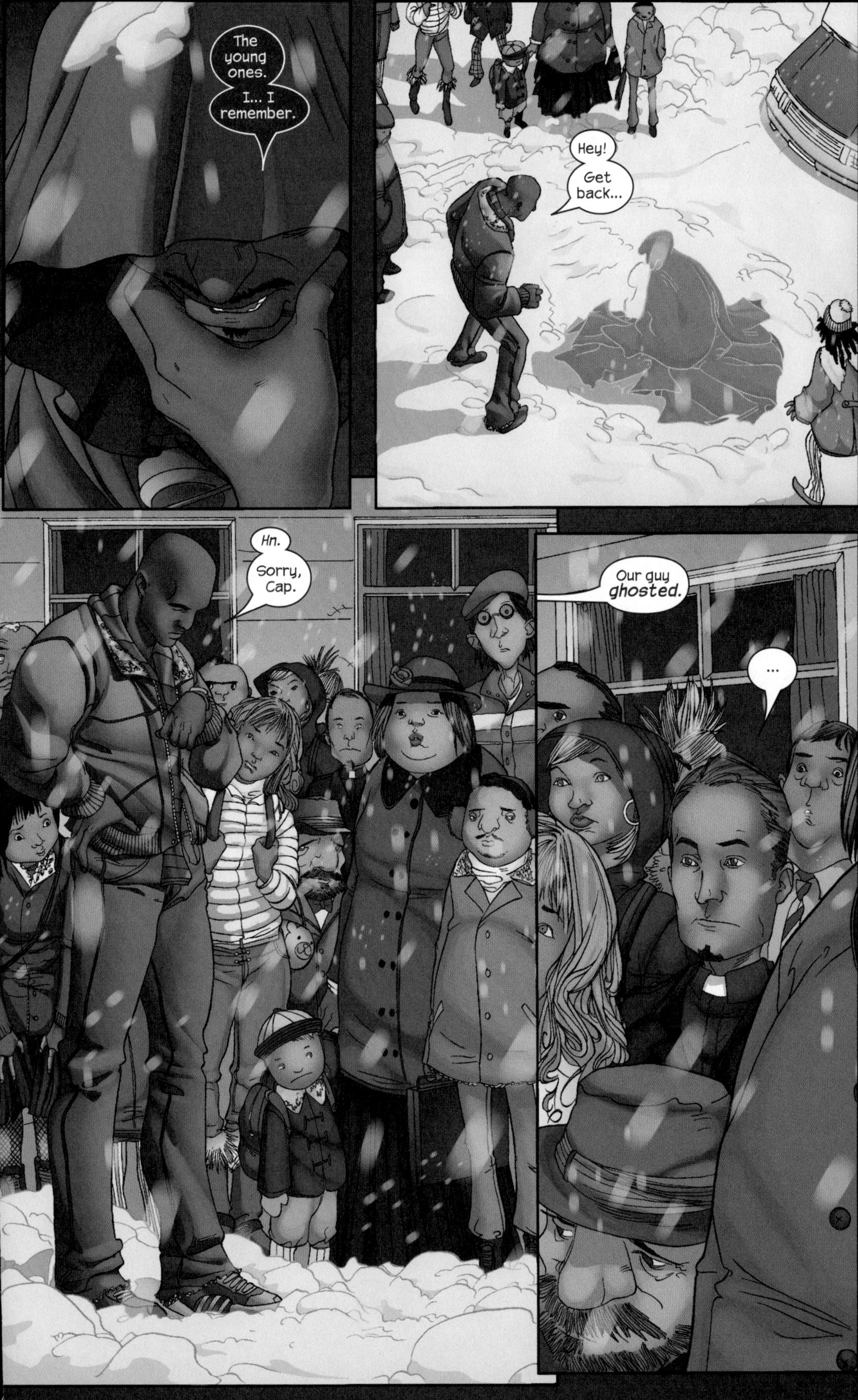
The young ones.
I... I remember.
Hey! Get back...
Hn.
Sorry, Cap.
Our guy *ghosted.*
...

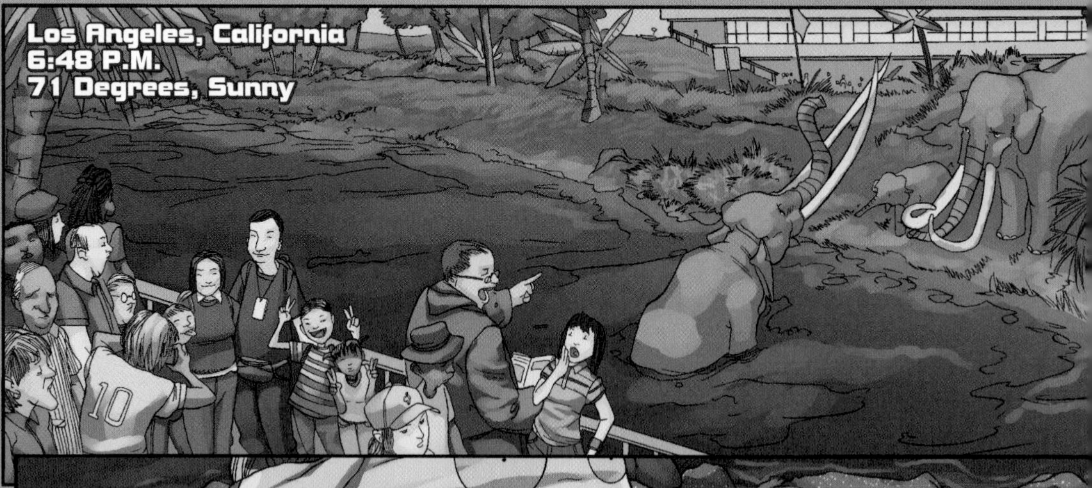
Los Angeles, California
6:48 P.M.
71 Degrees, Sunny

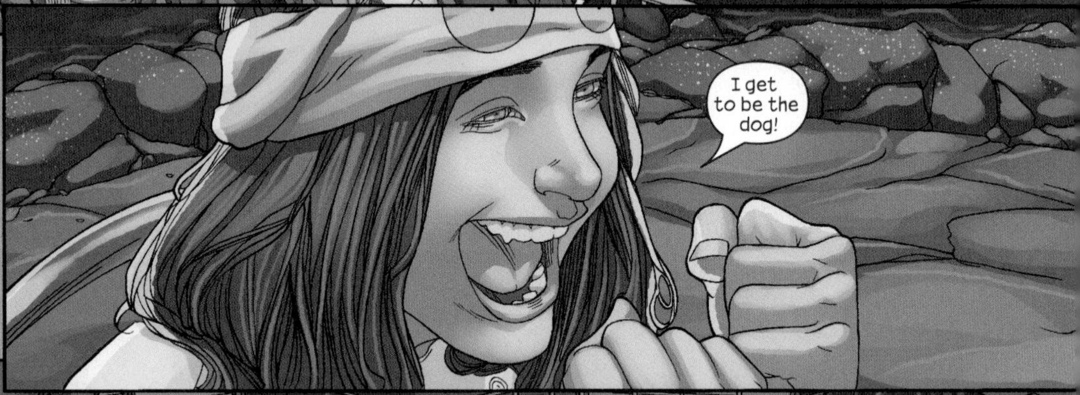
I get to be the dog!

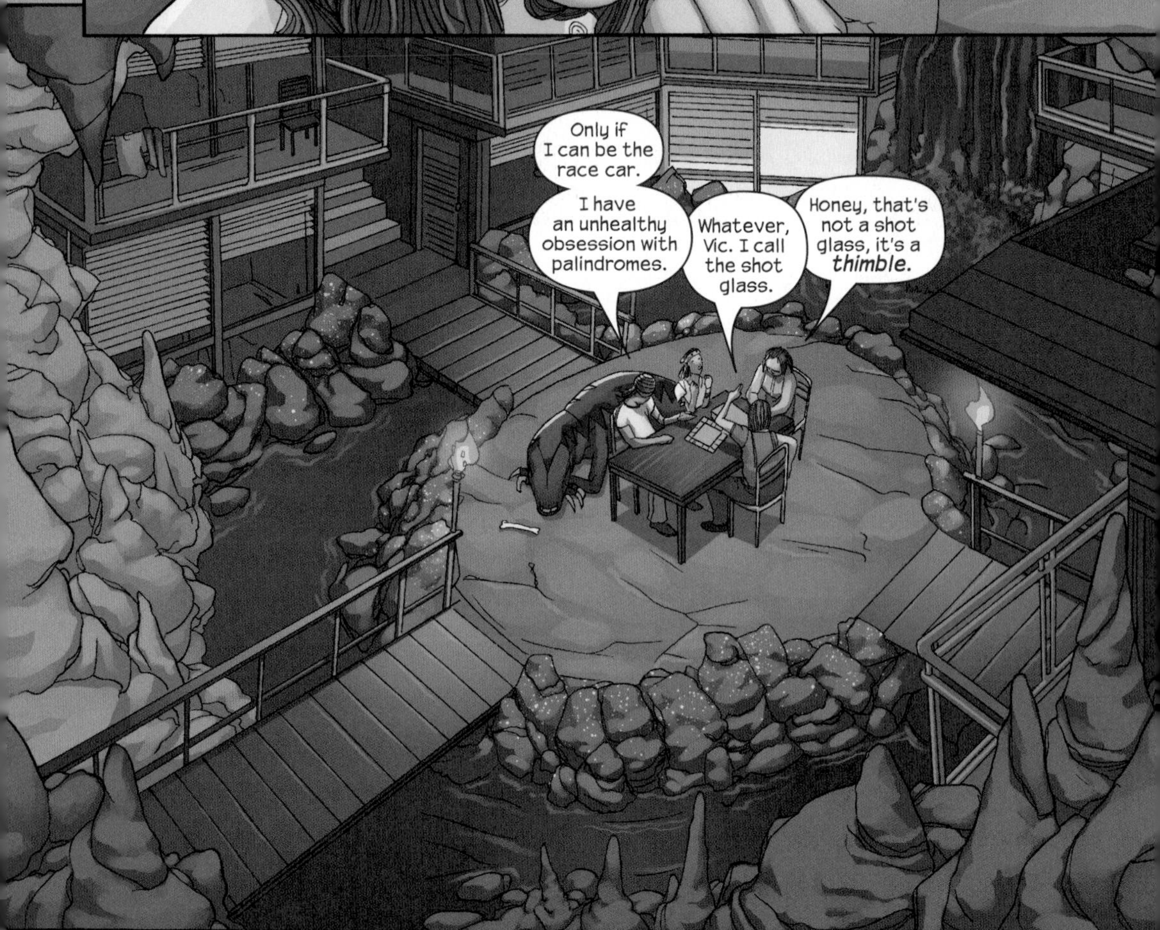
Only if I can be the race car.
I have an unhealthy obsession with palindromes.
Whatever, Vic. I call the shot glass.
Honey, that's not a shot glass, it's a *thimble.*

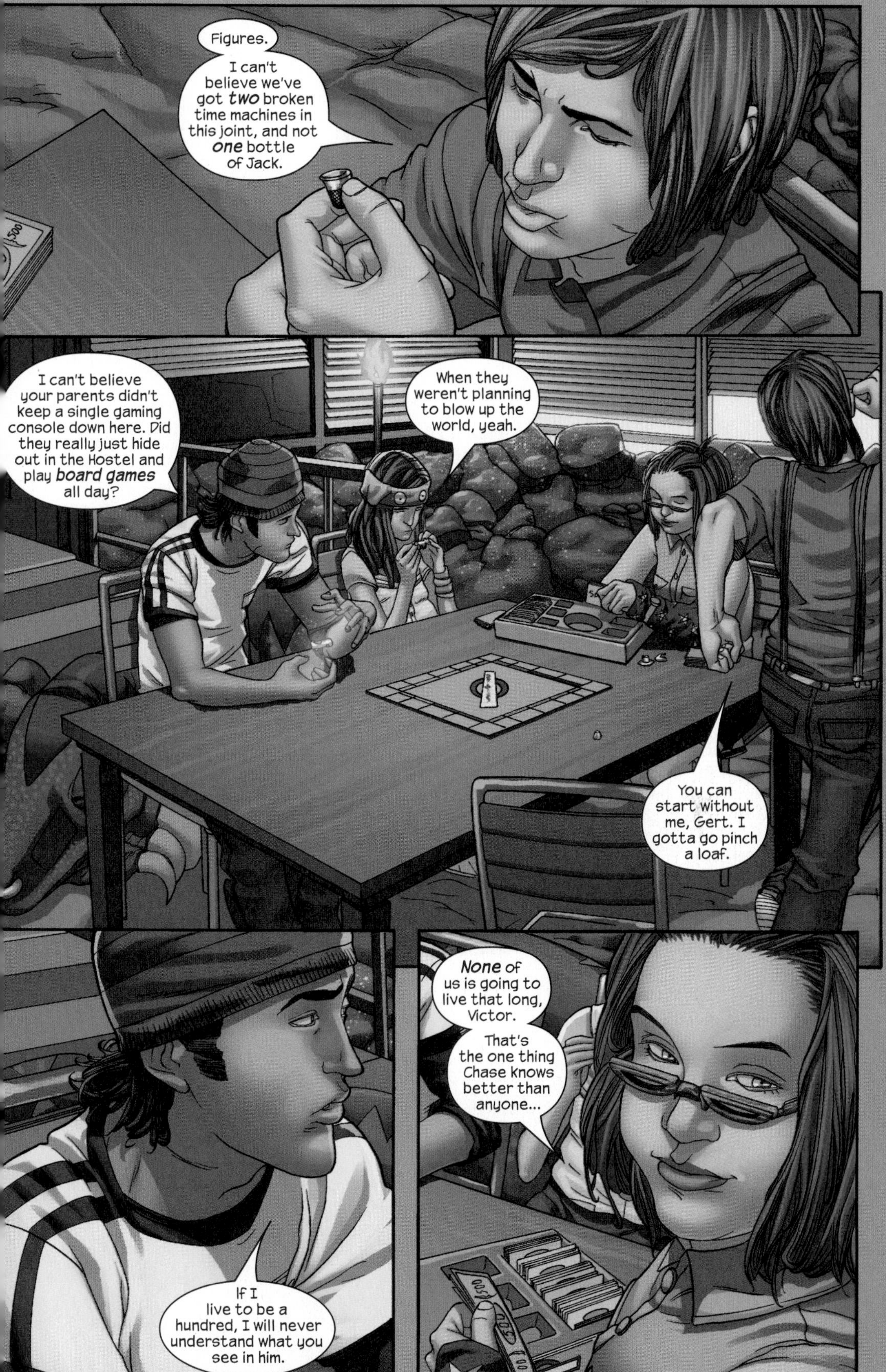
Figures.
I can't believe we've got *two* broken time machines in this joint, and not *one* bottle of Jack.
I can't believe your parents didn't keep a single gaming console down here. Did they really just hide out in the Hostel and play *board games* all day?
When they weren't planning to blow up the world, yeah.
You can start without me, Gert. I gotta go pinch a loaf.
If I live to be a hundred, I will never understand what you see in him.
None of us is going to live that long, Victor.
That's the one thing Chase knows better than anyone...

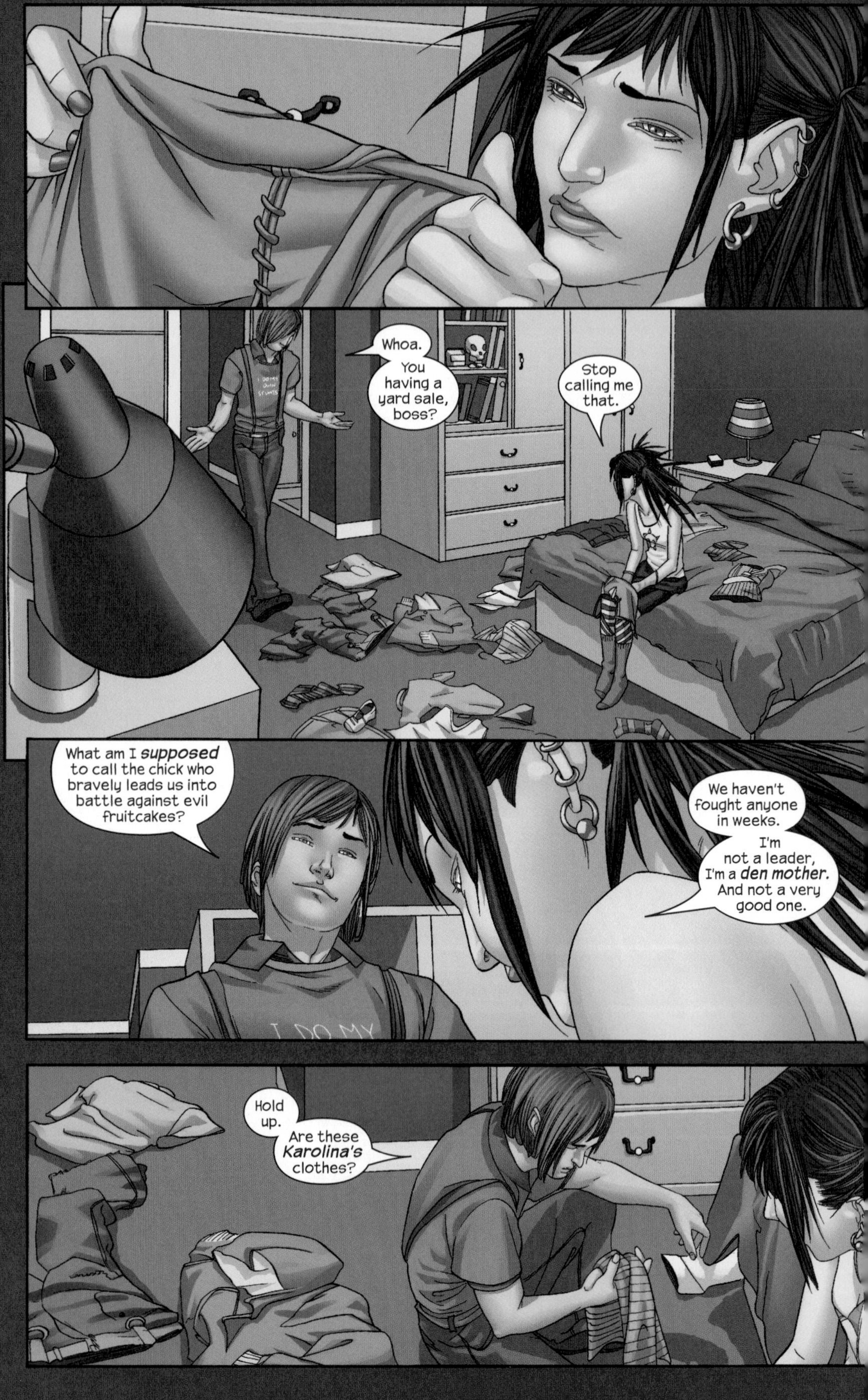
Whoa. You having a yard sale, boss?
Stop calling me that.
What am I *supposed* to call the chick who bravely leads us into battle against evil fruitcakes?
We haven't fought anyone in weeks.
I'm not a leader, I'm a *den mother.* And not a very good one.
Hold up.
Are these *Karolina's* clothes?

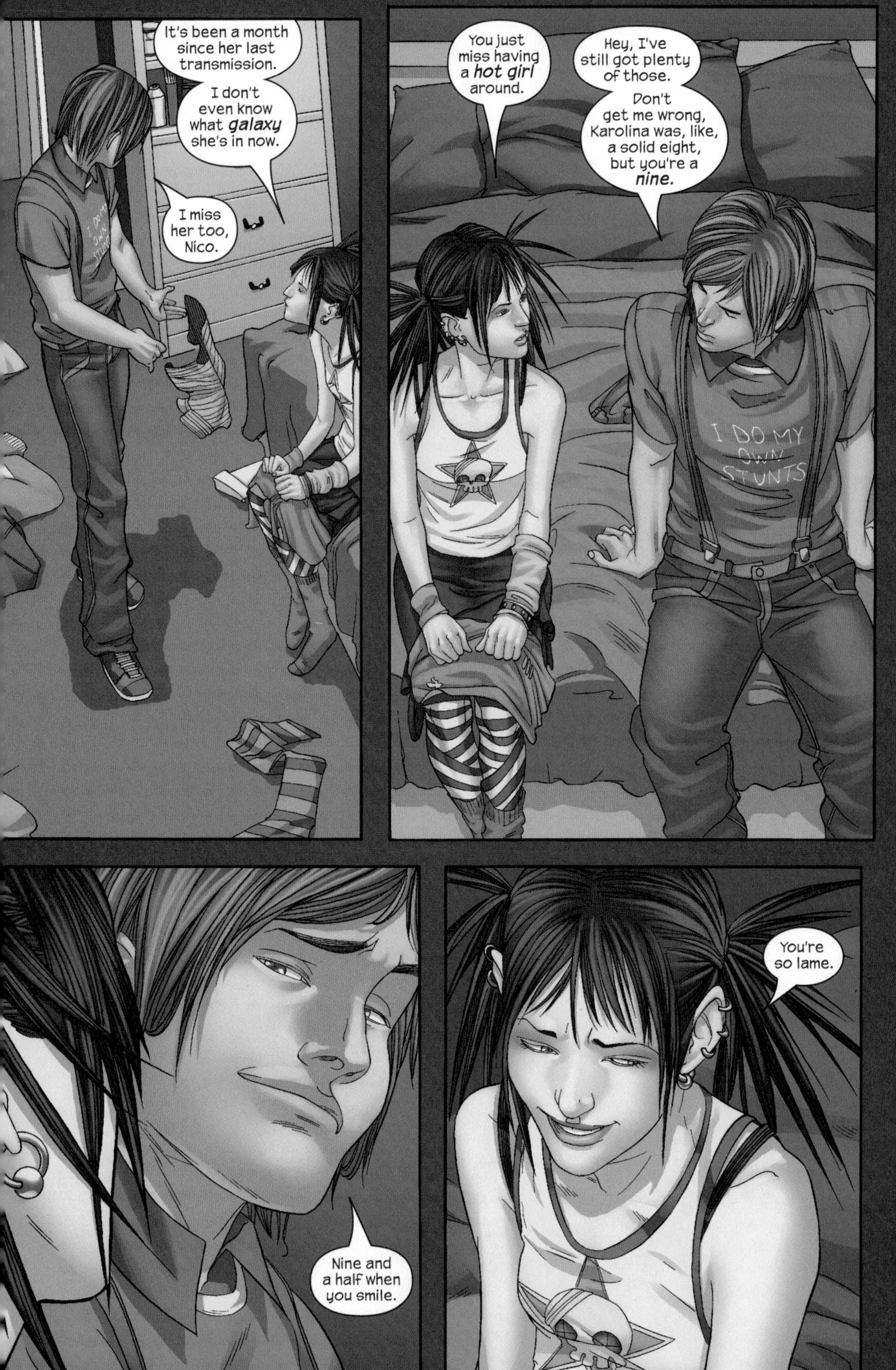
It's been a month since her last transmission.
I don't even know what *galaxy* she's in now.
I miss her too, Nico.
I DO MY OWN STUNTS
You just miss having a *hot girl* around.
Hey, I've still got plenty of those.
Don't get me wrong, Karolina was, like, a solid eight, but you're a *nine.*
I DO MY OWN STUNTS
Nine and a half when you smile.
You're so lame.

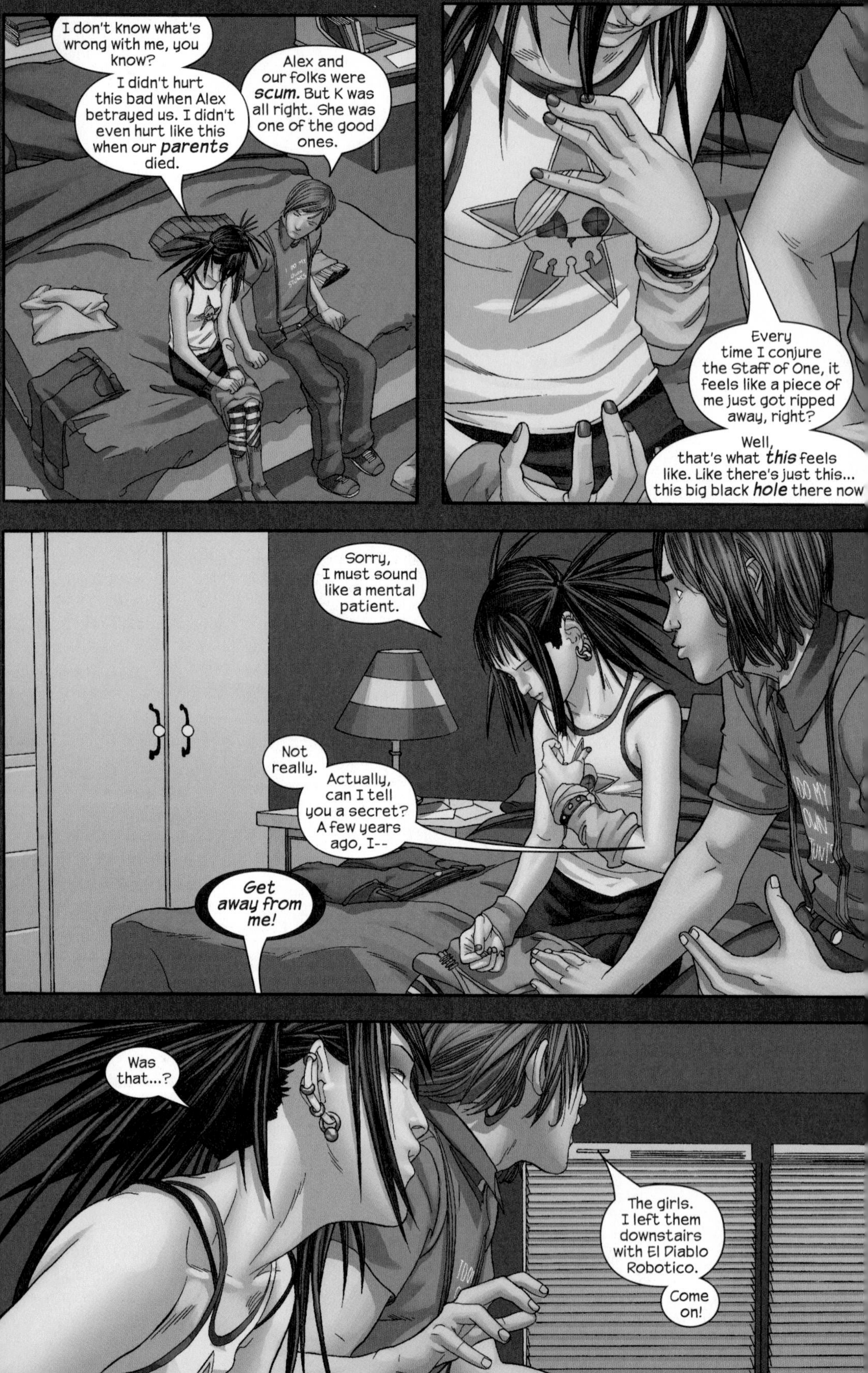
I don't know what's wrong with me, you know?
I didn't hurt this bad when Alex betrayed us. I didn't even hurt like this when our *parents* died.
Alex and our folks were ***scum.*** But K was all right. She was one of the good ones.
I DO MY OWN STUNTS
Every time I conjure the Staff of One, it feels like a piece of me just got ripped away, right?
Well, that's what ***this*** feels like. Like there's just this... this big black ***hole*** there now
Sorry, I must sound like a mental patient.
Not really.
Actually, can I tell you a secret? A few years ago, I--
Get away from me!
Was that...?
The girls. I left them downstairs with El Diablo Robotico.
Come on!

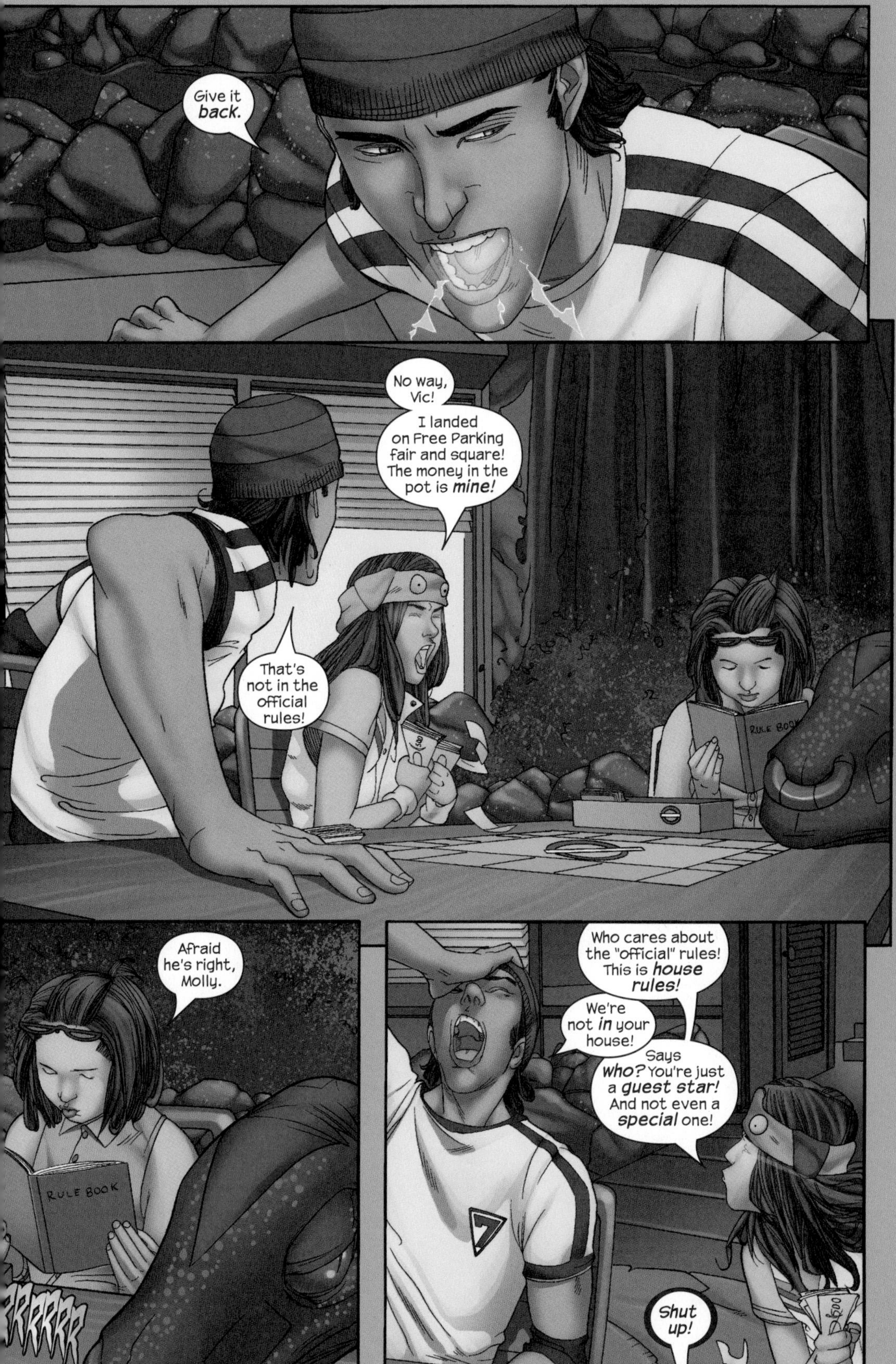
Give it back.
No way, Vic!
I landed on Free Parking fair and square! The money in the pot is mine!
That's not in the official rules!
RULE BOOK
Afraid he's right, Molly.
RULE BOOK
RRRRR
Who cares about the "official" rules! This is house rules!
We're not in your house!
Says who? You're just a guest star! And not even a special one!
Shut up!

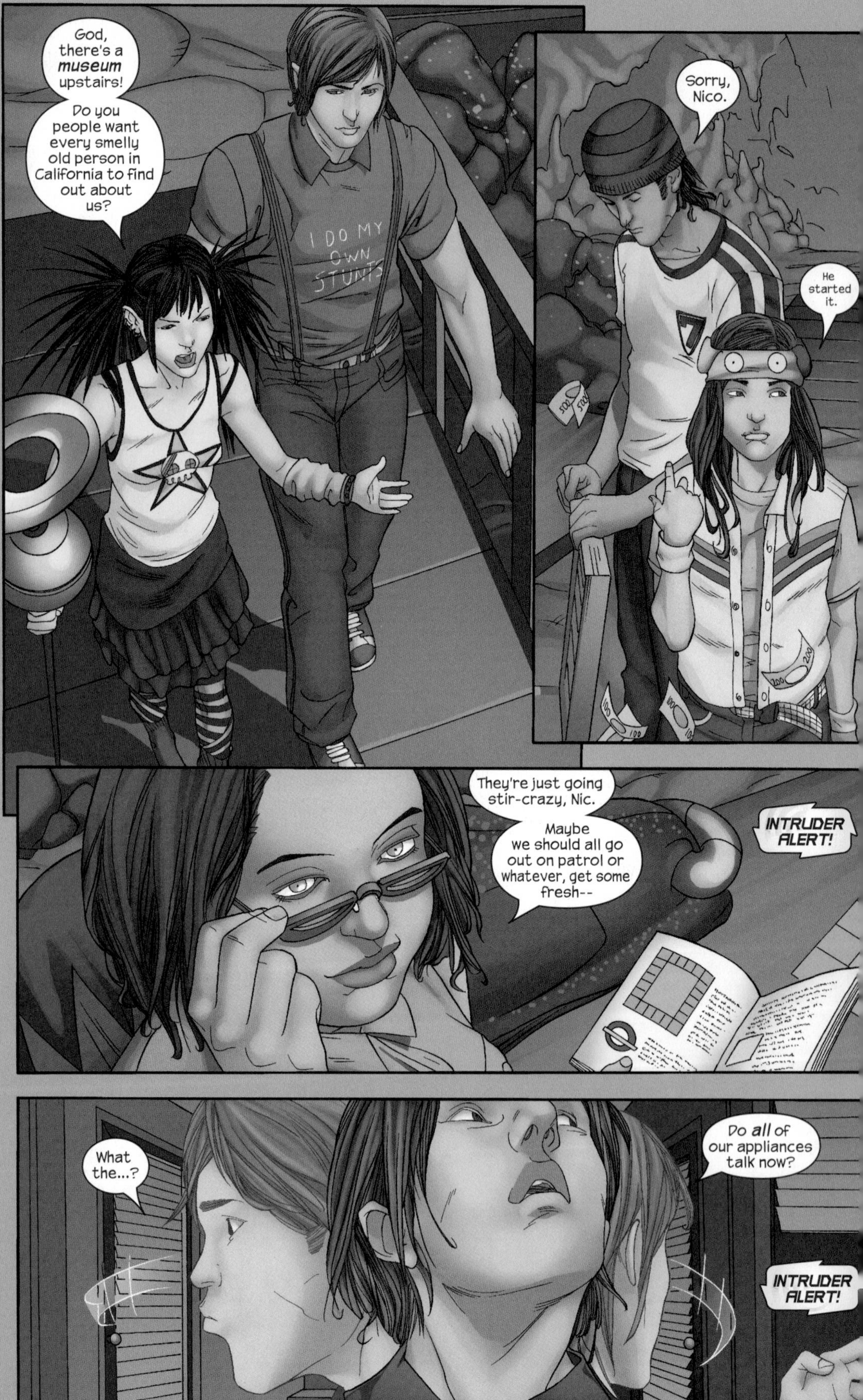
God, there's a **museum** upstairs!
Do you people want every smelly old person in California to find out about us?
I DO MY OWN STUNTS
Sorry, Nico.
He started it.
They're just going stir-crazy, Nic.
Maybe we should all go out on patrol or whatever, get some fresh--
INTRUDER ALERT!
What the...?
Do **all** of our appliances talk now?
INTRUDER ALERT!

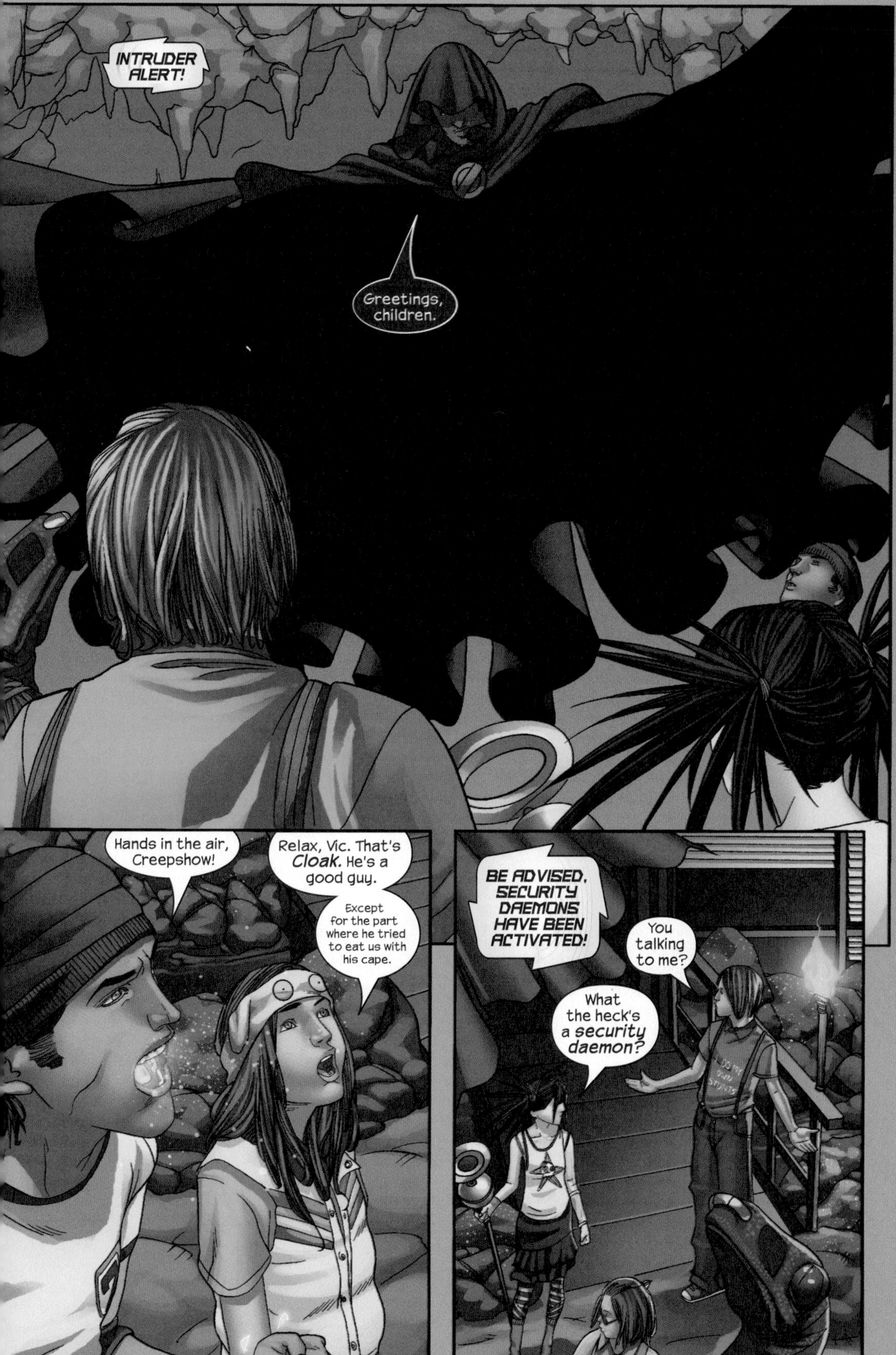
INTRUDER ALERT!
Greetings, children.
Hands in the air, Creepshow!
Relax, Vic. That's *Cloak*. He's a good guy.
Except for the part where he tried to eat us with his cape.
BE ADVISED. SECURITY DAEMONS HAVE BEEN ACTIVATED!
You talking to me?
What the heck's a *security daemon?*

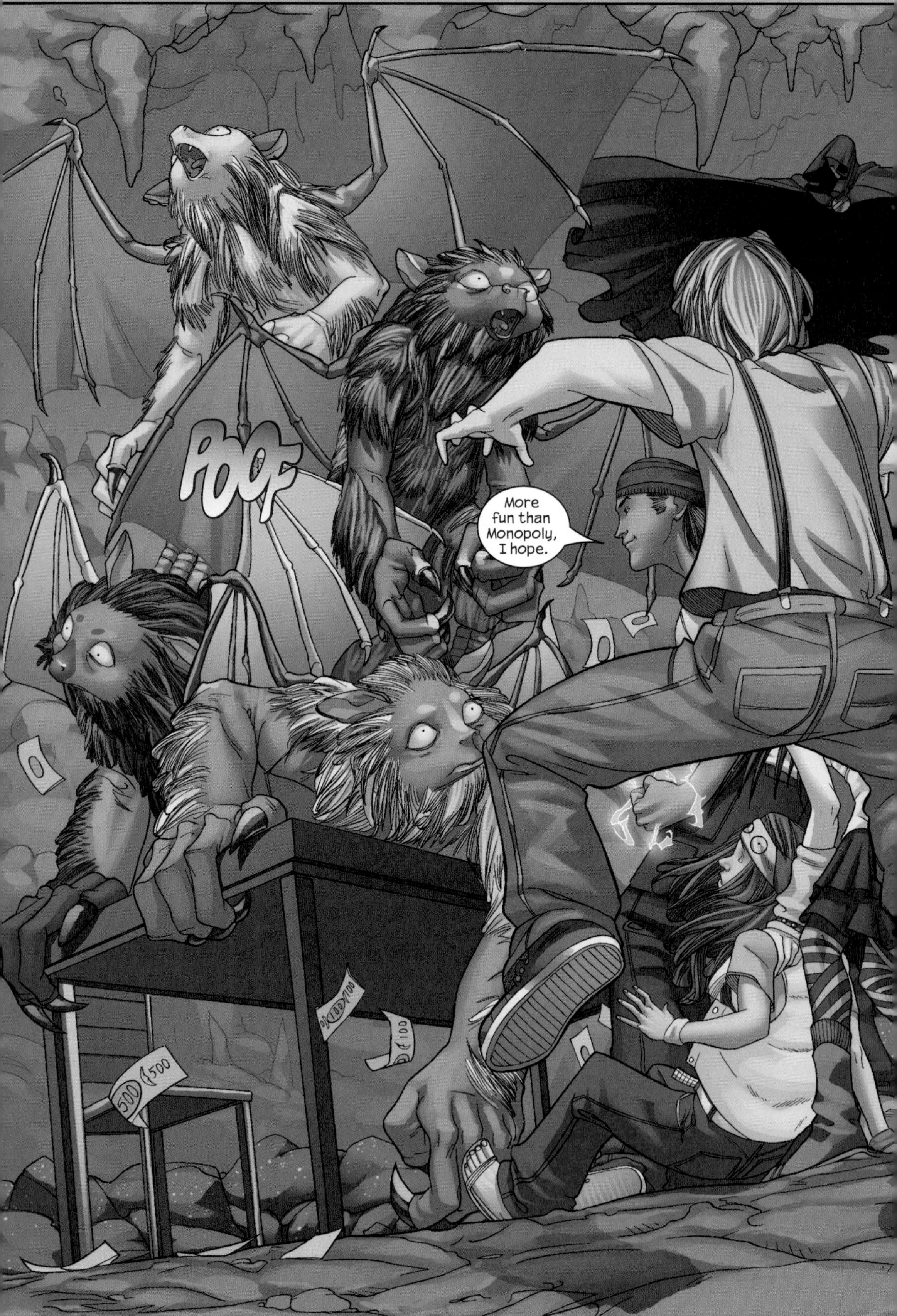
POOF
More fun than Monopoly, I hope.

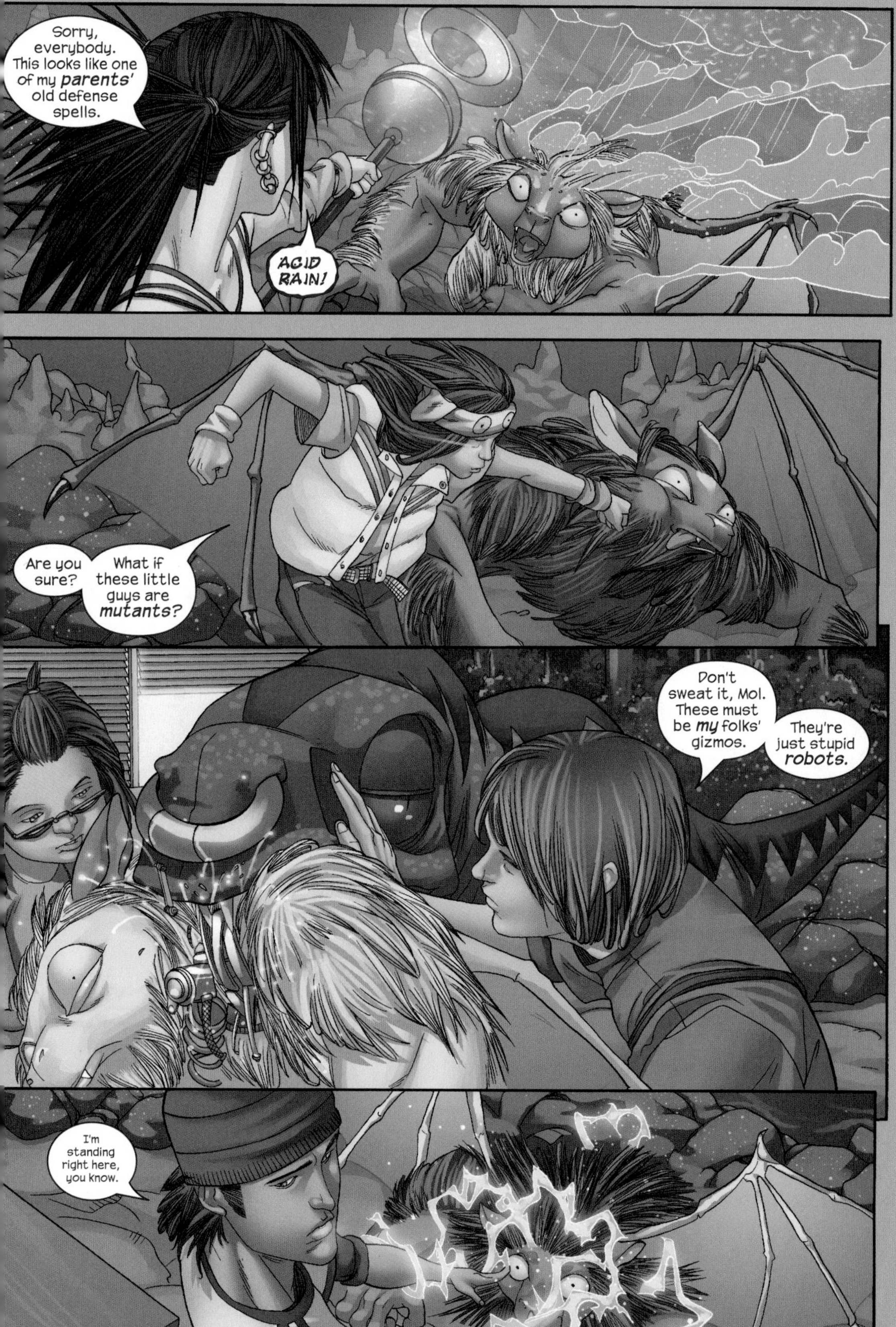

Sorry, everybody. This looks like one of my *parents'* old defense spells.
ACID RAIN!
Are you sure?
What if these little guys are *mutants*?
Don't sweat it, Mol. These must be *my* folks' gizmos.
They're just stupid *robots.*
I'm standing right here, you know.

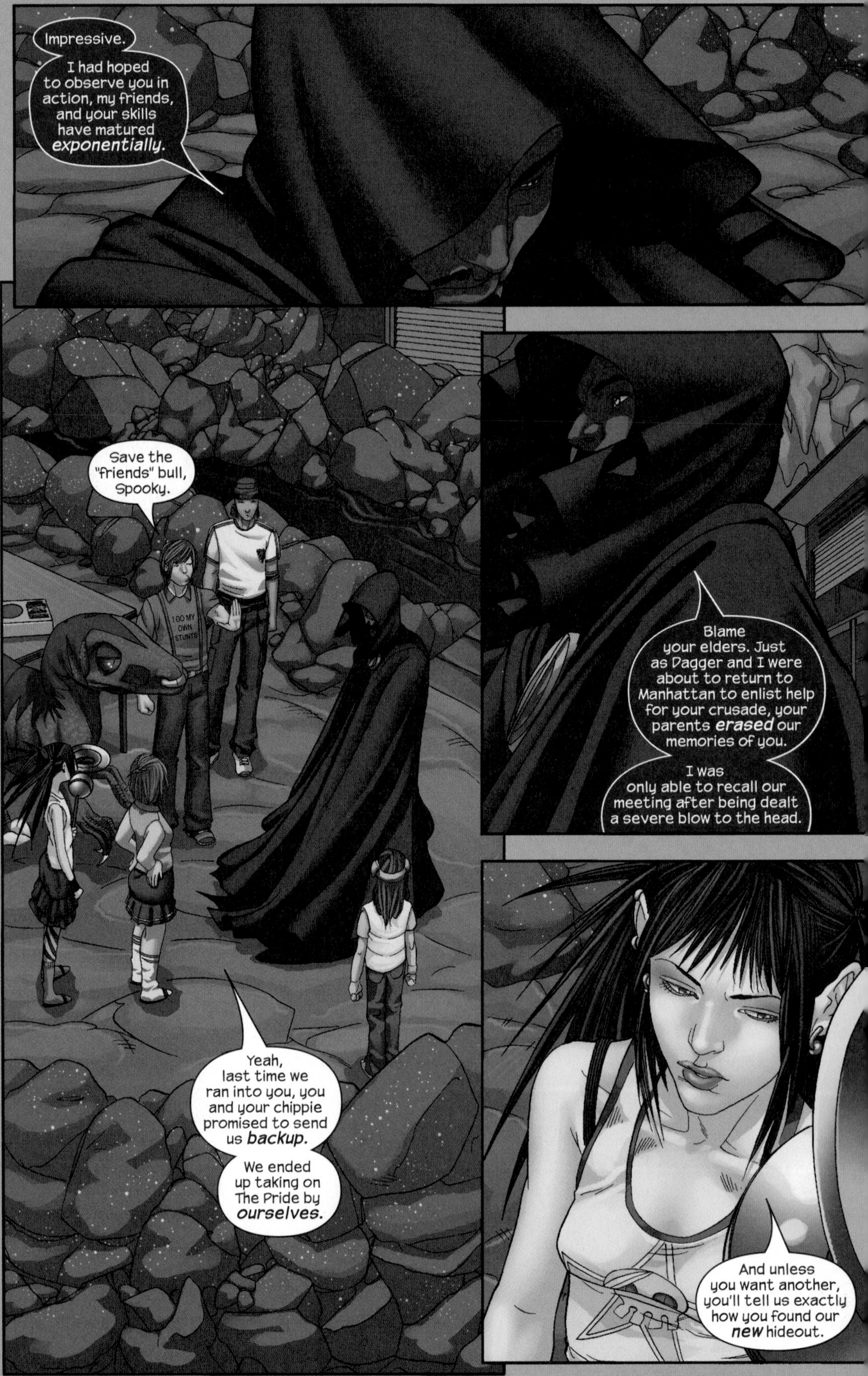
Impressive.
I had hoped to observe you in action, my friends, and your skills have matured *exponentially*.
Save the "friends" bull, Spooky.
I DO MY OWN STUNTS
Yeah, last time we ran into you, you and your chippie promised to send us *backup*.
We ended up taking on The Pride by *ourselves*.
Blame your elders. Just as Dagger and I were about to return to Manhattan to enlist help for your crusade, your parents *erased* our memories of you.
I was only able to recall our meeting after being dealt a severe blow to the head.
And unless you want another, you'll tell us exactly how you found our *new* hideout.

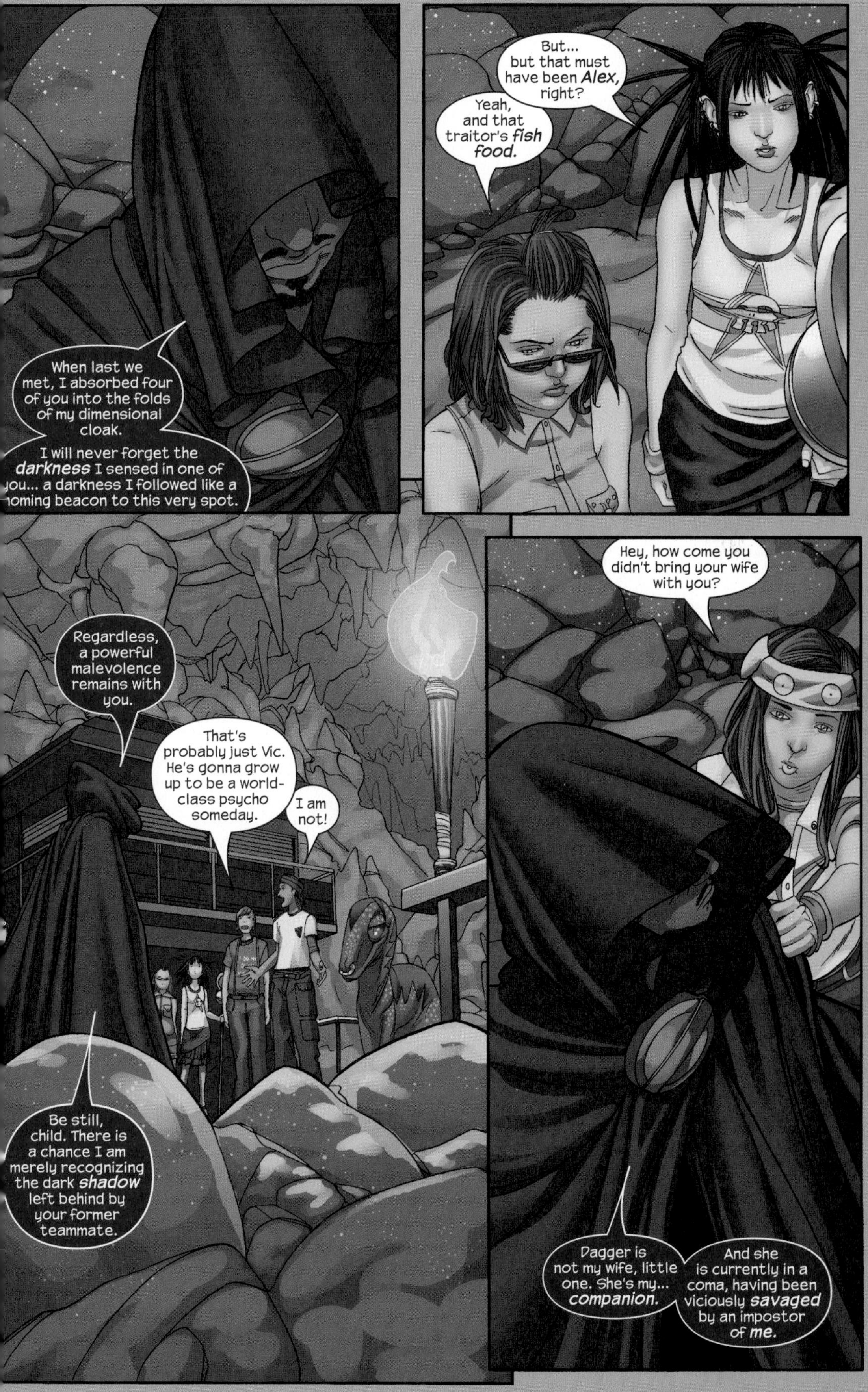

When last we met, I absorbed four of you into the folds of my dimensional cloak.
I will never forget the *darkness* I sensed in one of you... a darkness I followed like a homing beacon to this very spot.
But... but that must have been *Alex,* right?
Yeah, and that traitor's *fish food.*
Regardless, a powerful malevolence remains with you.
That's probably just Vic. He's gonna grow up to be a world-class psycho someday.
I am not!
Be still, child. There is a chance I am merely recognizing the dark *shadow* left behind by your former teammate.
Hey, how come you didn't bring your wife with you?
Dagger is not my wife, little one. She's my... *companion.*
And she is currently in a coma, having been viciously *savaged* by an impostor of *me.*

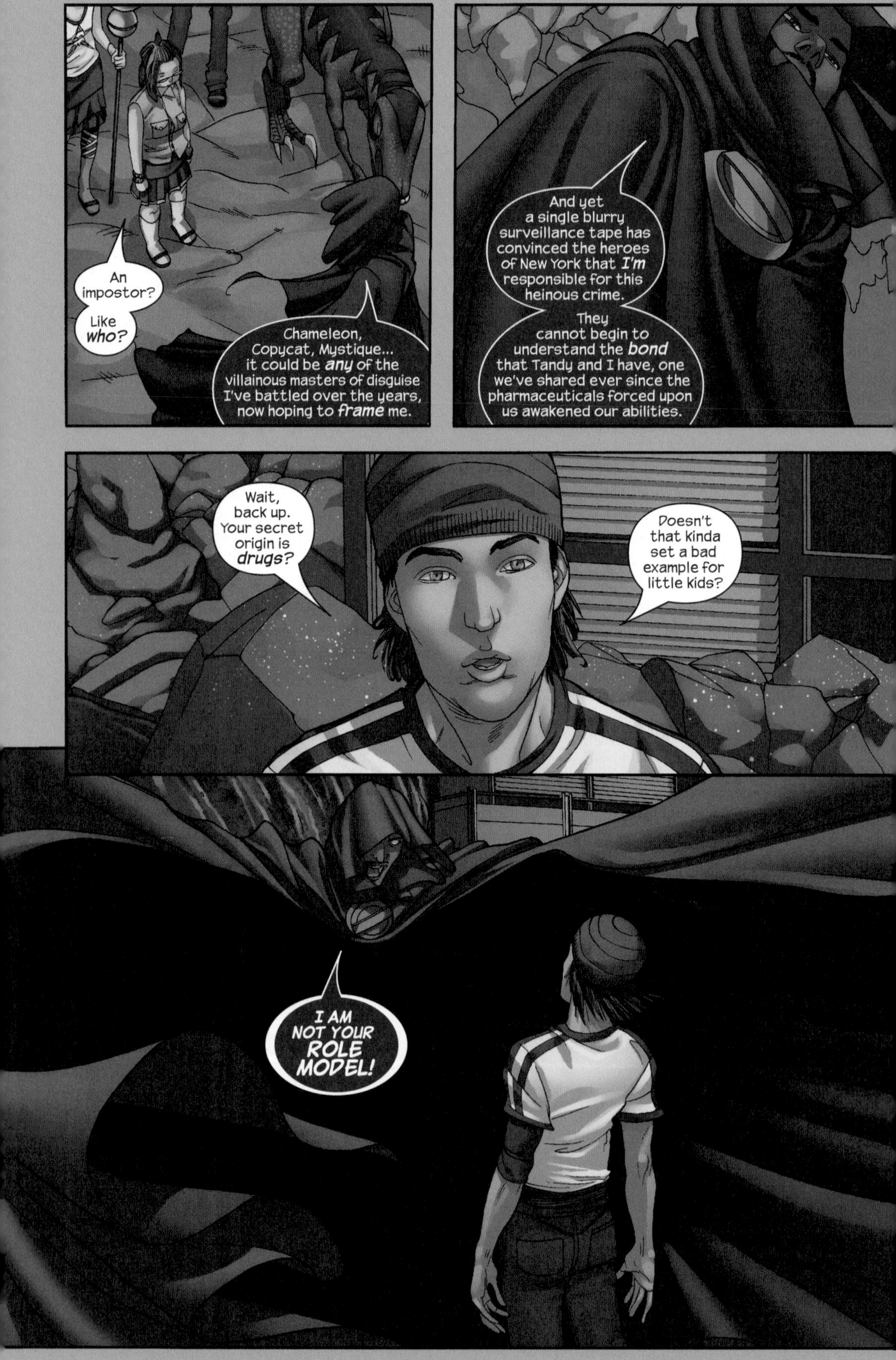
An impostor?
Like who?
Chameleon, Copycat, Mystique... it could be any of the villainous masters of disguise I've battled over the years, now hoping to frame me.
And yet a single blurry surveillance tape has convinced the heroes of New York that I'm responsible for this heinous crime.
They cannot begin to understand the bond that Tandy and I have, one we've shared ever since the pharmaceuticals forced upon us awakened our abilities.
Wait, back up. Your secret origin is drugs?
Doesn't that kinda set a bad example for little kids?
I AM NOT YOUR ROLE MODEL!

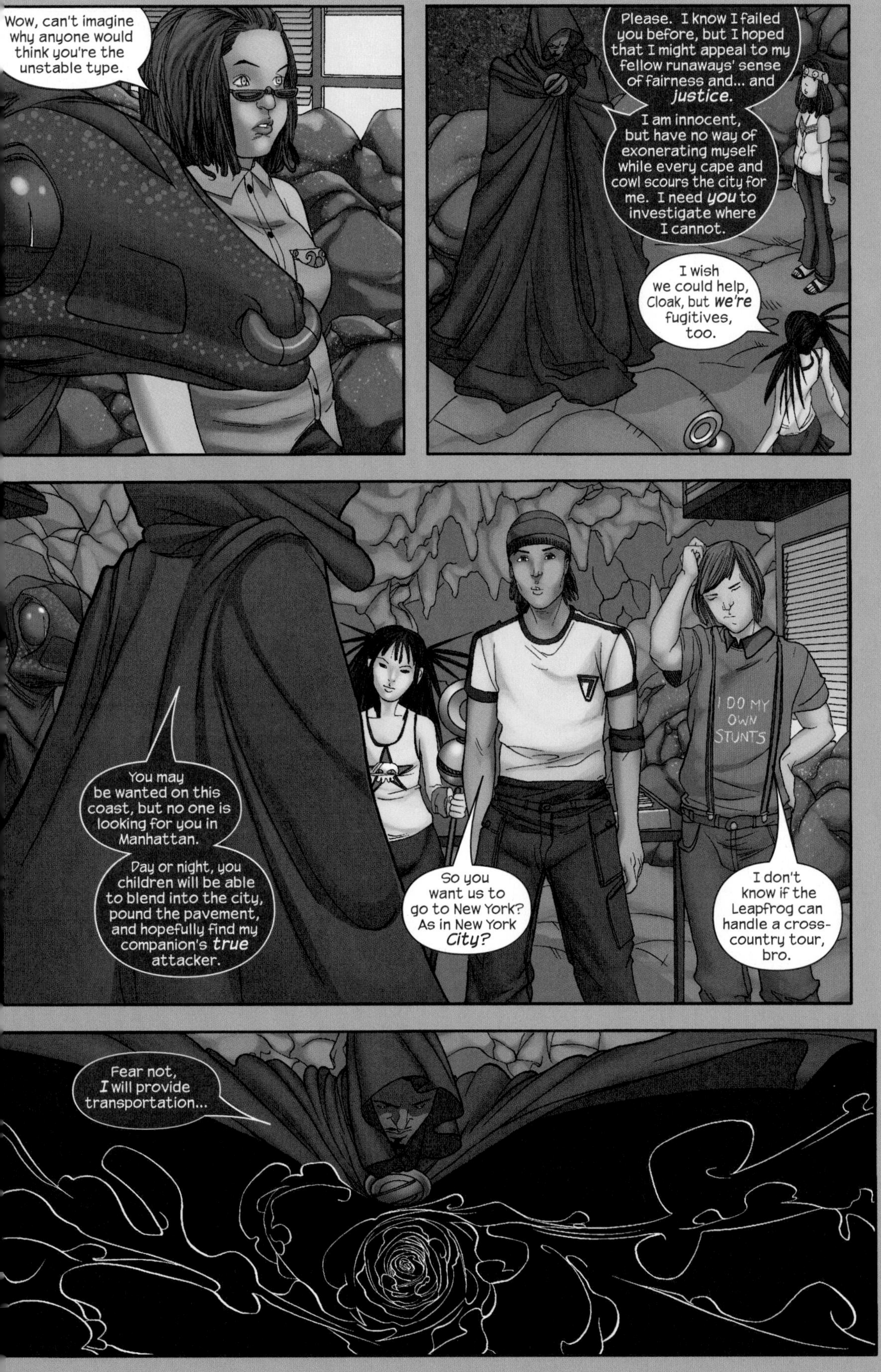
Wow, can't imagine why anyone would think you're the unstable type.
Please. I know I failed you before, but I hoped that I might appeal to my fellow runaways' sense of fairness and... and *justice*.
I am innocent, but have no way of exonerating myself while every cape and cowl scours the city for me. I need *you* to investigate where I cannot.
I wish we could help, Cloak, but *we're* fugitives, too.
I DO MY OWN STUNTS
You may be wanted on this coast, but no one is looking for you in Manhattan.
Day or night, you children will be able to blend into the city, pound the pavement, and hopefully find my companion's *true* attacker.
So you want us to go to New York? As in New York *City?*
I don't know if the Leapfrog can handle a cross-country tour, bro.
Fear not, *I* will provide transportation...

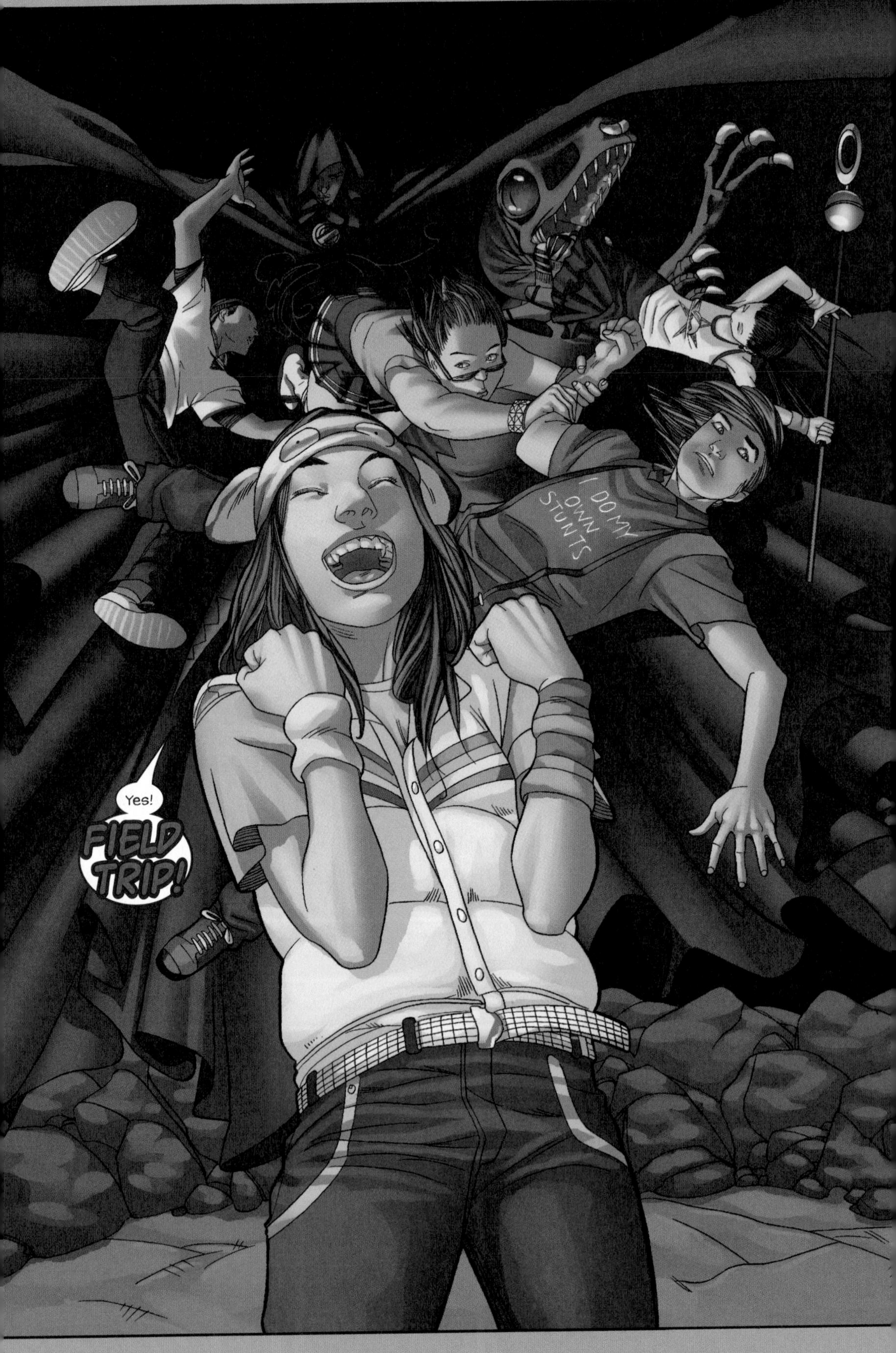
I DO MY OWN STUNTS
Yes!
FIELD TRIP!

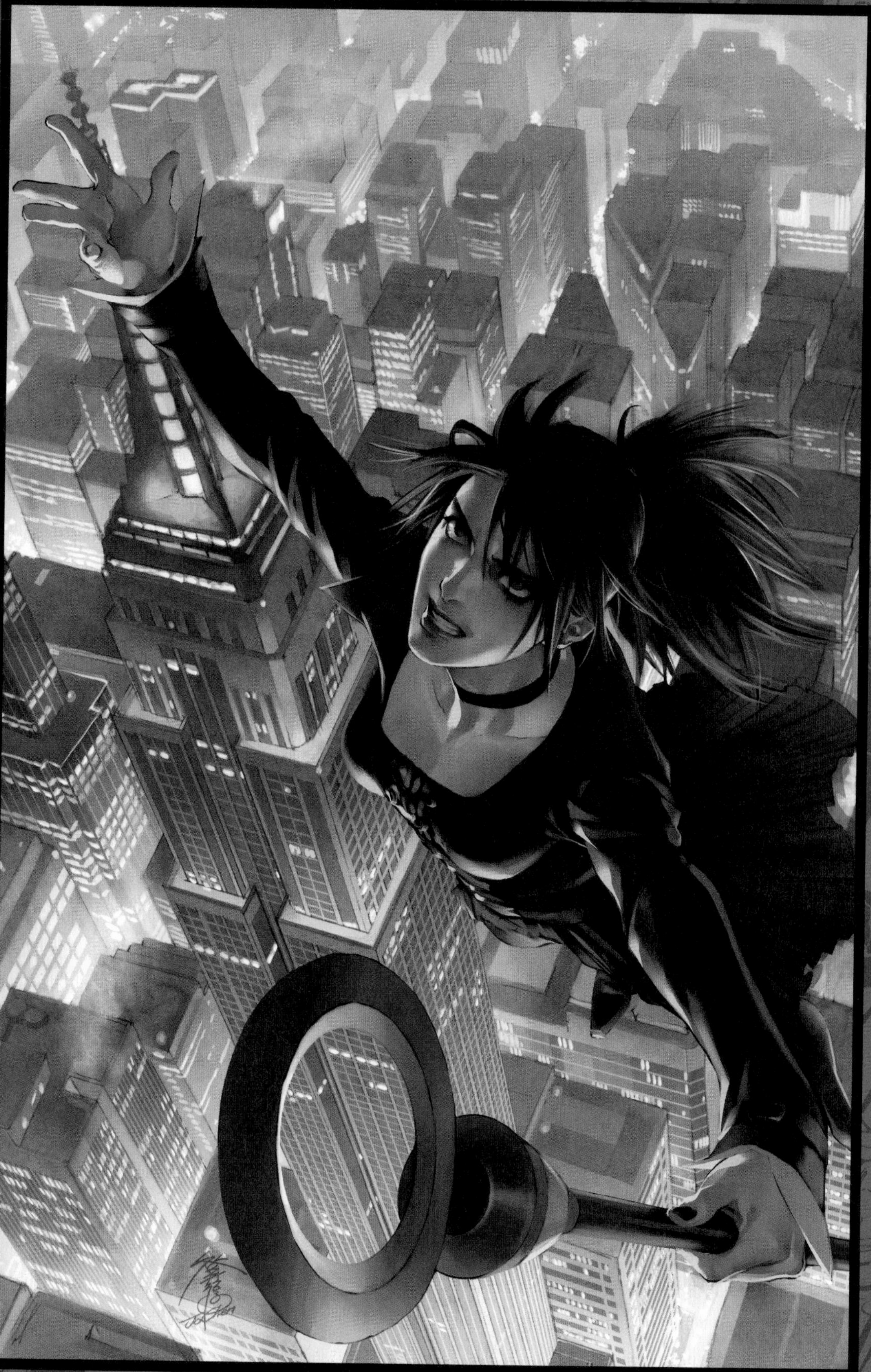

***RUNAWAYS* (2005) #10**
"EAST COAST/WEST COAST, PART 2"

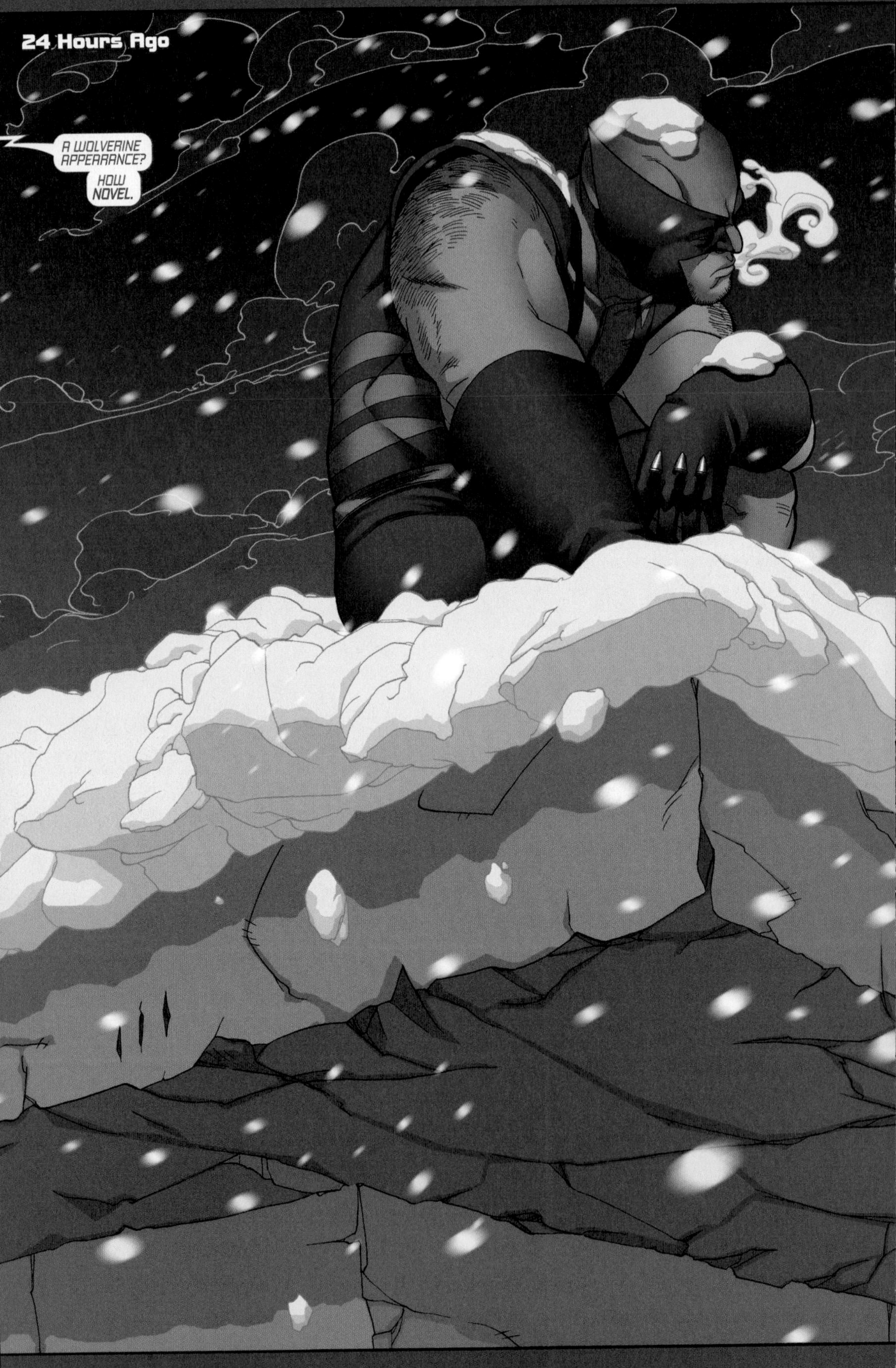
24 Hours Ago
A WOLVERINE APPEARANCE?
HOW NOVEL.

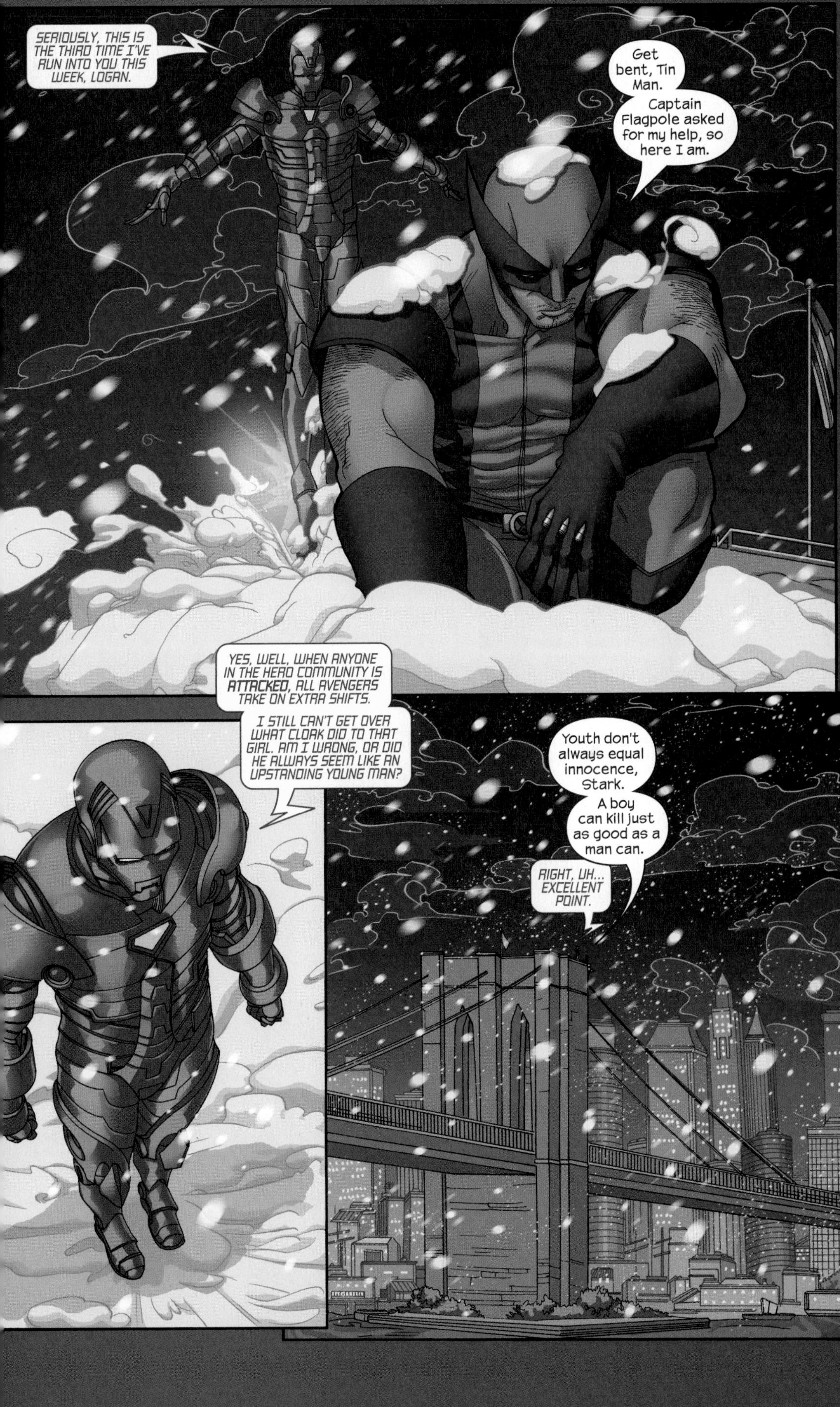
SERIOUSLY, THIS IS THE THIRD TIME I'VE RUN INTO YOU THIS WEEK, LOGAN.
Get bent, Tin Man.
Captain Flagpole asked for my help, so here I am.
YES, WELL, WHEN ANYONE IN THE HERO COMMUNITY IS **ATTACKED**, ALL AVENGERS TAKE ON EXTRA SHIFTS.
I STILL CAN'T GET OVER WHAT CLOAK DID TO THAT GIRL. AM I WRONG, OR DID HE ALWAYS SEEM LIKE AN UPSTANDING YOUNG MAN?
Youth don't always equal innocence, Stark.
A boy can kill just as good as a man can.
RIGHT, UH... EXCELLENT POINT.

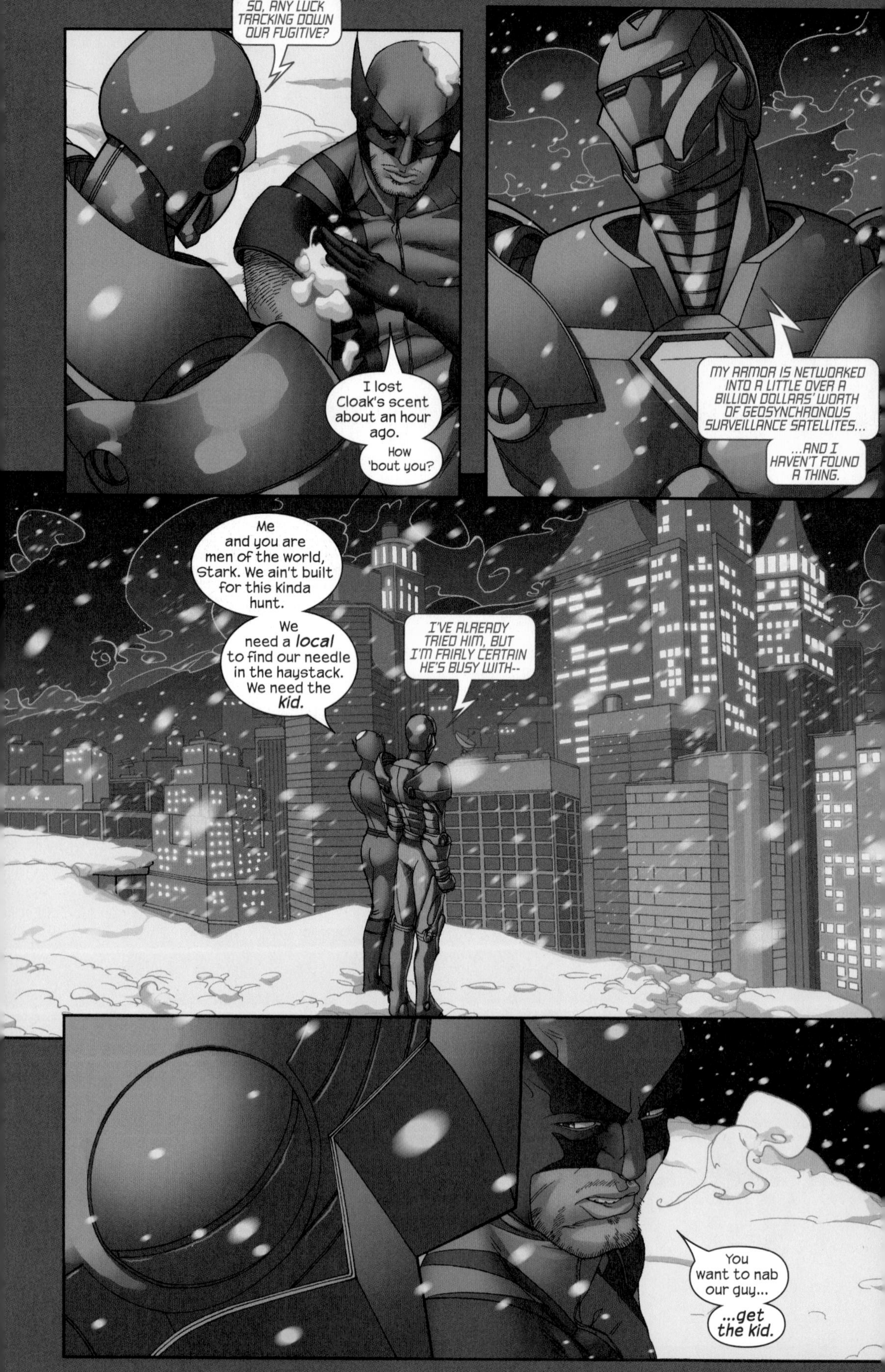
SO, ANY LUCK TRACKING DOWN OUR FUGITIVE?
I lost Cloak's scent about an hour ago.
How 'bout you?
MY ARMOR IS NETWORKED INTO A LITTLE OVER A BILLION DOLLARS' WORTH OF GEOSYNCHRONOUS SURVEILLANCE SATELLITES...
...AND I HAVEN'T FOUND A THING.
Me and you are men of the world, Stark. We ain't built for this kinda hunt.
We need a *local* to find our needle in the haystack. We need the ***kid.***
I'VE ALREADY TRIED HIM, BUT I'M FAIRLY CERTAIN HE'S BUSY WITH--
You want to nab our guy...
...get the kid.

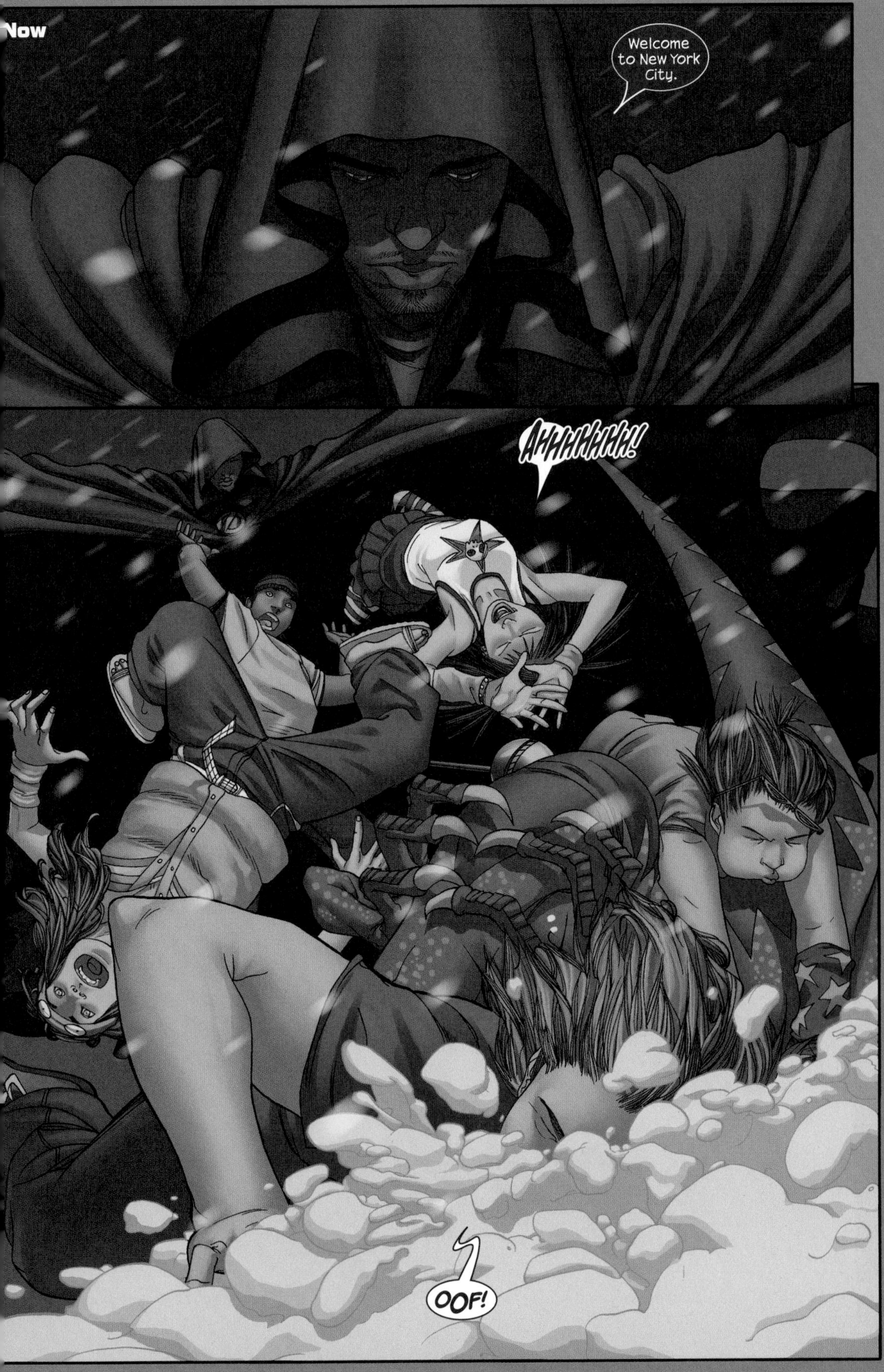
Now
Welcome to New York City.
AHHHHHHH!
OOF!

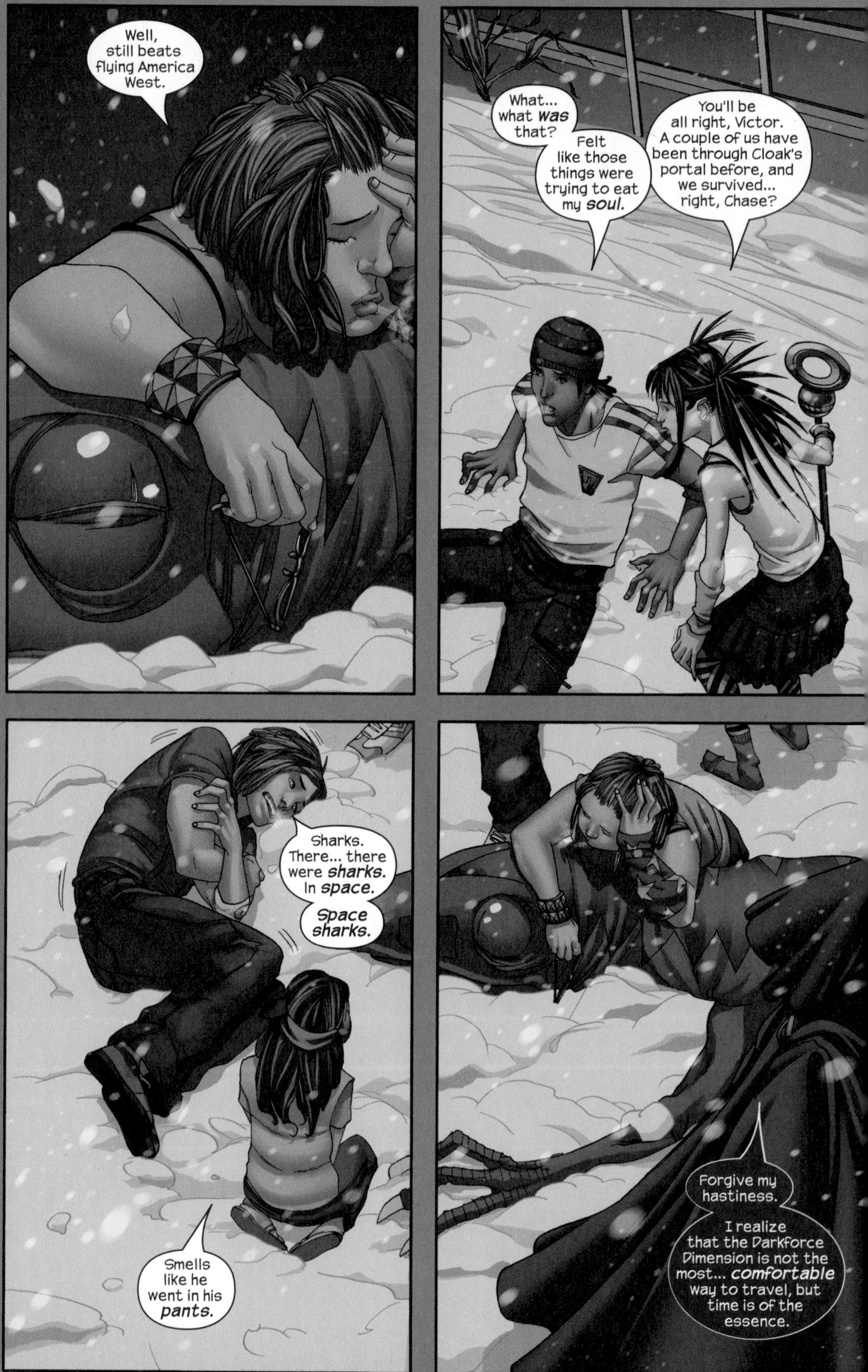

Well, still beats flying America West.
What... what *was* that?
Felt like those things were trying to eat my *soul.*
You'll be all right, Victor. A couple of us have been through Cloak's portal before, and we survived... right, Chase?
Sharks. There... there were *sharks.* In *space.*
Space sharks.
Smells like he went in his *pants.*
Forgive my hastiness.
I realize that the Darkforce Dimension is not the most... *comfortable* way to travel, but time is of the essence.

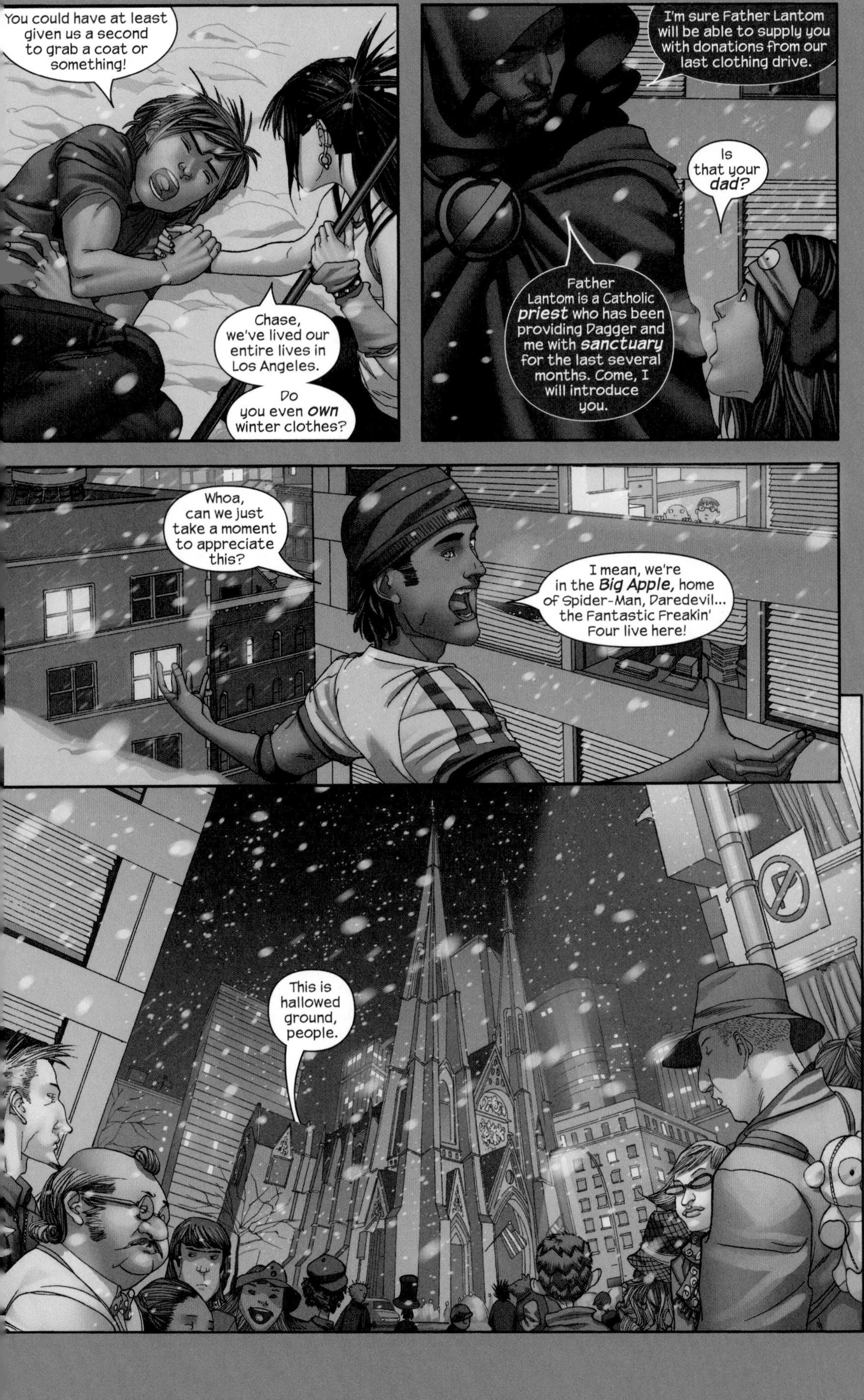
You could have at least given us a second to grab a coat or something!
Chase, we've lived our entire lives in Los Angeles.
Do you even *OWN* winter clothes?
I'm sure Father Lantom will be able to supply you with donations from our last clothing drive.
Is that your *dad?*
Father Lantom is a Catholic *priest* who has been providing Dagger and me with *sanctuary* for the last several months. Come, I will introduce you.
Whoa, can we just take a moment to appreciate this?
I mean, we're in the *Big Apple,* home of Spider-Man, Daredevil... the Fantastic Freakin' Four live here!
This is hallowed ground, people.

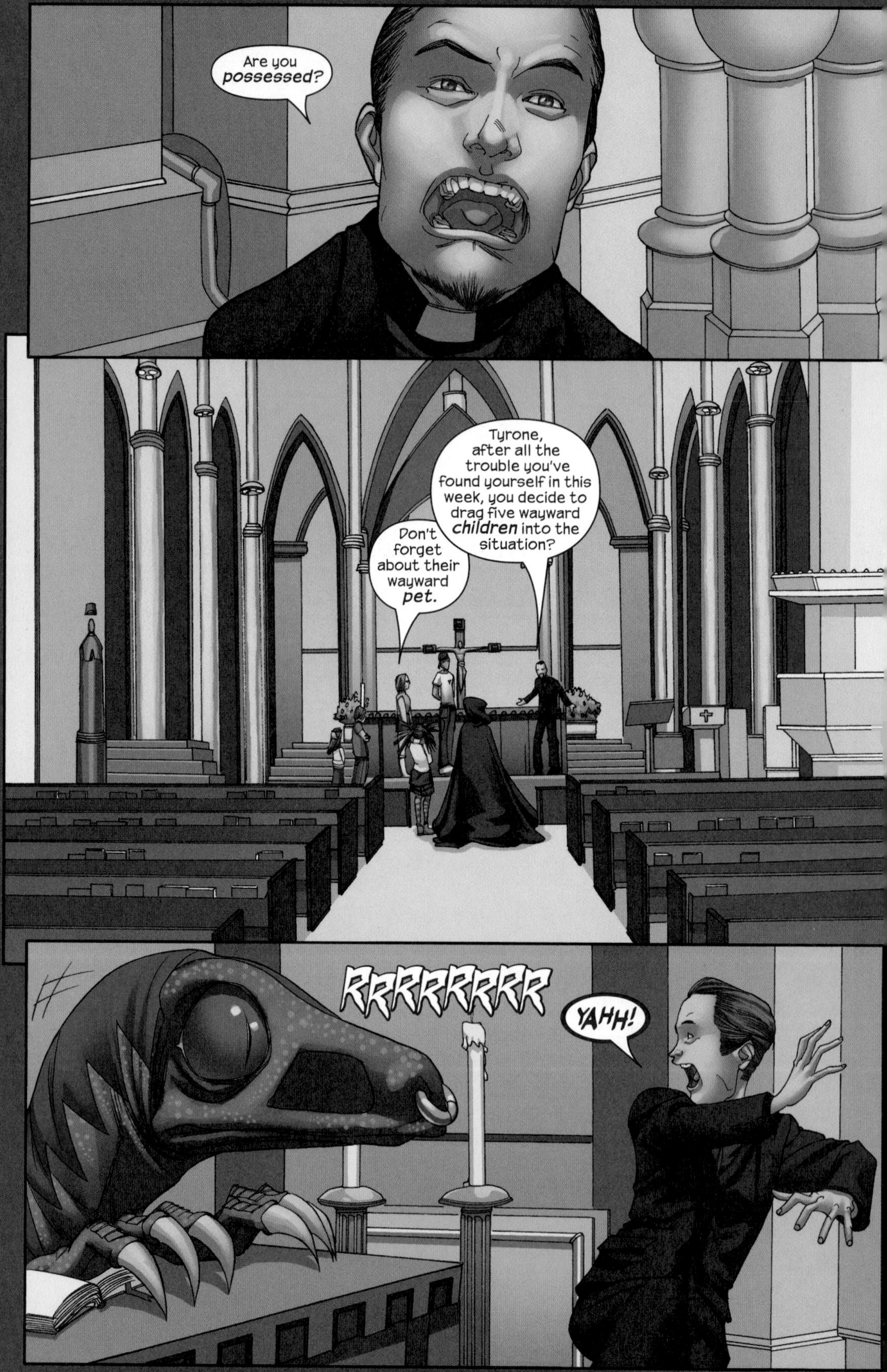
Are you *possessed?*
Don't forget about their wayward ***pet.***
Tyrone, after all the trouble you've found yourself in this week, you decide to drag five wayward ***children*** into the situation?
RRRRRRRR
YAHH!

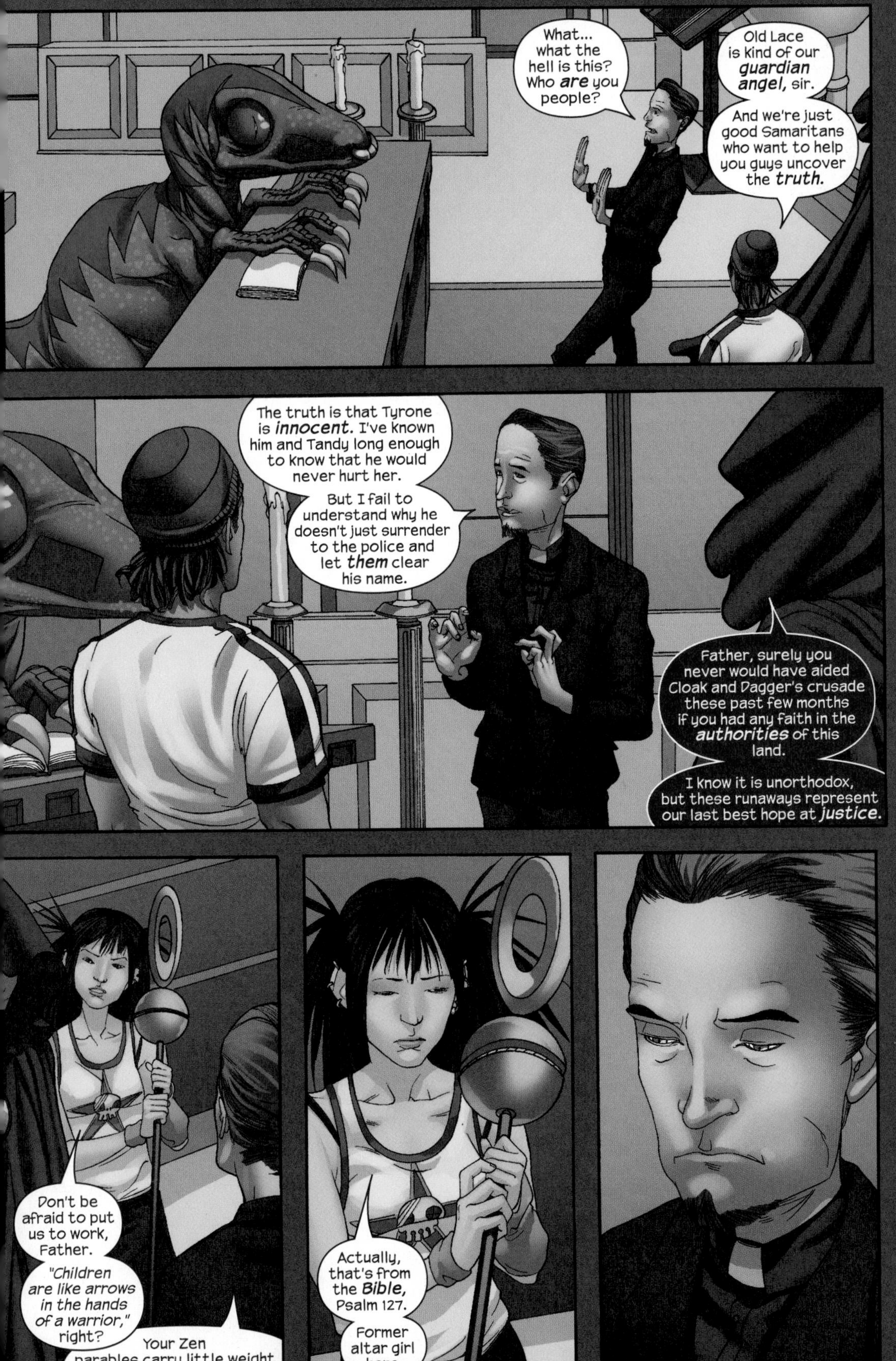

What... what the hell is this? Who *are* you people?
Old Lace is kind of our *guardian angel,* sir.
And we're just good Samaritans who want to help you guys uncover the *truth.*
The truth is that Tyrone is *innocent.* I've known him and Tandy long enough to know that he would never hurt her.
But I fail to understand why he doesn't just surrender to the police and let *them* clear his name.
Father, surely you never would have aided Cloak and Dagger's crusade these past few months if you had any faith in the *authorities* of this land.
I know it is unorthodox, but these runaways represent our last best hope at *justice.*
Don't be afraid to put us to work, Father.
"Children are like arrows in the hands of a warrior," right?
Your Zen parables carry little weight in this house, young lady.
Actually, that's from the *Bible,* Psalm 127.
Former altar girl here.

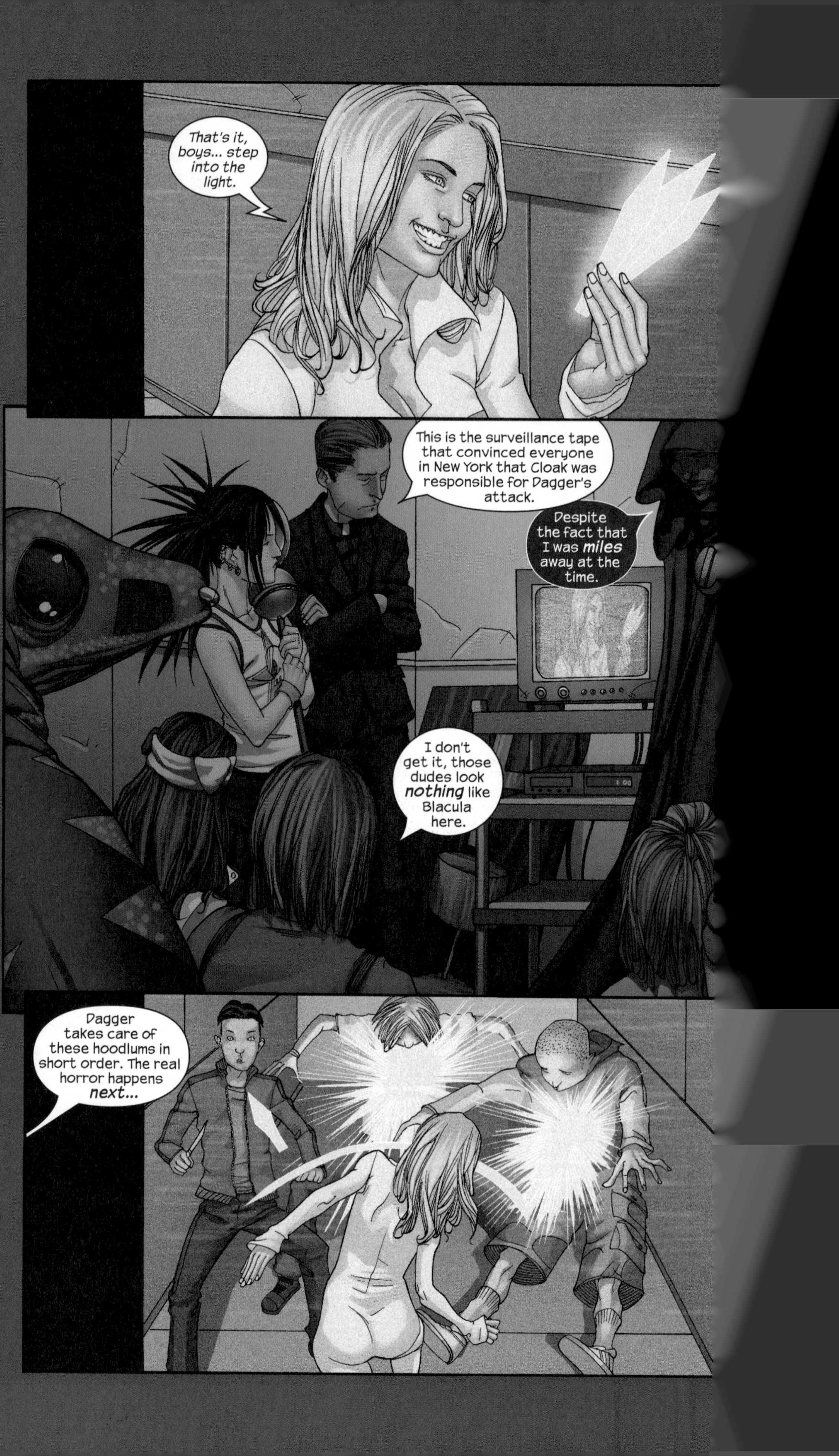
That's it, boys... step into the light.
This is the surveillance tape that convinced everyone in New York that Cloak was responsible for Dagger's attack.
Despite the fact that I was *miles* away at the time.
I don't get it, those dudes look **nothing** like Blacula here.
Dagger takes care of these hoodlums in short order. The real horror happens *next*...

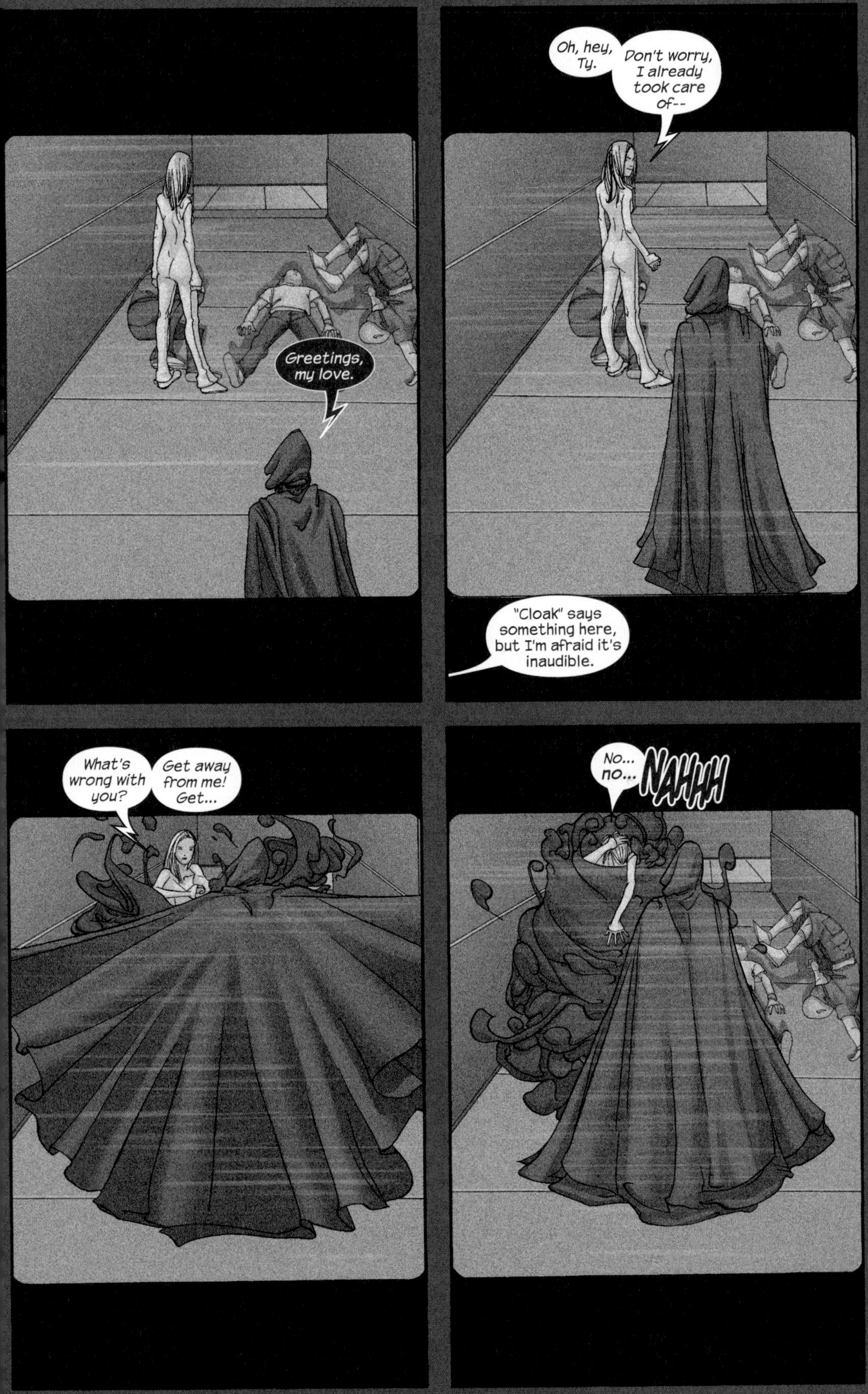
Greetings, my love.
Oh, hey, Ty.
Don't worry, I already took care of--
"Cloak" says something here, but I'm afraid it's inaudible.
What's wrong with you?
Get away from me! Get...
No... no...
NAHHH

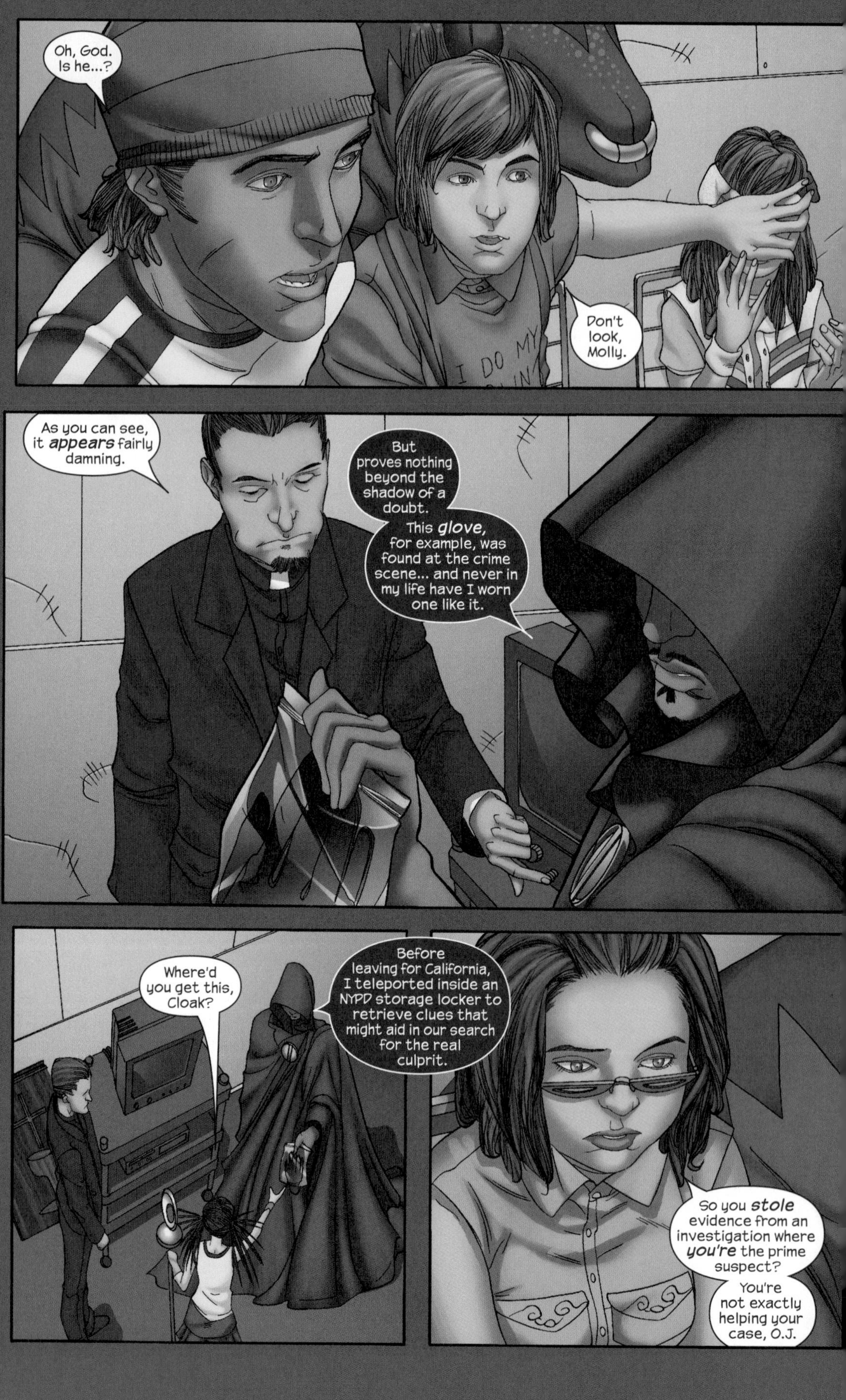

Oh, God. Is he...?
Don't look, Molly.
I DO MY
As you can see, it **appears** fairly damning.
But proves nothing beyond the shadow of a doubt.
This **glove,** for example, was found at the crime scene... and never in my life have I worn one like it.
Where'd you get this, Cloak?
Before leaving for California, I teleported inside an NYPD storage locker to retrieve clues that might aid in our search for the real culprit.
So you **stole** evidence from an investigation where **you're** the prime suspect?
You're not exactly helping your case, O.J.

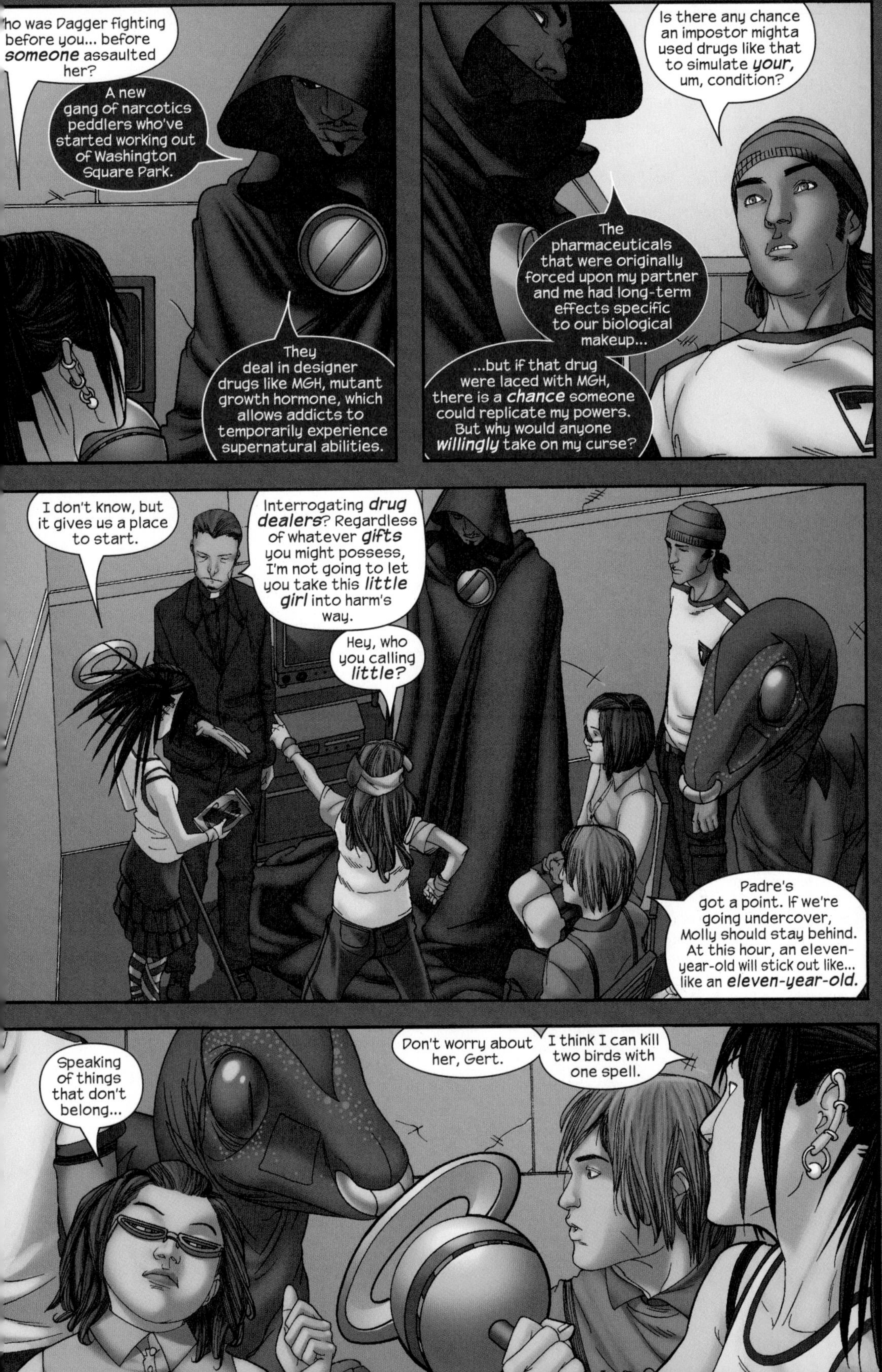

ho was Dagger fighting before you... before someone assaulted her?
A new gang of narcotics peddlers who've started working out of Washington Square Park.
They deal in designer drugs like MGH, mutant growth hormone, which allows addicts to temporarily experience supernatural abilities.
Is there any chance an impostor mighta used drugs like that to simulate your, um, condition?
The pharmaceuticals that were originally forced upon my partner and me had long-term effects specific to our biological makeup...
...but if that drug were laced with MGH, there is a chance someone could replicate my powers. But why would anyone willingly take on my curse?
I don't know, but it gives us a place to start.
Interrogating drug dealers? Regardless of whatever gifts you might possess, I'm not going to let you take this little girl into harm's way.
Hey, who you calling little?
Padre's got a point. If we're going undercover, Molly should stay behind. At this hour, an eleven-year-old will stick out like... like an eleven-year-old.
Speaking of things that don't belong...
Don't worry about her, Gert.
I think I can kill two birds with one spell.

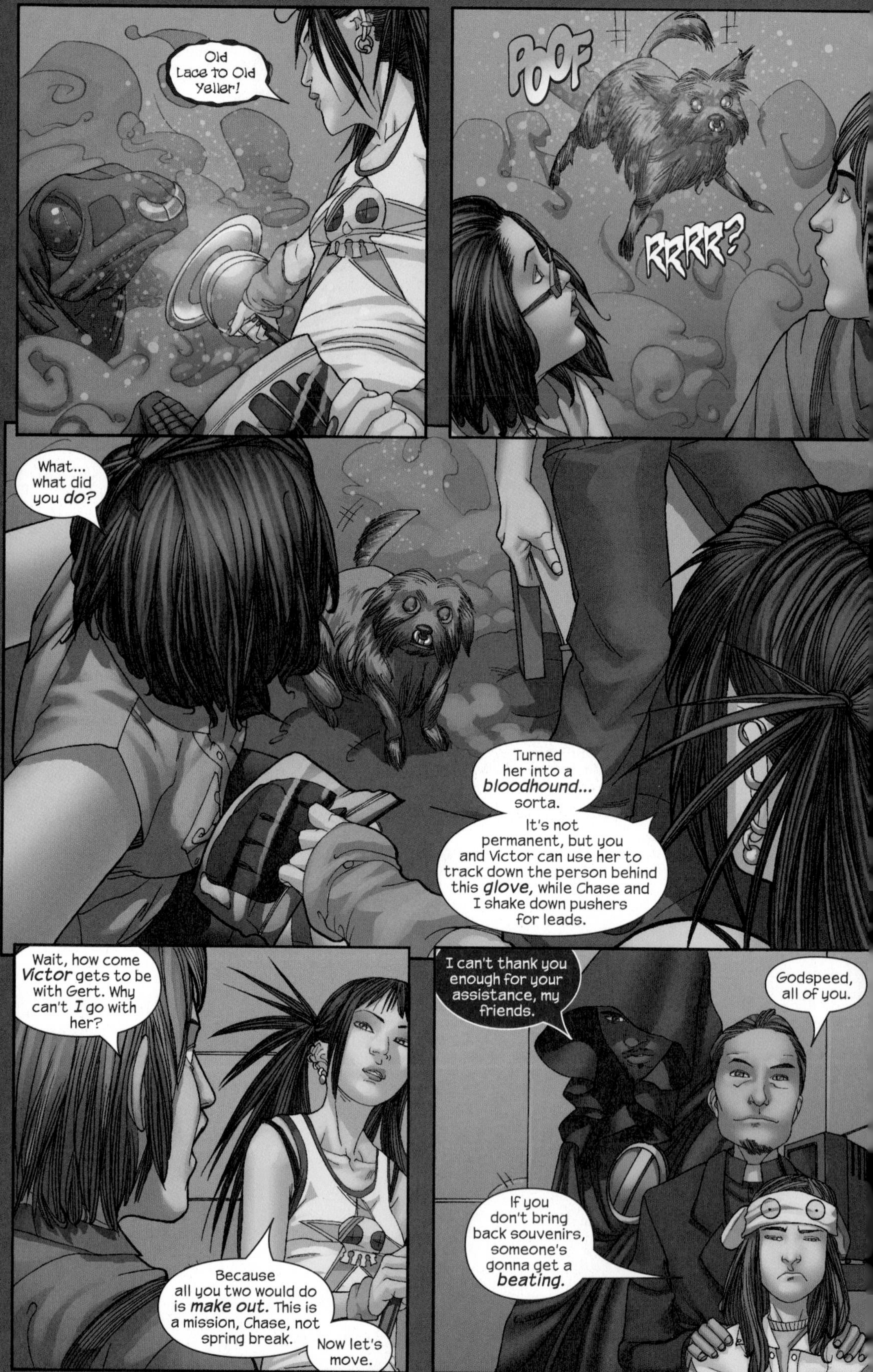
Old Lace to Old Yeller!
POOF
RRRR?
What... what did you **do**?
Turned her into a **bloodhound...** sorta.
It's not permanent, but you and Victor can use her to track down the person behind this ***glove,*** while Chase and I shake down pushers for leads.
Wait, how come ***Victor*** gets to be with Gert. Why can't ***I*** go with her?
Because all you two would do is ***make out.*** This is a mission, Chase, not spring break.
Now let's move.
I can't thank you enough for your assistance, my friends.
Godspeed, all of you.
If you don't bring back souvenirs, someone's gonna get a ***beating.***

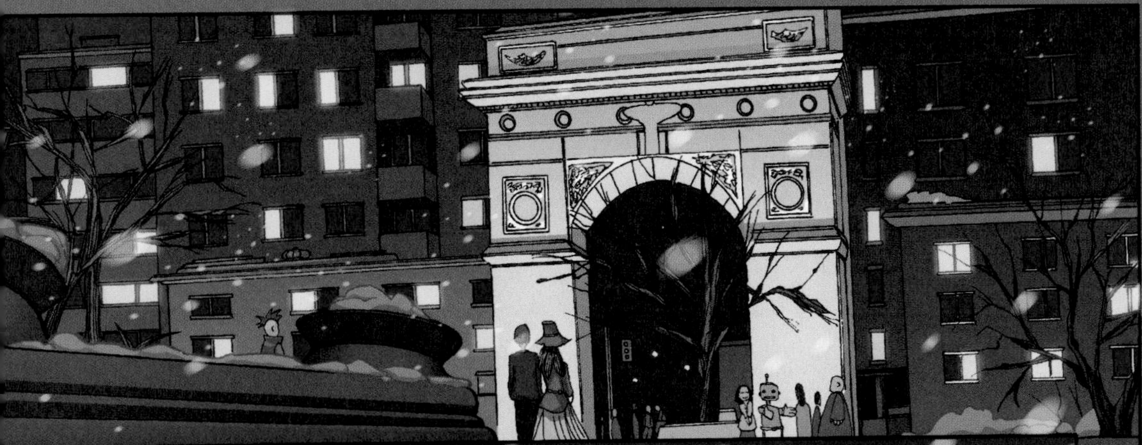
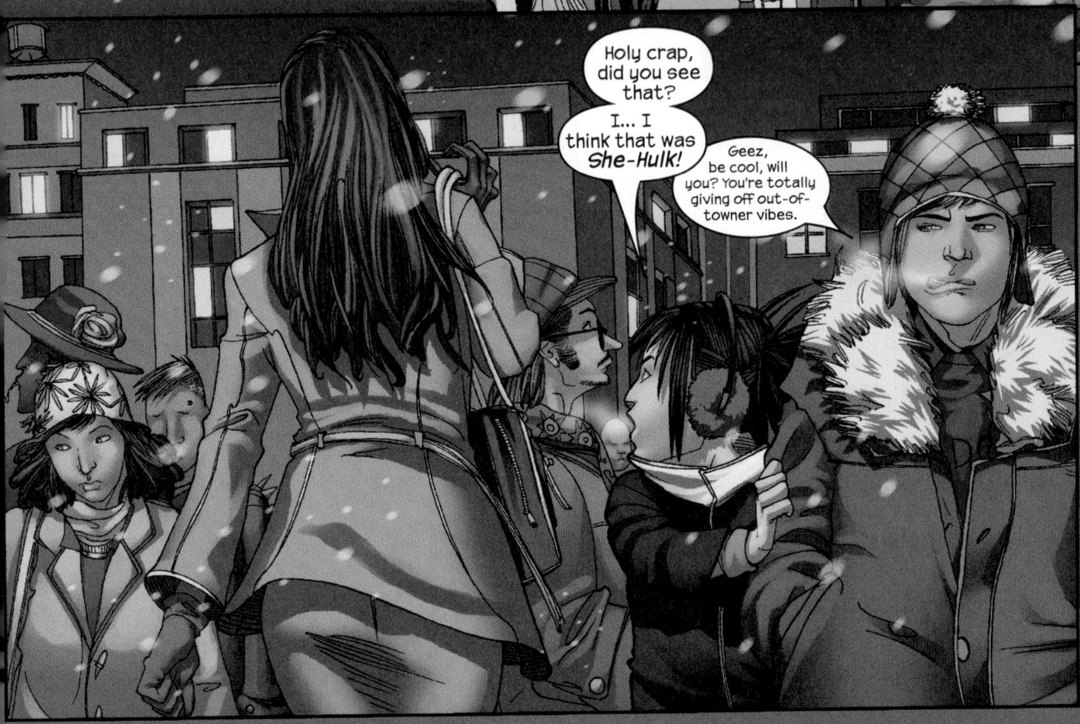
Holy crap, did you see that?
I... I think that was She-Hulk!
Geez, be cool, will you? You're totally giving off out-of-towner vibes.
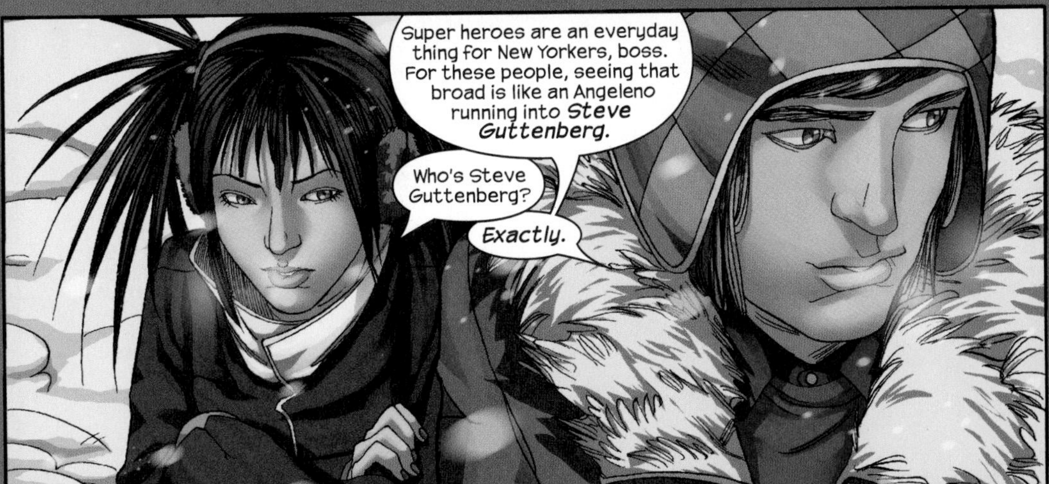
Super heroes are an everyday thing for New Yorkers, boss. For these people, seeing that broad is like an Angeleno running into Steve Guttenberg.
Who's Steve Guttenberg?
Exactly.

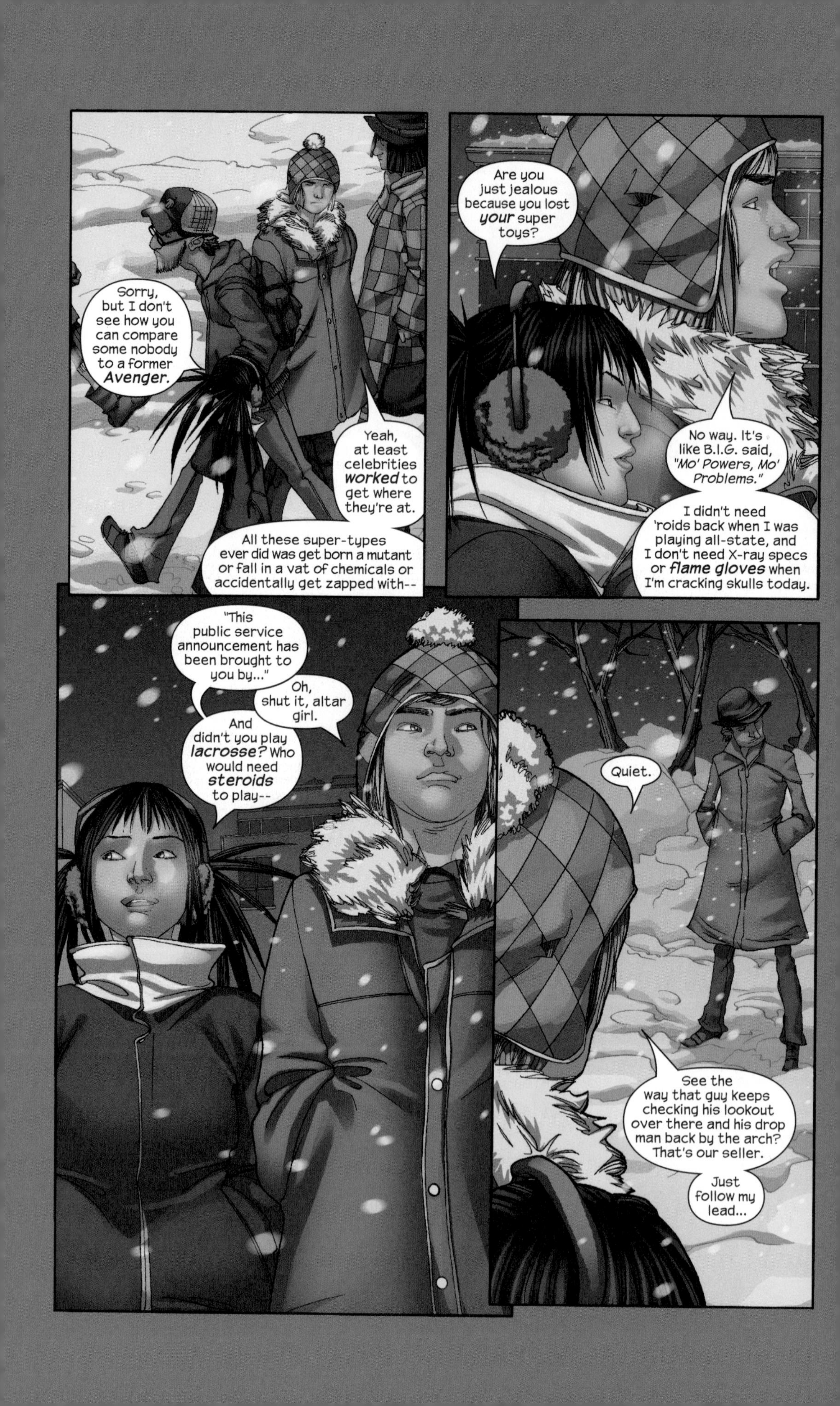
Sorry, but I don't see how you can compare some nobody to a former *Avenger.*
Yeah, at least celebrities ***worked*** to get where they're at.
All these super-types ever did was get born a mutant or fall in a vat of chemicals or accidentally get zapped with--
Are you just jealous because you lost ***your*** super toys?
No way. It's like B.I.G. said, *"Mo' Powers, Mo' Problems."*
I didn't need 'roids back when I was playing all-state, and I don't need X-ray specs or ***flame gloves*** when I'm cracking skulls today.
"This public service announcement has been brought to you by..."
Oh, shut it, altar girl.
And didn't you play ***lacrosse?*** Who would need ***steroids*** to play--
Quiet.
See the way that guy keeps checking his lookout over there and his drop man back by the arch? That's our seller.
Just follow my lead...

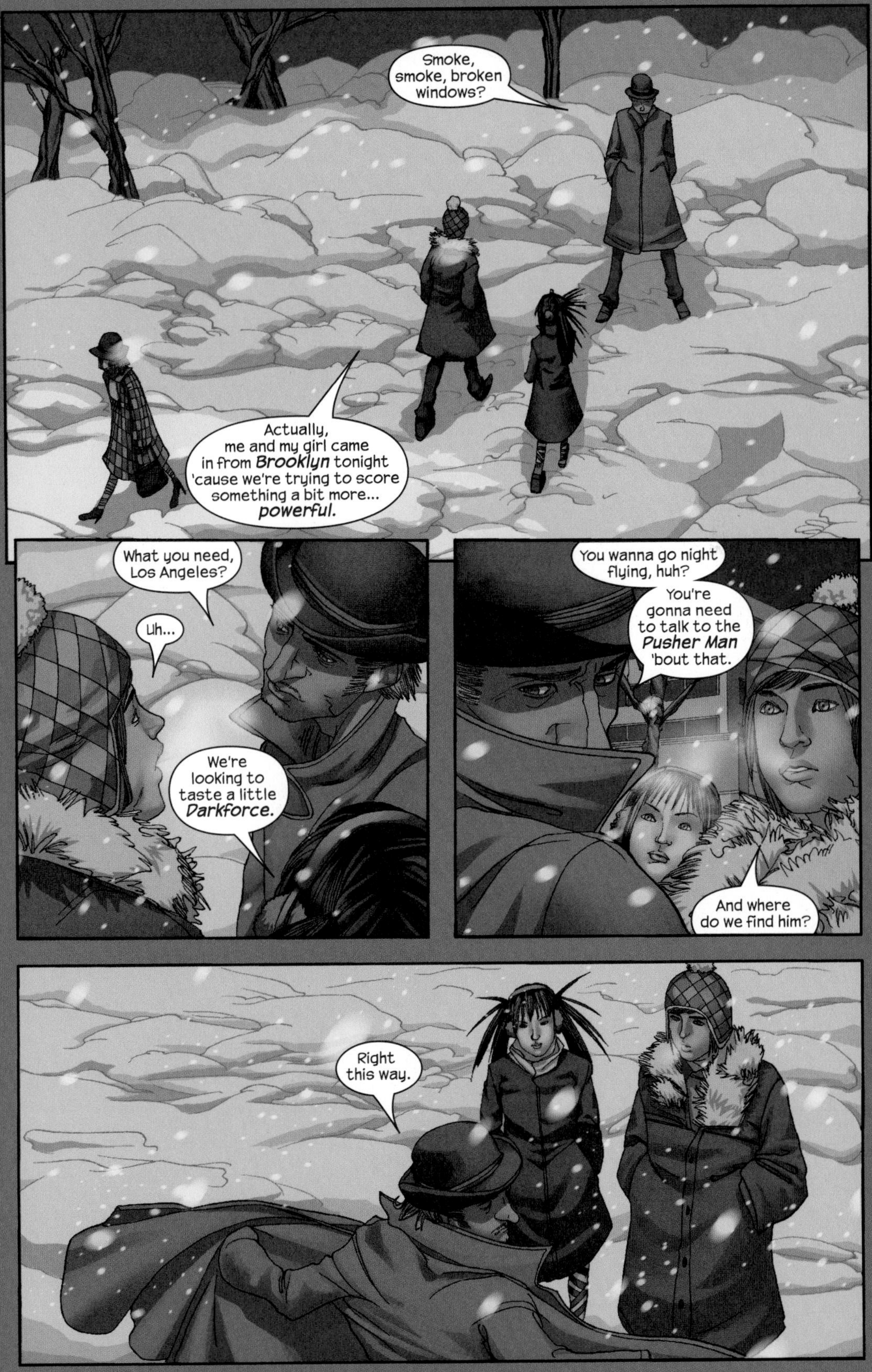
Smoke, smoke, broken windows?
Actually, me and my girl came in from Brooklyn tonight 'cause we're trying to score something a bit more... powerful.
What you need, Los Angeles?
Uh...
We're looking to taste a little Darkforce.
You wanna go night flying, huh?
You're gonna need to talk to the Pusher Man 'bout that.
And where do we find him?
Right this way.

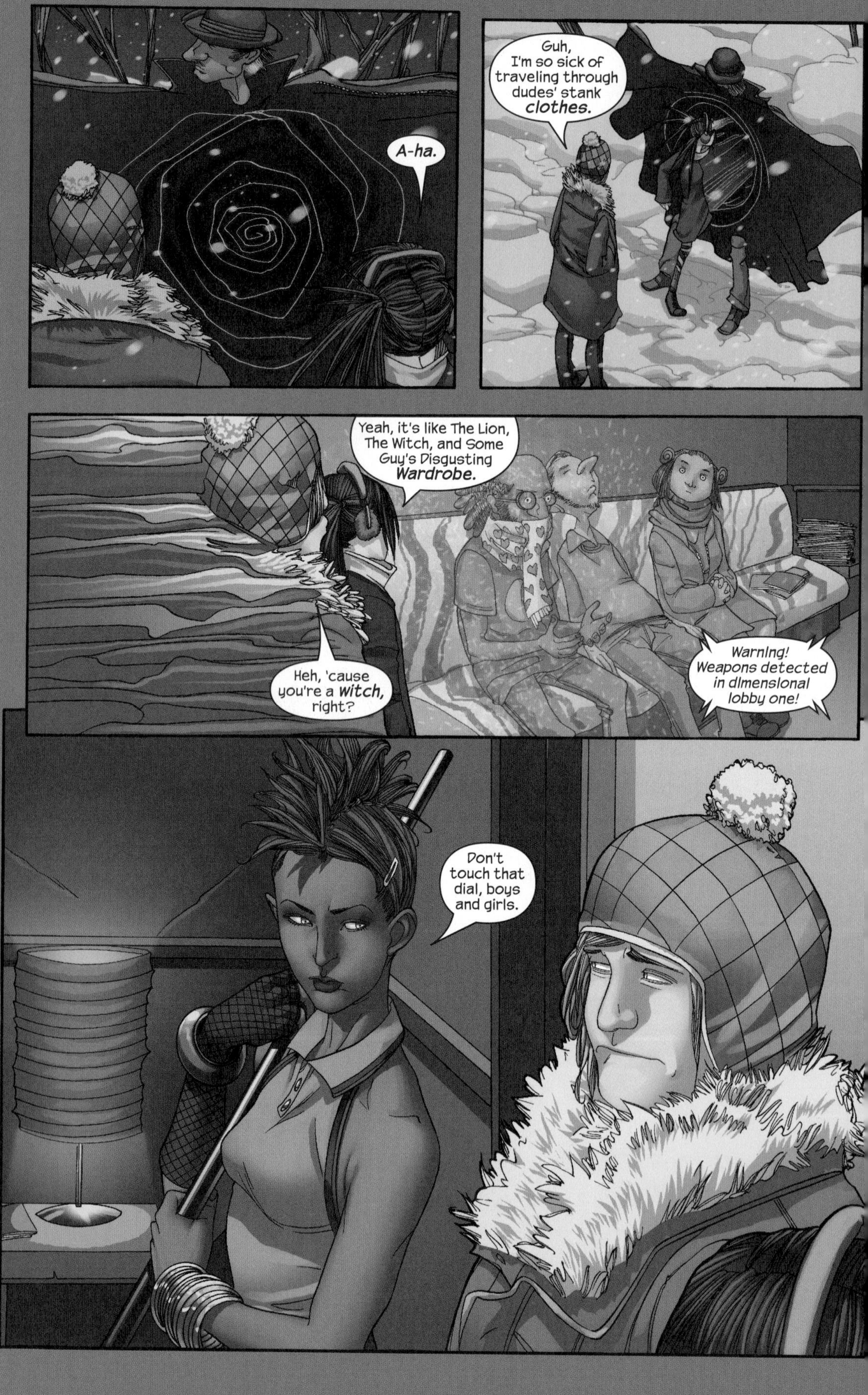

A-ha.
Guh, I'm so sick of traveling through dudes' stank *clothes.*
Yeah, it's like The Lion, The Witch, and Some Guy's Disgusting *Wardrobe.*
Heh, 'cause you're a *witch,* right?
Warning! Weapons detected in dimensional lobby one!
Don't touch that dial, boys and girls.

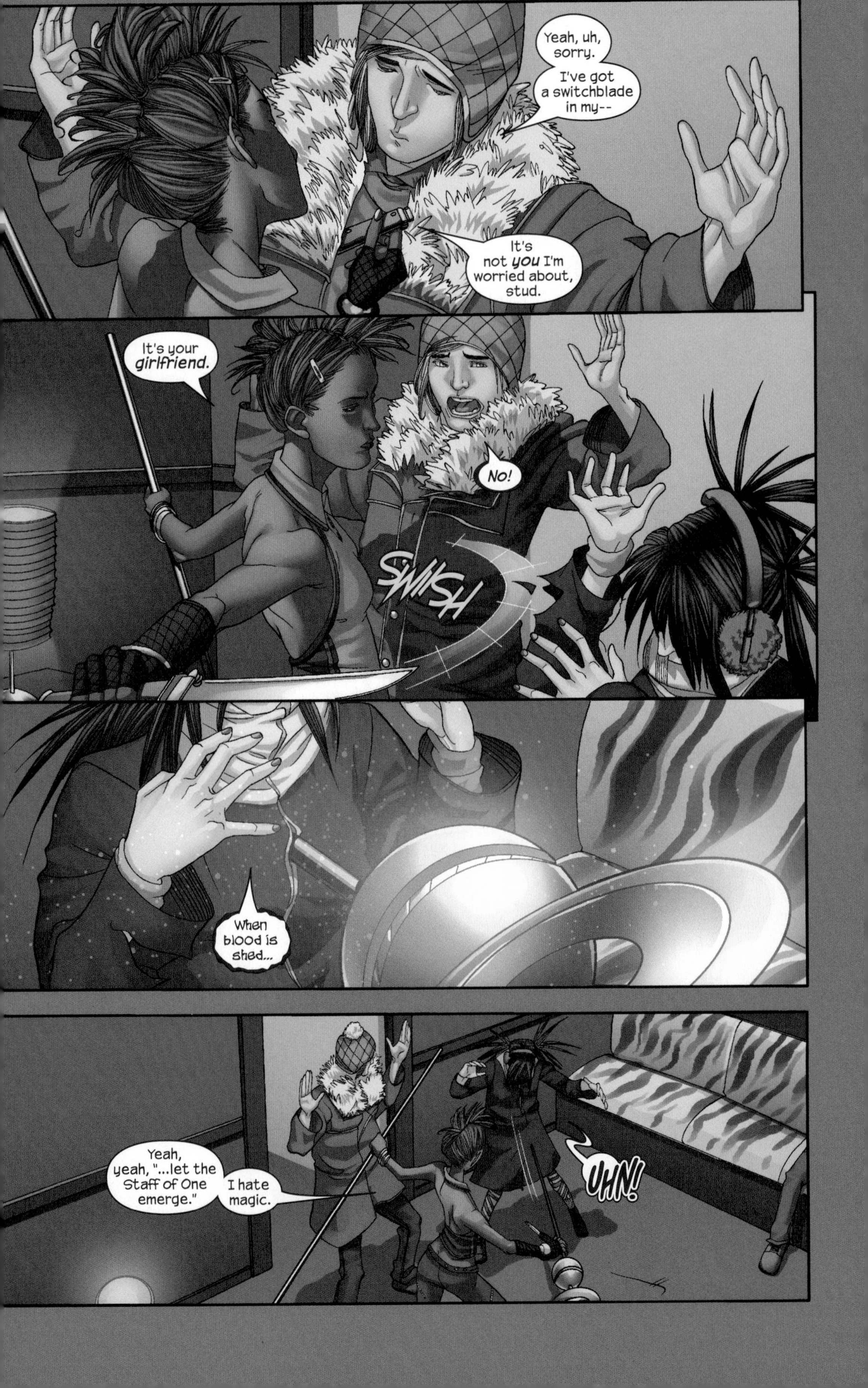
Yeah, uh, sorry.
I've got a switchblade in my--
It's not *you* I'm worried about, stud.
It's your *girlfriend*.
No!
SWISH
When blood is shed...
Yeah, yeah, "...let the Staff of One emerge."
I hate magic.
UHN!

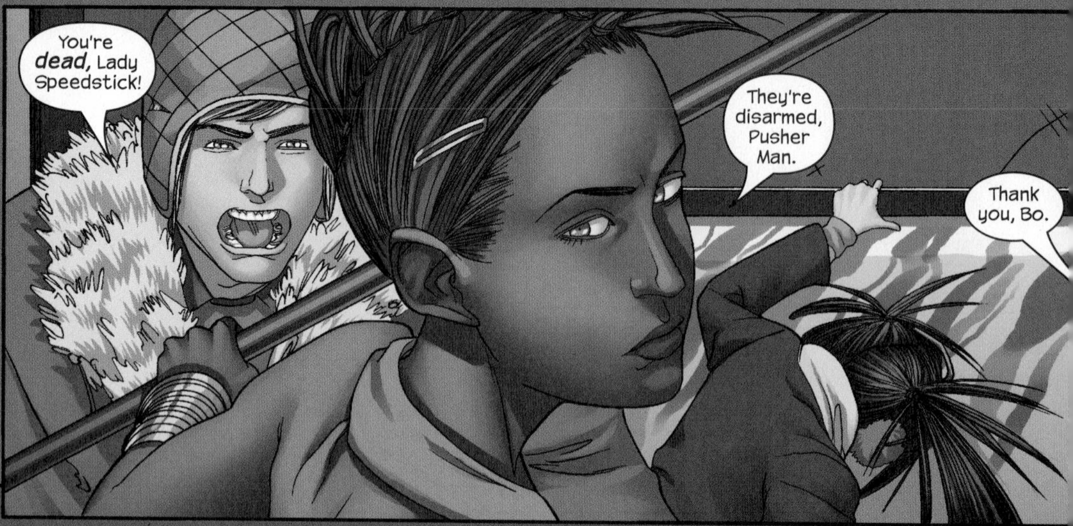
You're
dead, Lady
Speedstick!
They're
disarmed,
Pusher
Man.
Thank
you, Bo.
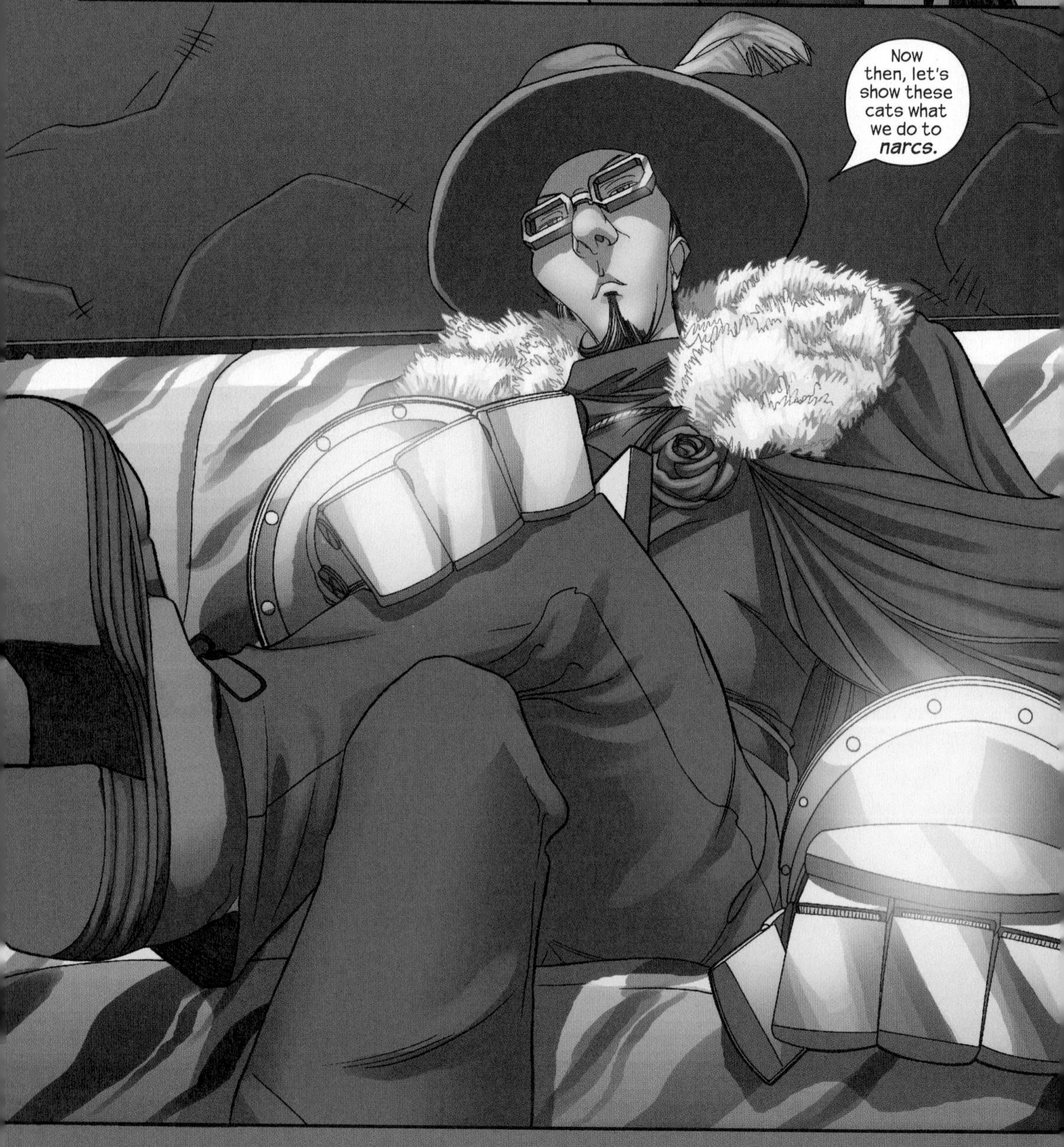
Now
then, let's
show these
cats what
we do to
narcs.

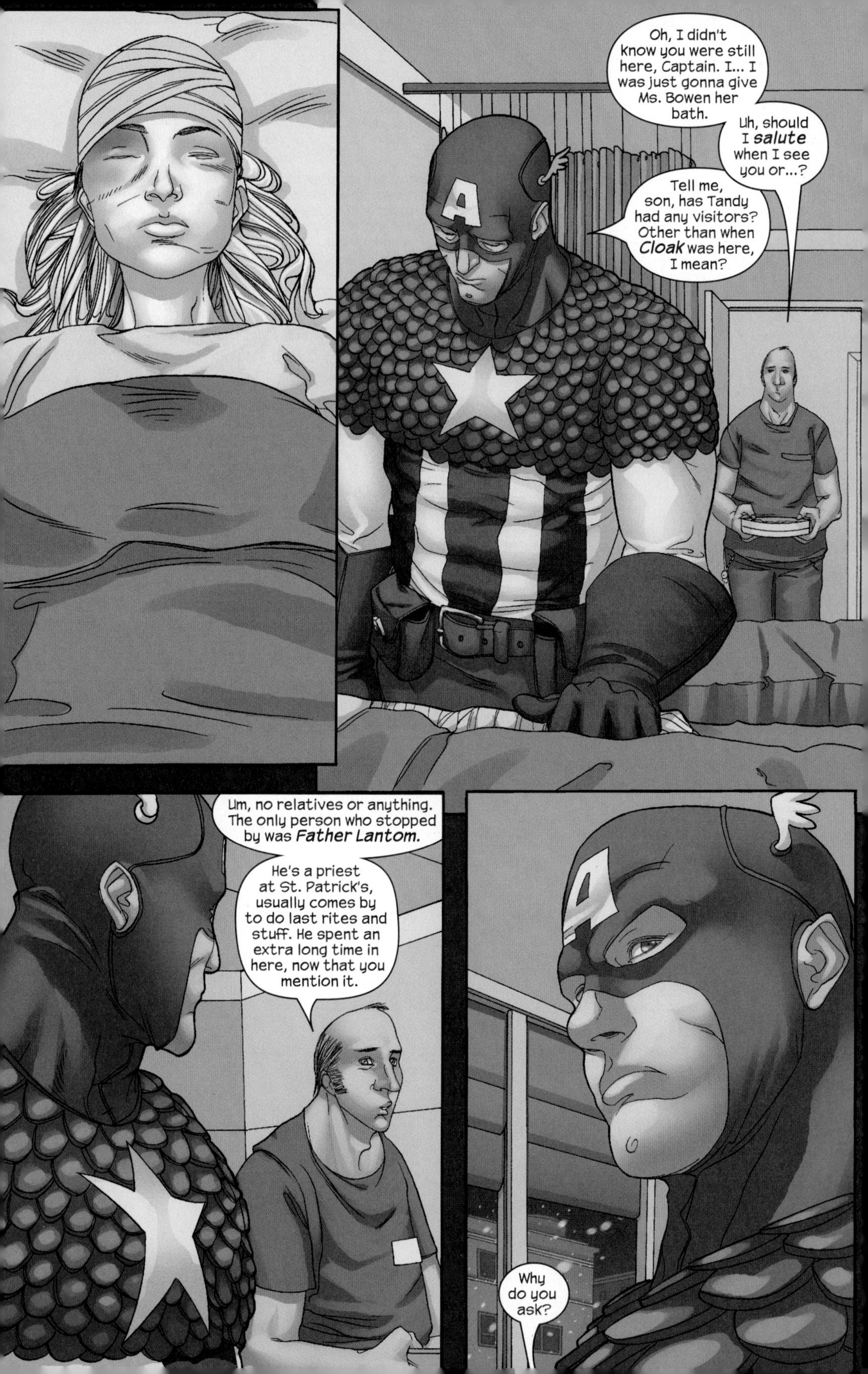
Oh, I didn't know you were still here, Captain. I... I was just gonna give Ms. Bowen her bath.
Uh, should I *salute* when I see you or...?
Tell me, son, has Tandy had any visitors? Other than when *Cloak* was here, I mean?
Um, no relatives or anything. The only person who stopped by was *Father Lantom.*
He's a priest at St. Patrick's, usually comes by to do last rites and stuff. He spent an extra long time in here, now that you mention it.
Why do you ask?

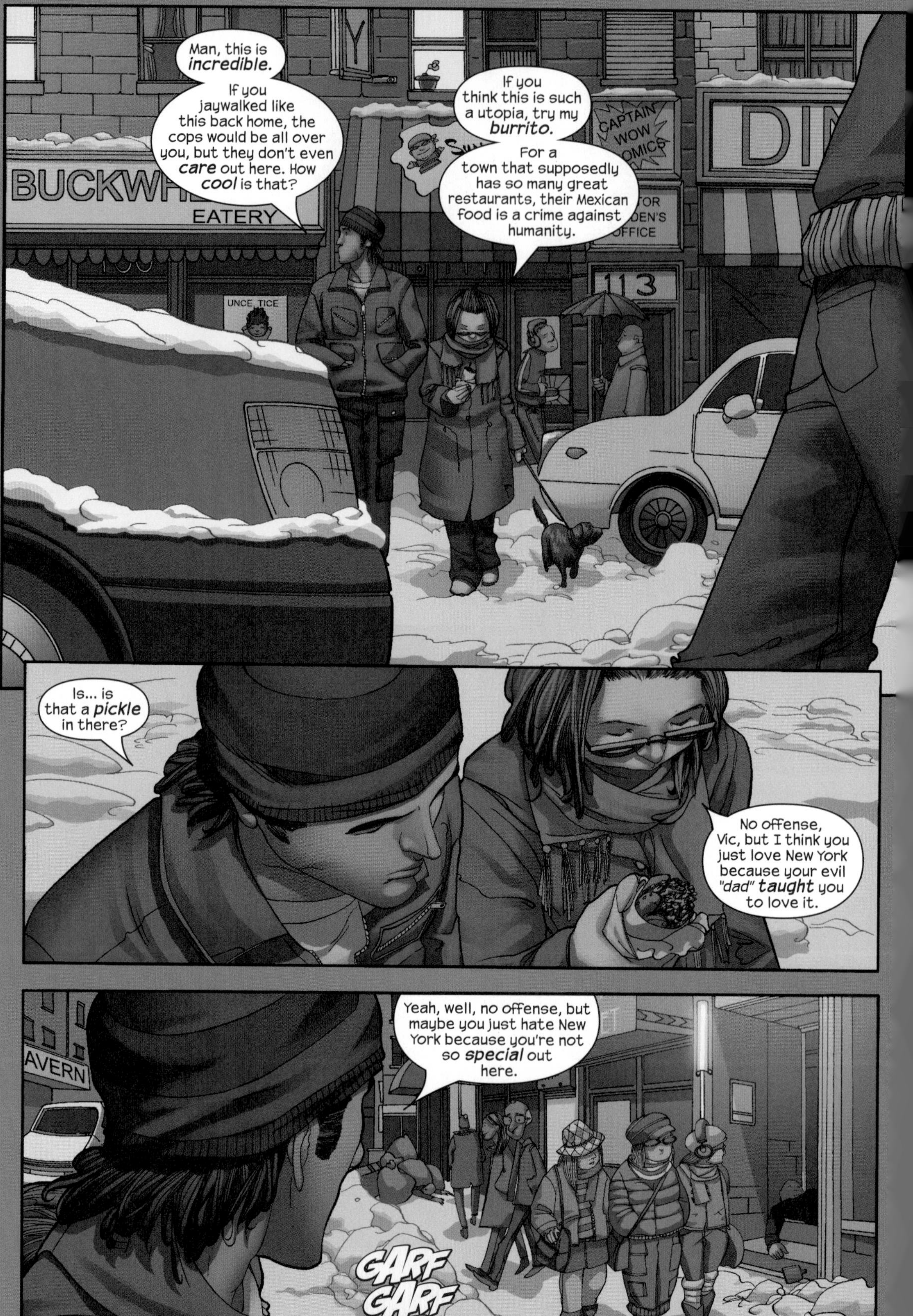
Man, this is *incredible.*
If you jaywalked like this back home, the cops would be all over you, but they don't even *care* out here. How *cool* is that?
If you think this is such a utopia, try my *burrito.*
For a town that supposedly has so many great restaurants, their Mexican food is a crime against humanity.
BUCKWH
EATERY
CAPTAIN WOW COMICS
113
Is... is that a *pickle* in there?
No offense, Vic, but I think you just love New York because your evil *"dad"* ***taught*** you to love it.
Yeah, well, no offense, but maybe you just hate New York because you're not so *special* out here.
AVERN
GARF
GARF
GARF

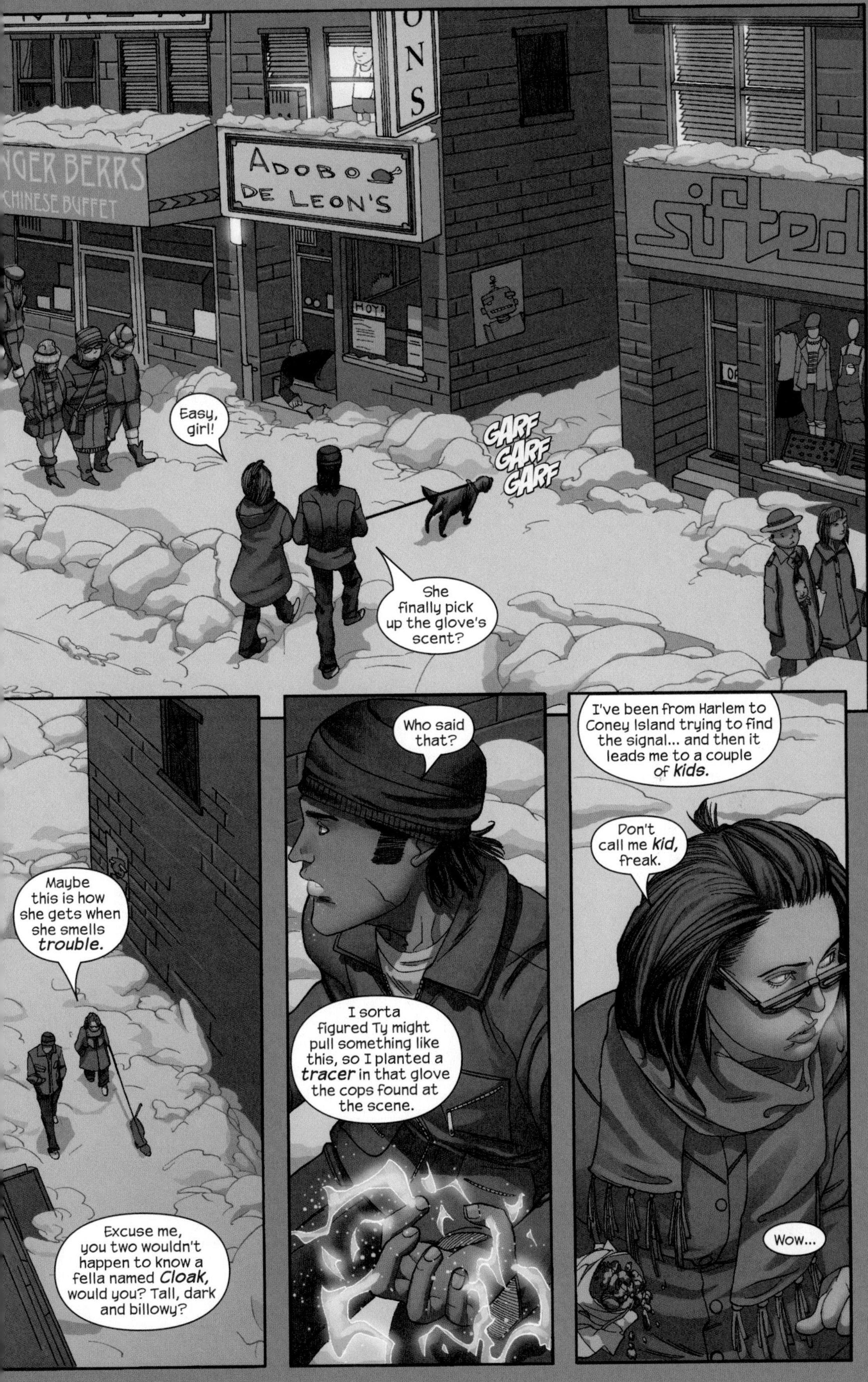
CHINESE BUFFET
ADOBO DE LEON'S
sifted
Easy, girl!
GARF GARF GARF
She finally pick up the glove's scent?
Maybe this is how she gets when she smells *trouble.*
Excuse me, you two wouldn't happen to know a fella named *Cloak,* would you? Tall, dark and billowy?
Who said that?
I sorta figured Ty might pull something like this, so I planted a *tracer* in that glove the cops found at the scene.
I've been from Harlem to Coney Island trying to find the signal... and then it leads me to a couple of *kids.*
Don't call me *kid,* freak.
Wow...

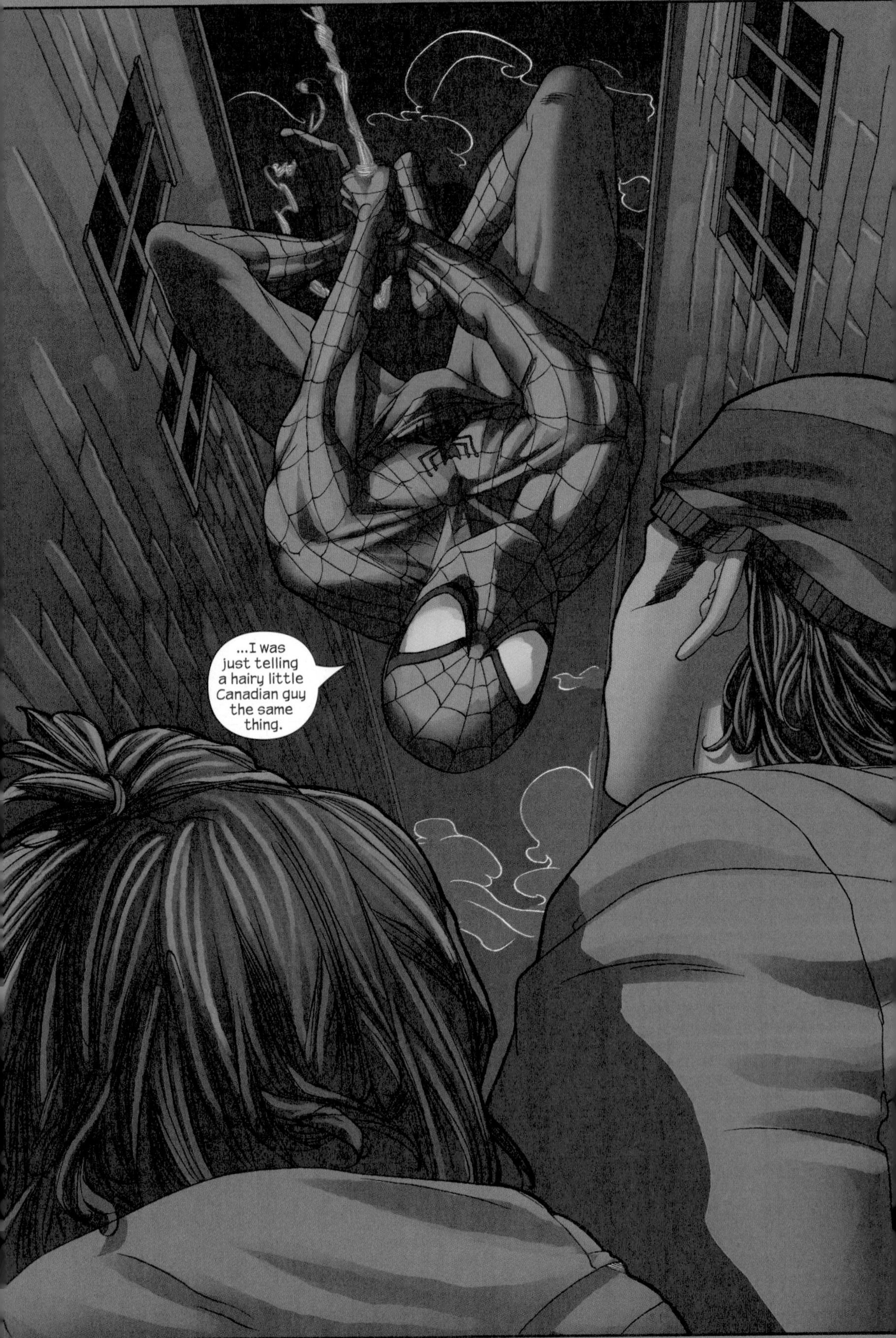
...I was just telling a hairy little Canadian guy the same thing.

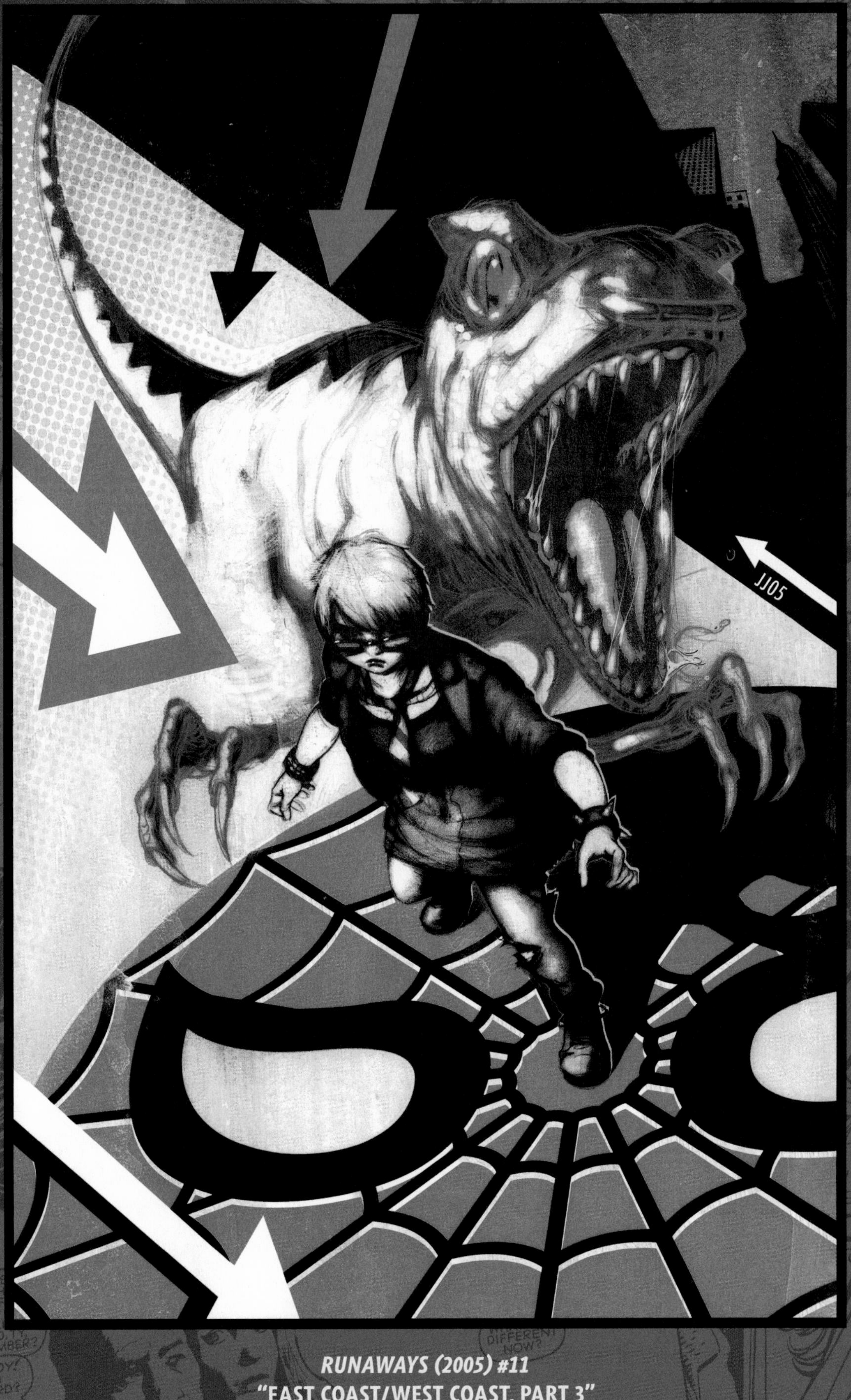
JJ05

***RUNAWAYS* (2005) #11**
"EAST COAST/WEST COAST, PART 3"

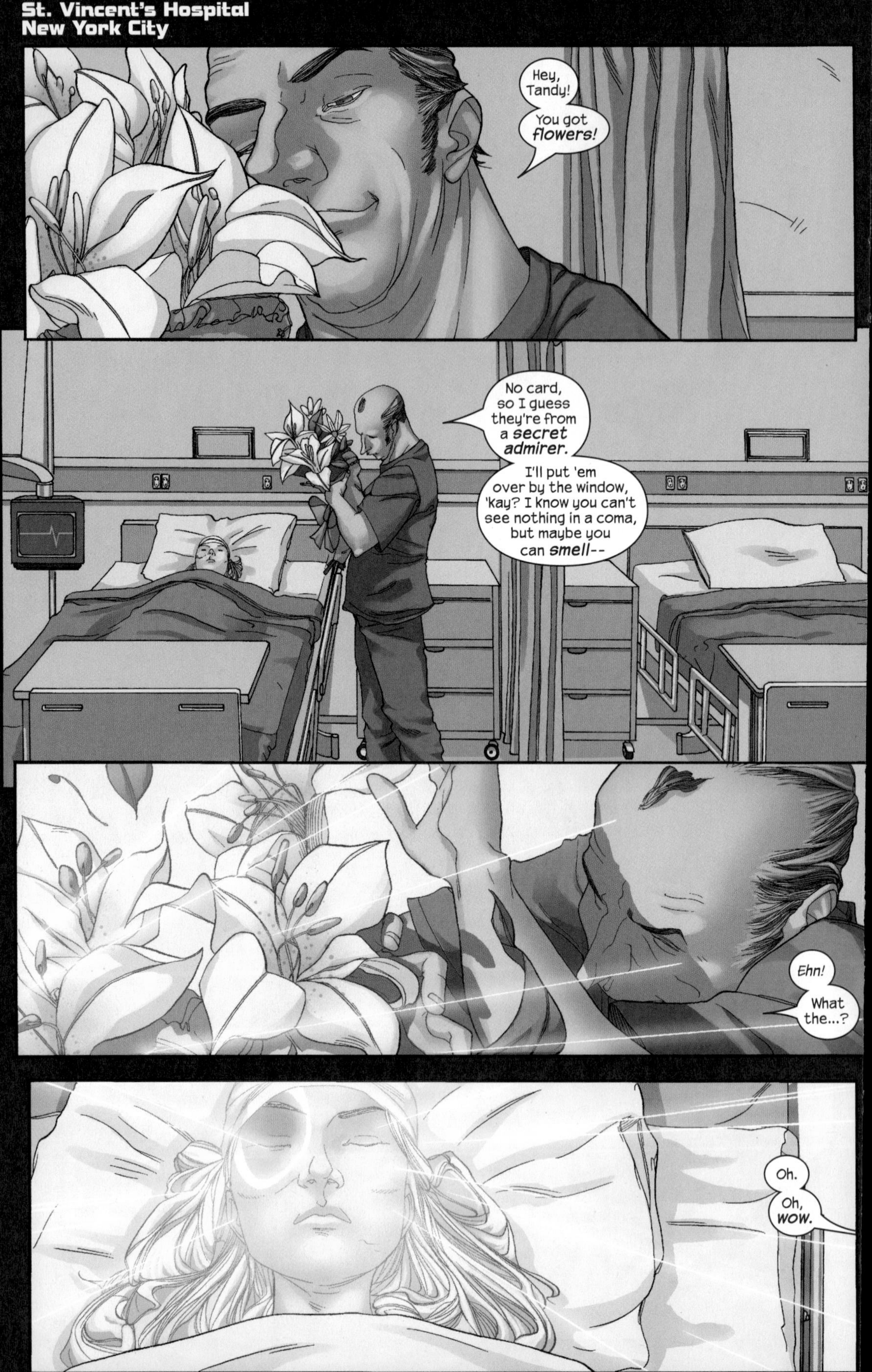
St. Vincent's Hospital
New York City
Hey, Tandy!
You got flowers!
No card, so I guess they're from a secret admirer.
I'll put 'em over by the window, 'kay? I know you can't see nothing in a coma, but maybe you can smell--
Ehn!
What the...?
Oh.
Oh, wow.

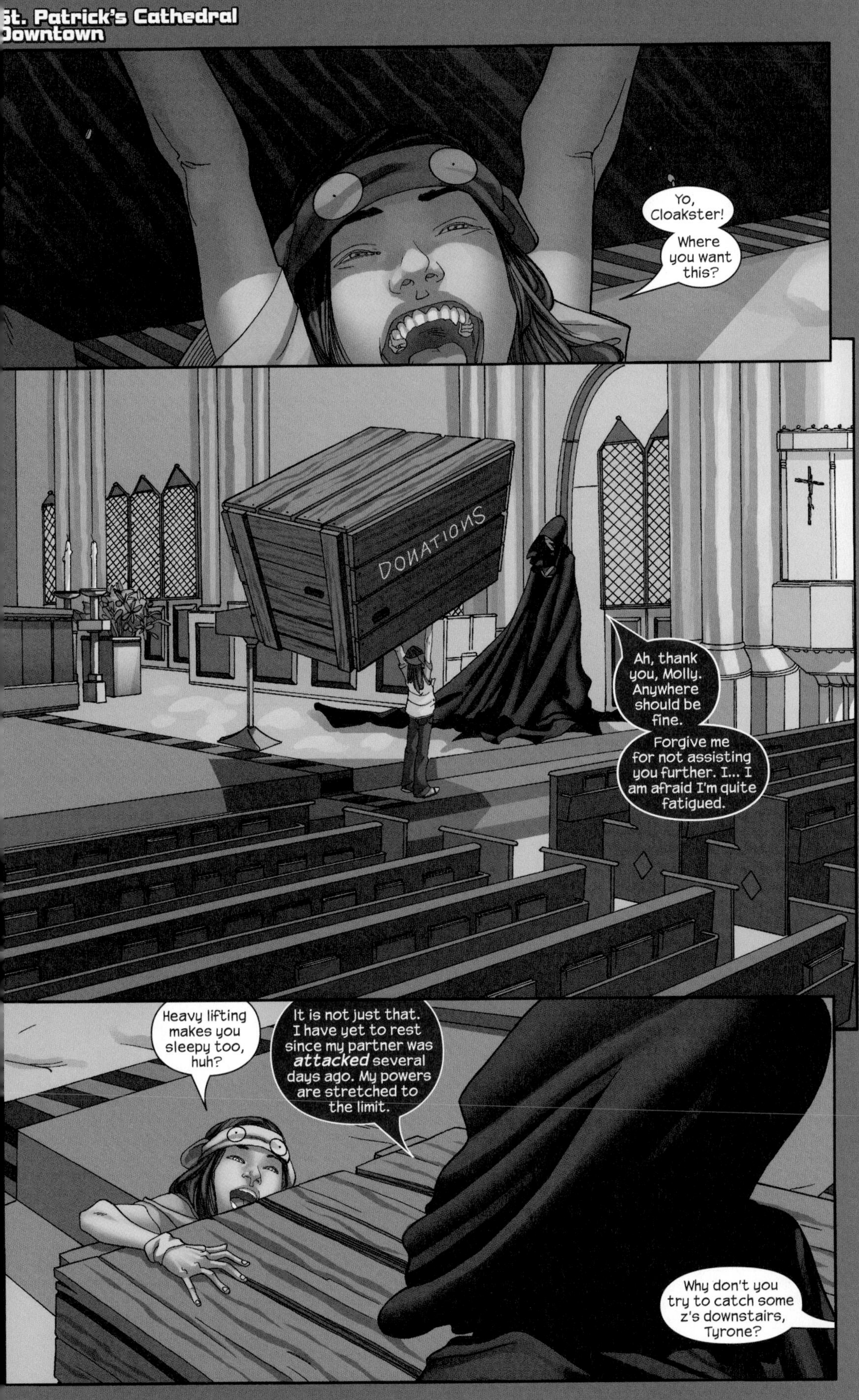
St. Patrick's Cathedral
Downtown
Yo, Cloakster!
Where you want this?
DONATIONS
Ah, thank you, Molly. Anywhere should be fine.
Forgive me for not assisting you further. I... I am afraid I'm quite fatigued.
Heavy lifting makes you sleepy too, huh?
It is not just that. I have yet to rest since my partner was *attacked* several days ago. My powers are stretched to the limit.
Why don't you try to catch some z's downstairs, Tyrone?

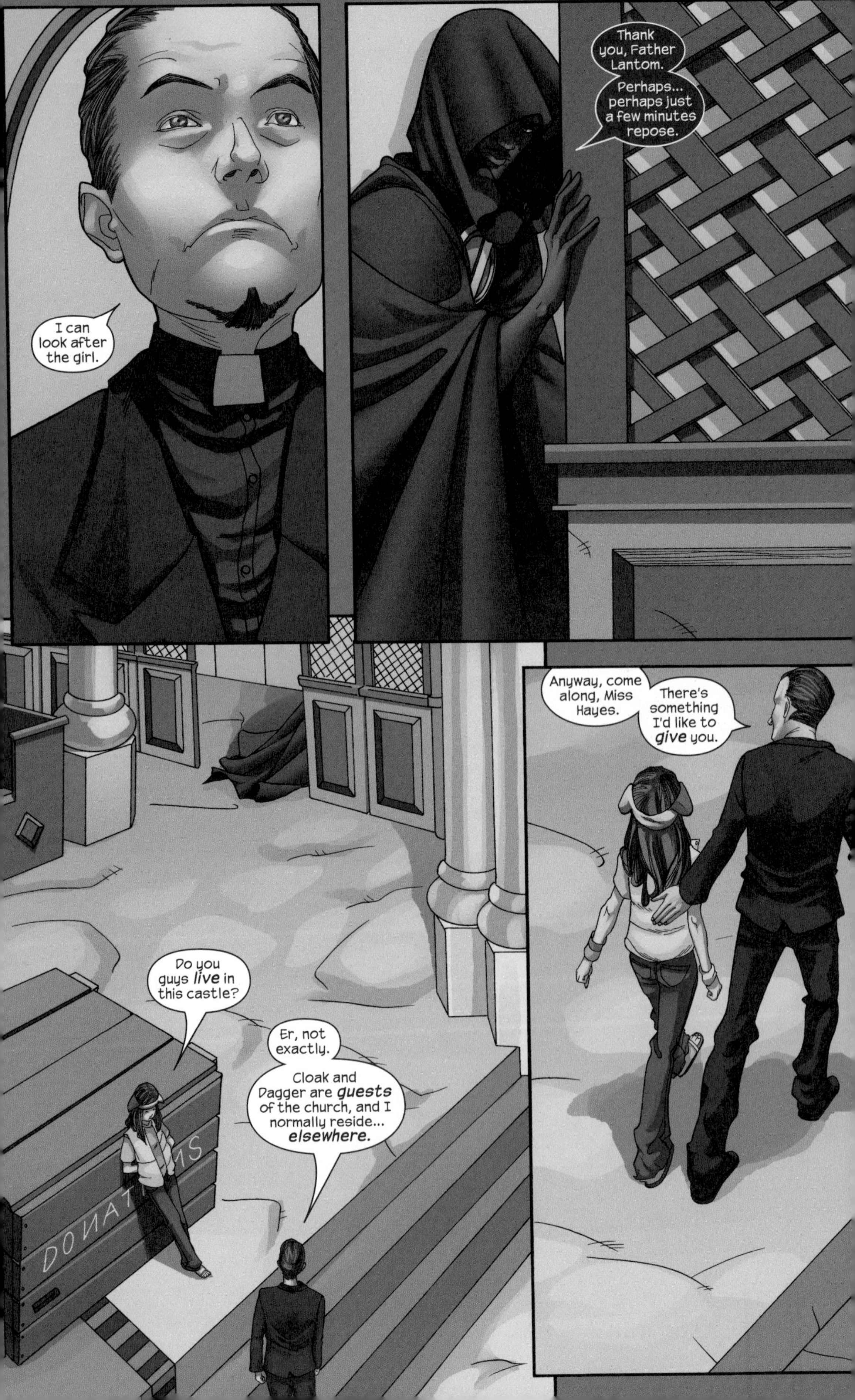

I can look after the girl.
Thank you, Father Lantom.
Perhaps... perhaps just a few minutes repose.
Do you guys live in this castle?
Er, not exactly.
Cloak and Dagger are guests of the church, and I normally reside... elsewhere.
DONATIONS
Anyway, come along, Miss Hayes.
There's something I'd like to give you.

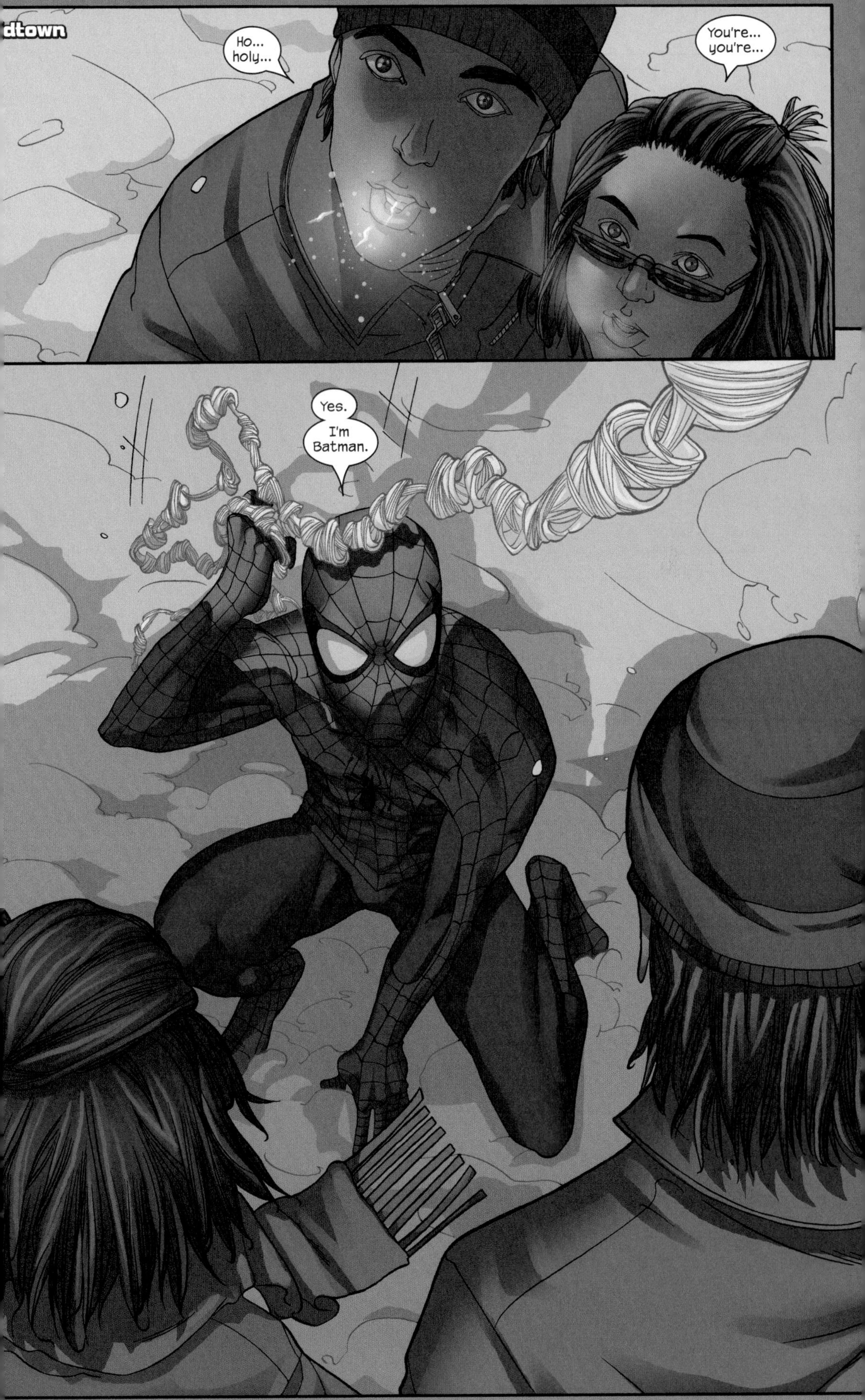
dtown
Ho... holy...
You're... you're...
Yes. I'm Batman.

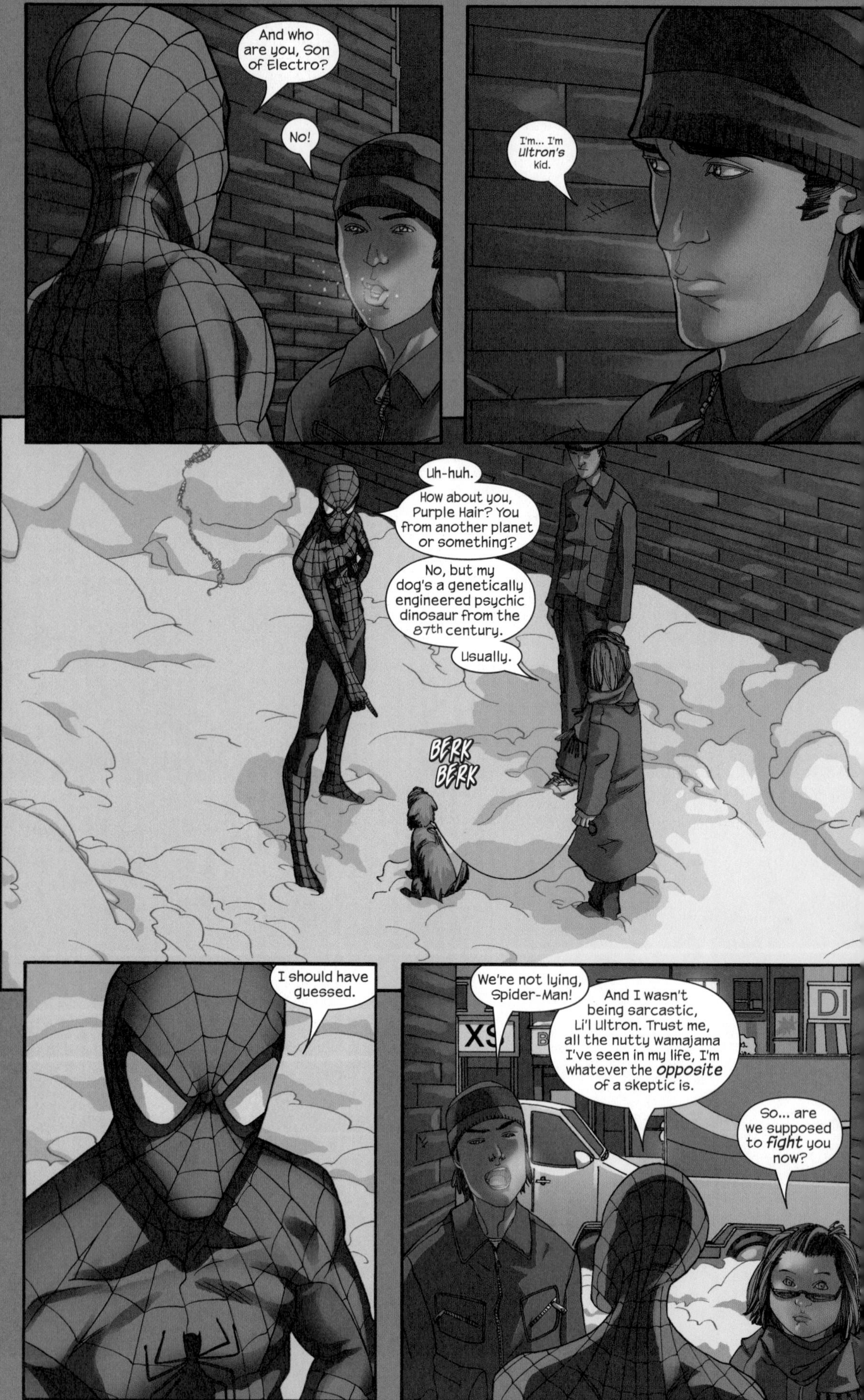

And who are you, Son of Electro?
No!
I'm... I'm Ultron's kid.
Uh-huh.
How about you, Purple Hair? You from another planet or something?
No, but my dog's a genetically engineered psychic dinosaur from the 87th century.
Usually.
BERK BERK
I should have guessed.
We're not lying, Spider-Man!
And I wasn't being sarcastic, Li'l Ultron. Trust me, all the nutty wamajama I've seen in my life, I'm whatever the *opposite* of a skeptic is.
So... are we supposed to *fight* you now?

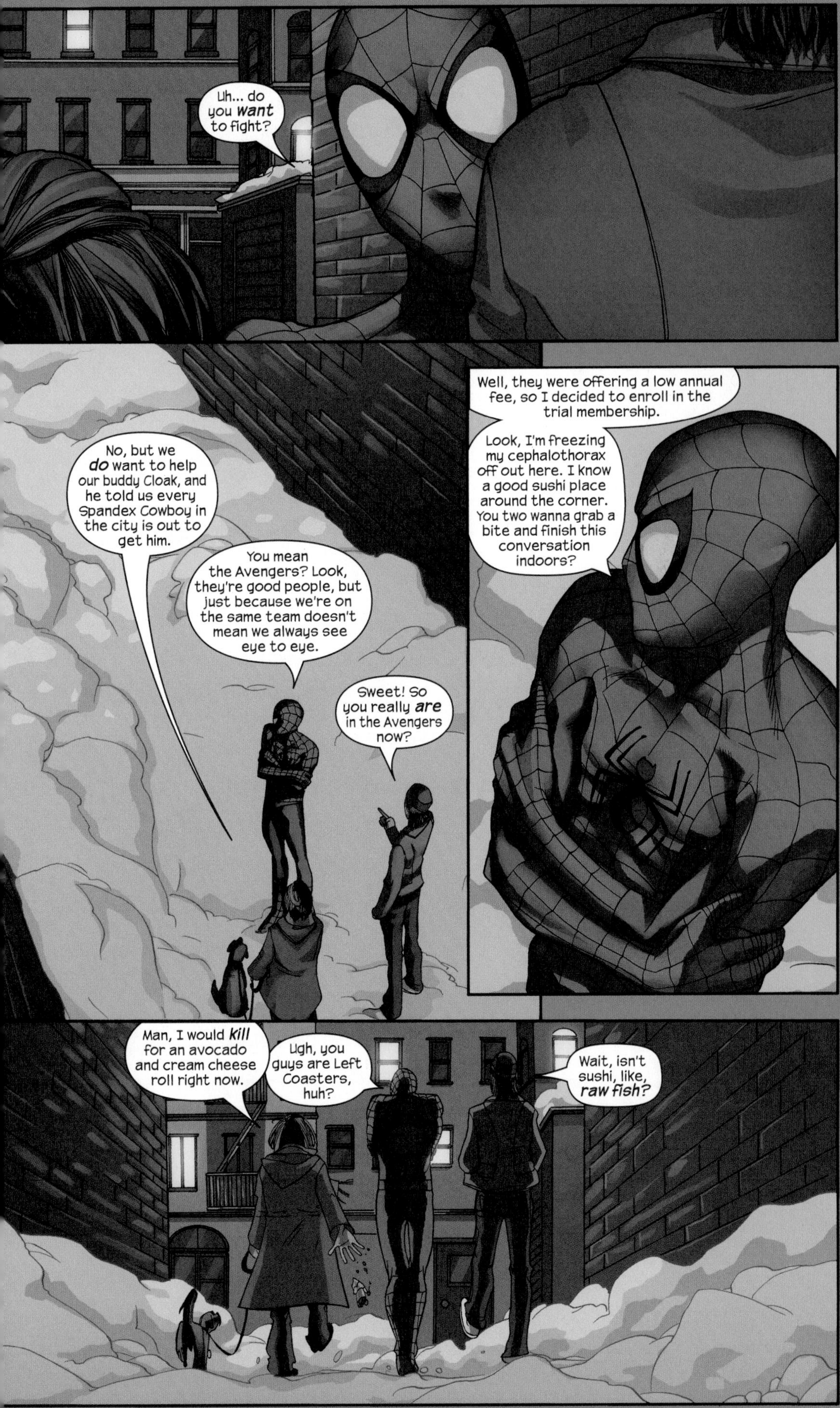
Uh... do you *want* to fight?
No, but we *do* want to help our buddy Cloak, and he told us every Spandex Cowboy in the city is out to get him.
You mean the Avengers? Look, they're good people, but just because we're on the same team doesn't mean we always see eye to eye.
Sweet! So you really *are* in the Avengers now?
Well, they were offering a low annual fee, so I decided to enroll in the trial membership.
Look, I'm freezing my cephalothorax off out here. I know a good sushi place around the corner. You two wanna grab a bite and finish this conversation indoors?
Man, I would *kill* for an avocado and cream cheese roll right now.
Ugh, you guys are Left Coasters, huh?
Wait, isn't sushi, like, *raw fish?*

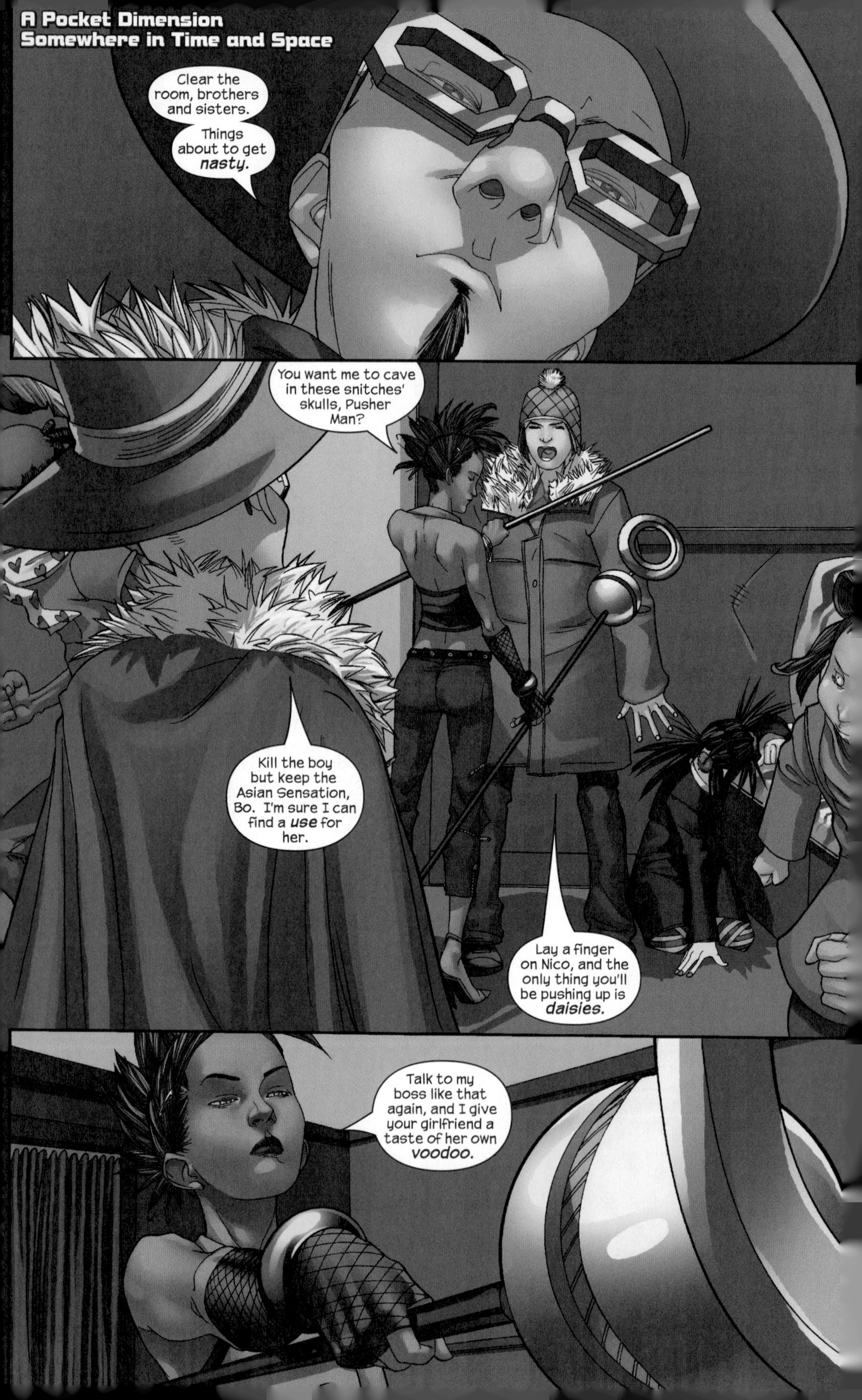
A Pocket Dimension
Somewhere in Time and Space
Clear the room, brothers and sisters.
Things about to get *nasty.*
You want me to cave in these snitches' skulls, Pusher Man?
Kill the boy but keep the Asian Sensation, Bo. I'm sure I can find a *use* for her.
Lay a finger on Nico, and the only thing you'll be pushing up is *daisies.*
Talk to my boss like that again, and I give your girlfriend a taste of her own *voodoo.*

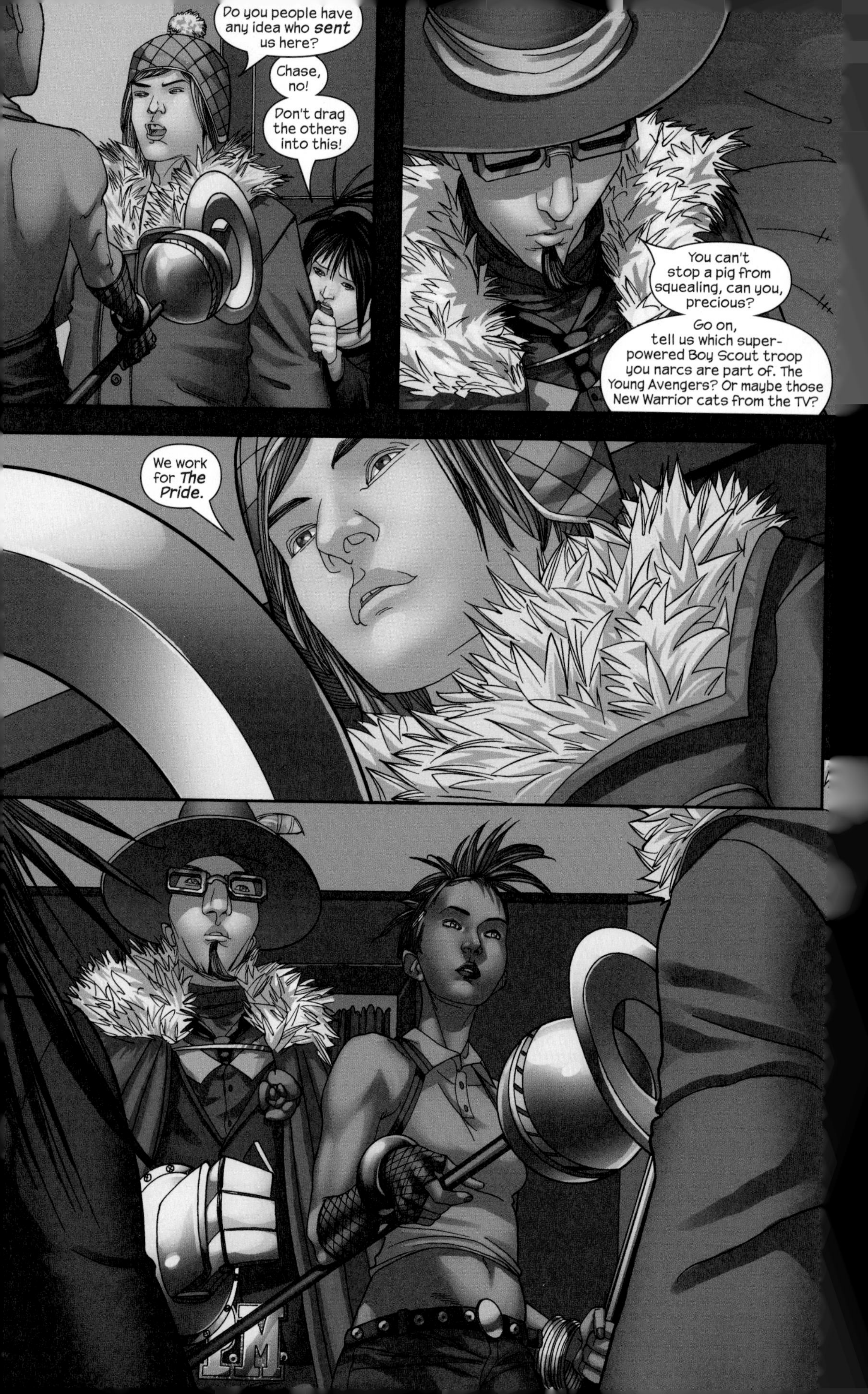
Do you people have any idea who *sent* us here?
Chase, no!
Don't drag the others into this!
You can't stop a pig from squealing, can you, precious?
Go on, tell us which super-powered Boy Scout troop you narcs are part of. The Young Avengers? Or maybe those New Warrior cats from the TV?
We work for *The Pride.*

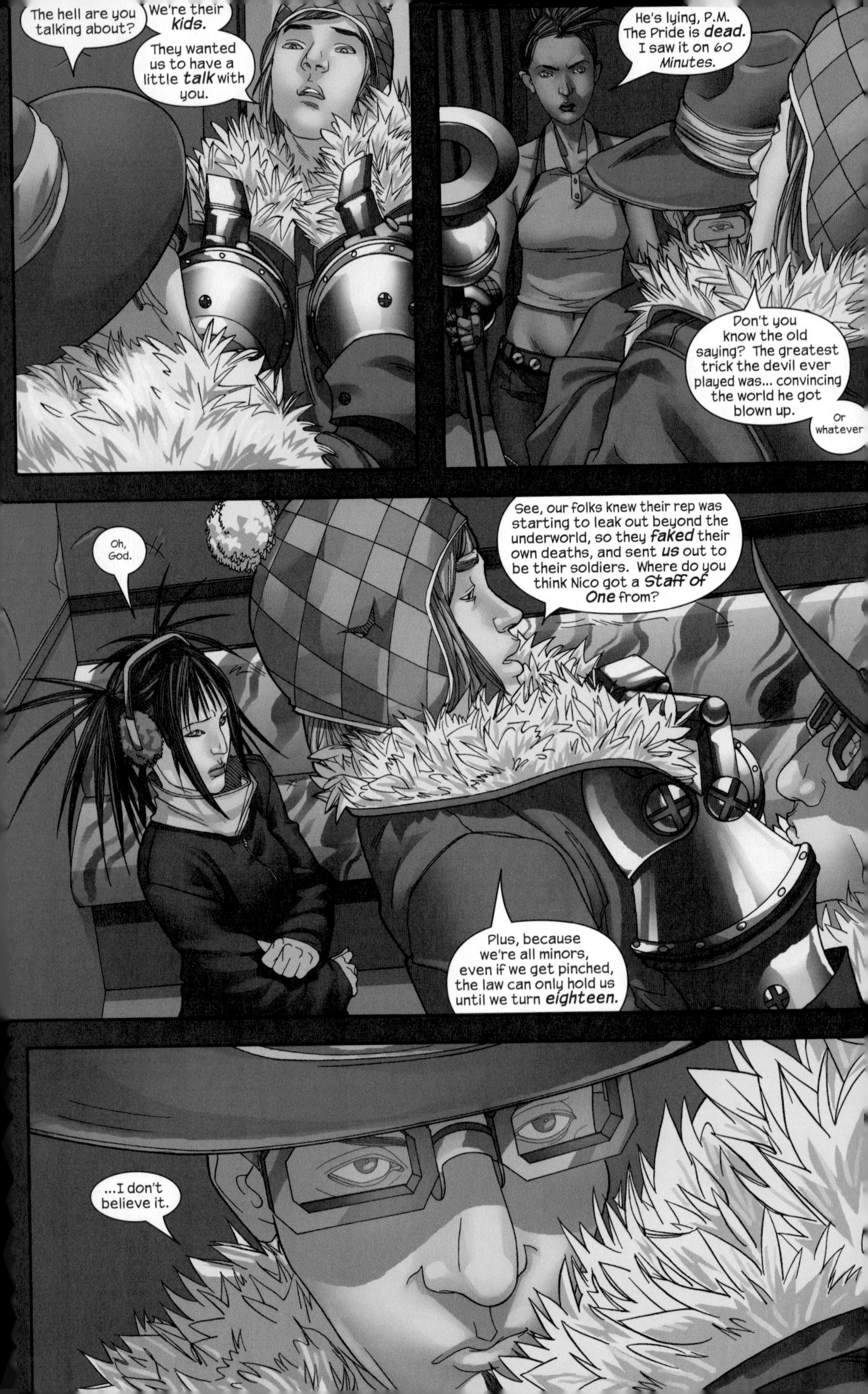
The hell are you talking about?
We're their *kids.*
They wanted us to have a little *talk* with you.
He's lying, P.M. The Pride is *dead.* I saw it on *60 Minutes.*
Don't you know the old saying? The greatest trick the devil ever played was... convincing the world he got blown up.
Or whatever
Oh, God.
See, our folks knew their rep was starting to leak out beyond the underworld, so they *faked* their own deaths, and sent *us* out to be their soldiers. Where do you think Nico got a *Staff of One* from?
Plus, because we're all minors, even if we get pinched, the law can only hold us until we turn *eighteen.*
...I don't believe it.

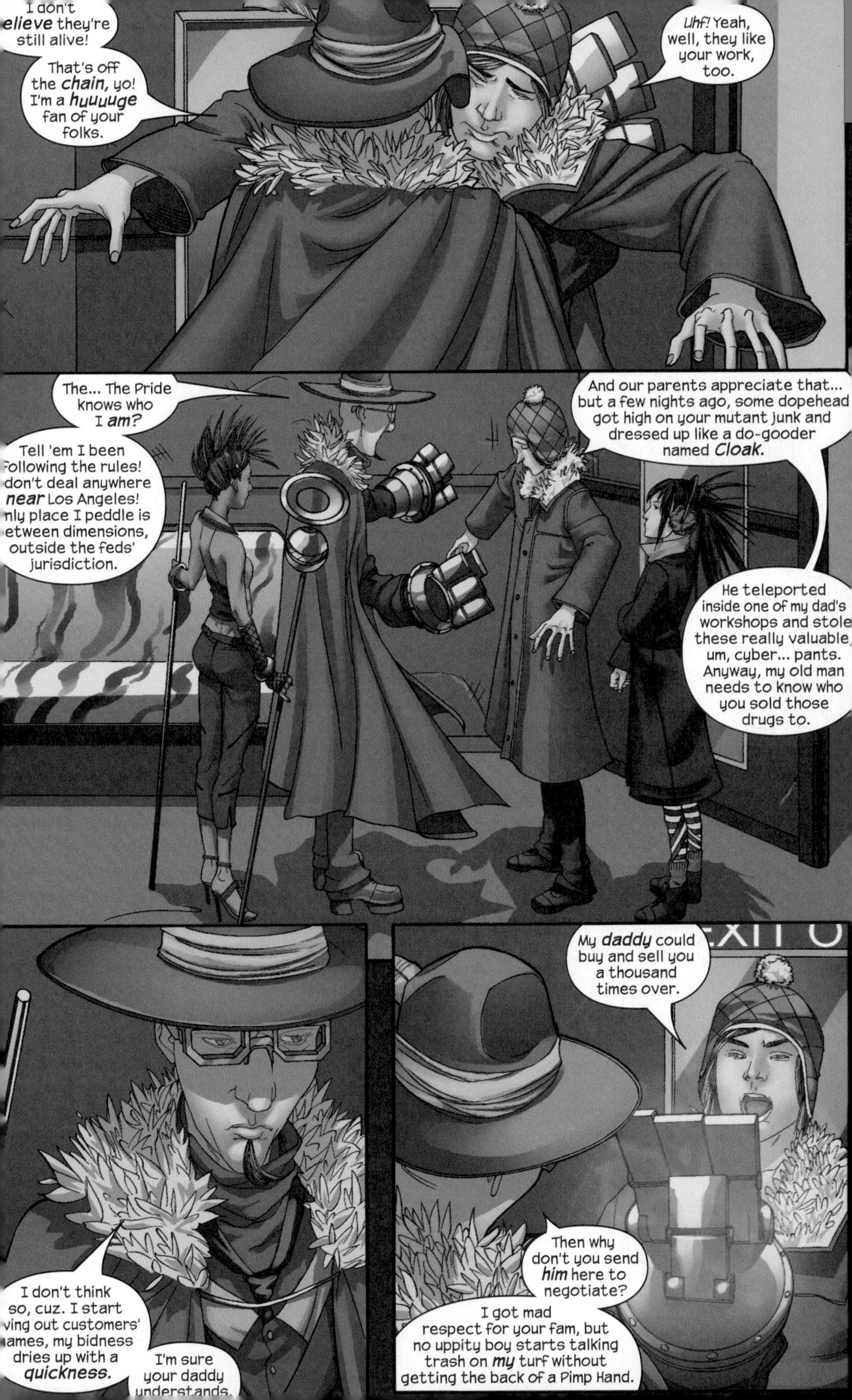
I don't elieve they're still alive!
That's off the chain, yo! I'm a huuuuge fan of your folks.
Uhf! Yeah, well, they like your work, too.
The... The Pride knows who I am?
Tell 'em I been following the rules! don't deal anywhere near Los Angeles! nly place I peddle is etween dimensions, outside the feds' jurisdiction.
And our parents appreciate that... but a few nights ago, some dopehead got high on your mutant junk and dressed up like a do-gooder named Cloak.
He teleported inside one of my dad's workshops and stole these really valuable, um, cyber... pants. Anyway, my old man needs to know who you sold those drugs to.
I don't think so, cuz. I start ving out customers' ames, my bidness dries up with a quickness.
I'm sure your daddy understands.
EXIT
My daddy could buy and sell you a thousand times over.
Then why don't you send him here to negotiate?
I got mad respect for your fam, but no uppity boy starts talking trash on my turf without getting the back of a Pimp Hand.

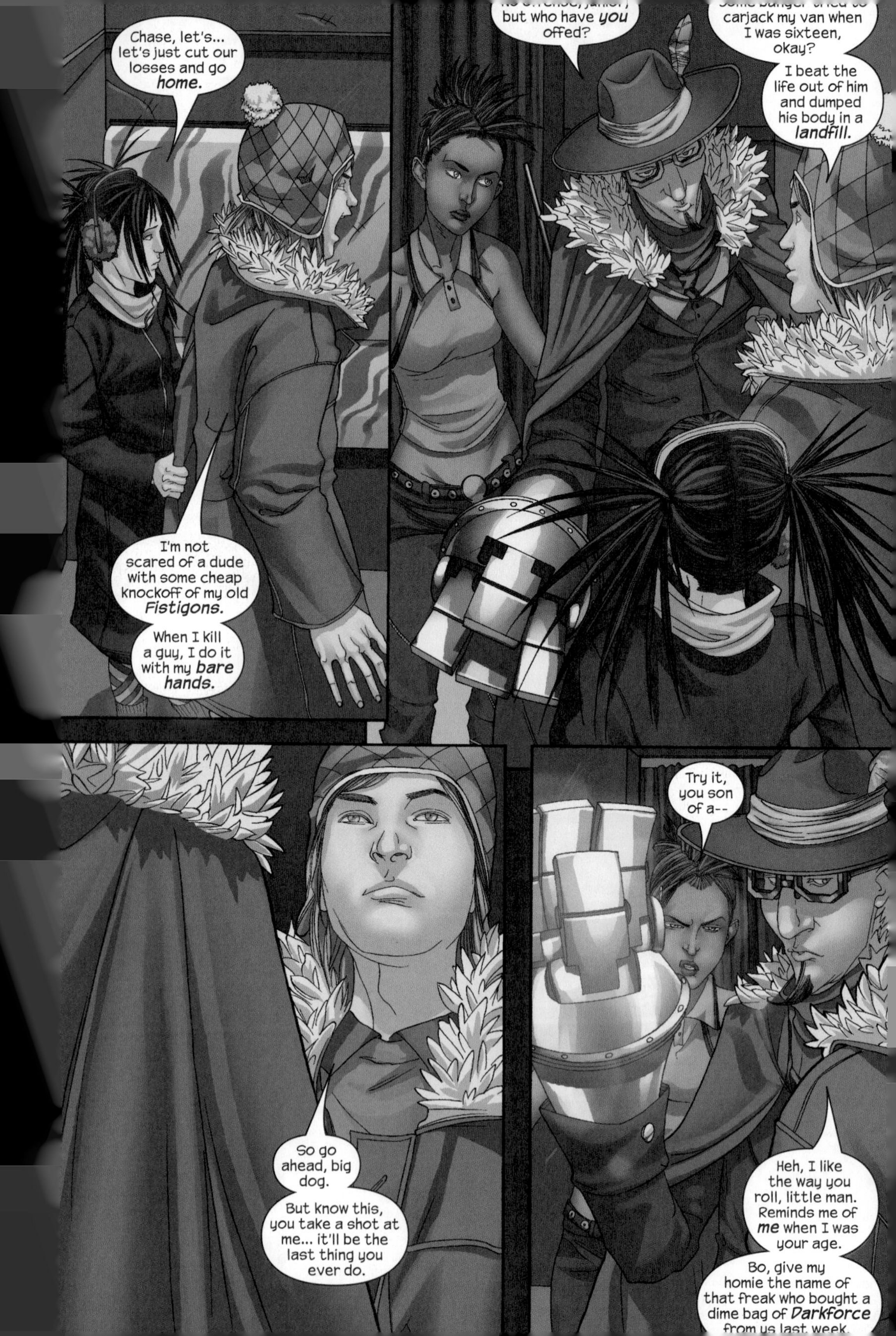
Chase, let's... let's just cut our losses and go home.
I'm not scared of a dude with some cheap knockoff of my old Fistigons.
When I kill a guy, I do it with my bare hands.
but who have you offed?
carjack my van when I was sixteen, okay?
I beat the life out of him and dumped his body in a landfill.
So go ahead, big dog.
But know this, you take a shot at me... it'll be the last thing you ever do.
Try it, you son of a--
Heh, I like the way you roll, little man. Reminds me of me when I was your age.
Bo, give my homie the name of that freak who bought a dime bag of Darkforce from us last week.

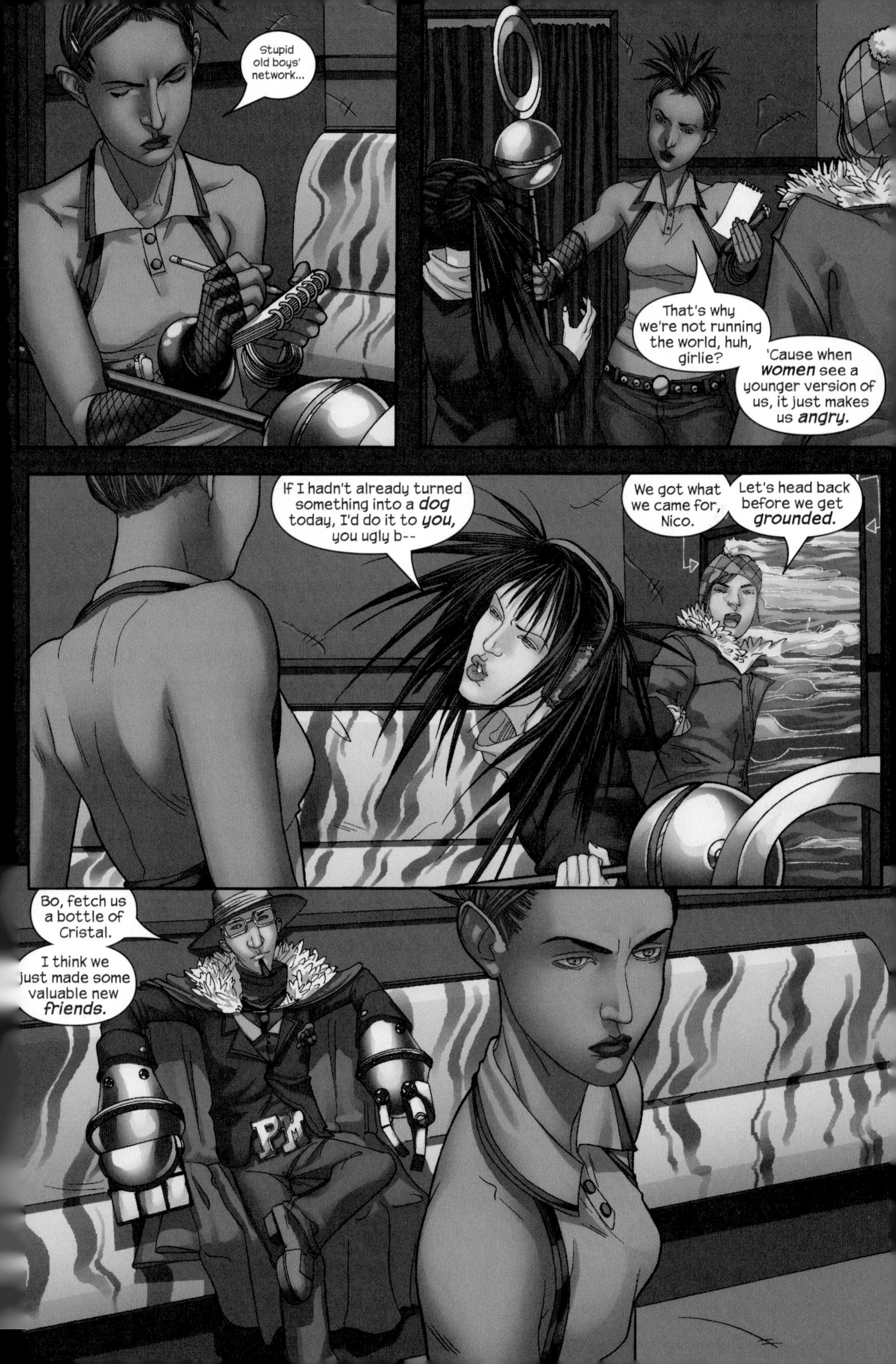

Stupid old boys' network...
That's why we're not running the world, huh, girlie?
'Cause when **women** see a younger version of us, it just makes us ***angry.***
If I hadn't already turned something into a ***dog*** today, I'd do it to ***you,*** you ugly b--
We got what we came for, Nico.
Let's head back before we get ***grounded.***
Bo, fetch us a bottle of Cristal.
I think we just made some valuable new ***friends.***

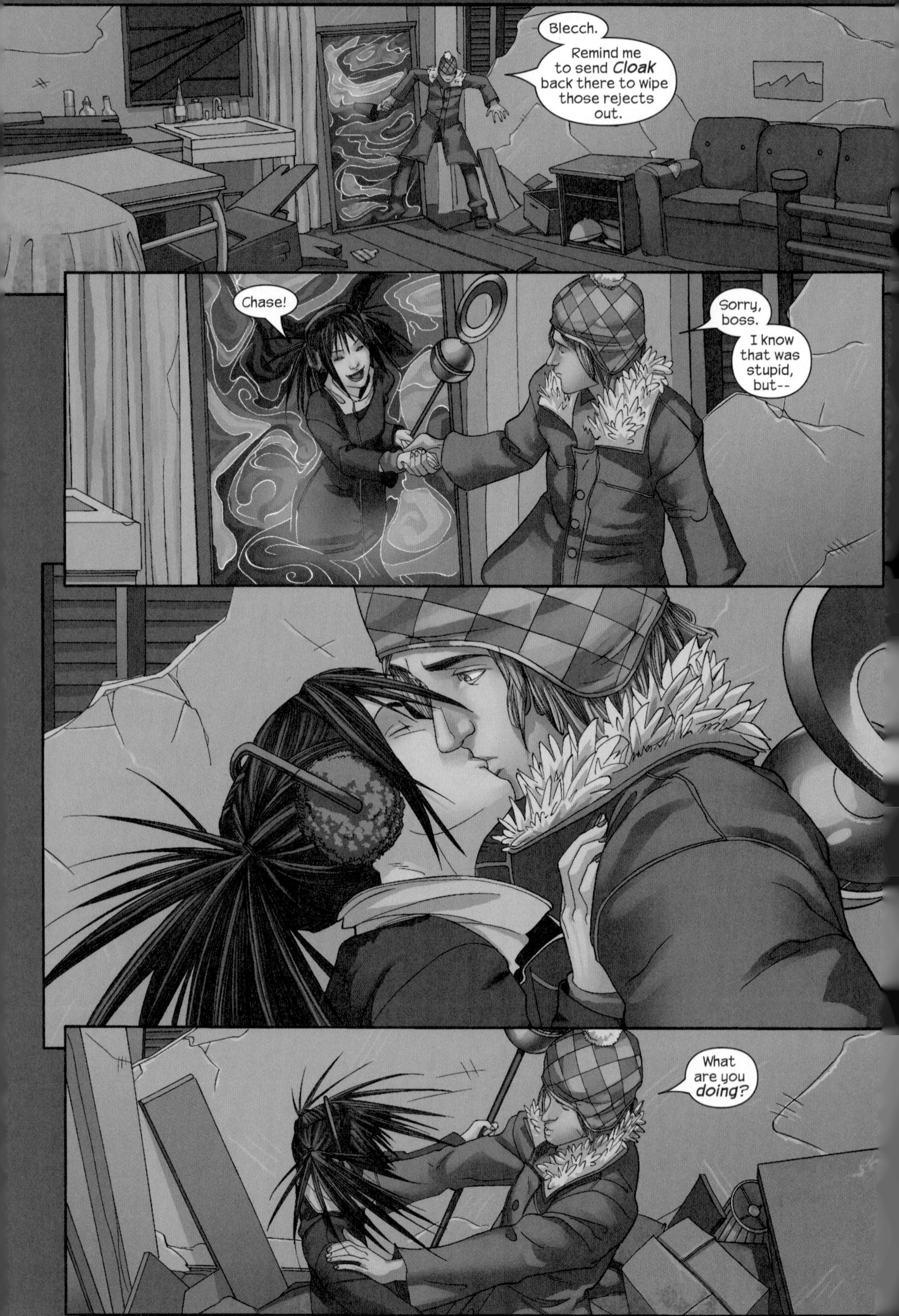
Blecch.
Remind me to send *Cloak* back there to wipe those rejects out.
Chase!
Sorry, boss.
I know that was stupid, but--
What are you *doing*?

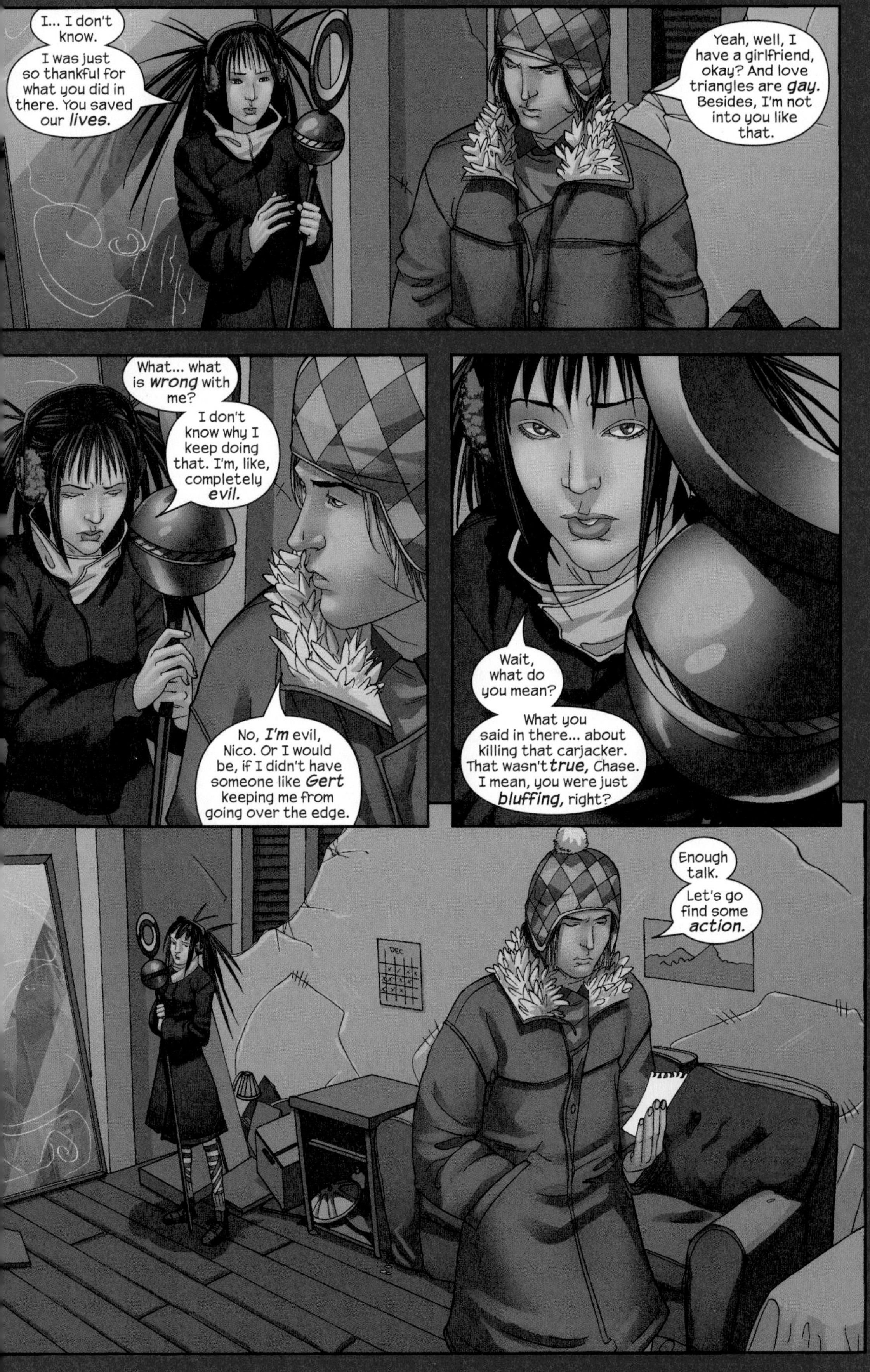
I... I don't know.
I was just so thankful for what you did in there. You saved our lives.
Yeah, well, I have a girlfriend, okay? And love triangles are gay. Besides, I'm not into you like that.
What... what is wrong with me?
I don't know why I keep doing that. I'm, like, completely evil.
No, I'm evil, Nico. Or I would be, if I didn't have someone like Gert keeping me from going over the edge.
Wait, what do you mean?
What you said in there... about killing that carjacker. That wasn't true, Chase. I mean, you were just bluffing, right?
DEC
Enough talk.
Let's go find some action.

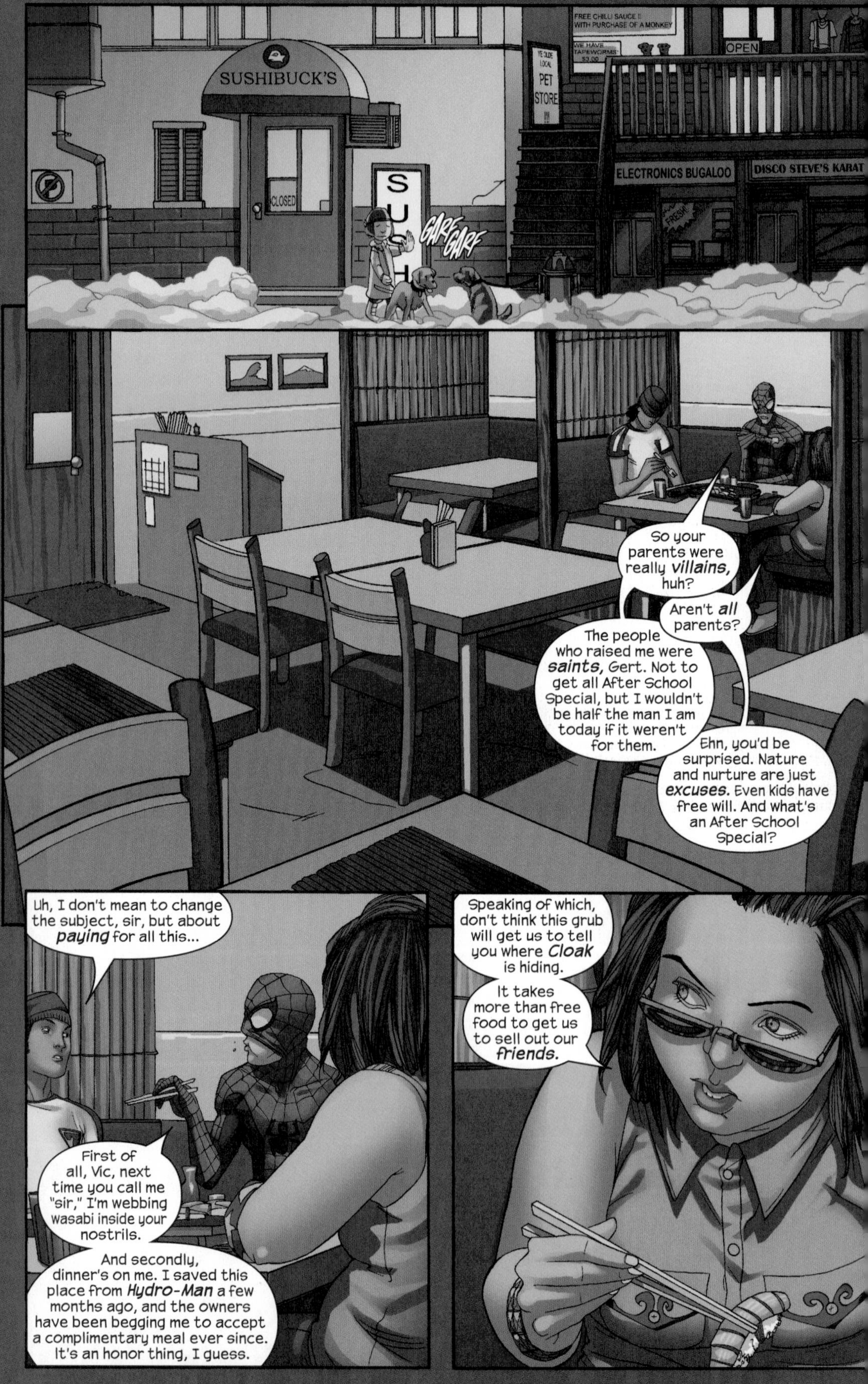

SUSHIBUCK'S
CLOSED
FREE CHILI SAUCE!! WITH PURCHASE OF A MONKEY
WE HAVE TAPEWORMS! $3.00
OPEN
YE OLDE LOCAL PET STORE !!!
ELECTRONICS BUGALOO
DISCO STEVE'S KARAT
FRESH!
GARF GARF
So your parents were really *villains*, huh?
Aren't *all* parents?
The people who raised me were *saints*, Gert. Not to get all After School Special, but I wouldn't be half the man I am today if it weren't for them.
Ehn, you'd be surprised. Nature and nurture are just *excuses*. Even kids have free will. And what's an After School Special?
Uh, I don't mean to change the subject, sir, but about *paying* for all this...
First of all, Vic, next time you call me "sir," I'm webbing wasabi inside your nostrils.
And secondly, dinner's on me. I saved this place from *Hydro-Man* a few months ago, and the owners have been begging me to accept a complimentary meal ever since. It's an honor thing, I guess.
Speaking of which, don't think this grub will get us to tell you where *Cloak* is hiding.
It takes more than free food to get us to sell out our *friends*.

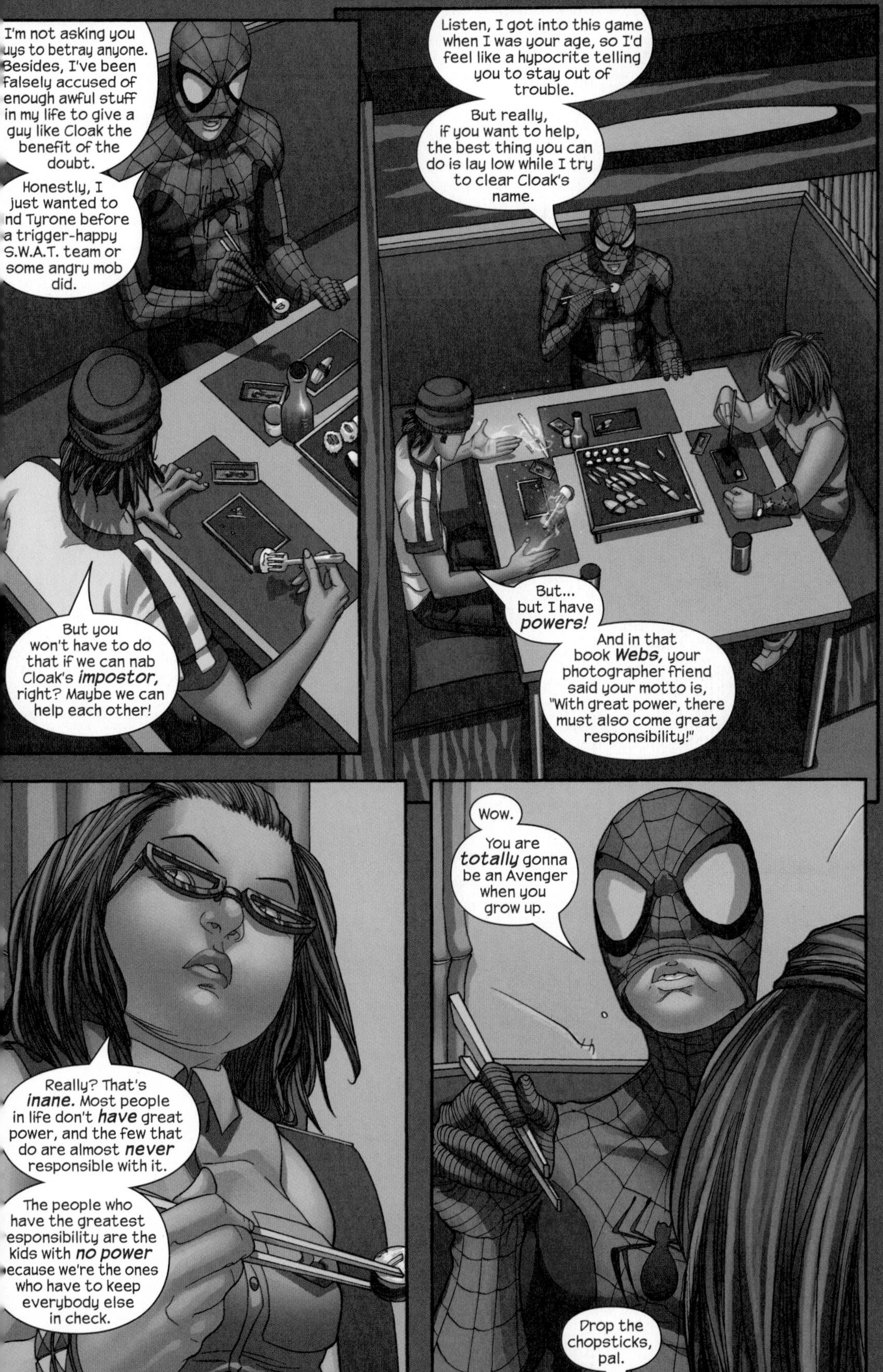

I'm not asking you uys to betray anyone. esides, I've been falsely accused of enough awful stuff in my life to give a guy like Cloak the benefit of the doubt.
Honestly, I just wanted to nd Tyrone before a trigger-happy S.W.A.T. team or some angry mob did.
But you won't have to do that if we can nab Cloak's *impostor*, right? Maybe we can help each other!
Listen, I got into this game when I was your age, so I'd feel like a hypocrite telling you to stay out of trouble.
But really, if you want to help, the best thing you can do is lay low while I try to clear Cloak's name.
But... but I have *powers!*
And in that book *Webs,* your photographer friend said your motto is, "With great power, there must also come great responsibility!"
Really? That's *inane.* Most people in life don't *have* great power, and the few that do are almost *never* responsible with it.
The people who have the greatest esponsibility are the kids with *no power* ecause we're the ones who have to keep everybody else in check.
Wow.
You are *totally* gonna be an Avenger when you grow up.
Drop the chopsticks, pal.

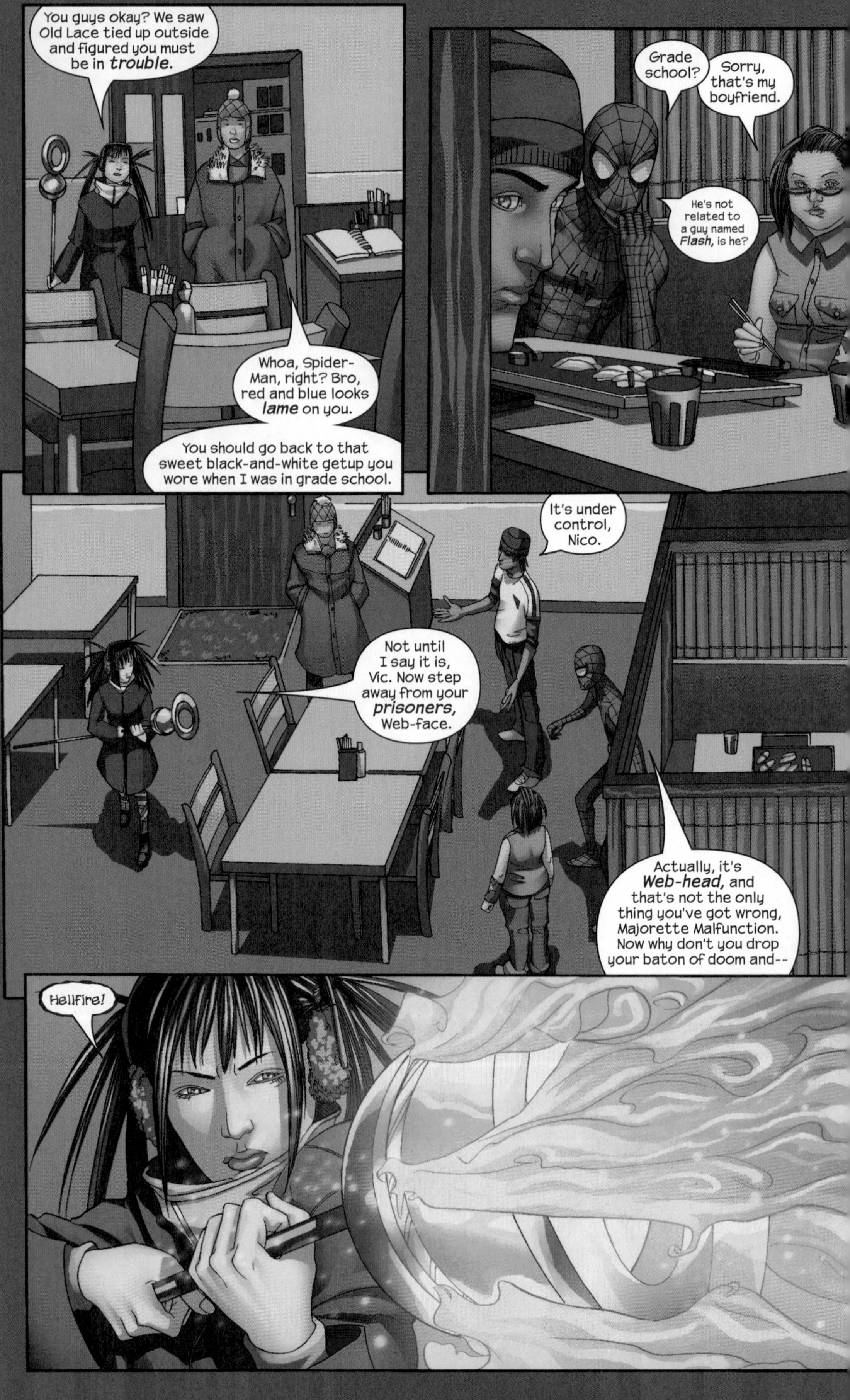
You guys okay? We saw Old Lace tied up outside and figured you must be in *trouble.*
Whoa, Spider-Man, right? Bro, red and blue looks *lame* on you.
You should go back to that sweet black-and-white getup you wore when I was in grade school.
Grade school?
Sorry, that's my boyfriend.
He's not related to a guy named *Flash,* is he?
It's under control, Nico.
Not until I say it is, Vic. Now step away from your *prisoners,* Web-face.
Actually, it's *Web-head,* and that's not the only thing you've got wrong, Majorette Malfunction. Now why don't you drop your baton of doom and--
Hellfire!

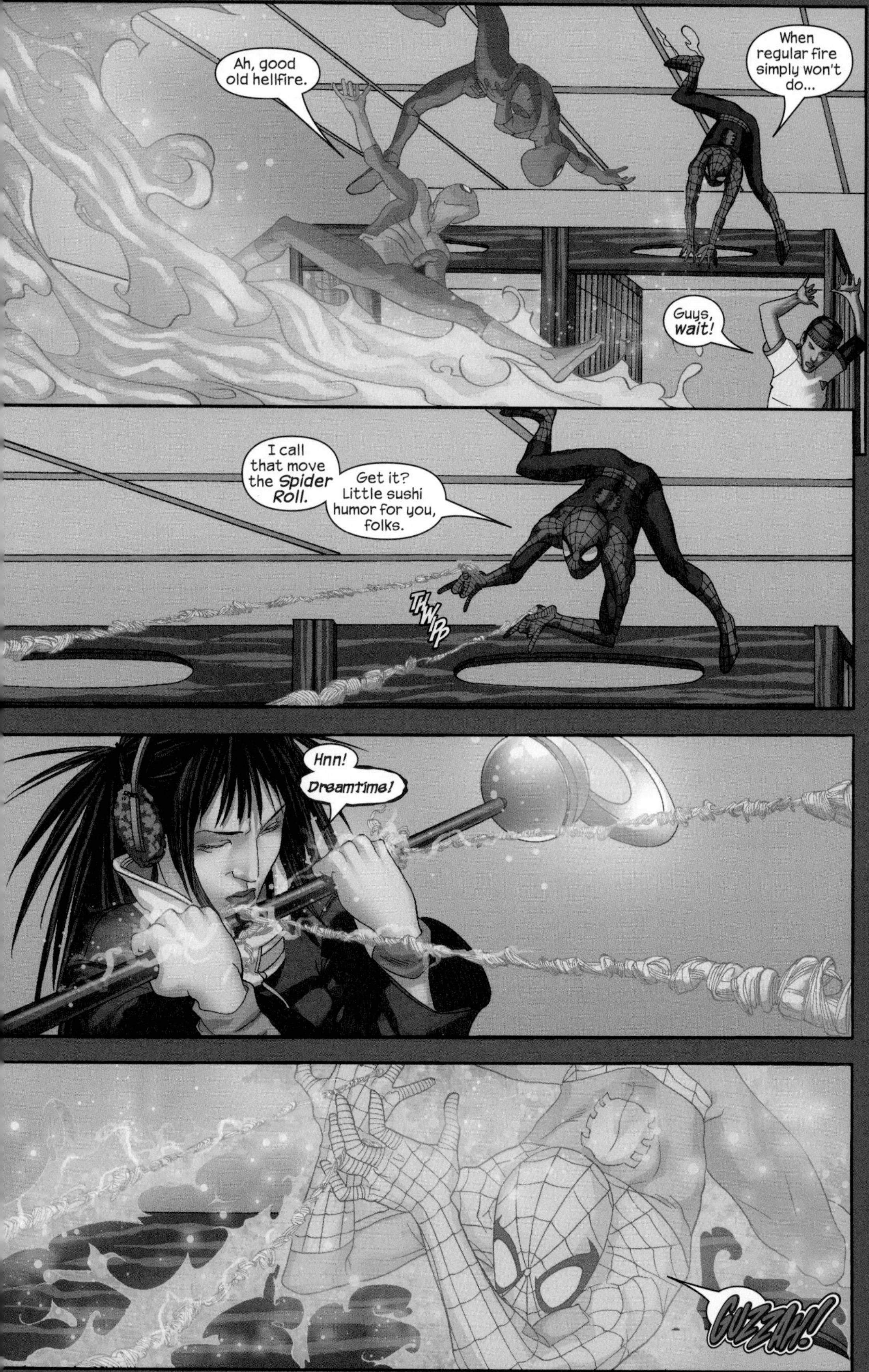
Ah, good old hellfire.
When regular fire simply won't do...
Guys, wait!
I call that move the Spider Roll.
Get it? Little sushi humor for you, folks.
THWIPP
Hnn!
Dreamtime!
GUZZAH!

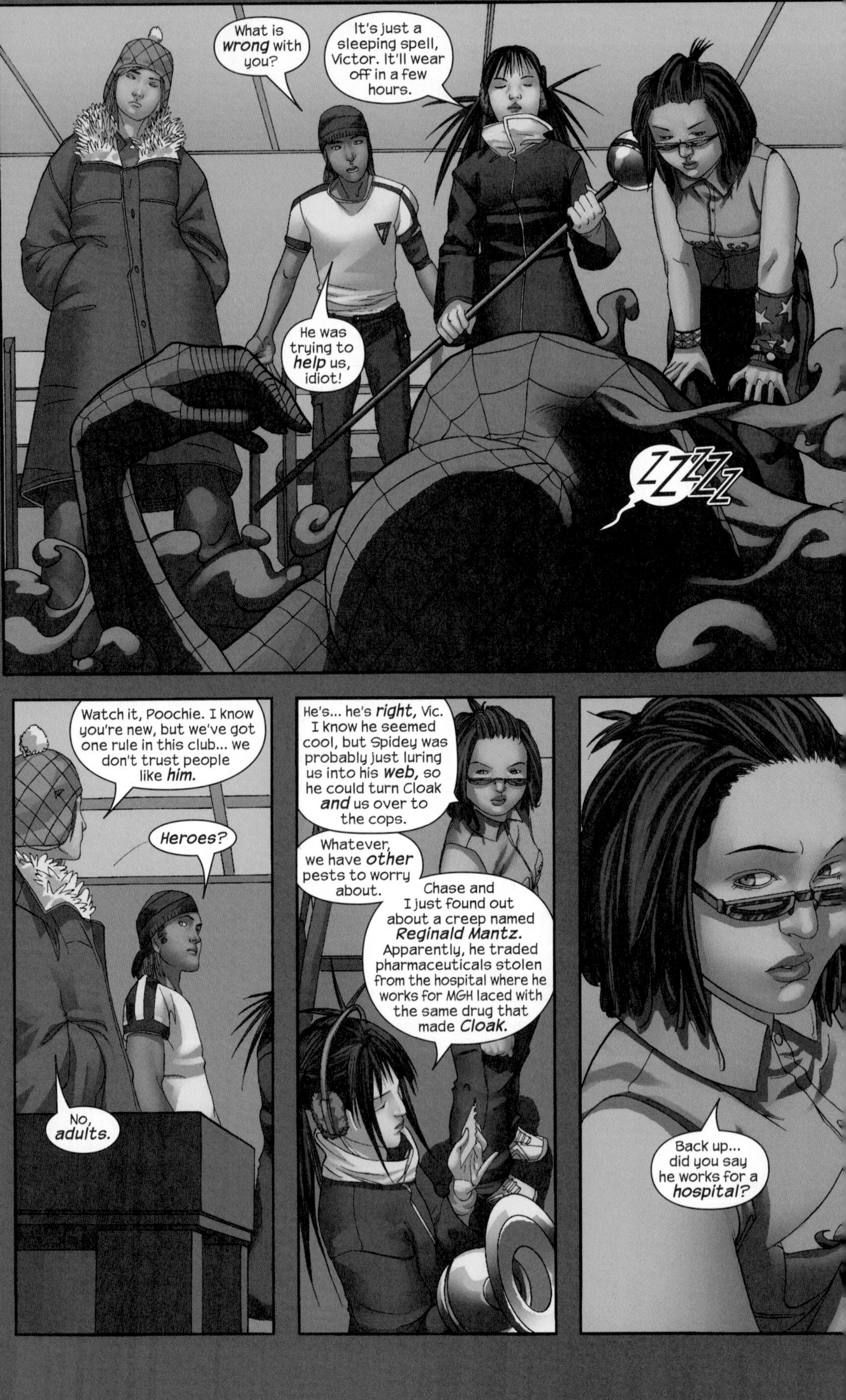
What is wrong with you?
It's just a sleeping spell, Victor. It'll wear off in a few hours.
He was trying to help us, idiot!
ZZZZZ
Watch it, Poochie. I know you're new, but we've got one rule in this club... we don't trust people like him.
Heroes?
No, adults.
He's... he's right, Vic. I know he seemed cool, but Spidey was probably just luring us into his web, so he could turn Cloak and us over to the cops.
Whatever, we have other pests to worry about.
Chase and I just found out about a creep named Reginald Mantz. Apparently, he traded pharmaceuticals stolen from the hospital where he works for MGH laced with the same drug that made Cloak.
Back up... did you say he works for a hospital?

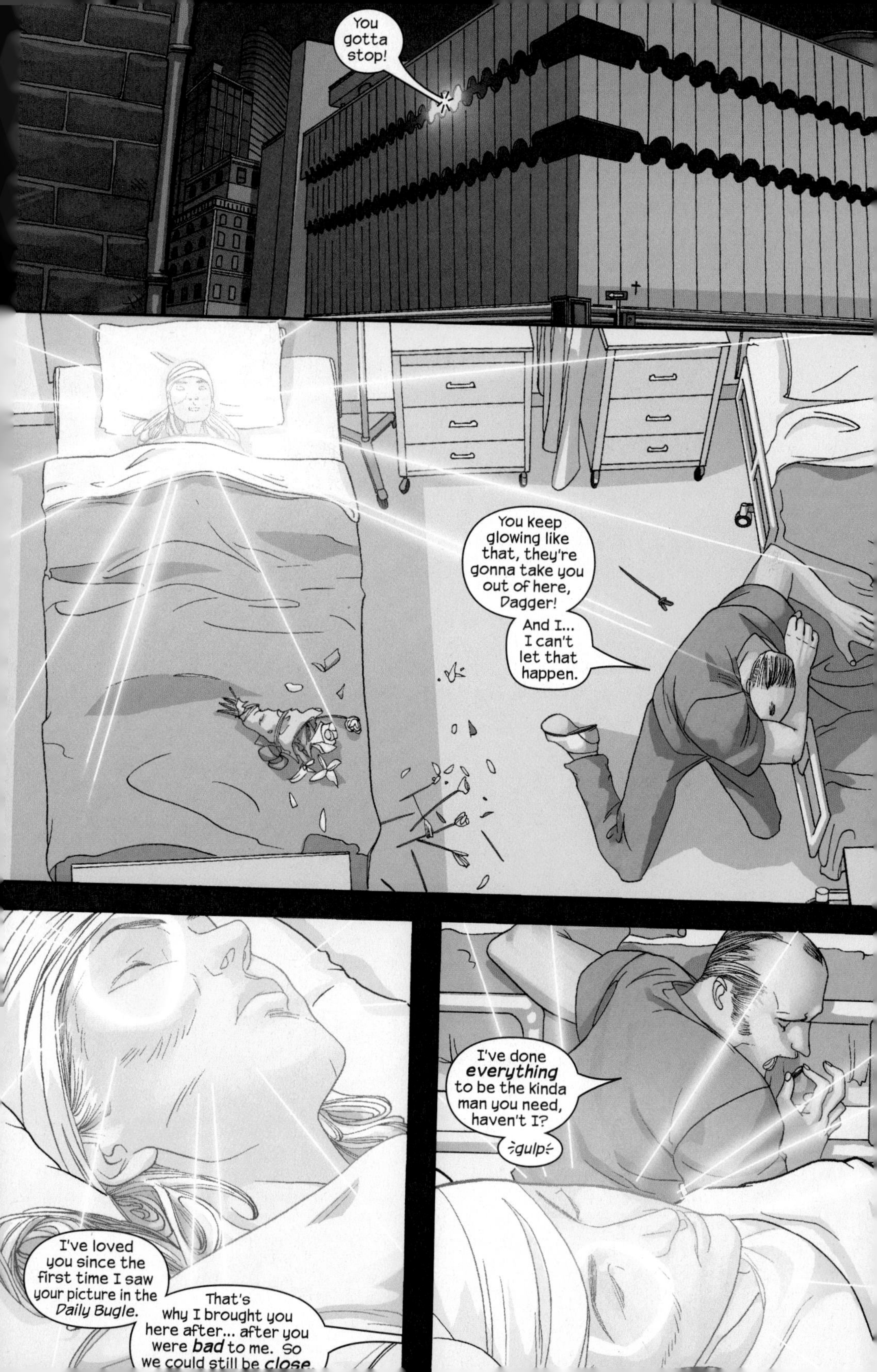
You gotta stop!
You keep glowing like that, they're gonna take you out of here, Dagger!
And I... I can't let that happen.
I've loved you since the first time I saw your picture in the Daily Bugle.
That's why I brought you here after... after you were bad to me. So we could still be close.
I've done everything to be the kinda man you need, haven't I?
gulp

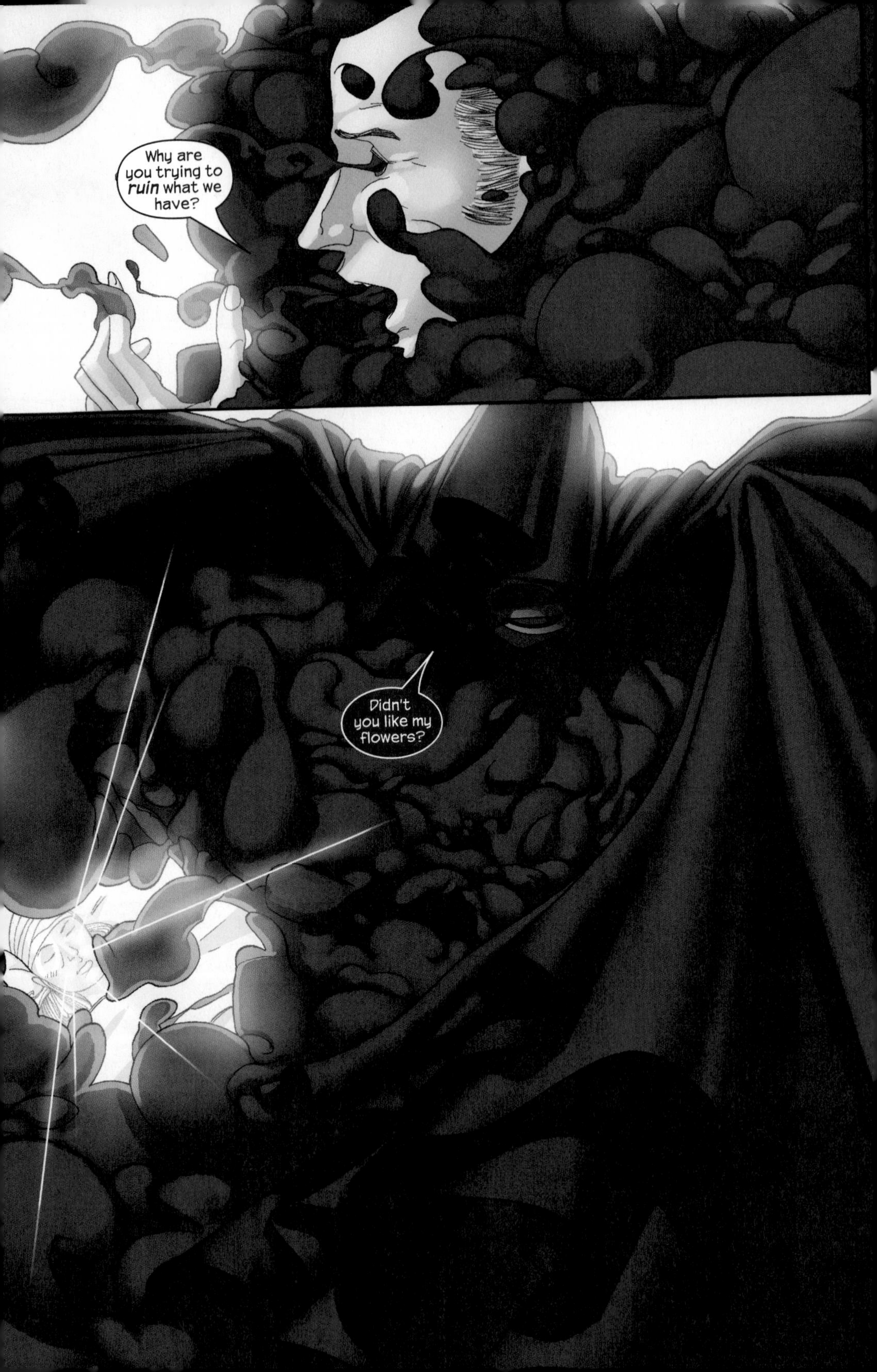
Why are you trying to *ruin* what we have?
Didn't you like my flowers?

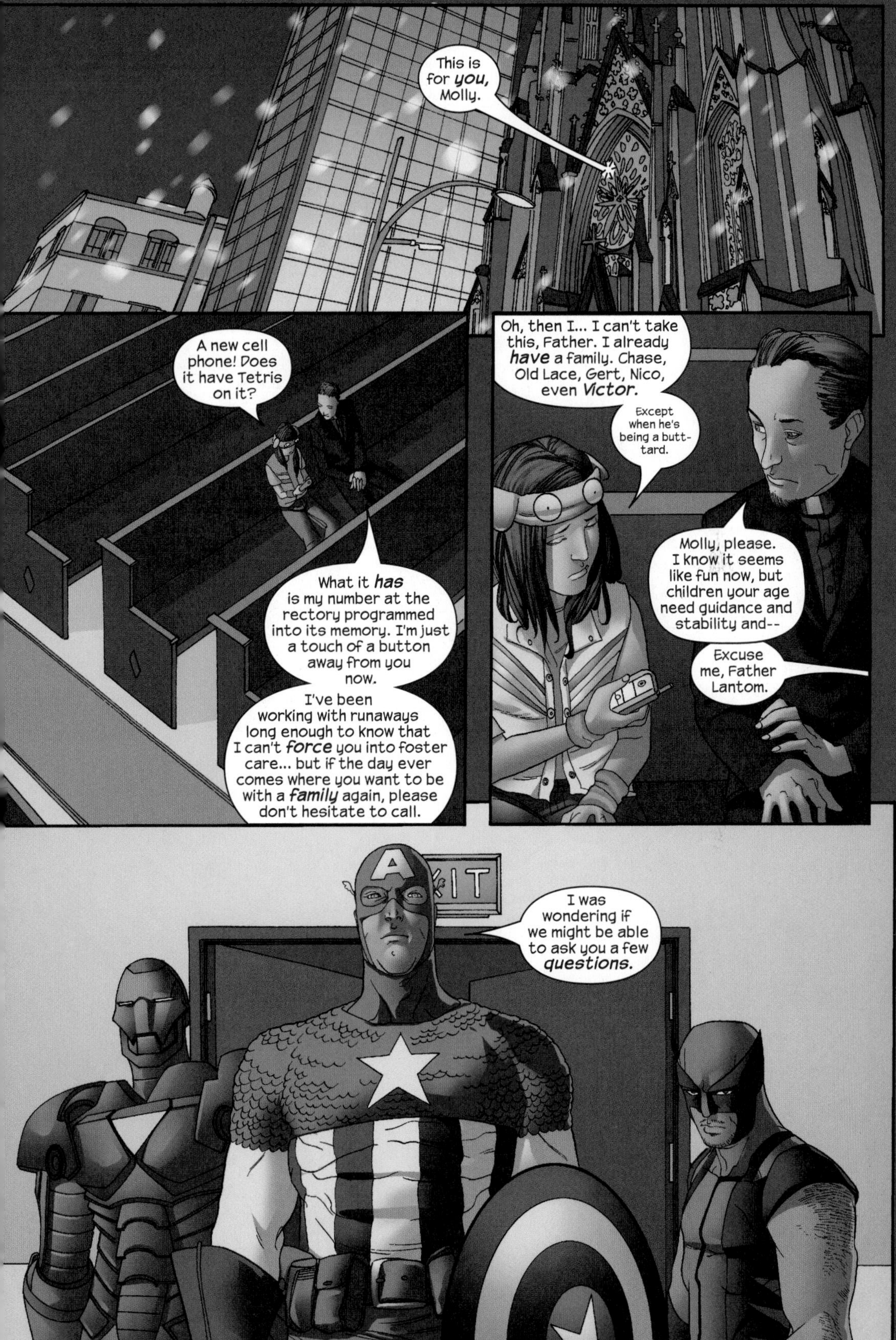
This is for you, Molly.
A new cell phone! Does it have Tetris on it?
What it has is my number at the rectory programmed into its memory. I'm just a touch of a button away from you now.
I've been working with runaways long enough to know that I can't force you into foster care... but if the day ever comes where you want to be with a family again, please don't hesitate to call.
Oh, then I... I can't take this, Father. I already have a family. Chase, Old Lace, Gert, Nico, even Victor.
Except when he's being a butt-tard.
Molly, please. I know it seems like fun now, but children your age need guidance and stability and--
Excuse me, Father Lantom.
XIT
I was wondering if we might be able to ask you a few questions.

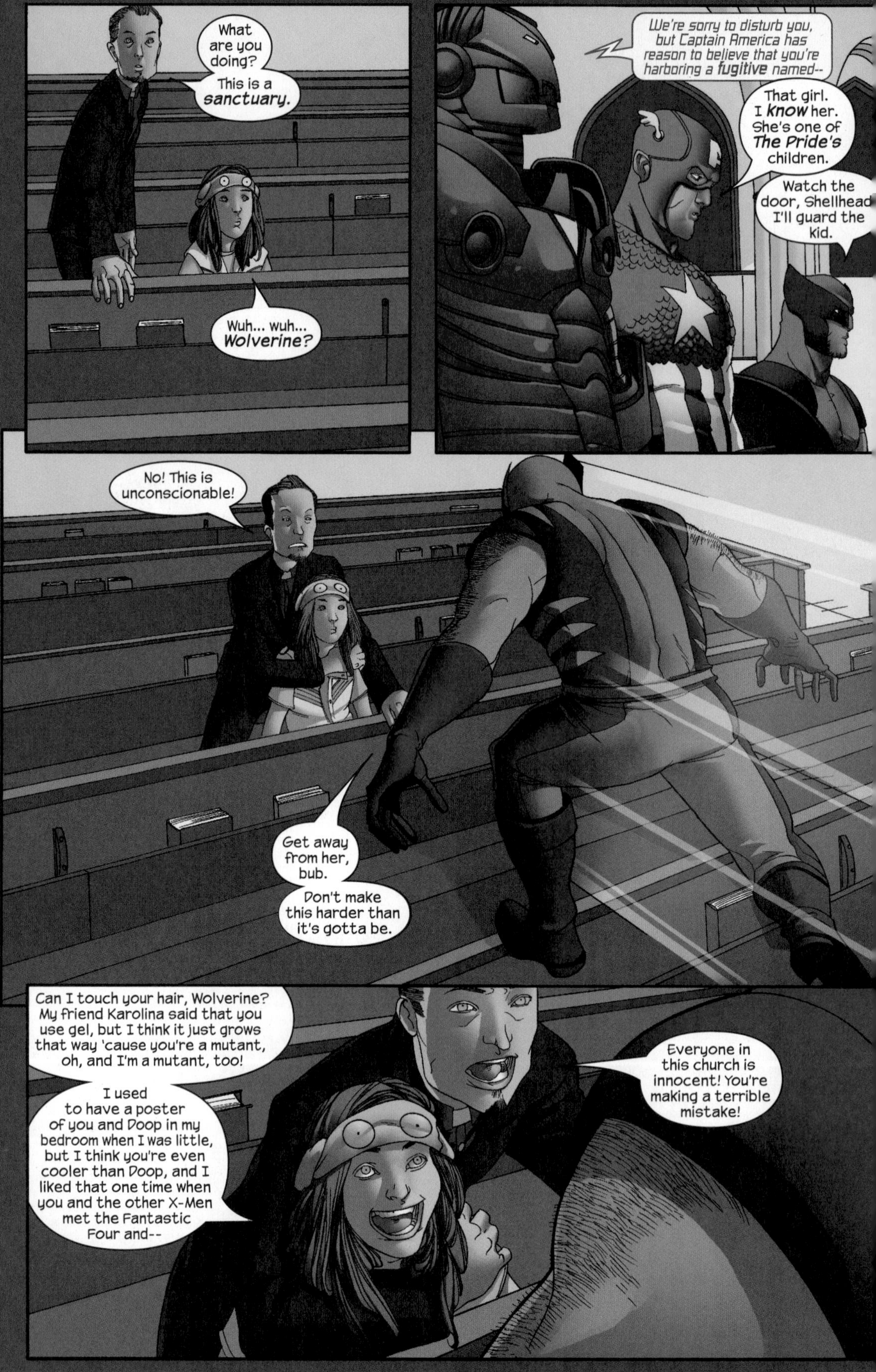
What are you doing? This is a sanctuary.
Wuh... wuh... Wolverine?
We're sorry to disturb you, but Captain America has reason to believe that you're harboring a fugitive named--
That girl. I know her. She's one of The Pride's children.
Watch the door, Shellhead. I'll guard the kid.
No! This is unconscionable!
Get away from her, bub.
Don't make this harder than it's gotta be.
Can I touch your hair, Wolverine? My friend Karolina said that you use gel, but I think it just grows that way 'cause you're a mutant, oh, and I'm a mutant, too!
I used to have a poster of you and Doop in my bedroom when I was little, but I think you're even cooler than Doop, and I liked that one time when you and the other X-Men met the Fantastic Four and--
Everyone in this church is innocent! You're making a terrible mistake!

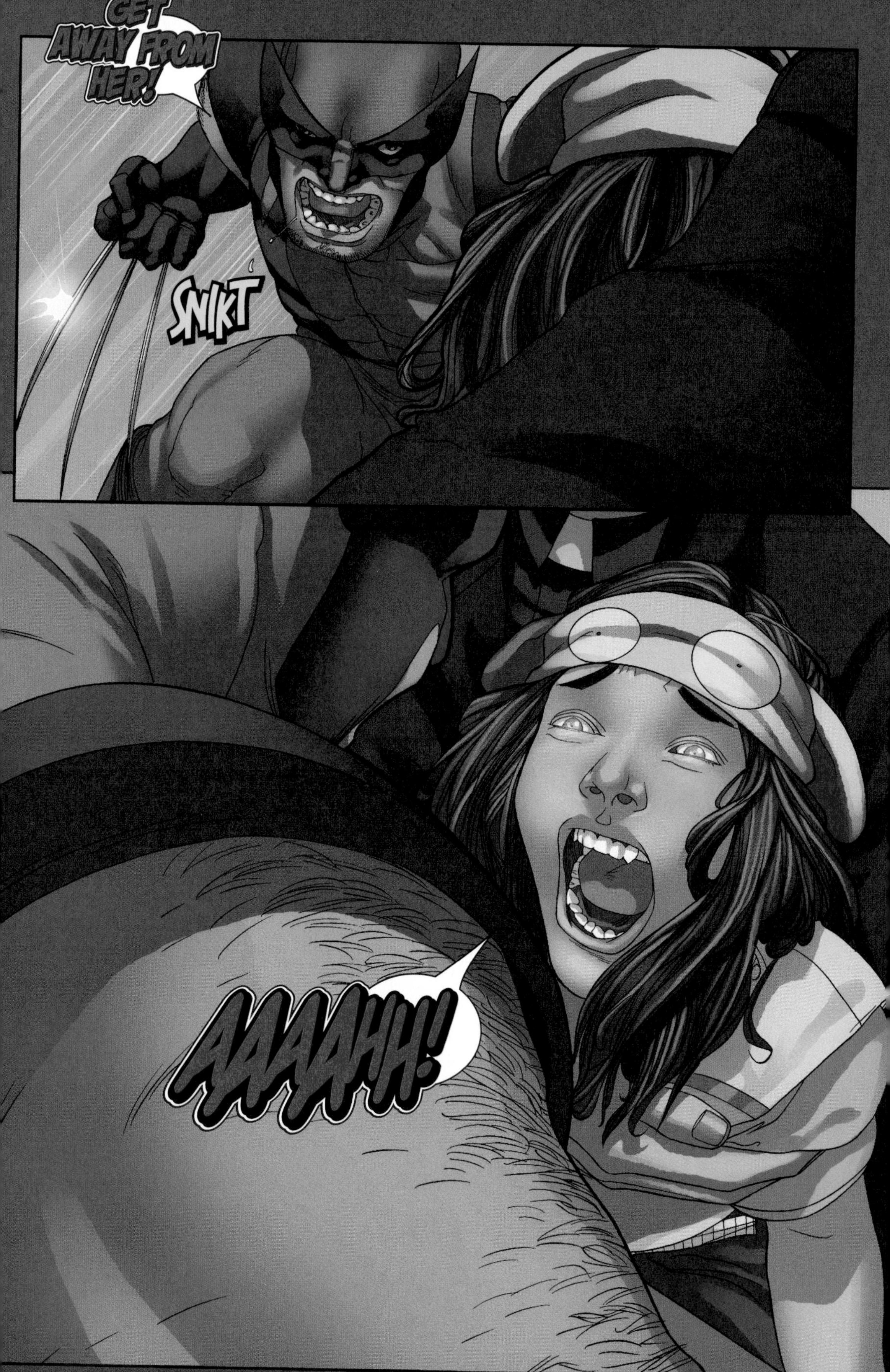
GET AWAY FROM HER!
SNIKT
AAAAHH!

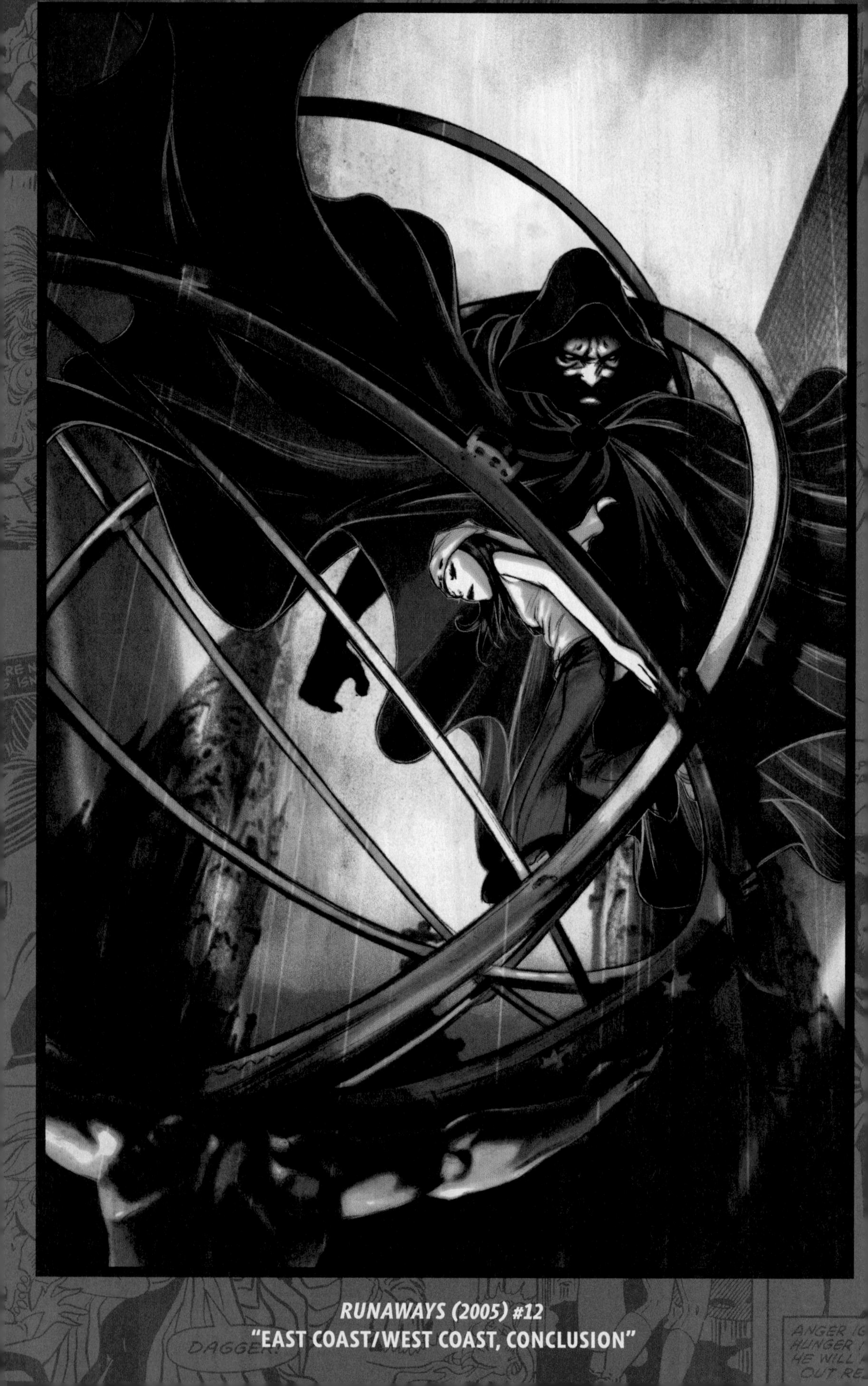

RUNAWAYS (2005) #12
"EAST COAST/WEST COAST, CONCLUSION"

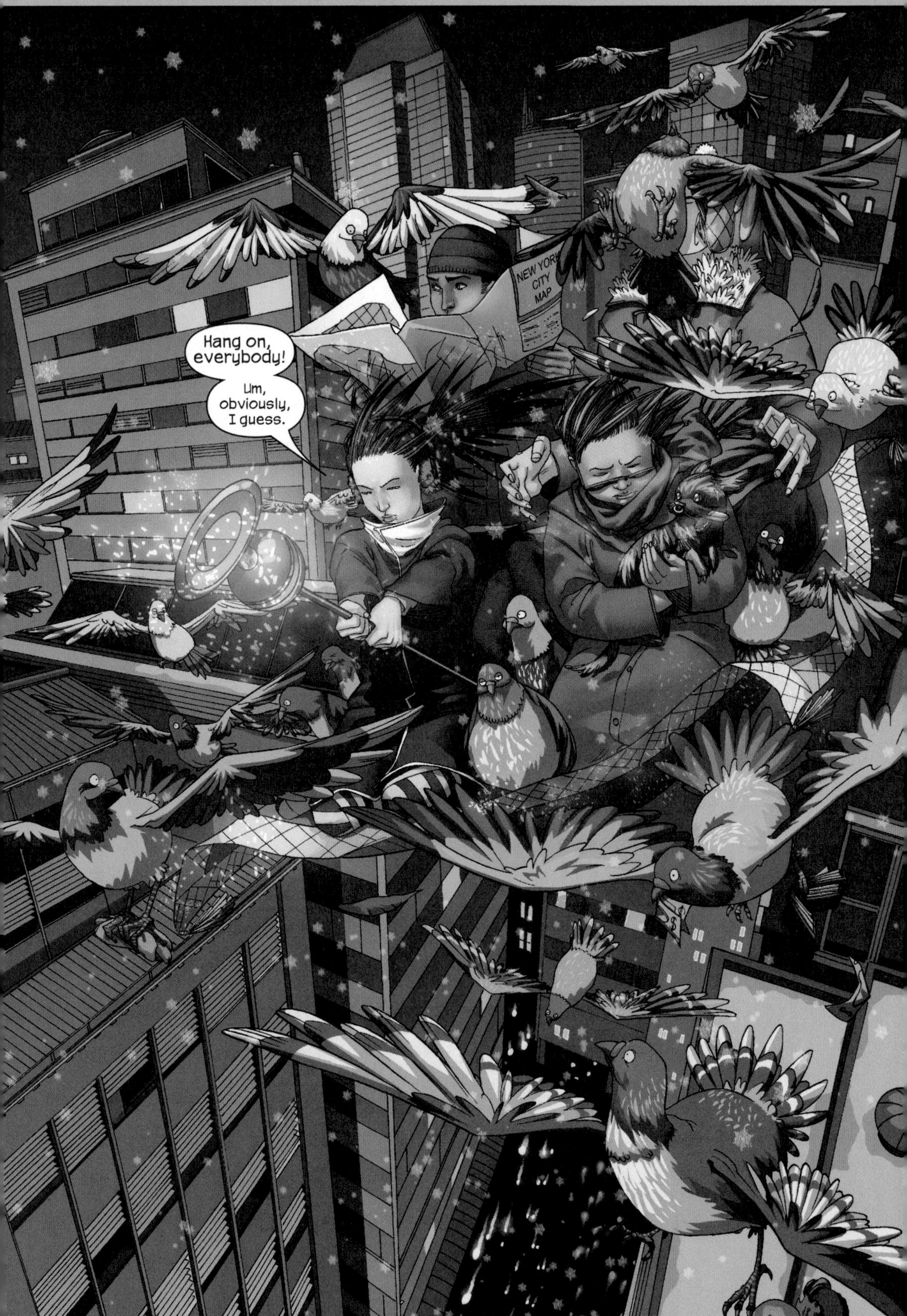
NEW YORK CITY MAP
Hang on, everybody!
Um, obviously, I guess.

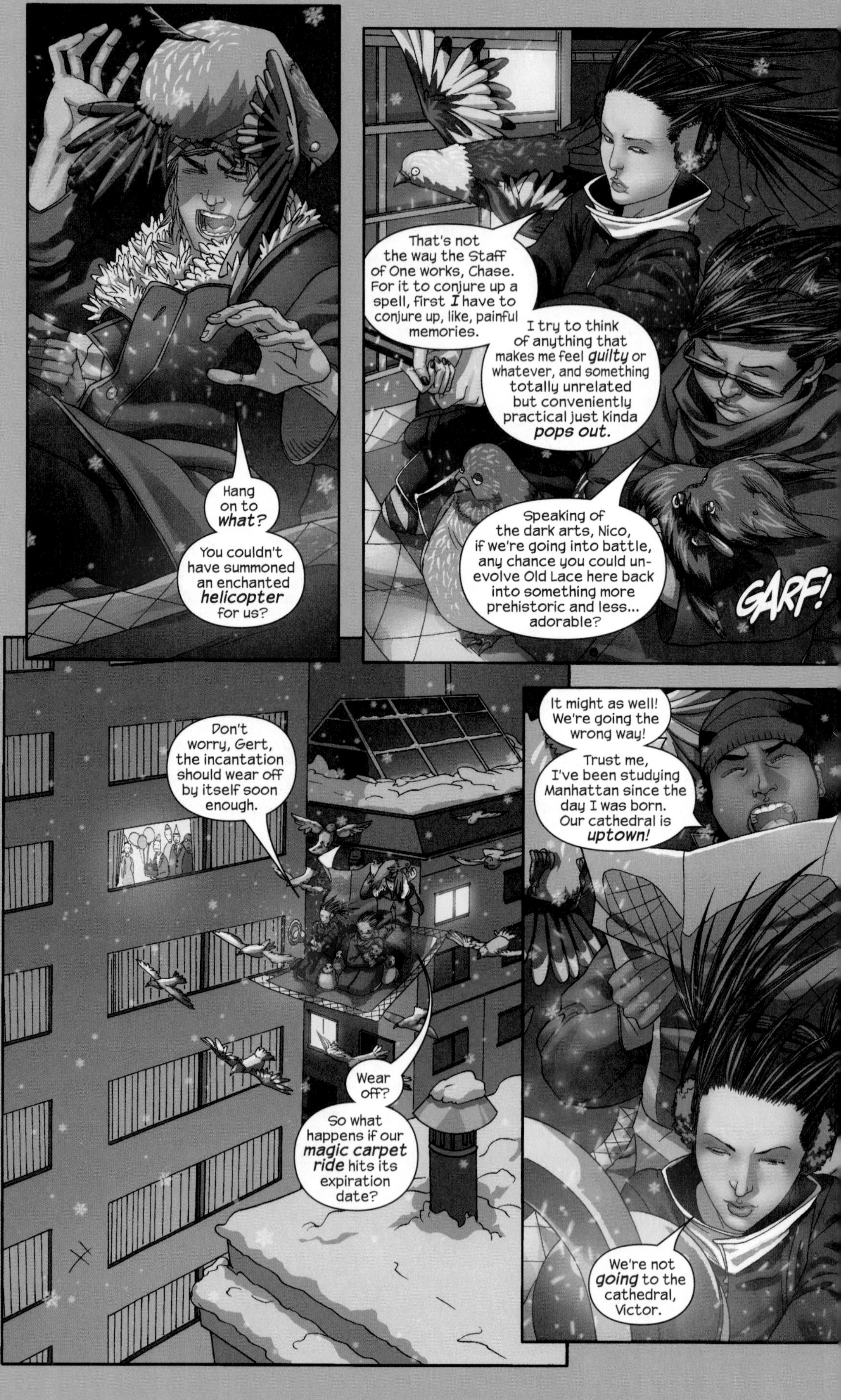
Hang on to what?
You couldn't have summoned an enchanted helicopter for us?
That's not the way the Staff of One works, Chase. For it to conjure up a spell, first I have to conjure up, like, painful memories.
I try to think of anything that makes me feel guilty or whatever, and something totally unrelated but conveniently practical just kinda pops out.
Speaking of the dark arts, Nico, if we're going into battle, any chance you could un-evolve Old Lace here back into something more prehistoric and less... adorable?
GARF!
Don't worry, Gert, the incantation should wear off by itself soon enough.
Wear off?
So what happens if our magic carpet ride hits its expiration date?
It might as well! We're going the wrong way!
Trust me, I've been studying Manhattan since the day I was born. Our cathedral is uptown!
We're not going to the cathedral, Victor.

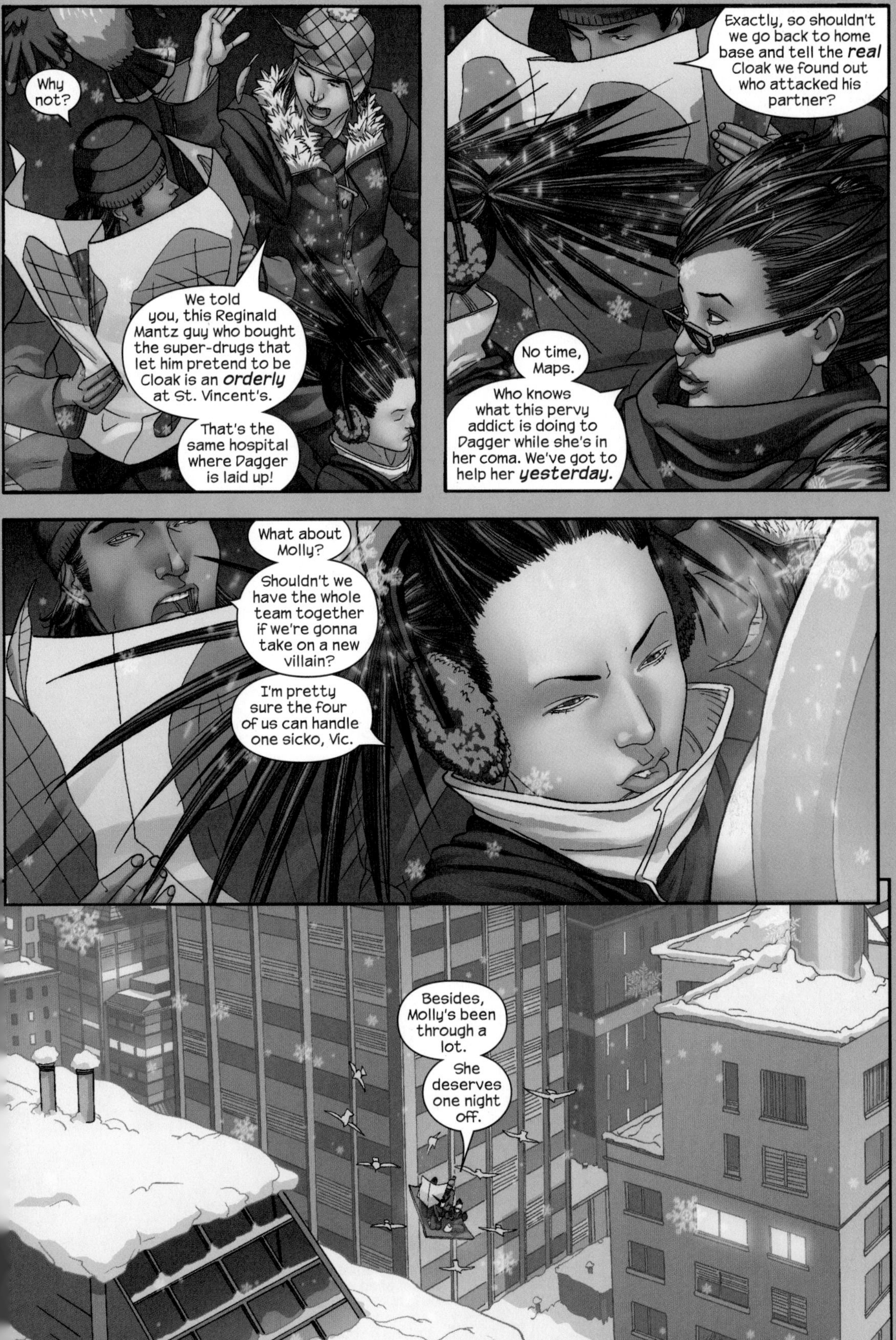

Why not?
We told you, this Reginald Mantz guy who bought the super-drugs that let him pretend to be Cloak is an *orderly* at St. Vincent's.
That's the same hospital where Dagger is laid up!
Exactly, so shouldn't we go back to home base and tell the *real* Cloak we found out who attacked his partner?
No time, Maps.
Who knows what this pervy addict is doing to Dagger while she's in her coma. We've got to help her *yesterday.*
What about Molly?
Shouldn't we have the whole team together if we're gonna take on a new villain?
I'm pretty sure the four of us can handle one sicko, Vic.
Besides, Molly's been through a lot.
She deserves one night off.

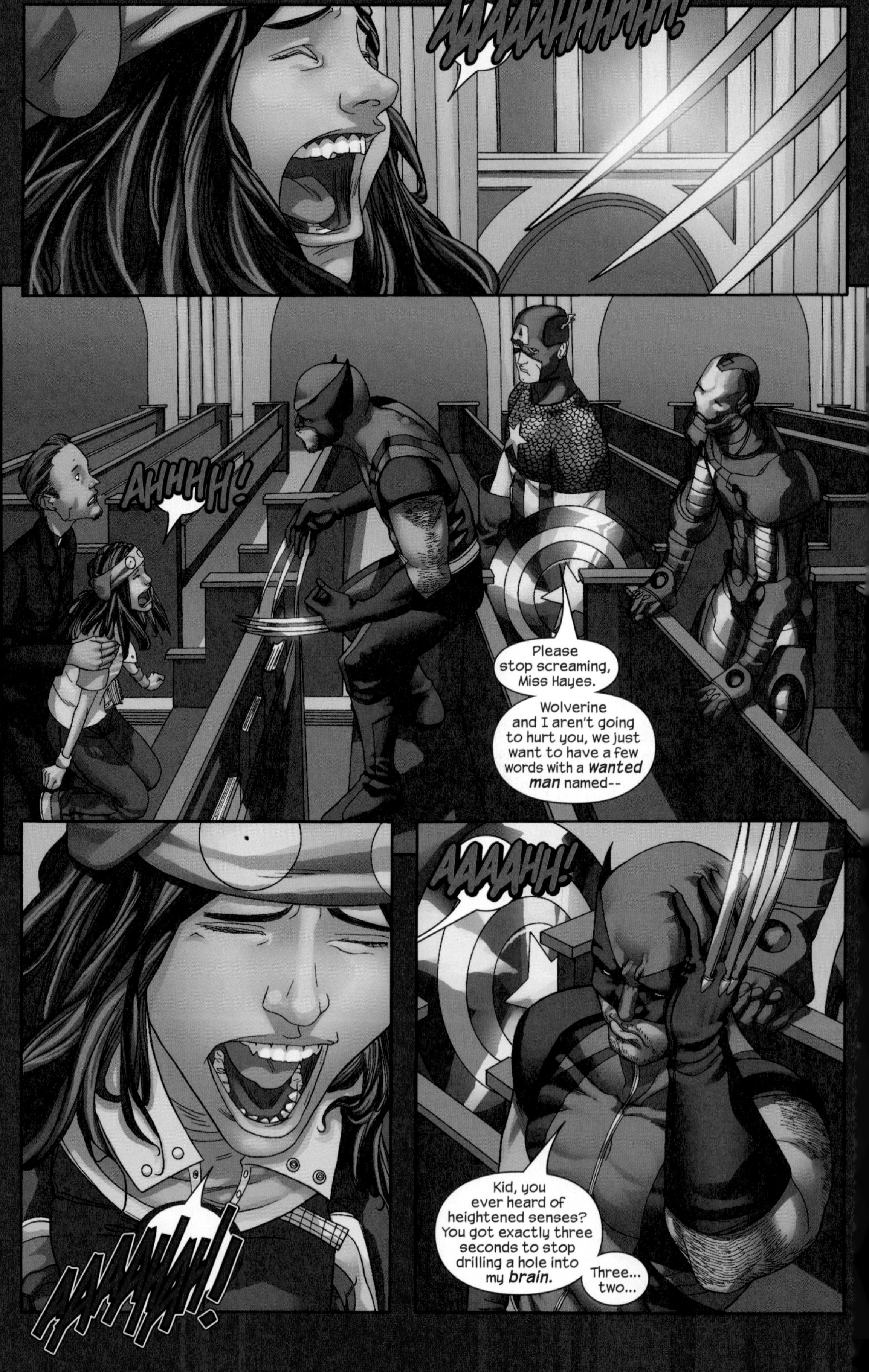
AAAAAHHHHHH!
AHHHH!
Please stop screaming, Miss Hayes.
Wolverine and I aren't going to hurt you, we just want to have a few words with a *wanted man* named--
AAAAHH!
Kid, you ever heard of heightened senses? You got exactly three seconds to stop drilling a hole into my *brain.*
Three... two...

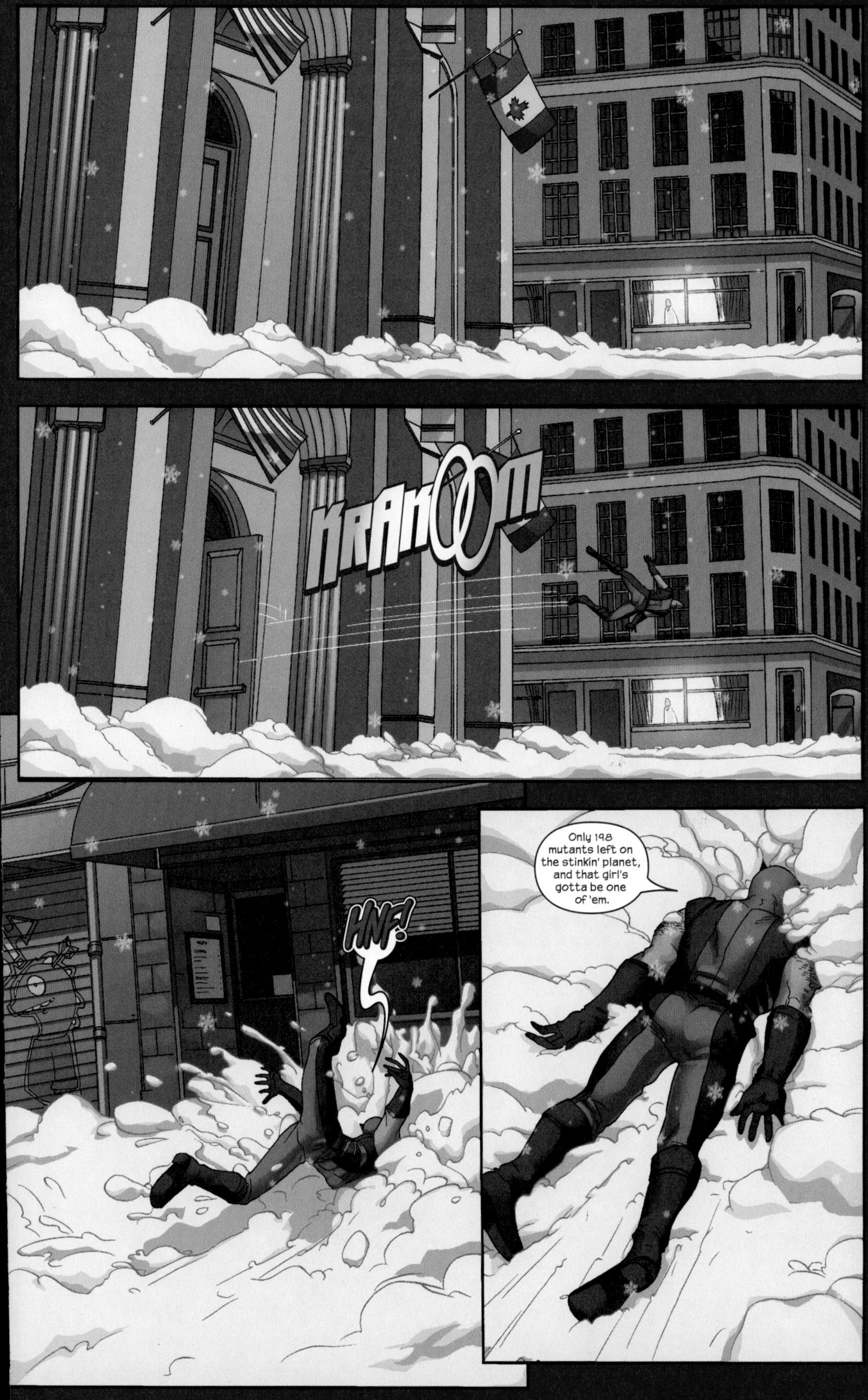
KRAKOOM
HNF!
Only 198 mutants left on the stinkin' planet, and that girl's gotta be one of 'em.

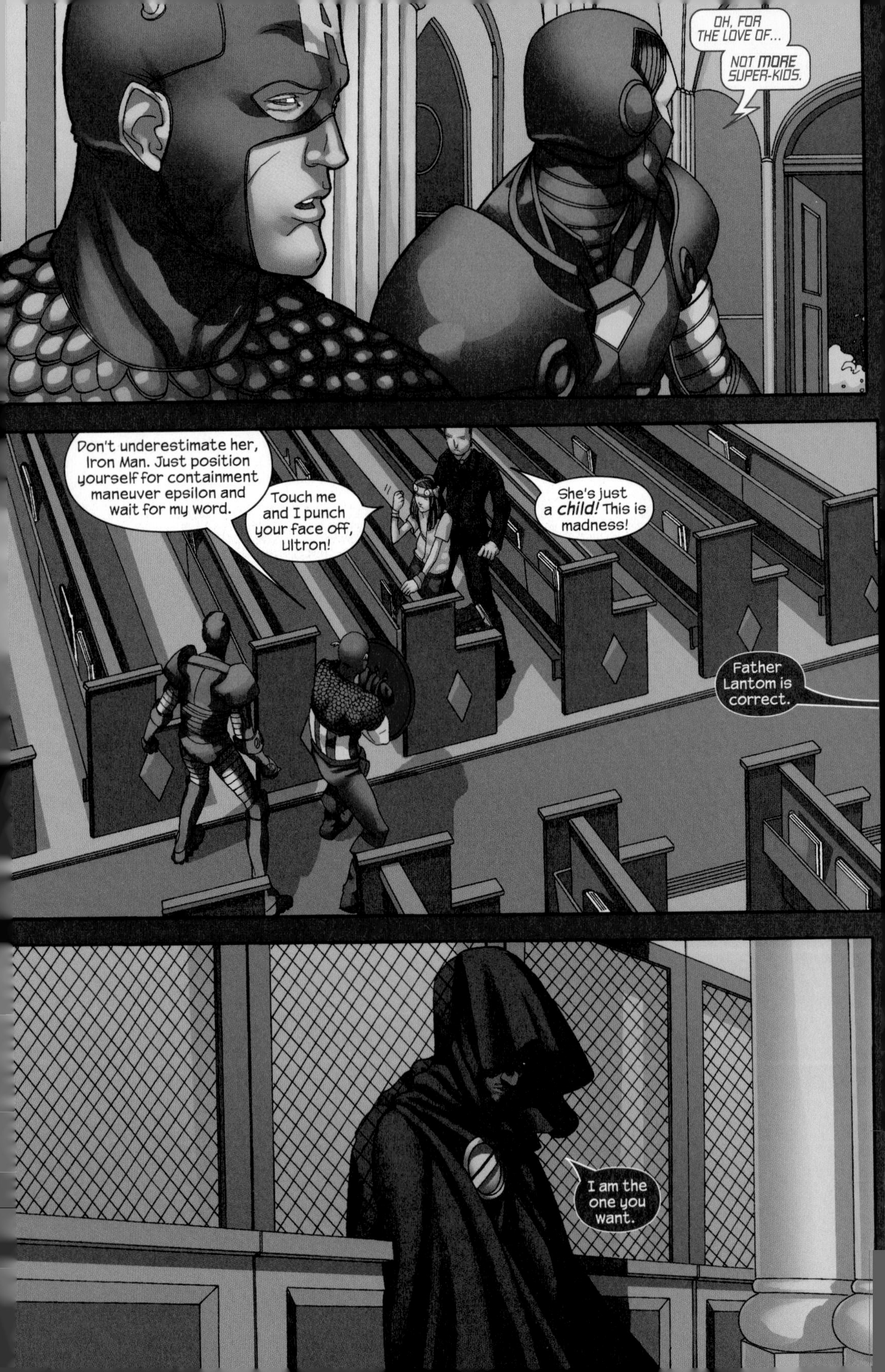

OH, FOR THE LOVE OF...
NOT MORE SUPER-KIDS.
Don't underestimate her, Iron Man. Just position yourself for containment maneuver epsilon and wait for my word.
Touch me and I punch your face off, Ultron!
She's just a child! This is madness!
Father Lantom is correct.
I am the one you want.

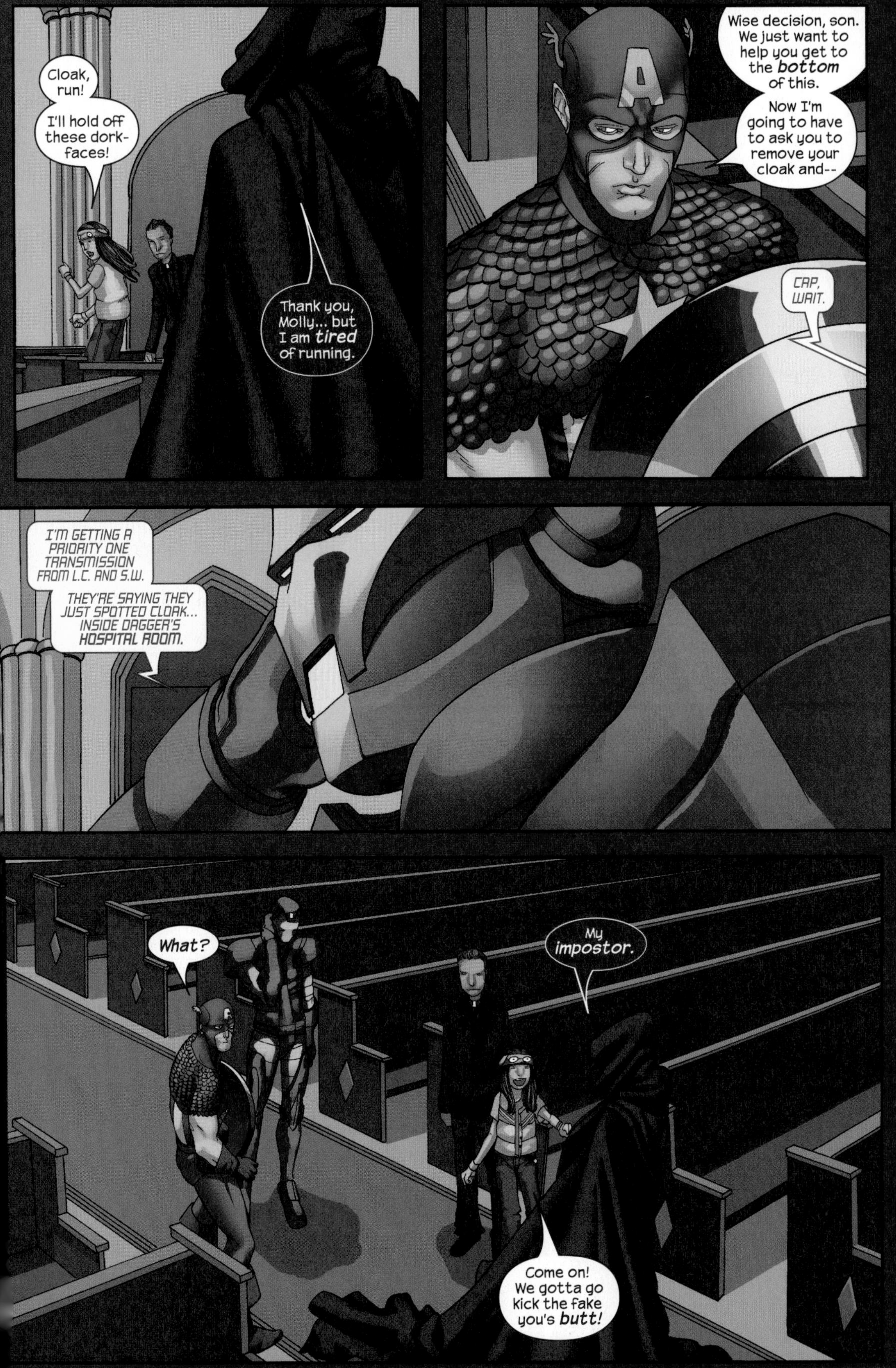
Cloak, run!
I'll hold off these dork-faces!
Thank you, Molly... but I am *tired* of running.
Wise decision, son. We just want to help you get to the *bottom* of this.
Now I'm going to have to ask you to remove your cloak and--
CAP, WAIT.
I'M GETTING A PRIORITY ONE TRANSMISSION FROM L.C. AND S.W.
THEY'RE SAYING THEY JUST SPOTTED CLOAK... INSIDE DAGGER'S *HOSPITAL ROOM.*
What?
My *impostor.*
Come on! We gotta go kick the fake you's *butt!*

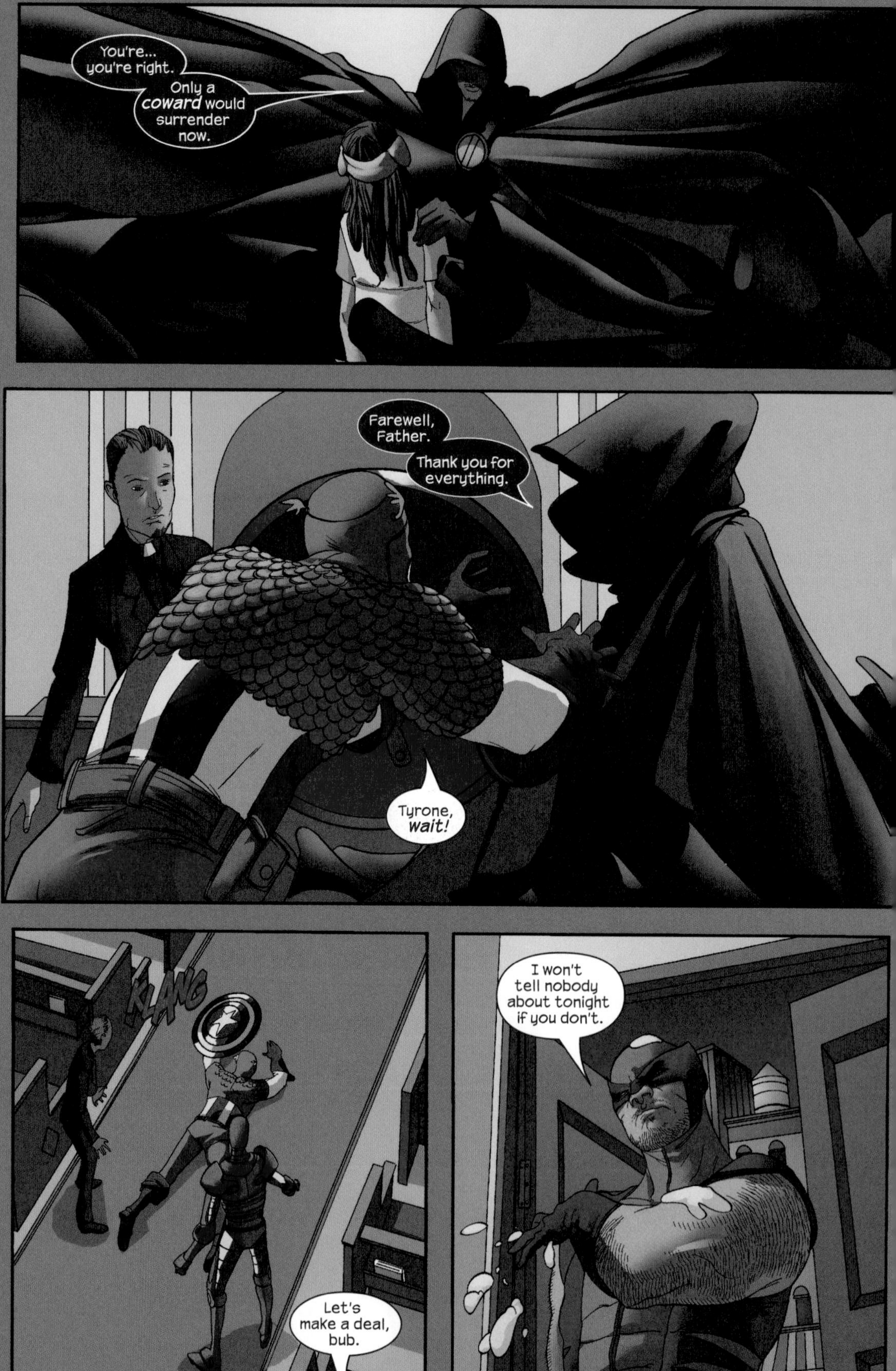
You're... you're right.
Only a coward would surrender now.
Farewell, Father.
Thank you for everything.
Tyrone, wait!
KLANG
Let's make a deal, bub.
I won't tell nobody about tonight if you don't.

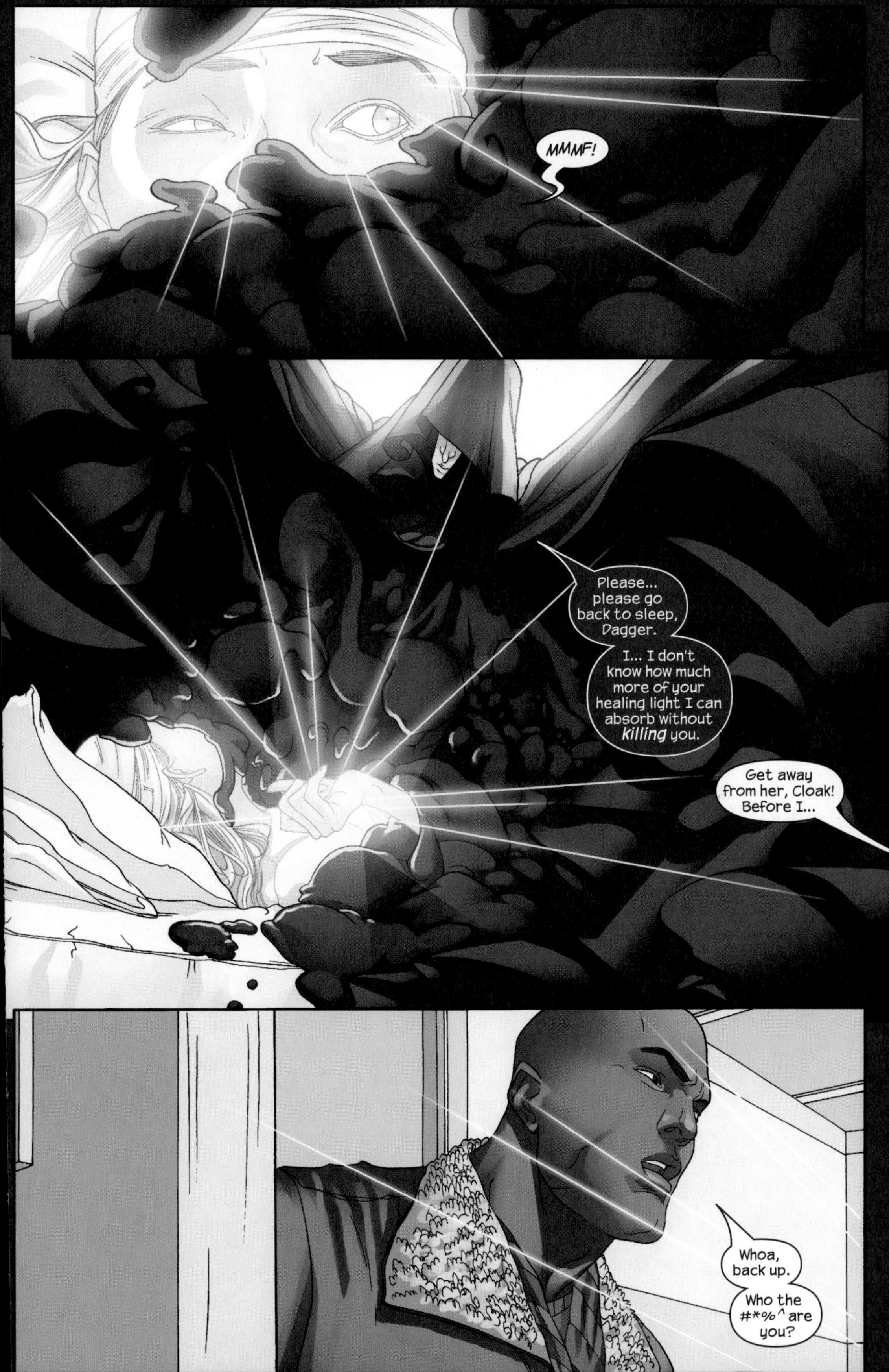
MMMF!
Please... please go back to sleep, Dagger.
I... I don't know how much more of your healing light I can absorb without *killing* you.
Get away from her, Cloak! Before I...
Whoa, back up.
Who the #*%^ are you?

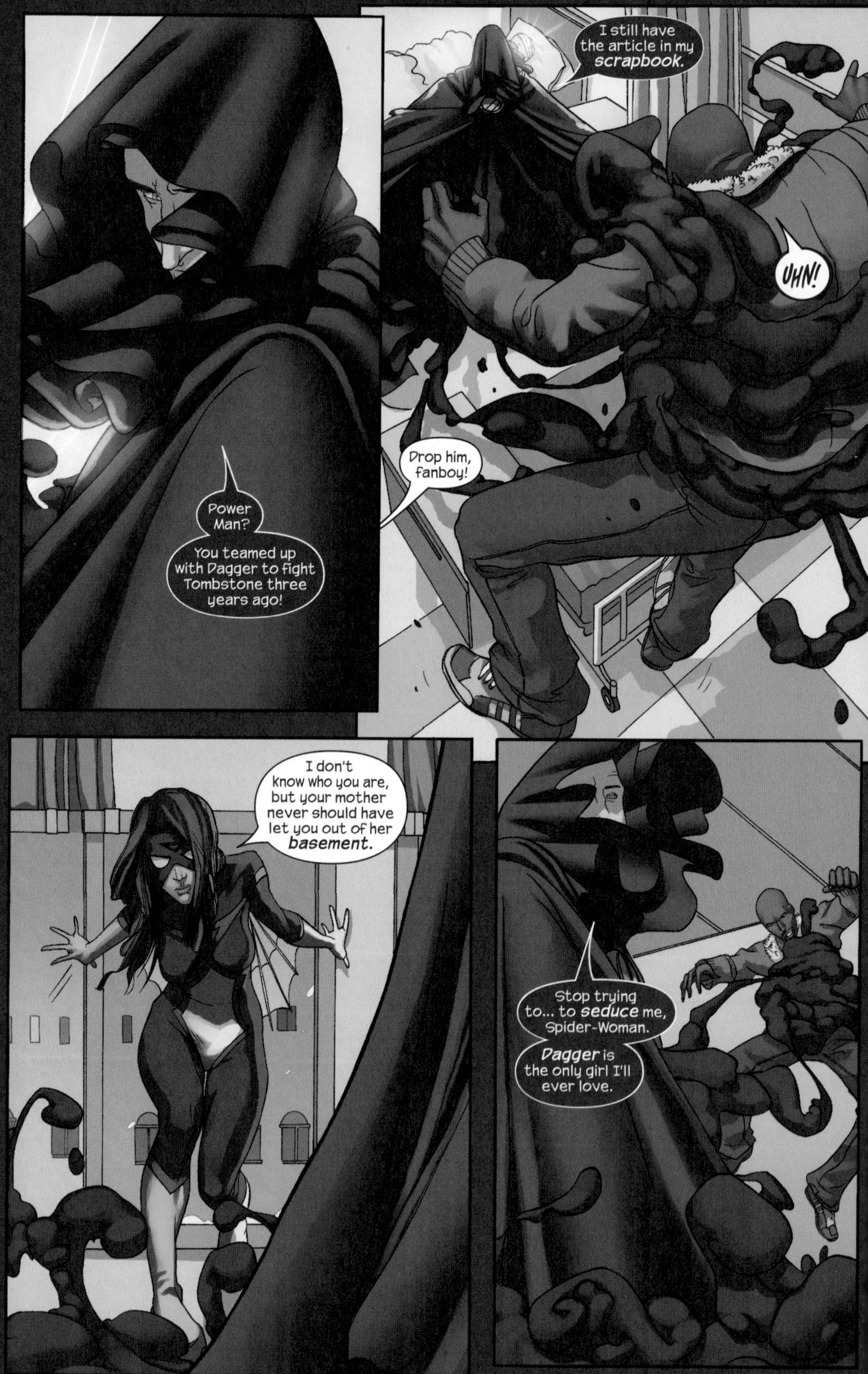
Power Man?
You teamed up with Dagger to fight Tombstone three years ago!
I still have the article in my *scrapbook.*
UHN!
Drop him, fanboy!
I don't know who you are, but your mother never should have let you out of her *basement.*
Stop trying to... to *seduce* me, Spider-Woman.
Dagger is the only girl I'll ever love.

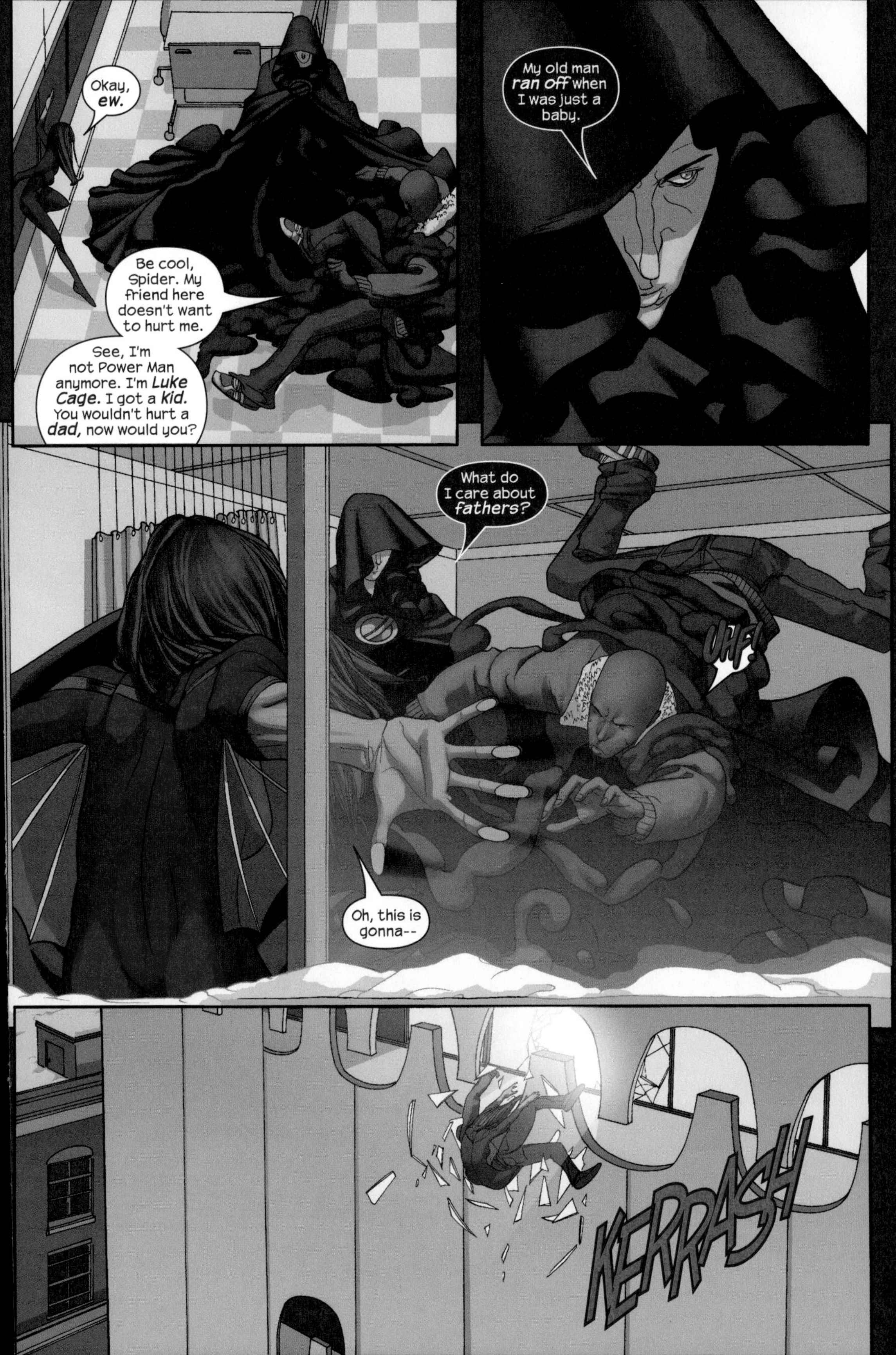
Okay, *ew.*
Be cool, Spider. My friend here doesn't want to hurt me.
See, I'm not Power Man anymore. I'm *Luke Cage.* I got a *kid.* You wouldn't hurt a *dad,* now would you?
My old man *ran off* when I was just a baby.
What do I care about *fathers?*
UHF!
Oh, this is gonna--
KERRASH

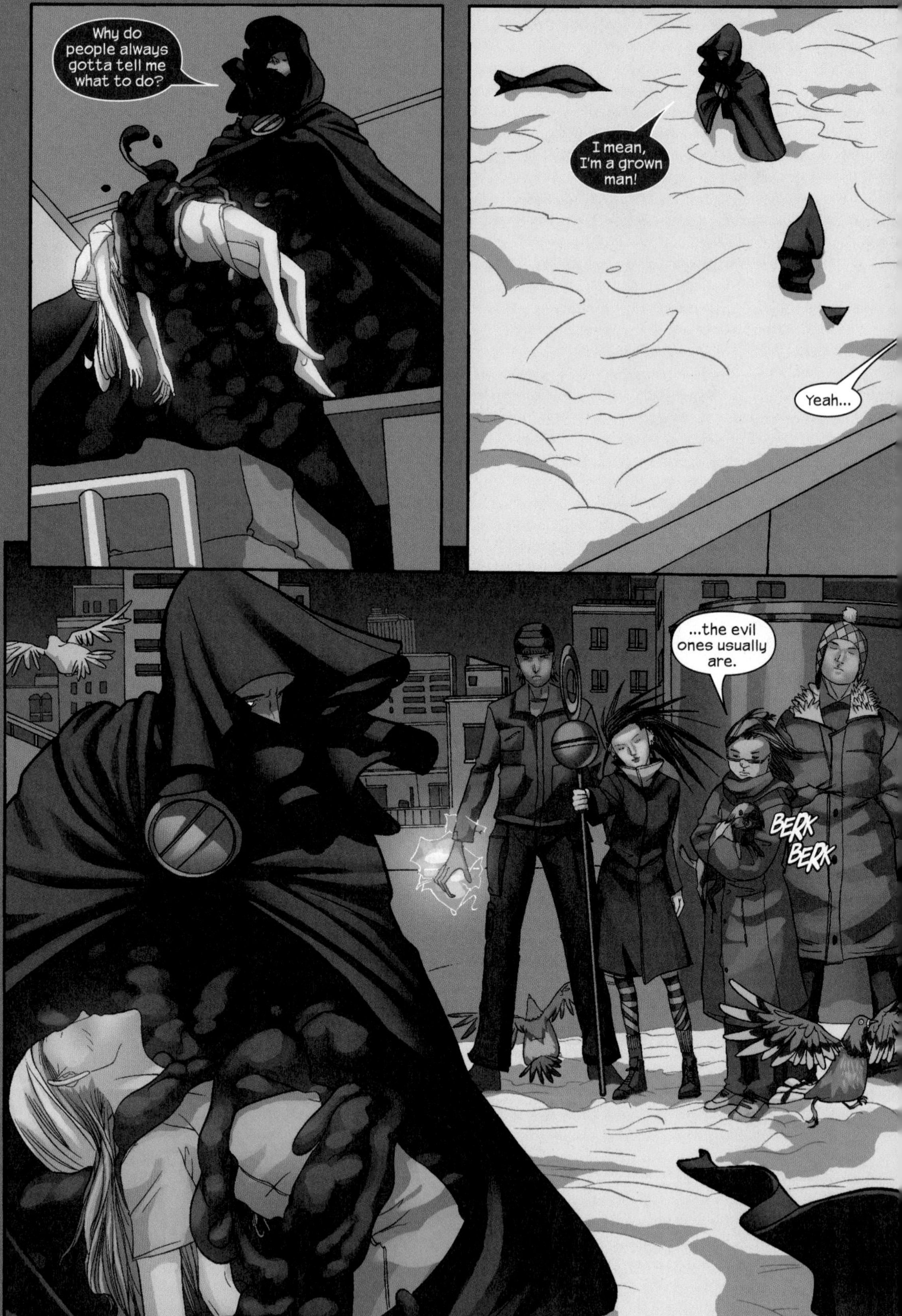
Why do people always gotta tell me what to do?
I mean, I'm a grown man!
Yeah...
...the evil ones usually are.
BERK BERK

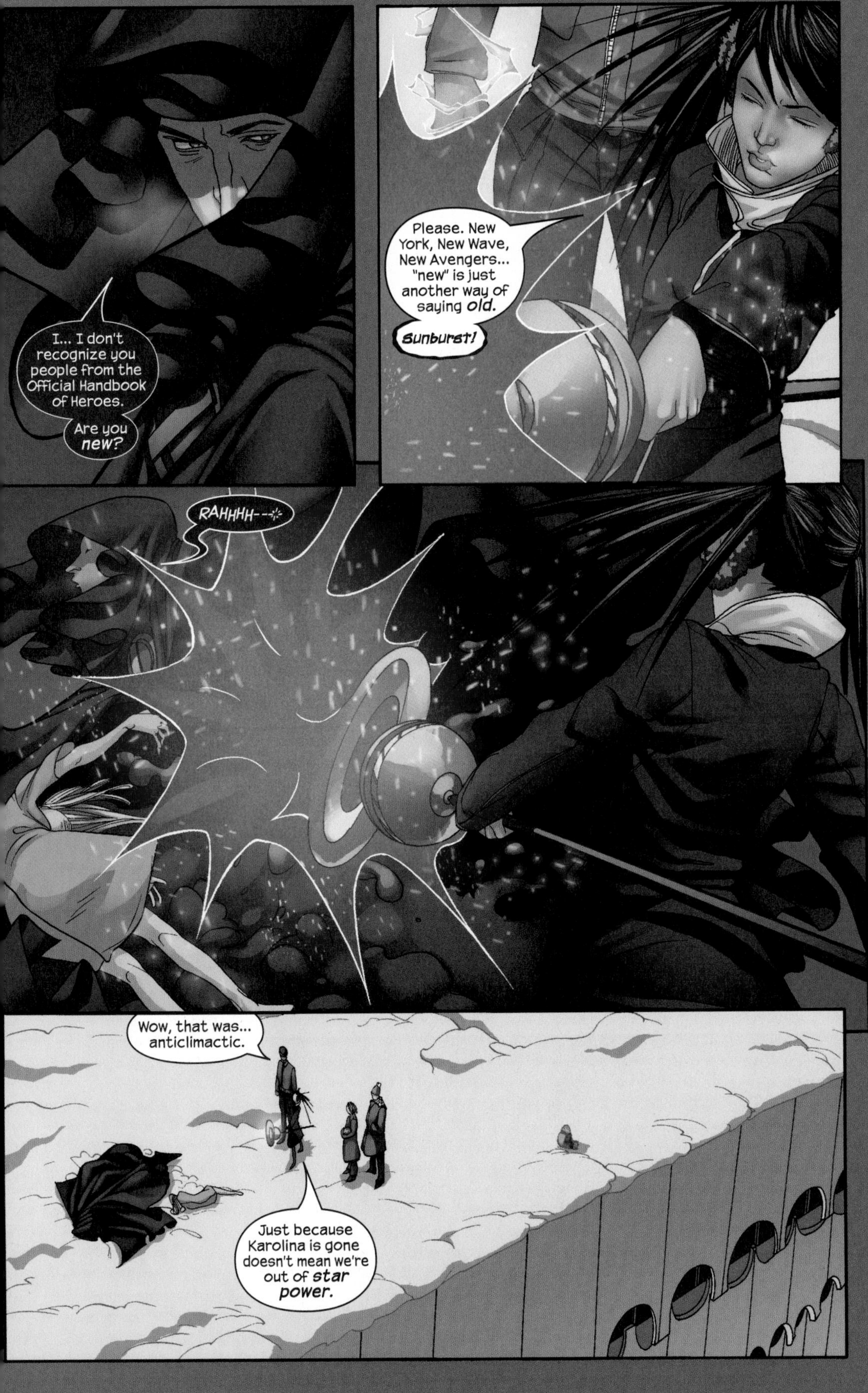
I... I don't recognize you people from the Official Handbook of Heroes.
Are you new?
Please. New York, New Wave, New Avengers... "new" is just another way of saying old.
Sunburst!
RAHHHH--
Wow, that was... anticlimactic.
Just because Karolina is gone doesn't mean we're out of star power.

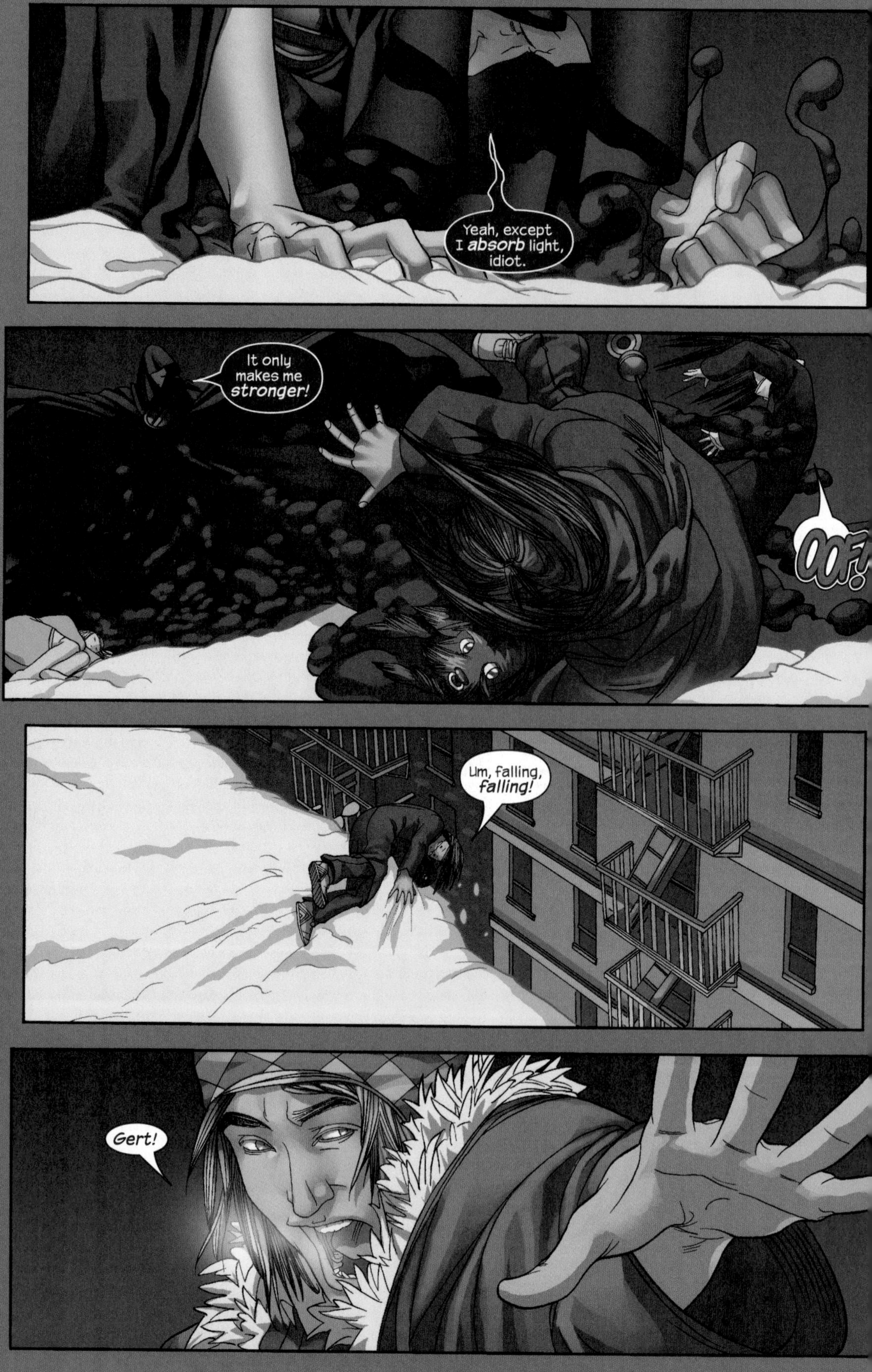
Yeah, except I *absorb* light, idiot.
It only makes me *stronger!*
OOF!
Um, falling, *falling!*
Gert!

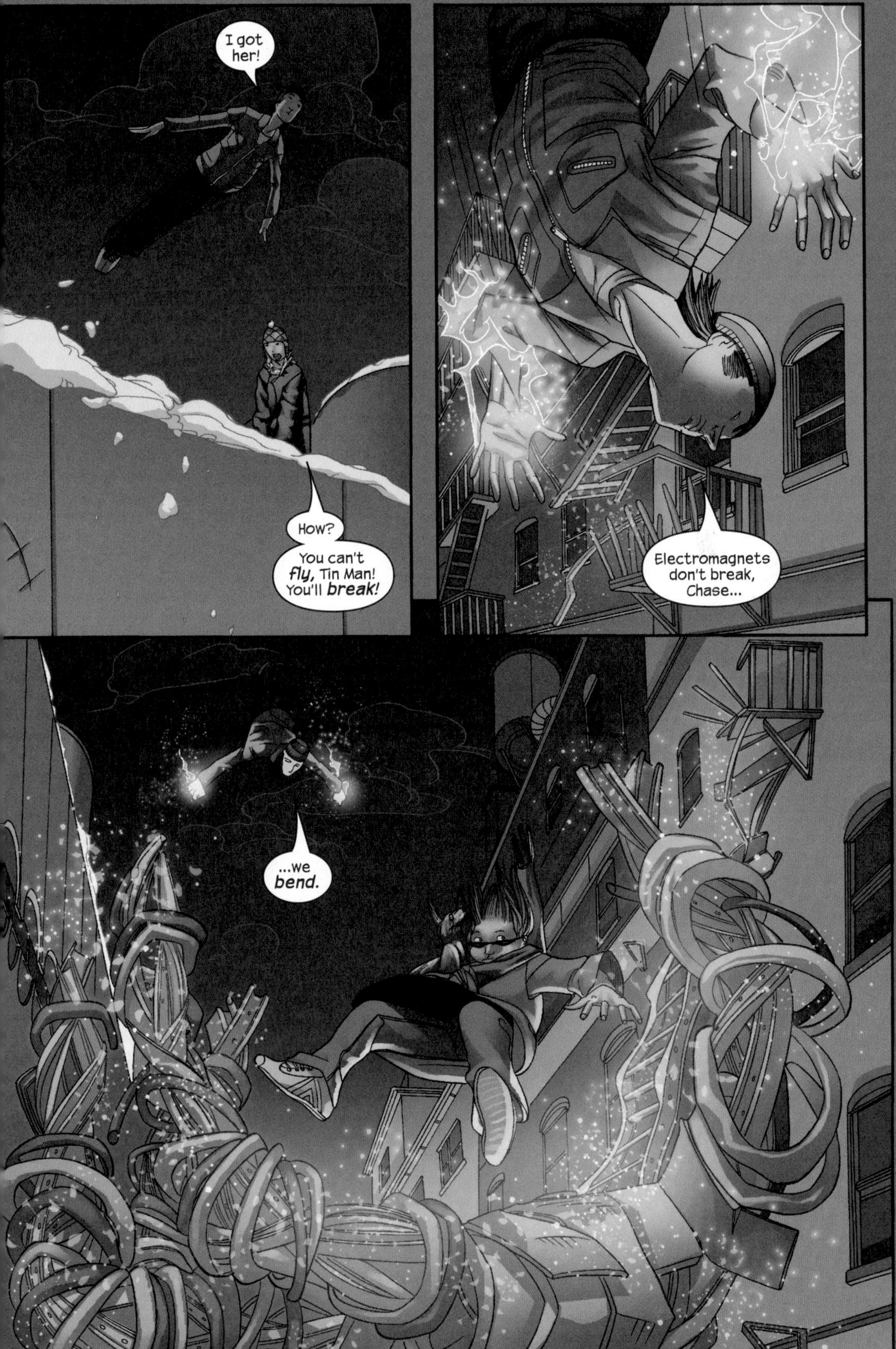
I got her!
How?
You can't *fly,* Tin Man! You'll *break!*
Electromagnets don't break, Chase...
...we *bend.*

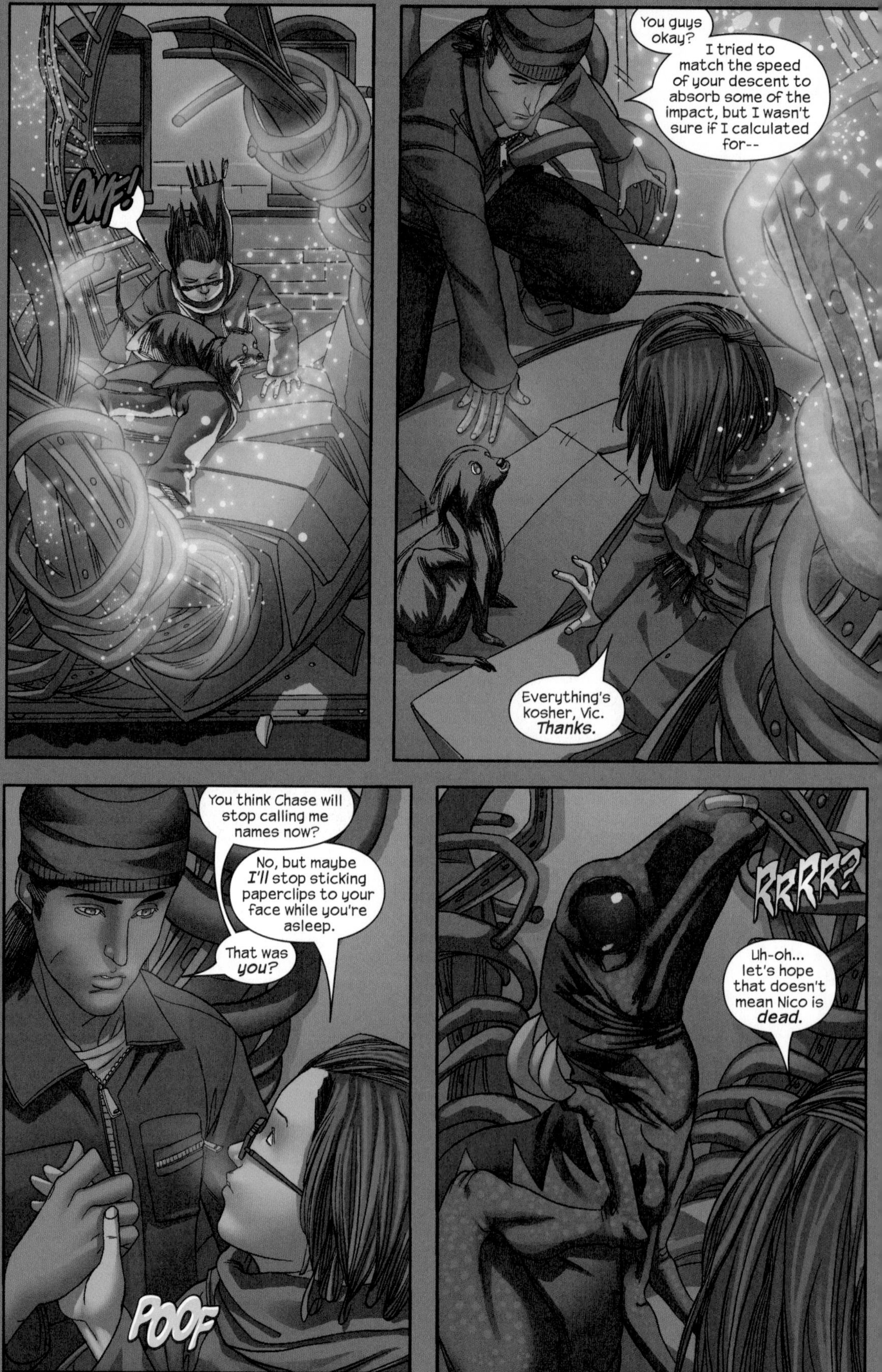
OWF!
You guys okay?
I tried to match the speed of your descent to absorb some of the impact, but I wasn't sure if I calculated for--
Everything's kosher, Vic. *Thanks.*
You think Chase will stop calling me names now?
No, but maybe *I'll* stop sticking paperclips to your face while you're asleep.
That was *you?*
POOF
RRRR?
Uh-oh... let's hope that doesn't mean Nico is *dead.*

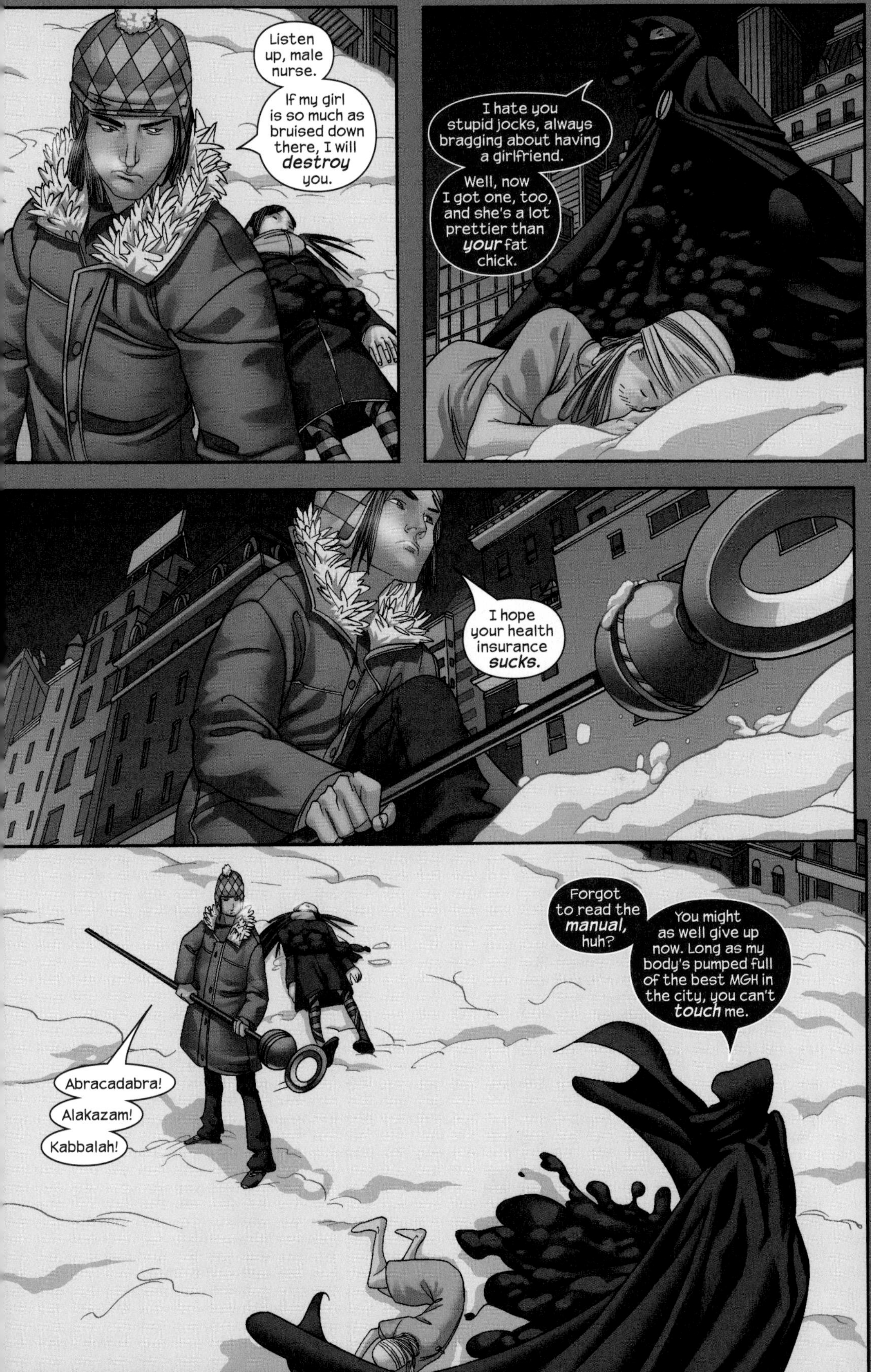
Listen up, male nurse.
If my girl is so much as bruised down there, I will destroy you.
I hate you stupid jocks, always bragging about having a girlfriend.
Well, now I got one, too, and she's a lot prettier than your fat chick.
I hope your health insurance sucks.
Abracadabra!
Alakazam!
Kabbalah!
Forgot to read the manual, huh?
You might as well give up now. Long as my body's pumped full of the best MGH in the city, you can't touch me.

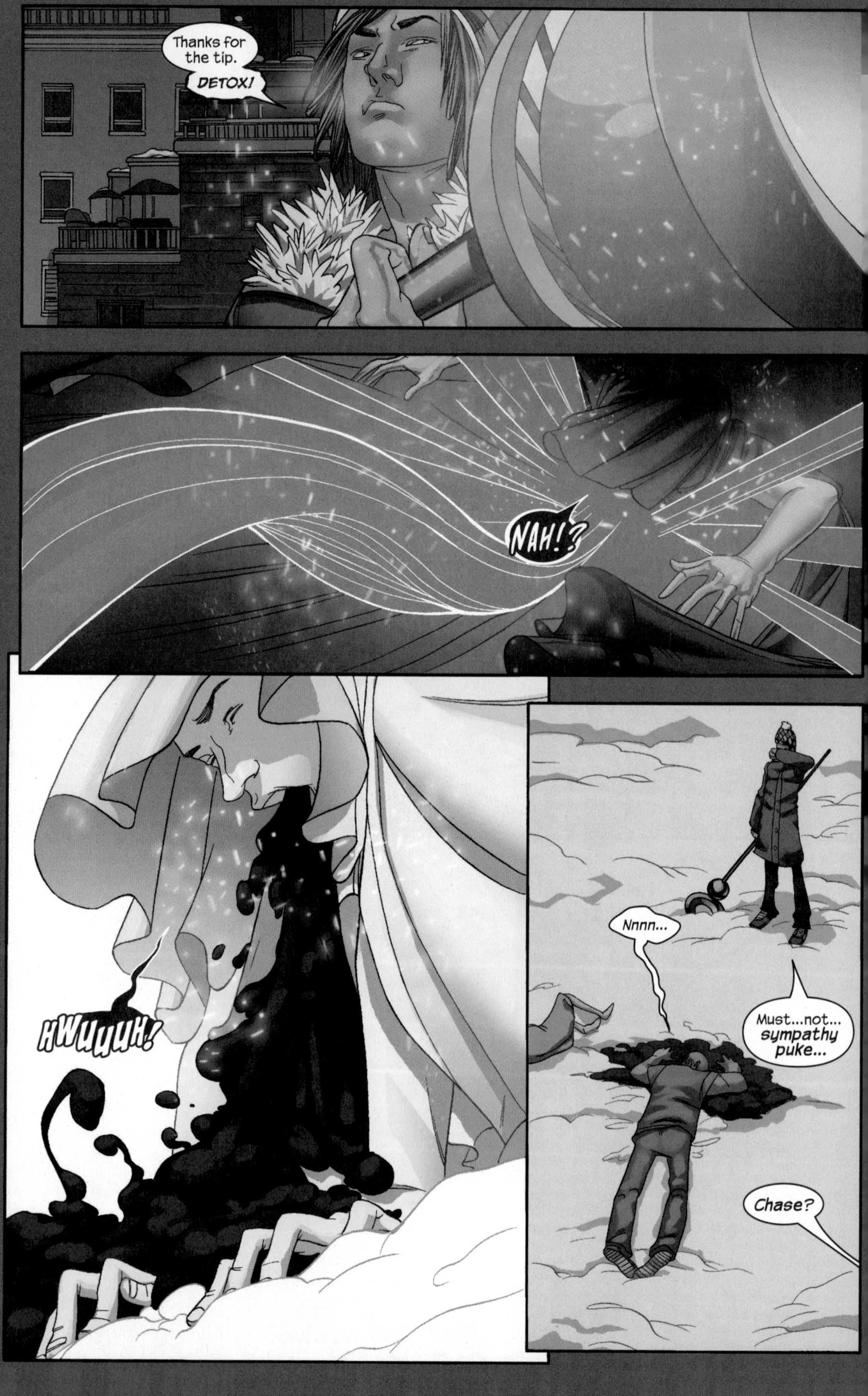
Thanks for the tip. DETOX!
NAH!?
HWUUUH!
Nnnn...
Must...not... sympathy puke...
Chase?

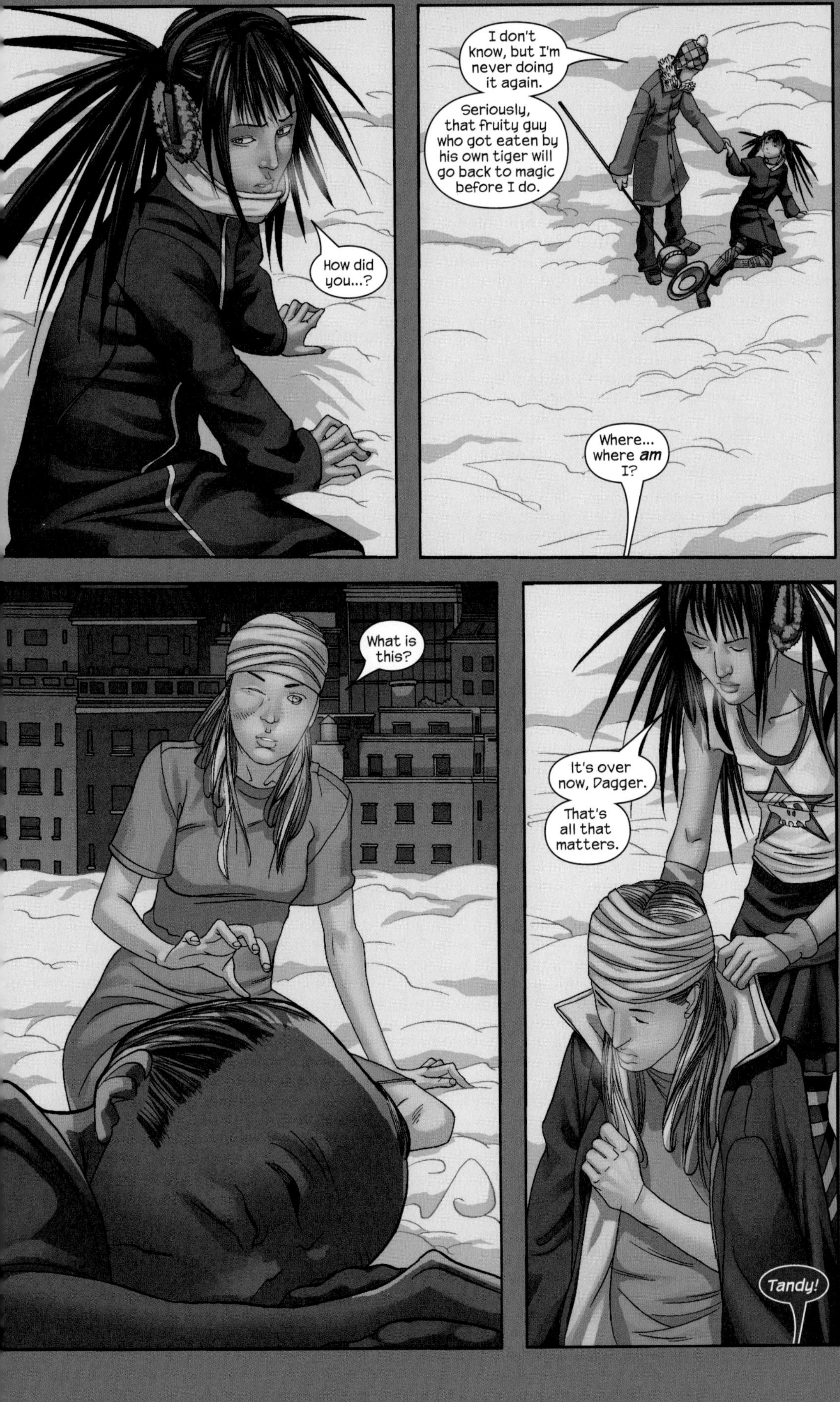
How did you...?
I don't know, but I'm never doing it again.
Seriously, that fruity guy who got eaten by his own tiger will go back to magic before I do.
Where... where *am* I?
What is this?
It's over now, Dagger.
That's all that matters.
Tandy!

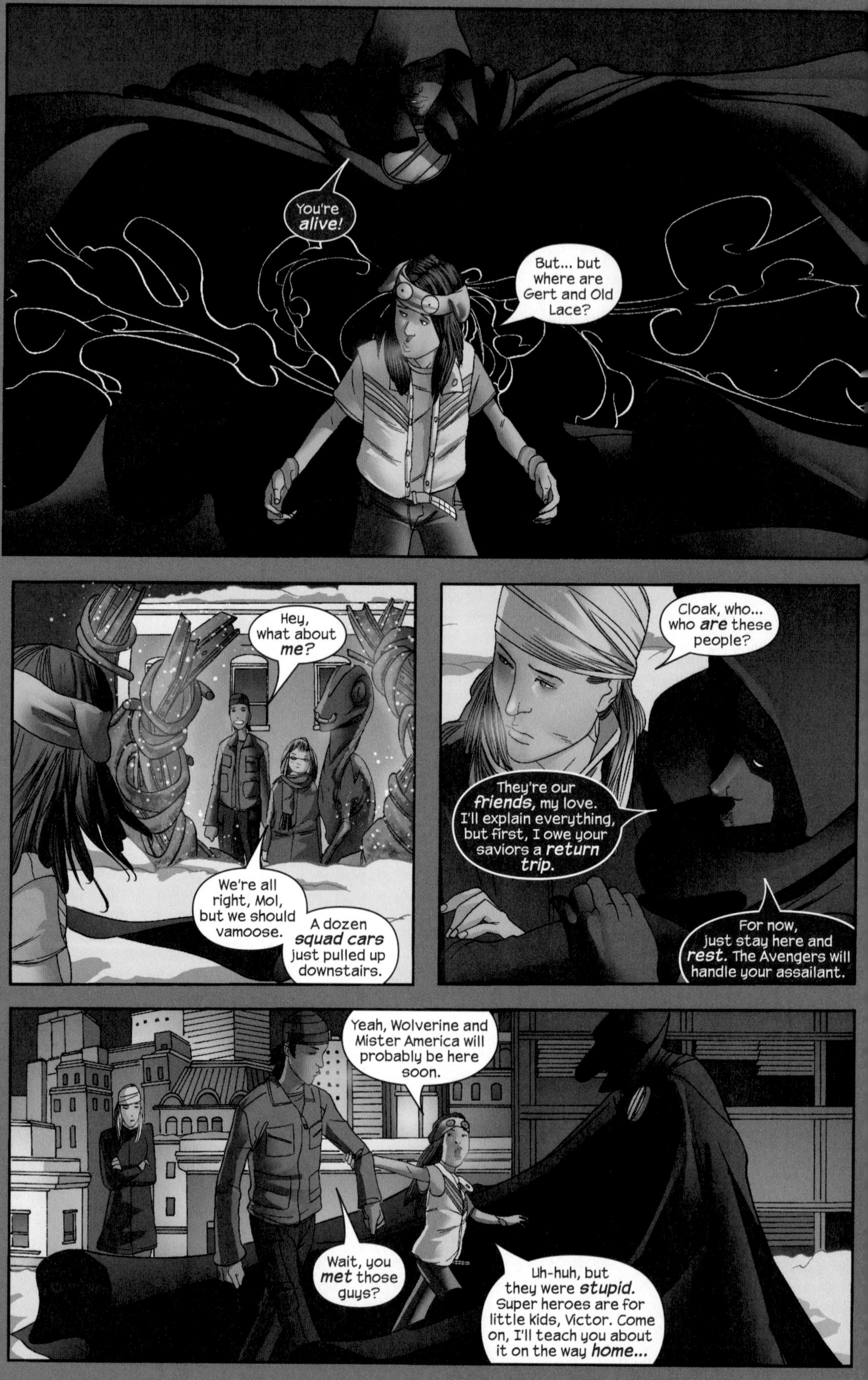
You're alive!
But... but where are Gert and Old Lace?
Hey, what about me?
We're all right, Mol, but we should vamoose.
A dozen squad cars just pulled up downstairs.
Cloak, who... who are these people?
They're our friends, my love. I'll explain everything, but first, I owe your saviors a return trip.
For now, just stay here and rest. The Avengers will handle your assailant.
Yeah, Wolverine and Mister America will probably be here soon.
Wait, you met those guys?
Uh-huh, but they were stupid. Super heroes are for little kids, Victor. Come on, I'll teach you about it on the way home...

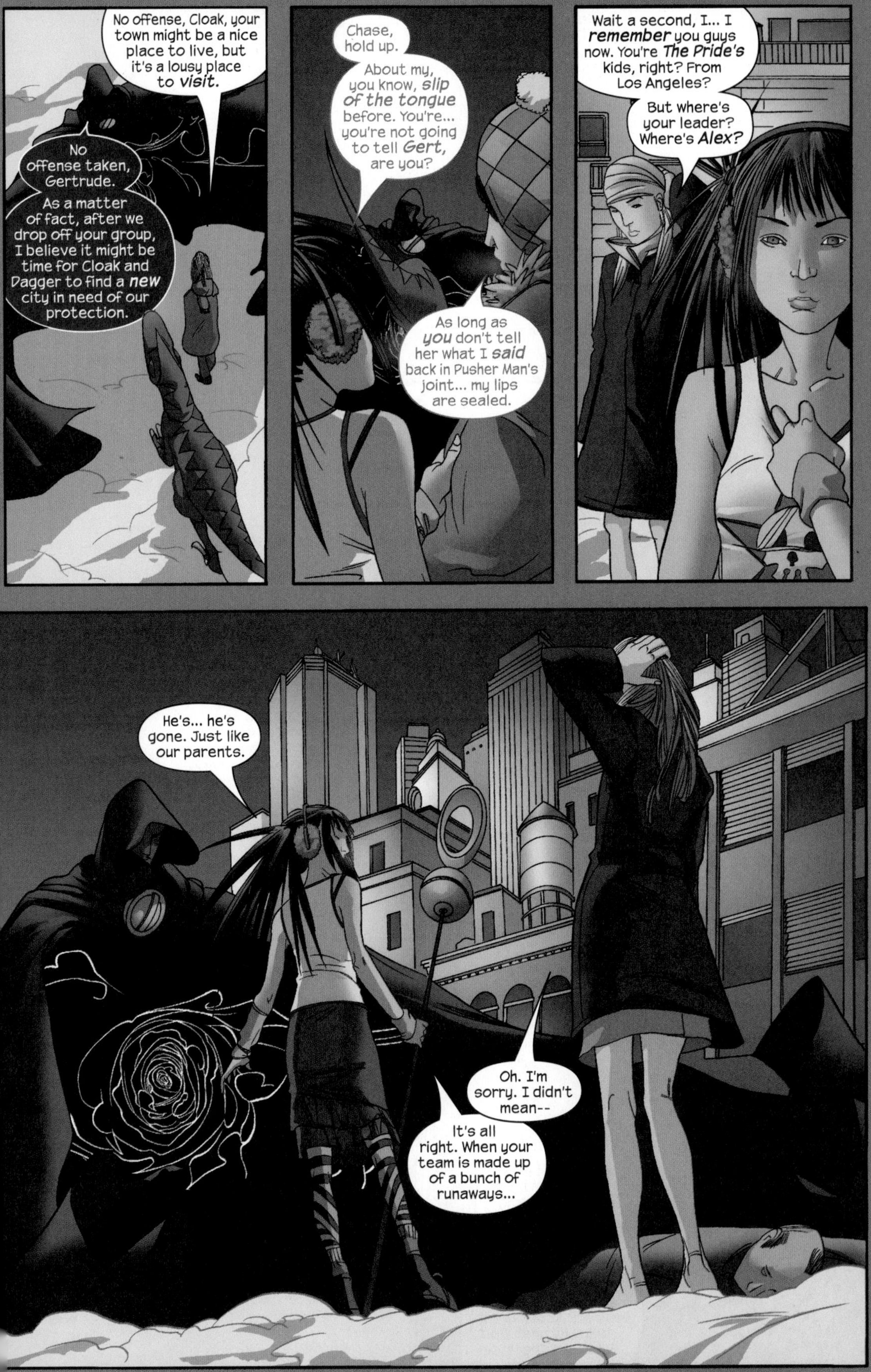
No offense, Cloak, your town might be a nice place to live, but it's a lousy place to *visit*.
No offense taken, Gertrude.
As a matter of fact, after we drop off your group, I believe it might be time for Cloak and Dagger to find a *new* city in need of our protection.
Chase, hold up.
About my, you know, *slip of the tongue* before. You're... you're not going to tell *Gert*, are you?
As long as *you* don't tell her what I *said* back in Pusher Man's joint... my lips are sealed.
Wait a second, I... I *remember* you guys now. You're *The Pride's* kids, right? From Los Angeles?
But where's your leader? Where's *Alex*?
He's... he's gone. Just like our parents.
Oh. I'm sorry. I didn't mean--
It's all right. When your team is made up of a bunch of runaways...

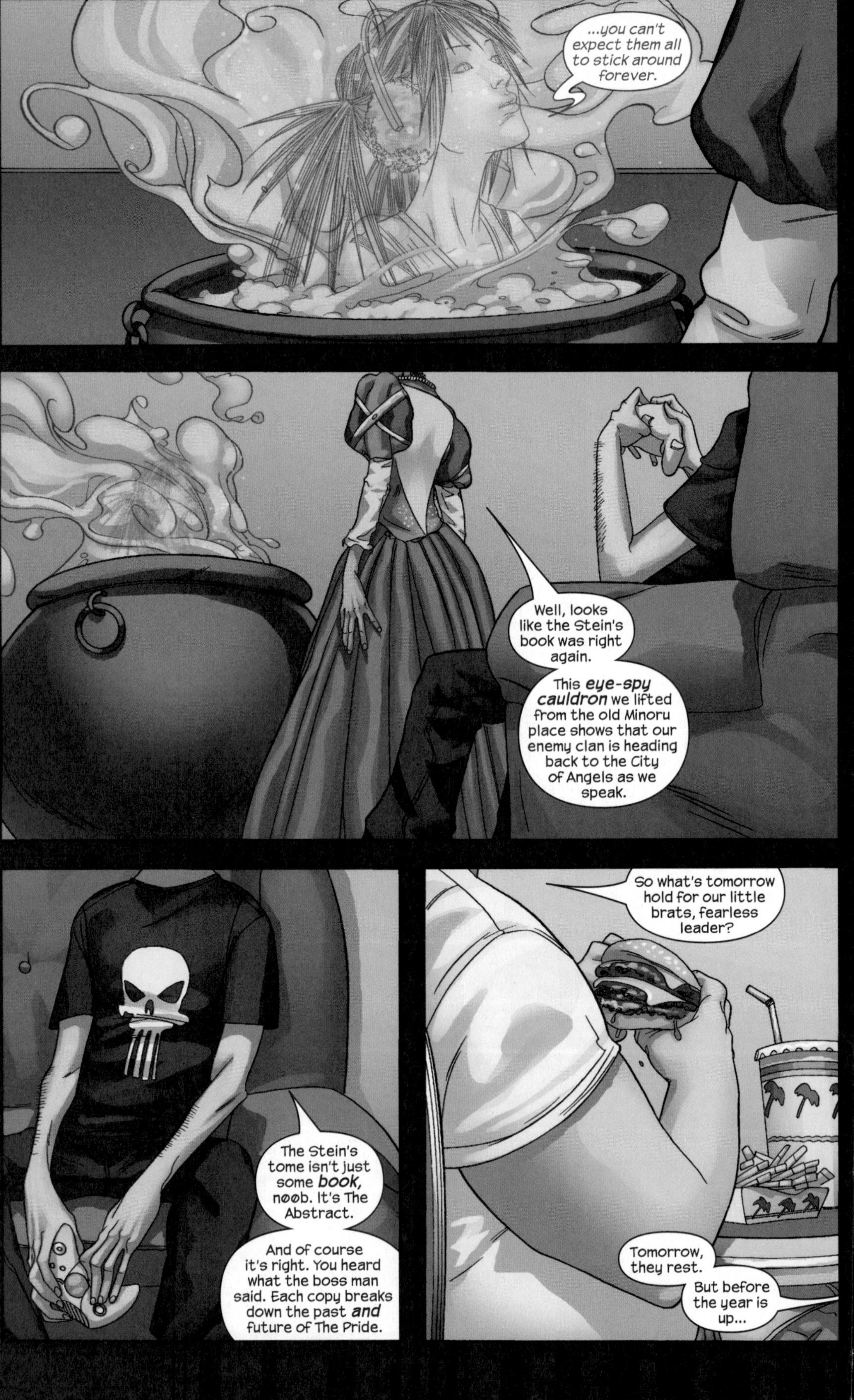
...you can't expect them all to stick around forever.
Well, looks like the Stein's book was right again.
This *eye-spy cauldron* we lifted from the old Minoru place shows that our enemy clan is heading back to the City of Angels as we speak.
The Stein's tome isn't just some *book,* nøøb. It's The Abstract.
And of course it's right. You heard what the boss man said. Each copy breaks down the past *and* future of The Pride.
So what's tomorrow hold for our little brats, fearless leader?
Tomorrow, they rest.
But before the year is up...

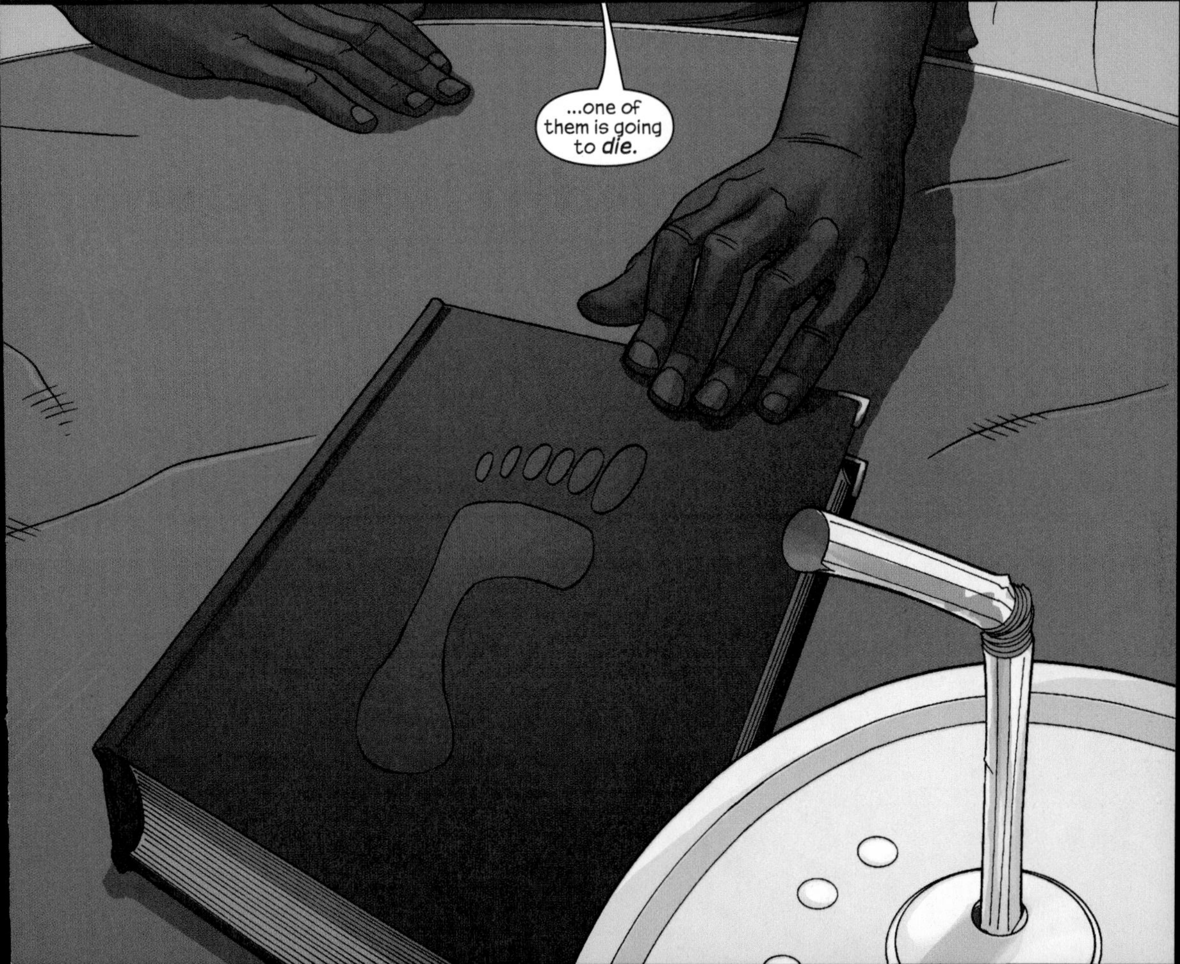
...one of them is going to *die.*

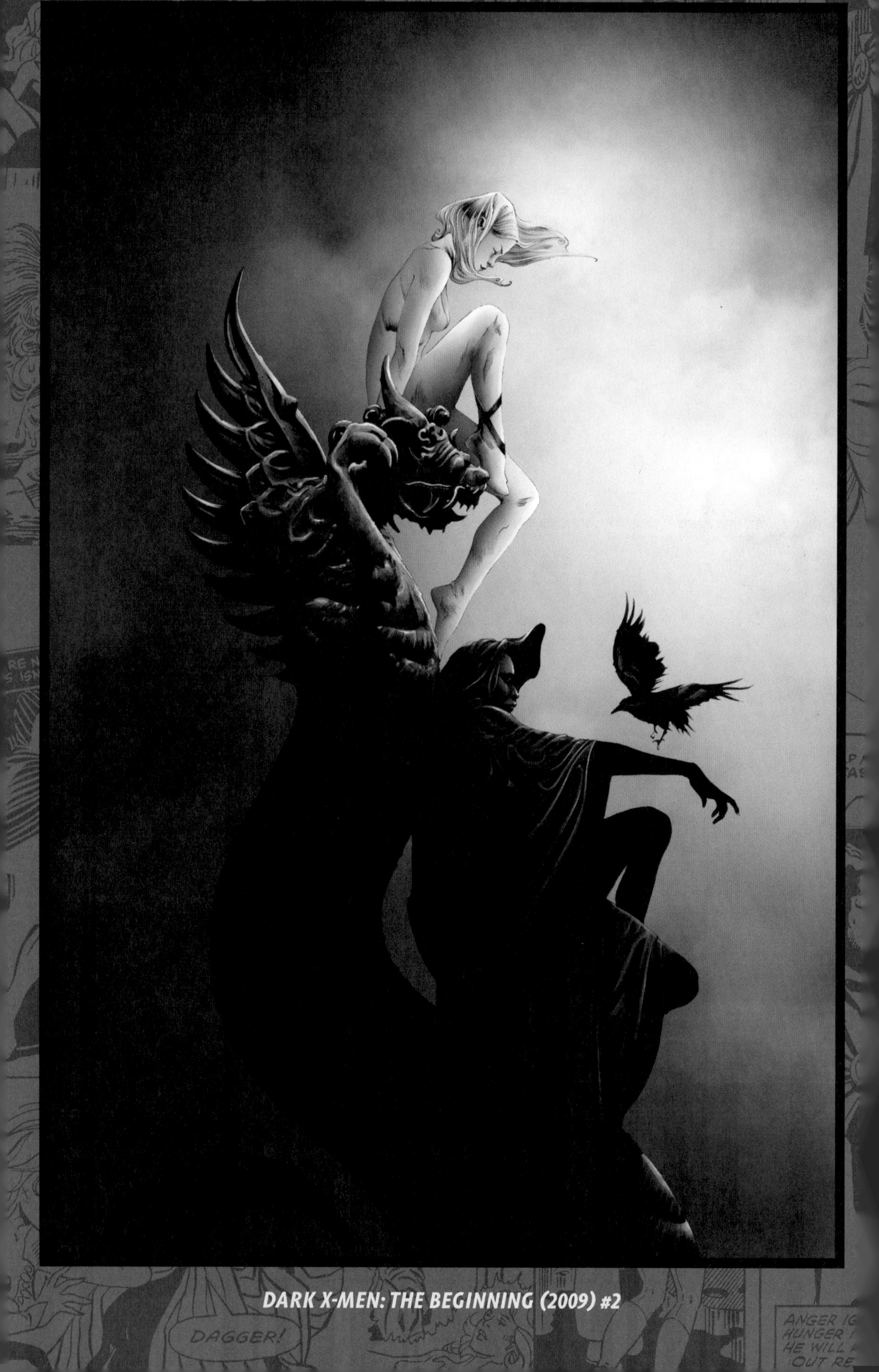

DARK X-MEN: THE BEGINNING (2009) #2

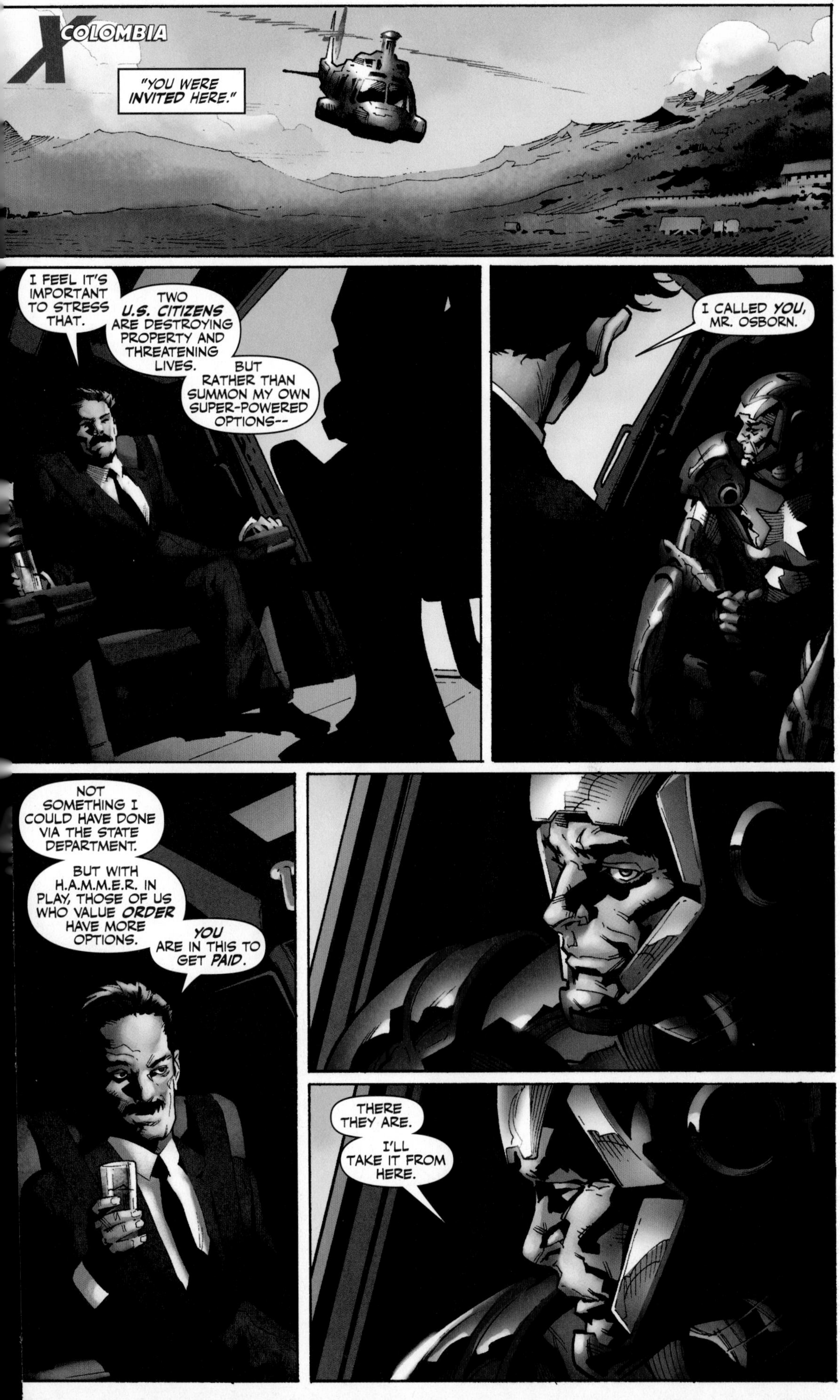
COLOMBIA
"YOU WERE INVITED HERE."
I FEEL IT'S IMPORTANT TO STRESS THAT.
TWO U.S. CITIZENS ARE DESTROYING PROPERTY AND THREATENING LIVES.
BUT RATHER THAN SUMMON MY OWN SUPER-POWERED OPTIONS--
I CALLED YOU, MR. OSBORN.
NOT SOMETHING I COULD HAVE DONE VIA THE STATE DEPARTMENT.
BUT WITH H.A.M.M.E.R. IN PLAY, THOSE OF US WHO VALUE ORDER HAVE MORE OPTIONS.
YOU ARE IN THIS TO GET PAID.
THERE THEY ARE.
I'LL TAKE IT FROM HERE.

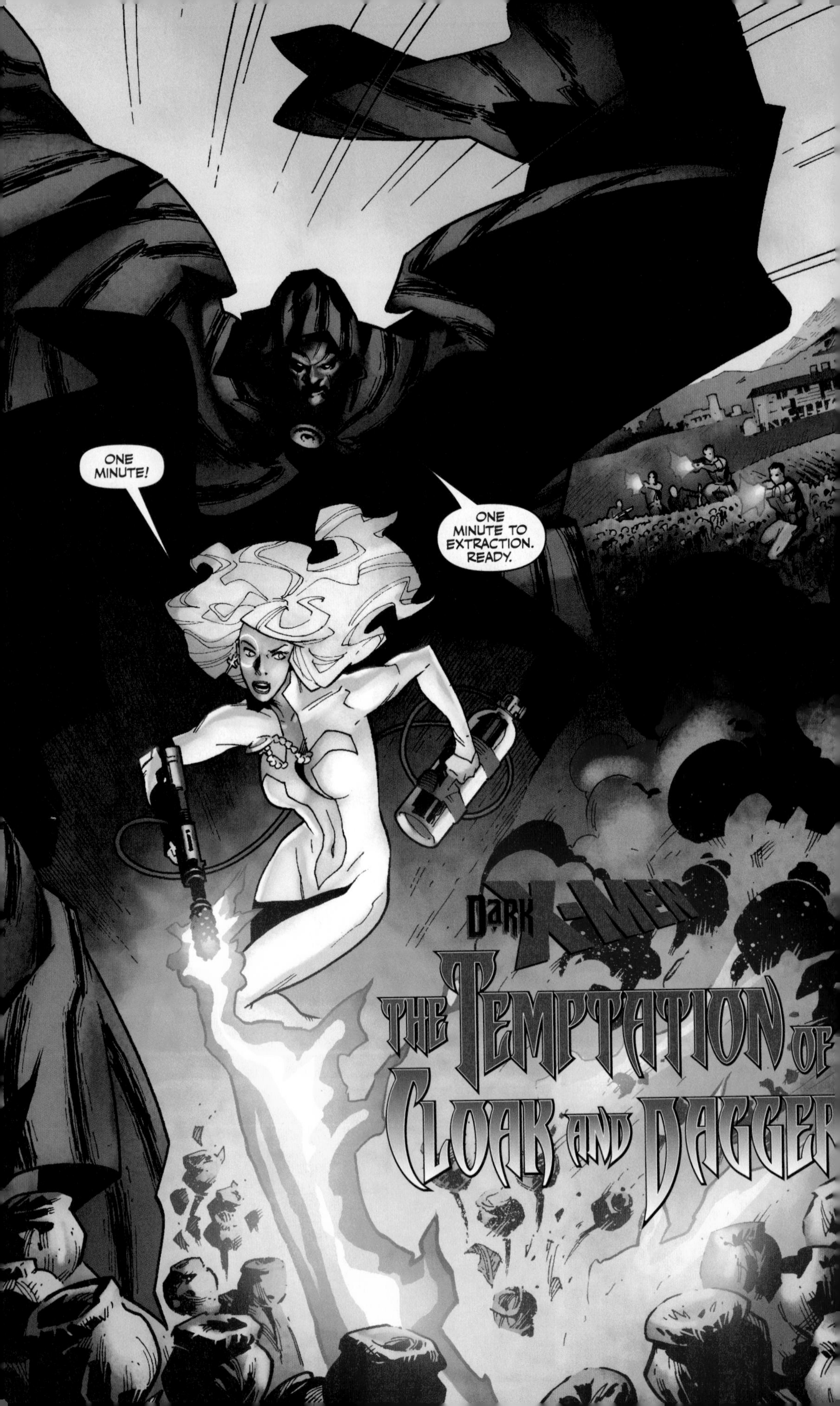
ONE MINUTE!
ONE MINUTE TO EXTRACTION. READY.
DARK X-MEN
THE TEMPTATION OF CLOAK AND DAGGER

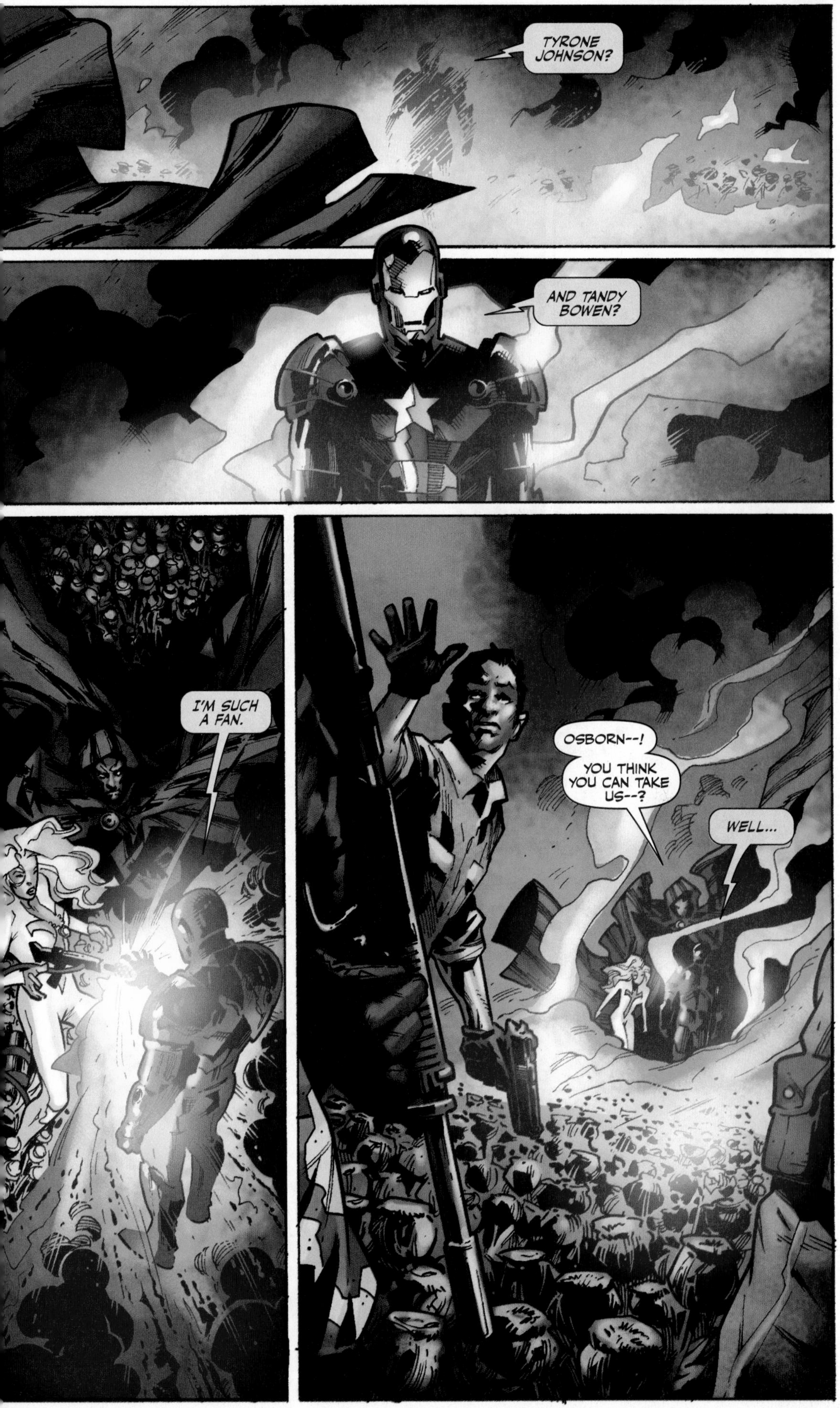
TYRONE JOHNSON?
AND TANDY BOWEN?
I'M SUCH A FAN.
OSBORN--! YOU THINK YOU CAN TAKE US--?
WELL...

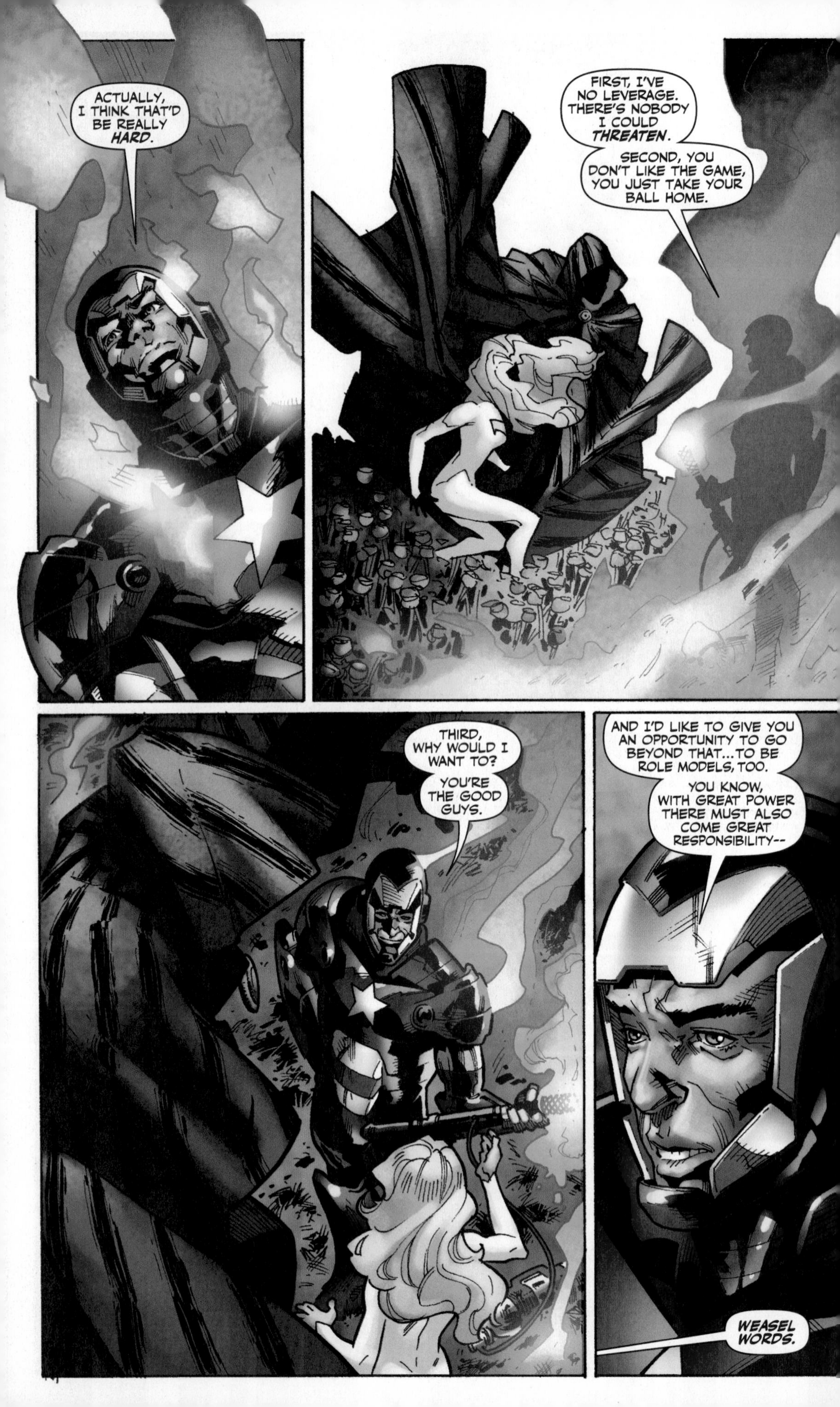
ACTUALLY, I THINK THAT'D BE REALLY *HARD*.
FIRST, I'VE NO LEVERAGE. THERE'S NOBODY I COULD *THREATEN*.
SECOND, YOU DON'T LIKE THE GAME, YOU JUST TAKE YOUR BALL HOME.
THIRD, WHY WOULD I WANT TO?
YOU'RE THE GOOD GUYS.
AND I'D LIKE TO GIVE YOU AN OPPORTUNITY TO GO BEYOND THAT...TO BE ROLE MODELS, TOO.
YOU KNOW, WITH GREAT POWER THERE MUST ALSO COME GREAT RESPONSIBILITY--
WEASEL WORDS.

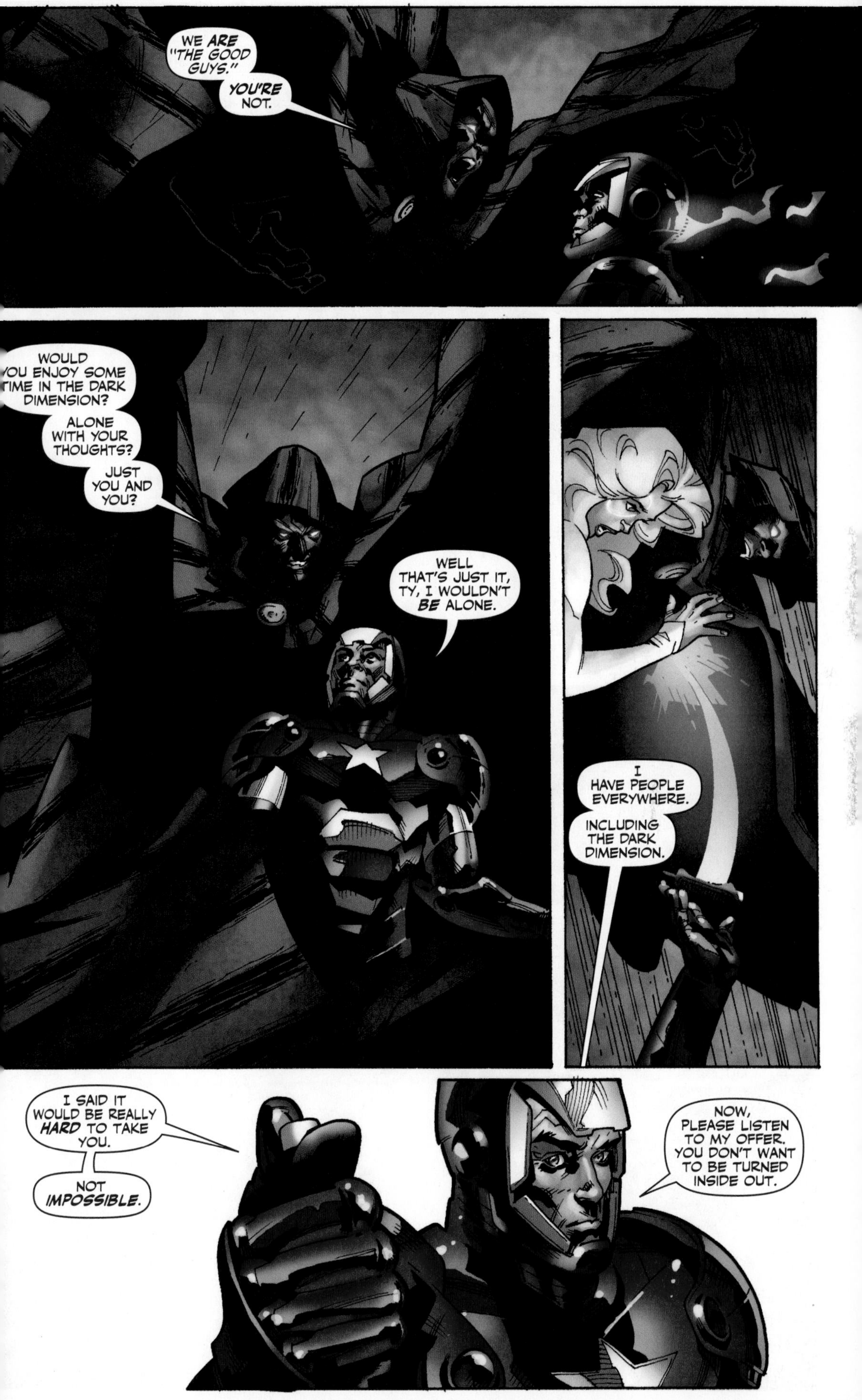
WE ARE "THE GOOD GUYS."
YOU'RE NOT.
WOULD YOU ENJOY SOME TIME IN THE DARK DIMENSION?
ALONE WITH YOUR THOUGHTS?
JUST YOU AND YOU?
WELL THAT'S JUST IT, TY, I WOULDN'T BE ALONE.
I HAVE PEOPLE EVERYWHERE.
INCLUDING THE DARK DIMENSION.
I SAID IT WOULD BE REALLY HARD TO TAKE YOU.
NOT IMPOSSIBLE.
NOW, PLEASE LISTEN TO MY OFFER. YOU DON'T WANT TO BE TURNED INSIDE OUT.

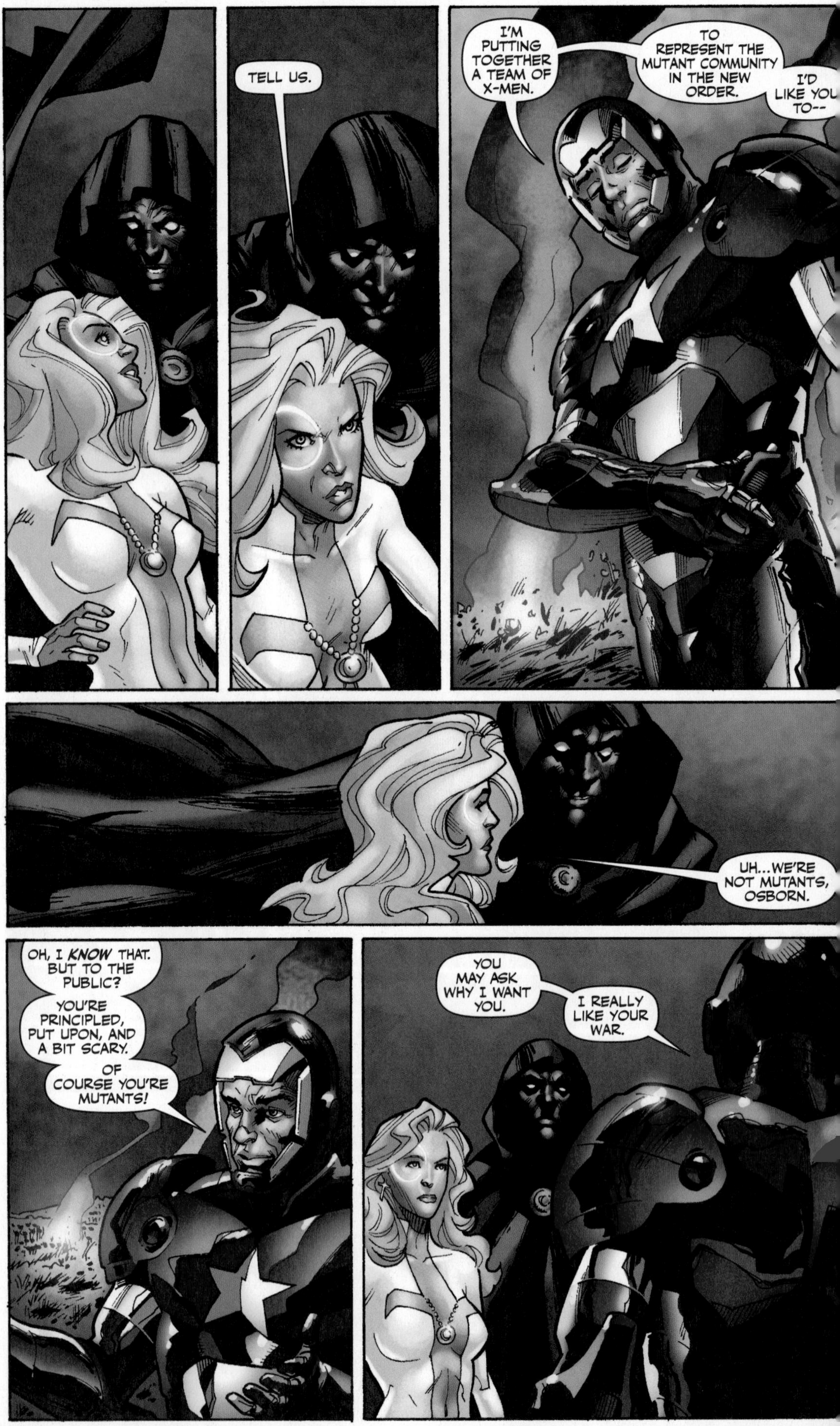
TELL US.
I'M PUTTING TOGETHER A TEAM OF X-MEN.
TO REPRESENT THE MUTANT COMMUNITY IN THE NEW ORDER.
I'D LIKE YOU TO--
UH...WE'RE NOT MUTANTS, OSBORN.
OH, I *KNOW* THAT. BUT TO THE PUBLIC?
YOU'RE PRINCIPLED, PUT UPON, AND A BIT SCARY.
OF COURSE YOU'RE MUTANTS!
YOU MAY ASK WHY I WANT YOU.
I REALLY LIKE YOUR WAR.

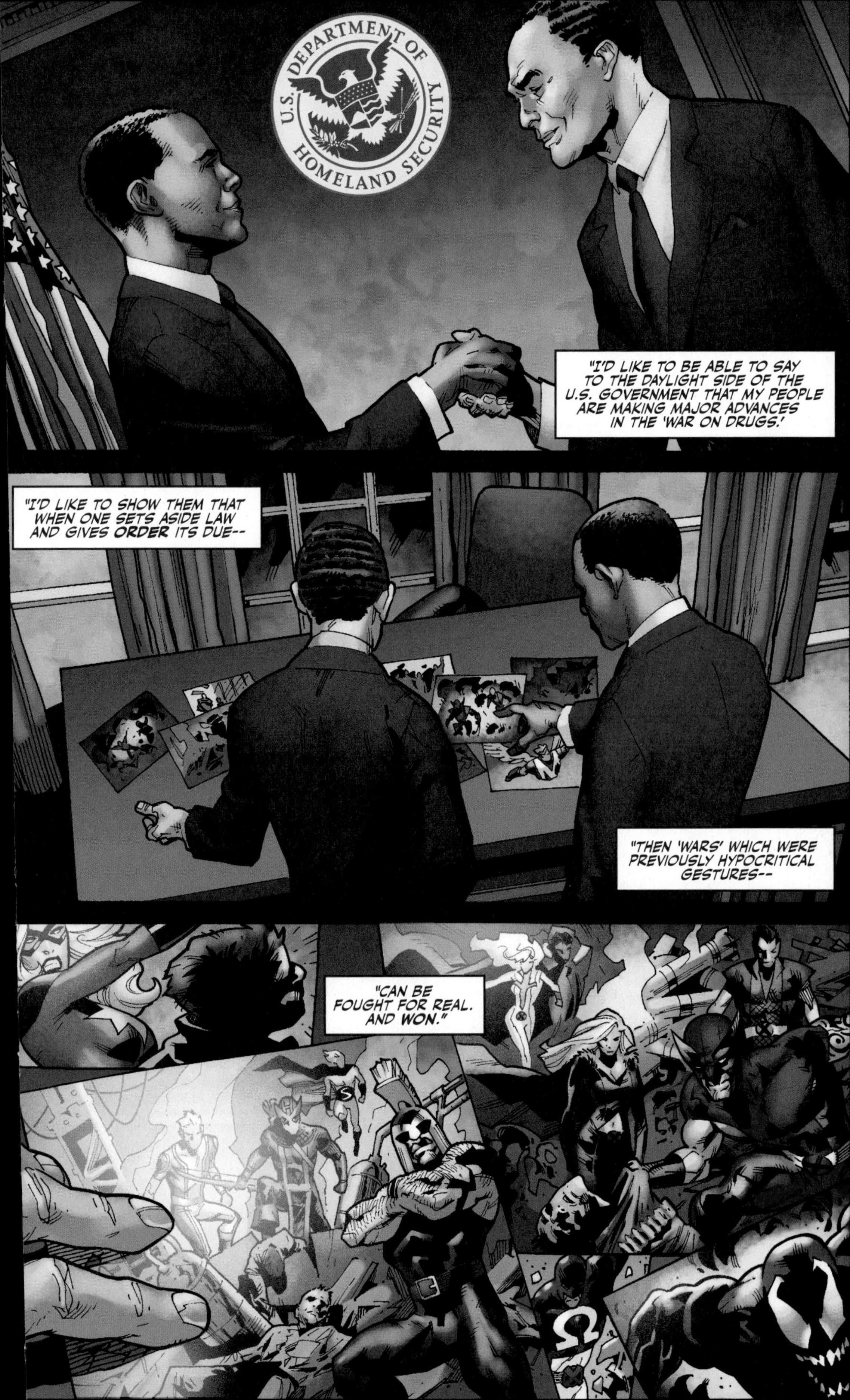
U.S. DEPARTMENT OF HOMELAND SECURITY
"I'D LIKE TO BE ABLE TO SAY TO THE DAYLIGHT SIDE OF THE U.S. GOVERNMENT THAT MY PEOPLE ARE MAKING MAJOR ADVANCES IN THE 'WAR ON DRUGS.'
"I'D LIKE TO SHOW THEM THAT WHEN ONE SETS ASIDE LAW AND GIVES ORDER ITS DUE--
"THEN 'WARS' WHICH WERE PREVIOUSLY HYPOCRITICAL GESTURES--
"CAN BE FOUGHT FOR REAL. AND WON."

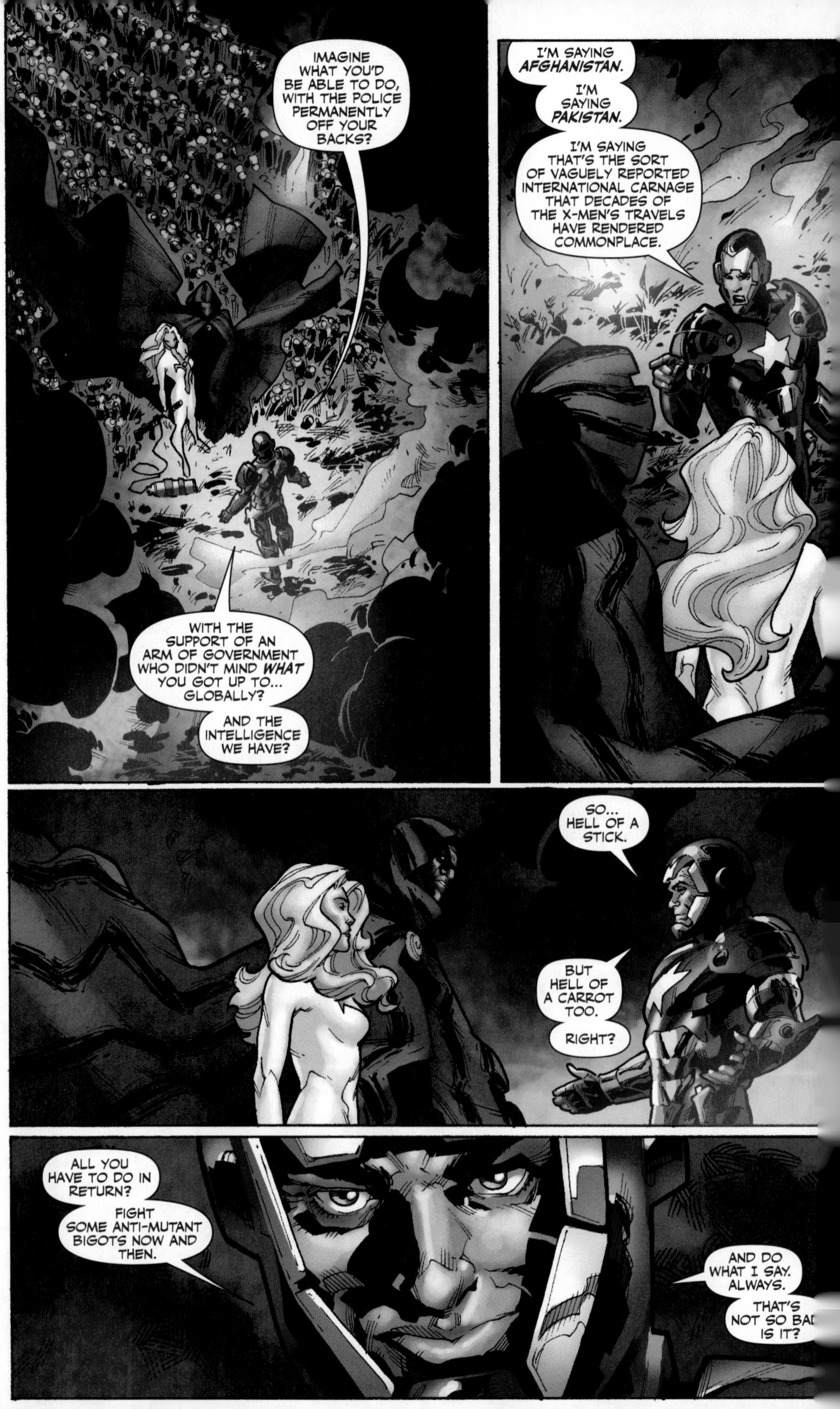
IMAGINE WHAT YOU'D BE ABLE TO DO, WITH THE POLICE PERMANENTLY OFF YOUR BACKS?
WITH THE SUPPORT OF AN ARM OF GOVERNMENT WHO DIDN'T MIND *WHAT* YOU GOT UP TO... GLOBALLY?
AND THE INTELLIGENCE WE HAVE?
I'M SAYING *AFGHANISTAN*.
I'M SAYING *PAKISTAN*.
I'M SAYING THAT'S THE SORT OF VAGUELY REPORTED INTERNATIONAL CARNAGE THAT DECADES OF THE X-MEN'S TRAVELS HAVE RENDERED COMMONPLACE.
SO... HELL OF A STICK.
BUT HELL OF A CARROT TOO.
RIGHT?
ALL YOU HAVE TO DO IN RETURN?
FIGHT SOME ANTI-MUTANT BIGOTS NOW AND THEN.
AND DO WHAT I SAY. ALWAYS.
THAT'S NOT SO BAD IS IT?

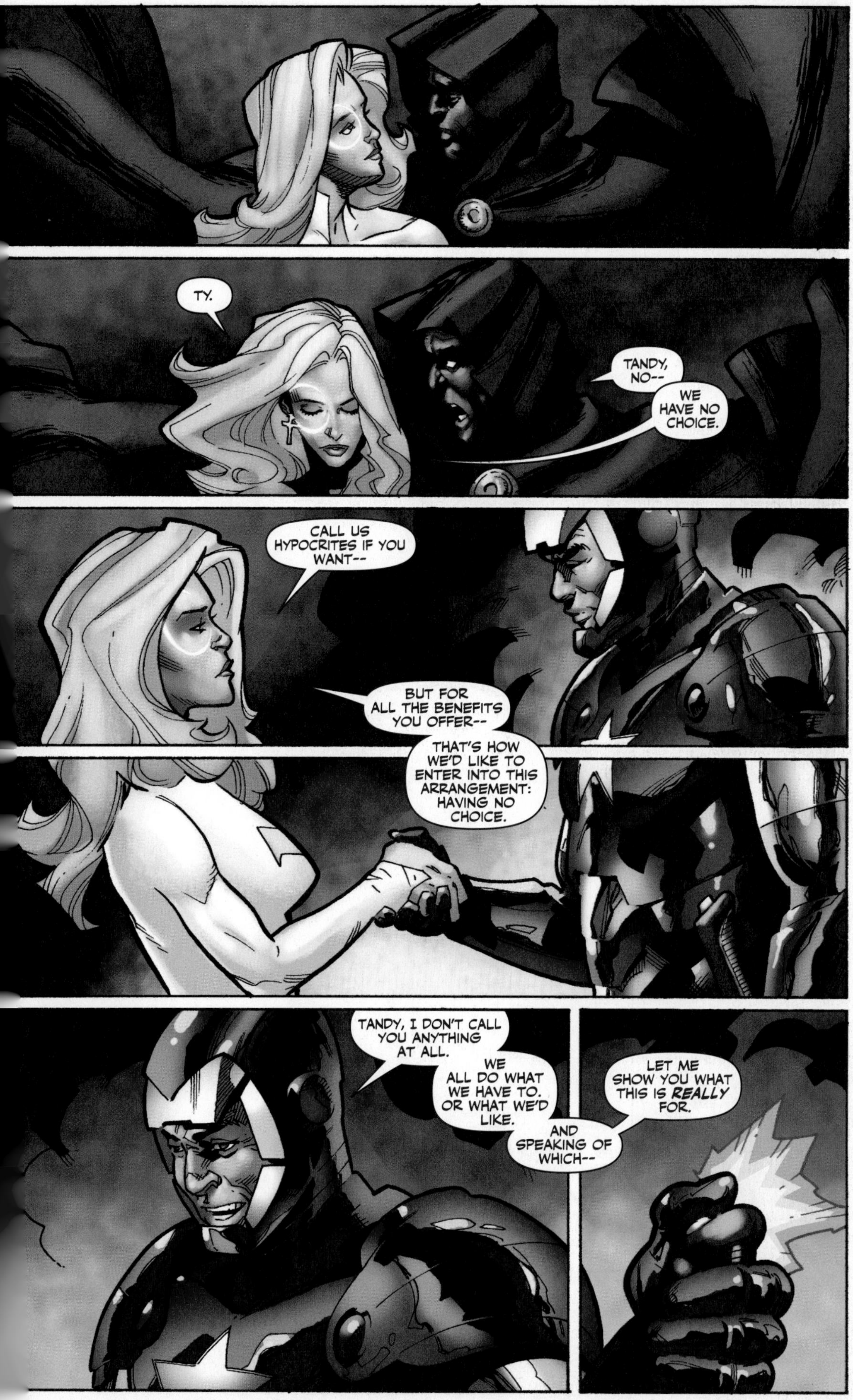
TY.
TANDY, NO--
WE HAVE NO CHOICE.
CALL US HYPOCRITES IF YOU WANT--
BUT FOR ALL THE BENEFITS YOU OFFER--
THAT'S HOW WE'D LIKE TO ENTER INTO THIS ARRANGEMENT: HAVING NO CHOICE.
TANDY, I DON'T CALL YOU ANYTHING AT ALL.
WE ALL DO WHAT WE HAVE TO. OR WHAT WE'D LIKE.
AND SPEAKING OF WHICH--
LET ME SHOW YOU WHAT THIS IS REALLY FOR.

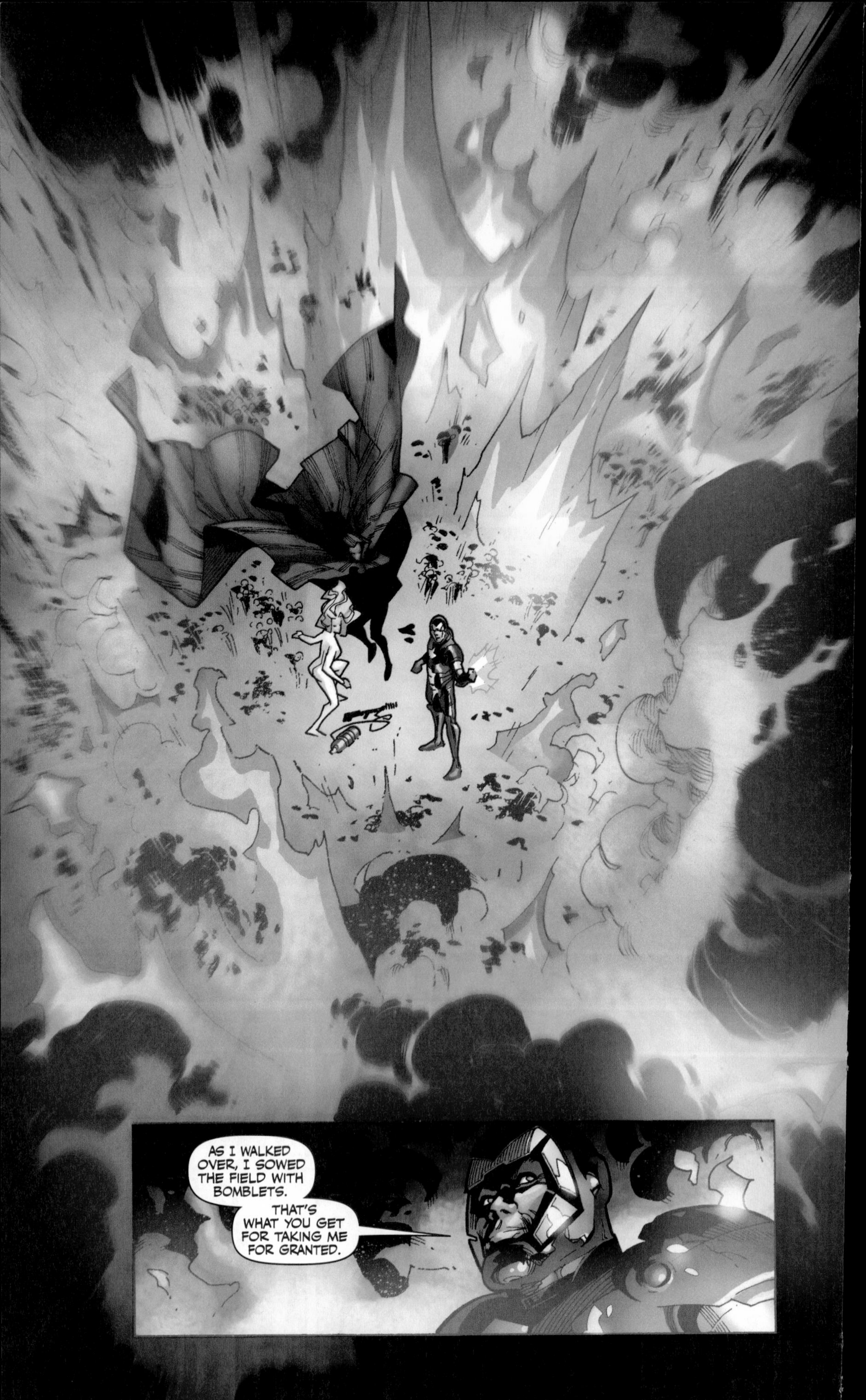
AS I WALKED OVER, I SOWED THE FIELD WITH BOMBLETS.
THAT'S WHAT YOU GET FOR TAKING ME FOR GRANTED.

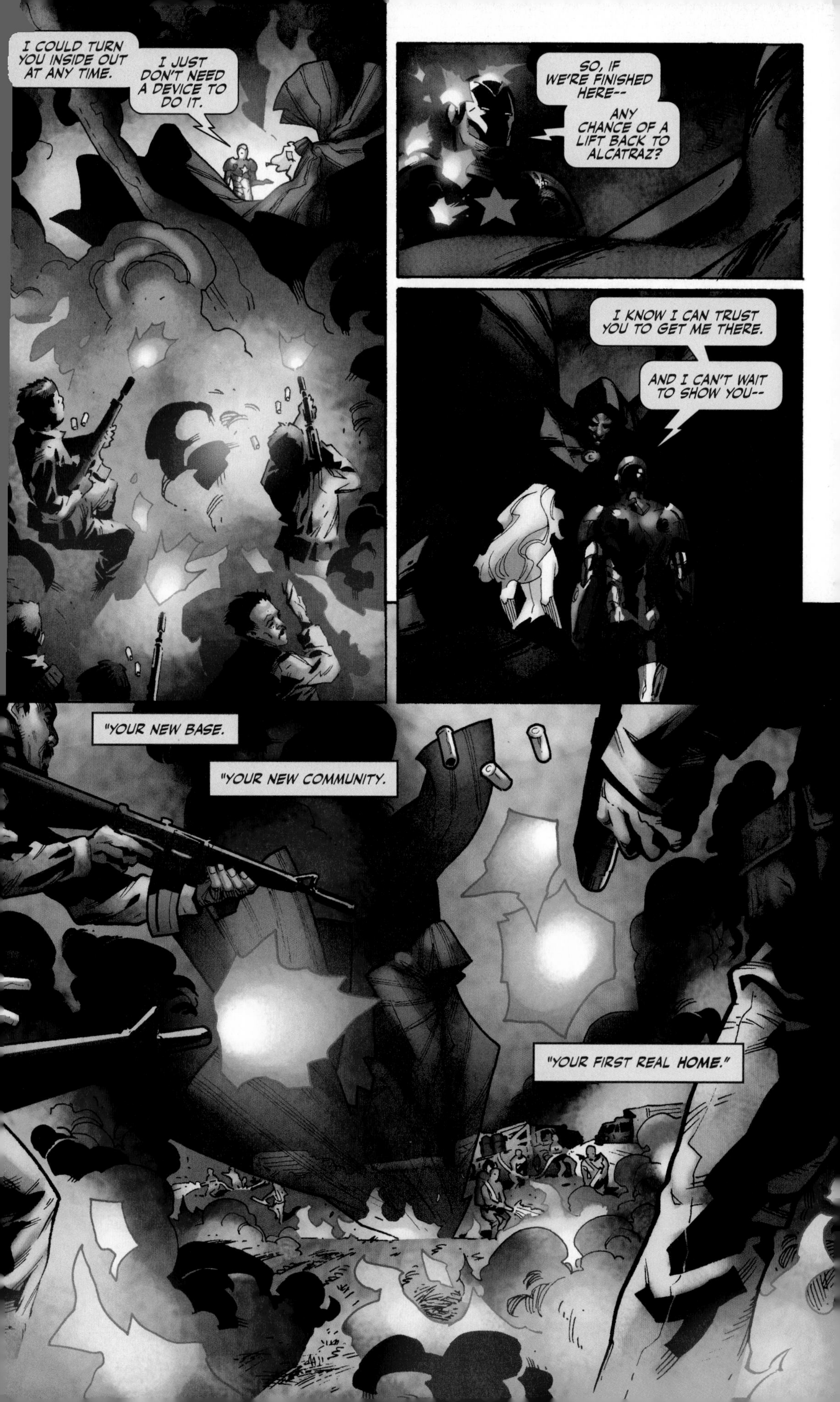
I COULD TURN YOU INSIDE OUT AT ANY TIME.
I JUST DON'T NEED A DEVICE TO DO IT.
SO, IF WE'RE FINISHED HERE--
ANY CHANCE OF A LIFT BACK TO ALCATRAZ?
I KNOW I CAN TRUST YOU TO GET ME THERE.
AND I CAN'T WAIT TO SHOW YOU--
"YOUR NEW BASE.
"YOUR NEW COMMUNITY.
"YOUR FIRST REAL HOME."

IN THE "UTOPIA" CROSSOVER, NORMAN OSBORN, MANIPULATIVE DIRECTOR OF H.A.M.M.E.R., PLOTTED TO PUBLICLY DISCREDIT THE X-MEN AND OFFER HIS OWN TEAM — INCLUDING CLOAK AND DAGGER — AS LAW-AND-ORDER ALTERNATIVES. RIOTS IN SAN FRANCISCO TURNED PUBLIC OPINION AGAINST THE X-MEN, BUT CYCLOPS TRANSFORMED THE REMAINS OF ASTEROID M INTO A FLOATING ISLAND AND PROCLAIMED IT A MUTANT SANCTUARY. AS SCORES OF MUTANTS FLOCKED TO CYCLOPS' ISLAND UTOPIA, CLOAK AND DAGGER BETRAYED OSBORN AND DEFECTED TO THE REAL X-MEN.

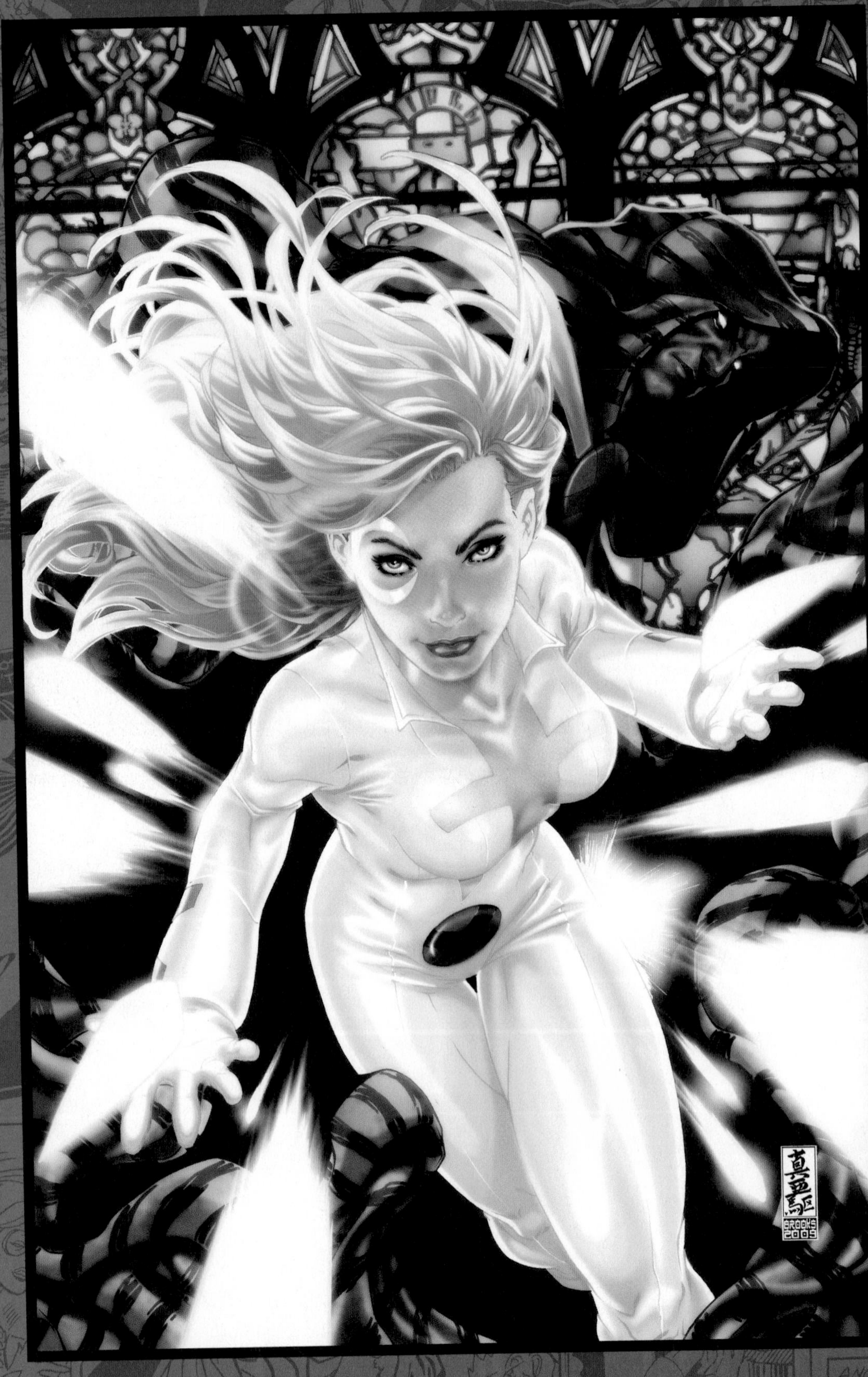
BROOKS 2009

CLOAK AND DAGGER (2010) #1

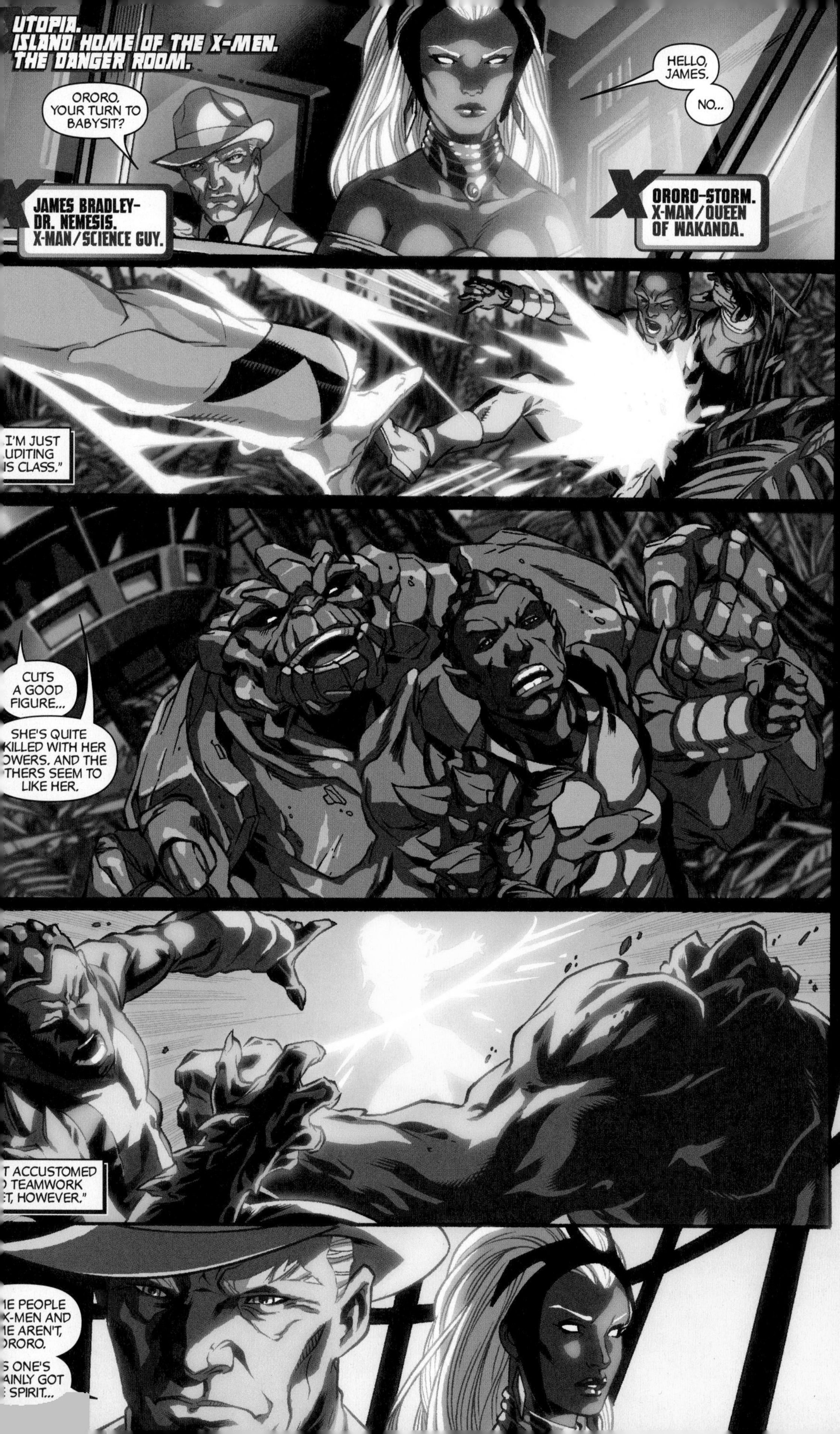
UTOPIA.
ISLAND HOME OF THE X-MEN.
THE DANGER ROOM.
ORORO. YOUR TURN TO BABYSIT?
HELLO, JAMES.
NO...
JAMES BRADLEY- DR. NEMESIS. X-MAN/SCIENCE GUY.
ORORO-STORM. X-MAN/QUEEN OF WAKANDA.
I'M JUST UDITING IS CLASS."
CUTS A GOOD FIGURE...
SHE'S QUITE KILLED WITH HER OWERS. AND THE THERS SEEM TO LIKE HER.
T ACCUSTOMED TEAMWORK ET, HOWEVER."
IE PEOPLE X-MEN AND IE AREN'T, ORORO.
S ONE'S AINLY GOT E SPIRIT...

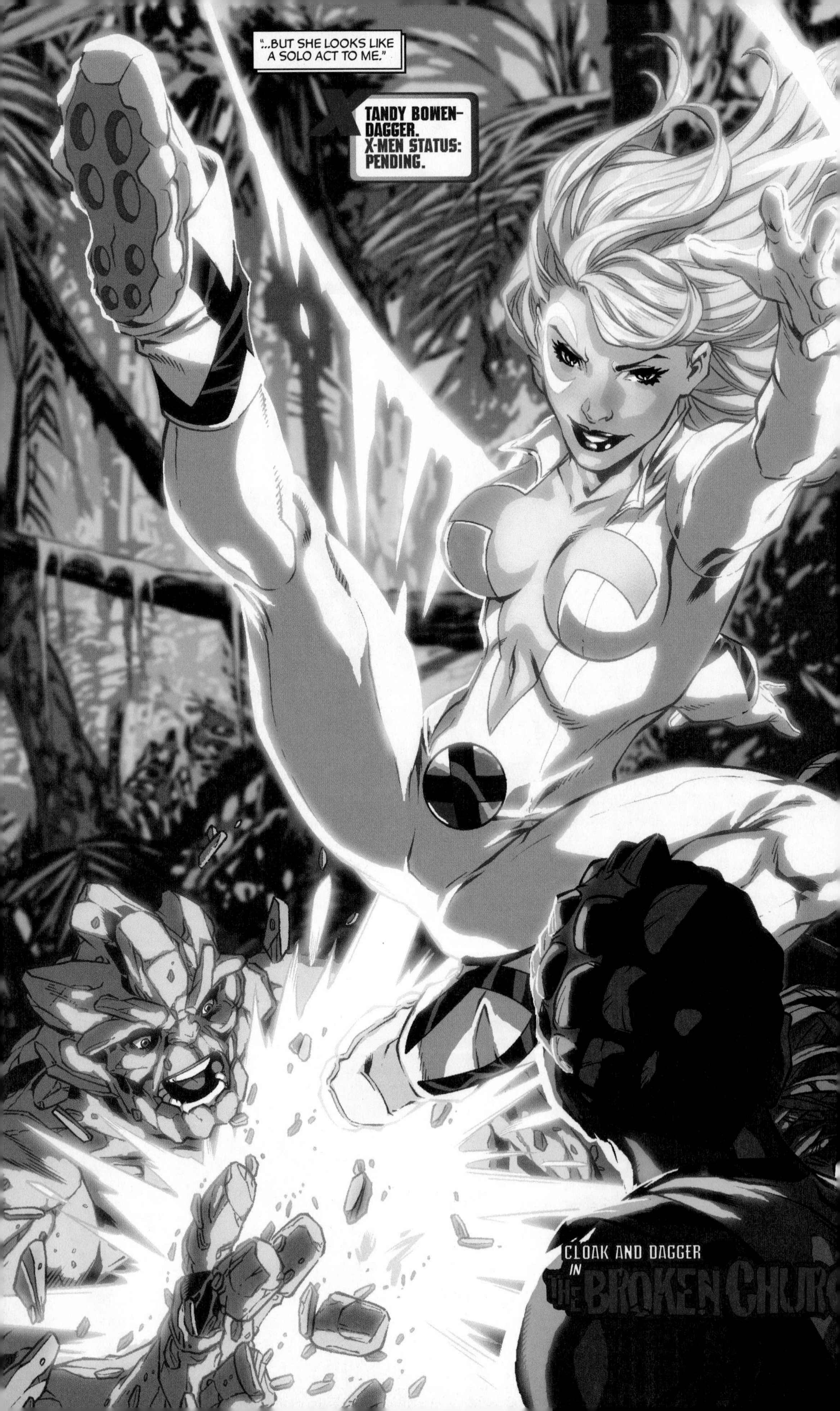
"...BUT SHE LOOKS LIKE A SOLO ACT TO ME."
TANDY BOWEN-DAGGER. X-MEN STATUS: PENDING.
CLOAK AND DAGGER IN
THE BROKEN CHURC

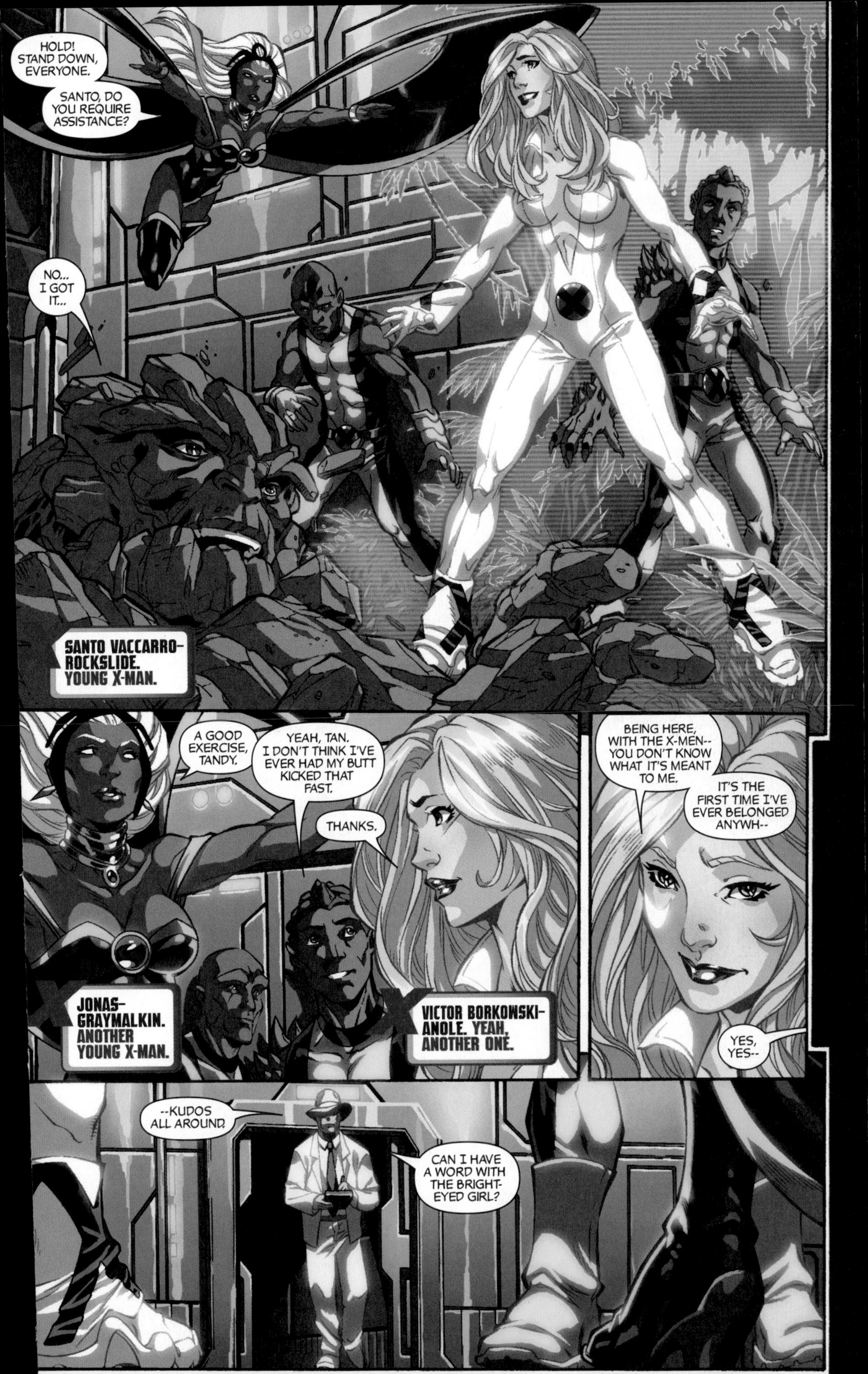
HOLD! STAND DOWN, EVERYONE.
SANTO, DO YOU REQUIRE ASSISTANCE?
NO... I GOT IT...
SANTO VACCARRO- ROCKSLIDE. YOUNG X-MAN.
A GOOD EXERCISE, TANDY.
YEAH, TAN. I DON'T THINK I'VE EVER HAD MY BUTT KICKED THAT FAST.
THANKS.
JONAS- GRAYMALKIN. ANOTHER YOUNG X-MAN.
VICTOR BORKOWSKI- ANOLE. YEAH, ANOTHER ONE.
BEING HERE, WITH THE X-MEN-- YOU DON'T KNOW WHAT IT'S MEANT TO ME.
IT'S THE FIRST TIME I'VE EVER BELONGED ANYWH--
YES, YES--
--KUDOS ALL AROUND.
CAN I HAVE A WORD WITH THE BRIGHT-EYED GIRL?

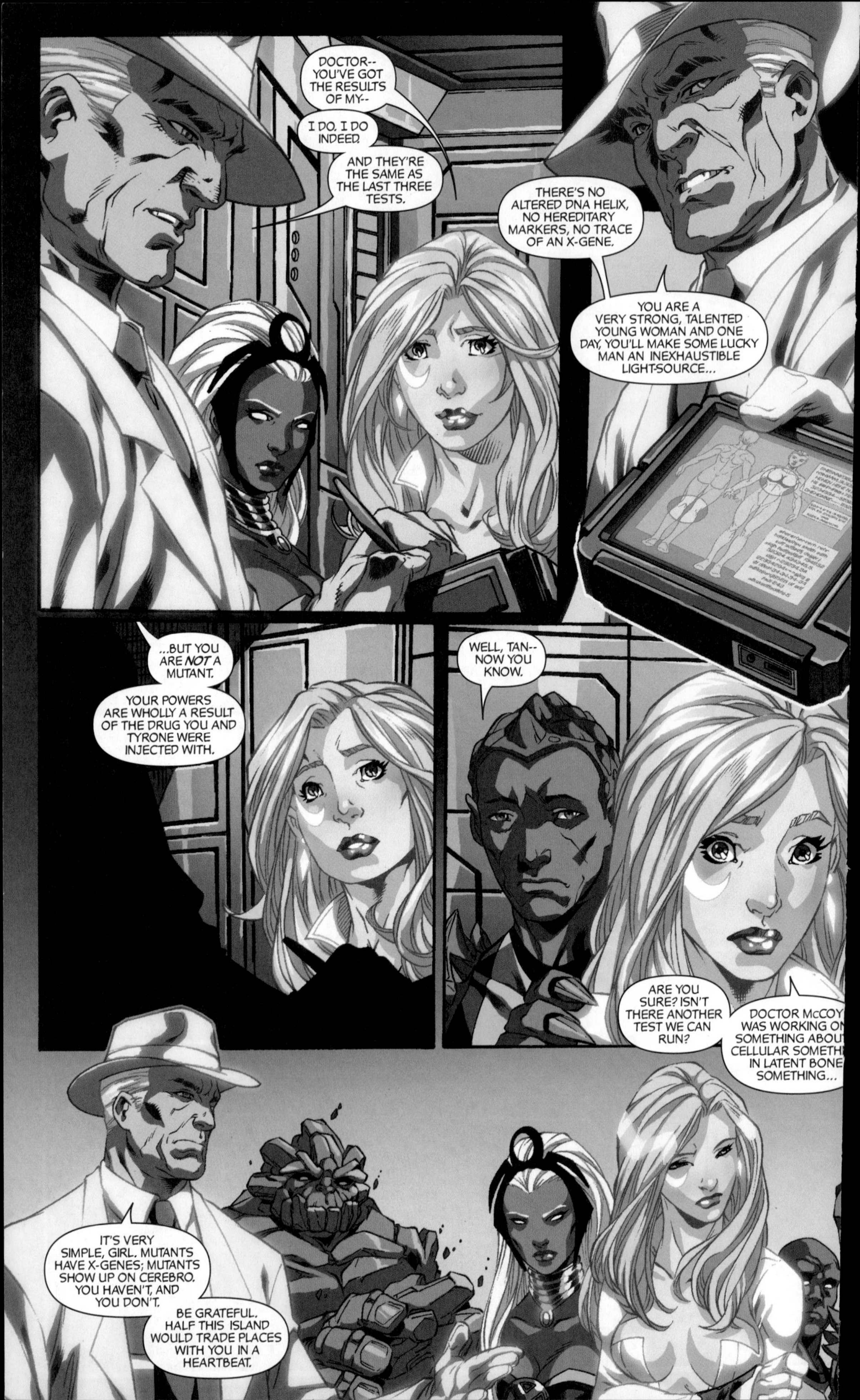
DOCTOR-- YOU'VE GOT THE RESULTS OF MY--
I DO. I DO INDEED.
AND THEY'RE THE SAME AS THE LAST THREE TESTS.
THERE'S NO ALTERED DNA HELIX, NO HEREDITARY MARKERS, NO TRACE OF AN X-GENE.
YOU ARE A VERY STRONG, TALENTED YOUNG WOMAN AND ONE DAY, YOU'LL MAKE SOME LUCKY MAN AN INEXHAUSTIBLE LIGHT-SOURCE...
...BUT YOU ARE *NOT* A MUTANT.
YOUR POWERS ARE WHOLLY A RESULT OF THE DRUG YOU AND TYRONE WERE INJECTED WITH.
WELL, TAN-- NOW YOU KNOW.
ARE YOU SURE? ISN'T THERE ANOTHER TEST WE CAN RUN?
DOCTOR McCOY WAS WORKING ON SOMETHING ABOUT CELLULAR SOMETH IN LATENT BONE SOMETHING...
IT'S VERY SIMPLE, GIRL. MUTANTS HAVE X-GENES; MUTANTS SHOW UP ON CEREBRO. YOU HAVEN'T, AND YOU DON'T.
BE GRATEFUL. HALF THIS ISLAND WOULD TRADE PLACES WITH YOU IN A HEARTBEAT.

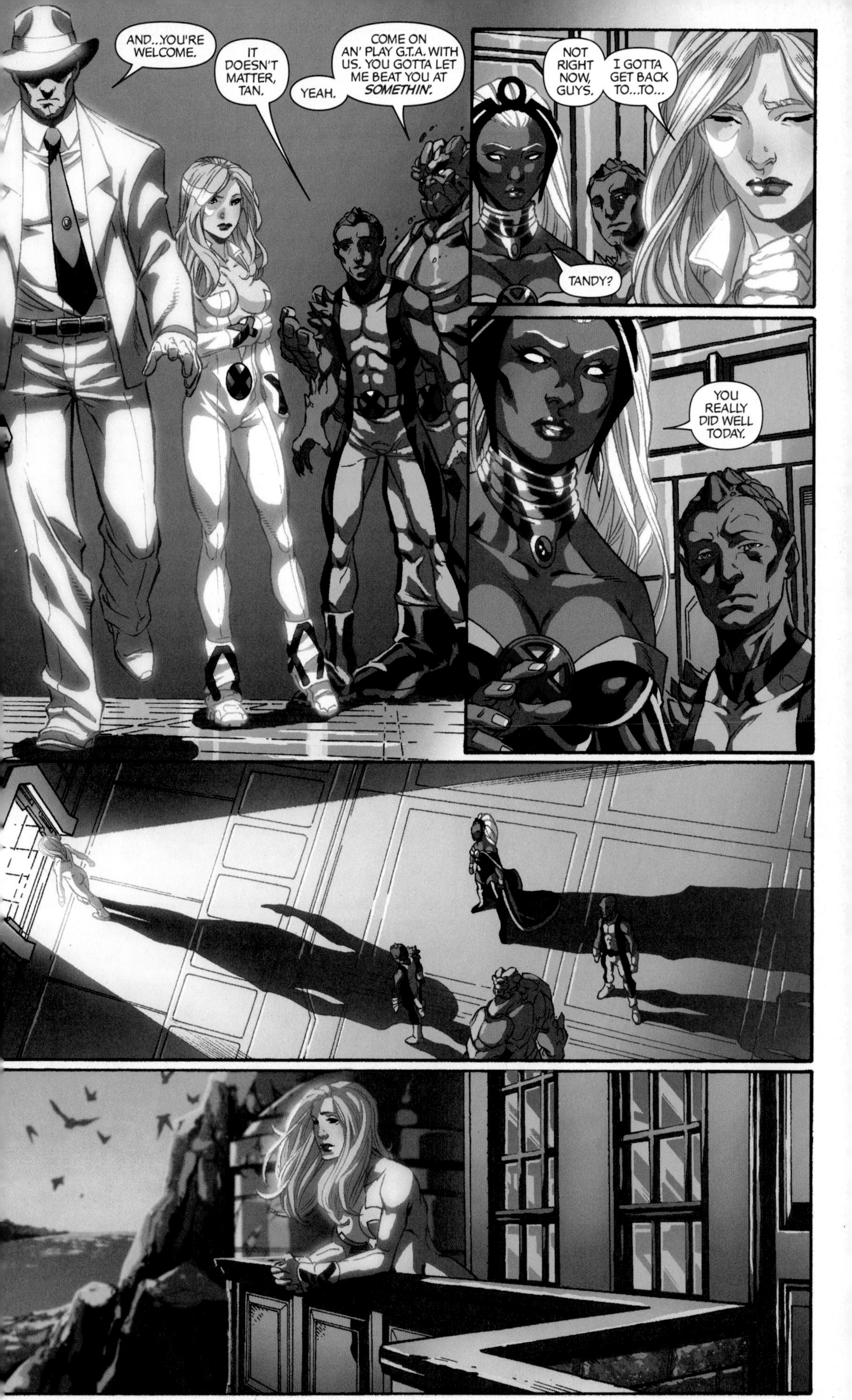
AND...YOU'RE WELCOME.
IT DOESN'T MATTER, TAN.
YEAH.
COME ON AN' PLAY G.T.A. WITH US. YOU GOTTA LET ME BEAT YOU AT SOMETHIN'.
NOT RIGHT NOW, GUYS.
I GOTTA GET BACK TO...TO...
TANDY?
YOU REALLY DID WELL TODAY.

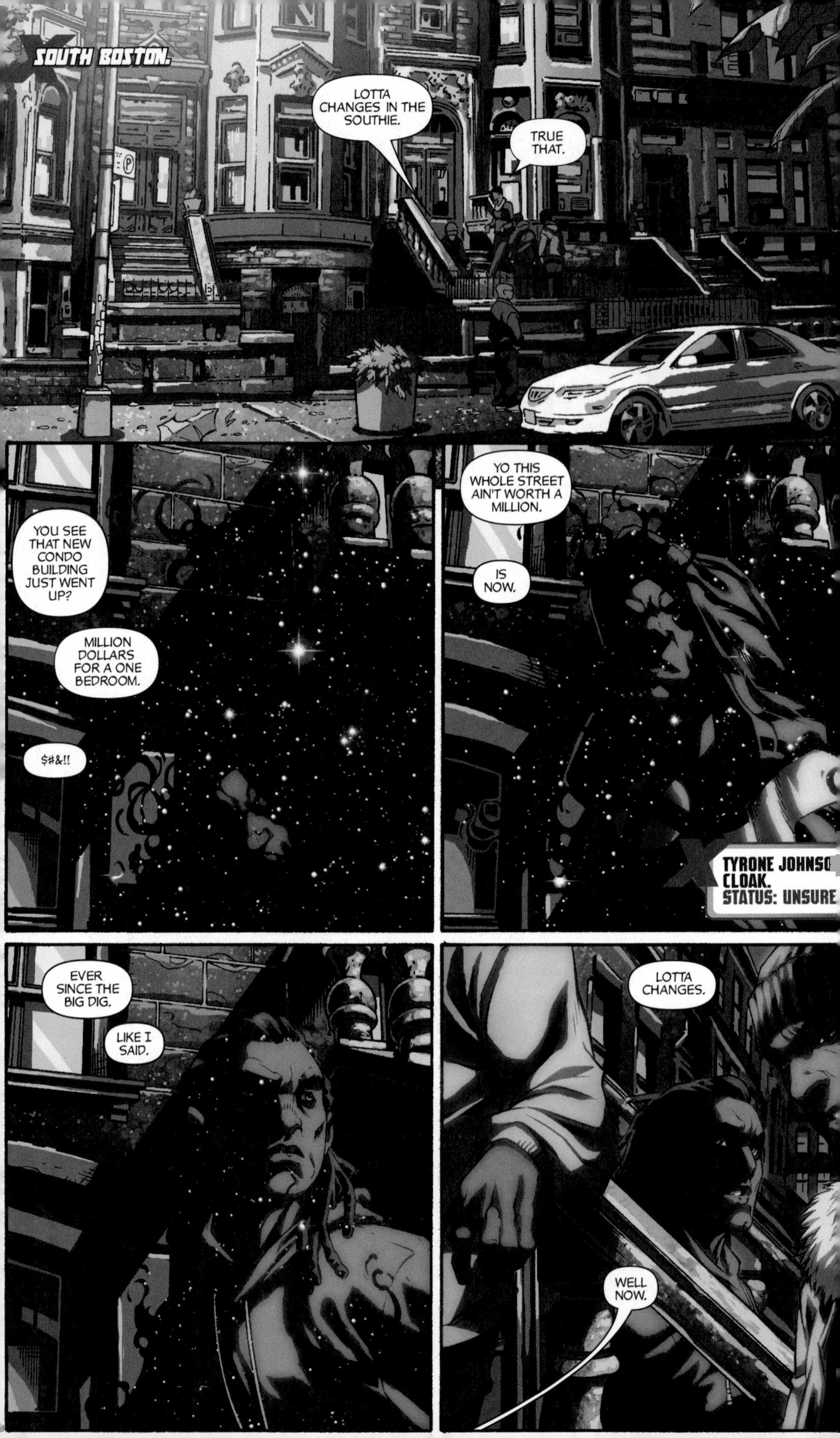
SOUTH BOSTON.
LOTTA CHANGES IN THE SOUTHIE.
TRUE THAT.
YOU SEE THAT NEW CONDO BUILDING JUST WENT UP?
MILLION DOLLARS FOR A ONE BEDROOM.
$#&!!
YO THIS WHOLE STREET AIN'T WORTH A MILLION.
IS NOW.
TYRONE JOHNSO
CLOAK.
STATUS: UNSURE
EVER SINCE THE BIG DIG.
LIKE I SAID.
LOTTA CHANGES.
WELL NOW.

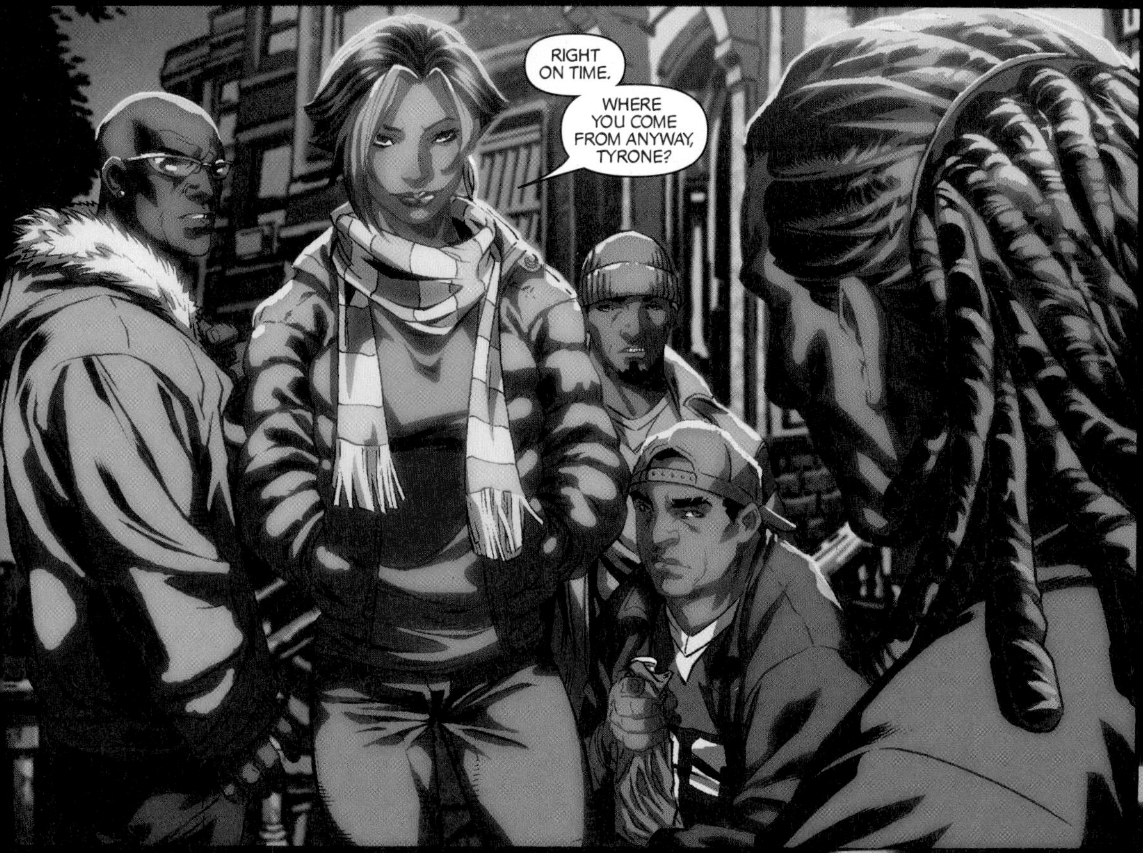
RIGHT ON TIME.
WHERE YOU COME FROM ANYWAY, TYRONE?

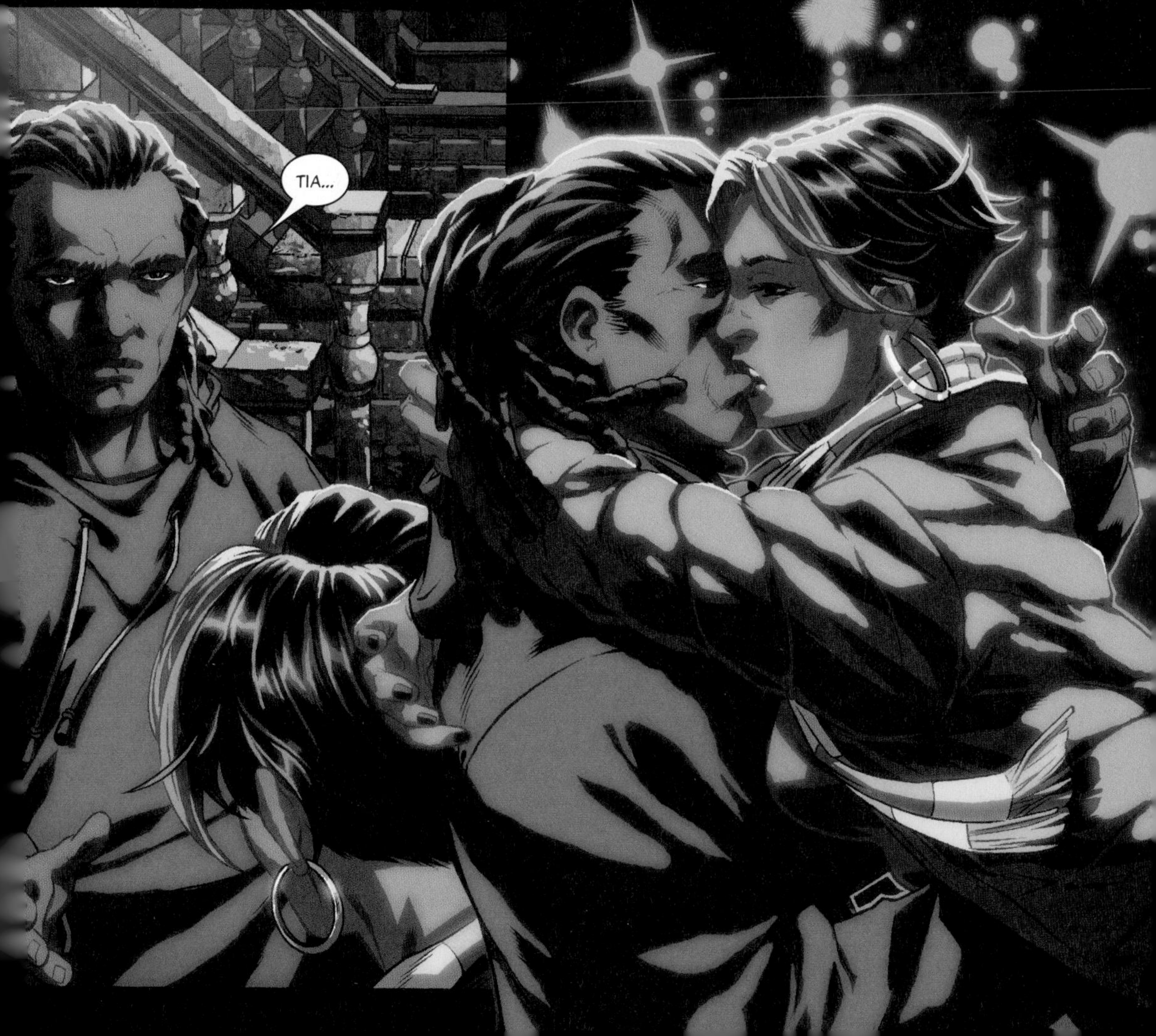
TIA...

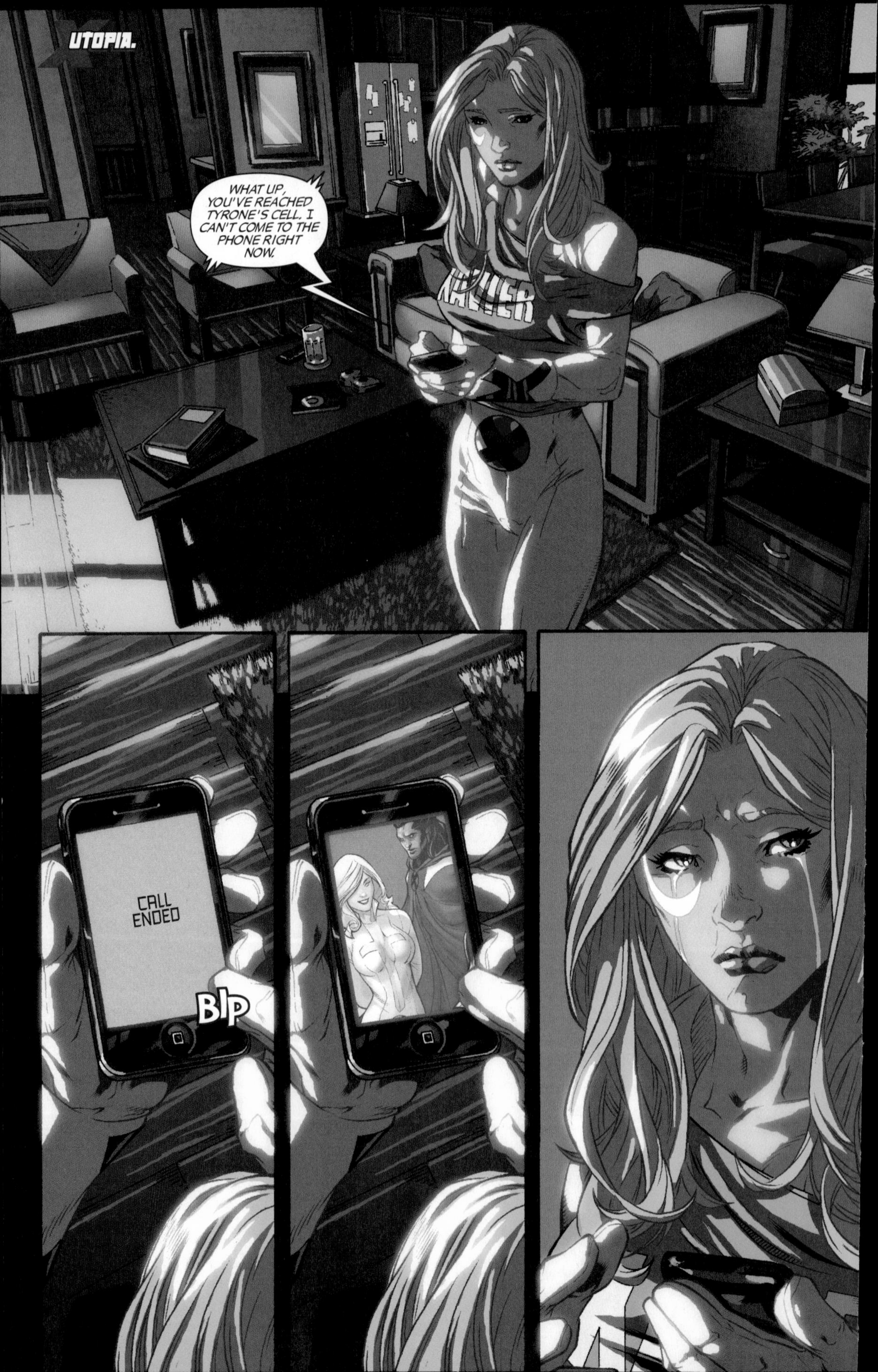
UTOPIA.
WHAT UP, YOU'VE REACHED TYRONE'S CELL. I CAN'T COME TO THE PHONE RIGHT NOW.
CALL ENDED
BIP

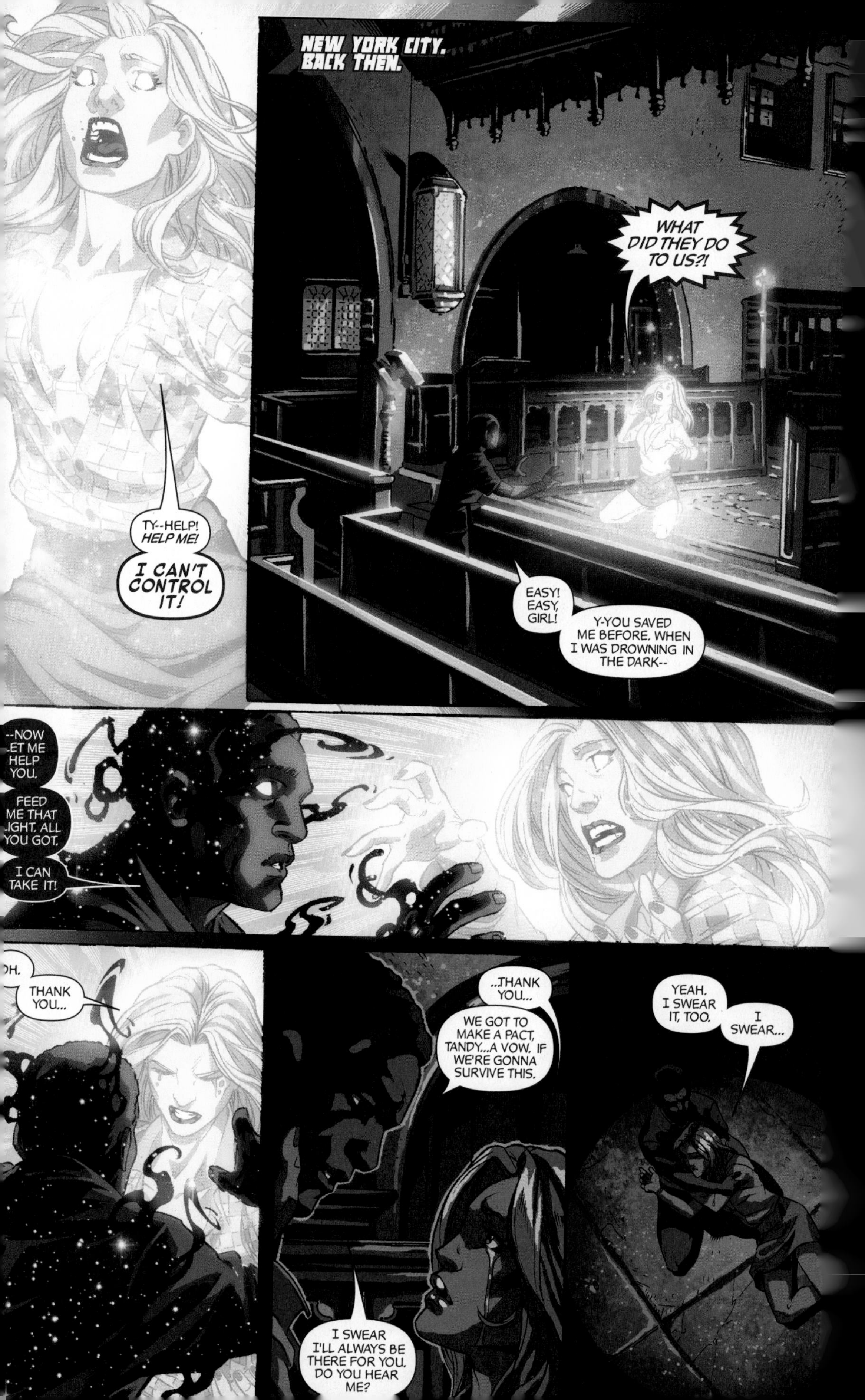
TY--HELP! HELP ME!
I CAN'T CONTROL IT!
NEW YORK CITY. BACK THEN.
WHAT DID THEY DO TO US?!
EASY! EASY, GIRL!
Y-YOU SAVED ME BEFORE. WHEN I WAS DROWNING IN THE DARK--
--NOW LET ME HELP YOU.
FEED ME THAT LIGHT. ALL YOU GOT.
I CAN TAKE IT!
OH.
THANK YOU...
...THANK YOU...
WE GOT TO MAKE A PACT, TANDY...A VOW, IF WE'RE GONNA SURVIVE THIS.
I SWEAR I'LL ALWAYS BE THERE FOR YOU. DO YOU HEAR ME?
YEAH. I SWEAR IT, TOO.
I SWEAR...

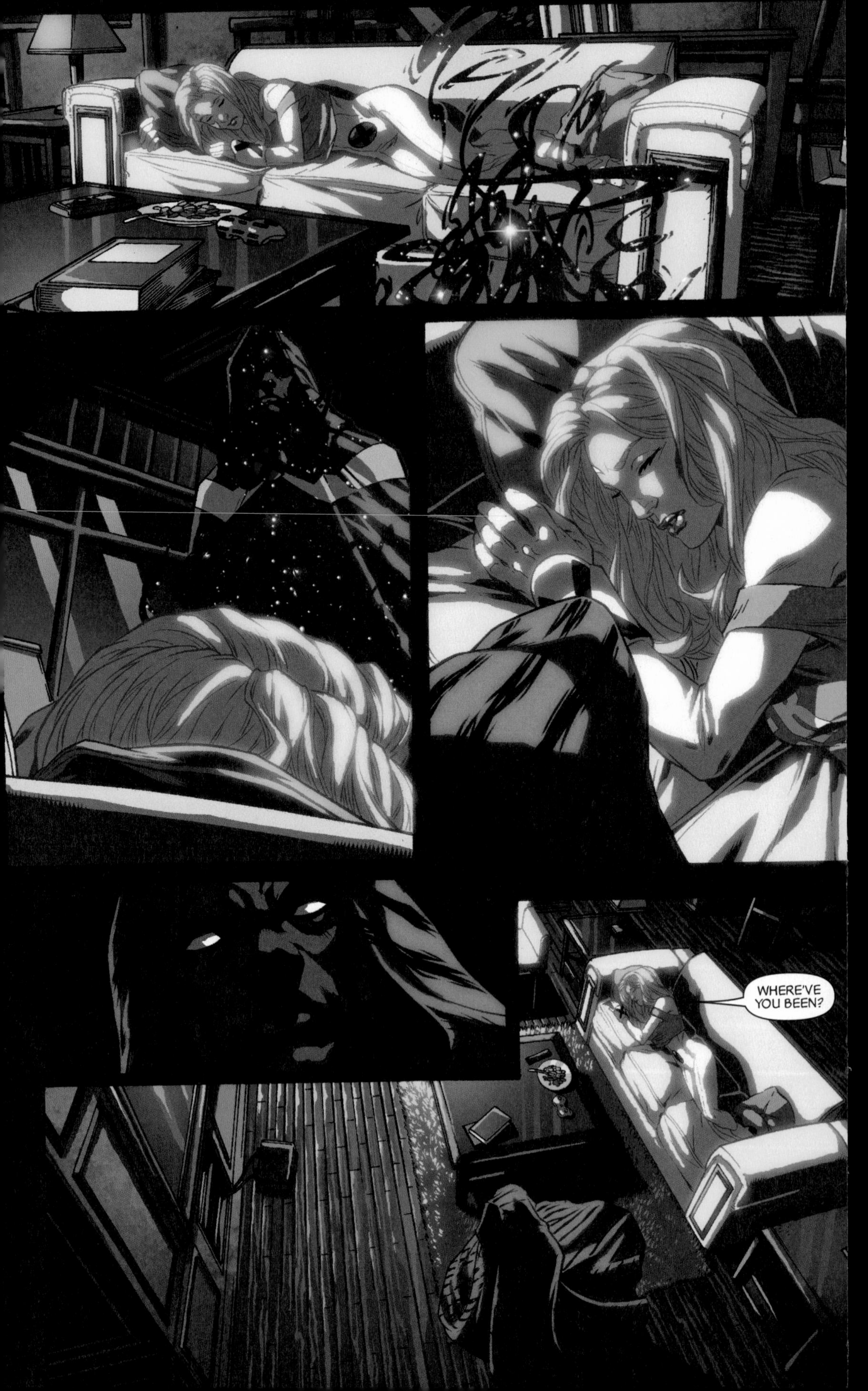
WHERE'VE YOU BEEN?

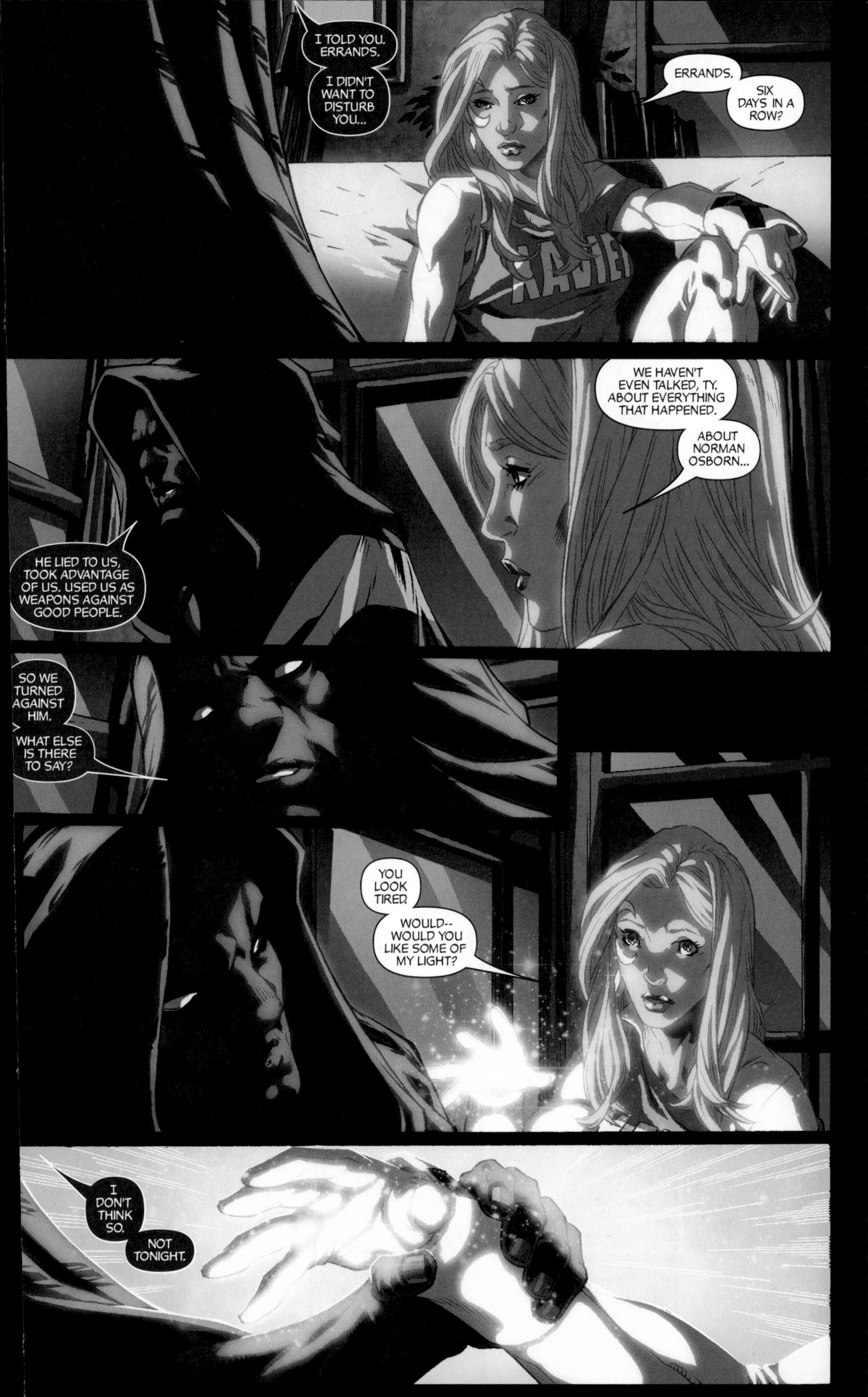
I TOLD YOU. ERRANDS.
I DIDN'T WANT TO DISTURB YOU...
ERRANDS.
SIX DAYS IN A ROW?
WE HAVEN'T EVEN TALKED, TY. ABOUT EVERYTHING THAT HAPPENED.
ABOUT NORMAN OSBORN...
HE LIED TO US, TOOK ADVANTAGE OF US. USED US AS WEAPONS AGAINST GOOD PEOPLE.
SO WE TURNED AGAINST HIM.
WHAT ELSE IS THERE TO SAY?
YOU LOOK TIRED.
WOULD-- WOULD YOU LIKE SOME OF MY LIGHT?
I DON'T THINK SO.
NOT TONIGHT.

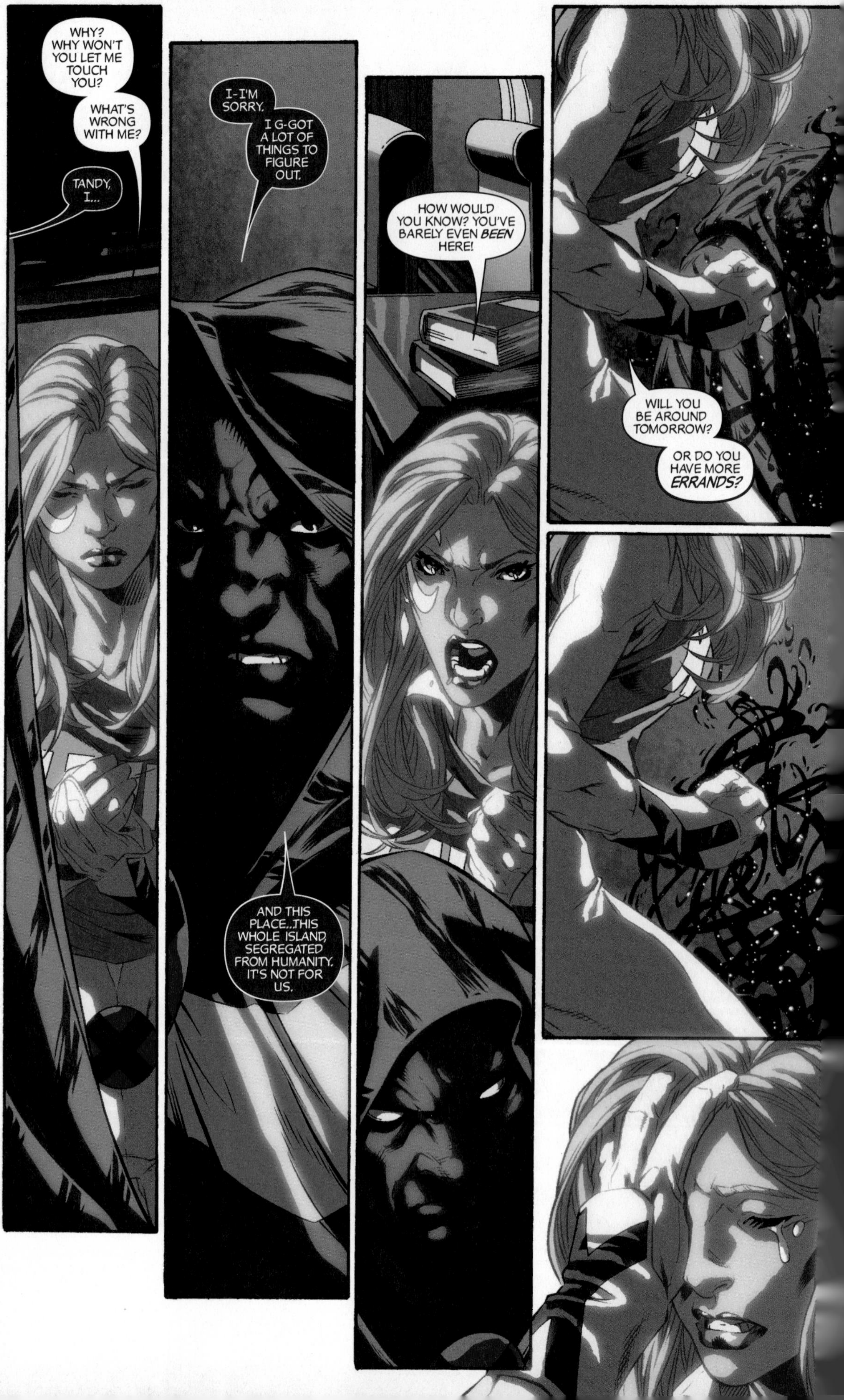
WHY? WHY WON'T YOU LET ME TOUCH YOU?
WHAT'S WRONG WITH ME?
TANDY, I...
I-I'M SORRY.
I G-GOT A LOT OF THINGS TO FIGURE OUT.
AND THIS PLACE...THIS WHOLE ISLAND, SEGREGATED FROM HUMANITY. IT'S NOT FOR US.
HOW WOULD YOU KNOW? YOU'VE BARELY EVEN *BEEN* HERE!
WILL YOU BE AROUND TOMORROW?
OR DO YOU HAVE MORE *ERRANDS?*

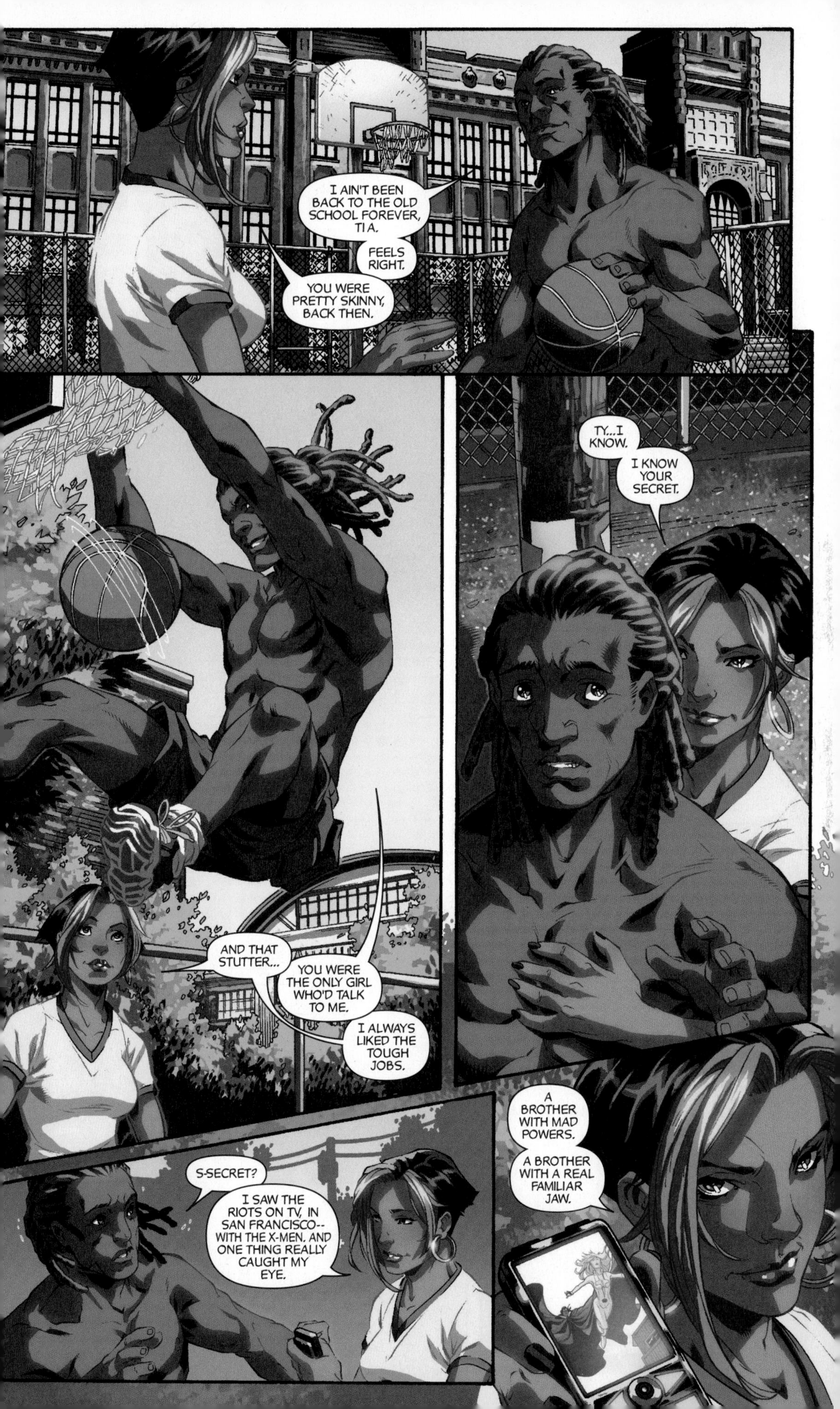
I AIN'T BEEN BACK TO THE OLD SCHOOL FOREVER, TIA.
FEELS RIGHT.
YOU WERE PRETTY SKINNY, BACK THEN.
AND THAT STUTTER...
YOU WERE THE ONLY GIRL WHO'D TALK TO ME.
I ALWAYS LIKED THE TOUGH JOBS.
TY...I KNOW.
I KNOW YOUR SECRET.
S-SECRET?
I SAW THE RIOTS ON TV, IN SAN FRANCISCO-- WITH THE X-MEN. AND ONE THING REALLY CAUGHT MY EYE.
A BROTHER WITH MAD POWERS.
A BROTHER WITH A REAL FAMILIAR JAW.

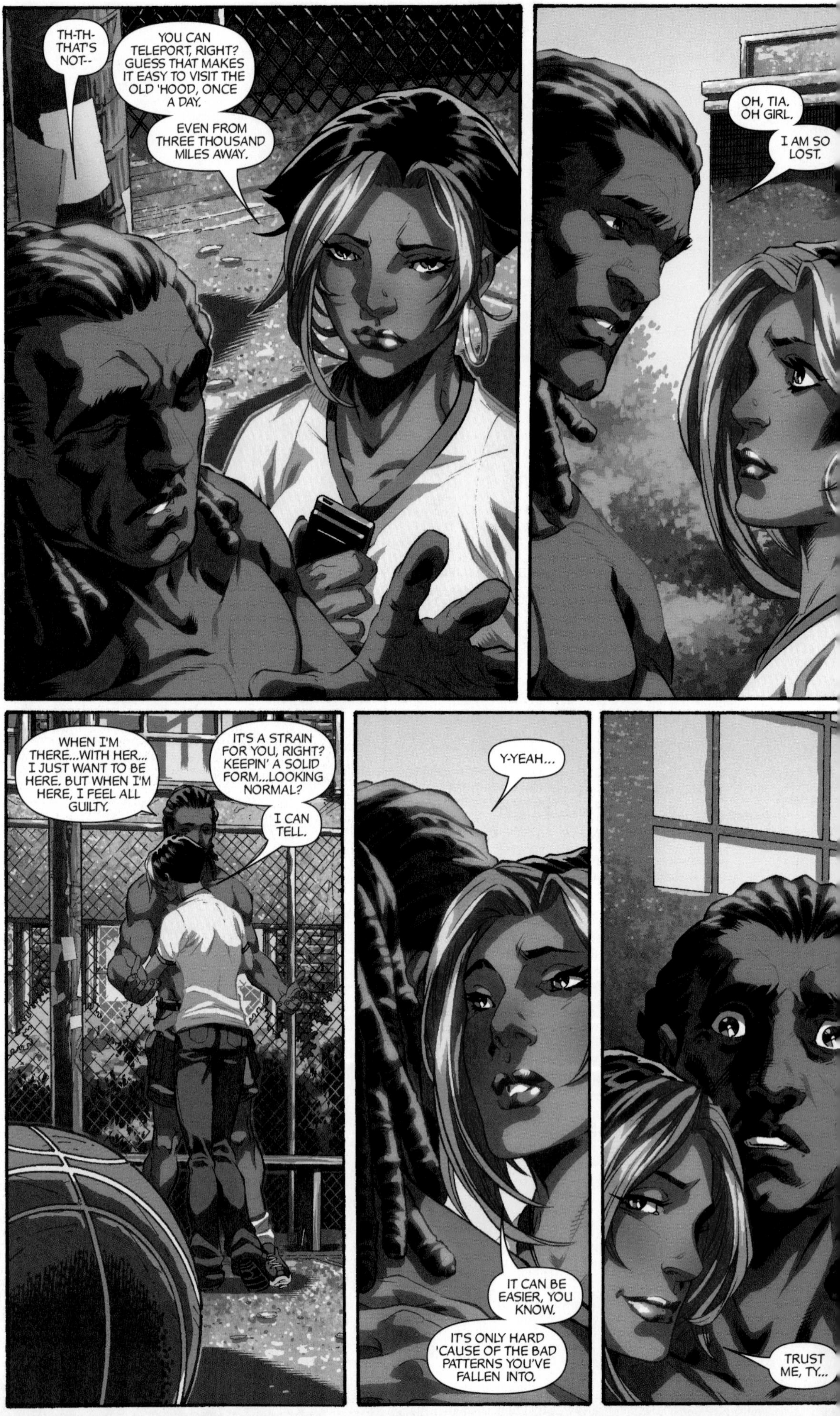
TH-TH-THAT'S NOT--
YOU CAN TELEPORT, RIGHT? GUESS THAT MAKES IT EASY TO VISIT THE OLD 'HOOD, ONCE A DAY.
EVEN FROM THREE THOUSAND MILES AWAY.
OH, TIA. OH GIRL.
I AM SO LOST.
WHEN I'M THERE...WITH HER... I JUST WANT TO BE HERE. BUT WHEN I'M HERE, I FEEL ALL GUILTY.
IT'S A STRAIN FOR YOU, RIGHT? KEEPIN' A SOLID FORM...LOOKING NORMAL?
I CAN TELL.
Y-YEAH...
IT CAN BE EASIER, YOU KNOW.
IT'S ONLY HARD 'CAUSE OF THE BAD PATTERNS YOU'VE FALLEN INTO.
TRUST ME, TY...

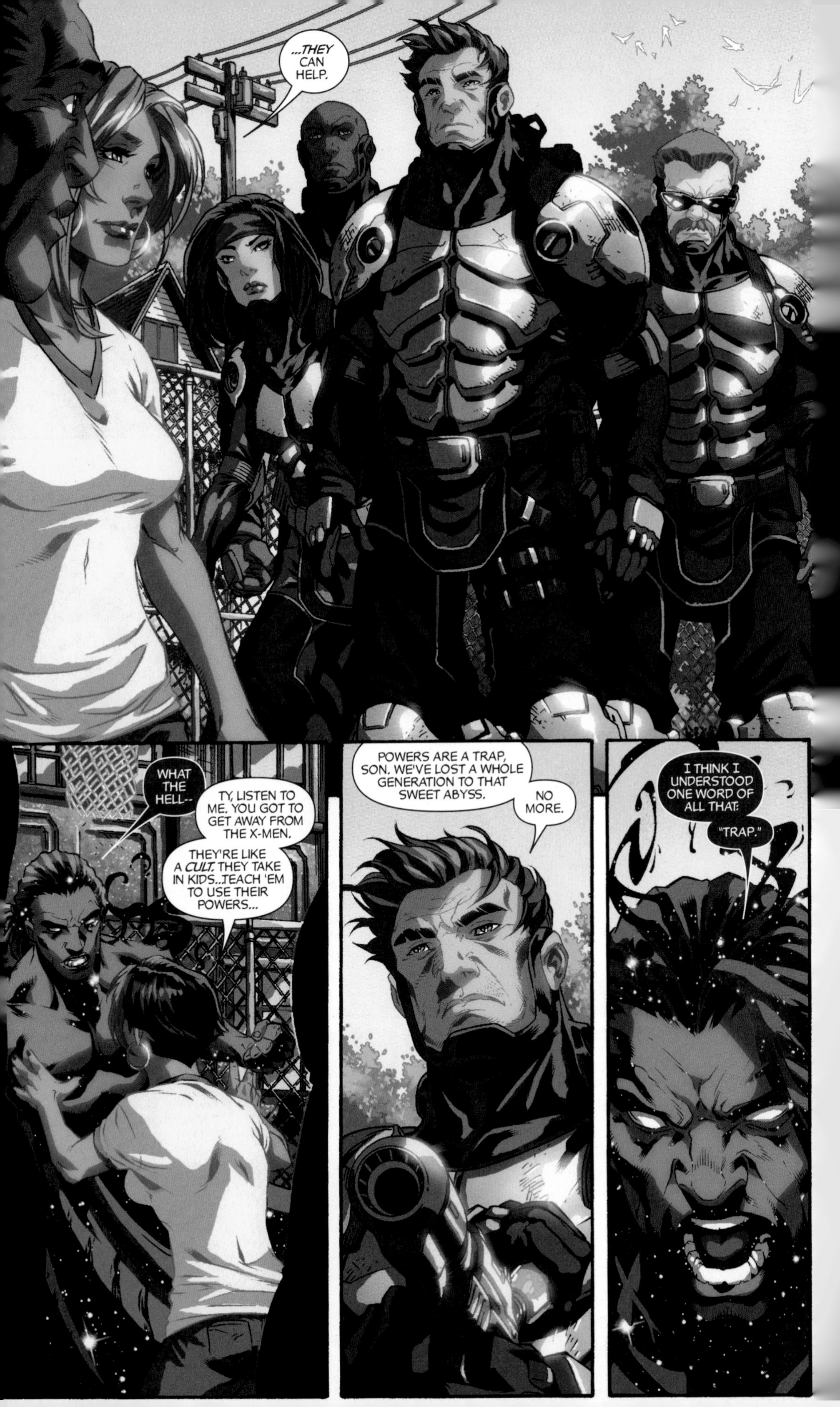
...THEY CAN HELP.
WHAT THE HELL--
TY, LISTEN TO ME. YOU GOT TO GET AWAY FROM THE X-MEN.
THEY'RE LIKE A *CULT*. THEY TAKE IN KIDS...TEACH 'EM TO USE THEIR POWERS...
POWERS ARE A TRAP, SON. WE'VE LOST A WHOLE GENERATION TO THAT SWEET ABYSS.
NO MORE.
I THINK I UNDERSTOOD ONE WORD OF ALL THAT:
"TRAP."

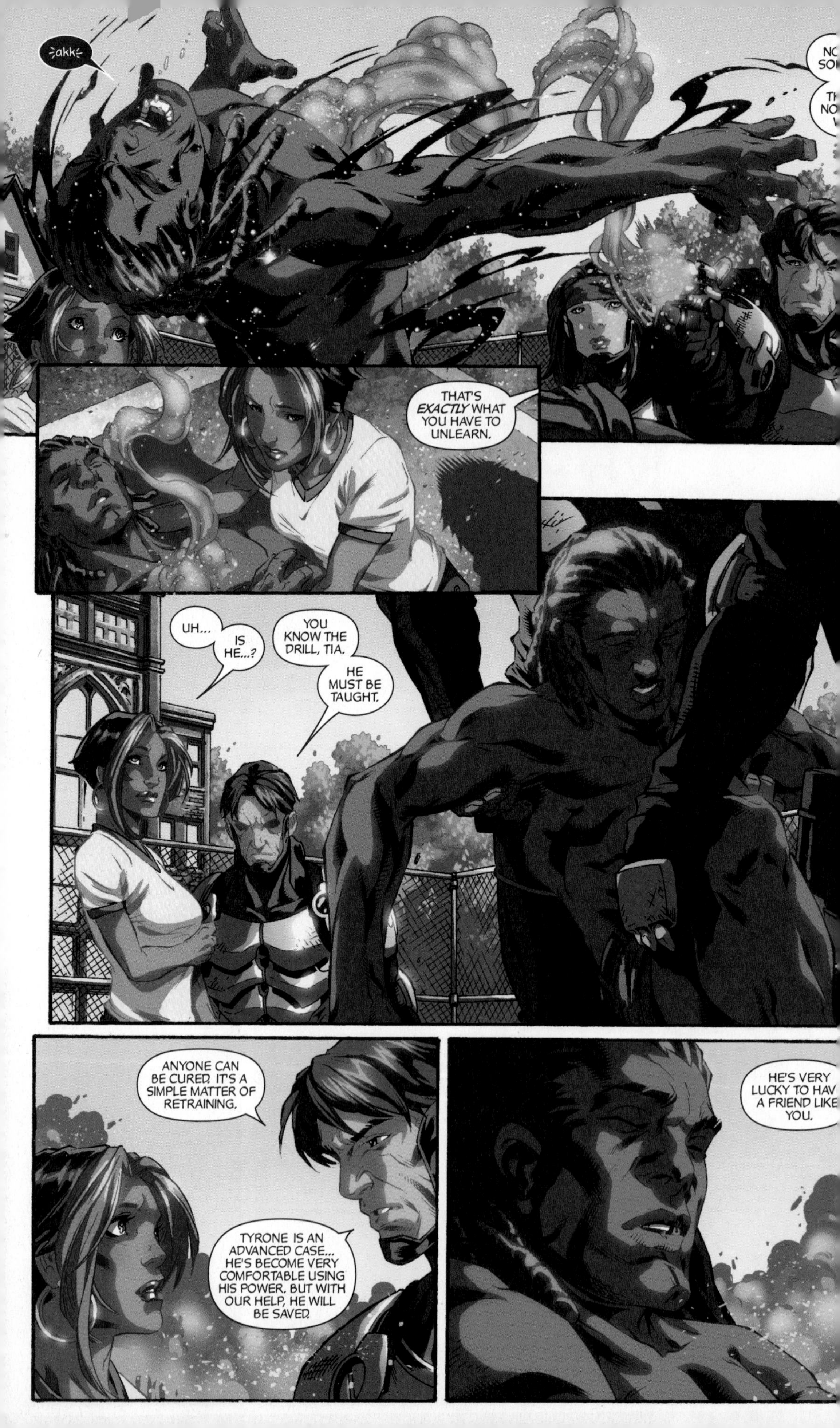

akk
THAT'S *EXACTLY* WHAT YOU HAVE TO UNLEARN.
UH...
IS HE...?
YOU KNOW THE DRILL, TIA.
HE MUST BE TAUGHT.
ANYONE CAN BE CURED. IT'S A SIMPLE MATTER OF RETRAINING.
TYRONE IS AN ADVANCED CASE... HE'S BECOME VERY COMFORTABLE USING HIS POWER. BUT WITH OUR HELP, HE WILL BE SAVED.
HE'S VERY LUCKY TO HAV A FRIEND LIKE YOU.

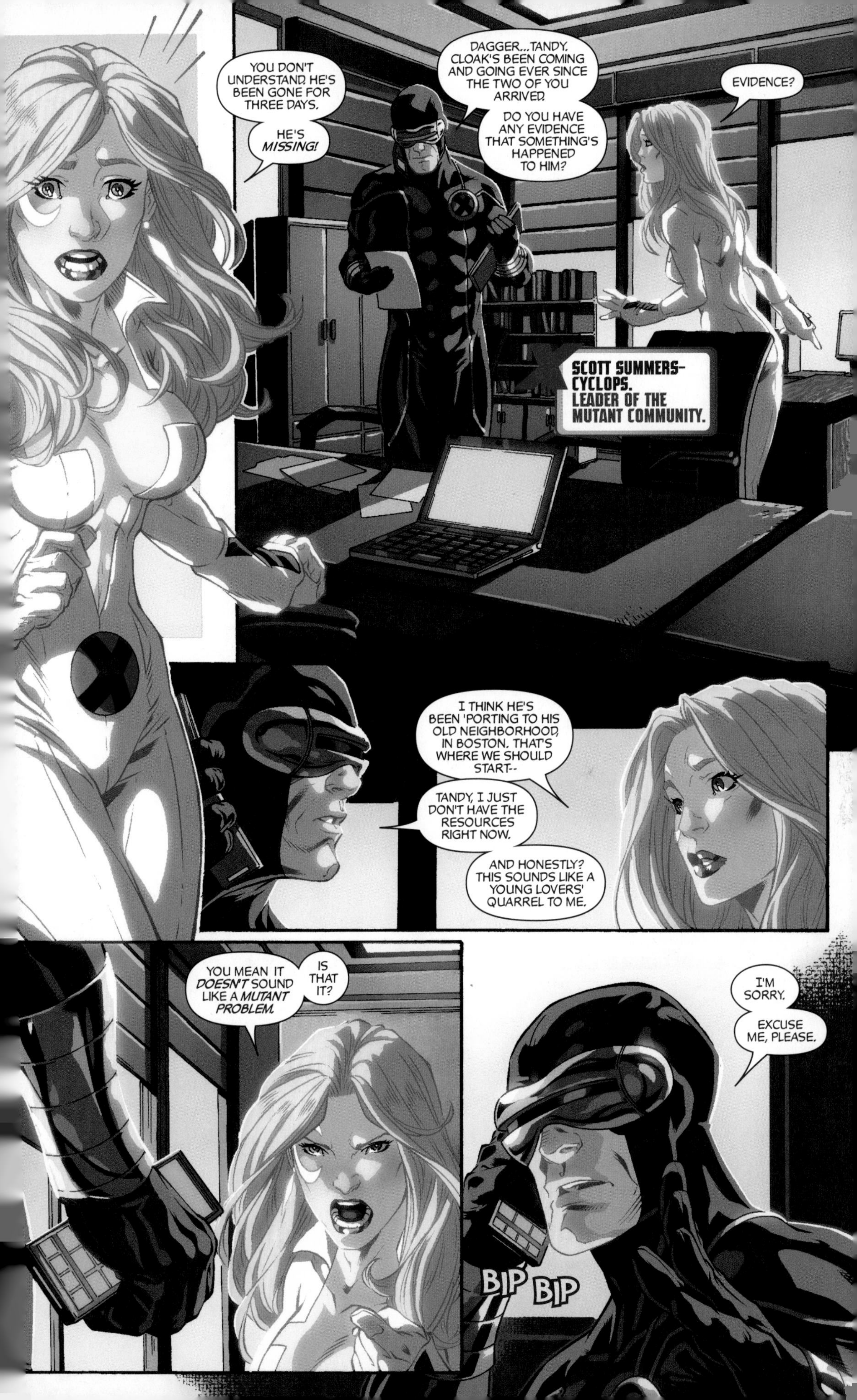
YOU DON'T UNDERSTAND. HE'S BEEN GONE FOR THREE DAYS.
HE'S *MISSING!*
DAGGER...TANDY. CLOAK'S BEEN COMING AND GOING EVER SINCE THE TWO OF YOU ARRIVED.
DO YOU HAVE ANY EVIDENCE THAT SOMETHING'S HAPPENED TO HIM?
EVIDENCE?
SCOTT SUMMERS-CYCLOPS. LEADER OF THE MUTANT COMMUNITY.
I THINK HE'S BEEN 'PORTING TO HIS OLD NEIGHBORHOOD, IN BOSTON. THAT'S WHERE WE SHOULD START--
TANDY, I JUST DON'T HAVE THE RESOURCES RIGHT NOW.
AND HONESTLY? THIS SOUNDS LIKE A YOUNG LOVERS' QUARREL TO ME.
YOU MEAN IT *DOESN'T* SOUND LIKE A *MUTANT PROBLEM.*
IS THAT IT?
I'M SORRY.
EXCUSE ME, PLEASE.
BIP BIP

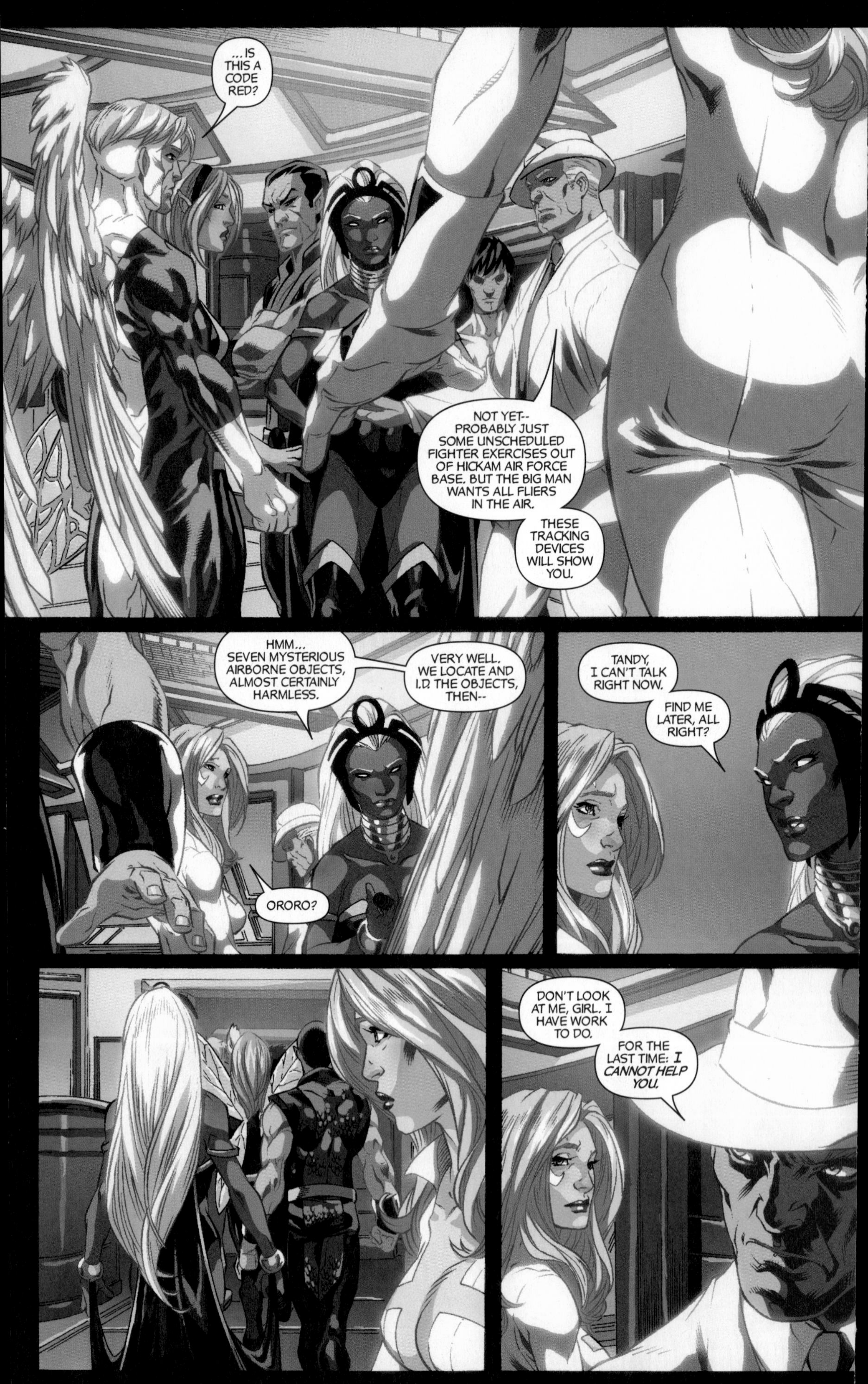
...IS THIS A CODE RED?
NOT YET-- PROBABLY JUST SOME UNSCHEDULED FIGHTER EXERCISES OUT OF HICKAM AIR FORCE BASE. BUT THE BIG MAN WANTS ALL FLIERS IN THE AIR.
THESE TRACKING DEVICES WILL SHOW YOU.
HMM... SEVEN MYSTERIOUS AIRBORNE OBJECTS, ALMOST CERTAINLY HARMLESS.
VERY WELL. WE LOCATE AND I.D. THE OBJECTS, THEN--
ORORO?
TANDY, I CAN'T TALK RIGHT NOW.
FIND ME LATER, ALL RIGHT?
DON'T LOOK AT ME, GIRL. I HAVE WORK TO DO.
FOR THE LAST TIME: *I CANNOT HELP YOU.*

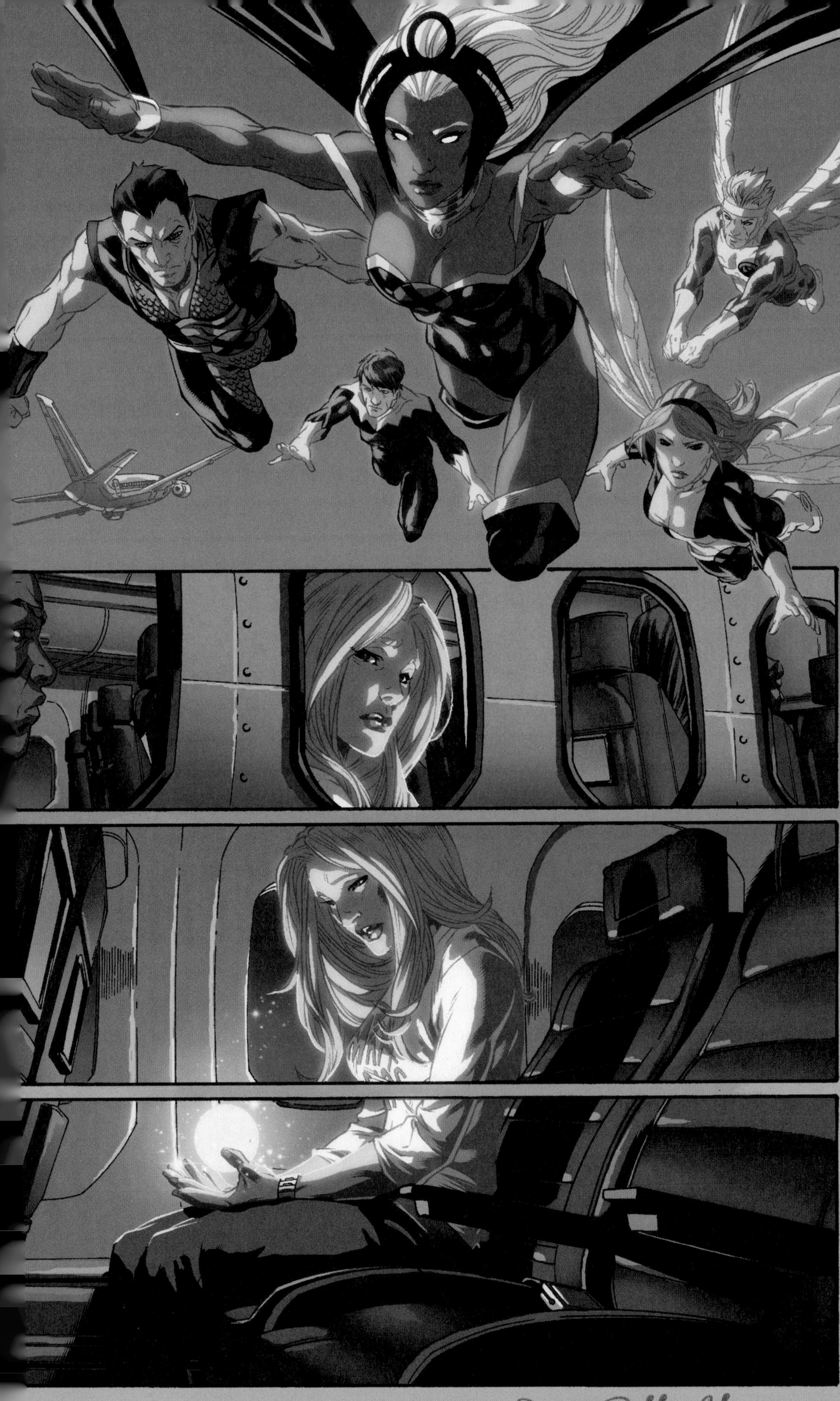

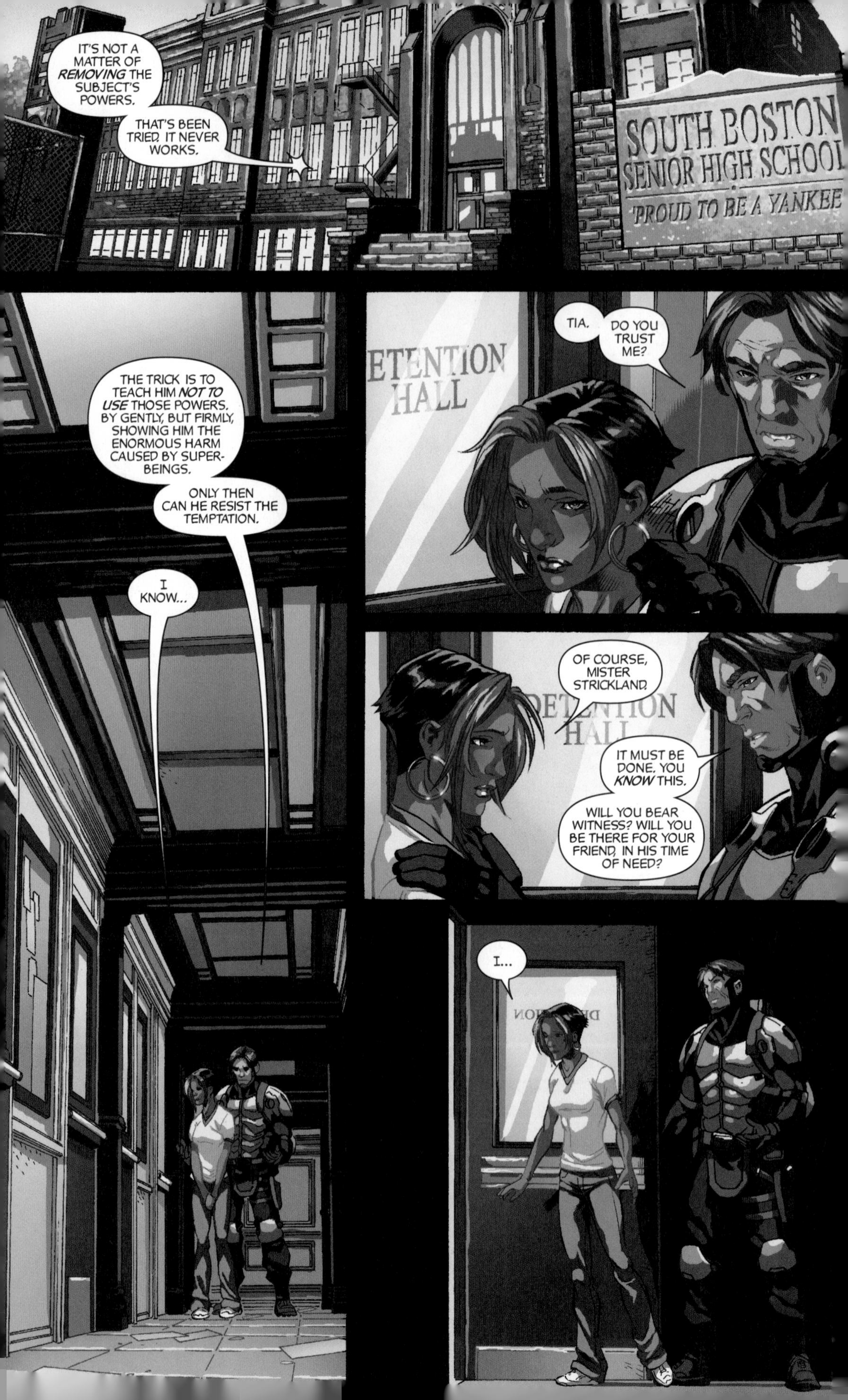
IT'S NOT A MATTER OF *REMOVING* THE SUBJECT'S POWERS.
THAT'S BEEN TRIED. IT NEVER WORKS.
SOUTH BOSTON SENIOR HIGH SCHOOL
PROUD TO BE A YANKEE
THE TRICK IS TO TEACH HIM *NOT TO USE* THOSE POWERS. BY GENTLY, BUT FIRMLY, SHOWING HIM THE ENORMOUS HARM CAUSED BY SUPER-BEINGS.
ONLY THEN CAN HE RESIST THE TEMPTATION.
I KNOW...
DETENTION HALL
TIA.
DO YOU TRUST ME?
OF COURSE, MISTER STRICKLAND.
IT MUST BE DONE. YOU *KNOW* THIS.
WILL YOU BEAR WITNESS? WILL YOU BE THERE FOR YOUR FRIEND, IN HIS TIME OF NEED?
I...

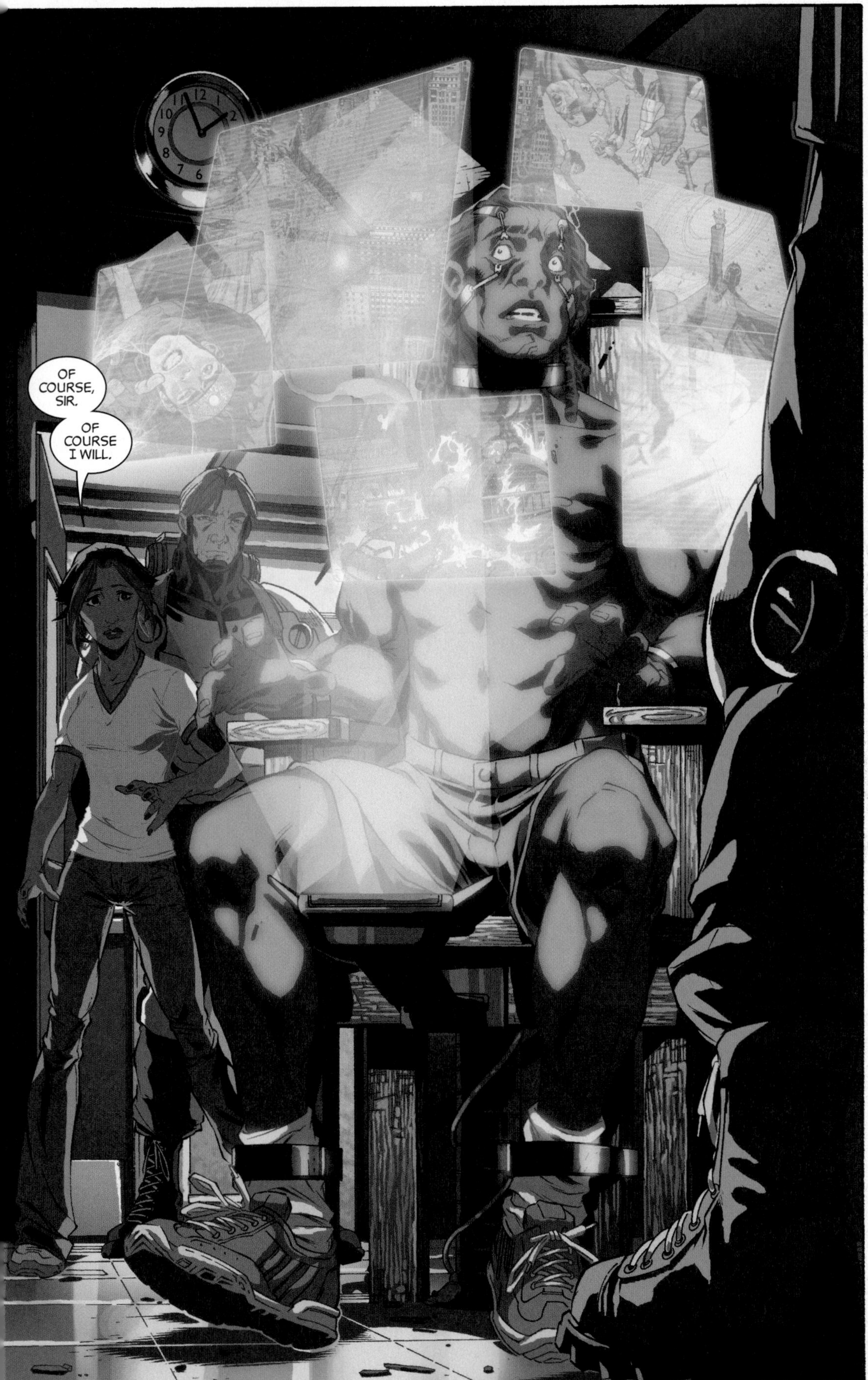
OF COURSE, SIR.
OF COURSE I WILL.

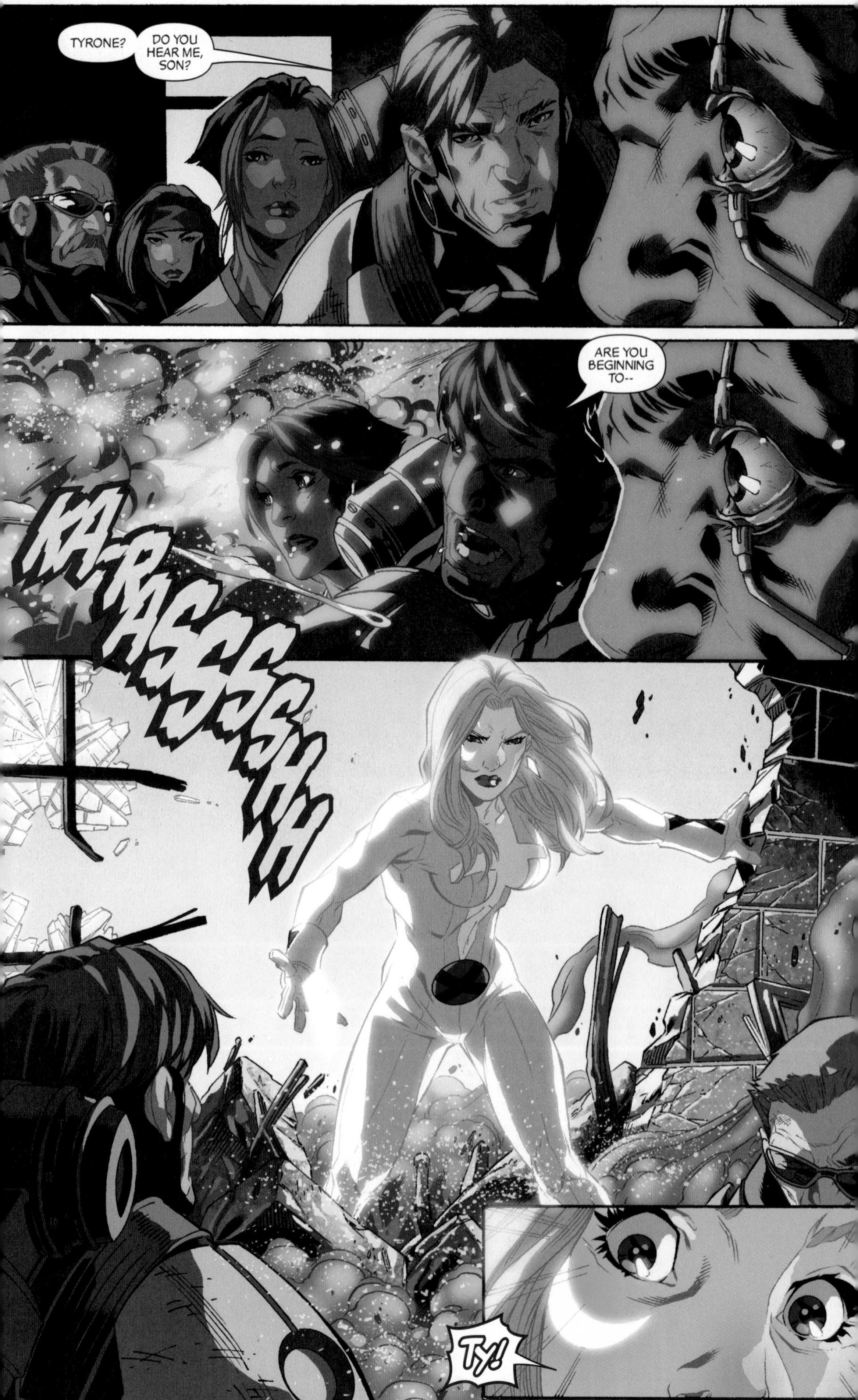
TYRONE?
DO YOU HEAR ME, SON?
ARE YOU BEGINNING TO--
KA-RASSSHH
TY!

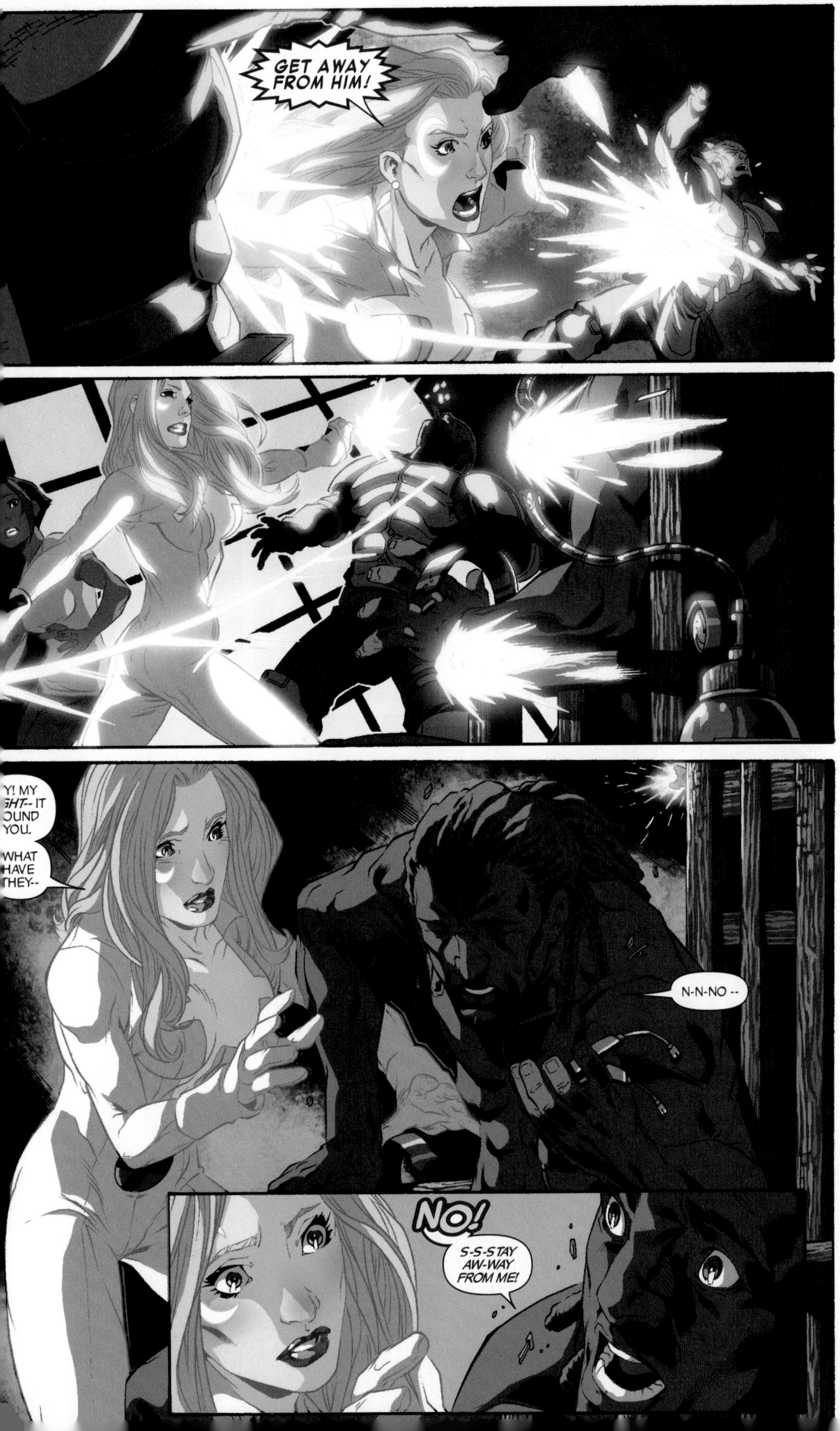
GET AWAY FROM HIM!
Y! MY GHT-- IT OUND YOU.
WHAT HAVE THEY--
N-N-NO --
NO!
S-S-STAY AW-WAY FROM ME!

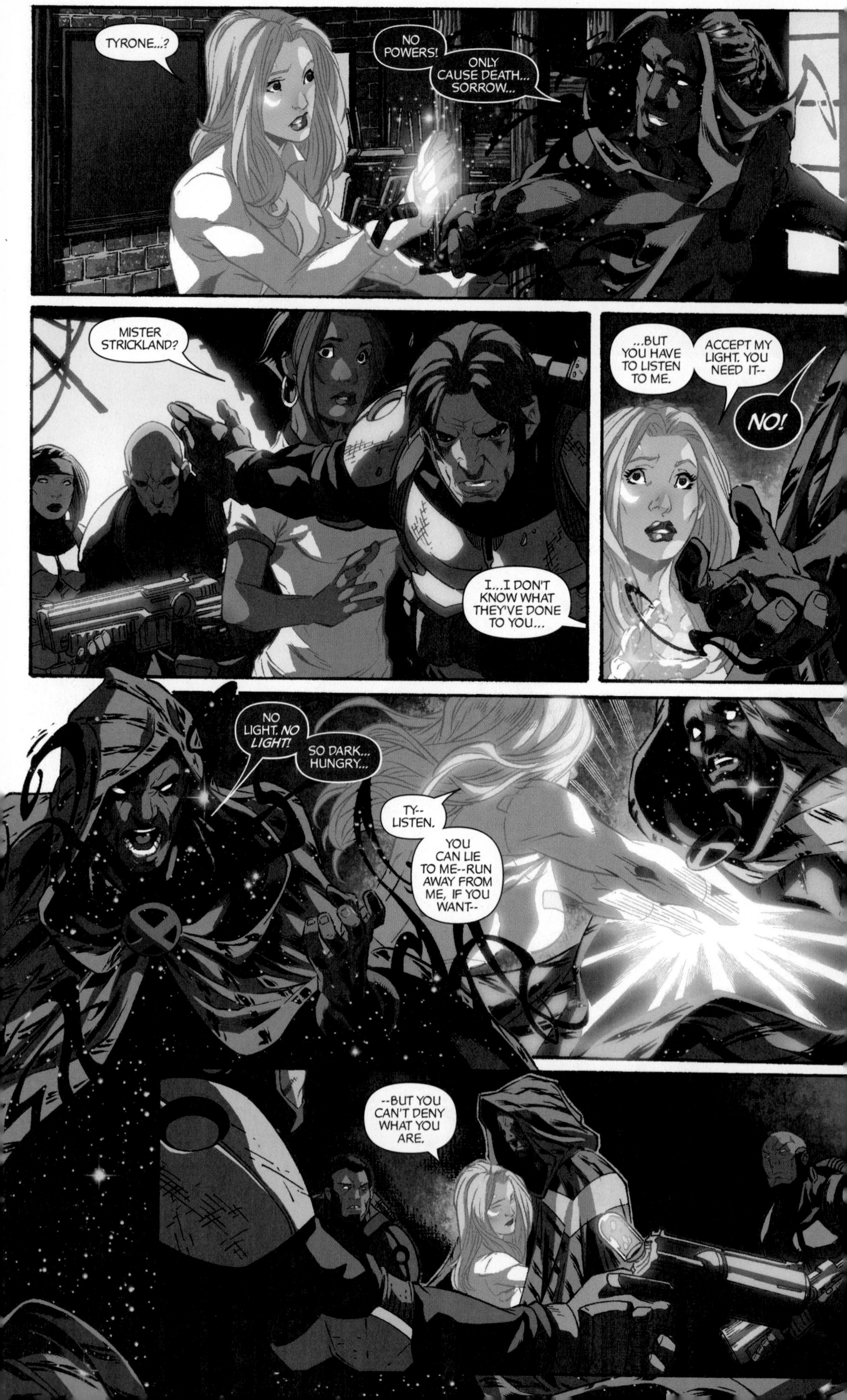
TYRONE...?
NO POWERS!
ONLY CAUSE DEATH... SORROW...
MISTER STRICKLAND?
I...I DON'T KNOW WHAT THEY'VE DONE TO YOU...
...BUT YOU HAVE TO LISTEN TO ME.
ACCEPT MY LIGHT. YOU NEED IT--
NO!
NO LIGHT. NO LIGHT!
SO DARK... HUNGRY...
TY-- LISTEN.
YOU CAN LIE TO ME--RUN AWAY FROM ME, IF YOU WANT--
--BUT YOU CAN'T DENY WHAT YOU ARE.

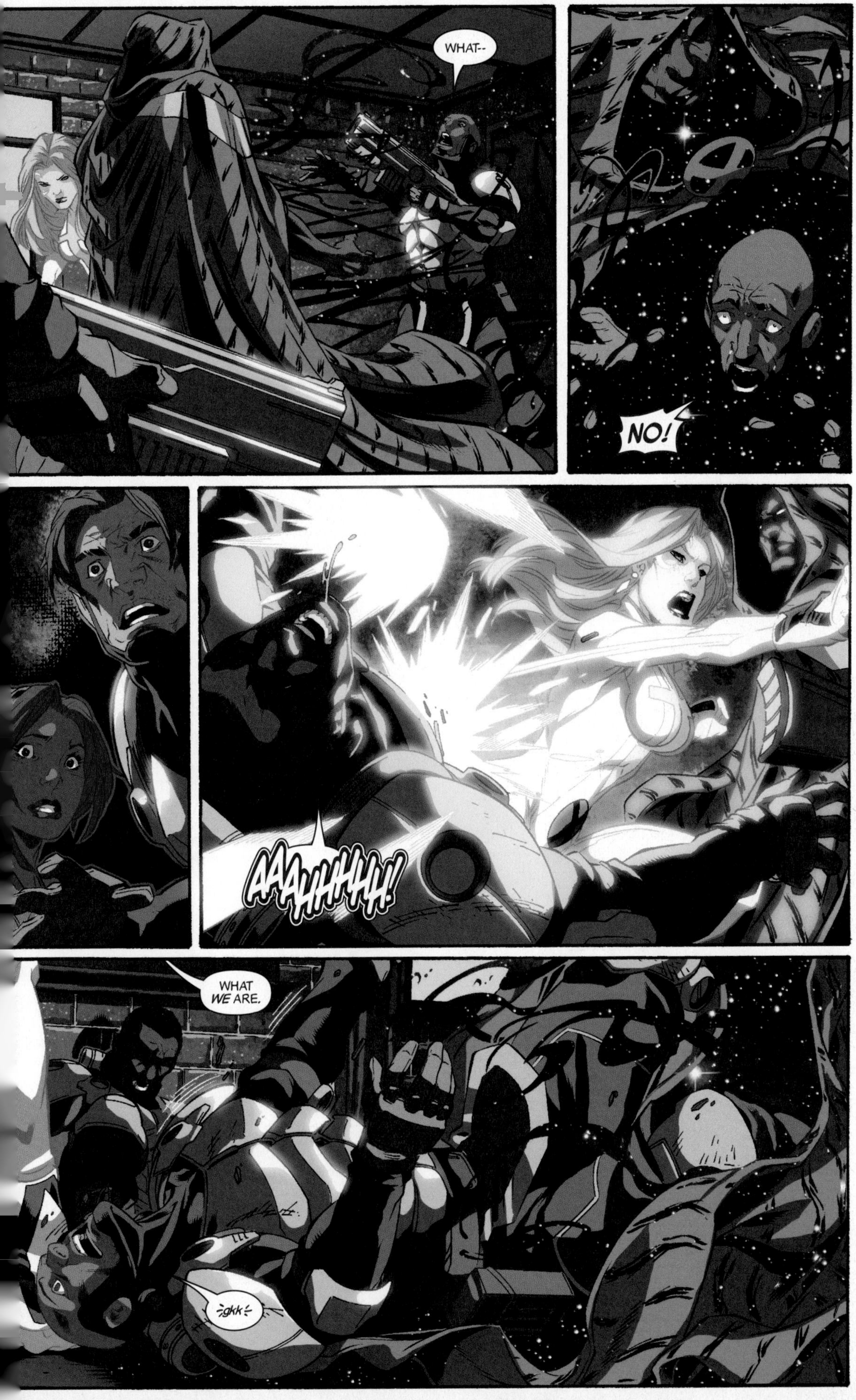
WHAT--
NO!
AAAHHHHH!
WHAT WE ARE.
gkk

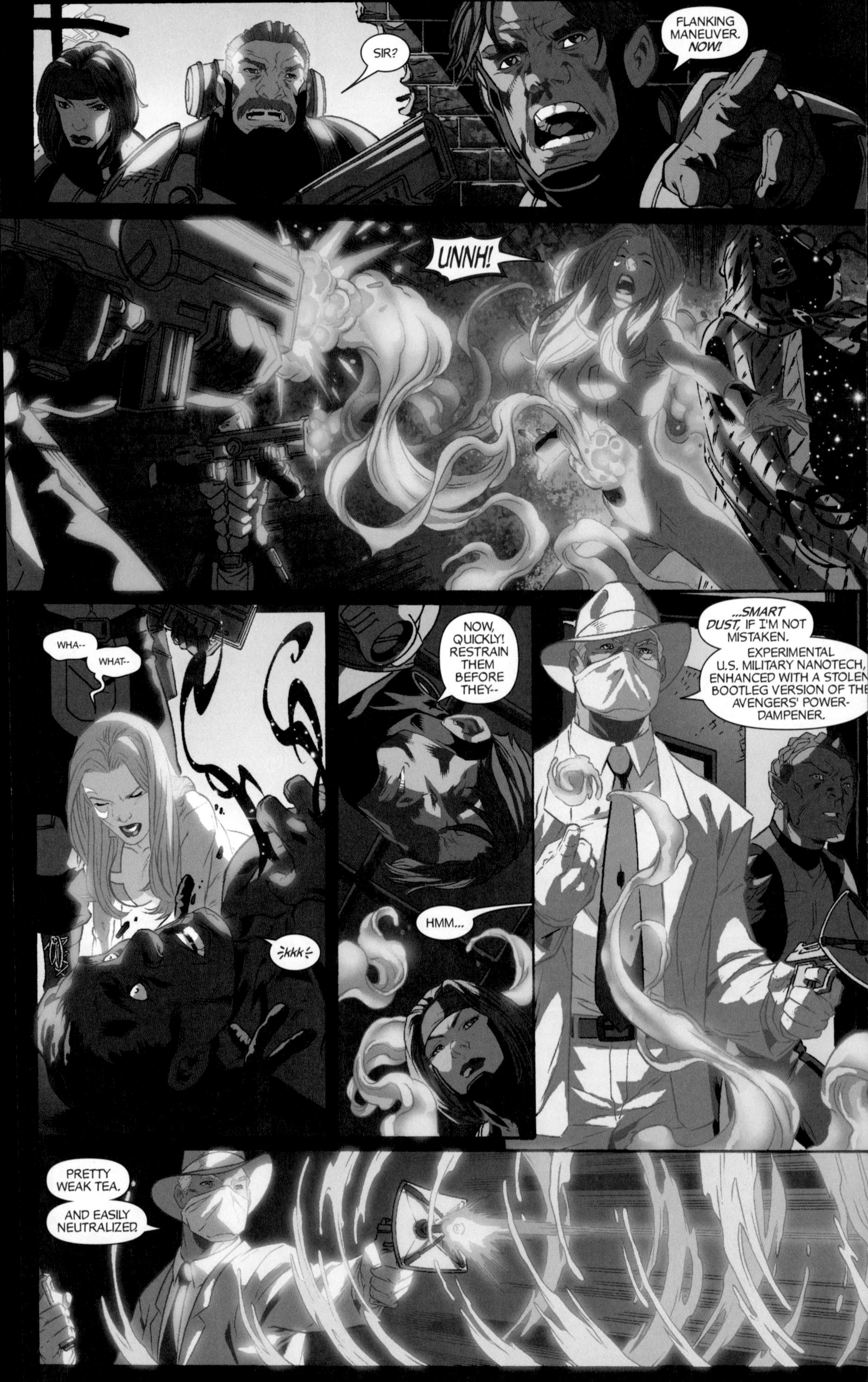
SIR?
FLANKING MANEUVER. NOW!
UNNH!
WHA--
WHAT--
KKK
NOW, QUICKLY! RESTRAIN THEM BEFORE THEY--
HMM...
...SMART DUST, IF I'M NOT MISTAKEN.
EXPERIMENTAL U.S. MILITARY NANOTECH, ENHANCED WITH A STOLEN BOOTLEG VERSION OF THE AVENGERS' POWER-DAMPENER.
PRETTY WEAK TEA.
AND EASILY NEUTRALIZED.

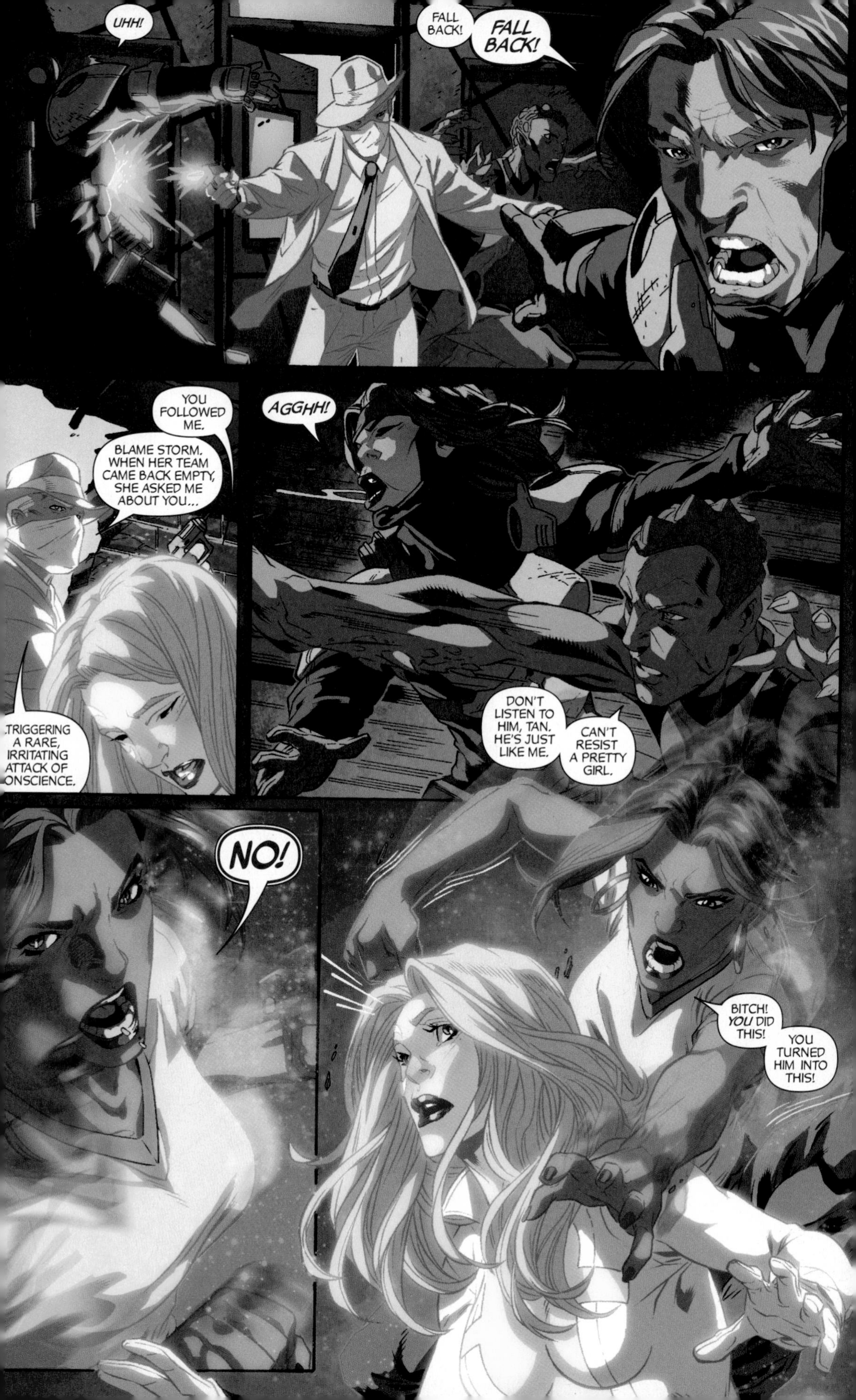
UHH!
FALL BACK!
FALL BACK!
YOU FOLLOWED ME.
BLAME STORM. WHEN HER TEAM CAME BACK EMPTY, SHE ASKED ME ABOUT YOU...
...TRIGGERING A RARE, IRRITATING ATTACK OF ...ONSCIENCE.
AGGHH!
DON'T LISTEN TO HIM, TAN. HE'S JUST LIKE ME.
CAN'T RESIST A PRETTY GIRL.
NO!
BITCH! YOU DID THIS!
YOU TURNED HIM INTO THIS!

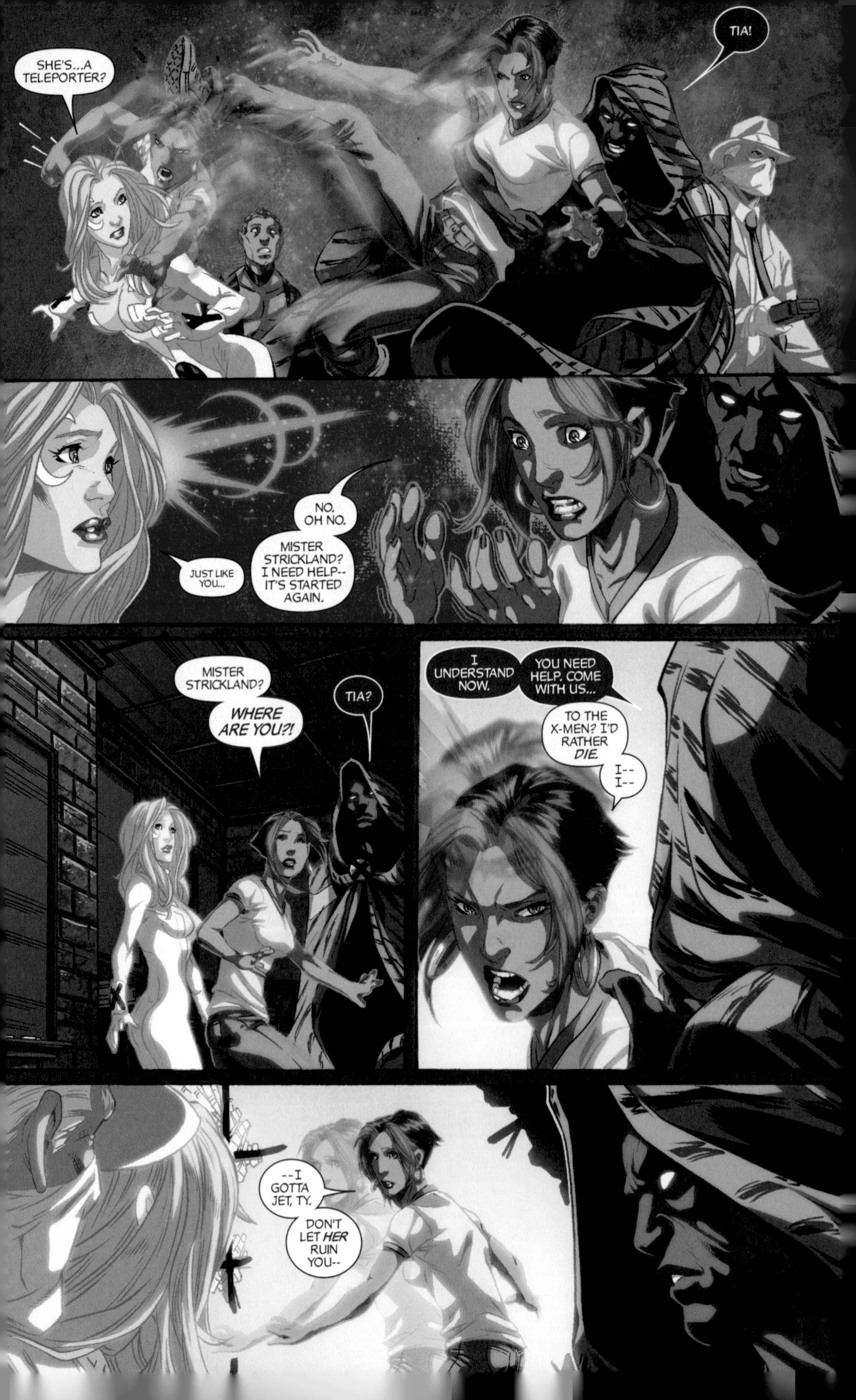
SHE'S...A TELEPORTER?
TIA!
NO. OH NO.
MISTER STRICKLAND? I NEED HELP-- IT'S STARTED AGAIN.
JUST LIKE YOU...
MISTER STRICKLAND?
WHERE ARE YOU?!
TIA?
I UNDERSTAND NOW.
YOU NEED HELP. COME WITH US...
TO THE X-MEN? I'D RATHER *DIE.*
I-- I--
--I GOTTA JET, TY.
DON'T LET *HER* RUIN YOU--

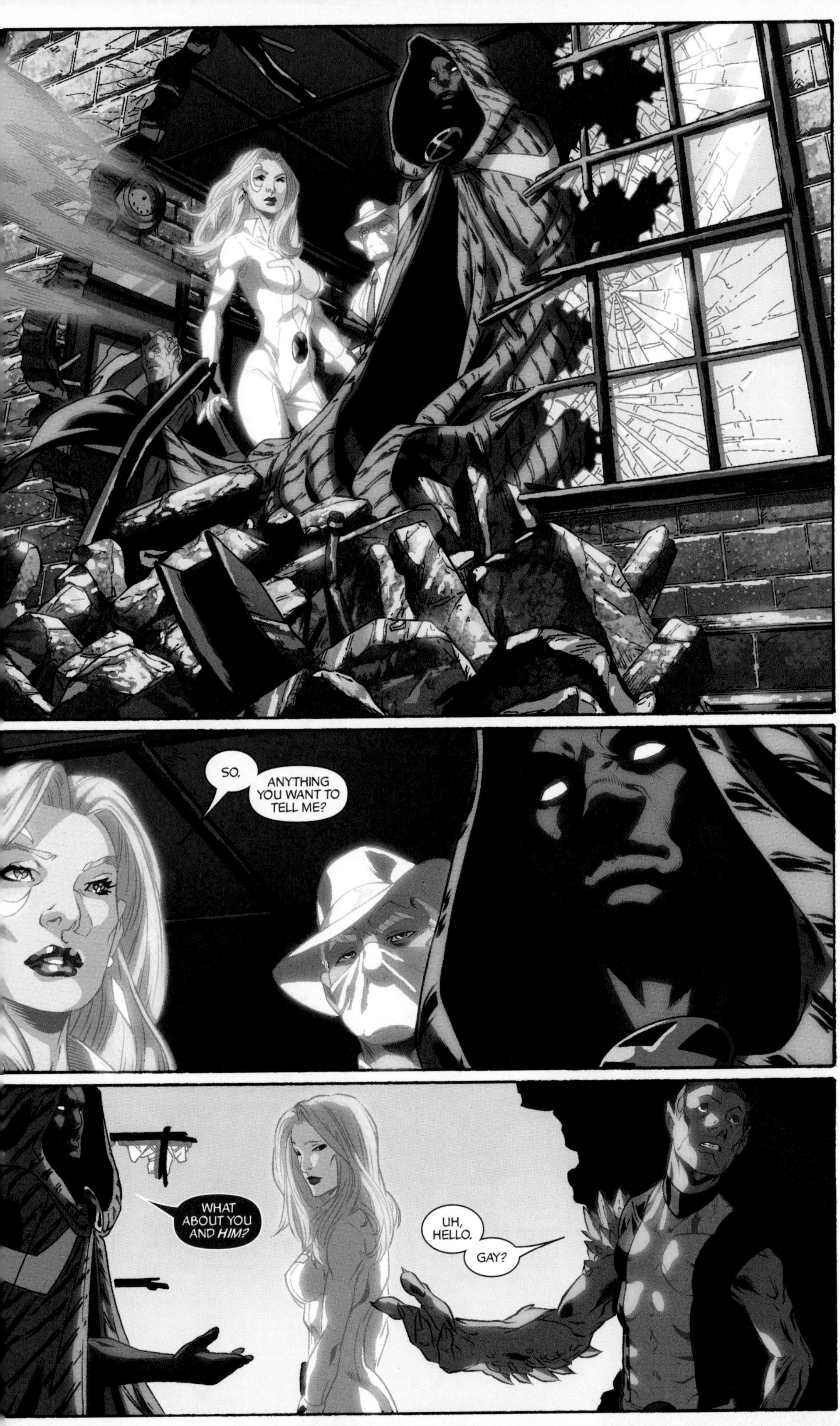
SO.
ANYTHING YOU WANT TO TELL ME?
WHAT ABOUT YOU AND *HIM?*
UH, HELLO.
GAY?

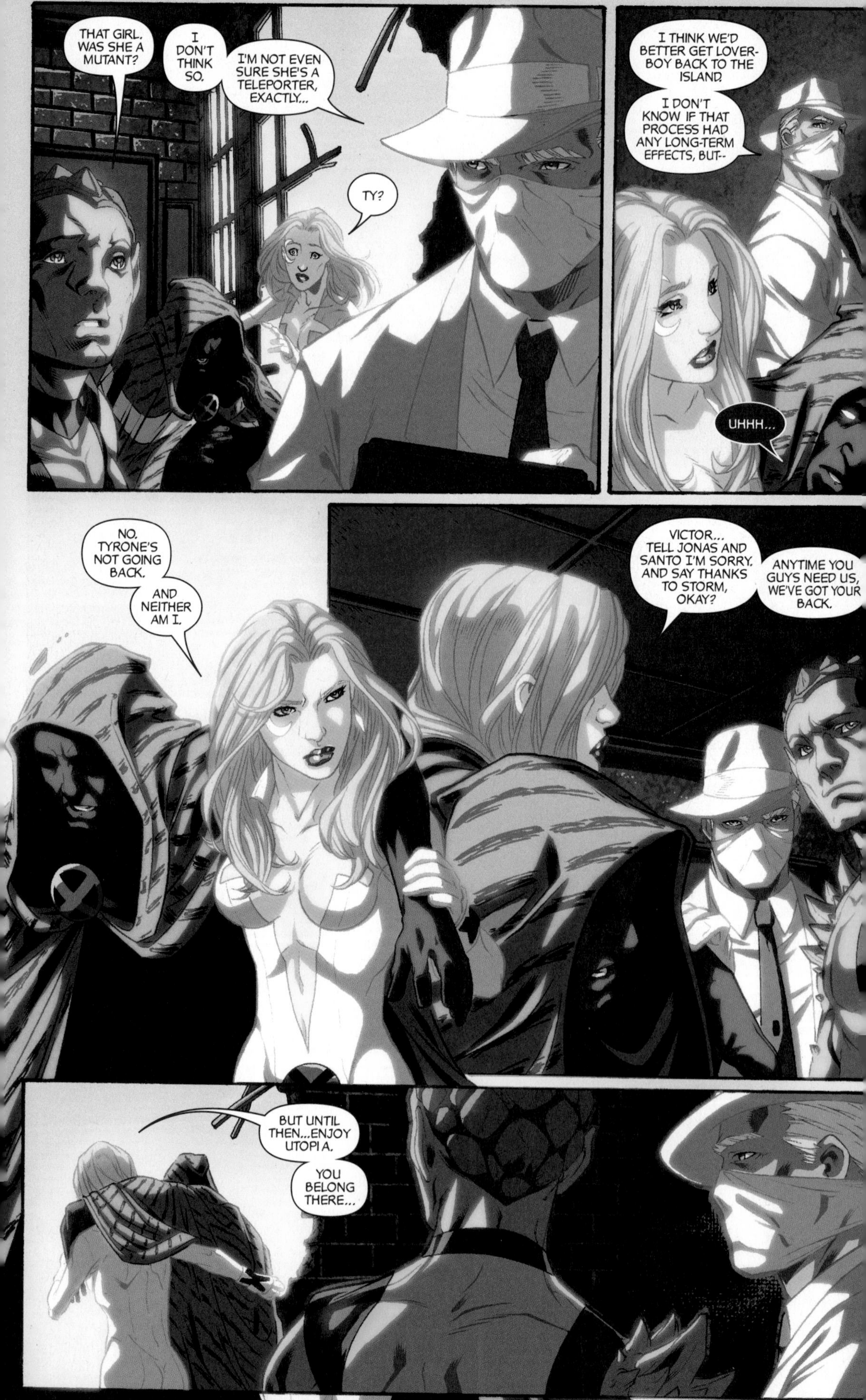
THAT GIRL. WAS SHE A MUTANT?
I DON'T THINK SO.
I'M NOT EVEN SURE SHE'S A TELEPORTER, EXACTLY...
TY?
I THINK WE'D BETTER GET LOVER-BOY BACK TO THE ISLAND.
I DON'T KNOW IF THAT PROCESS HAD ANY LONG-TERM EFFECTS, BUT--
UHHH...
NO. TYRONE'S NOT GOING BACK.
AND NEITHER AM I.
VICTOR... TELL JONAS AND SANTO I'M SORRY. AND SAY THANKS TO STORM, OKAY?
ANYTIME YOU GUYS NEED US, WE'VE GOT YOUR BACK.
BUT UNTIL THEN...ENJOY UTOPIA.
YOU BELONG THERE...

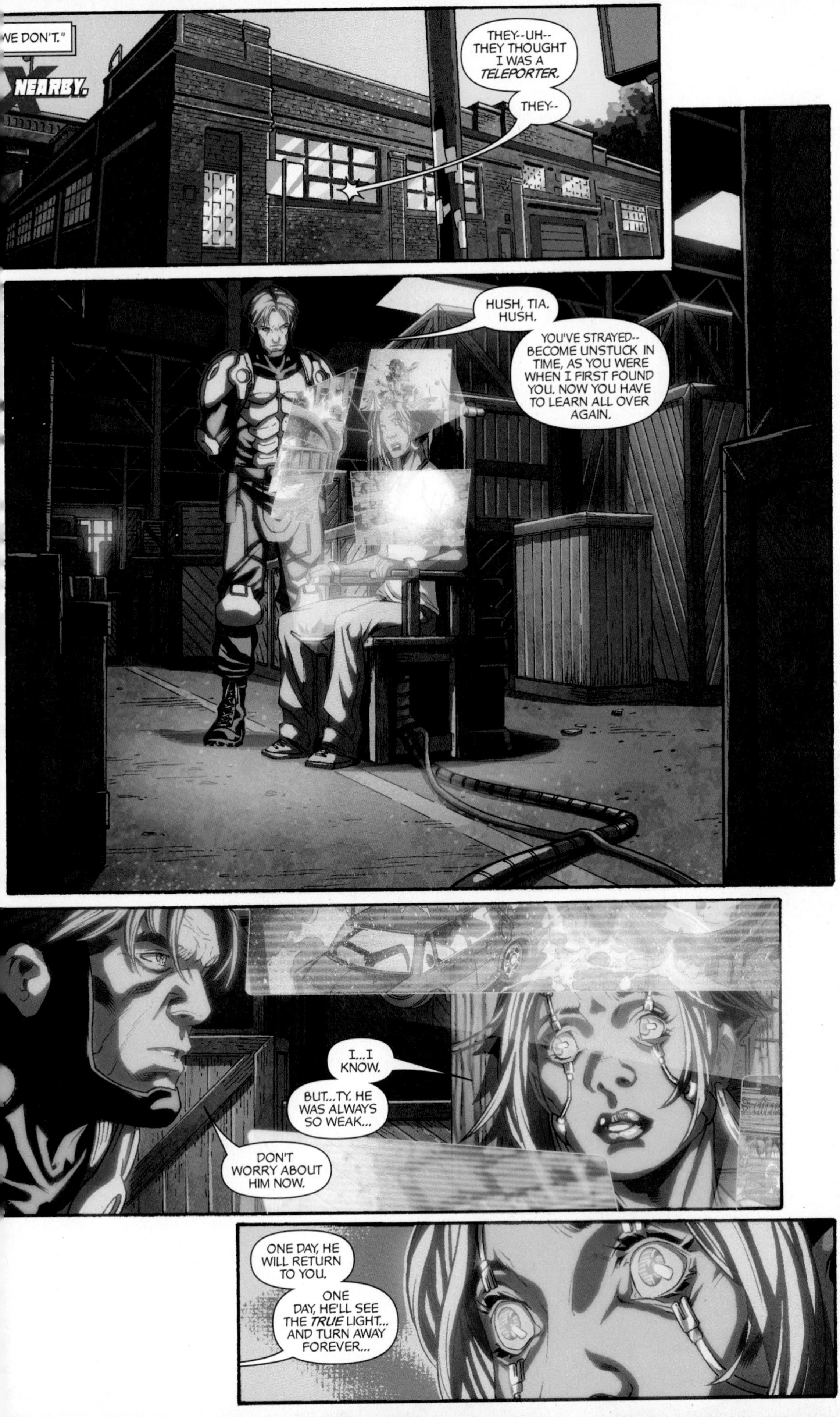
WE DON'T."
NEARBY.
THEY--UH-- THEY THOUGHT I WAS A *TELEPORTER.*
THEY--
HUSH, TIA. HUSH.
YOU'VE STRAYED-- BECOME UNSTUCK IN TIME, AS YOU WERE WHEN I FIRST FOUND YOU. NOW YOU HAVE TO LEARN ALL OVER AGAIN.
I...I KNOW.
BUT...TY. HE WAS ALWAYS SO WEAK...
DON'T WORRY ABOUT HIM NOW.
ONE DAY, HE WILL RETURN TO YOU.
ONE DAY, HE'LL SEE THE *TRUE* LIGHT... AND TURN AWAY FOREVER...

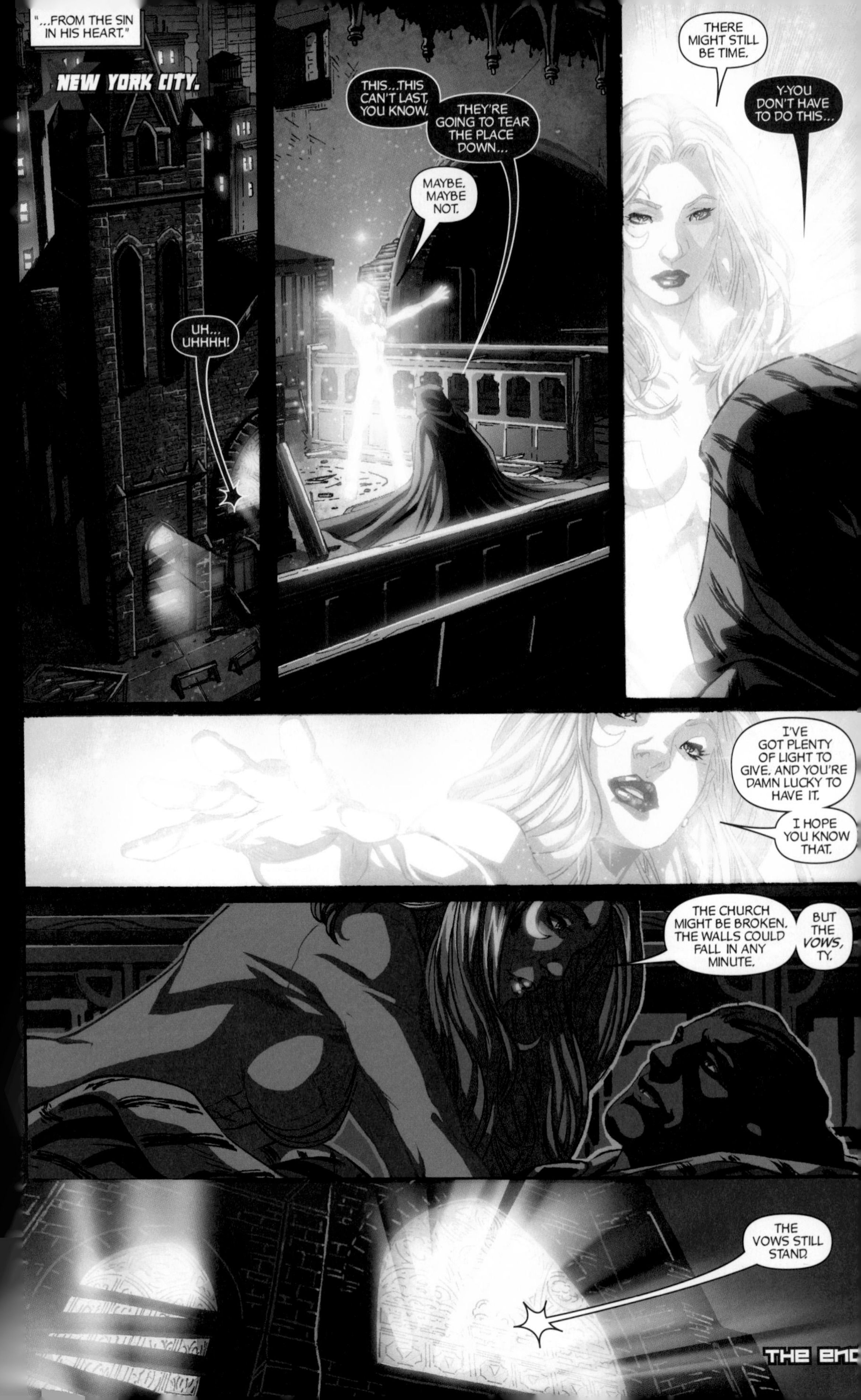
"...FROM THE SIN IN HIS HEART."
NEW YORK CITY.
UH... UHHHH!
THIS...THIS CAN'T LAST, YOU KNOW.
THEY'RE GOING TO TEAR THE PLACE DOWN...
MAYBE. MAYBE NOT.
THERE MIGHT STILL BE TIME.
Y-YOU DON'T HAVE TO DO THIS...
I'VE GOT PLENTY OF LIGHT TO GIVE. AND YOU'RE DAMN LUCKY TO HAVE IT.
I HOPE YOU KNOW THAT.
THE CHURCH MIGHT BE BROKEN. THE WALLS COULD FALL IN ANY MINUTE.
BUT THE *VOWS*, TY.
THE VOWS STILL STAND.
THE END

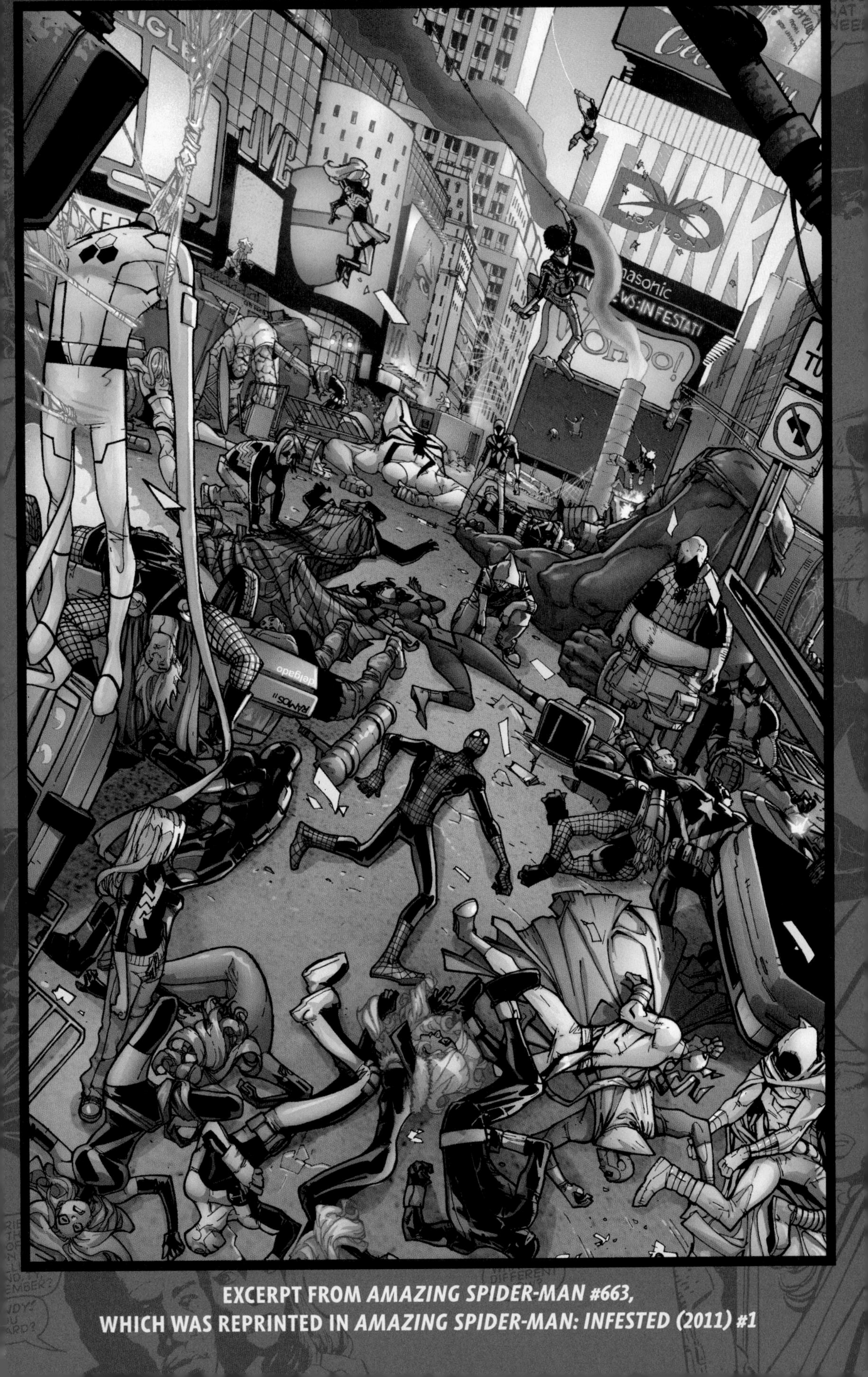
JVC
delgado
RAMOS

EXCERPT FROM *AMAZING SPIDER-MAN* #663,
WHICH WAS REPRINTED IN *AMAZING SPIDER-MAN: INFESTED* (2011) #1

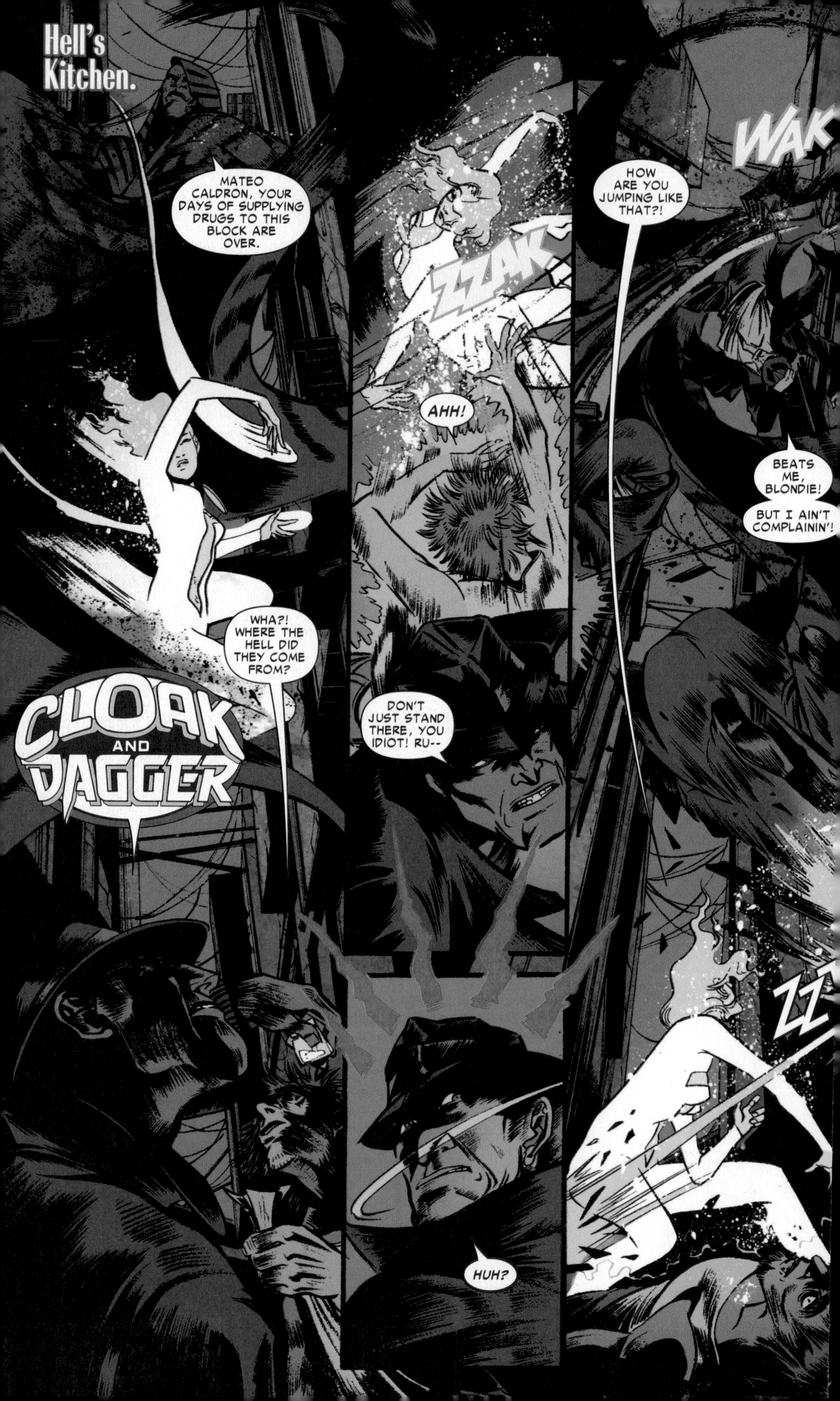
Hell's Kitchen.
MATEO CALDRON, YOUR DAYS OF SUPPLYING DRUGS TO THIS BLOCK ARE OVER.
WHA?! WHERE THE HELL DID THEY COME FROM?
CLOAK AND DAGGER
ZZAK
AHH!
DON'T JUST STAND THERE, YOU IDIOT! RU--
HUH?
WAK
HOW ARE YOU JUMPING LIKE THAT?!
BEATS ME, BLONDIE!
BUT I AIN'T COMPLAININ'!

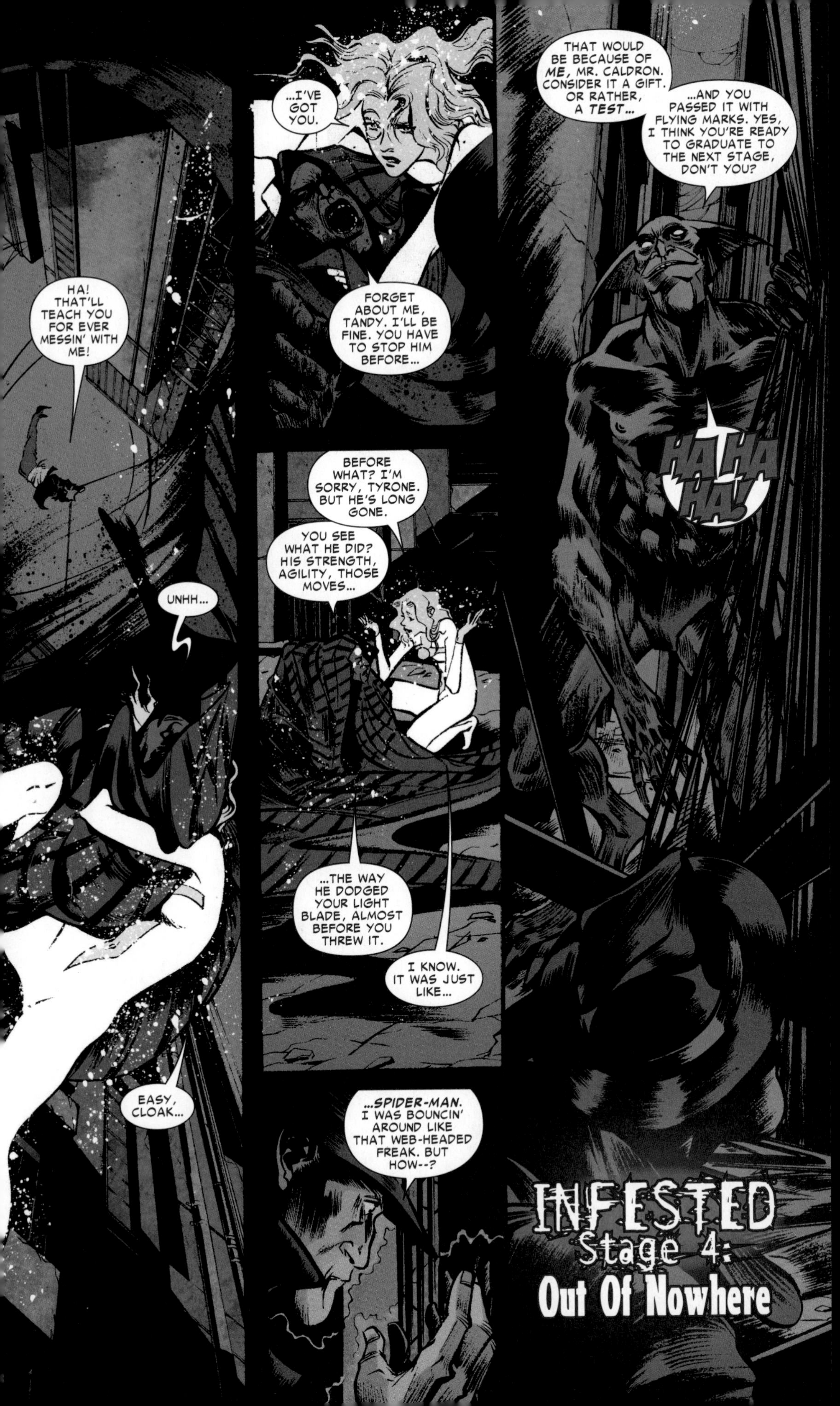
HA! THAT'LL TEACH YOU FOR EVER MESSIN' WITH ME!
UNHH...
EASY, CLOAK...
...I'VE GOT YOU.
FORGET ABOUT ME, TANDY. I'LL BE FINE. YOU HAVE TO STOP HIM BEFORE...
BEFORE WHAT? I'M SORRY, TYRONE. BUT HE'S LONG GONE.
YOU SEE WHAT HE DID? HIS STRENGTH, AGILITY, THOSE MOVES...
...THE WAY HE DODGED YOUR LIGHT BLADE, ALMOST BEFORE YOU THREW IT.
I KNOW. IT WAS JUST LIKE...
...SPIDER-MAN. I WAS BOUNCIN' AROUND LIKE THAT WEB-HEADED FREAK. BUT HOW--?
THAT WOULD BE BECAUSE OF ME, MR. CALDRON. CONSIDER IT A GIFT. OR RATHER, A TEST...
...AND YOU PASSED IT WITH FLYING MARKS. YES, I THINK YOU'RE READY TO GRADUATE TO THE NEXT STAGE, DON'T YOU?
HA HA HA!
INFESTED
Stage 4:
Out Of Nowhere

PREVIOUSLY IN "SPIDER-ISLAND": MANHATTAN IS INFESTED. THE VILLAINOUS JACKAL HAS GENETICALLY ENGINEERED BEDBUGS TO SPREAD SPIDEY-POWERS WITH THEIR BITE. BUT NOT EVERYONE WITH GREAT POWER HAS THE SAME GREAT RESPONSIBILITY AS SPIDER-MAN, AND MANHATTAN IS QUICKLY OVERRUN WITH SPIDER-POWERED, JOYRIDING BULLIES AND THUGS. NOW THE SUPER HEROES OF NEW YORK HAVE COME TOGETHER TO COMBAT THE RIOTS...

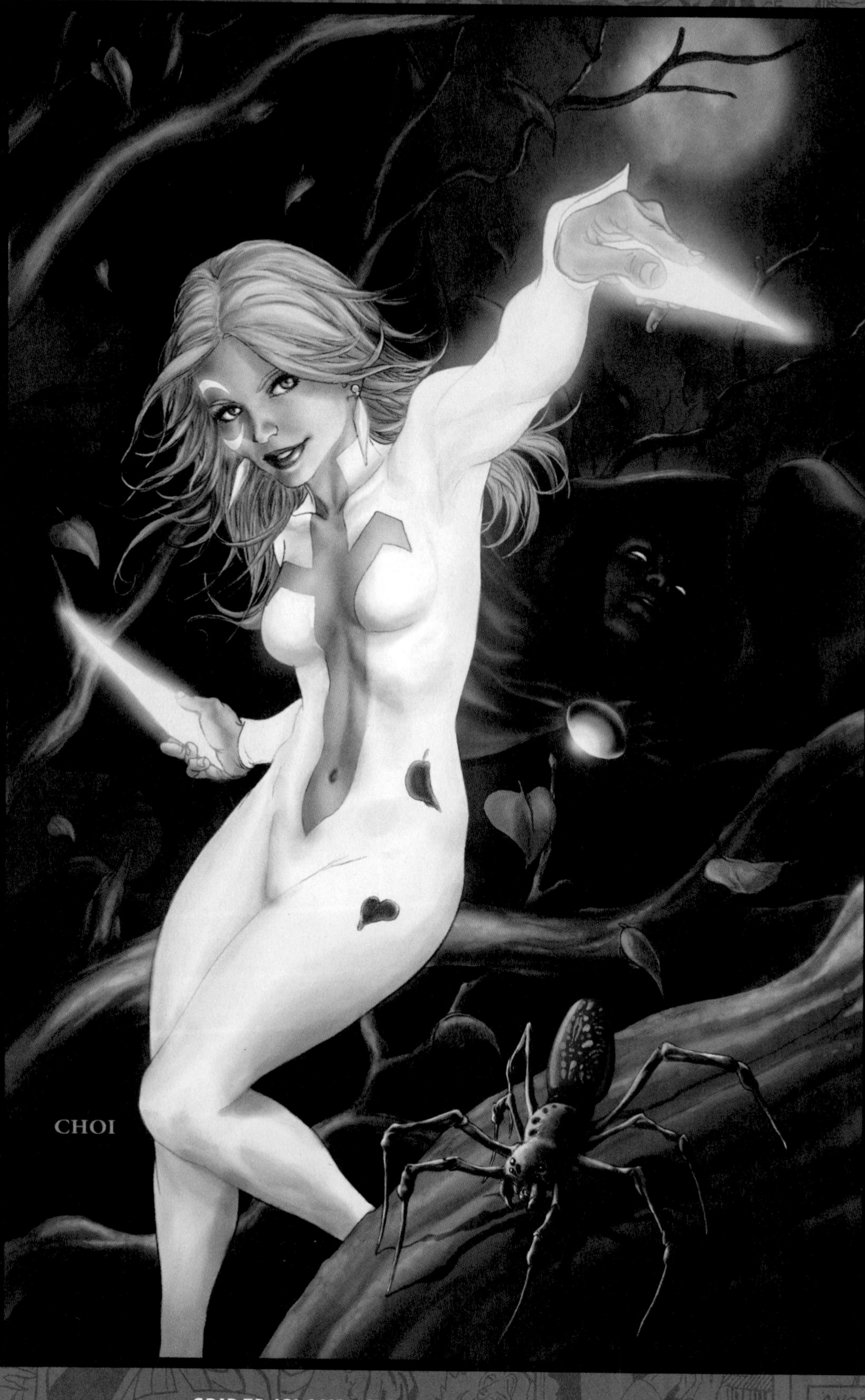
CHOI

SPIDER-ISLAND: CLOAK AND DAGGER (2011) #1

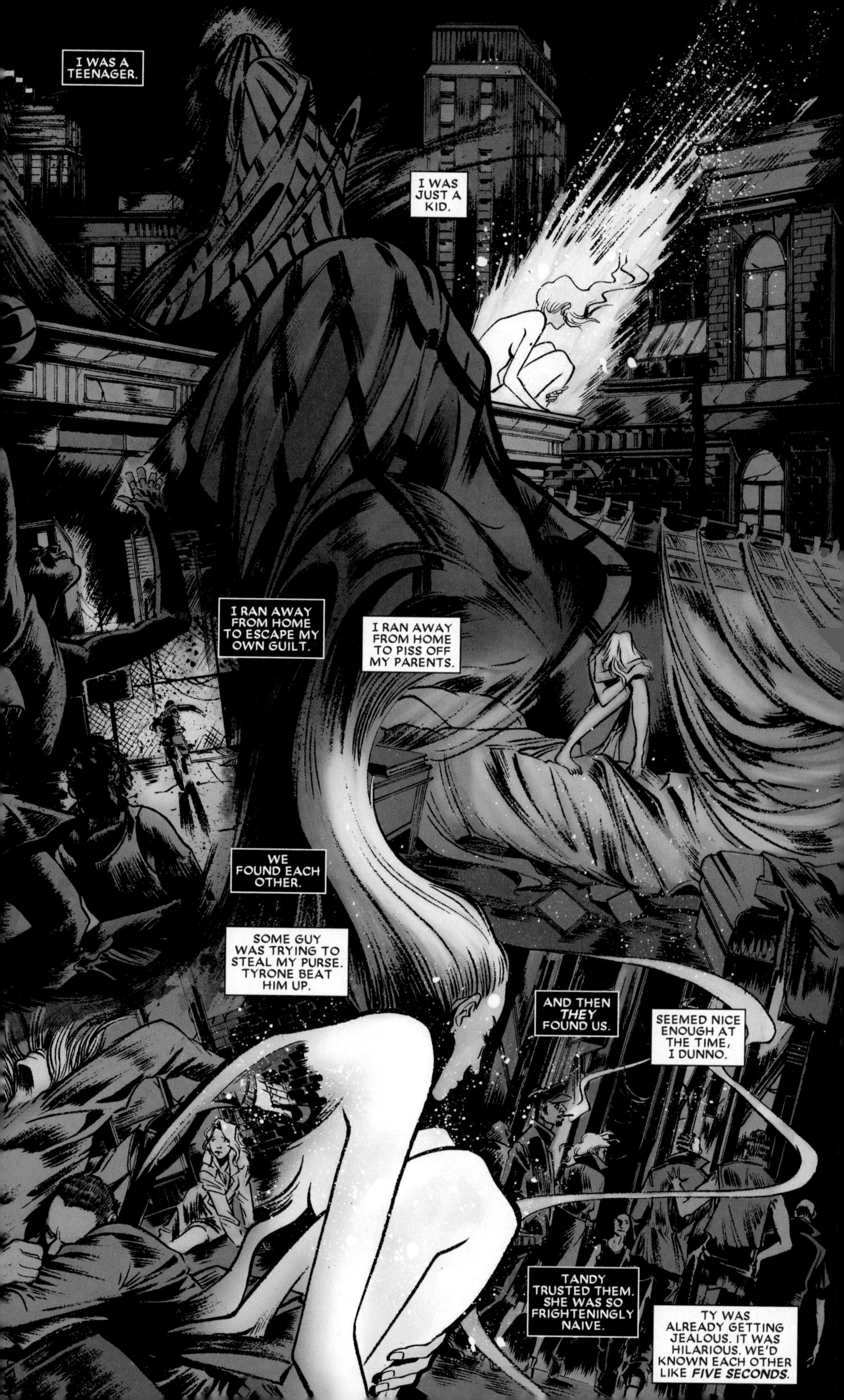
I WAS A TEENAGER.
I WAS JUST A KID.
I RAN AWAY FROM HOME TO ESCAPE MY OWN GUILT.
I RAN AWAY FROM HOME TO PISS OFF MY PARENTS.
WE FOUND EACH OTHER.
SOME GUY WAS TRYING TO STEAL MY PURSE. TYRONE BEAT HIM UP.
AND THEN *THEY* FOUND US.
SEEMED NICE ENOUGH AT THE TIME, I DUNNO.
TANDY TRUSTED THEM. SHE WAS SO FRIGHTENINGLY NAIVE.
TY WAS ALREADY GETTING JEALOUS. IT WAS HILARIOUS. WE'D KNOWN EACH OTHER LIKE *FIVE SECONDS*.

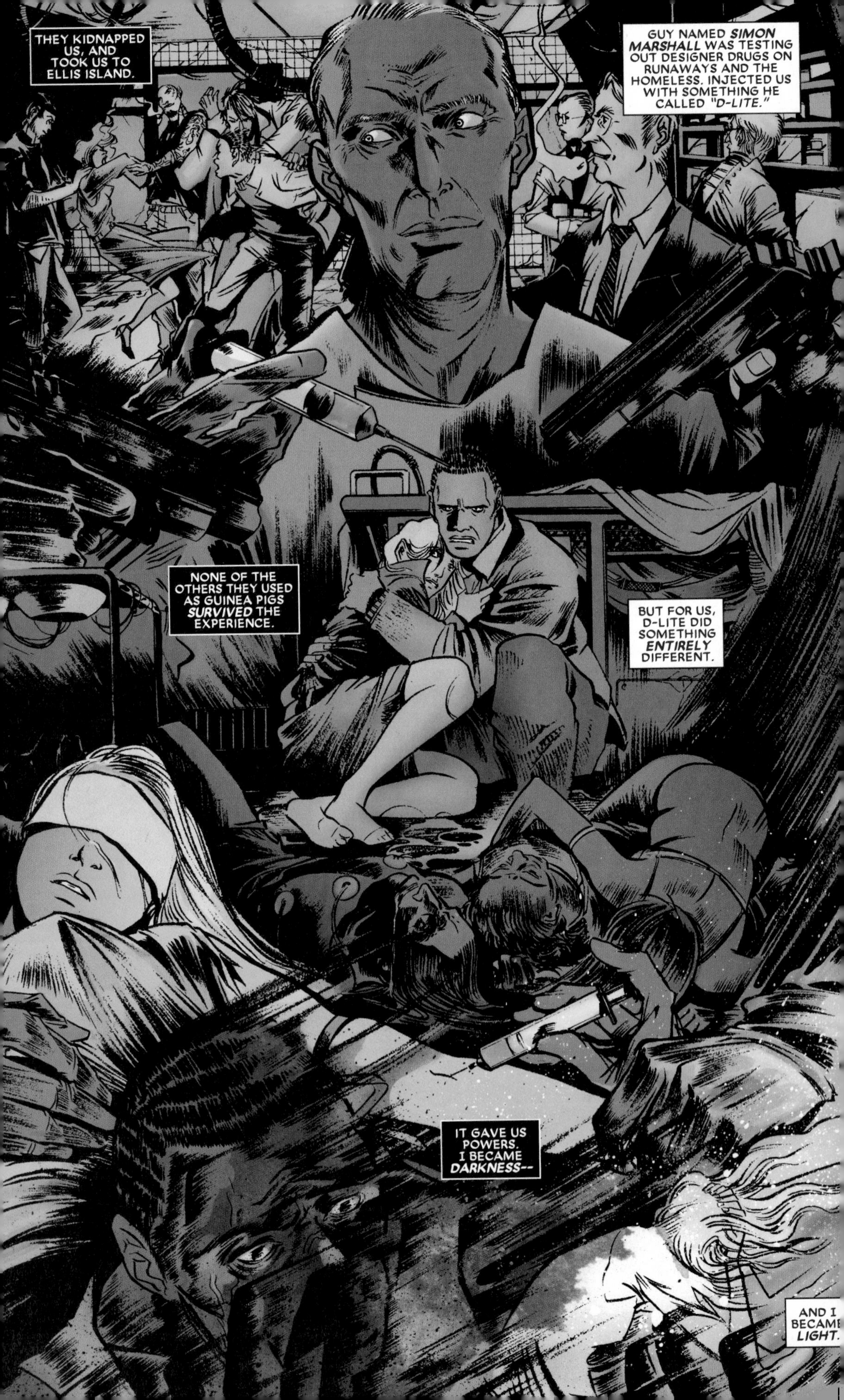
THEY KIDNAPPED US, AND TOOK US TO ELLIS ISLAND.
GUY NAMED *SIMON MARSHALL* WAS TESTING OUT DESIGNER DRUGS ON RUNAWAYS AND THE HOMELESS. INJECTED US WITH SOMETHING HE CALLED *"D-LITE."*
NONE OF THE OTHERS THEY USED AS GUINEA PIGS *SURVIVED* THE EXPERIENCE.
BUT FOR US, D-LITE DID SOMETHING *ENTIRELY* DIFFERENT.
IT GAVE US POWERS. I BECAME *DARKNESS--*
AND I BECAME *LIGHT.*

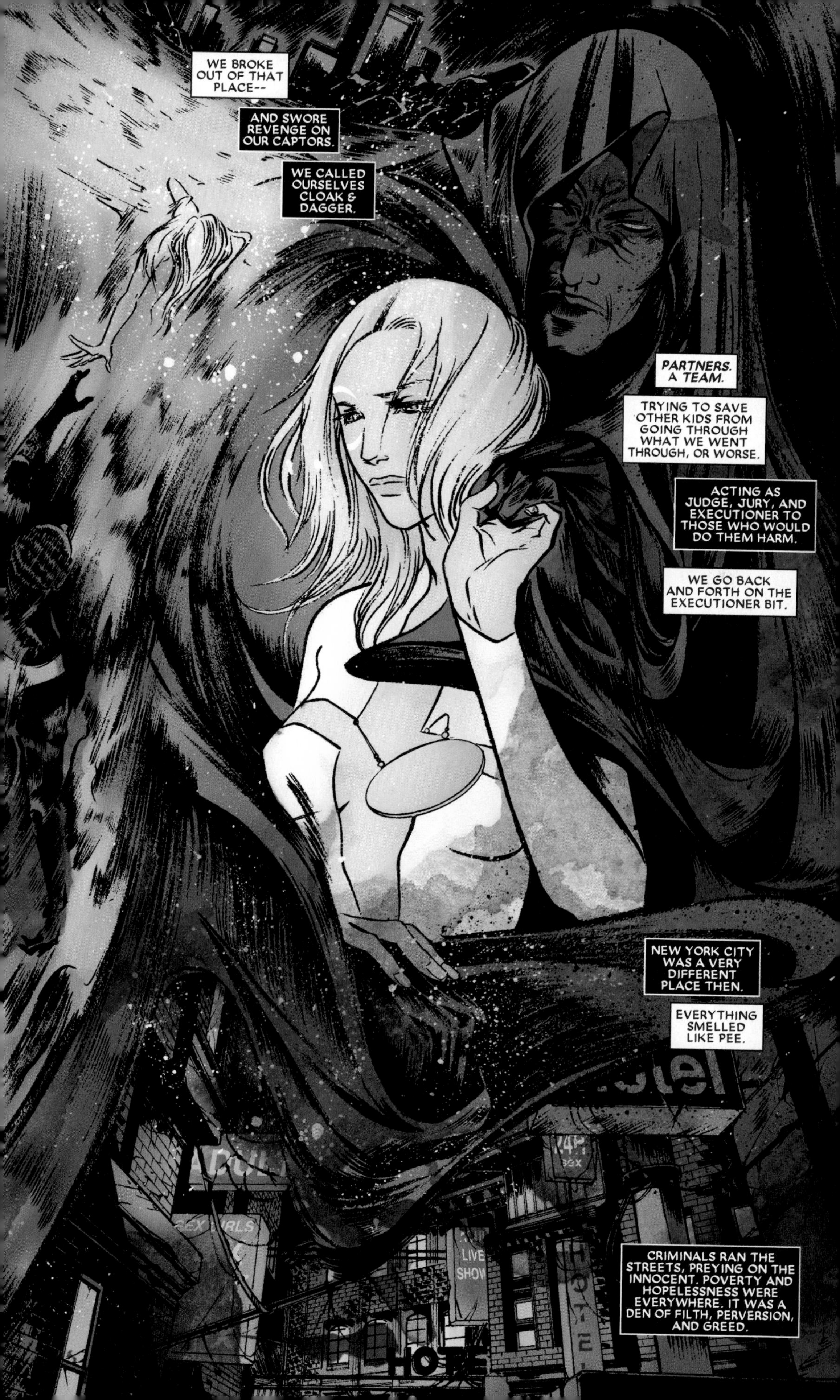
WE BROKE OUT OF THAT PLACE--
AND SWORE REVENGE ON OUR CAPTORS.
WE CALLED OURSELVES CLOAK & DAGGER.
PARTNERS. A *TEAM.*
TRYING TO SAVE OTHER KIDS FROM GOING THROUGH WHAT WE WENT THROUGH, OR WORSE.
ACTING AS JUDGE, JURY, AND EXECUTIONER TO THOSE WHO WOULD DO THEM HARM.
WE GO BACK AND FORTH ON THE EXECUTIONER BIT.
NEW YORK CITY WAS A VERY DIFFERENT PLACE THEN.
EVERYTHING SMELLED LIKE PEE.
SEX GIRLS
LIVE SHOW
CRIMINALS RAN THE STREETS, PREYING ON THE INNOCENT. POVERTY AND HOPELESSNESS WERE EVERYWHERE. IT WAS A DEN OF FILTH, PERVERSION, AND GREED.

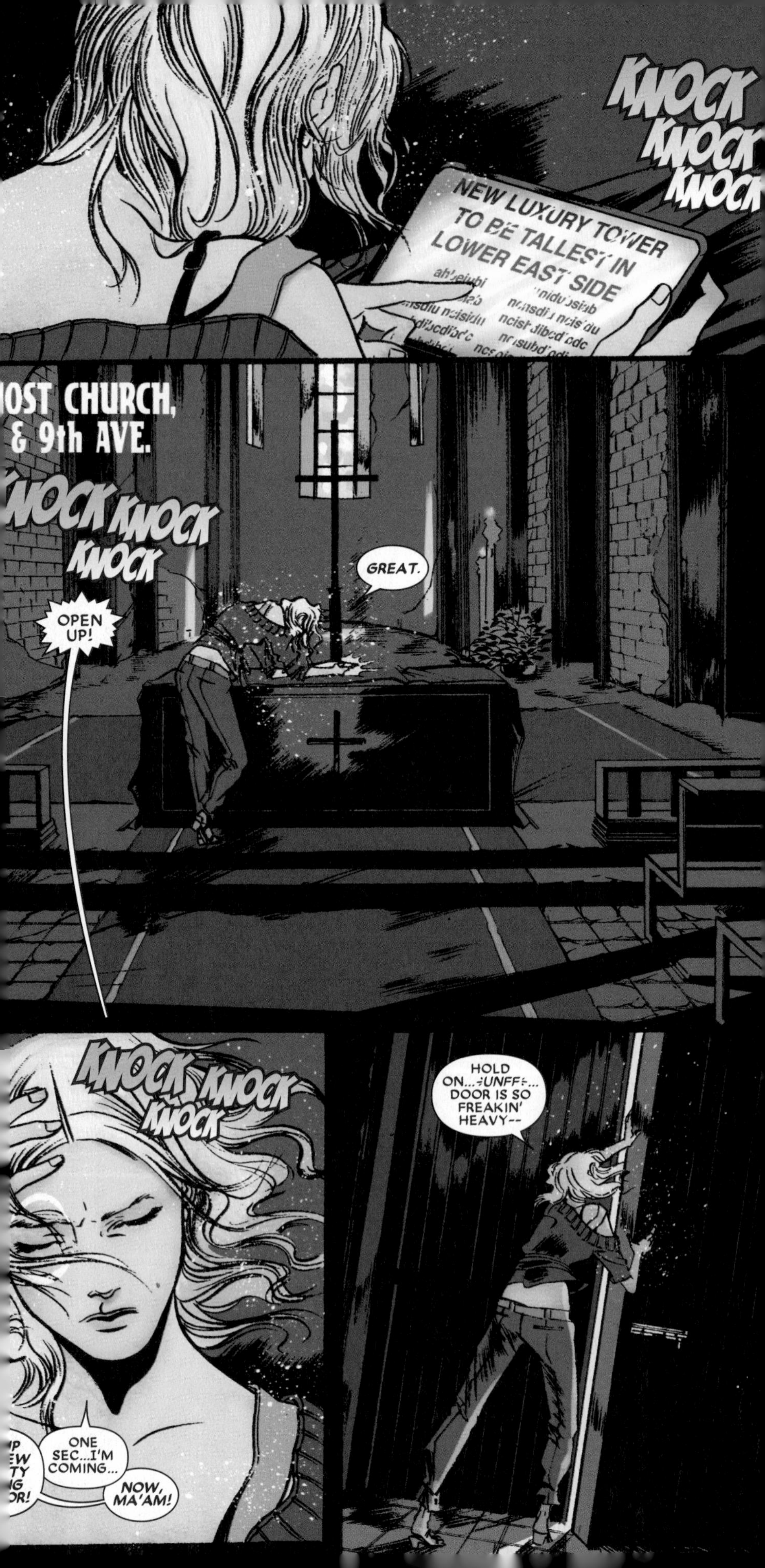
KNOCK KNOCK KNOCK
NEW LUXURY TOWER TO BE TALLEST IN LOWER EAST SIDE
OST CHURCH, & 9th AVE.
KNOCK KNOCK KNOCK
OPEN UP!
GREAT.
KNOCK KNOCK KNOCK
ONE SEC...I'M COMING...
NOW, MA'AM!
HOLD ON... *UNFF*... DOOR IS SO FREAKIN' HEAVY--

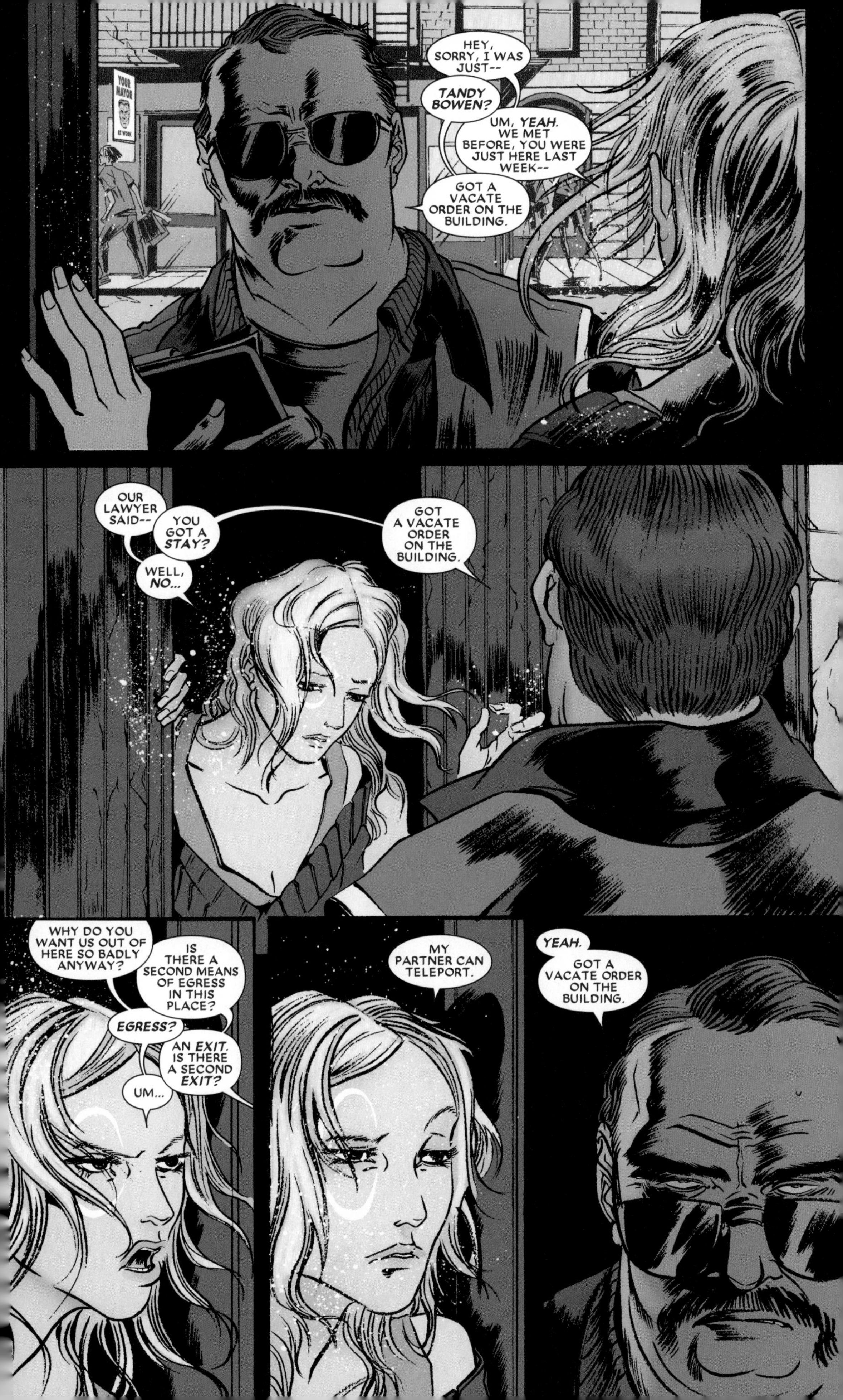
YOUR MAYOR AT WORK
HEY, SORRY, I WAS JUST--
TANDY BOWEN?
UM, YEAH. WE MET BEFORE, YOU WERE JUST HERE LAST WEEK--
GOT A VACATE ORDER ON THE BUILDING.
OUR LAWYER SAID--
YOU GOT A STAY?
WELL, NO...
GOT A VACATE ORDER ON THE BUILDING.
WHY DO YOU WANT US OUT OF HERE SO BADLY ANYWAY?
IS THERE A SECOND MEANS OF EGRESS IN THIS PLACE?
EGRESS?
AN EXIT. IS THERE A SECOND EXIT?
UM...
MY PARTNER CAN TELEPORT.
YEAH.
GOT A VACATE ORDER ON THE BUILDING.

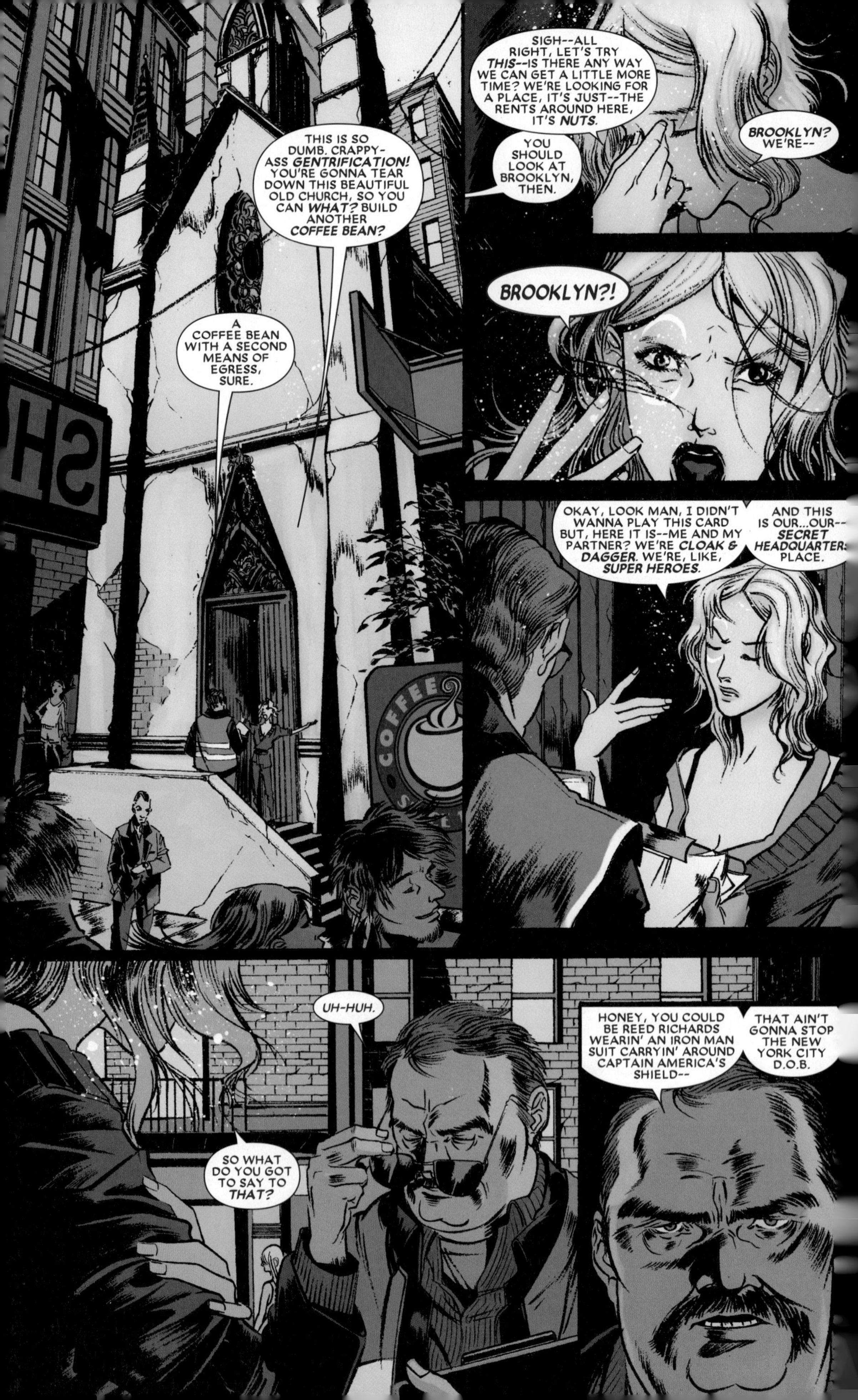
THIS IS SO DUMB. CRAPPY-ASS GENTRIFICATION! YOU'RE GONNA TEAR DOWN THIS BEAUTIFUL OLD CHURCH, SO YOU CAN WHAT? BUILD ANOTHER COFFEE BEAN?
A COFFEE BEAN WITH A SECOND MEANS OF EGRESS, SURE.
SIGH--ALL RIGHT, LET'S TRY THIS--IS THERE ANY WAY WE CAN GET A LITTLE MORE TIME? WE'RE LOOKING FOR A PLACE, IT'S JUST--THE RENTS AROUND HERE, IT'S NUTS.
YOU SHOULD LOOK AT BROOKLYN, THEN.
BROOKLYN? WE'RE--
BROOKLYN?!
OKAY, LOOK MAN, I DIDN'T WANNA PLAY THIS CARD BUT, HERE IT IS--ME AND MY PARTNER? WE'RE CLOAK & DAGGER. WE'RE, LIKE, SUPER HEROES.
AND THIS IS OUR...OUR--SECRET HEADQUARTERS PLACE.
UH-HUH.
SO WHAT DO YOU GOT TO SAY TO THAT?
HONEY, YOU COULD BE REED RICHARDS WEARIN' AN IRON MAN SUIT CARRYIN' AROUND CAPTAIN AMERICA'S SHIELD--
THAT AIN'T GONNA STOP THE NEW YORK CITY D.O.B.

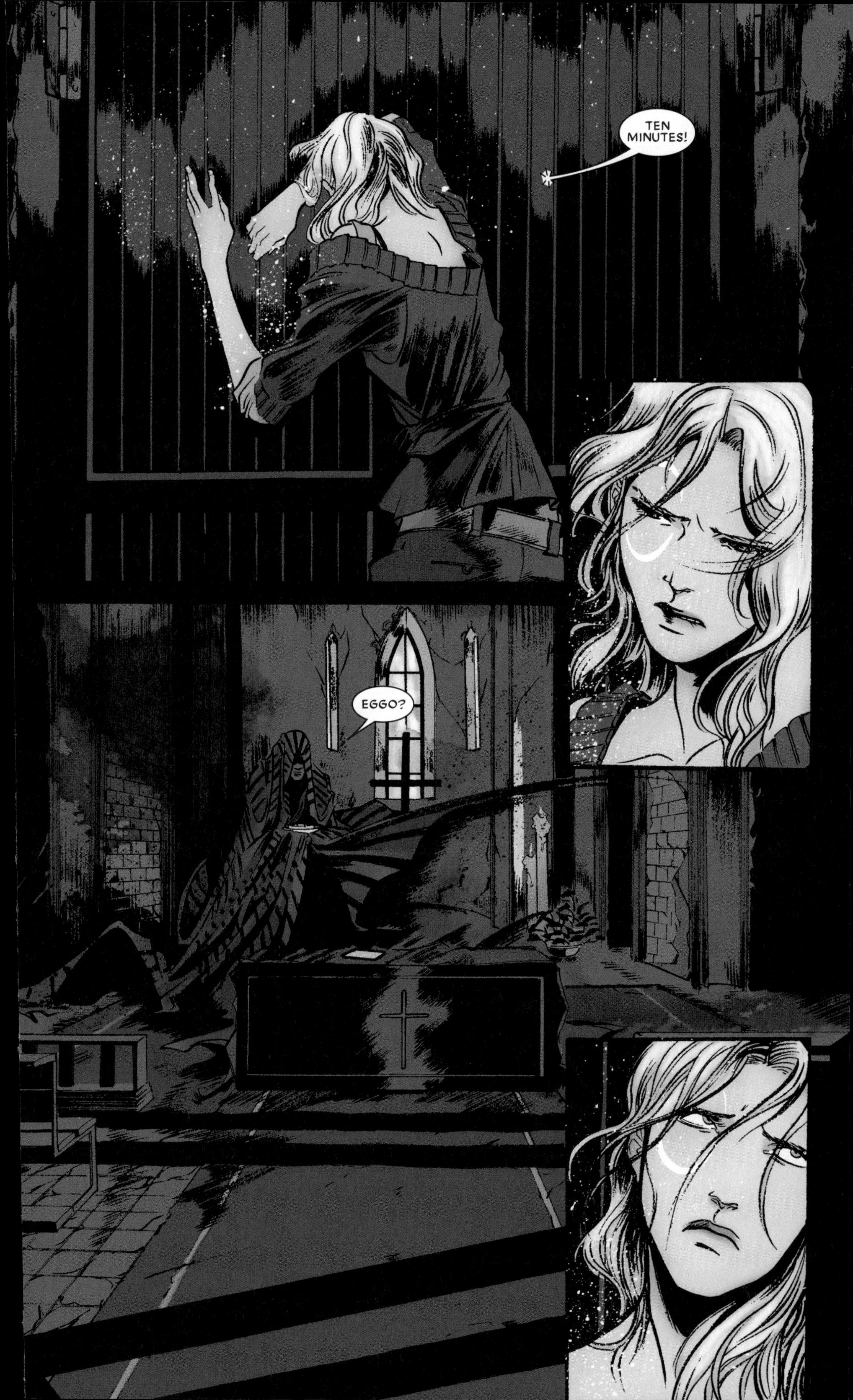
TEN MINUTES!
EGGO?

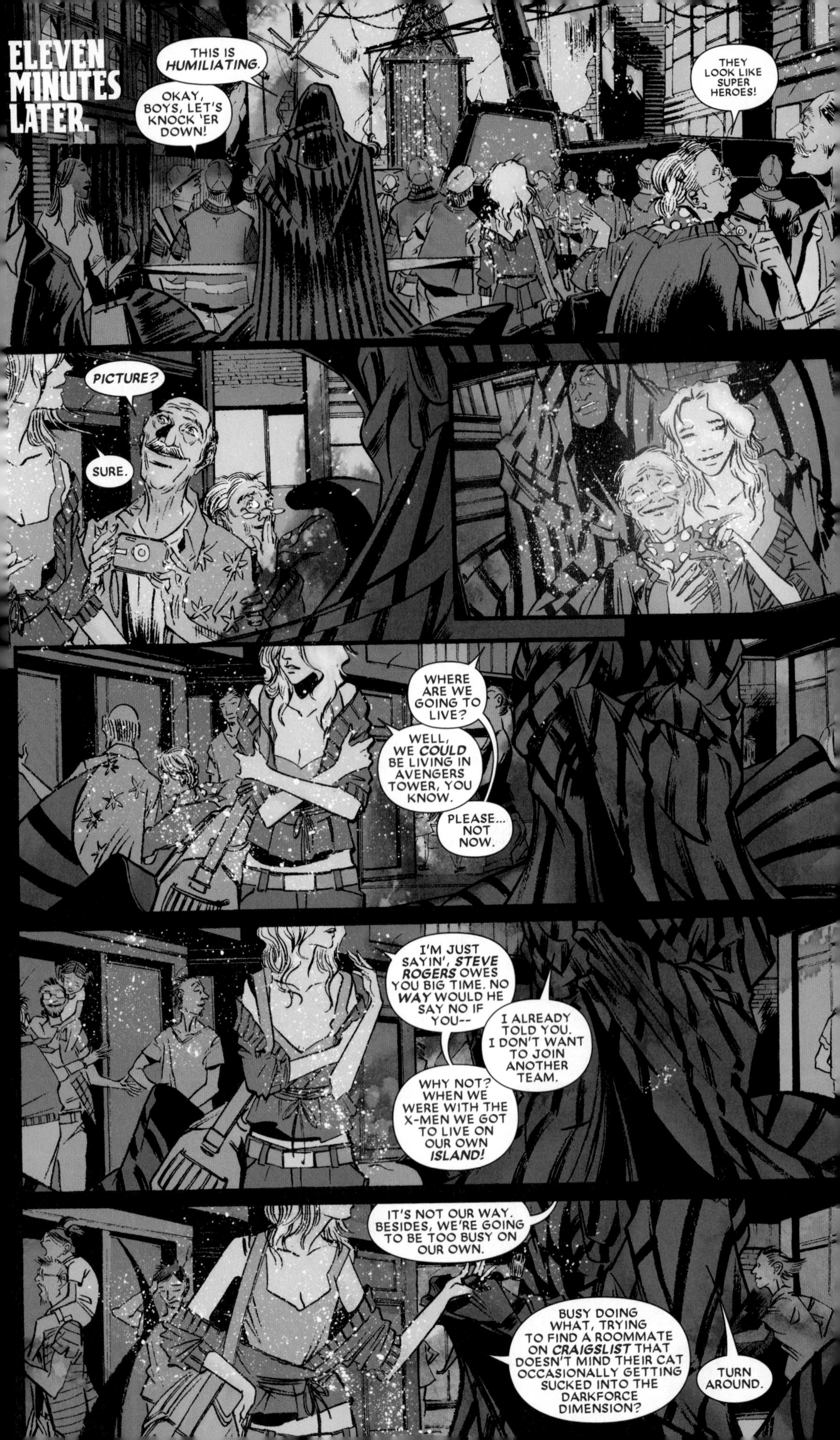
ELEVEN MINUTES LATER.
THIS IS HUMILIATING.
OKAY, BOYS, LET'S KNOCK 'ER DOWN!
THEY LOOK LIKE SUPER HEROES!
PICTURE?
SURE.
WHERE ARE WE GOING TO LIVE?
WELL, WE COULD BE LIVING IN AVENGERS TOWER, YOU KNOW.
PLEASE... NOT NOW.
I'M JUST SAYIN', STEVE ROGERS OWES YOU BIG TIME. NO WAY WOULD HE SAY NO IF YOU--
I ALREADY TOLD YOU. I DON'T WANT TO JOIN ANOTHER TEAM.
WHY NOT? WHEN WE WERE WITH THE X-MEN WE GOT TO LIVE ON OUR OWN ISLAND!
IT'S NOT OUR WAY. BESIDES, WE'RE GOING TO BE TOO BUSY ON OUR OWN.
BUSY DOING WHAT, TRYING TO FIND A ROOMMATE ON CRAIGSLIST THAT DOESN'T MIND THEIR CAT OCCASIONALLY GETTING SUCKED INTO THE DARKFORCE DIMENSION?
TURN AROUND.

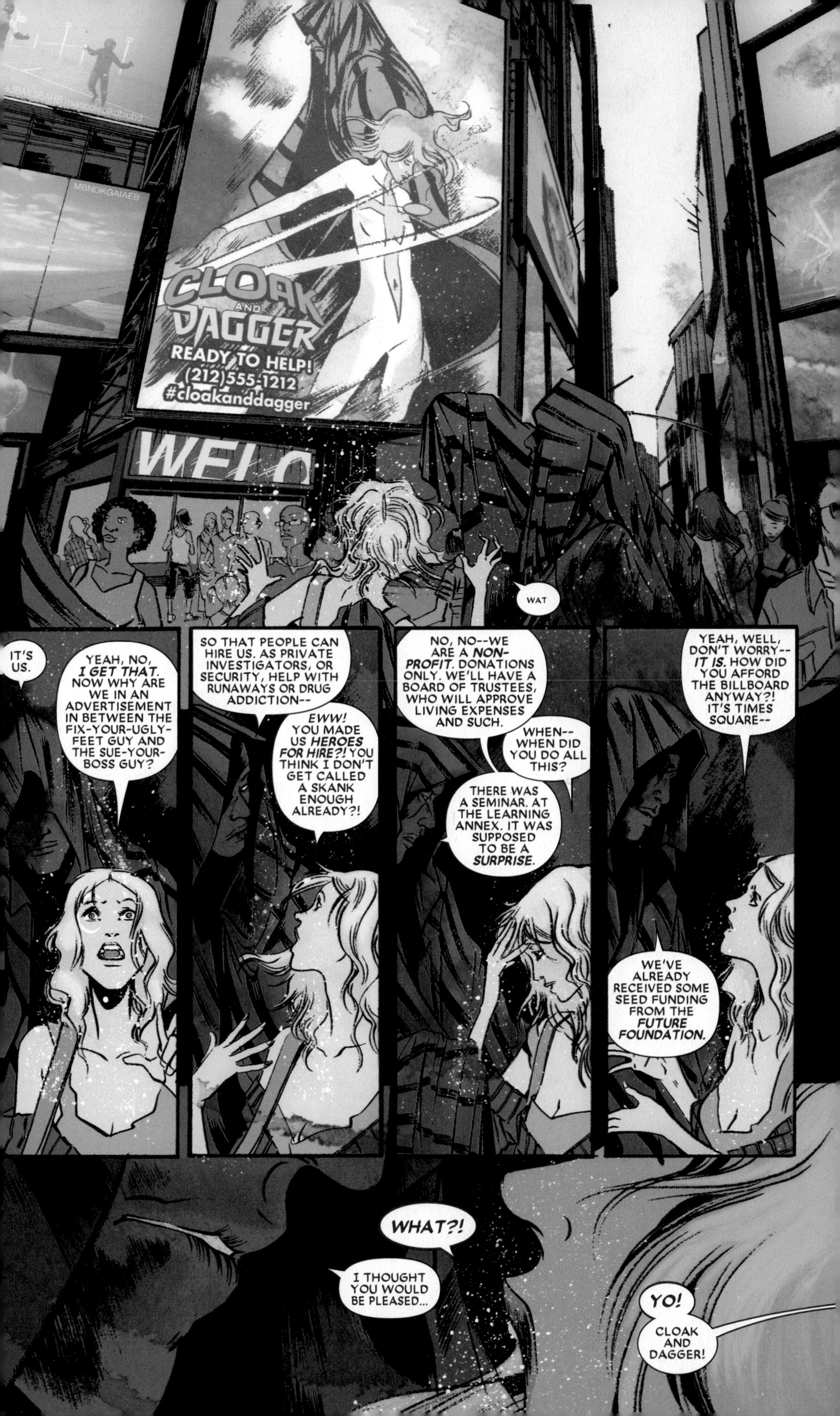
CLOAK AND DAGGER
READY TO HELP!
(212)555-1212
#cloakanddagger
WAT
IT'S US.
YEAH, NO, *I GET THAT*. NOW WHY ARE WE IN AN ADVERTISEMENT IN BETWEEN THE FIX-YOUR-UGLY-FEET GUY AND THE SUE-YOUR-BOSS GUY?
SO THAT PEOPLE CAN HIRE US. AS PRIVATE INVESTIGATORS, OR SECURITY, HELP WITH RUNAWAYS OR DRUG ADDICTION--
EWW! YOU MADE US *HEROES FOR HIRE?!* YOU THINK I DON'T GET CALLED A SKANK ENOUGH ALREADY?!
NO, NO--WE ARE A *NON-PROFIT*. DONATIONS ONLY. WE'LL HAVE A BOARD OF TRUSTEES, WHO WILL APPROVE LIVING EXPENSES AND SUCH.
WHEN--WHEN DID YOU DO ALL THIS?
THERE WAS A SEMINAR. AT THE LEARNING ANNEX. IT WAS SUPPOSED TO BE A *SURPRISE*.
YEAH, WELL, DON'T WORRY--*IT IS.* HOW DID YOU AFFORD THE BILLBOARD ANYWAY?! IT'S TIMES SQUARE--
WE'VE ALREADY RECEIVED SOME SEED FUNDING FROM THE *FUTURE FOUNDATION*.
WHAT?!
I THOUGHT YOU WOULD BE PLEASED...
YO!
CLOAK AND DAGGER!

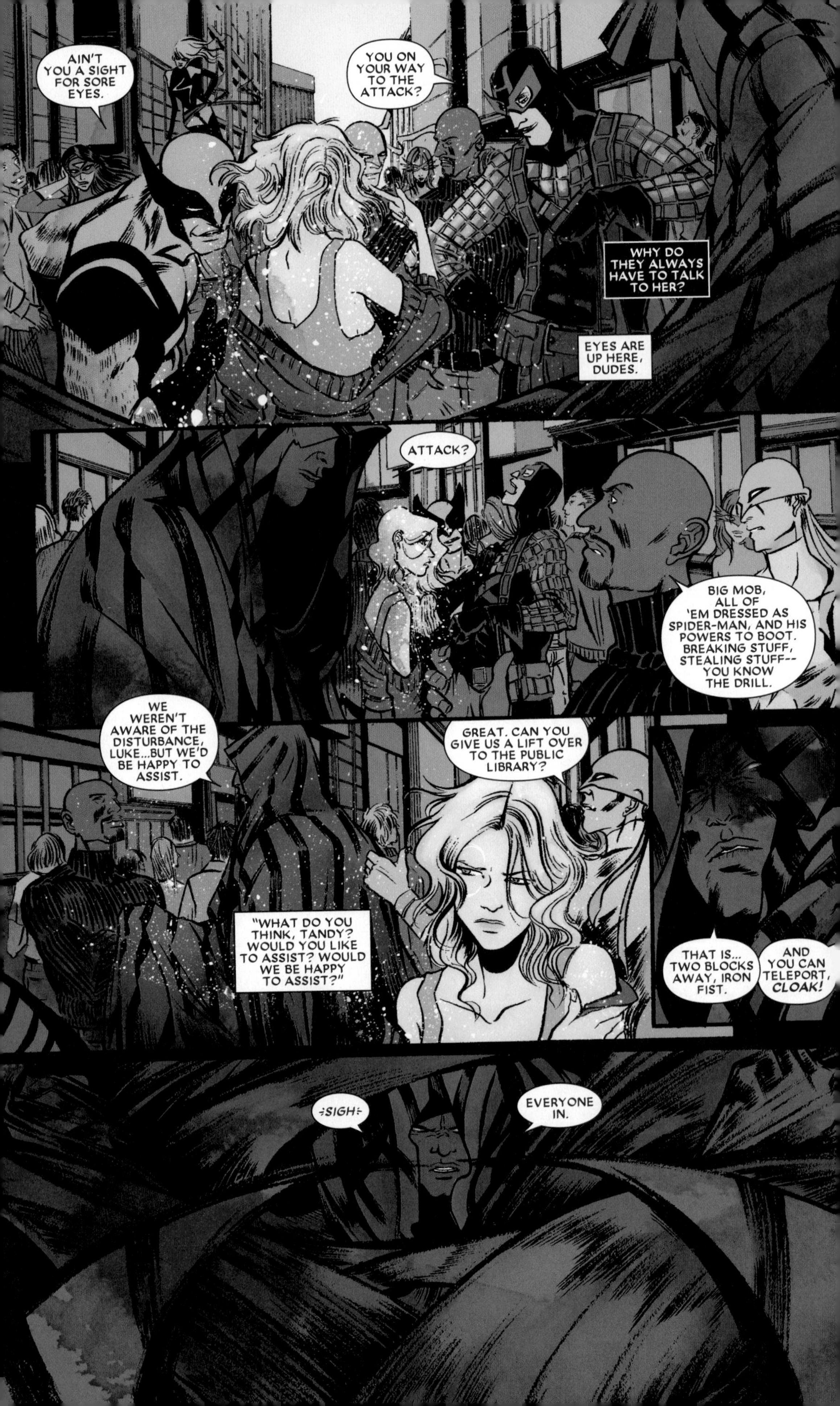
AIN'T YOU A SIGHT FOR SORE EYES.
YOU ON YOUR WAY TO THE ATTACK?
WHY DO THEY ALWAYS HAVE TO TALK TO HER?
EYES ARE UP HERE, DUDES.
ATTACK?
BIG MOB, ALL OF 'EM DRESSED AS SPIDER-MAN, AND HIS POWERS TO BOOT. BREAKING STUFF, STEALING STUFF--YOU KNOW THE DRILL.
WE WEREN'T AWARE OF THE DISTURBANCE, LUKE...BUT WE'D BE HAPPY TO ASSIST.
GREAT. CAN YOU GIVE US A LIFT OVER TO THE PUBLIC LIBRARY?
"WHAT DO YOU THINK, TANDY? WOULD YOU LIKE TO ASSIST? WOULD WE BE HAPPY TO ASSIST?"
THAT IS... TWO BLOCKS AWAY, IRON FIST.
AND YOU CAN TELEPORT, CLOAK!
⸗SIGH⸗
EVERYONE IN.

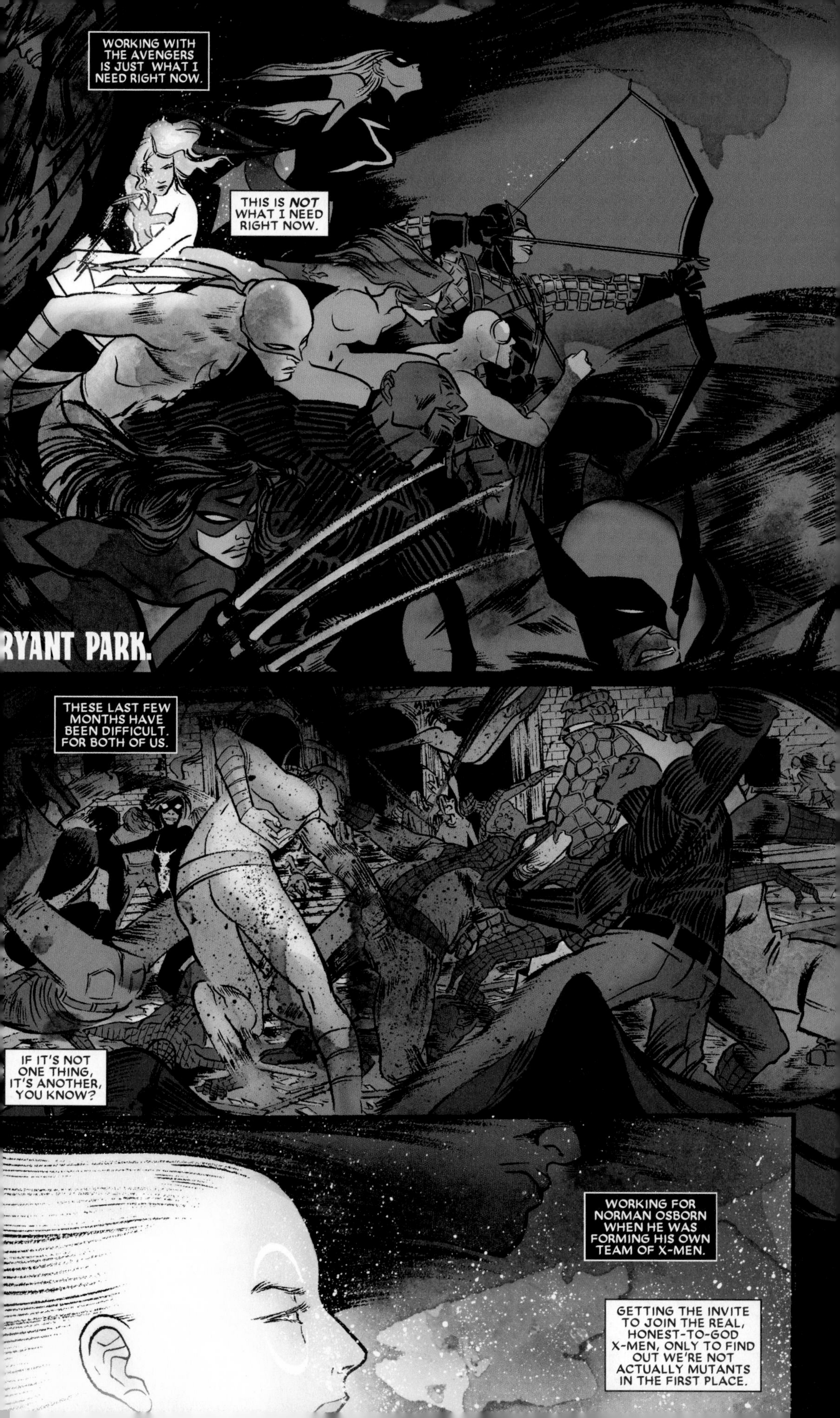
WORKING WITH THE AVENGERS IS JUST WHAT I NEED RIGHT NOW.
THIS IS *NOT* WHAT I NEED RIGHT NOW.
RYANT PARK.
THESE LAST FEW MONTHS HAVE BEEN DIFFICULT. FOR BOTH OF US.
IF IT'S NOT ONE THING, IT'S ANOTHER, YOU KNOW?
WORKING FOR NORMAN OSBORN WHEN HE WAS FORMING HIS OWN TEAM OF X-MEN.
GETTING THE INVITE TO JOIN THE REAL, HONEST-TO-GOD X-MEN, ONLY TO FIND OUT WE'RE NOT ACTUALLY MUTANTS IN THE FIRST PLACE.

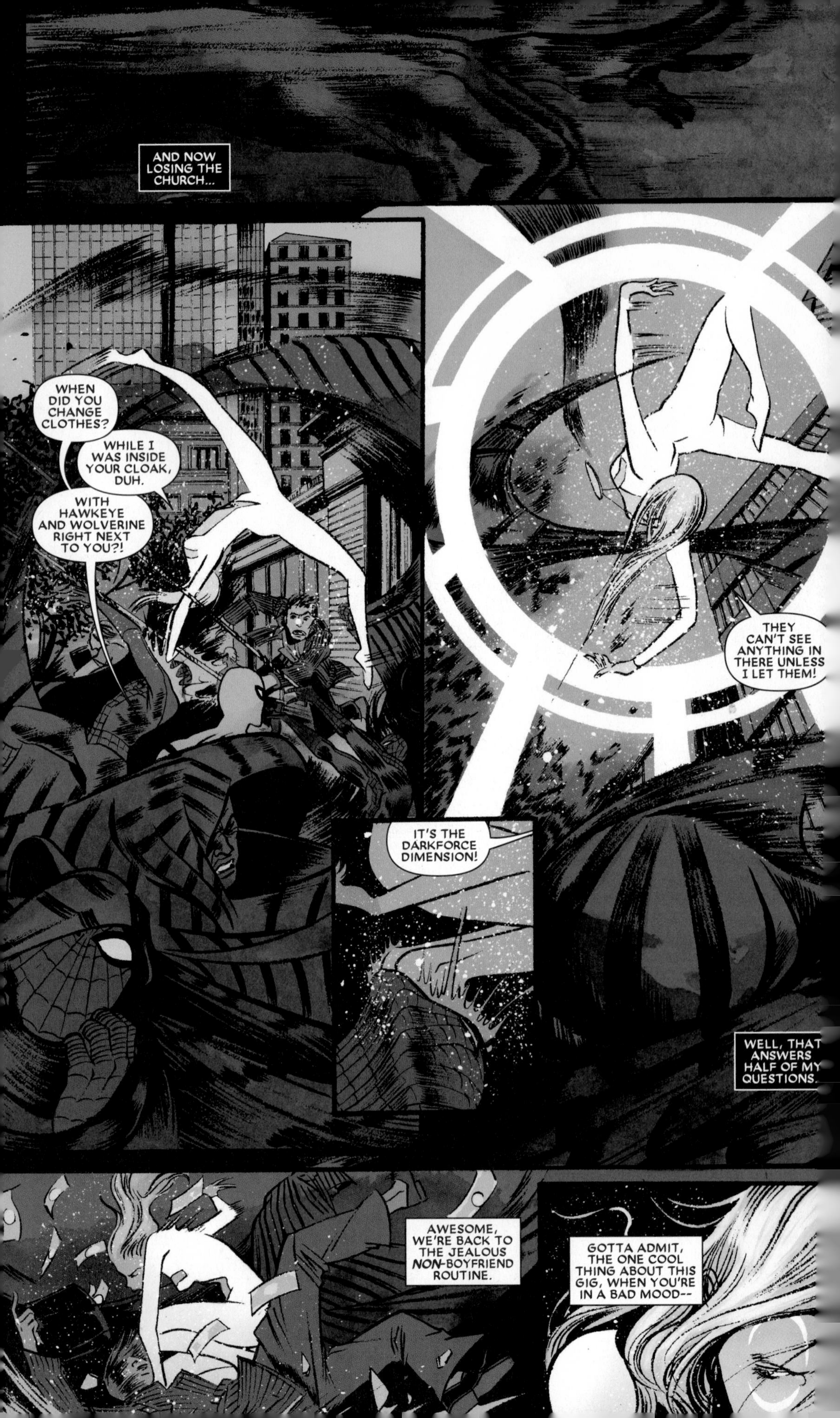
AND NOW LOSING THE CHURCH...
WHEN DID YOU CHANGE CLOTHES?
WHILE I WAS INSIDE YOUR CLOAK, DUH.
WITH HAWKEYE AND WOLVERINE RIGHT NEXT TO YOU?!
THEY CAN'T SEE ANYTHING IN THERE UNLESS I LET THEM!
IT'S THE DARKFORCE DIMENSION!
WELL, THAT ANSWERS HALF OF MY QUESTIONS.
AWESOME, WE'RE BACK TO THE JEALOUS NON-BOYFRIEND ROUTINE.
GOTTA ADMIT, THE ONE COOL THING ABOUT THIS GIG, WHEN YOU'RE IN A BAD MOOD--

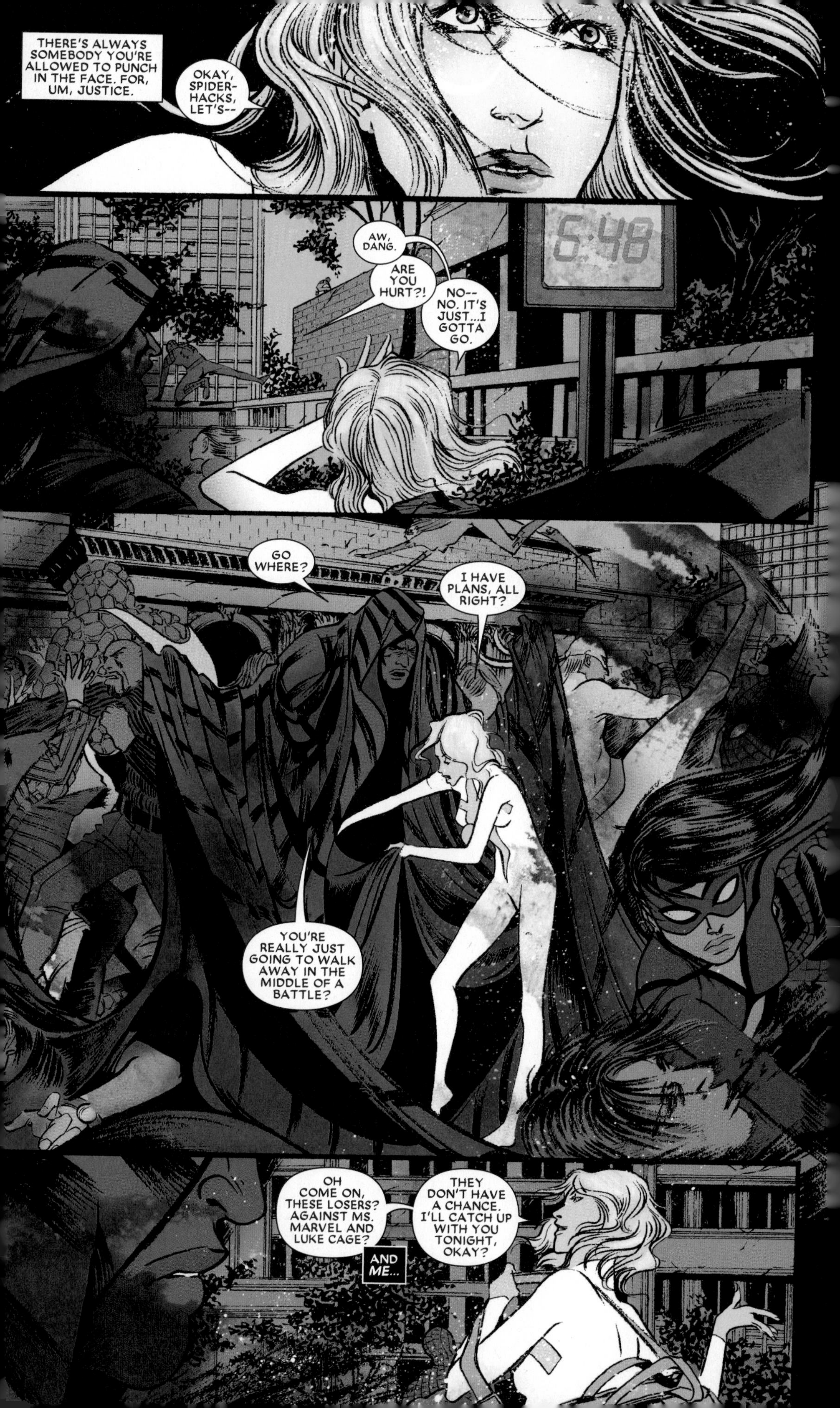
THERE'S ALWAYS SOMEBODY YOU'RE ALLOWED TO PUNCH IN THE FACE. FOR, UM, JUSTICE.
OKAY, SPIDER-HACKS, LET'S--
6:48
AW, DANG.
ARE YOU HURT?!
NO--NO. IT'S JUST...I GOTTA GO.
GO WHERE?
I HAVE PLANS, ALL RIGHT?
YOU'RE REALLY JUST GOING TO WALK AWAY IN THE MIDDLE OF A BATTLE?
OH COME ON, THESE LOSERS? AGAINST MS. MARVEL AND LUKE CAGE?
AND ME...
THEY DON'T HAVE A CHANCE. I'LL CATCH UP WITH YOU TONIGHT, OKAY?

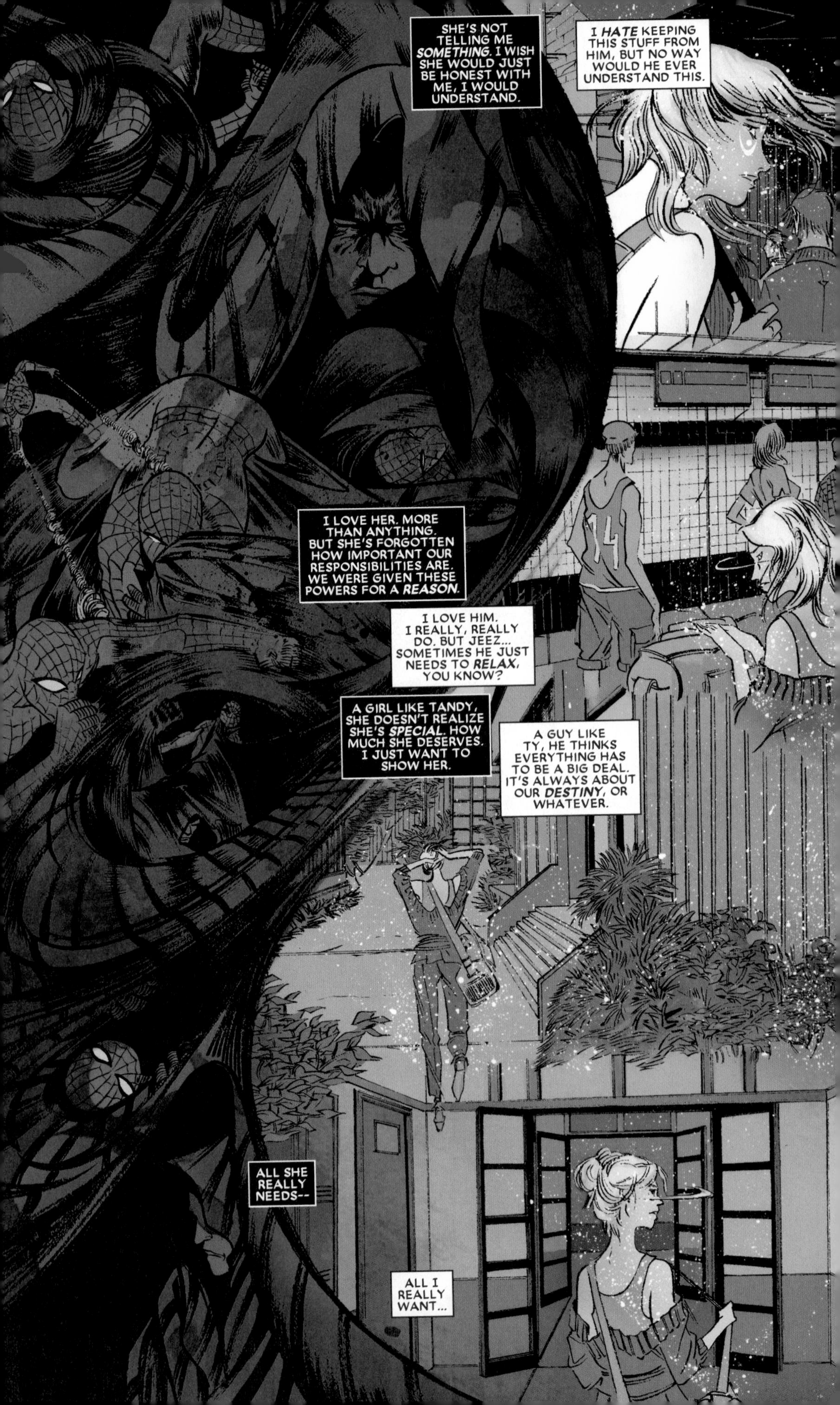

SHE'S NOT TELLING ME *SOMETHING*. I WISH SHE WOULD JUST BE HONEST WITH ME, I WOULD UNDERSTAND.
I *HATE* KEEPING THIS STUFF FROM HIM, BUT NO WAY WOULD HE EVER UNDERSTAND THIS.
I LOVE HER. MORE THAN ANYTHING. BUT SHE'S FORGOTTEN HOW IMPORTANT OUR RESPONSIBILITIES ARE. WE WERE GIVEN THESE POWERS FOR A *REASON*.
I LOVE HIM. I REALLY, REALLY DO. BUT JEEZ... SOMETIMES HE JUST NEEDS TO *RELAX*, YOU KNOW?
A GIRL LIKE TANDY, SHE DOESN'T REALIZE SHE'S *SPECIAL*. HOW MUCH SHE DESERVES. I JUST WANT TO SHOW HER.
A GUY LIKE TY, HE THINKS EVERYTHING HAS TO BE A BIG DEAL. IT'S ALWAYS ABOUT OUR *DESTINY*, OR WHATEVER.
ALL SHE REALLY NEEDS--
ALL I REALLY WANT...

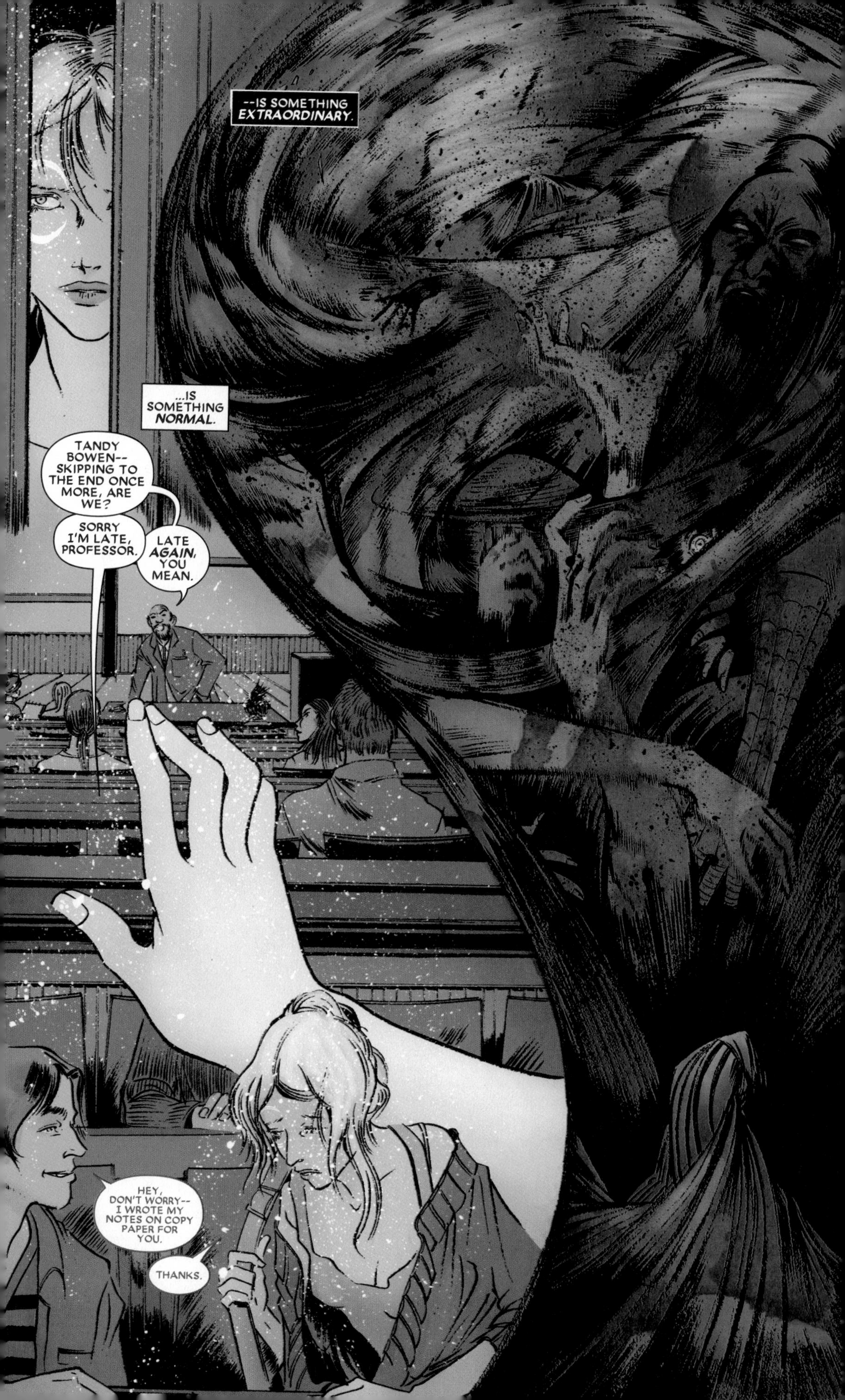
--IS SOMETHING EXTRAORDINARY.
...IS SOMETHING NORMAL.
TANDY BOWEN--SKIPPING TO THE END ONCE MORE, ARE WE?
SORRY I'M LATE, PROFESSOR.
LATE AGAIN, YOU MEAN.
HEY, DON'T WORRY--I WROTE MY NOTES ON COPY PAPER FOR YOU.
THANKS.

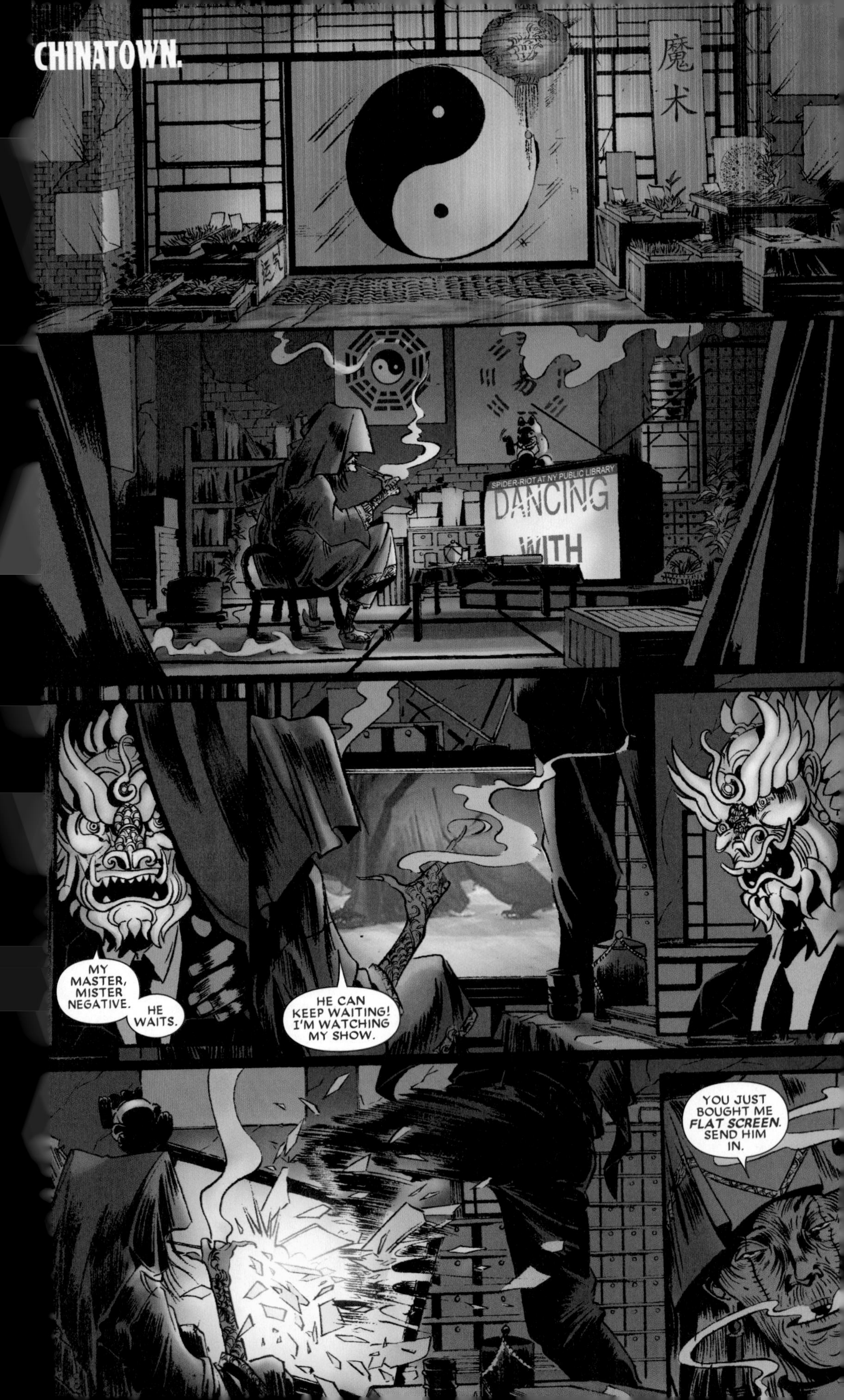
CHINATOWN.
魔术
SPIDER-RIOT AT NY PUBLIC LIBRARY
DANCING WITH
MY MASTER, MISTER NEGATIVE.
HE WAITS.
HE CAN KEEP WAITING! I'M WATCHING MY SHOW.
YOU JUST BOUGHT ME FLAT SCREEN. SEND HIM IN.

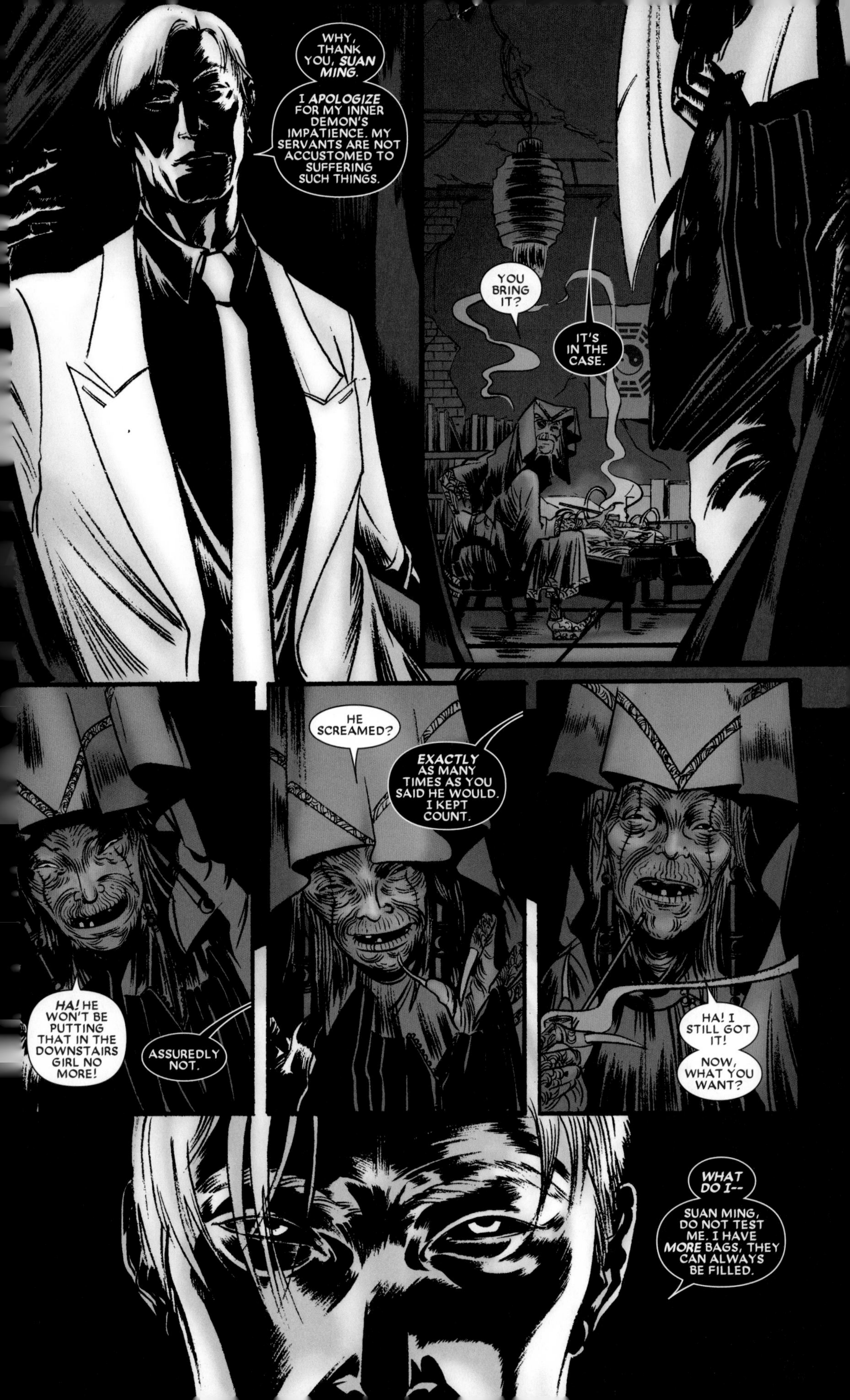
WHY, THANK YOU, *SUAN MING*.
I *APOLOGIZE* FOR MY INNER DEMON'S IMPATIENCE. MY SERVANTS ARE NOT ACCUSTOMED TO SUFFERING SUCH THINGS.
YOU BRING IT?
IT'S IN THE CASE.
HA! HE WON'T BE PUTTING THAT IN THE DOWNSTAIRS GIRL NO MORE!
ASSUREDLY NOT.
HE SCREAMED?
EXACTLY AS MANY TIMES AS YOU SAID HE WOULD. I KEPT COUNT.
HA! I STILL GOT IT!
NOW, WHAT YOU WANT?
WHAT DO I--
SUAN MING, DO NOT TEST ME. I HAVE *MORE* BAGS, THEY CAN ALWAYS BE FILLED.

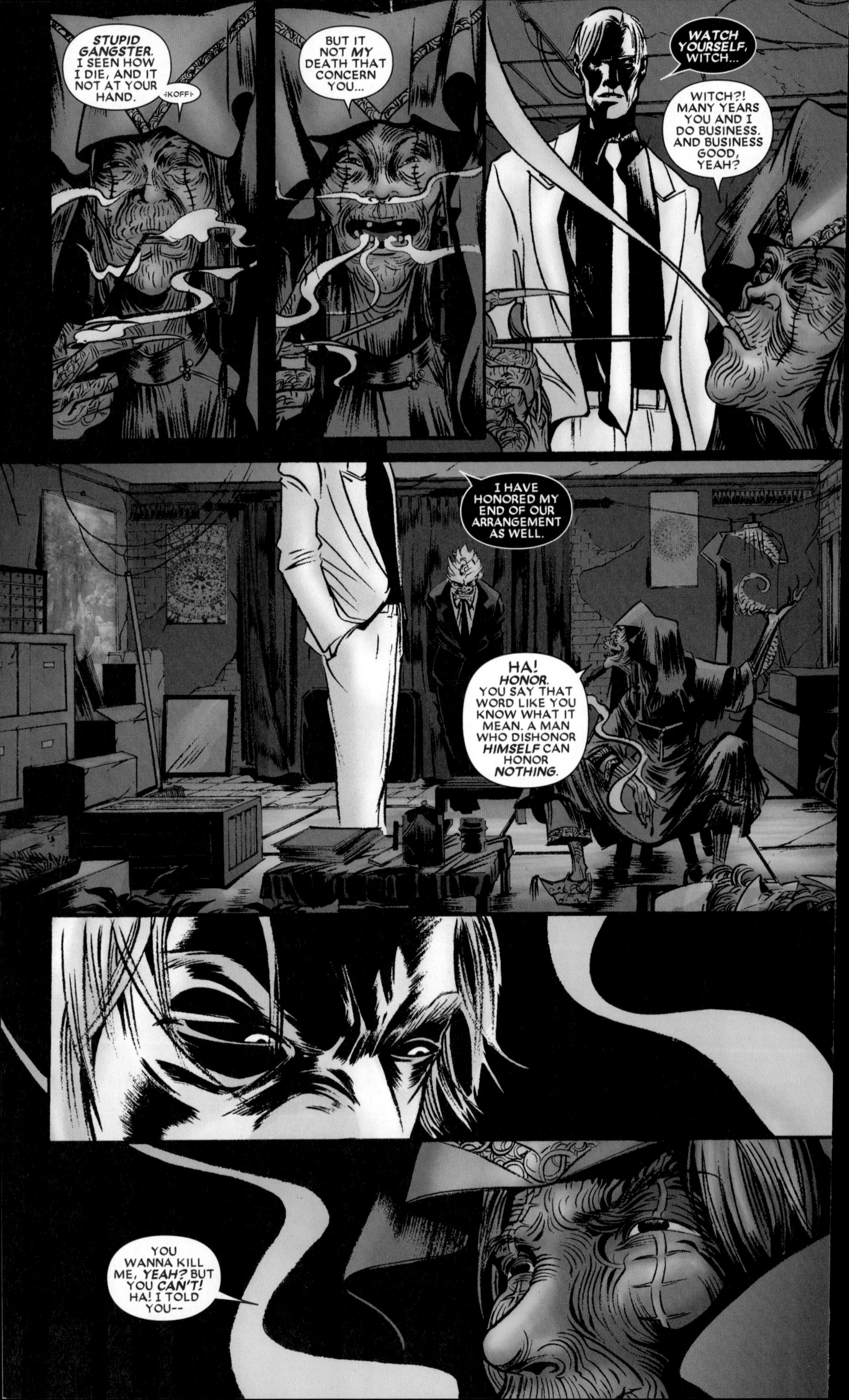
STUPID GANGSTER. I SEEN HOW I DIE, AND IT NOT AT YOUR HAND.
KOFF
BUT IT NOT MY DEATH THAT CONCERN YOU...
WATCH YOURSELF, WITCH...
WITCH?! MANY YEARS YOU AND I DO BUSINESS. AND BUSINESS GOOD, YEAH?
I HAVE HONORED MY END OF OUR ARRANGEMENT AS WELL.
HA! HONOR. YOU SAY THAT WORD LIKE YOU KNOW WHAT IT MEAN. A MAN WHO DISHONOR HIMSELF CAN HONOR NOTHING.
YOU WANNA KILL ME, YEAH? BUT YOU CAN'T! HA! I TOLD YOU--

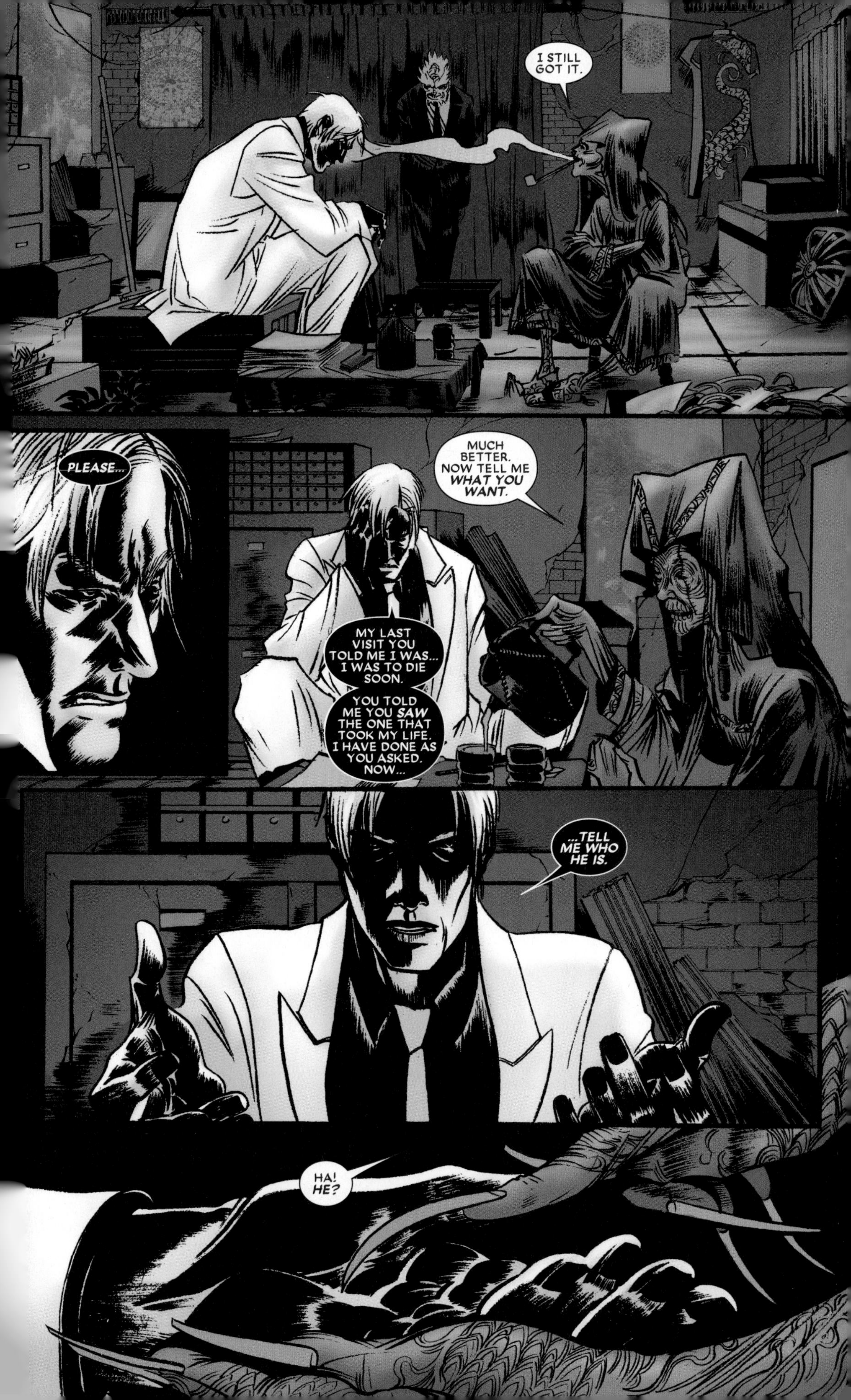
I STILL GOT IT.
PLEASE...
MUCH BETTER. NOW TELL ME WHAT YOU WANT.
MY LAST VISIT YOU TOLD ME I WAS... I WAS TO DIE SOON.
YOU TOLD ME YOU SAW THE ONE THAT TOOK MY LIFE. I HAVE DONE AS YOU ASKED. NOW...
...TELL ME WHO HE IS.
HA! HE?

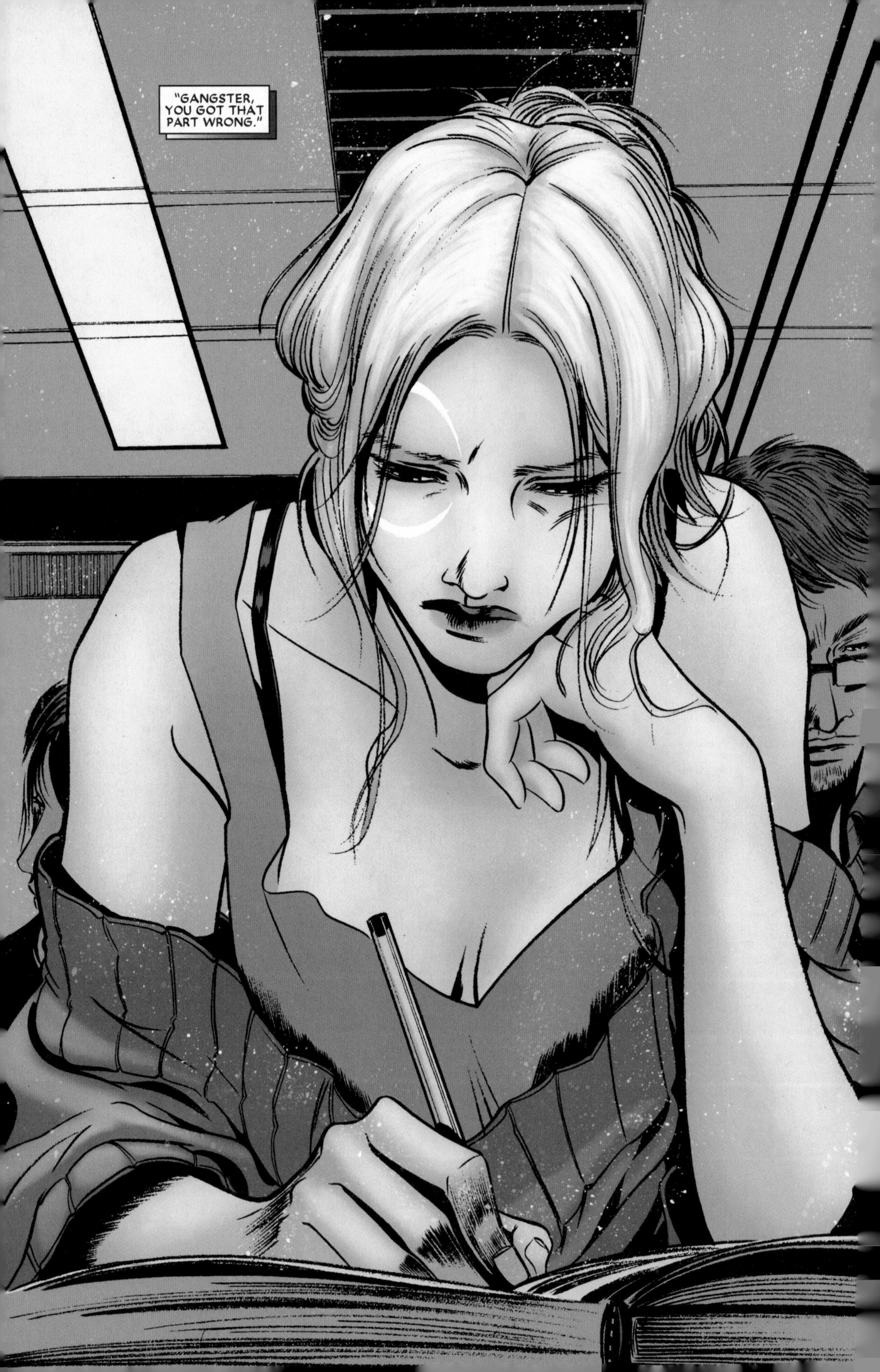
"GANGSTER, YOU GOT THAT PART WRONG."

SPIDER-ISLAND: CLOAK AND DAGGER #1 2ND-PRINTING VARIANT BY **MIKE CHOI**

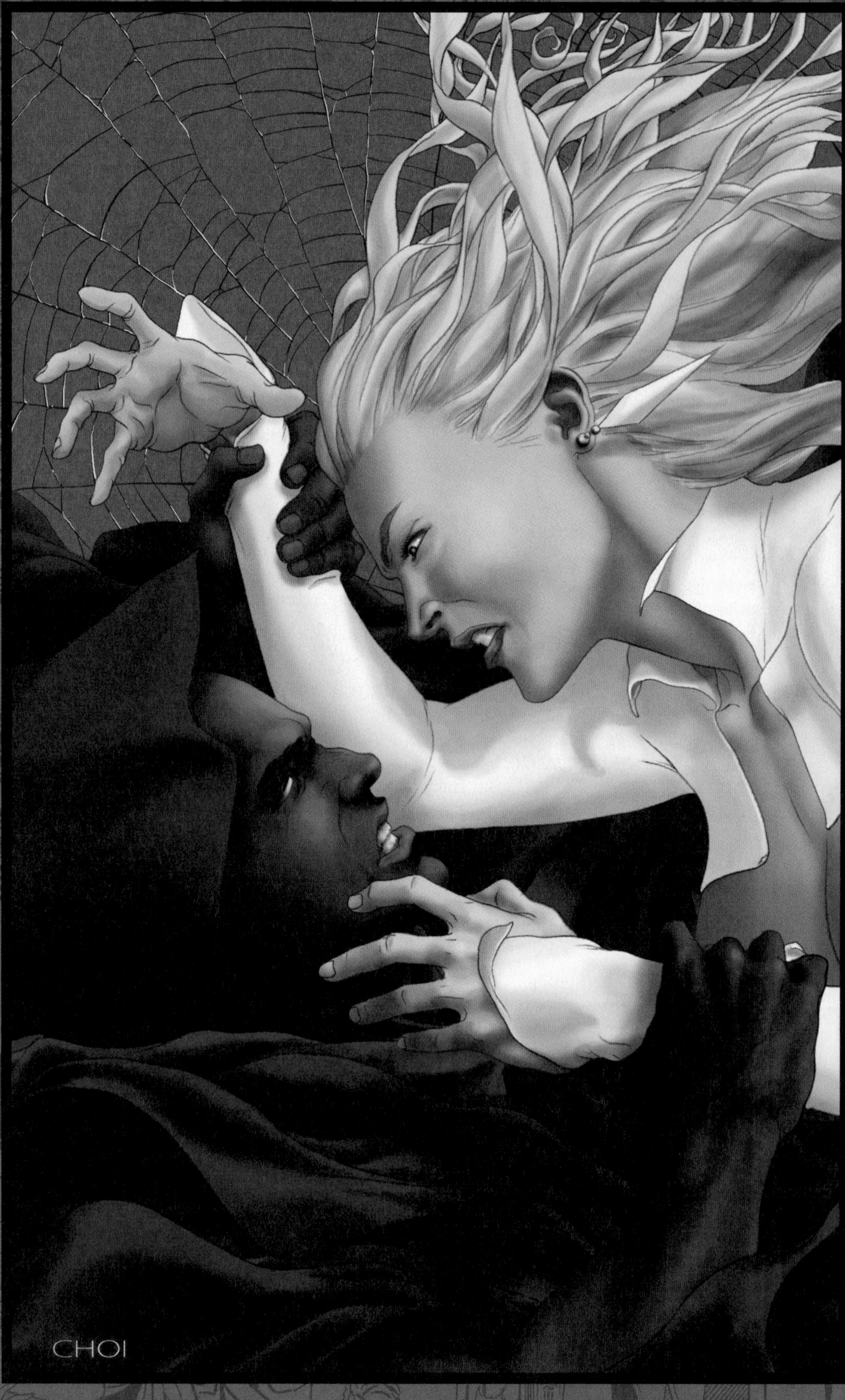
CHOI

SPIDER-ISLAND: CLOAK AND DAGGER (2011) #2

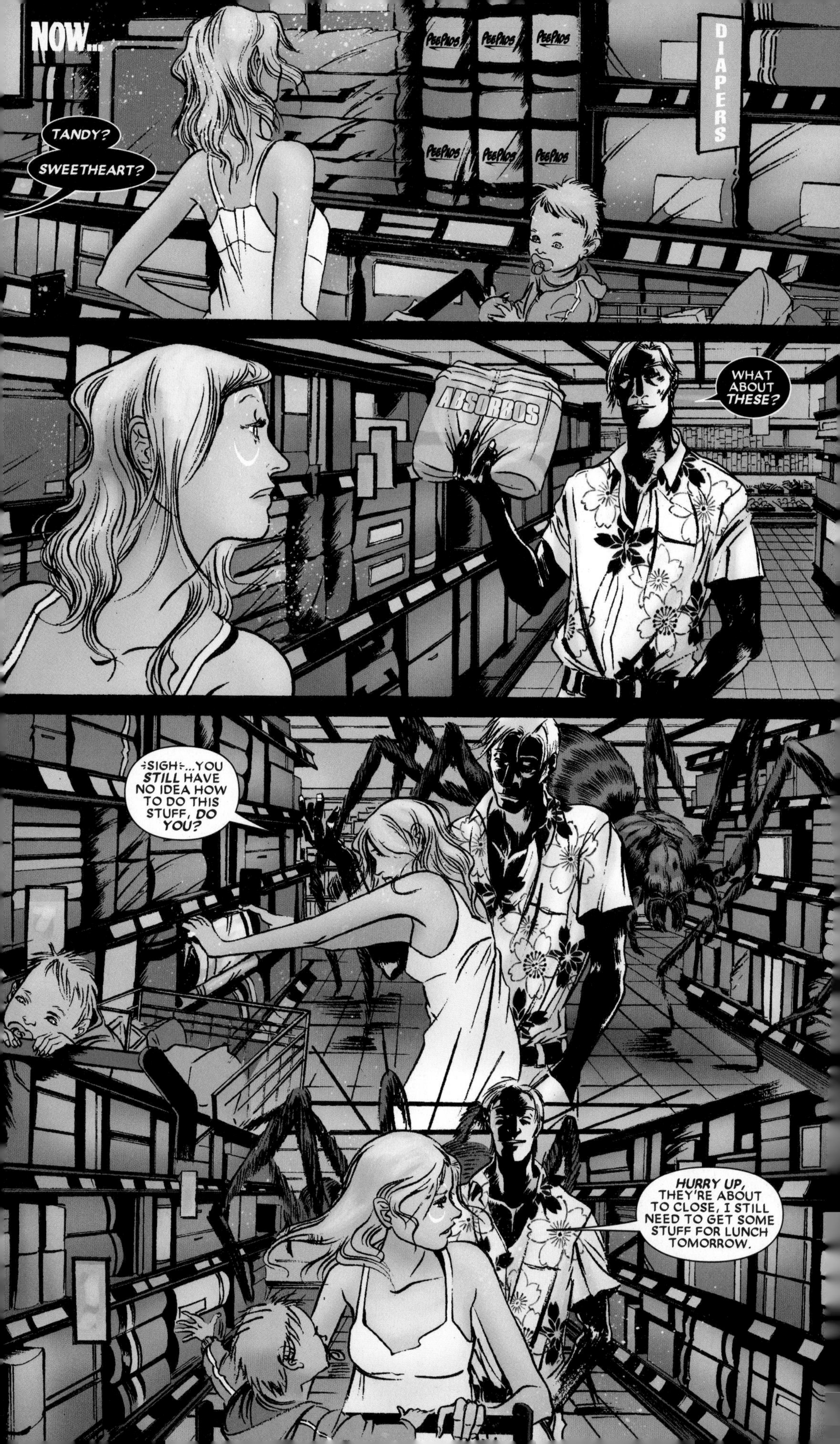
NOW...
TANDY?
SWEETHEART?
PEEPAOS
DIAPERS
ABSORBOS
WHAT ABOUT THESE?
⸗SIGH⸗...YOU STILL HAVE NO IDEA HOW TO DO THIS STUFF, DO YOU?
HURRY UP, THEY'RE ABOUT TO CLOSE, I STILL NEED TO GET SOME STUFF FOR LUNCH TOMORROW.

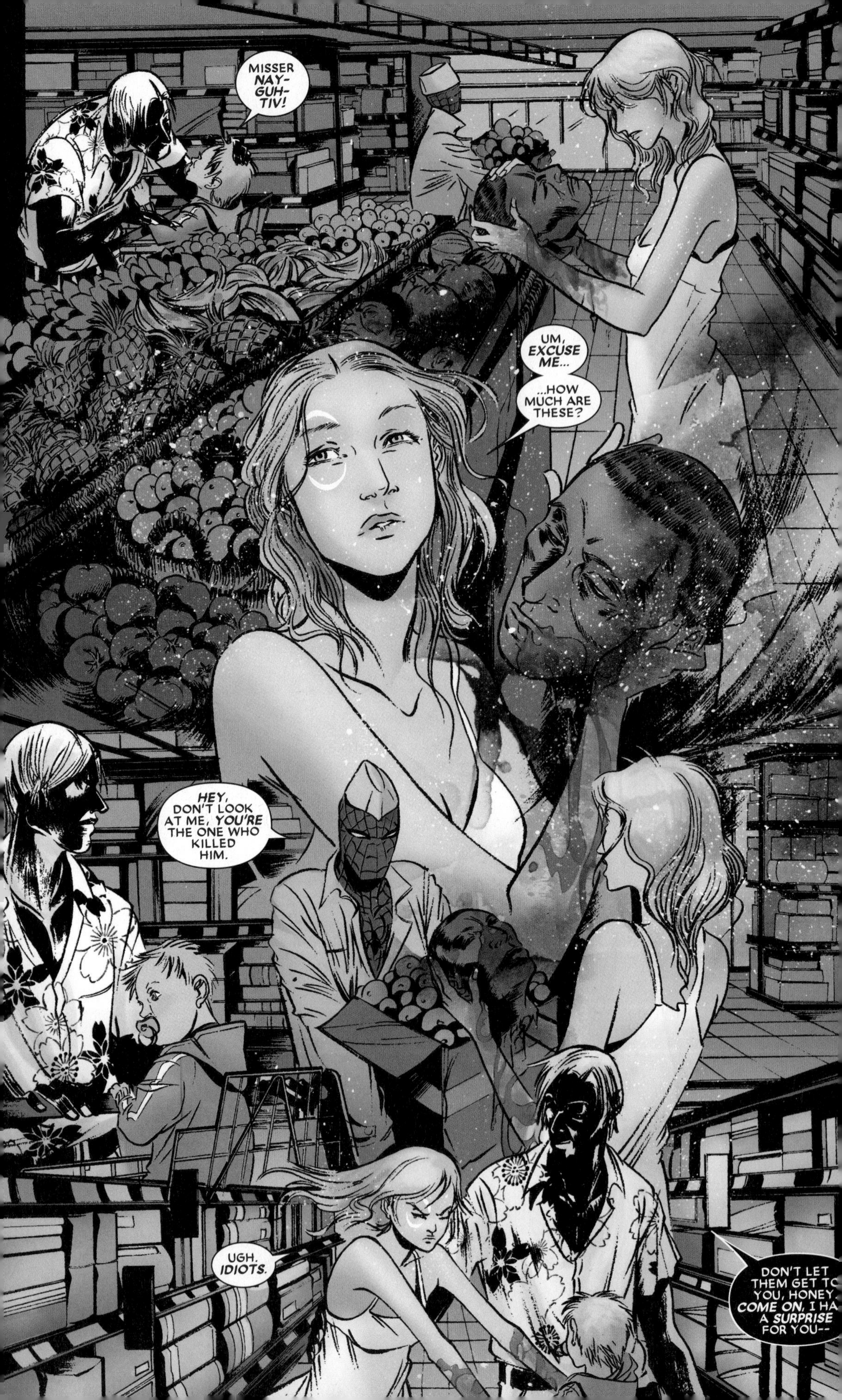
MISSER NAY-GUH-TIV!
UM, EXCUSE ME...
...HOW MUCH ARE THESE?
HEY, DON'T LOOK AT ME, YOU'RE THE ONE WHO KILLED HIM.
UGH. IDIOTS.
DON'T LET THEM GET TO YOU, HONEY COME ON, I HA A SURPRISE FOR YOU--

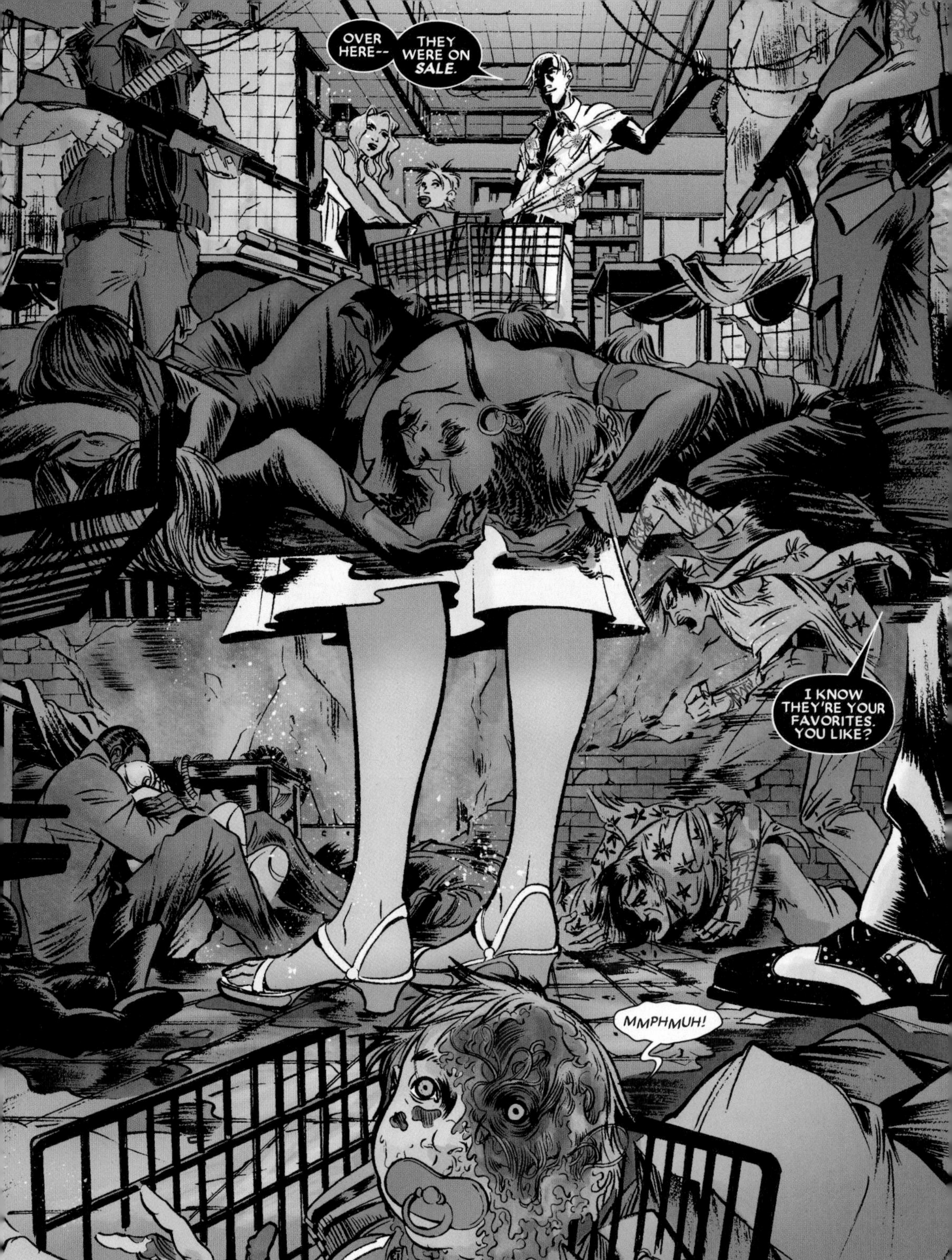
OVER HERE--
THEY WERE ON SALE.
I KNOW THEY'RE YOUR FAVORITES. YOU LIKE?
MMPHMUH!
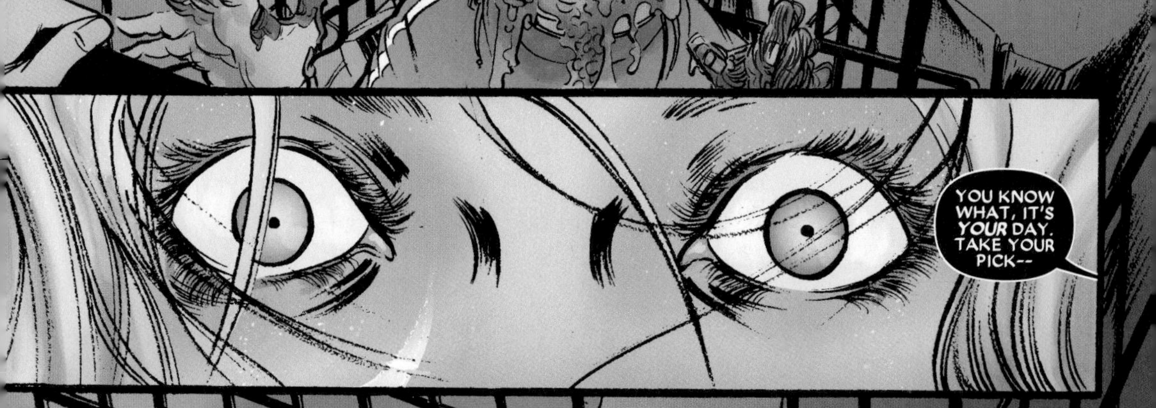
YOU KNOW WHAT, IT'S YOUR DAY. TAKE YOUR PICK--

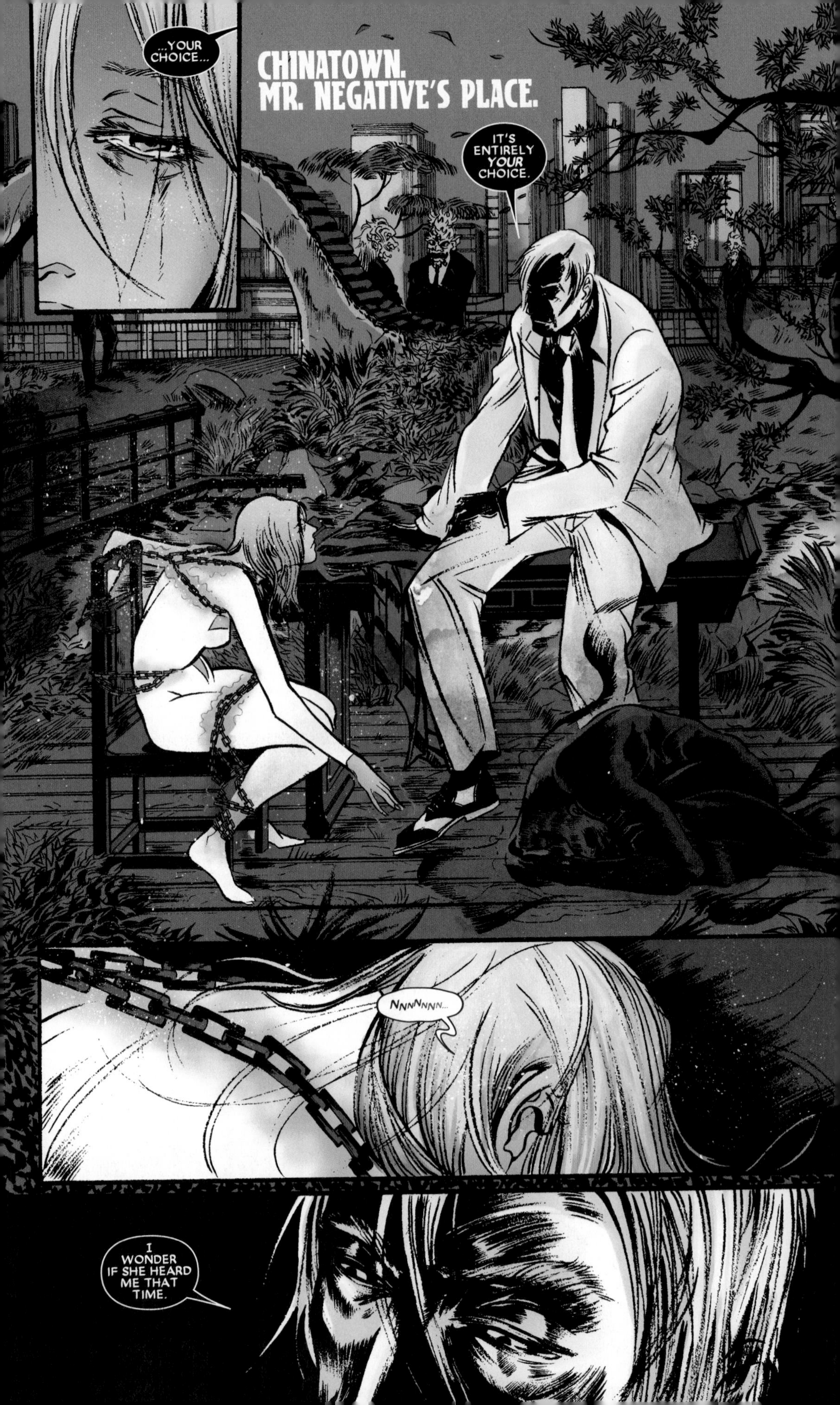
...YOUR CHOICE...
CHINATOWN. MR. NEGATIVE'S PLACE.
IT'S ENTIRELY *YOUR* CHOICE.
NNNNNNN...
I WONDER IF SHE HEARD ME THAT TIME.

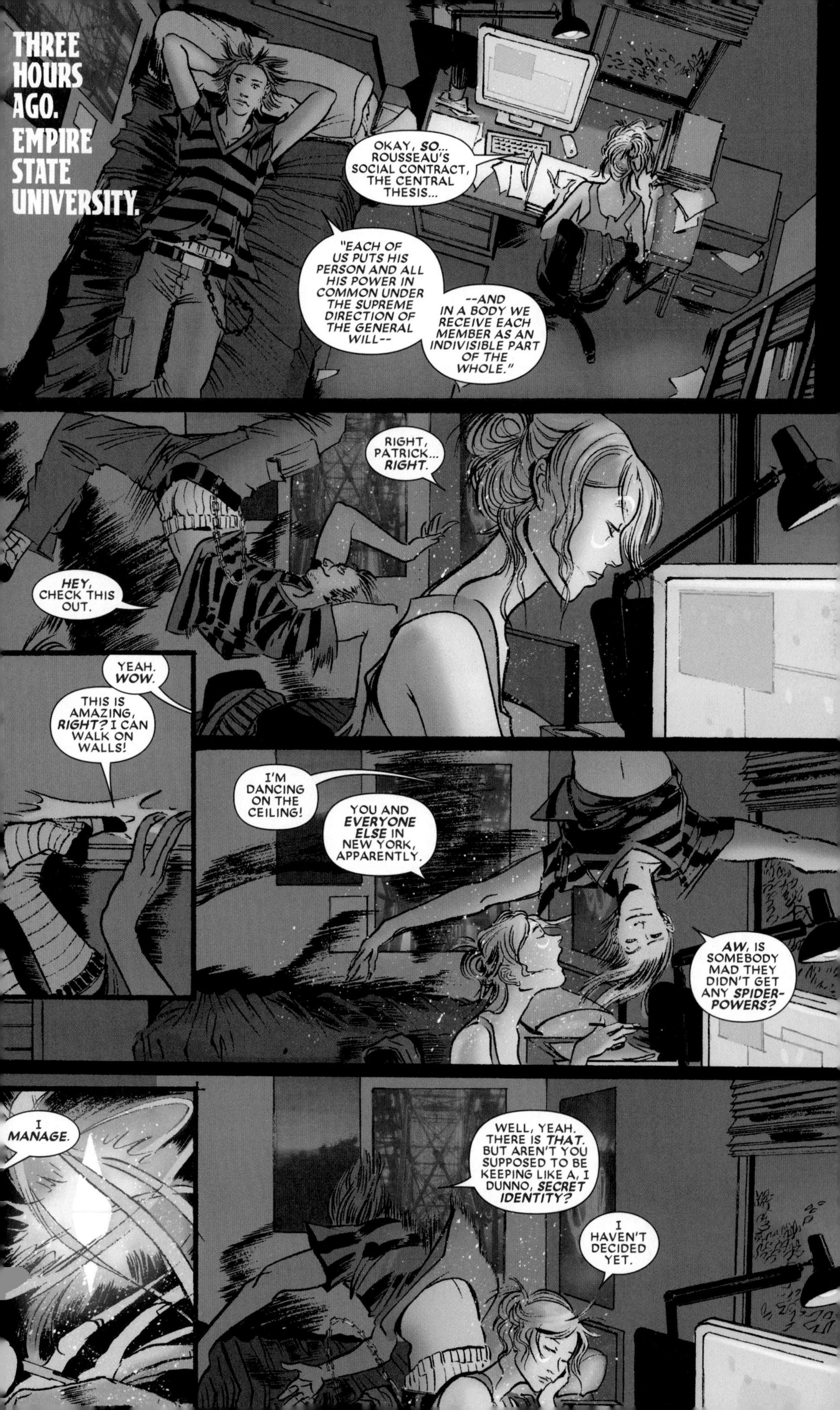
THREE HOURS AGO. EMPIRE STATE UNIVERSITY.
OKAY, SO... ROUSSEAU'S SOCIAL CONTRACT, THE CENTRAL THESIS...
"EACH OF US PUTS HIS PERSON AND ALL HIS POWER IN COMMON UNDER THE SUPREME DIRECTION OF THE GENERAL WILL--
--AND IN A BODY WE RECEIVE EACH MEMBER AS AN INDIVISIBLE PART OF THE WHOLE."
RIGHT, PATRICK... RIGHT.
HEY, CHECK THIS OUT.
YEAH. WOW.
THIS IS AMAZING, RIGHT? I CAN WALK ON WALLS!
I'M DANCING ON THE CEILING!
YOU AND EVERYONE ELSE IN NEW YORK, APPARENTLY.
AW, IS SOMEBODY MAD THEY DIDN'T GET ANY SPIDER-POWERS?
I MANAGE.
WELL, YEAH. THERE IS THAT. BUT AREN'T YOU SUPPOSED TO BE KEEPING LIKE A, I DUNNO, SECRET IDENTITY?
I HAVEN'T DECIDED YET.

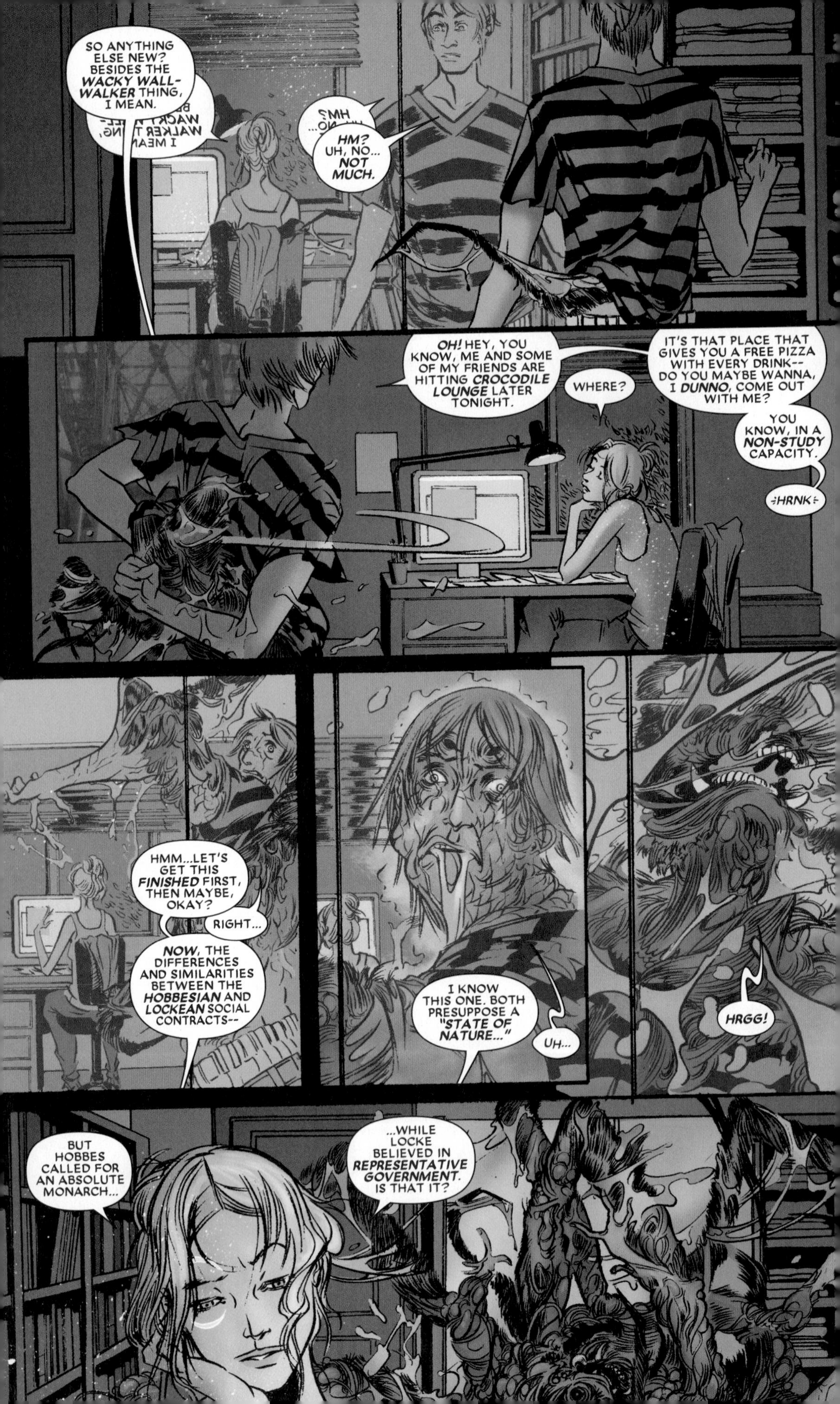

SO ANYTHING ELSE NEW? BESIDES THE *WACKY WALL-WALKER* THING, I MEAN.
HM? UH, NO... *NOT MUCH.*
OH! HEY, YOU KNOW, ME AND SOME OF MY FRIENDS ARE HITTING *CROCODILE LOUNGE* LATER TONIGHT.
WHERE?
IT'S THAT PLACE THAT GIVES YOU A FREE PIZZA WITH EVERY DRINK-- DO YOU MAYBE WANNA, I *DUNNO,* COME OUT WITH ME?
YOU KNOW, IN A *NON-STUDY* CAPACITY.
HRNK
HMM...LET'S GET THIS *FINISHED* FIRST, THEN MAYBE, OKAY?
RIGHT...
NOW, THE DIFFERENCES AND SIMILARITIES BETWEEN THE *HOBBESIAN* AND *LOCKEAN* SOCIAL CONTRACTS--
I KNOW THIS ONE. BOTH PRESUPPOSE A *"STATE OF NATURE..."*
UH...
HRGG!
BUT HOBBES CALLED FOR AN ABSOLUTE MONARCH...
...WHILE LOCKE BELIEVED IN *REPRESENTATIVE GOVERNMENT.* IS THAT IT?

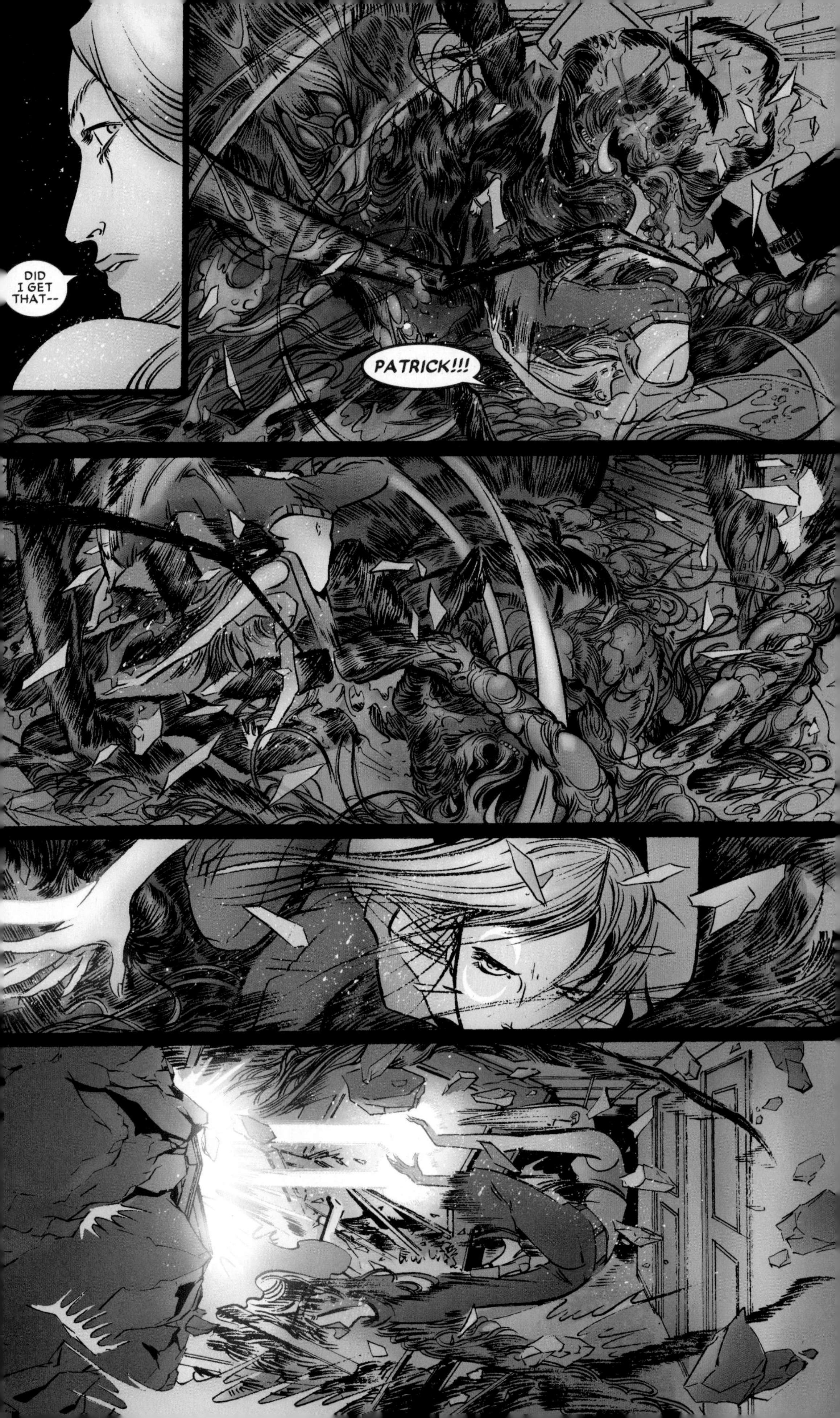
DID I GET THAT--
PATRICK!!!

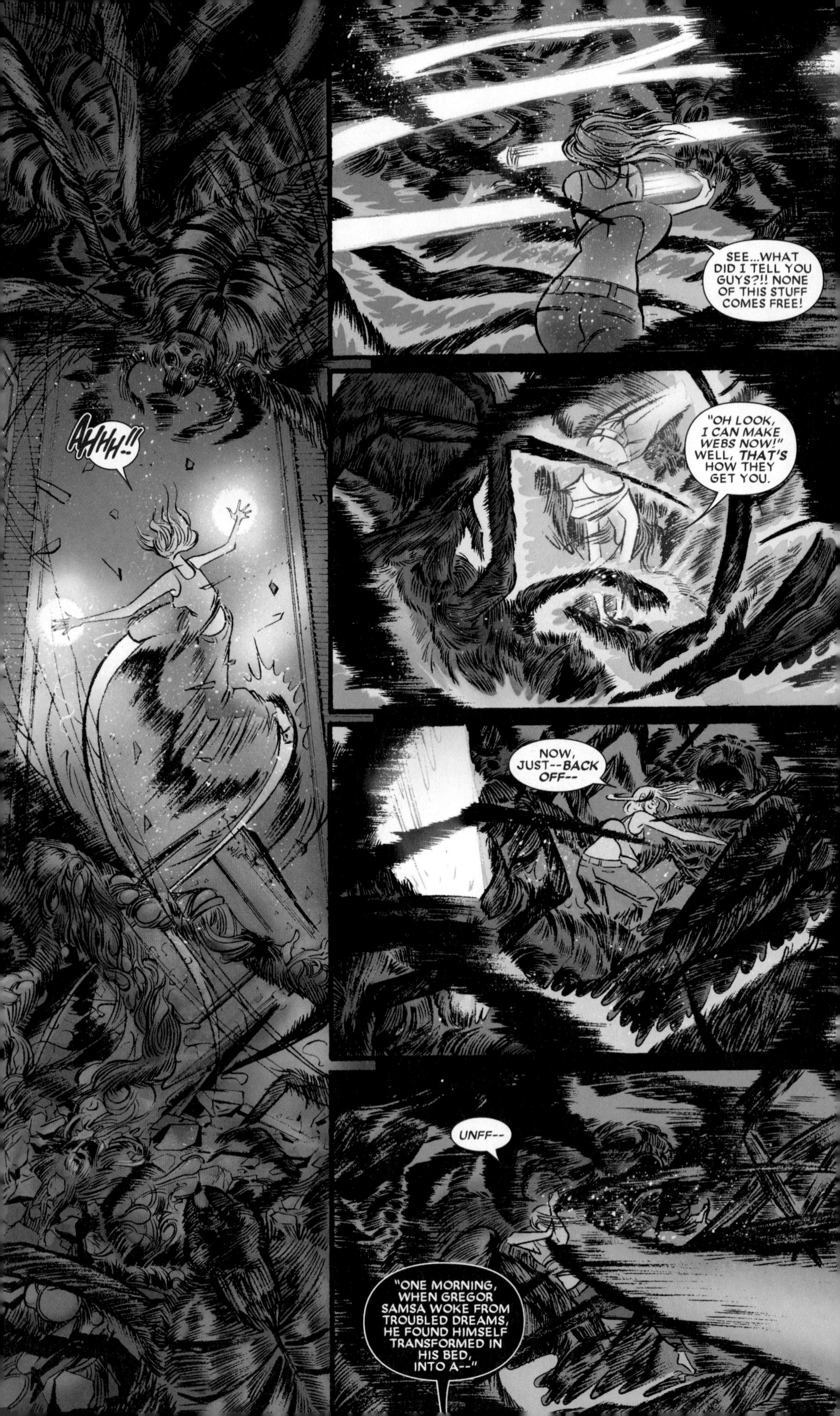
AHHH!!--
SEE...WHAT DID I TELL YOU GUYS?!! NONE OF THIS STUFF COMES FREE!
"OH LOOK, I CAN MAKE WEBS NOW!" WELL, THAT'S HOW THEY GET YOU.
NOW, JUST--BACK OFF--
UNFF--
"ONE MORNING, WHEN GREGOR SAMSA WOKE FROM TROUBLED DREAMS, HE FOUND HIMSELF TRANSFORMED IN HIS BED, INTO A--"

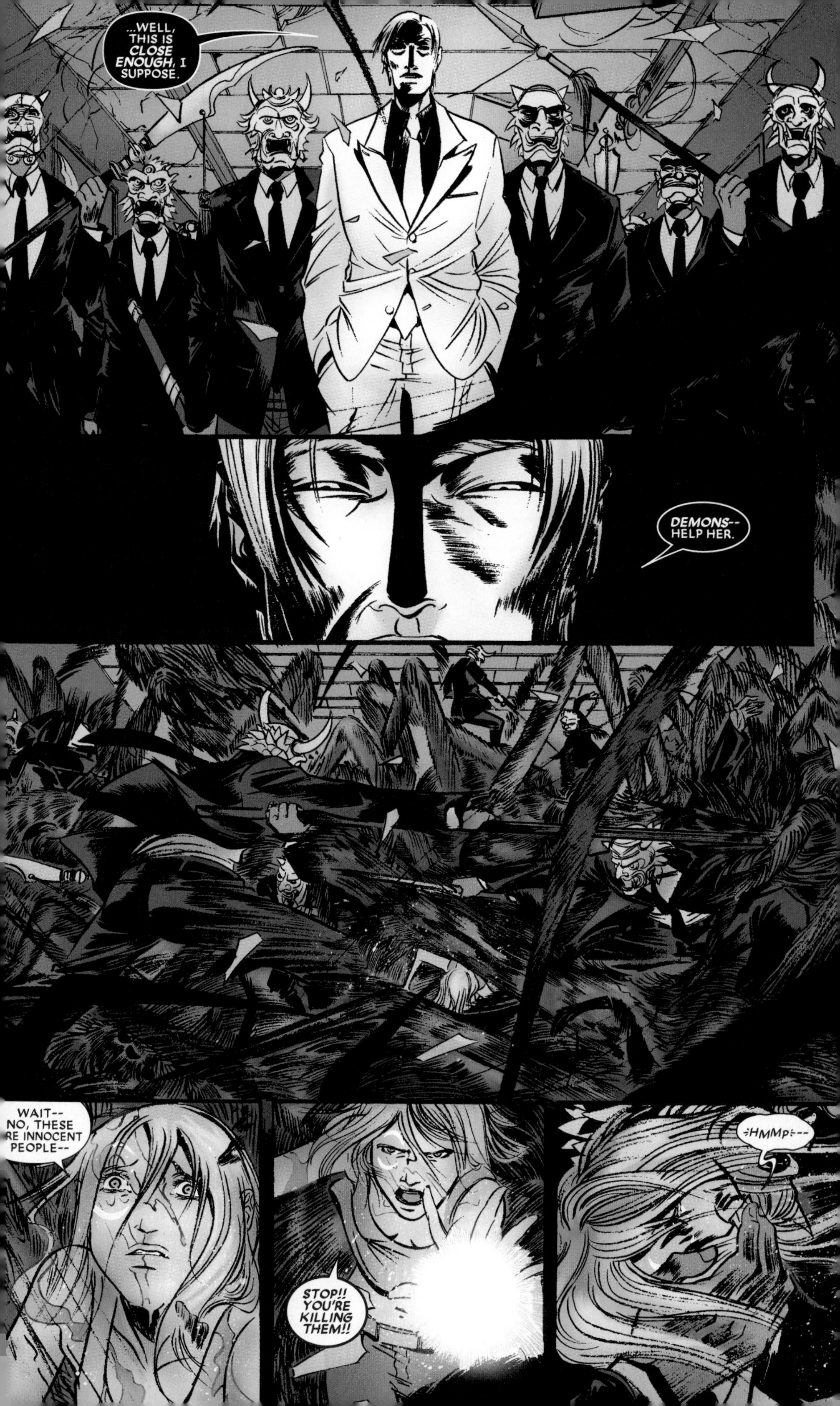
...WELL, THIS IS CLOSE ENOUGH, I SUPPOSE.
DEMONS-- HELP HER.
WAIT-- NO, THESE RE INNOCENT PEOPLE--
STOP!! YOU'RE KILLING THEM!!
HMMP---

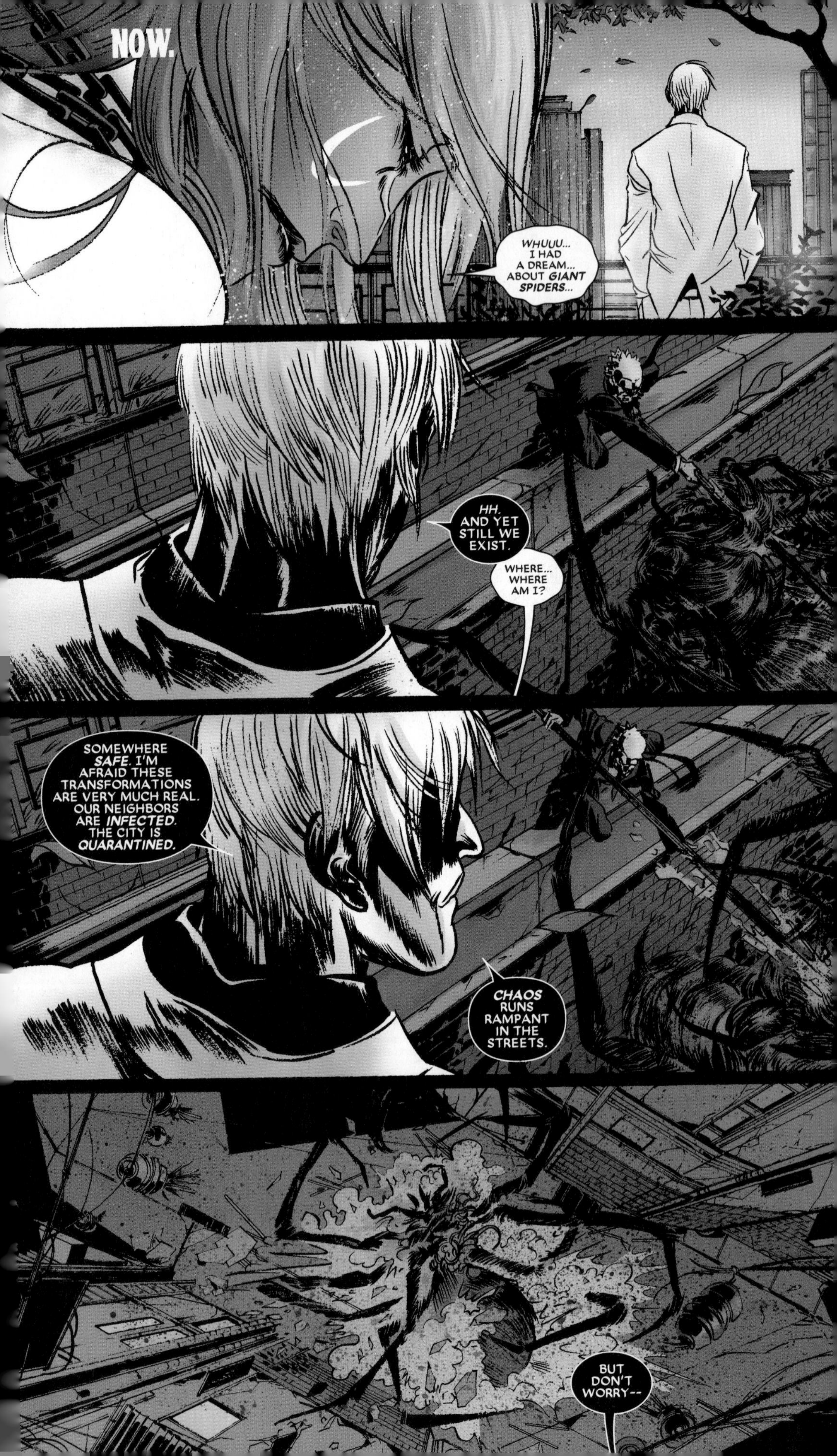
NOW.
WHUUU... I HAD A DREAM... ABOUT GIANT SPIDERS...
HH. AND YET STILL WE EXIST.
WHERE... WHERE AM I?
SOMEWHERE SAFE. I'M AFRAID THESE TRANSFORMATIONS ARE VERY MUCH REAL. OUR NEIGHBORS ARE INFECTED. THE CITY IS QUARANTINED.
CHAOS RUNS RAMPANT IN THE STREETS.
BUT DON'T WORRY--

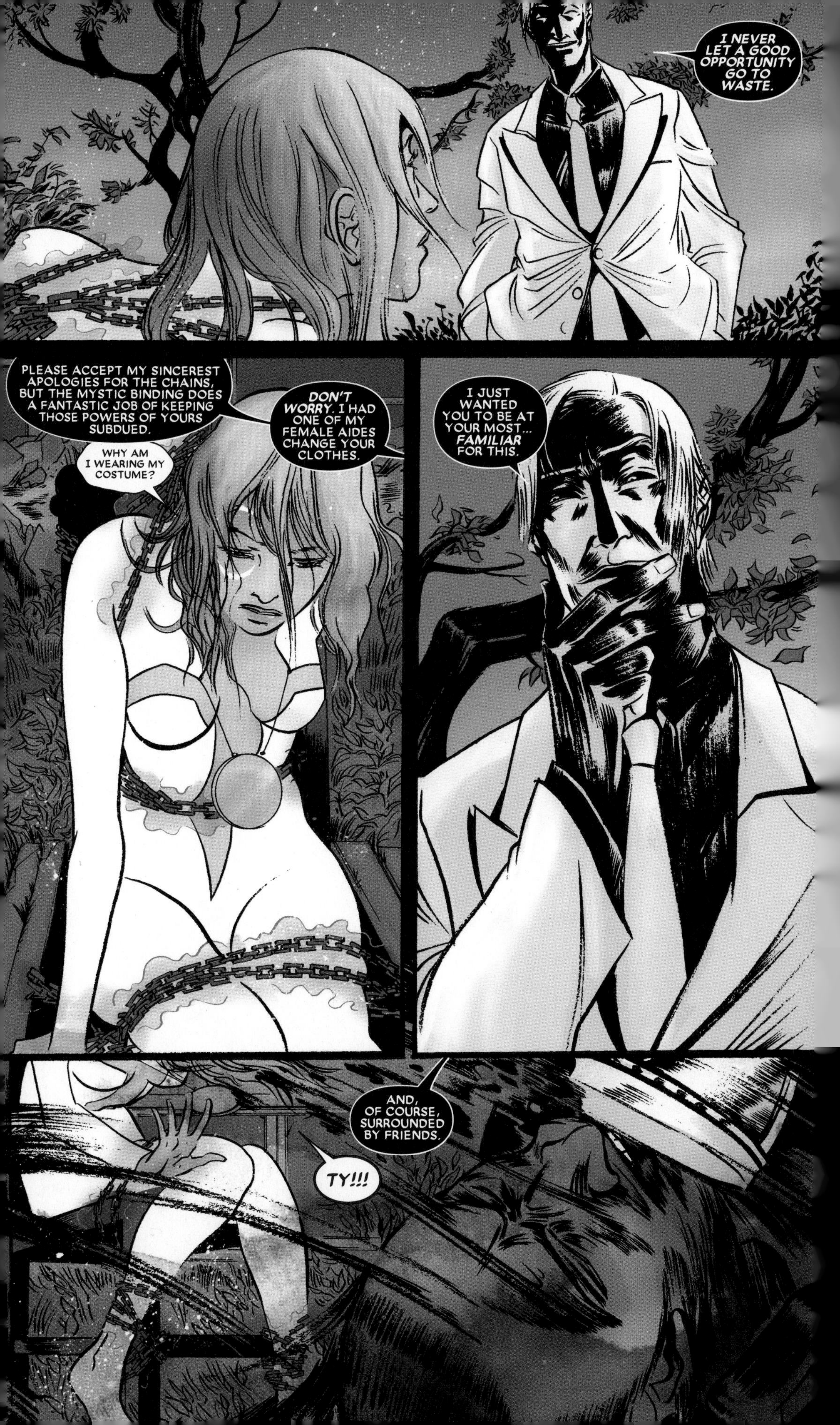
I NEVER LET A GOOD OPPORTUNITY GO TO WASTE.
PLEASE ACCEPT MY SINCEREST APOLOGIES FOR THE CHAINS, BUT THE MYSTIC BINDING DOES A FANTASTIC JOB OF KEEPING THOSE POWERS OF YOURS SUBDUED.
WHY AM I WEARING MY COSTUME?
DON'T WORRY. I HAD ONE OF MY FEMALE AIDES CHANGE YOUR CLOTHES.
I JUST WANTED YOU TO BE AT YOUR MOST... FAMILIAR FOR THIS.
AND, OF COURSE, SURROUNDED BY FRIENDS.
TY!!!

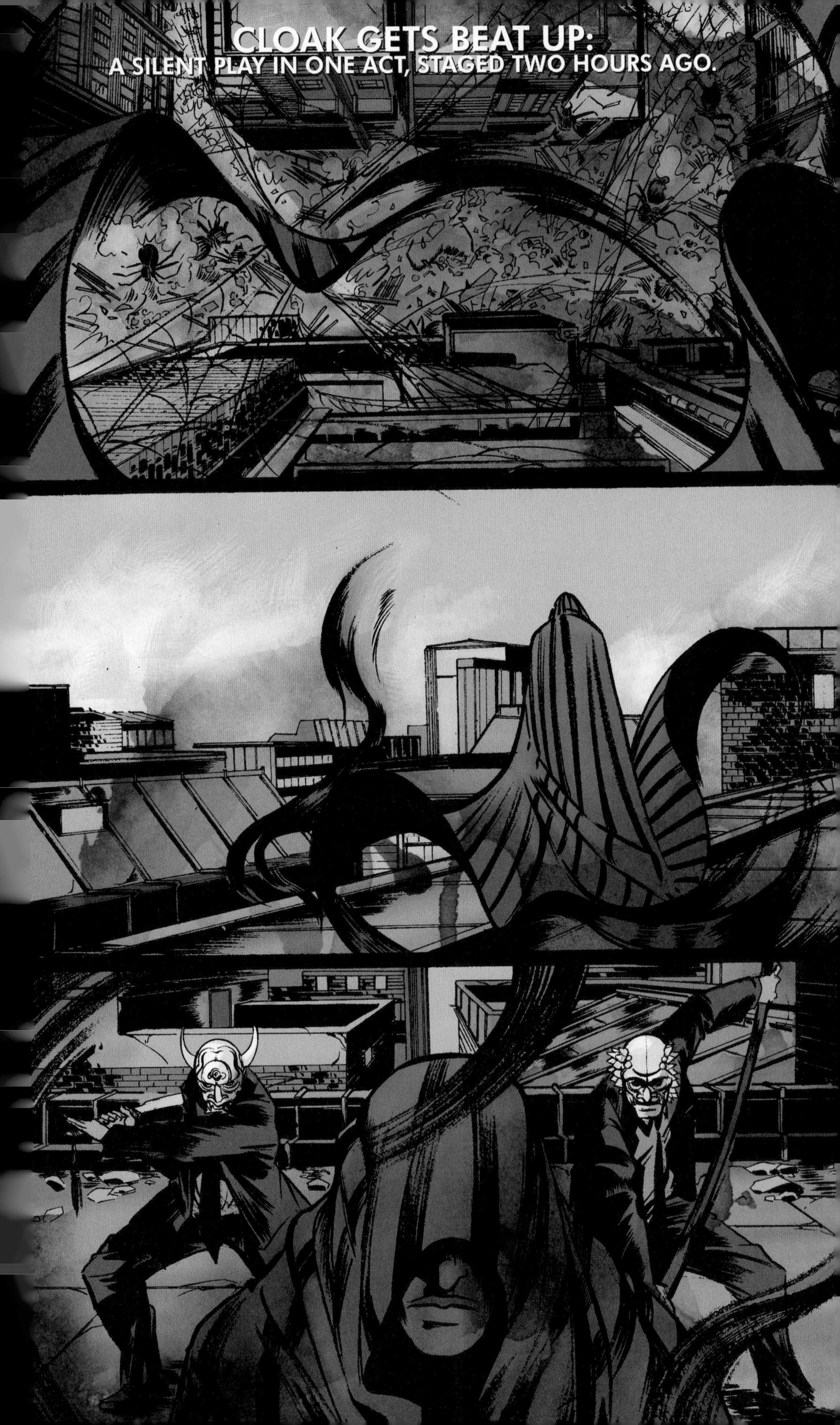
CLOAK GETS BEAT UP:
A SILENT PLAY IN ONE ACT, STAGED TWO HOURS AGO.

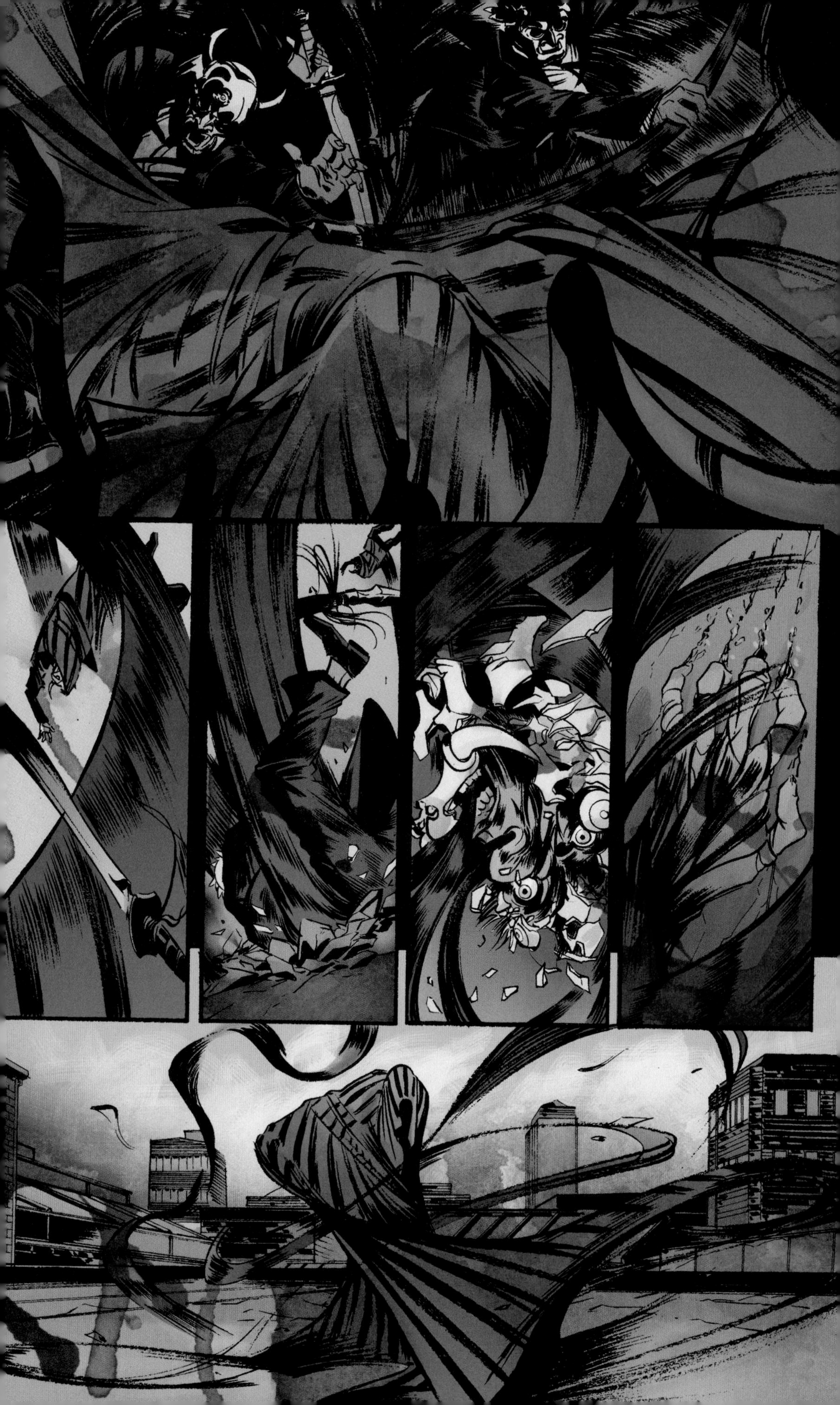

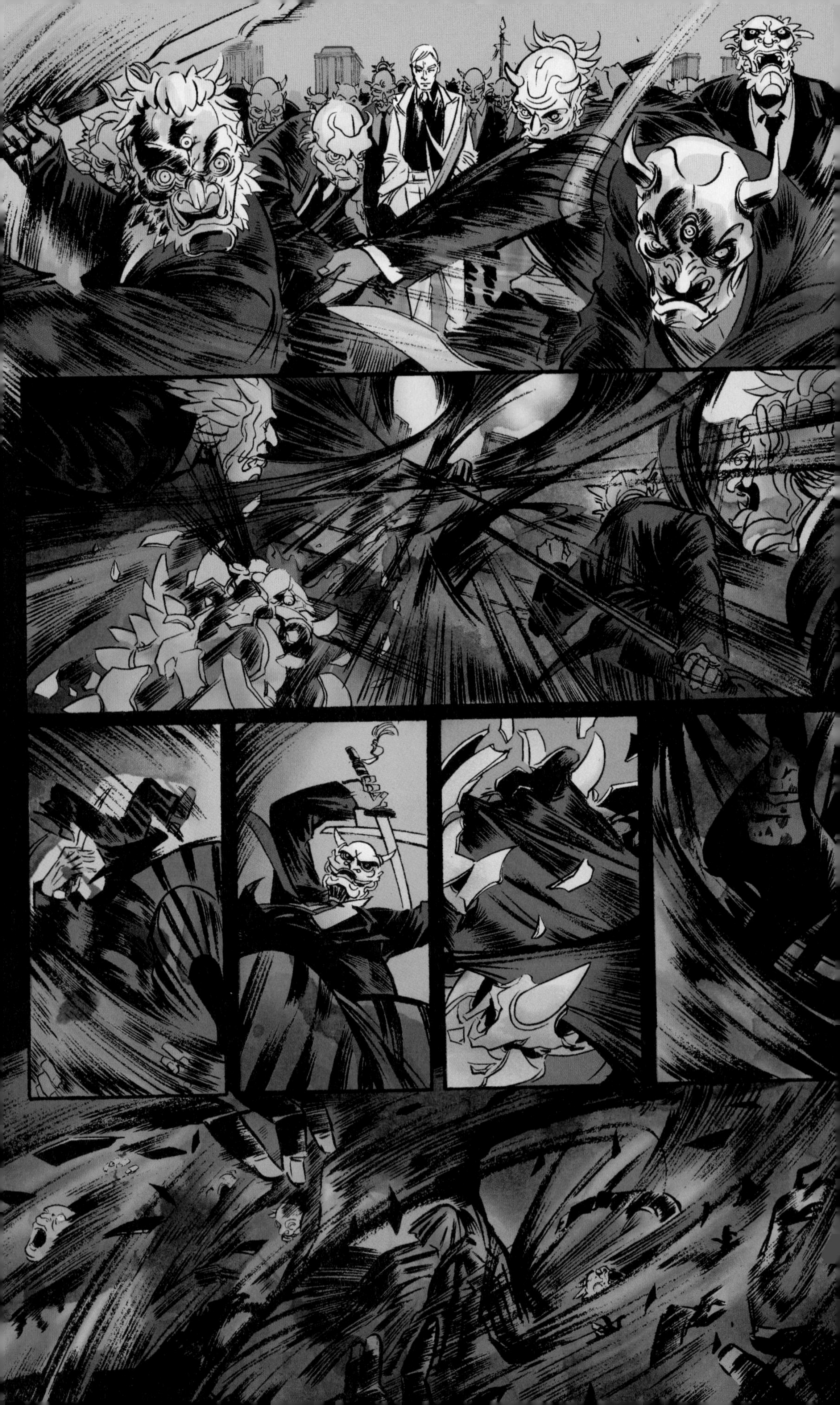

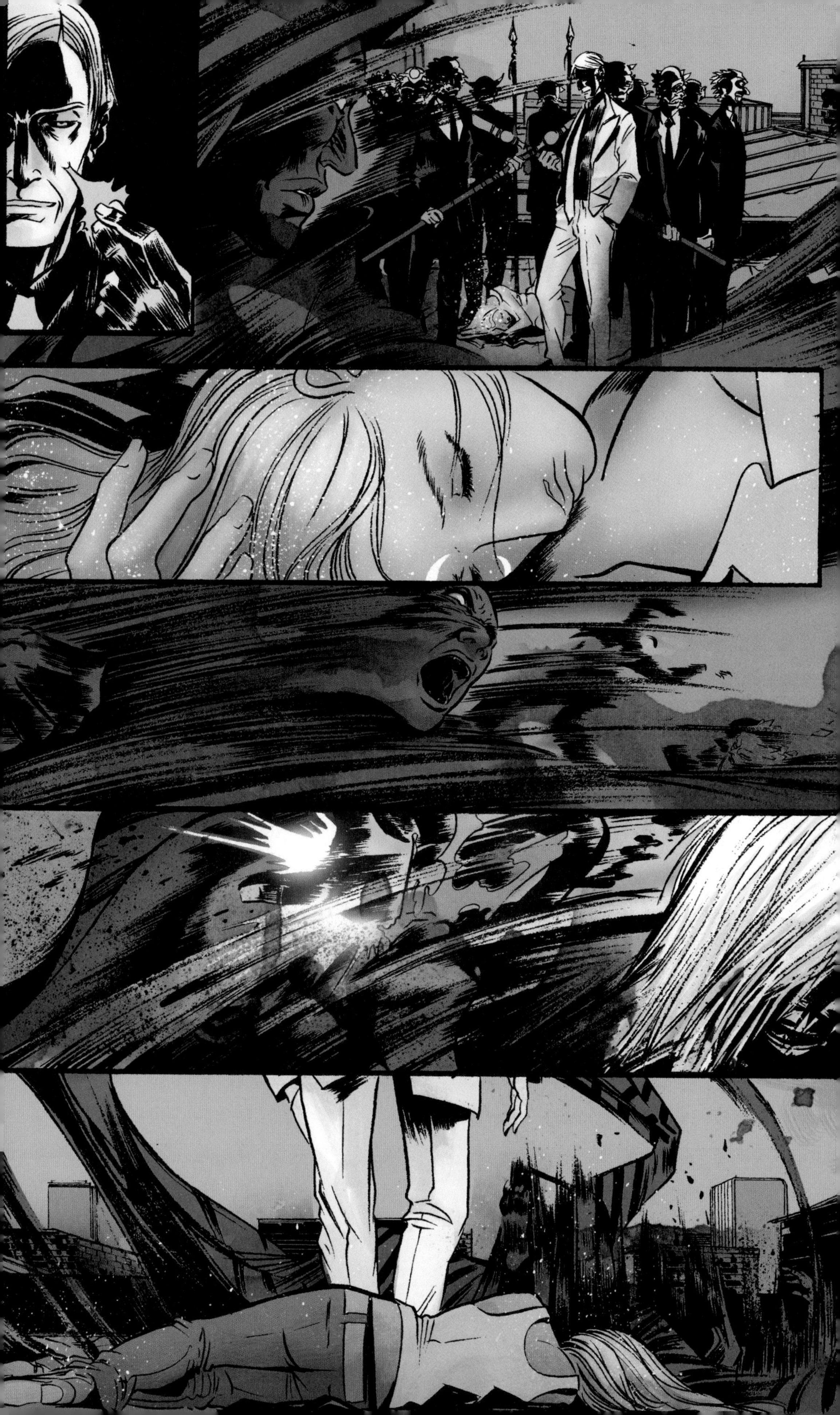

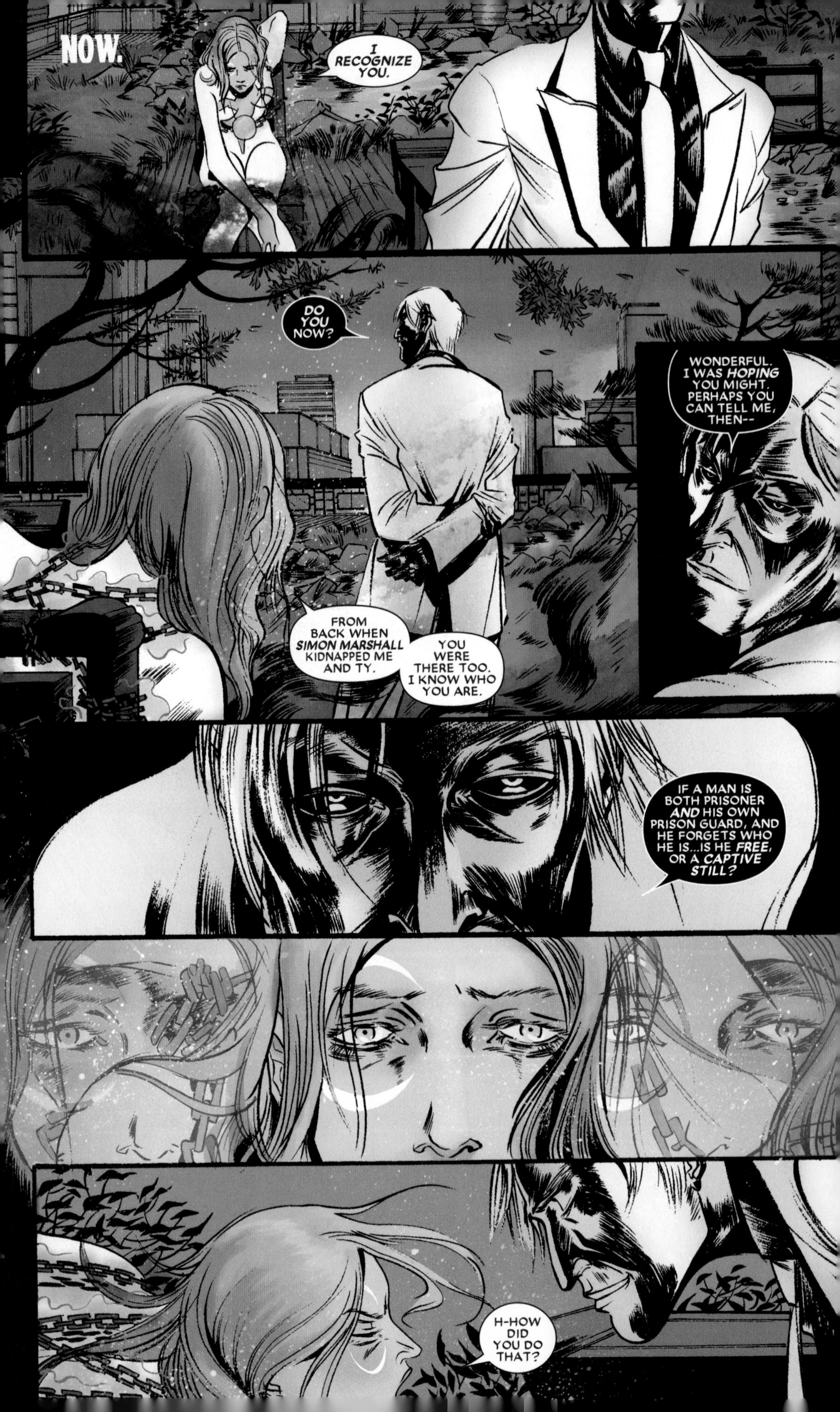
NOW.
I RECOGNIZE YOU.
DO YOU NOW?
WONDERFUL. I WAS HOPING YOU MIGHT. PERHAPS YOU CAN TELL ME, THEN--
FROM BACK WHEN SIMON MARSHALL KIDNAPPED ME AND TY.
YOU WERE THERE TOO. I KNOW WHO YOU ARE.
IF A MAN IS BOTH PRISONER AND HIS OWN PRISON GUARD, AND HE FORGETS WHO HE IS...IS HE FREE, OR A CAPTIVE STILL?
H-HOW DID YOU DO THAT?

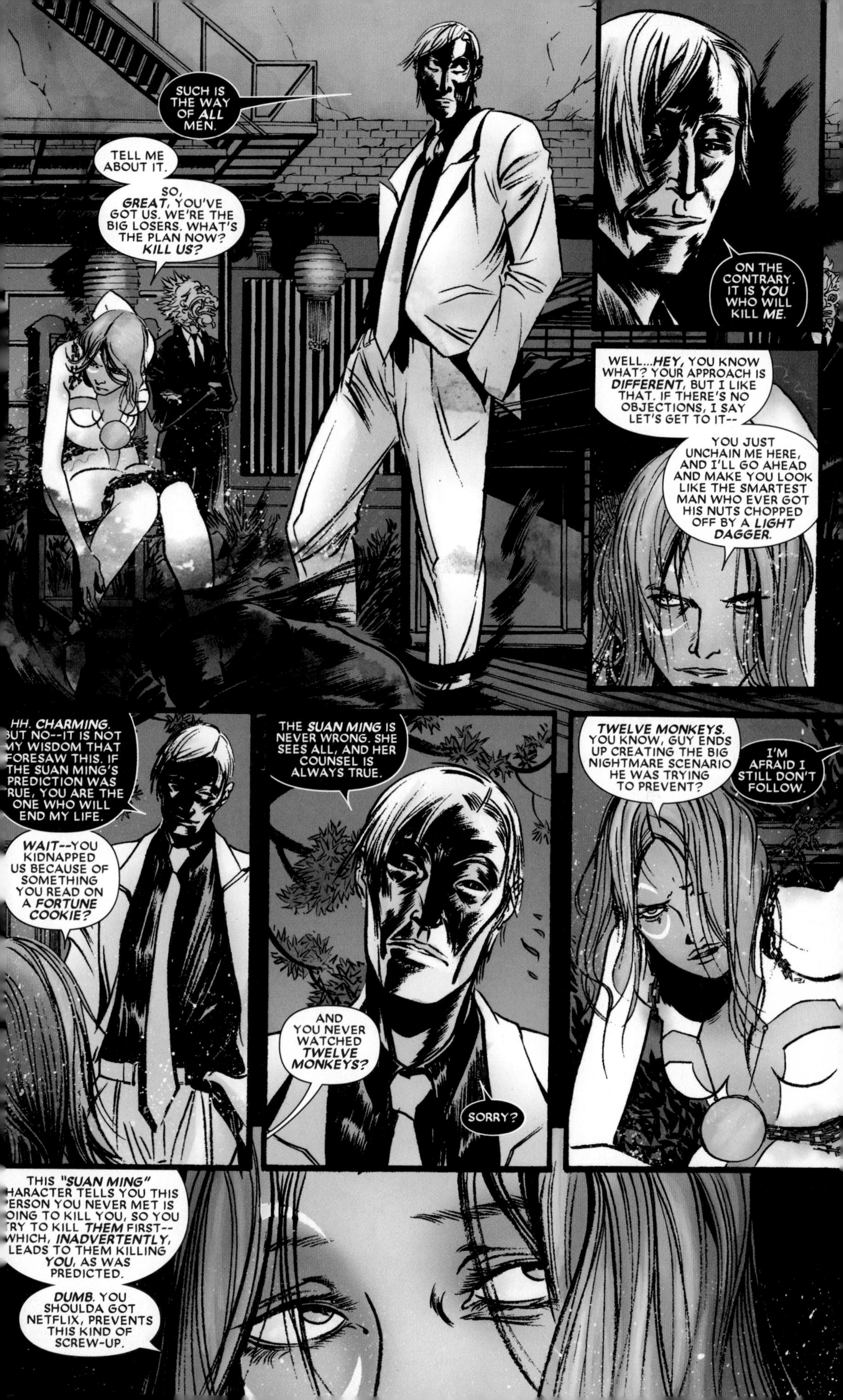
SUCH IS THE WAY OF *ALL* MEN.
TELL ME ABOUT IT.
SO, *GREAT*, YOU'VE GOT US. WE'RE THE BIG LOSERS. WHAT'S THE PLAN NOW? *KILL US?*
ON THE CONTRARY. IT IS *YOU* WHO WILL KILL *ME*.
WELL...*HEY*, YOU KNOW WHAT? YOUR APPROACH IS *DIFFERENT*, BUT I LIKE THAT. IF THERE'S NO OBJECTIONS, I SAY LET'S GET TO IT--
YOU JUST UNCHAIN ME HERE, AND I'LL GO AHEAD AND MAKE YOU LOOK LIKE THE SMARTEST MAN WHO EVER GOT HIS NUTS CHOPPED OFF BY A *LIGHT DAGGER*.
HH. *CHARMING*. UT NO--IT IS NOT MY WISDOM THAT FORESAW THIS. IF THE SUAN MING'S PREDICTION WAS RUE, YOU ARE THE ONE WHO WILL END MY LIFE.
*WAIT--*YOU KIDNAPPED US BECAUSE OF SOMETHING YOU READ ON A *FORTUNE COOKIE?*
THE *SUAN MING* IS NEVER WRONG. SHE SEES ALL, AND HER COUNSEL IS ALWAYS TRUE.
AND YOU NEVER WATCHED *TWELVE MONKEYS?*
SORRY?
TWELVE MONKEYS. YOU KNOW, GUY ENDS UP CREATING THE BIG NIGHTMARE SCENARIO HE WAS TRYING TO PREVENT?
I'M AFRAID I STILL DON'T FOLLOW.
THIS *"SUAN MING"* HARACTER TELLS YOU THIS ERSON YOU NEVER MET IS OING TO KILL YOU, SO YOU RY TO KILL *THEM* FIRST-- WHICH, *INADVERTENTLY*, LEADS TO THEM KILLING *YOU*, AS WAS PREDICTED.
DUMB. YOU SHOULDA GOT NETFLIX, PREVENTS THIS KIND OF SCREW-UP.

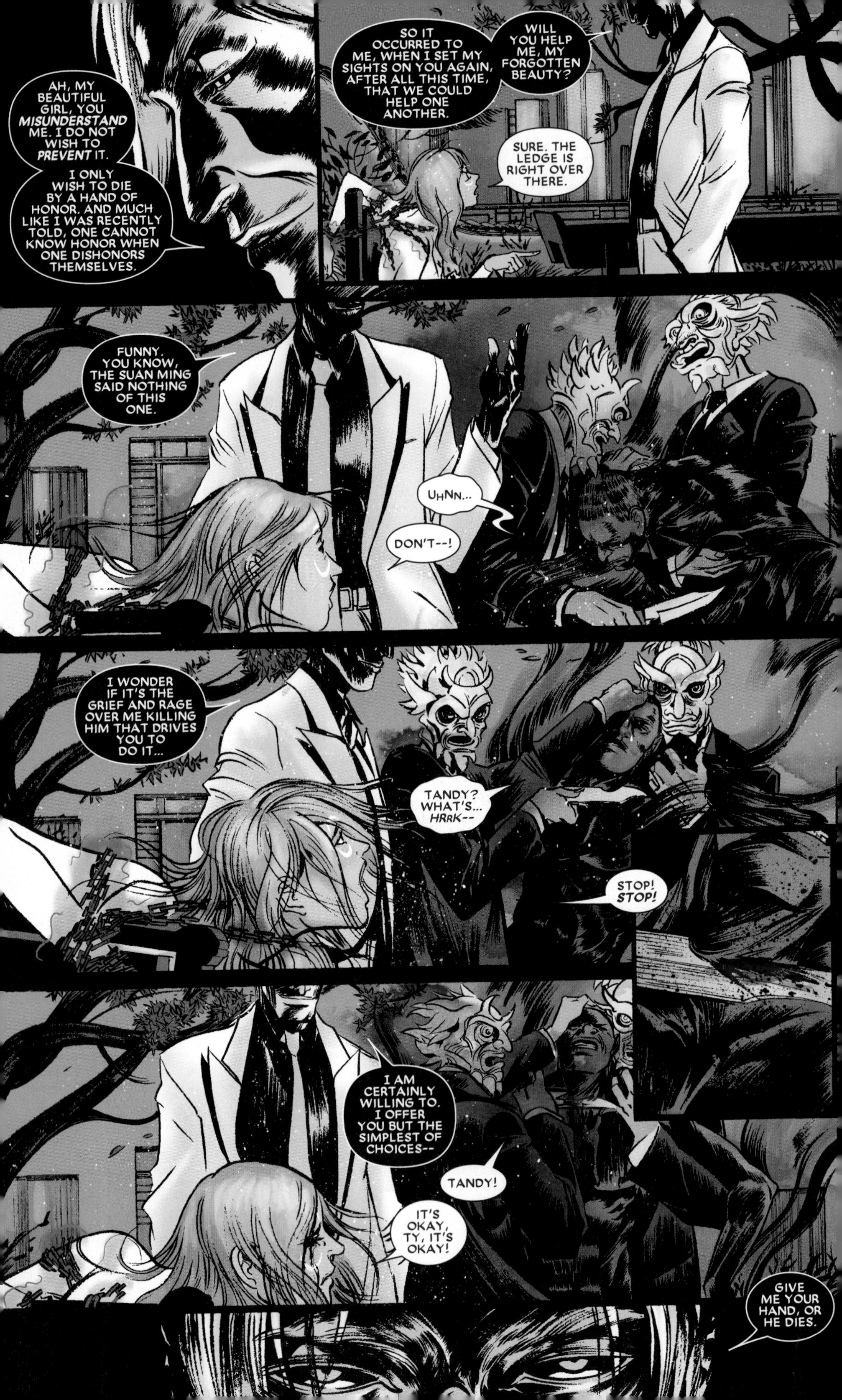
AH, MY BEAUTIFUL GIRL, YOU *MISUNDERSTAND* ME. I DO NOT WISH TO *PREVENT* IT.
I ONLY WISH TO DIE BY A HAND OF HONOR. AND MUCH LIKE I WAS RECENTLY TOLD, ONE CANNOT KNOW HONOR WHEN ONE DISHONORS THEMSELVES.
SO IT OCCURRED TO ME, WHEN I SET MY SIGHTS ON YOU AGAIN, AFTER ALL THIS TIME, THAT WE COULD HELP ONE ANOTHER.
WILL YOU HELP ME, MY FORGOTTEN BEAUTY?
SURE. THE LEDGE IS RIGHT OVER THERE.
FUNNY. YOU KNOW, THE SUAN MING SAID NOTHING OF THIS ONE.
UHNN...
DON'T--!
I WONDER IF IT'S THE GRIEF AND RAGE OVER ME KILLING HIM THAT DRIVES YOU TO DO IT...
TANDY? WHAT'S... *HRRK--*
STOP! **STOP!**
I AM CERTAINLY WILLING TO. I OFFER YOU BUT THE SIMPLEST OF CHOICES--
TANDY!
IT'S OKAY, TY, IT'S OKAY!
GIVE ME YOUR HAND, OR HE DIES.

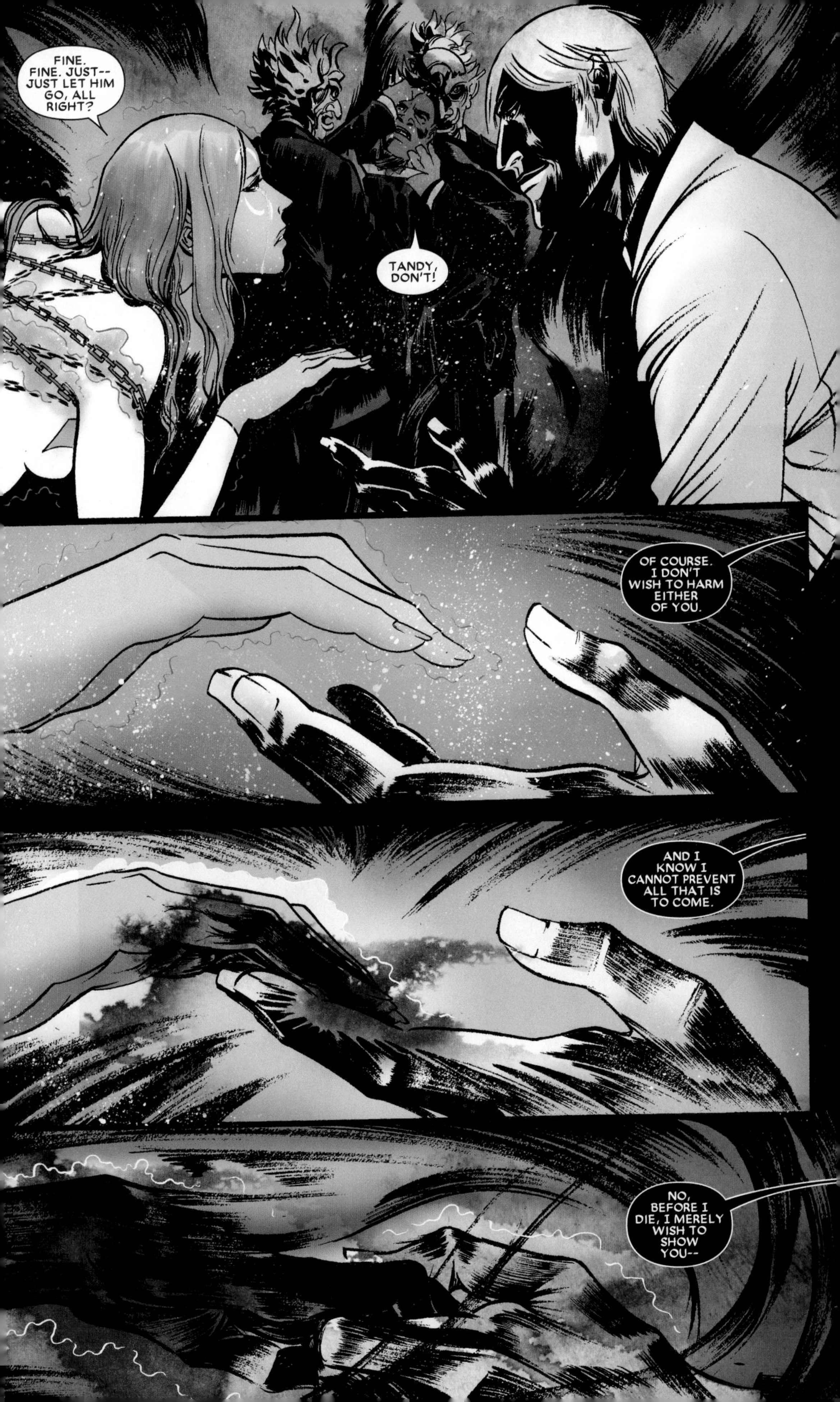
FINE. FINE. JUST-- JUST LET HIM GO, ALL RIGHT?
TANDY, DON'T!
OF COURSE. I DON'T WISH TO HARM EITHER OF YOU.
AND I KNOW I CANNOT PREVENT ALL THAT IS TO COME.
NO, BEFORE I DIE, I MERELY WISH TO SHOW YOU--

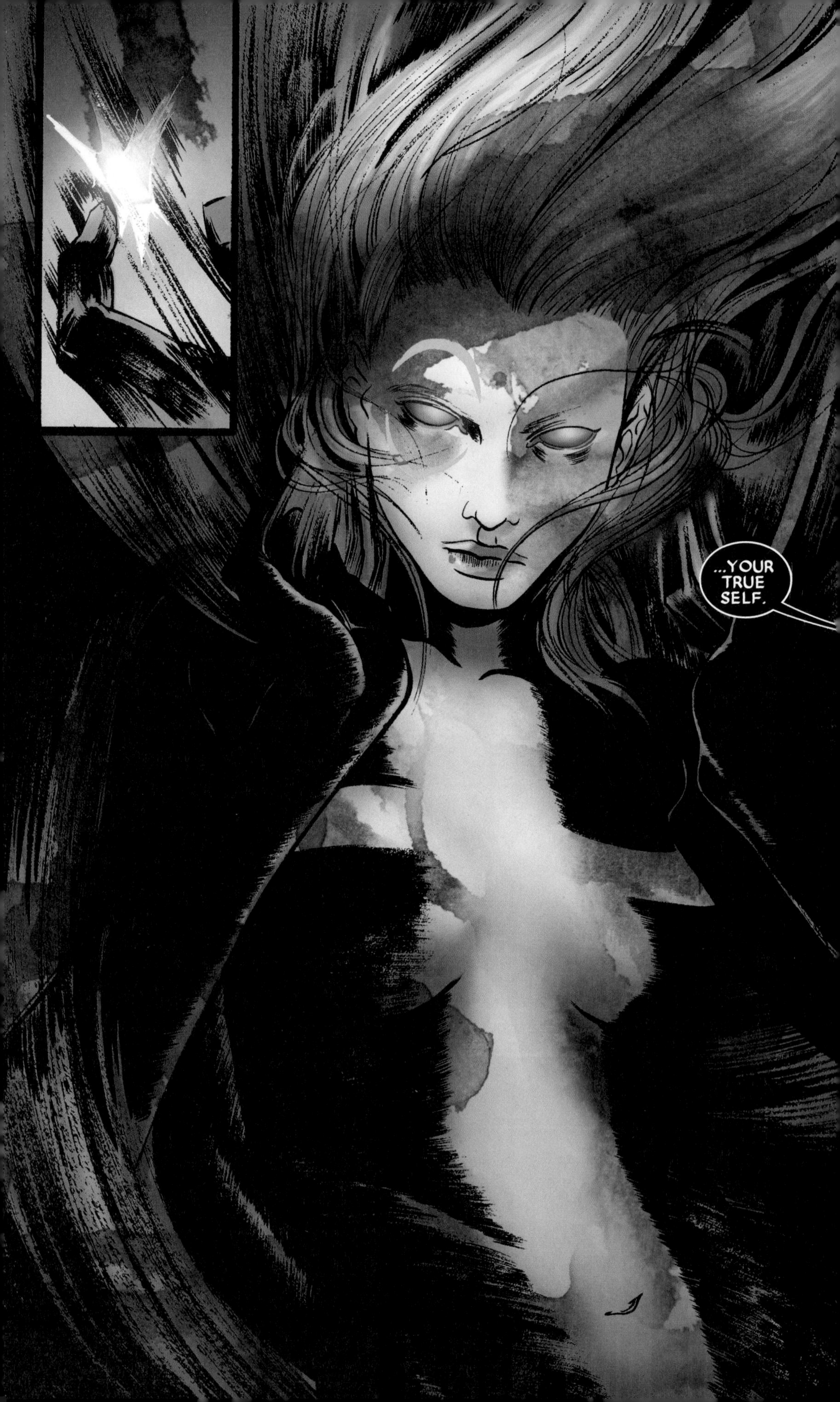
...YOUR TRUE SELF.

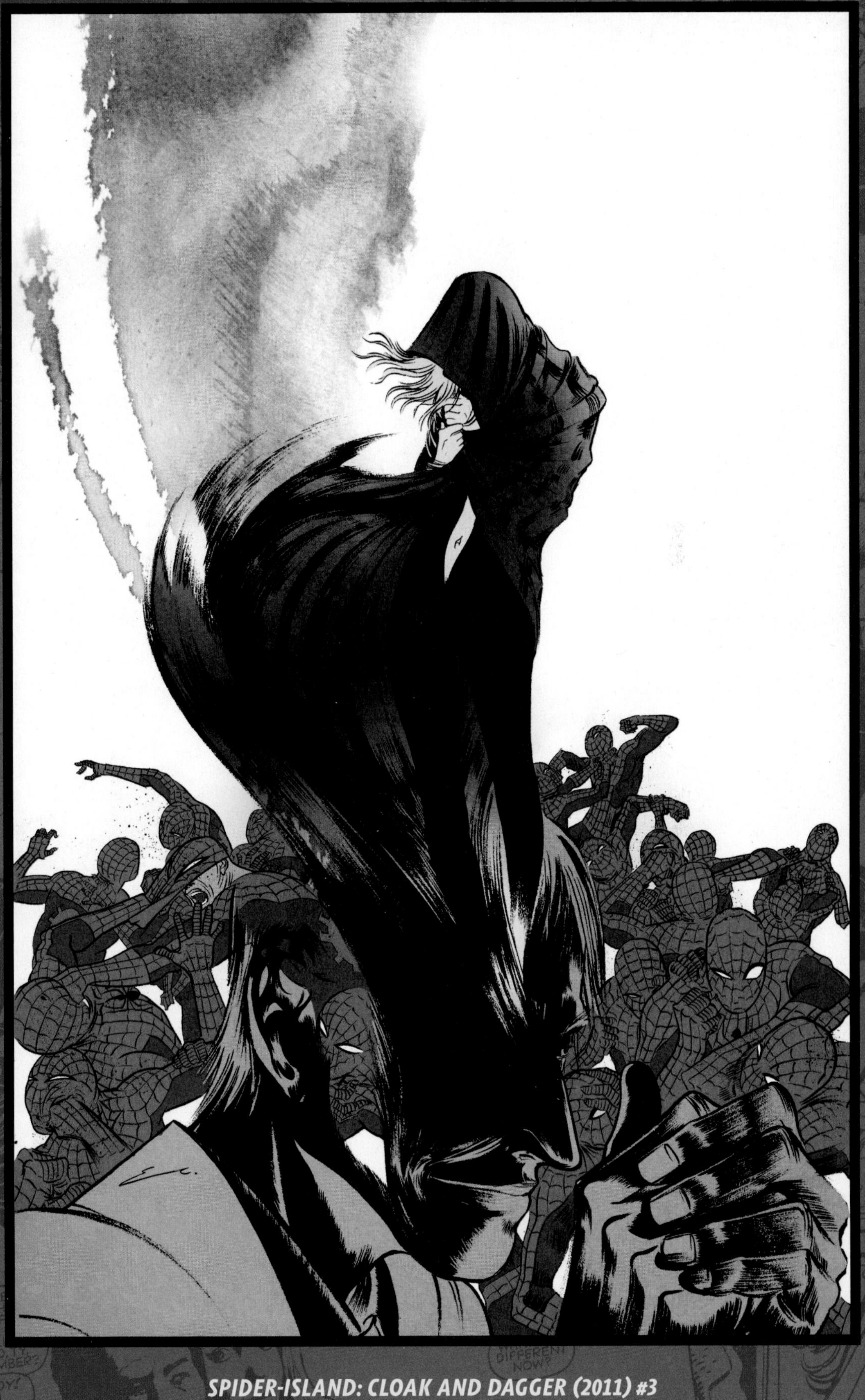

SPIDER-ISLAND: CLOAK AND DAGGER (2011) #3

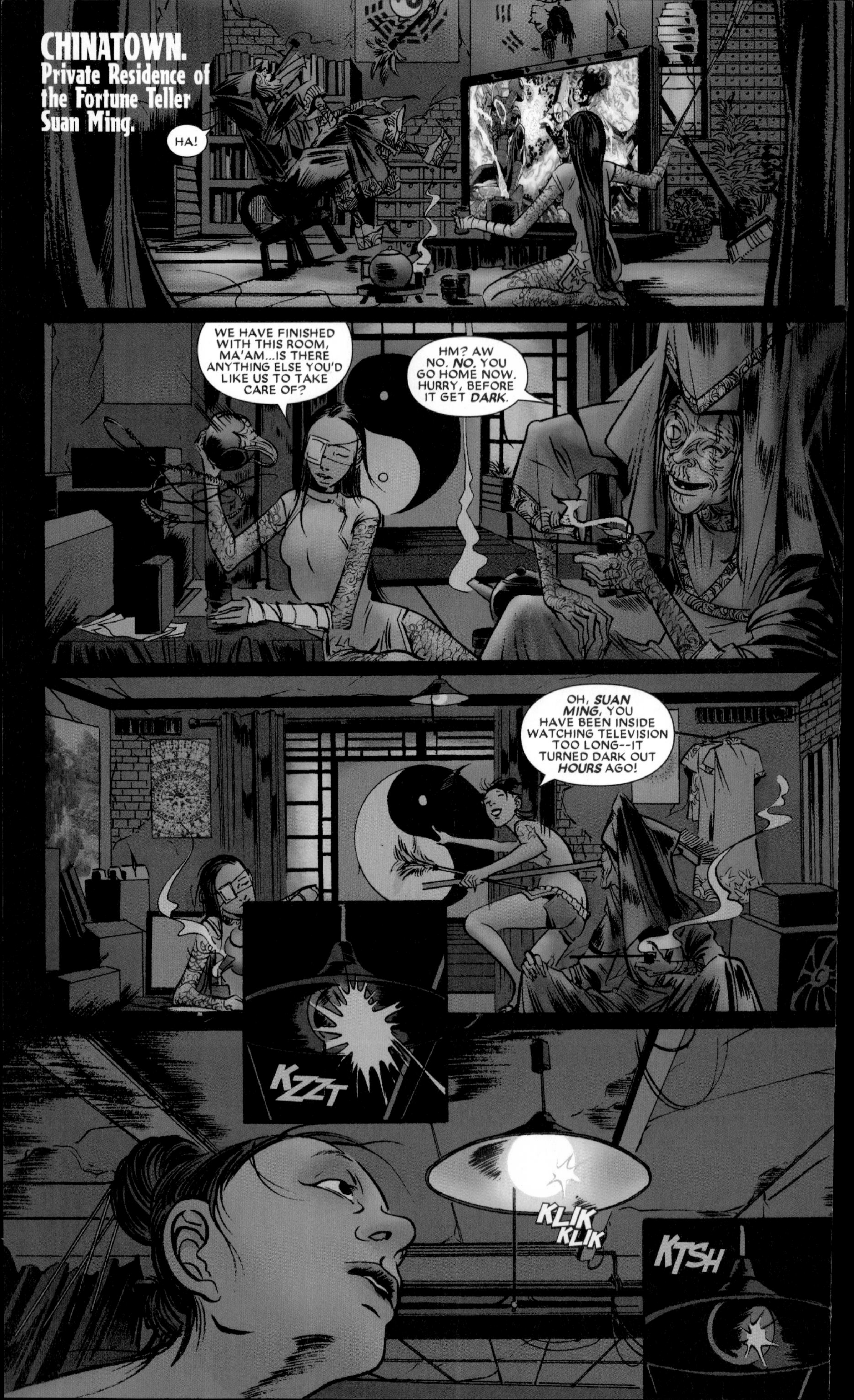
CHINATOWN.
Private Residence of the Fortune Teller Suan Ming.
HA!
WE HAVE FINISHED WITH THIS ROOM, MA'AM...IS THERE ANYTHING ELSE YOU'D LIKE US TO TAKE CARE OF?
HM? AW NO. NO. YOU GO HOME NOW. HURRY, BEFORE IT GET DARK.
OH, SUAN MING, YOU HAVE BEEN INSIDE WATCHING TELEVISION TOO LONG--IT TURNED DARK OUT HOURS AGO!
KZZT
KLIK KLIK
KTSH

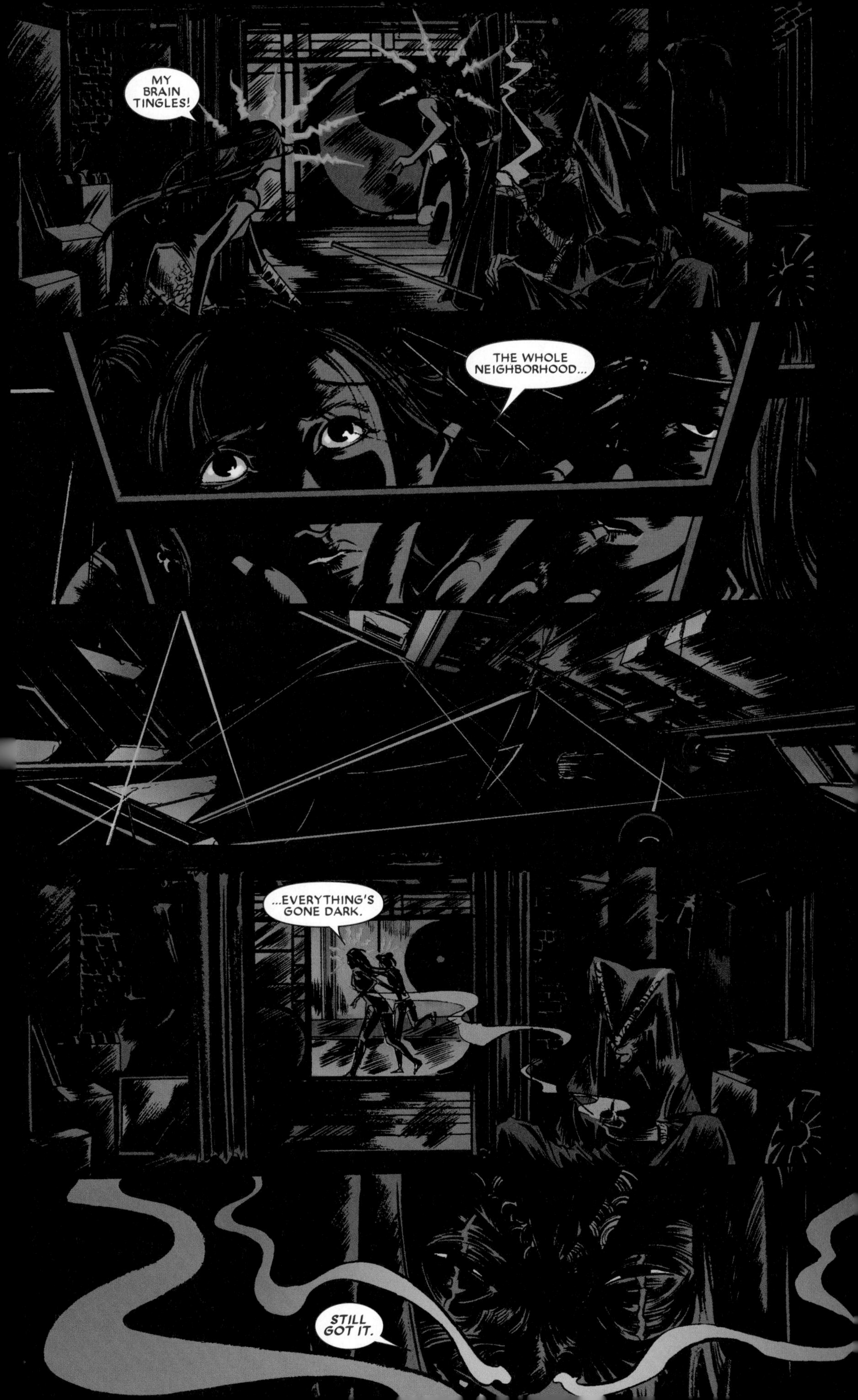
MY BRAIN TINGLES!
THE WHOLE NEIGHBORHOOD...
...EVERYTHING'S GONE DARK.
STILL GOT IT.

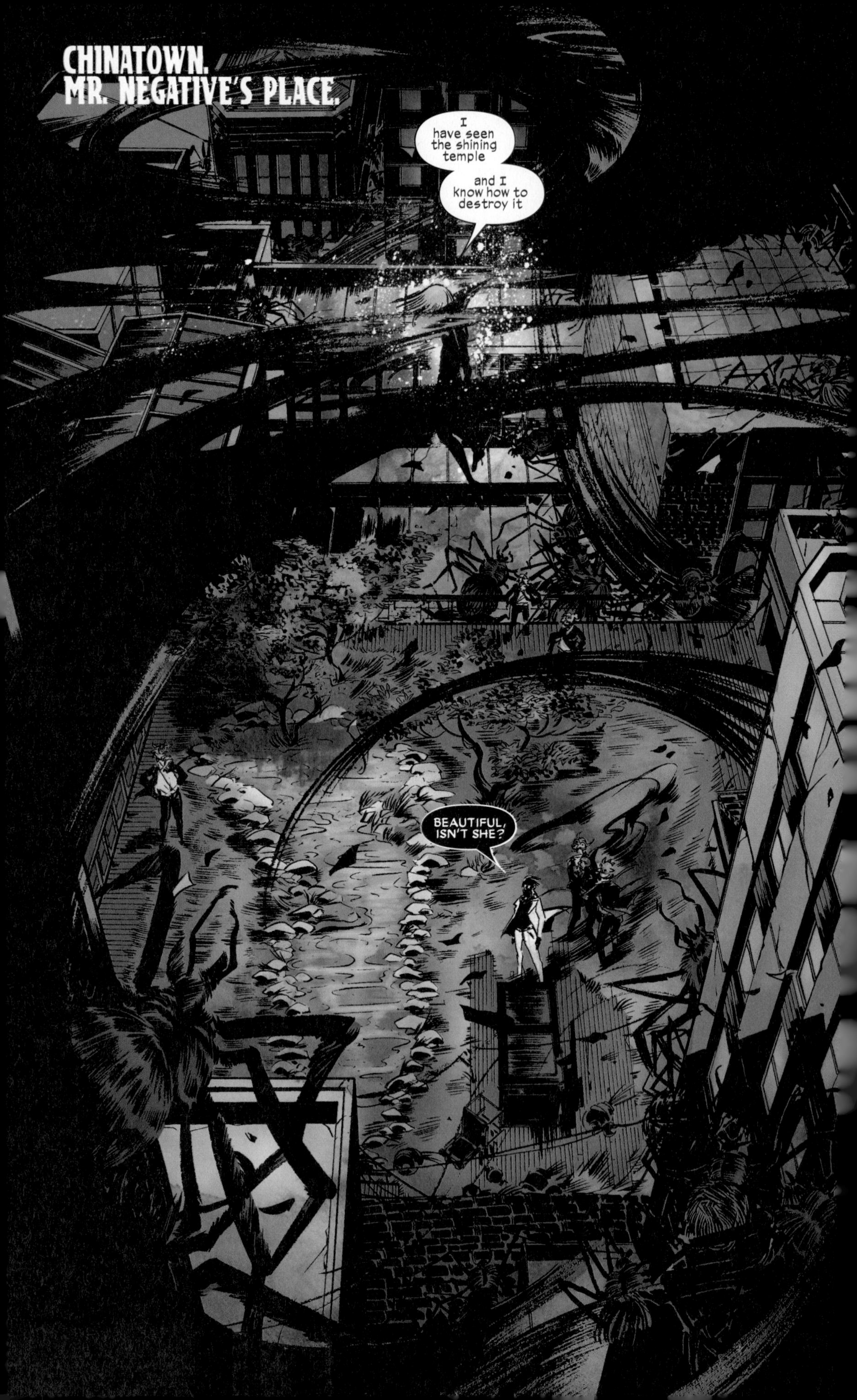
CHINATOWN.
MR. NEGATIVE'S PLACE.
I have seen the shining temple
and I know how to destroy it
BEAUTIFUL, ISN'T SHE?

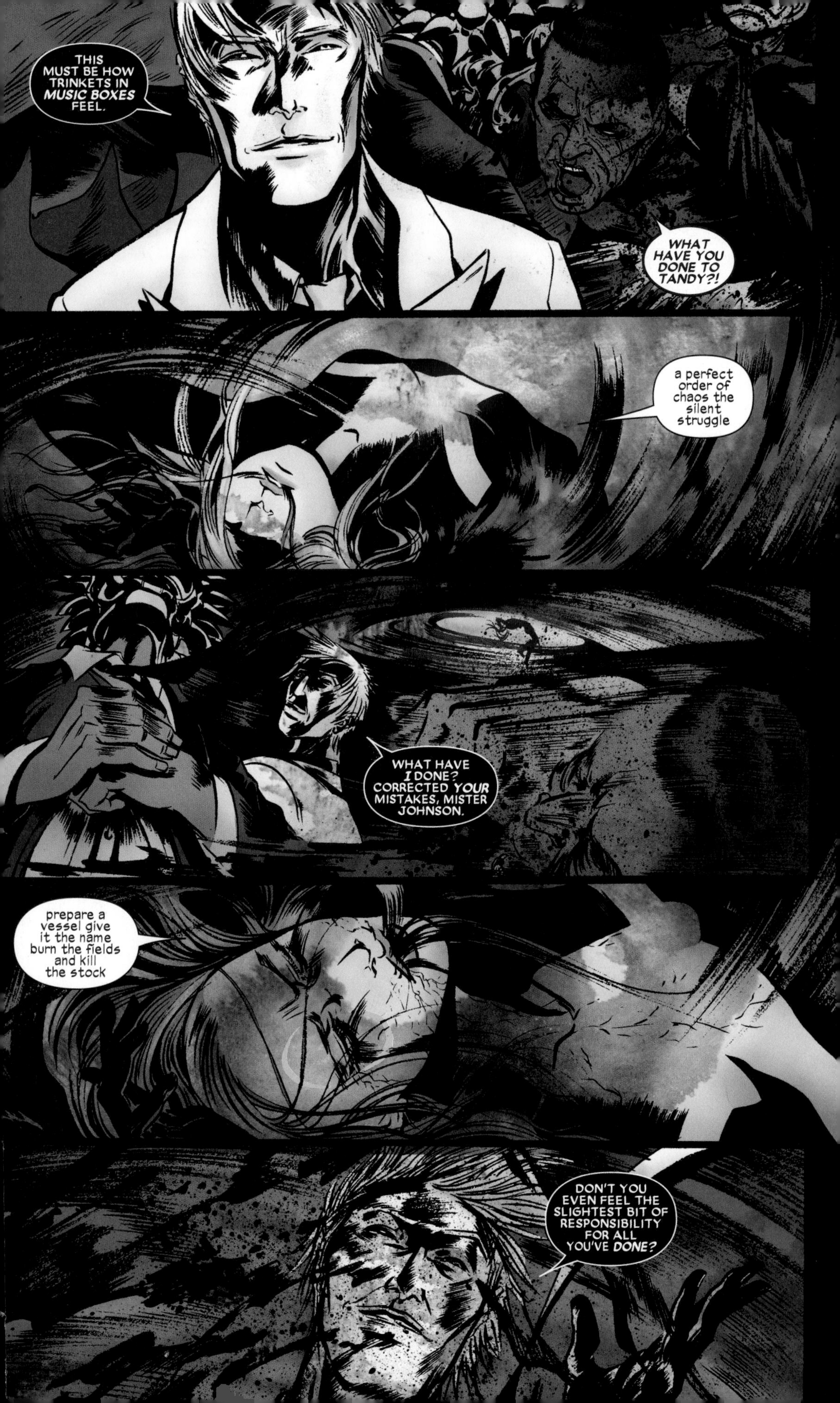
THIS MUST BE HOW TRINKETS IN *MUSIC BOXES* FEEL.
WHAT HAVE YOU DONE TO TANDY?!
a perfect order of chaos the silent struggle
WHAT HAVE *I* DONE? CORRECTED *YOUR* MISTAKES, MISTER JOHNSON.
prepare a vessel give it the name burn the fields and kill the stock
DON'T YOU EVEN FEEL THE SLIGHTEST BIT OF RESPONSIBILITY FOR ALL YOU'VE *DONE?*

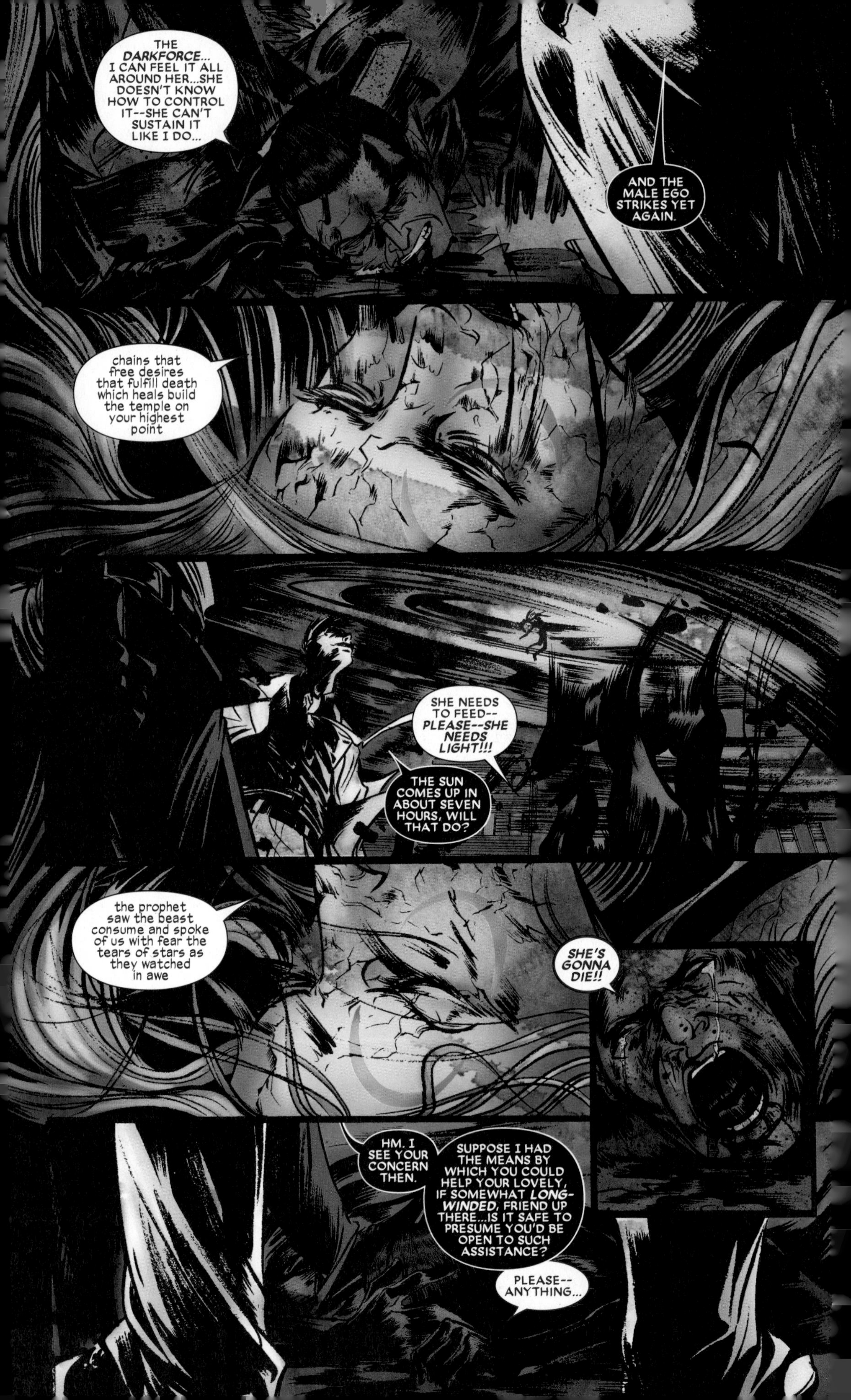
THE *DARKFORCE*... I CAN FEEL IT ALL AROUND HER...SHE DOESN'T KNOW HOW TO CONTROL IT--SHE CAN'T SUSTAIN IT LIKE I DO...
AND THE MALE EGO STRIKES YET AGAIN.
chains that free desires that fulfill death which heals build the temple on your highest point
SHE NEEDS TO FEED-- *PLEASE--SHE NEEDS LIGHT!!!*
THE SUN COMES UP IN ABOUT SEVEN HOURS, WILL THAT DO?
the prophet saw the beast consume and spoke of us with fear the tears of stars as they watched in awe
SHE'S GONNA DIE!!
HM. I SEE YOUR CONCERN THEN.
SUPPOSE I HAD THE MEANS BY WHICH YOU COULD HELP YOUR LOVELY, IF SOMEWHAT *LONG-WINDED*, FRIEND UP THERE...IS IT SAFE TO PRESUME YOU'D BE OPEN TO SUCH ASSISTANCE?
PLEASE-- ANYTHING...

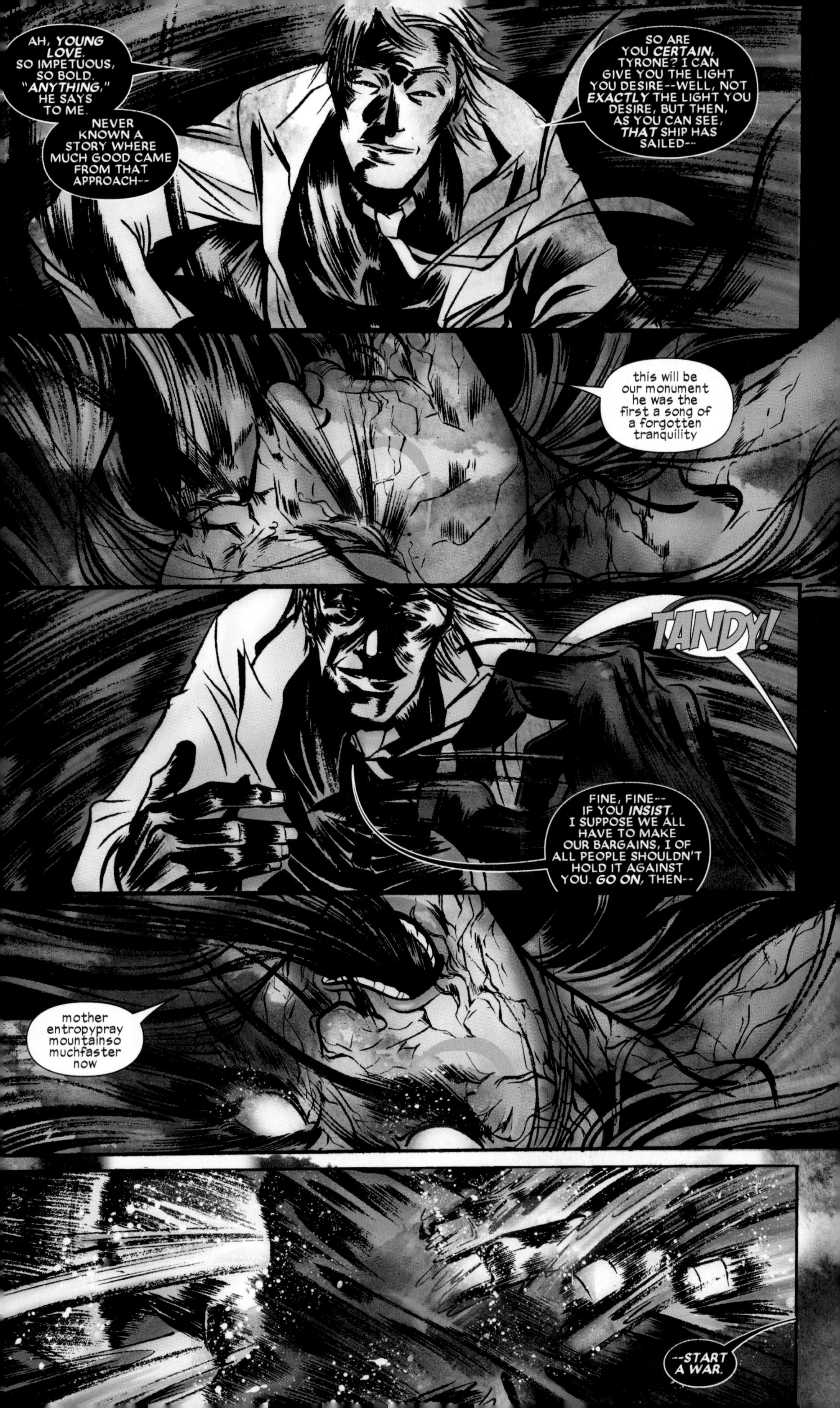
AH, YOUNG LOVE. SO IMPETUOUS, SO BOLD. "ANYTHING," HE SAYS TO ME.
NEVER KNOWN A STORY WHERE MUCH GOOD CAME FROM THAT APPROACH--
SO ARE YOU CERTAIN, TYRONE? I CAN GIVE YOU THE LIGHT YOU DESIRE--WELL, NOT EXACTLY THE LIGHT YOU DESIRE, BUT THEN, AS YOU CAN SEE, THAT SHIP HAS SAILED--
this will be our monument he was the first a song of a forgotten tranquility
TANDY!
FINE, FINE-- IF YOU INSIST. I SUPPOSE WE ALL HAVE TO MAKE OUR BARGAINS, I OF ALL PEOPLE SHOULDN'T HOLD IT AGAINST YOU. GO ON, THEN--
mother entropypray mountainso muchfaster now
--START A WAR.

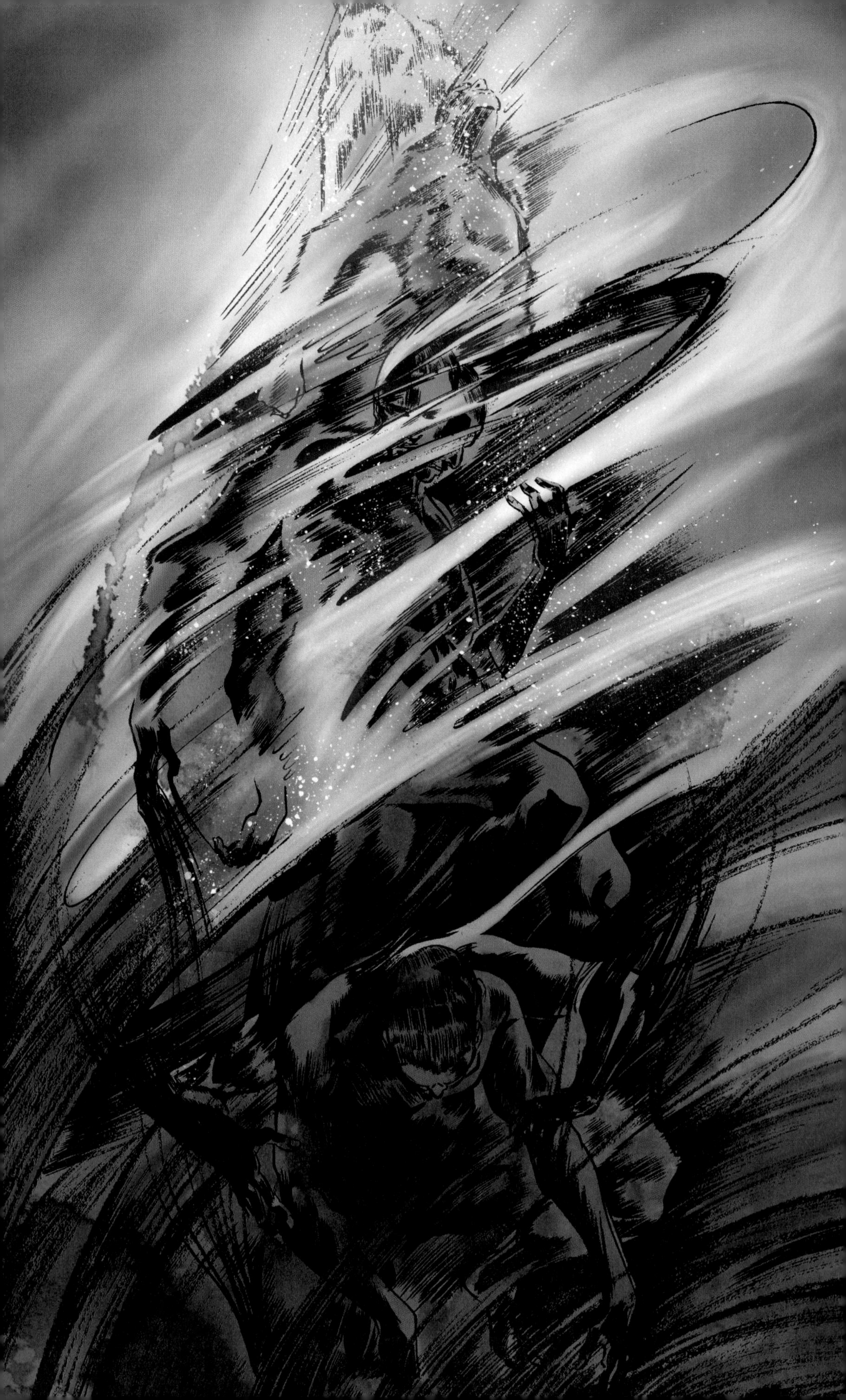

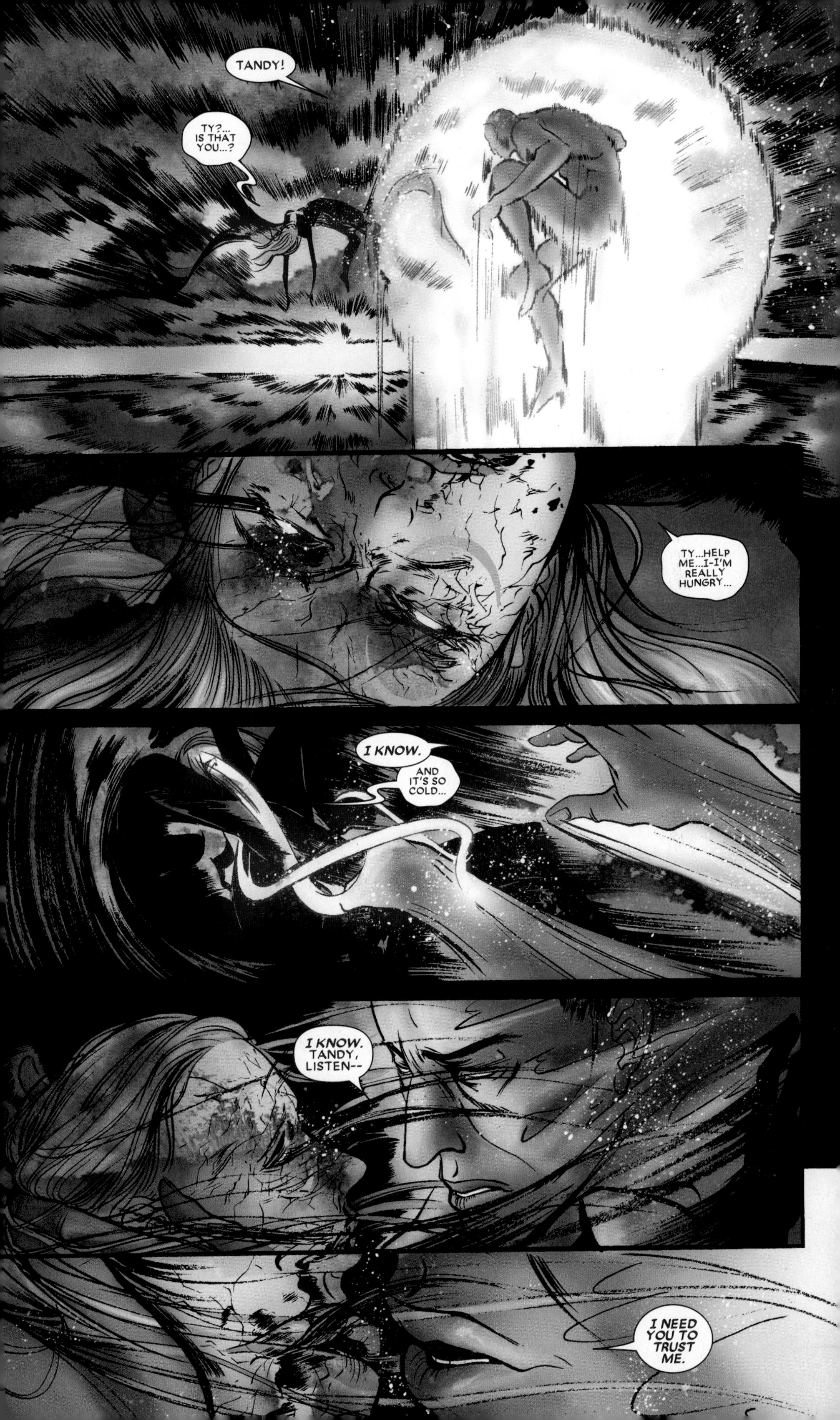

TANDY!
TY?... IS THAT YOU...?
TY...HELP ME...I-I'M REALLY HUNGRY...
I KNOW.
AND IT'S SO COLD...
I KNOW. TANDY, LISTEN--
I NEED YOU TO TRUST ME.

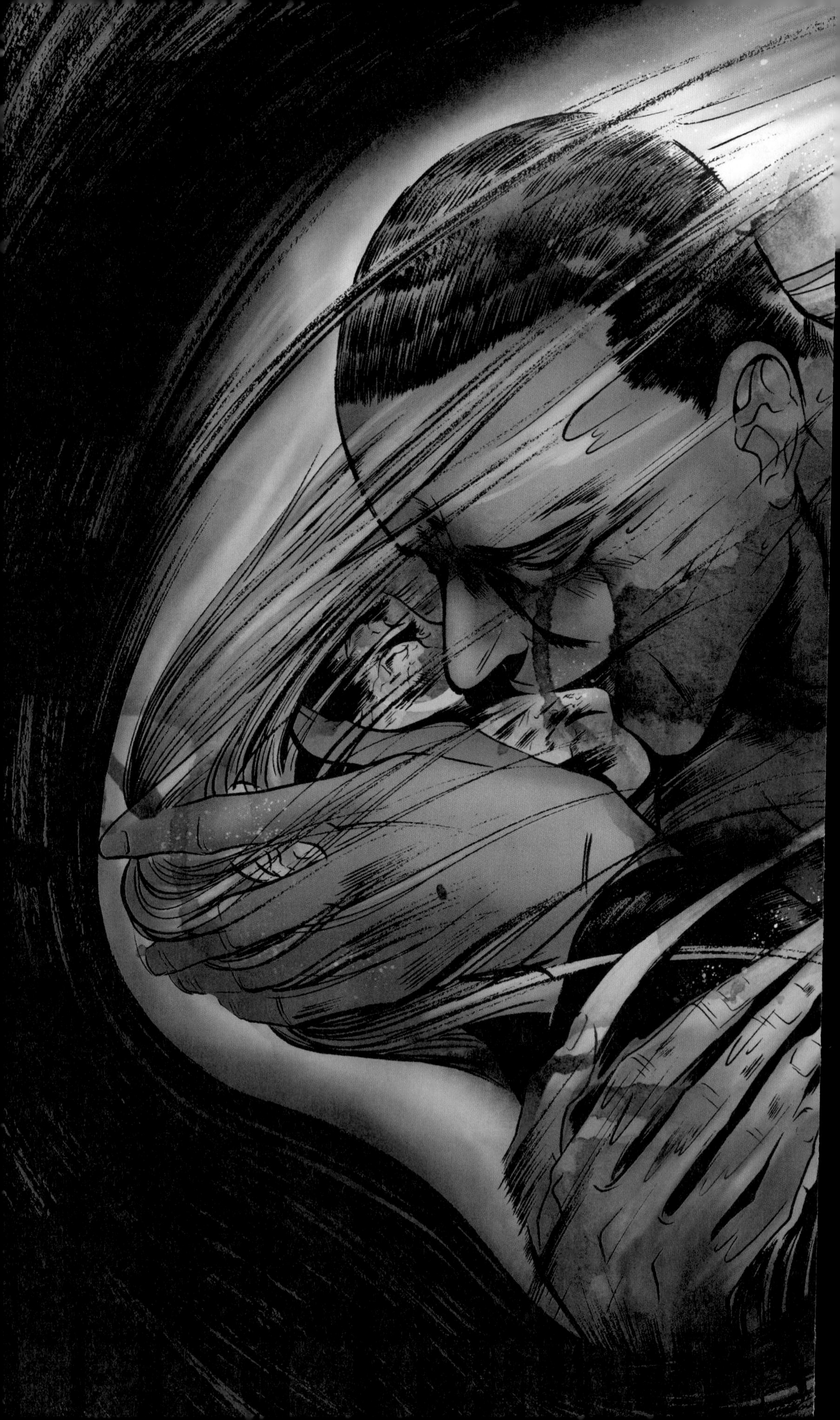

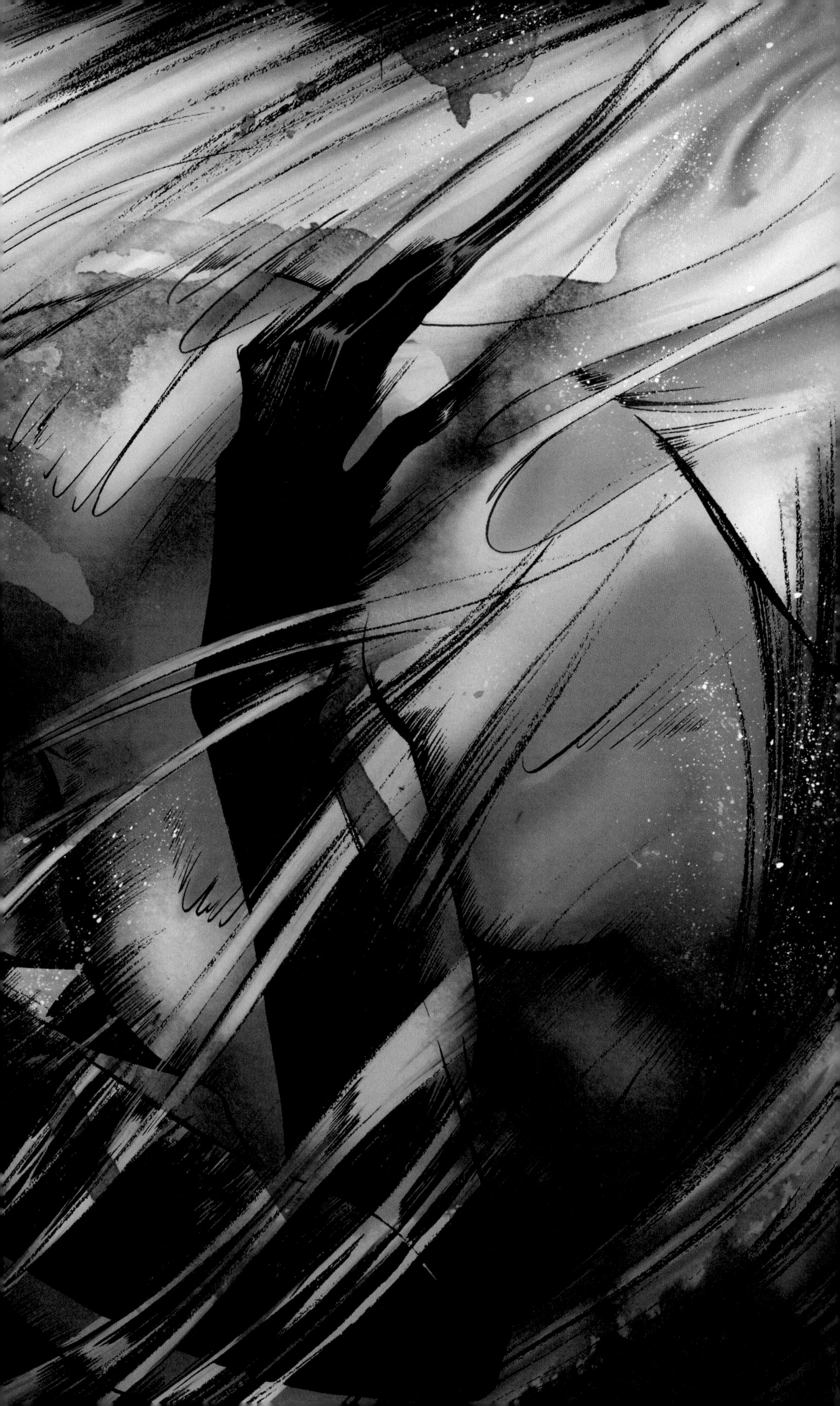

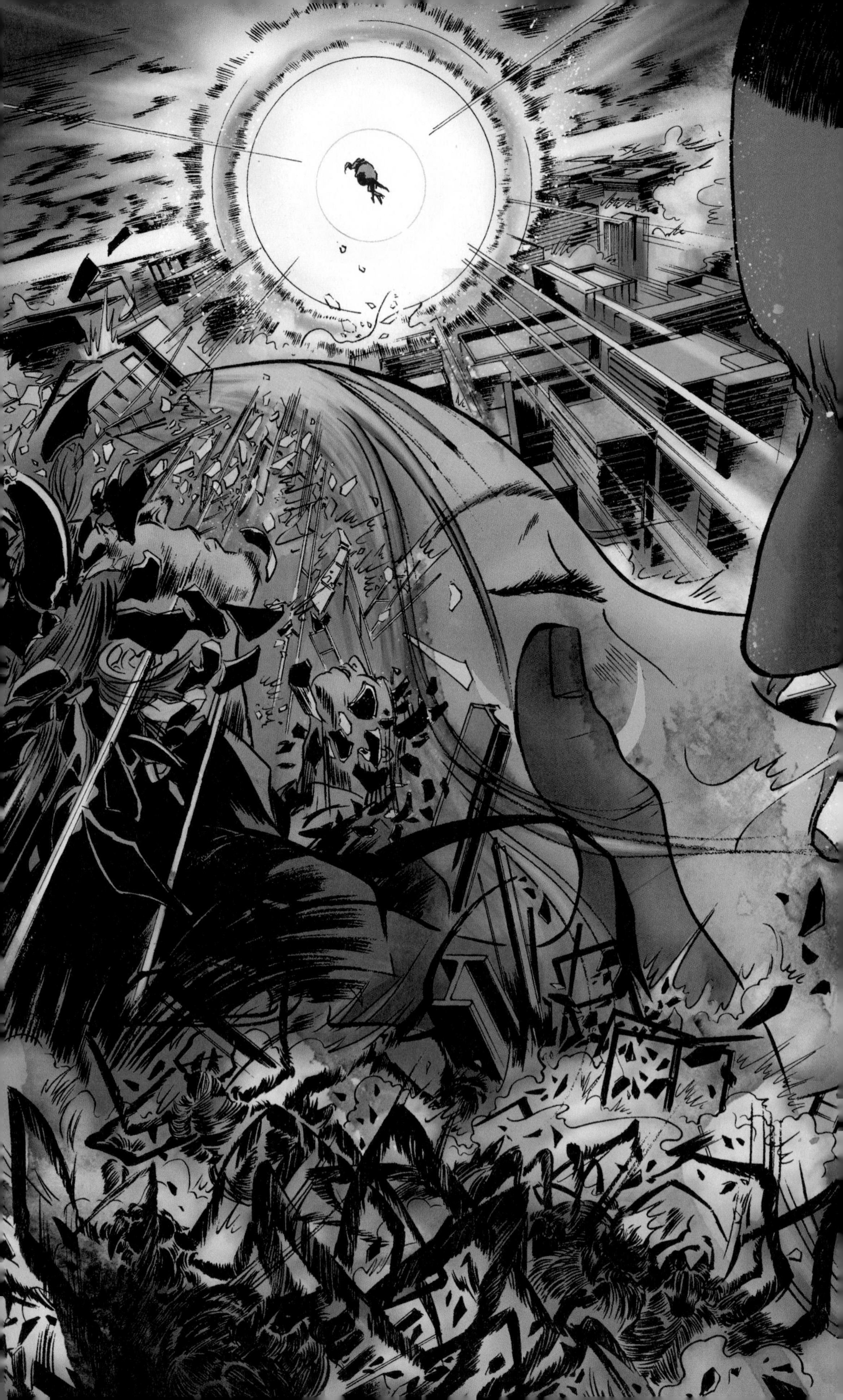

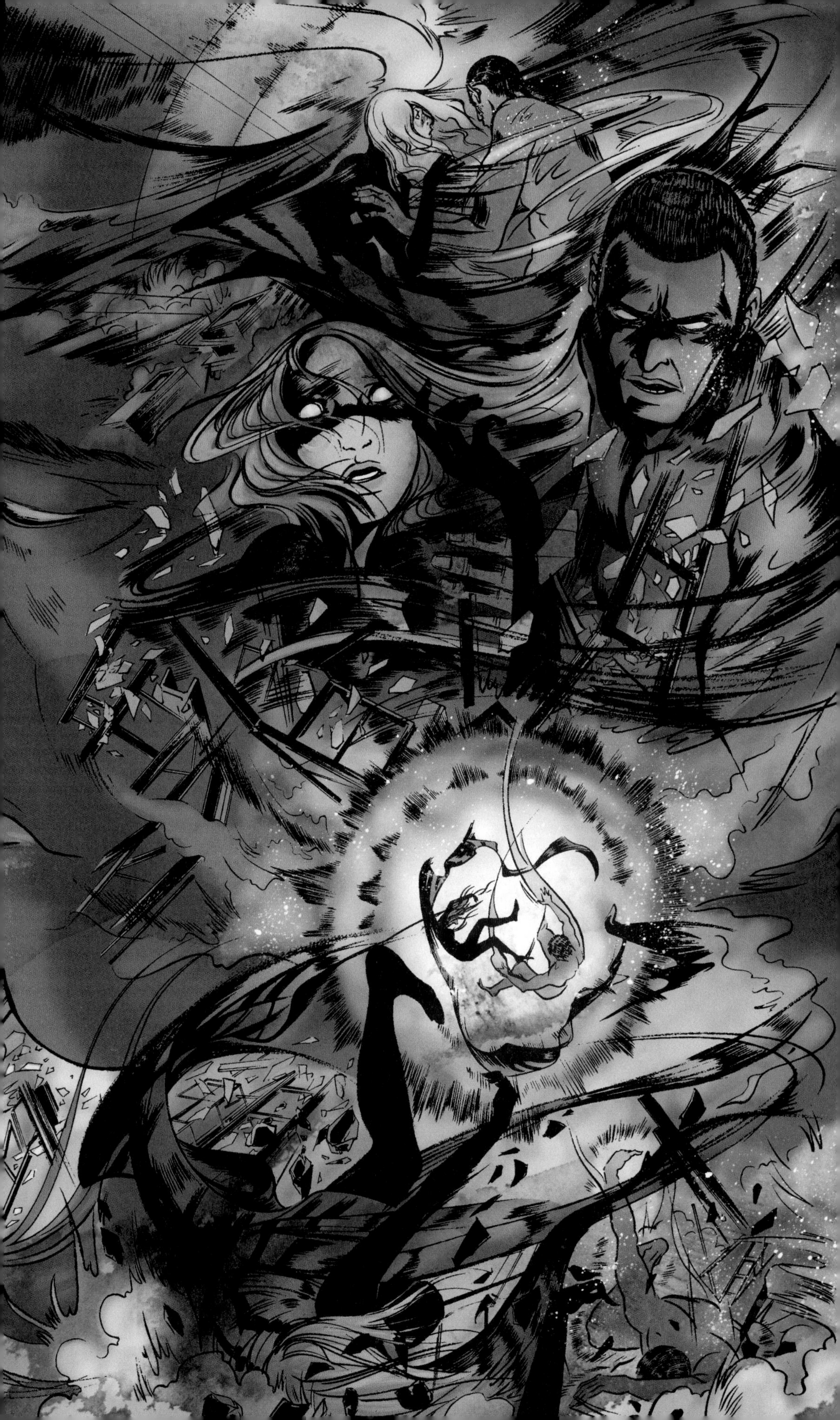

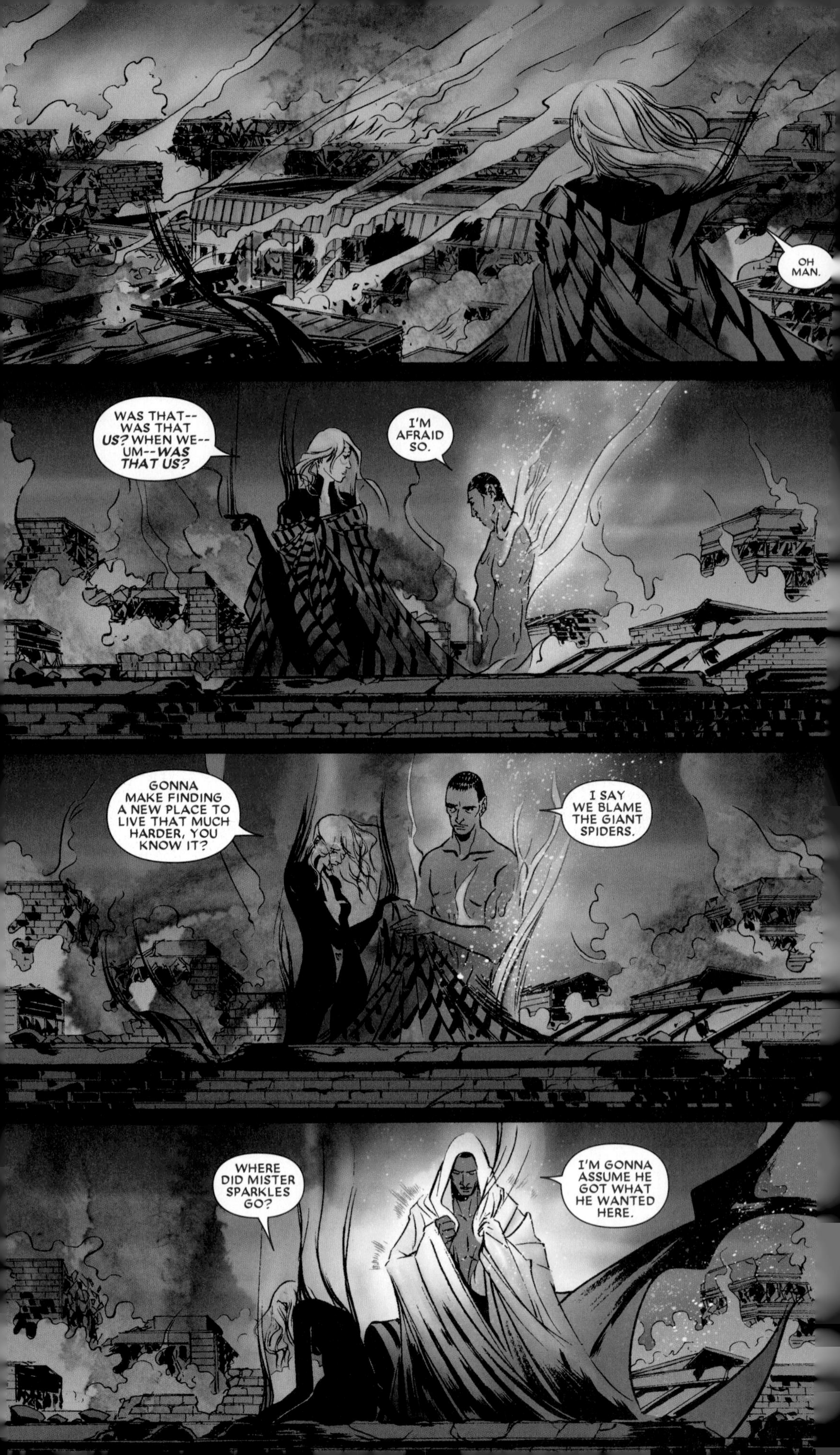
OH MAN.
WAS THAT-- WAS THAT *US?* WHEN WE-- UM--***WAS THAT US?***
I'M AFRAID SO.
GONNA MAKE FINDING A NEW PLACE TO LIVE THAT MUCH HARDER, YOU KNOW IT?
I SAY WE BLAME THE GIANT SPIDERS.
WHERE DID MISTER SPARKLES GO?
I'M GONNA ASSUME HE GOT WHAT HE WANTED HERE.

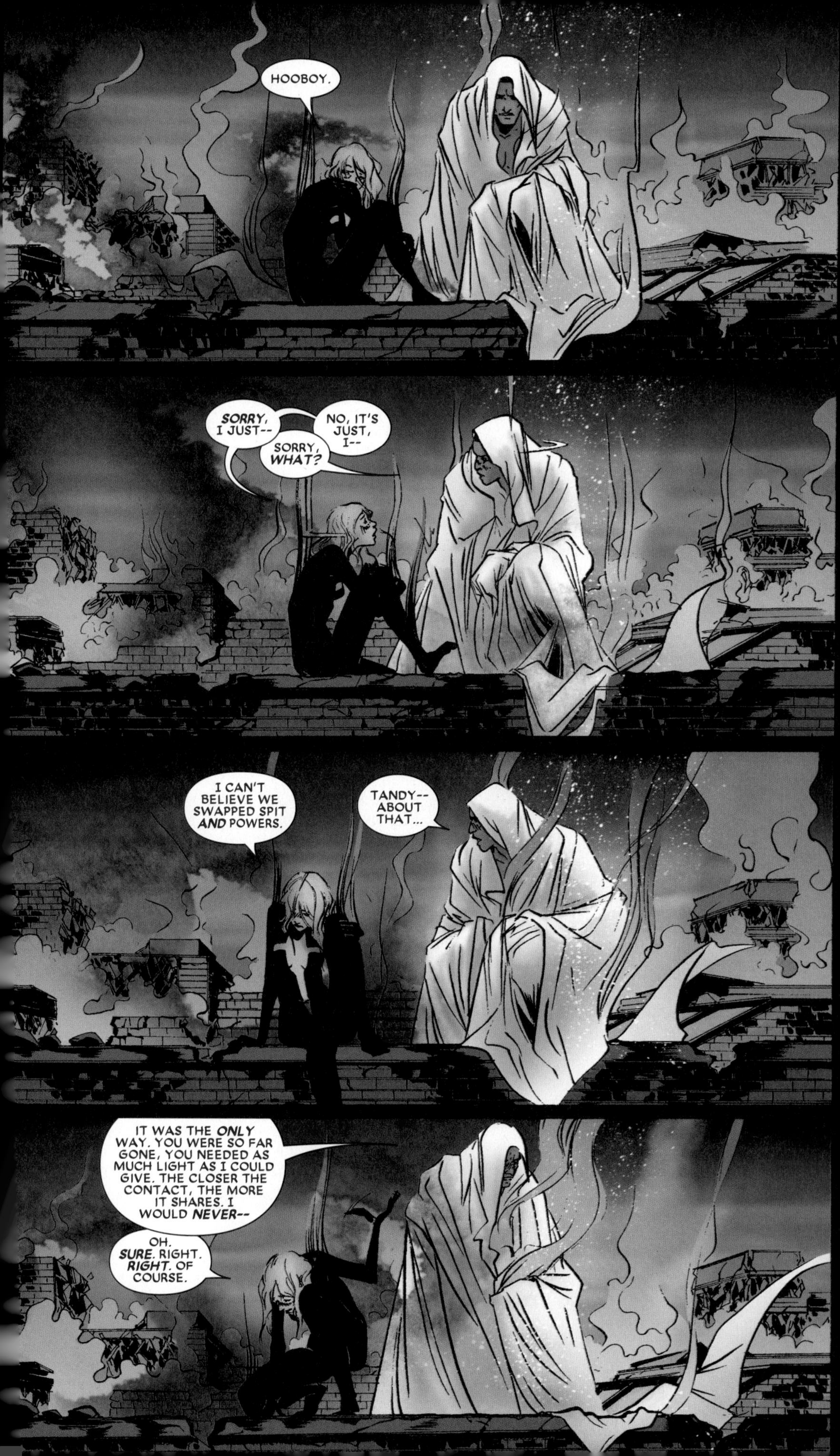
HOOBOY.
SORRY, I JUST--
NO, IT'S JUST, I--
SORRY, WHAT?
I CAN'T BELIEVE WE SWAPPED SPIT AND POWERS.
TANDY--ABOUT THAT...
IT WAS THE ONLY WAY. YOU WERE SO FAR GONE, YOU NEEDED AS MUCH LIGHT AS I COULD GIVE. THE CLOSER THE CONTACT, THE MORE IT SHARES. I WOULD NEVER--
OH. SURE. RIGHT. RIGHT. OF COURSE.

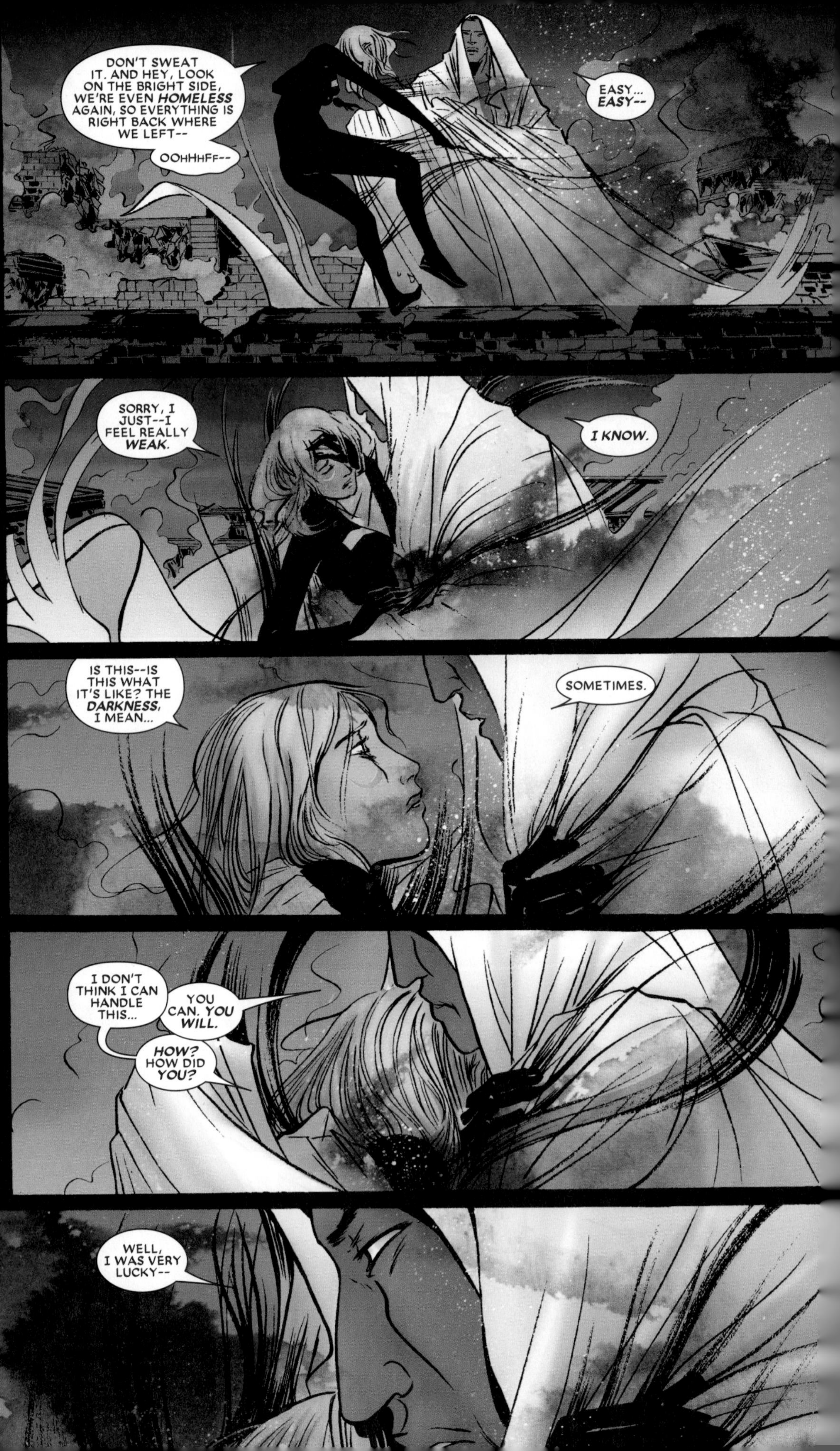
DON'T SWEAT IT. AND HEY, LOOK ON THE BRIGHT SIDE, WE'RE EVEN HOMELESS AGAIN, SO EVERYTHING IS RIGHT BACK WHERE WE LEFT--
OOHHHFF--
EASY... EASY--
SORRY, I JUST--I FEEL REALLY WEAK.
I KNOW.
IS THIS--IS THIS WHAT IT'S LIKE? THE DARKNESS, I MEAN...
SOMETIMES.
I DON'T THINK I CAN HANDLE THIS...
YOU CAN. YOU WILL.
HOW? HOW DID YOU?
WELL, I WAS VERY LUCKY--

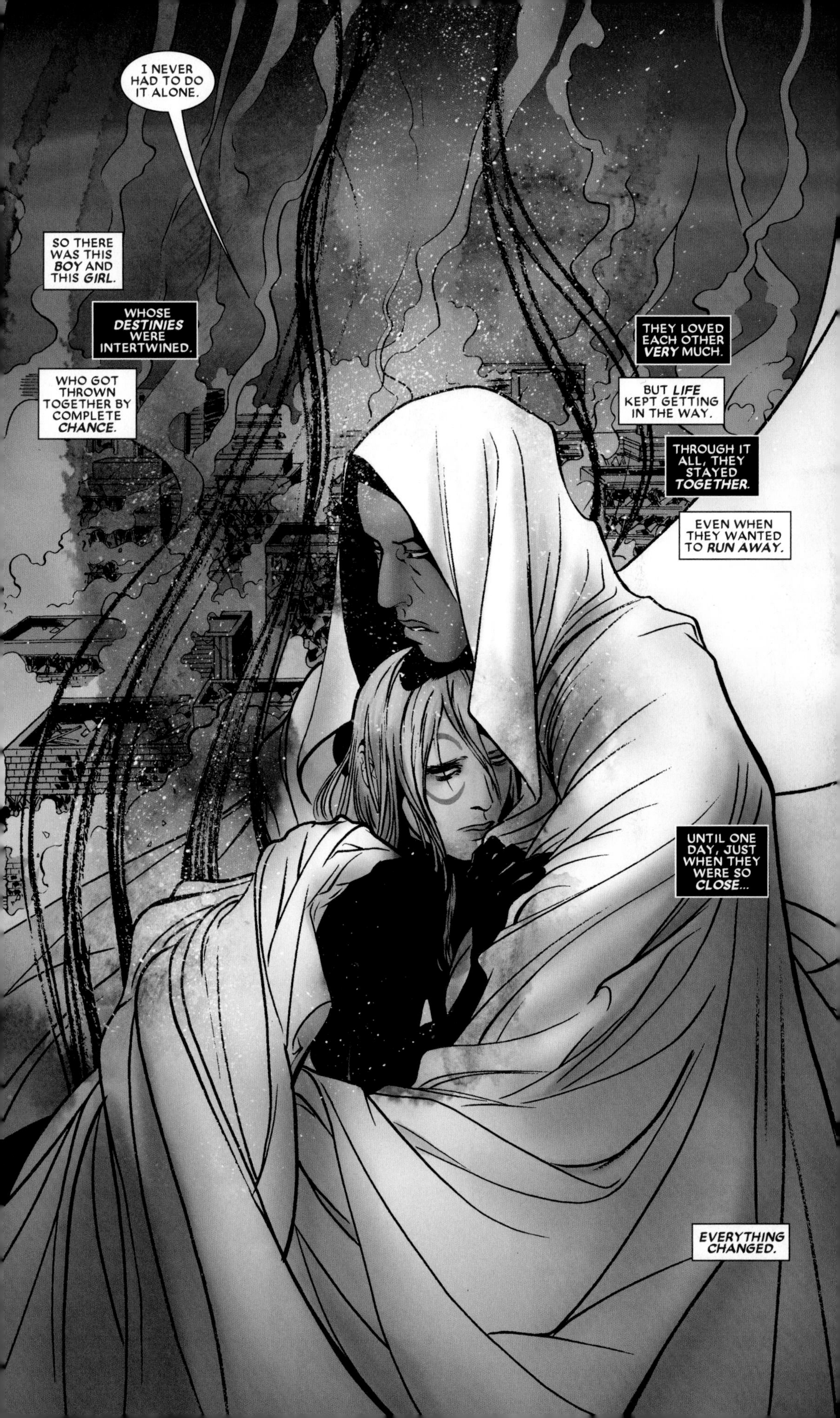
I NEVER HAD TO DO IT ALONE.
SO THERE WAS THIS *BOY* AND THIS *GIRL*.
WHOSE *DESTINIES* WERE INTERTWINED.
WHO GOT THROWN TOGETHER BY COMPLETE *CHANCE*.
THEY LOVED EACH OTHER *VERY* MUCH.
BUT *LIFE* KEPT GETTING IN THE WAY.
THROUGH IT ALL, THEY STAYED *TOGETHER*.
EVEN WHEN THEY WANTED TO *RUN AWAY*.
UNTIL ONE DAY, JUST WHEN THEY WERE SO *CLOSE*...
EVERYTHING CHANGED.

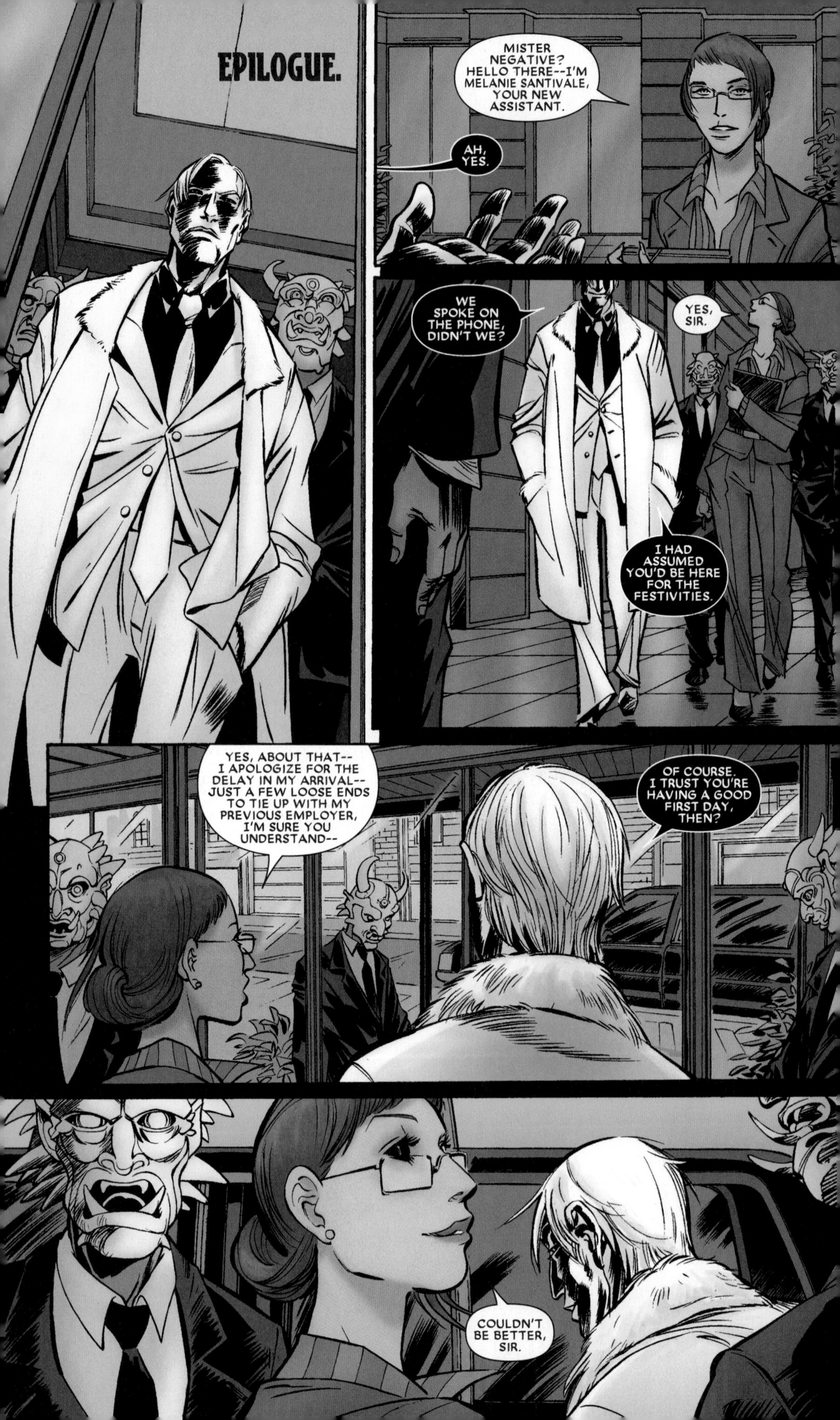
EPILOGUE.
MISTER NEGATIVE? HELLO THERE--I'M MELANIE SANTIVALE, YOUR NEW ASSISTANT.
AH, YES.
WE SPOKE ON THE PHONE, DIDN'T WE?
YES, SIR.
I HAD ASSUMED YOU'D BE HERE FOR THE FESTIVITIES.
YES, ABOUT THAT-- I APOLOGIZE FOR THE DELAY IN MY ARRIVAL--JUST A FEW LOOSE ENDS TO TIE UP WITH MY PREVIOUS EMPLOYER, I'M SURE YOU UNDERSTAND--
OF COURSE. I TRUST YOU'RE HAVING A GOOD FIRST DAY, THEN?
COULDN'T BE BETTER, SIR.

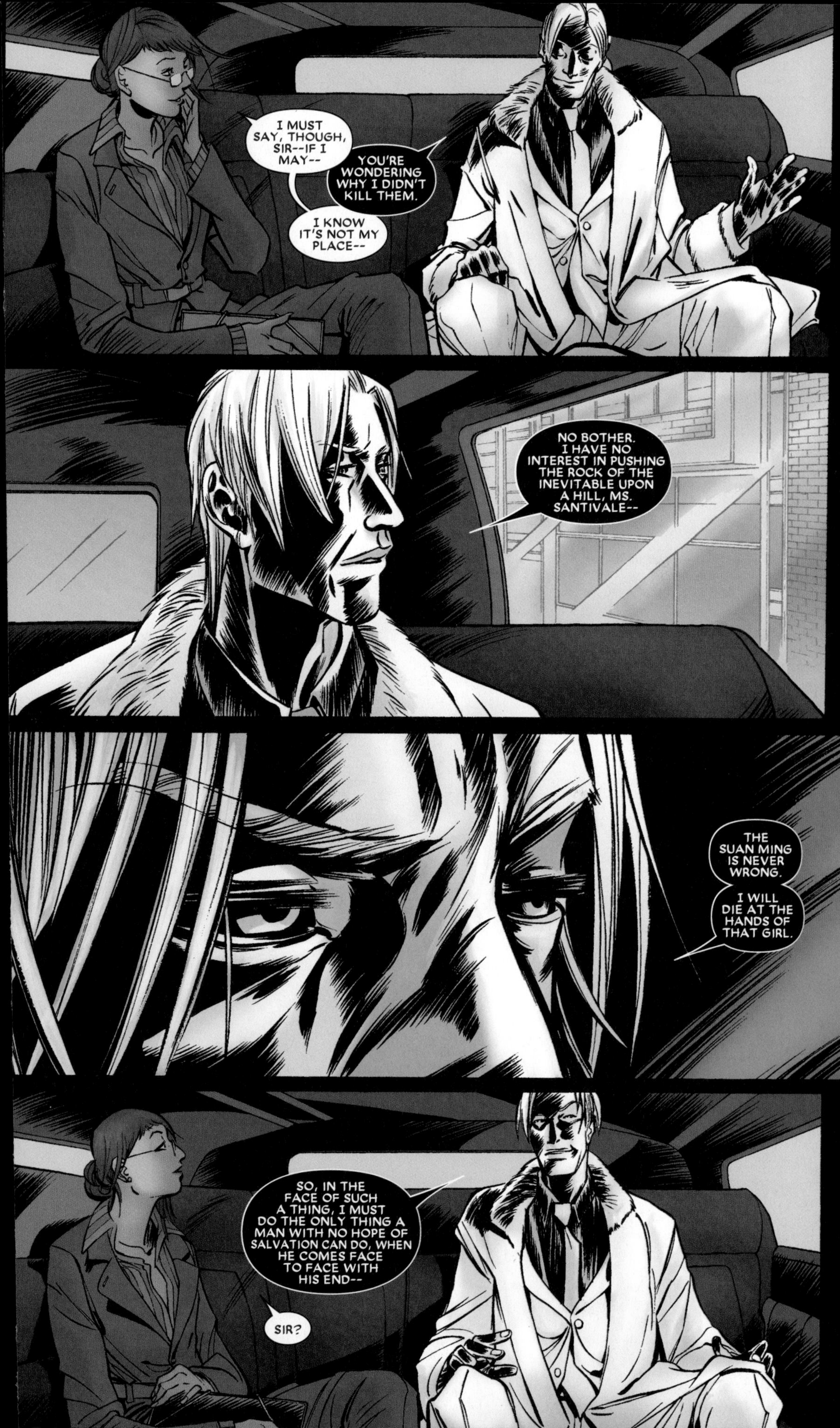
I MUST SAY, THOUGH, SIR--IF I MAY--
YOU'RE WONDERING WHY I DIDN'T KILL THEM.
I KNOW IT'S NOT MY PLACE--
NO BOTHER. I HAVE NO INTEREST IN PUSHING THE ROCK OF THE INEVITABLE UPON A HILL, MS. SANTIVALE--
THE SUAN MING IS NEVER WRONG.
I WILL DIE AT THE HANDS OF THAT GIRL.
SO, IN THE FACE OF SUCH A THING, I MUST DO THE ONLY THING A MAN WITH NO HOPE OF SALVATION CAN DO, WHEN HE COMES FACE TO FACE WITH HIS END--
SIR?

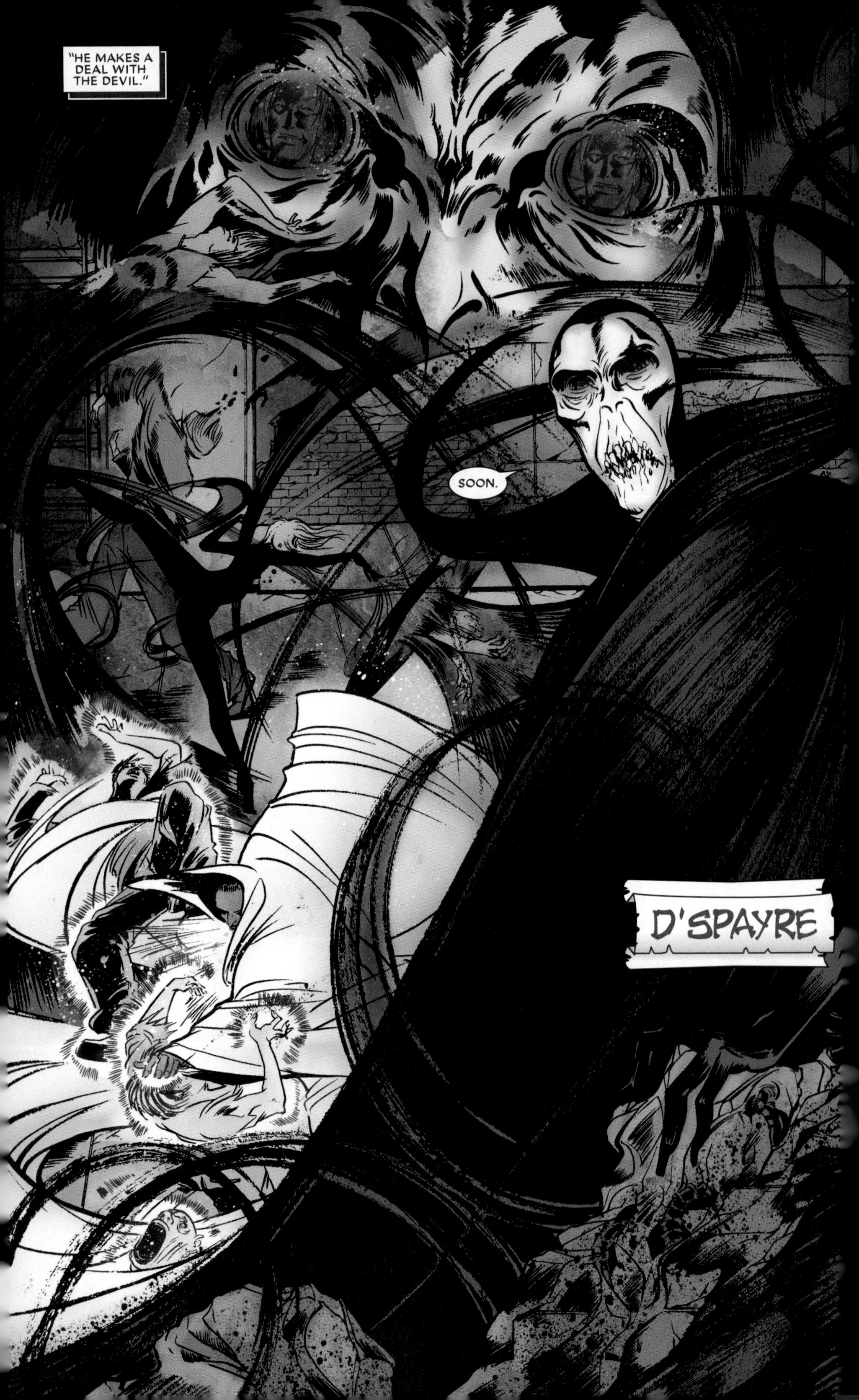
"HE MAKES A DEAL WITH THE DEVIL."
SOON.
D'SPAYRE

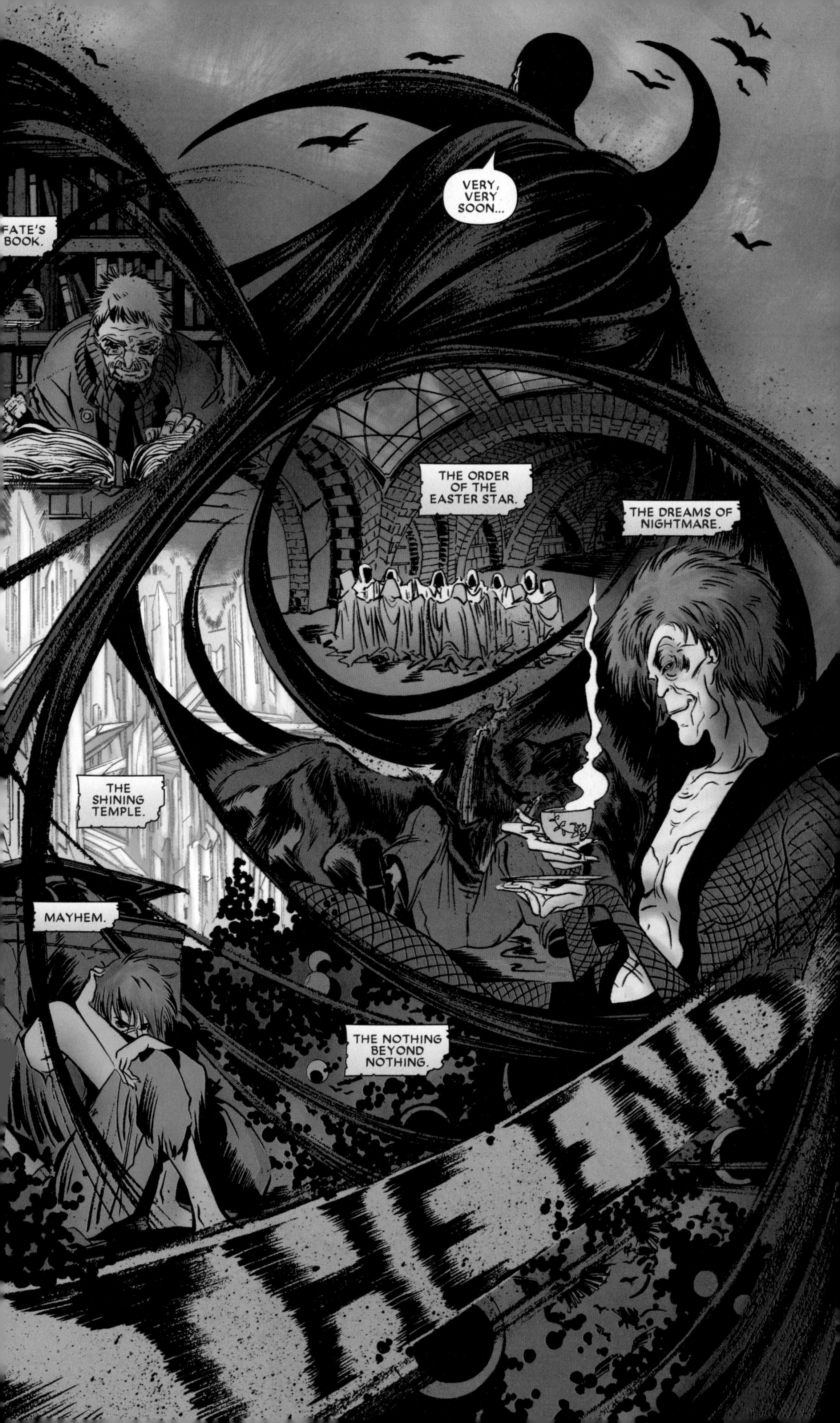
VERY, VERY SOON...
FATE'S BOOK.
THE ORDER OF THE EASTER STAR.
THE DREAMS OF NIGHTMARE.
THE SHINING TEMPLE.
MAYHEM.
THE NOTHING BEYOND NOTHING.
THE END

IN THE MONTHS FOLLOWING "SPIDER-ISLAND," PETER PARKER'S FRIENDLY NEIGHBORHOOD HAS GOTTEN A WHOLE LOT BIGGER. HIS COMPANY, PARKER INDUSTRIES, IS CHANGING THE WORLD WITH CUTTING-EDGE TECHNOLOGY AND HAS OFFICES ALL OVER THE WORLD, INCLUDING SHANGHAI, CHINA. BUT PARKER'S GLOBAL PRESENCE HAS ALSO PUT HIS ALTER EGO, THE AMAZING SPIDER-MAN, FACE-TO-FACE WITH DEADLY THREATS FROM ACROSS THE WORLD…

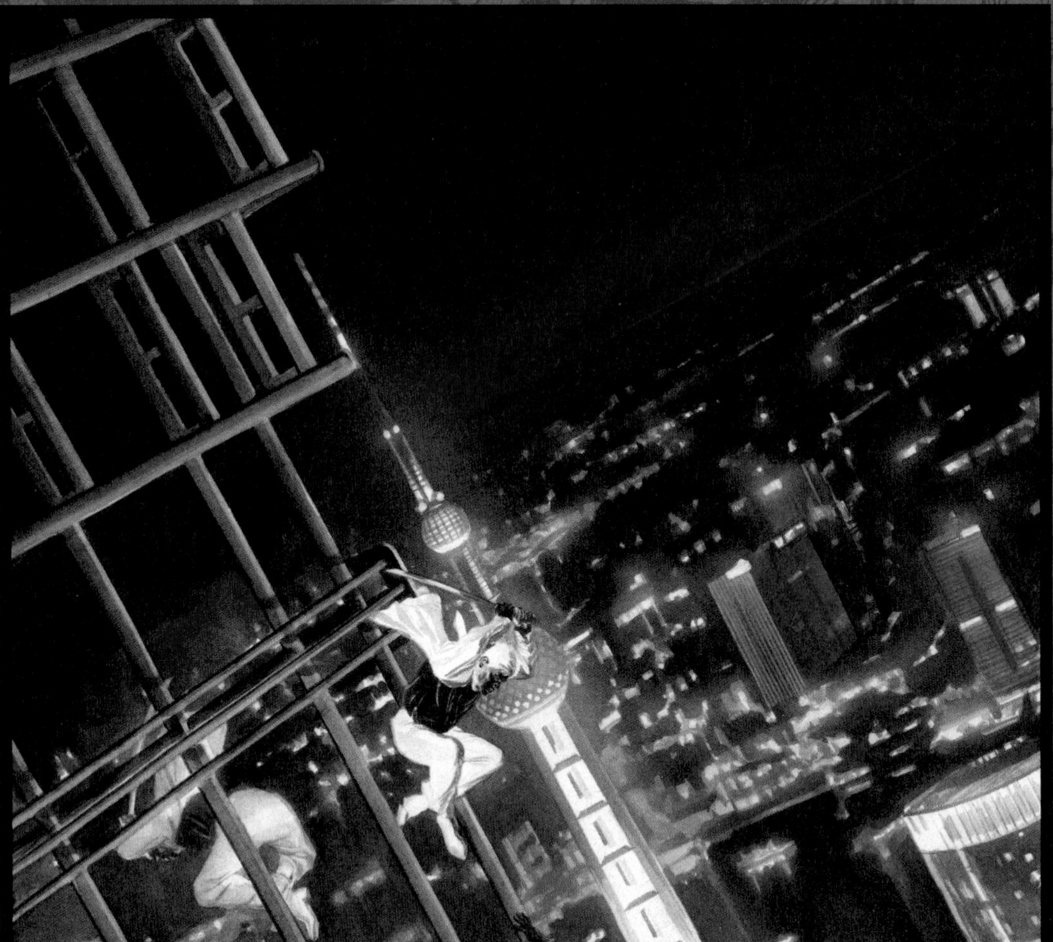

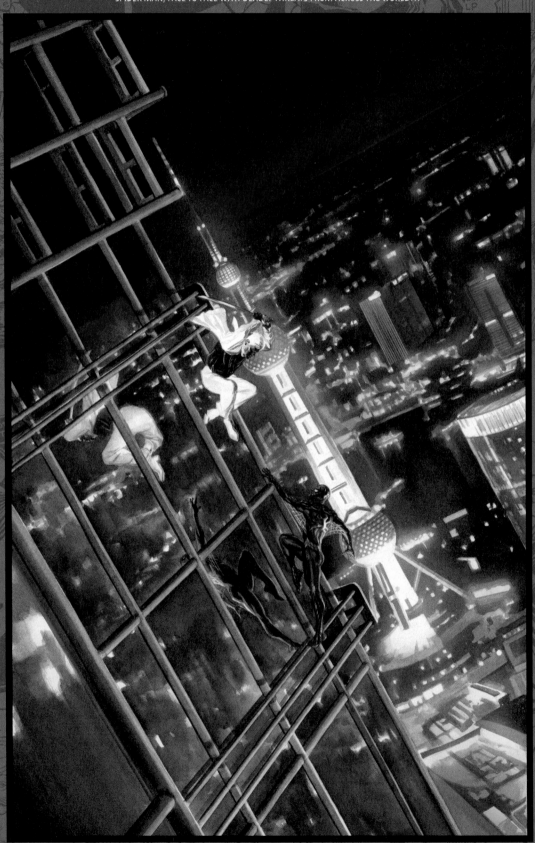

***AMAZING SPIDER-MAN* (2015) #6**

"THE DARK KINGDOM, PART 1: TURNABOUT"

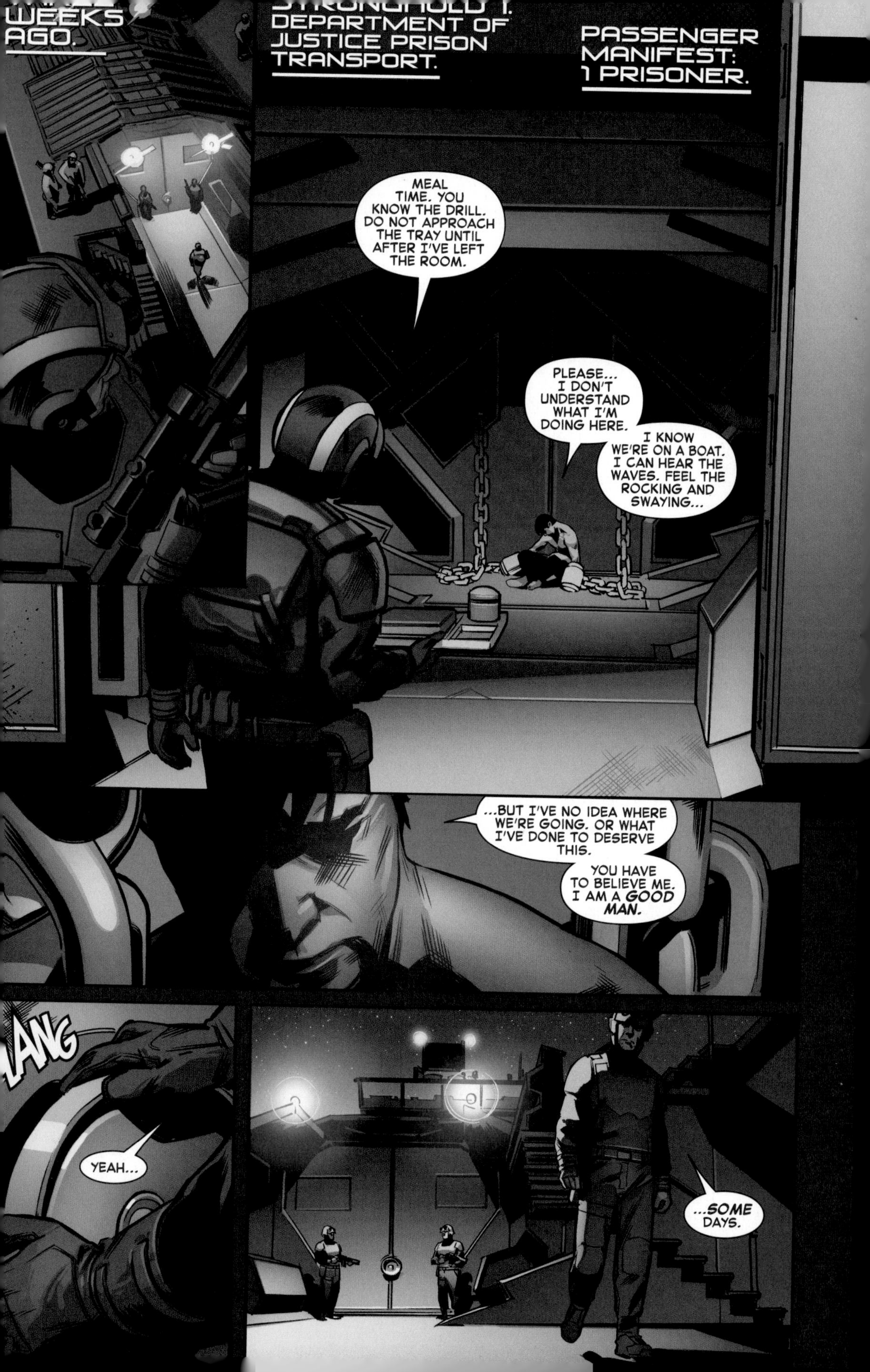

WEEKS AGO.
DEPARTMENT OF JUSTICE PRISON TRANSPORT.
PASSENGER MANIFEST: 1 PRISONER.
MEAL TIME. YOU KNOW THE DRILL. DO NOT APPROACH THE TRAY UNTIL AFTER I'VE LEFT THE ROOM.
PLEASE... I DON'T UNDERSTAND WHAT I'M DOING HERE.
I KNOW WE'RE ON A BOAT. I CAN HEAR THE WAVES. FEEL THE ROCKING AND SWAYING...
...BUT I'VE NO IDEA WHERE WE'RE GOING. OR WHAT I'VE DONE TO DESERVE THIS.
YOU HAVE TO BELIEVE ME. I AM A *GOOD MAN.*
LANG
YEAH...
...*SOME* DAYS.

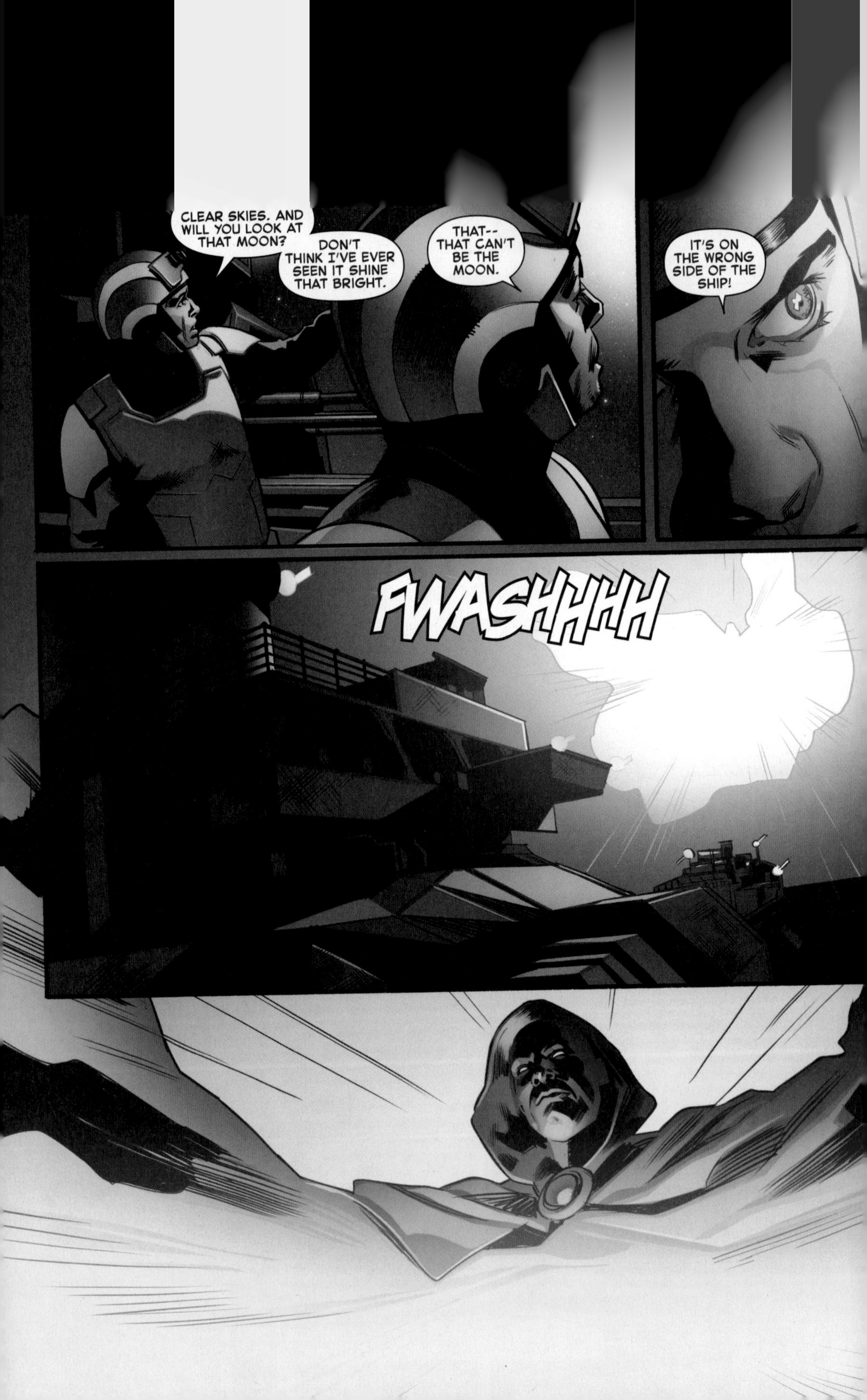
CLEAR SKIES. AND WILL YOU LOOK AT THAT MOON?
DON'T THINK I'VE EVER SEEN IT SHINE THAT BRIGHT.
THAT-- THAT CAN'T BE THE MOON.
IT'S ON THE WRONG SIDE OF THE SHIP!
FWASHHHH

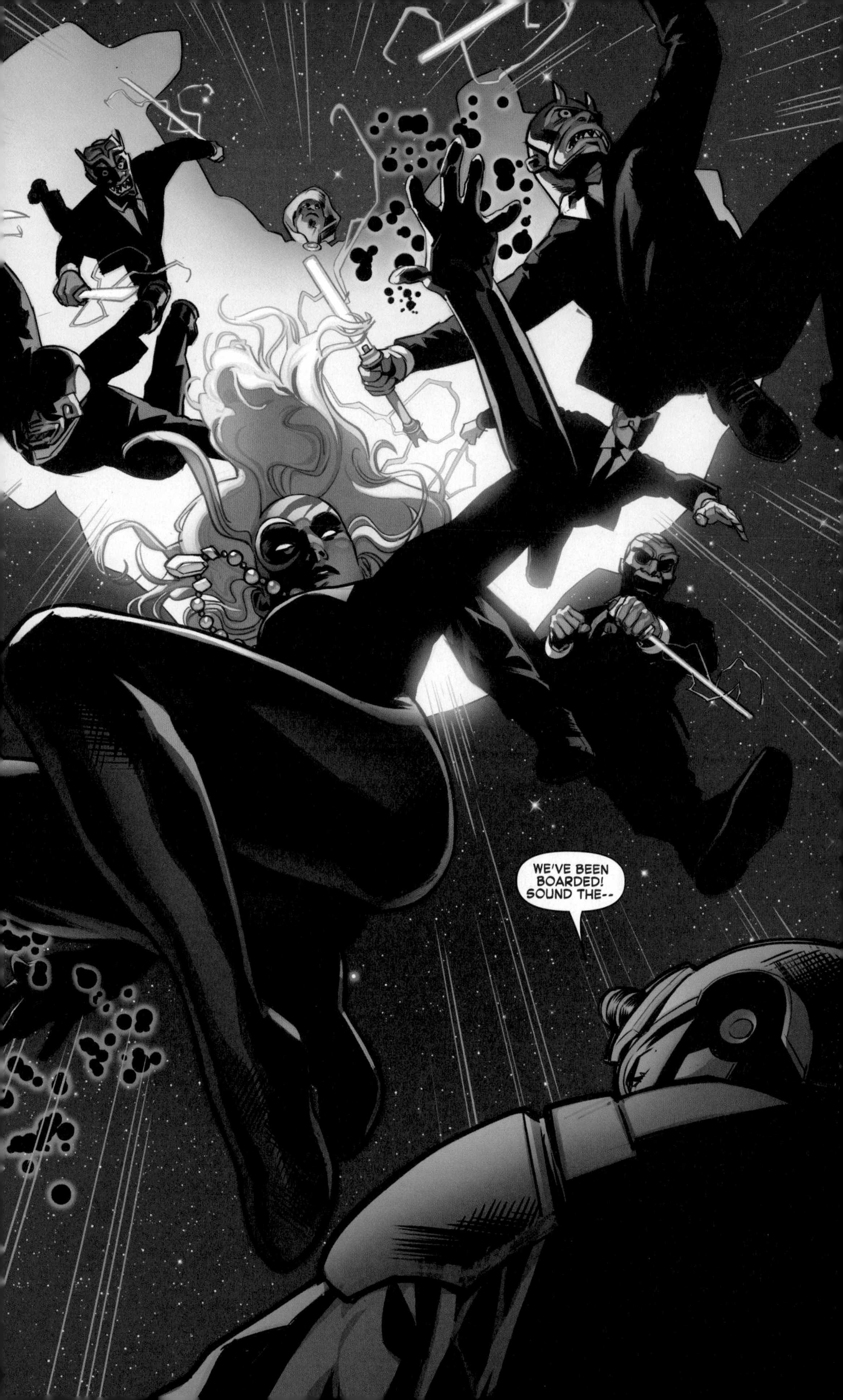
WE'VE BEEN BOARDED! SOUND THE--

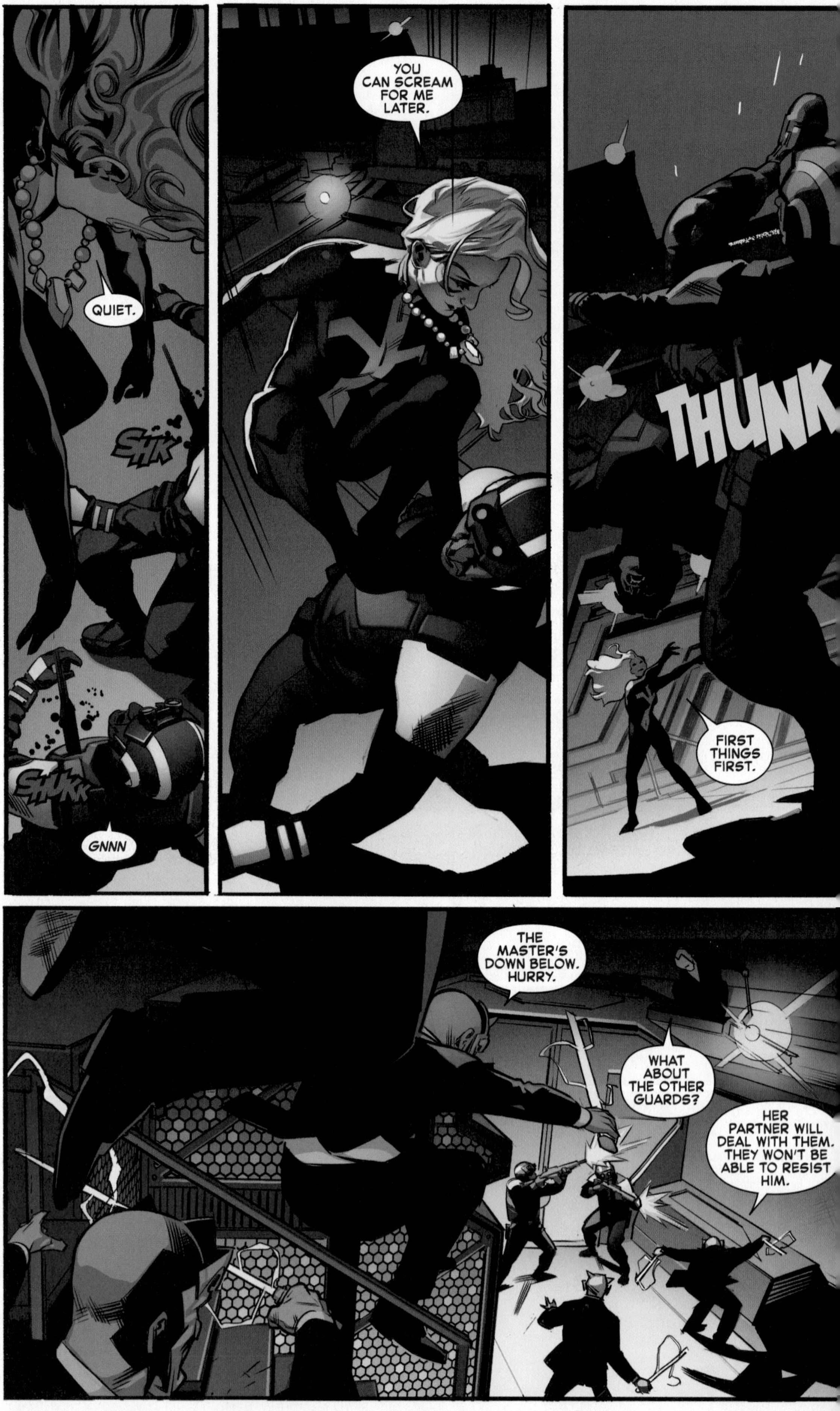
QUIET.
SHK
SHUKK
GNNN
YOU CAN SCREAM FOR ME LATER.
THUNK
FIRST THINGS FIRST.
THE MASTER'S DOWN BELOW. HURRY.
WHAT ABOUT THE OTHER GUARDS?
HER PARTNER WILL DEAL WITH THEM. THEY WON'T BE ABLE TO RESIST HIM.

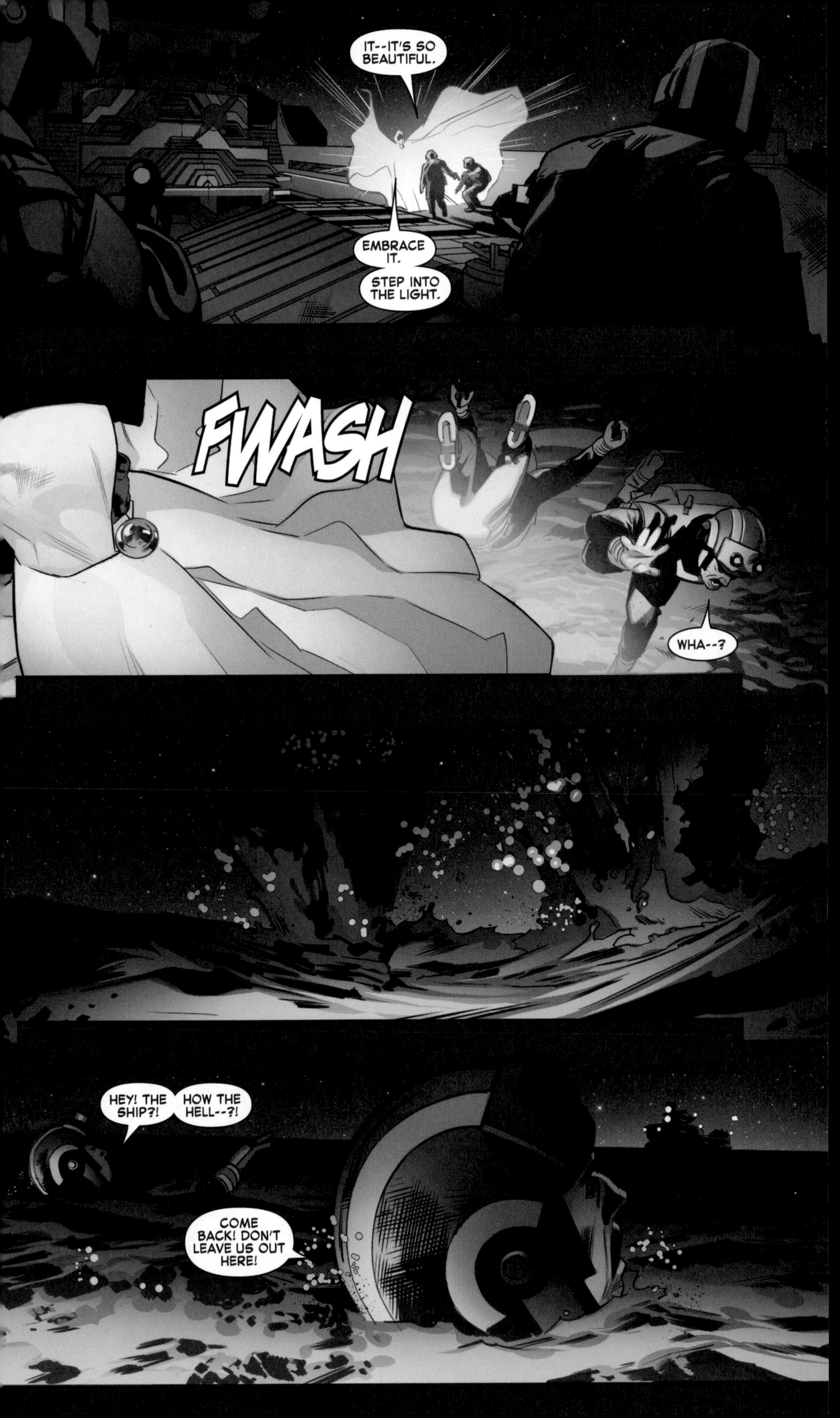
IT--IT'S SO BEAUTIFUL.
EMBRACE IT.
STEP INTO THE LIGHT.
FWASH
WHA--?
HEY! THE SHIP?!
HOW THE HELL--?!
COME BACK! DON'T LEAVE US OUT HERE!

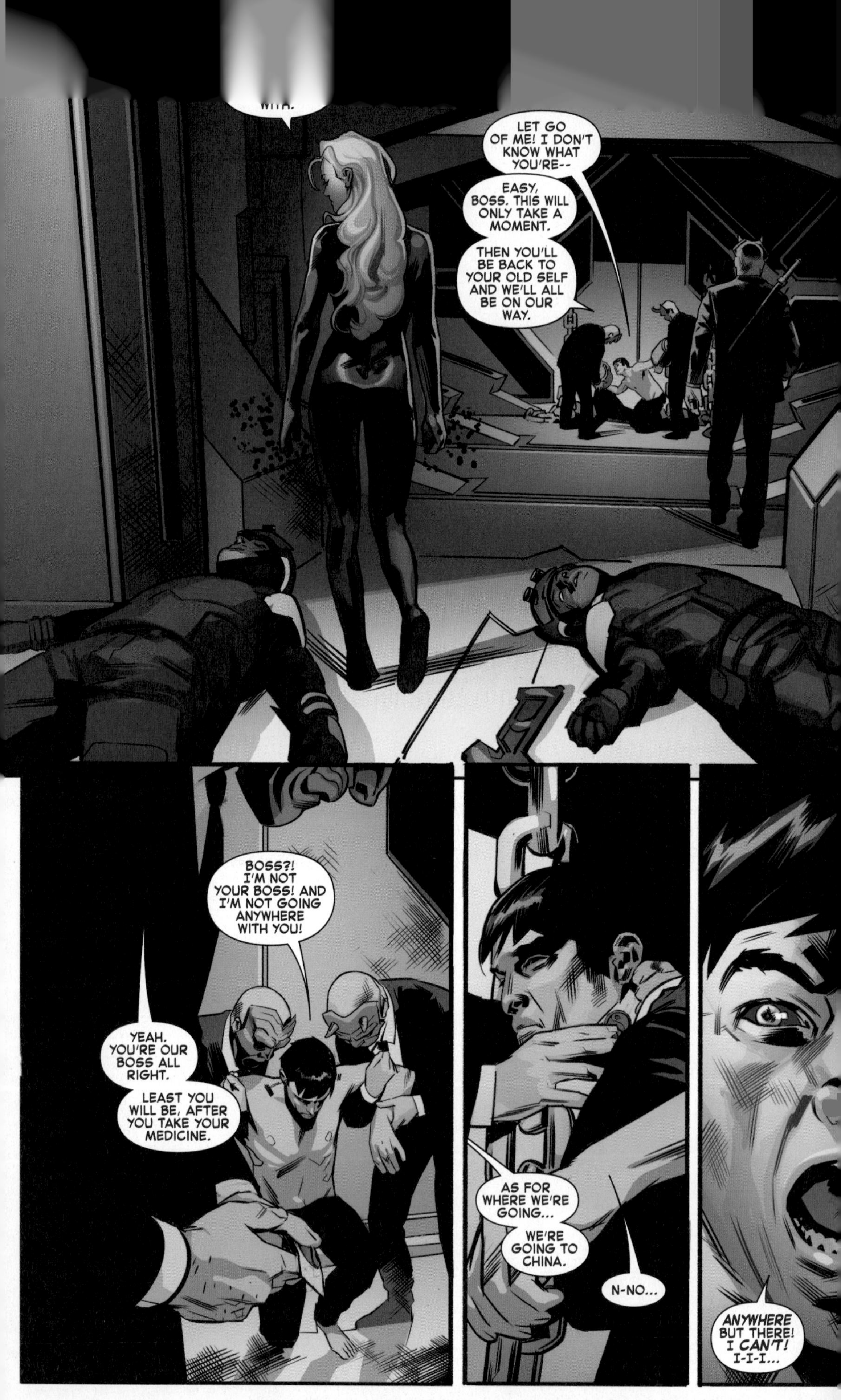

WITH.
LET GO OF ME! I DON'T KNOW WHAT YOU'RE--
EASY, BOSS. THIS WILL ONLY TAKE A MOMENT.
THEN YOU'LL BE BACK TO YOUR OLD SELF AND WE'LL ALL BE ON OUR WAY.
BOSS?! I'M NOT YOUR BOSS! AND I'M NOT GOING ANYWHERE WITH YOU!
YEAH. YOU'RE OUR BOSS ALL RIGHT.
LEAST YOU WILL BE, AFTER YOU TAKE YOUR MEDICINE.
AS FOR WHERE WE'RE GOING...
WE'RE GOING TO CHINA.
N-NO...
ANYWHERE BUT THERE! I CAN'T! I-I-I...

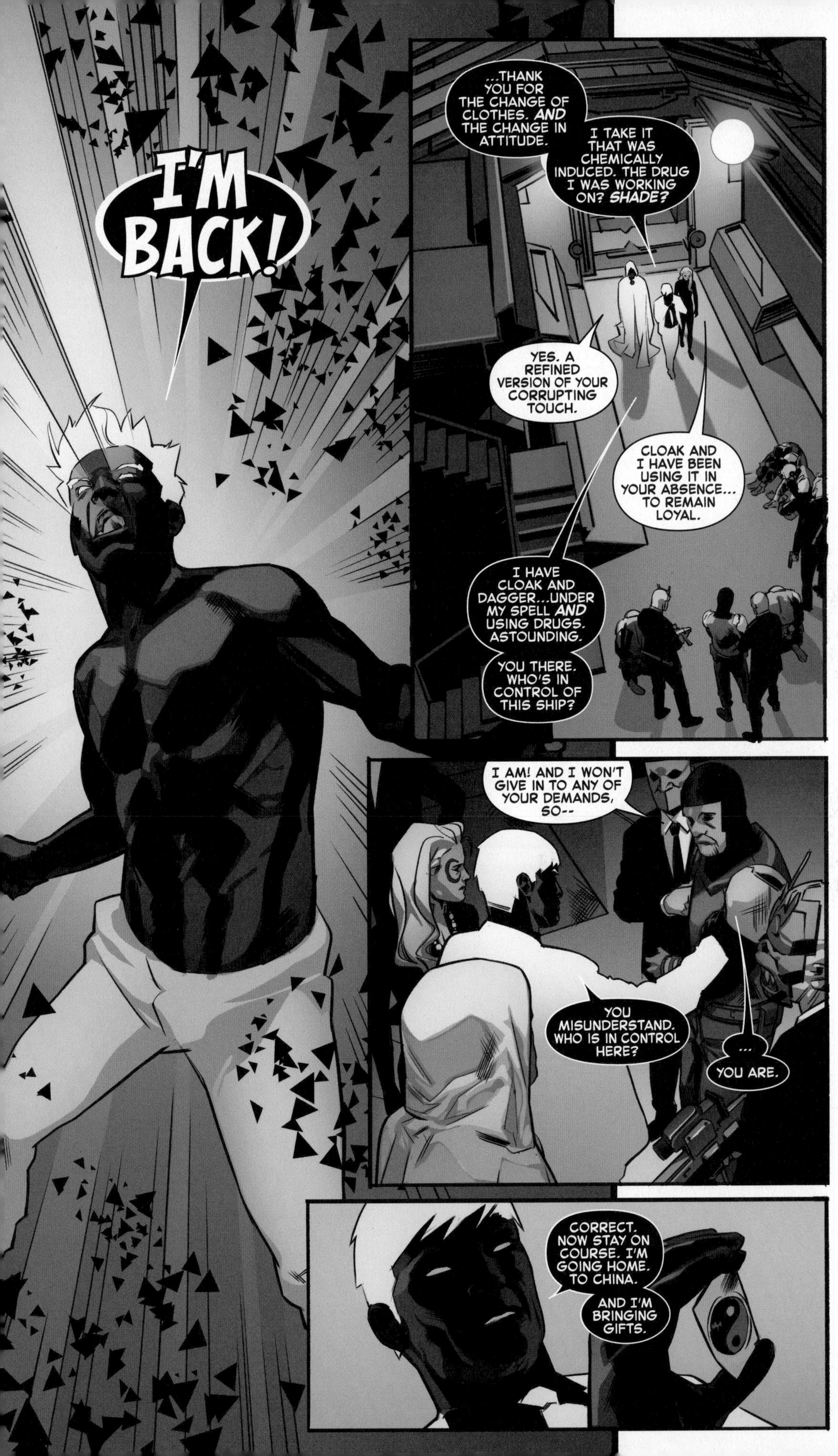
I'M BACK!
...THANK YOU FOR THE CHANGE OF CLOTHES. AND THE CHANGE IN ATTITUDE.
I TAKE IT THAT WAS CHEMICALLY INDUCED. THE DRUG I WAS WORKING ON? SHADE?
YES. A REFINED VERSION OF YOUR CORRUPTING TOUCH.
CLOAK AND I HAVE BEEN USING IT IN YOUR ABSENCE... TO REMAIN LOYAL.
I HAVE CLOAK AND DAGGER...UNDER MY SPELL AND USING DRUGS. ASTOUNDING.
YOU THERE. WHO'S IN CONTROL OF THIS SHIP?
I AM! AND I WON'T GIVE IN TO ANY OF YOUR DEMANDS, SO--
YOU MISUNDERSTAND. WHO IS IN CONTROL HERE?
...
YOU ARE.
CORRECT. NOW STAY ON COURSE. I'M GOING HOME. TO CHINA.
AND I'M BRINGING GIFTS.

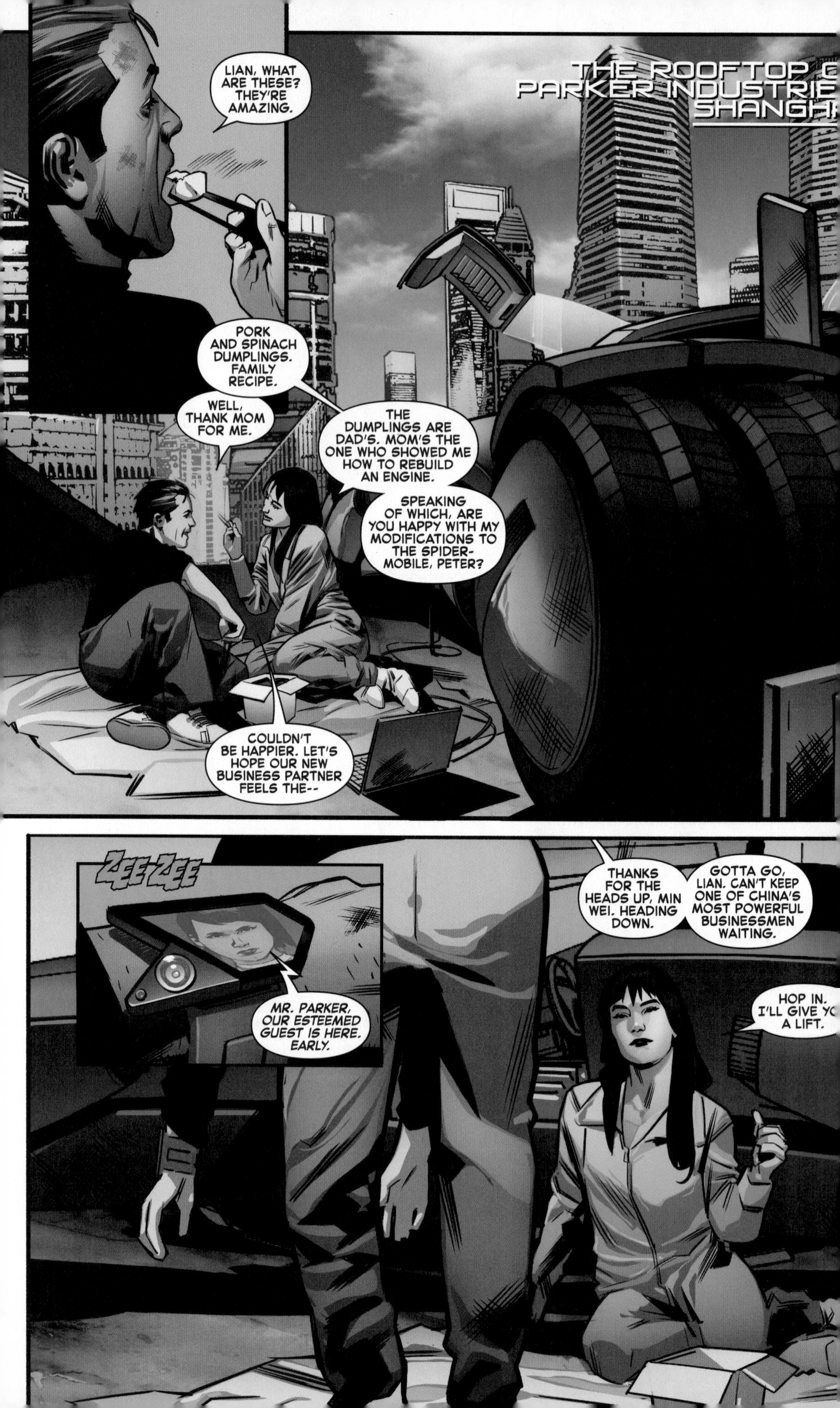
LIAN, WHAT ARE THESE? THEY'RE AMAZING.
THE ROOFTOP
PARKER INDUSTRIE
SHANGH
PORK AND SPINACH DUMPLINGS. FAMILY RECIPE.
WELL, THANK MOM FOR ME.
THE DUMPLINGS ARE DAD'S. MOM'S THE ONE WHO SHOWED ME HOW TO REBUILD AN ENGINE.
SPEAKING OF WHICH, ARE YOU HAPPY WITH MY MODIFICATIONS TO THE SPIDER-MOBILE, PETER?
COULDN'T BE HAPPIER. LET'S HOPE OUR NEW BUSINESS PARTNER FEELS THE--
ZEE-ZEE
MR. PARKER, OUR ESTEEMED GUEST IS HERE. EARLY.
THANKS FOR THE HEADS UP, MIN WEI. HEADING DOWN.
GOTTA GO, LIAN. CAN'T KEEP ONE OF CHINA'S MOST POWERFUL BUSINESSMEN WAITING.
HOP IN. I'LL GIVE Y
A LIFT.

YOU KNOW, I DO HAVE AN EXPRESS ELEVATOR, MS. TANG. THIS IS FASTER. TRUST ME.

ALL RIGHT. CAN I DRIVE?

HA. ONLY TWO PEOPLE CAN HANDLE THIS BABY: ME AND SPIDER-MAN.

AND THAT'S ONLY 'CAUSE HE HAS SPIDER-SENSE.

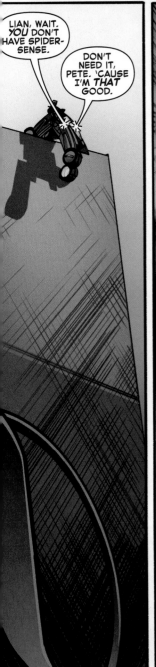

LIAN, WAIT. *YOU* DON'T HAVE SPIDER-SENSE.

DON'T NEED IT, PETE. 'CAUSE I'M *THAT* GOOD.

VRMM

MR. PARKER? COME ON! WHAT'S KEEPING YOU?

BE THERE IN A SEC, MIN.

MY STOMACH AND SOME PORK DUMPLINGS WILL BE THERE IN TWO.

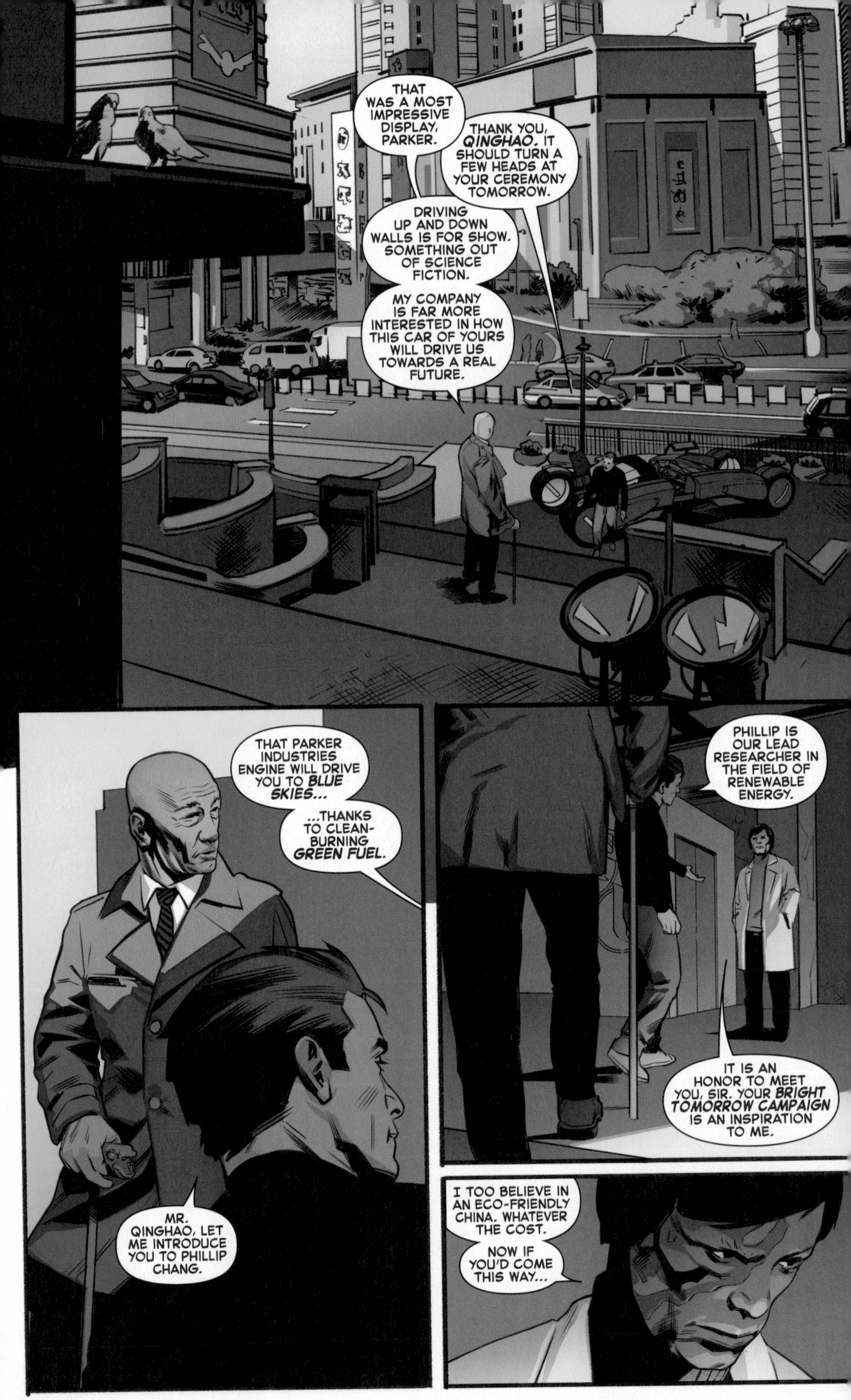
THAT WAS A MOST IMPRESSIVE DISPLAY, PARKER.
THANK YOU, QINGHAO. IT SHOULD TURN A FEW HEADS AT YOUR CEREMONY TOMORROW.
DRIVING UP AND DOWN WALLS IS FOR SHOW. SOMETHING OUT OF SCIENCE FICTION.
MY COMPANY IS FAR MORE INTERESTED IN HOW THIS CAR OF YOURS WILL DRIVE US TOWARDS A REAL FUTURE.
THAT PARKER INDUSTRIES ENGINE WILL DRIVE YOU TO BLUE SKIES...
...THANKS TO CLEAN-BURNING GREEN FUEL.
MR. QINGHAO, LET ME INTRODUCE YOU TO PHILLIP CHANG.
PHILLIP IS OUR LEAD RESEARCHER IN THE FIELD OF RENEWABLE ENERGY.
IT IS AN HONOR TO MEET YOU, SIR. YOUR BRIGHT TOMORROW CAMPAIGN IS AN INSPIRATION TO ME.
I TOO BELIEVE IN AN ECO-FRIENDLY CHINA. WHATEVER THE COST.
NOW IF YOU'D COME THIS WAY...

...WE CAN SHOW YOU THE PROCESS WE'RE USING TO PRODUCE OUR NEW ENVIRONMENTALLY CONSCIOUS FUELS.

WE BELIEVE WITH PARKER INDUSTRIES' CONCEPTS AND *BRIGHT TOMORROW'S* GOOD STANDING...

...WE COULD IMPROVE THE AIR QUALITY NOT JUST FOR CHINA BUT FOR--

YOU SENT FOR THE POLICE?

BUT WE HAD THIS MATTER UNDER CONTROL.

NO. WHAT WE HAD WAS FOREIGNERS SNOOPING AROUND. AS A CITIZEN IT'S BEEN MY DUTY TO REPORT OUR BREAK-IN* TO *LOCAL* AUTHORITIES.

BUT ON TODAY OF ALL DAYS--OH, MR. QINGHAO!

*BACK IN ASM #1! --NUDGING NICK

MR. PARKER? WHY ARE THE POLICE SEARCHING YOUR OFFICES?

EXTRA SECURITY FOR TOMORROW'S CELEBRATION, SIR. HERE, LET ME FINISH YOUR TOUR.

THANKS, MIN.

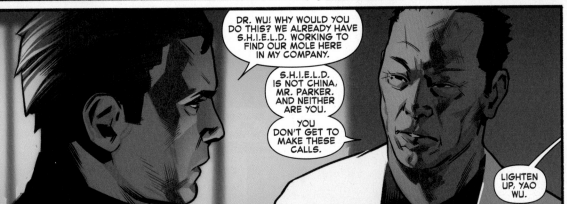

DR. WU! WHY WOULD YOU DO THIS? WE ALREADY HAVE S.H.I.E.L.D. WORKING TO FIND OUR MOLE HERE IN MY COMPANY.

S.H.I.E.L.D. IS NOT CHINA, MR. PARKER. AND NEITHER ARE YOU. YOU DON'T GET TO MAKE THESE CALLS.

LIGHTEN UP, YAO WU.

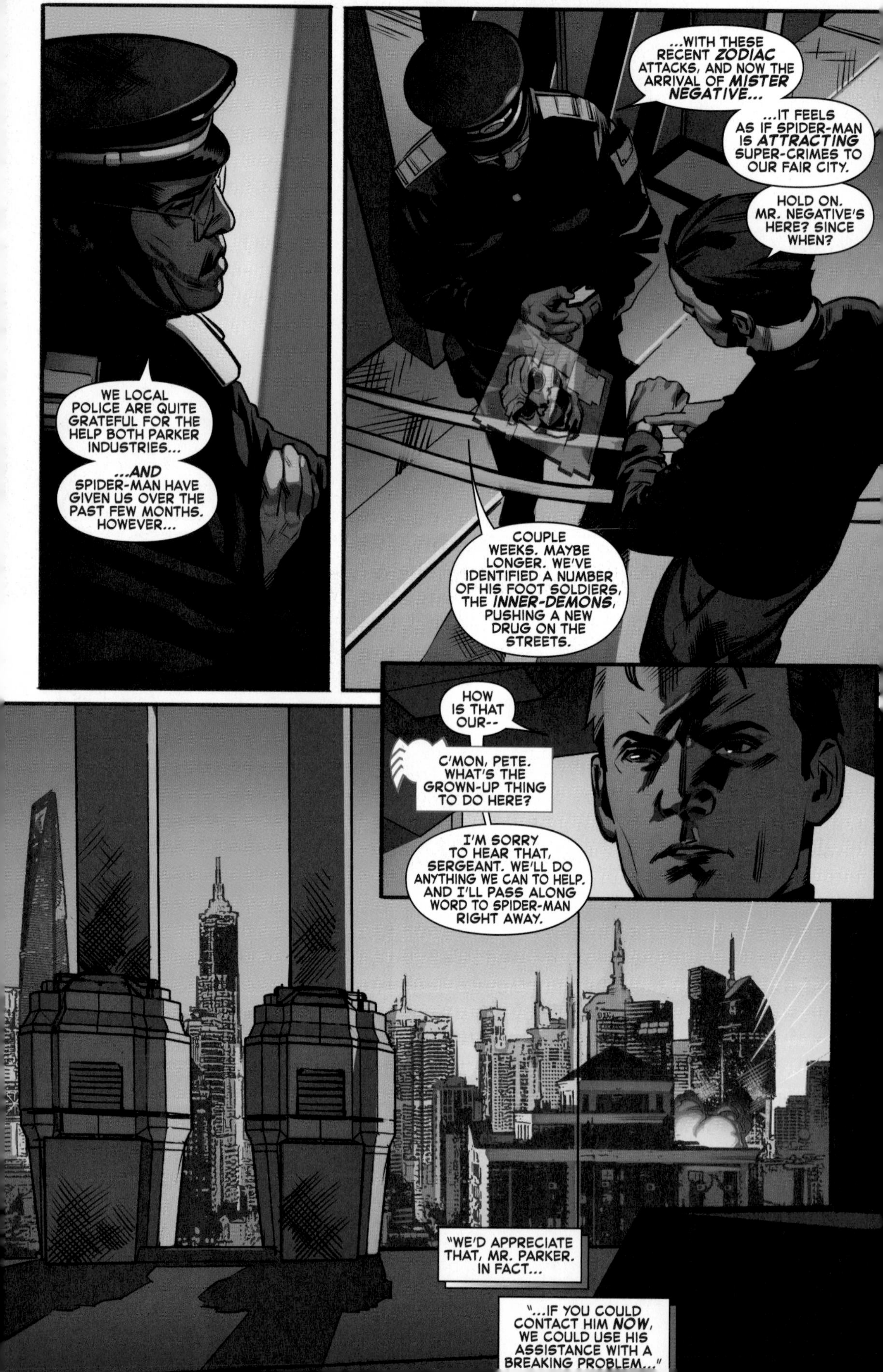
WE LOCAL POLICE ARE QUITE GRATEFUL FOR THE HELP BOTH PARKER INDUSTRIES...
...AND SPIDER-MAN HAVE GIVEN US OVER THE PAST FEW MONTHS. HOWEVER...
...WITH THESE RECENT ZODIAC ATTACKS, AND NOW THE ARRIVAL OF MISTER NEGATIVE...
...IT FEELS AS IF SPIDER-MAN IS ATTRACTING SUPER-CRIMES TO OUR FAIR CITY.
HOLD ON. MR. NEGATIVE'S HERE? SINCE WHEN?
COUPLE WEEKS. MAYBE LONGER. WE'VE IDENTIFIED A NUMBER OF HIS FOOT SOLDIERS, THE INNER-DEMONS, PUSHING A NEW DRUG ON THE STREETS.
HOW IS THAT OUR--
C'MON, PETE. WHAT'S THE GROWN-UP THING TO DO HERE?
I'M SORRY TO HEAR THAT, SERGEANT. WE'LL DO ANYTHING WE CAN TO HELP. AND I'LL PASS ALONG WORD TO SPIDER-MAN RIGHT AWAY.
"WE'D APPRECIATE THAT, MR. PARKER. IN FACT...
"...IF YOU COULD CONTACT HIM NOW, WE COULD USE HIS ASSISTANCE WITH A BREAKING PROBLEM..."

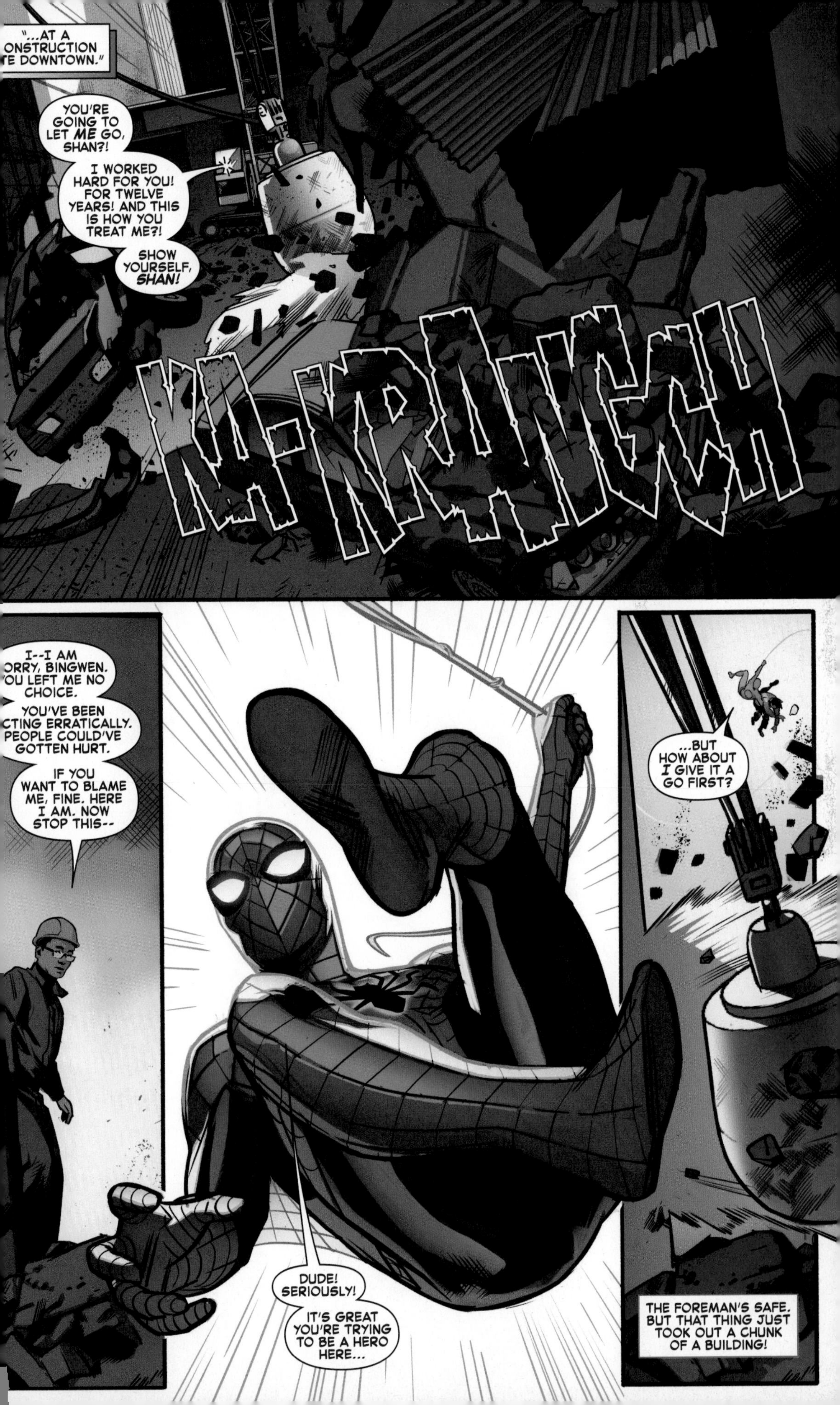
"...AT A
ONSTRUCTION
TE DOWNTOWN."
YOU'RE GOING TO LET *ME* GO, SHAN?!
I WORKED HARD FOR YOU! FOR TWELVE YEARS! AND THIS IS HOW YOU TREAT ME?!
SHOW YOURSELF, *SHAN!*
KA-KRANGCH
I--I AM ORRY, BINGWEN. OU LEFT ME NO CHOICE.
YOU'VE BEEN CTING ERRATICALLY. PEOPLE COULD'VE GOTTEN HURT.
IF YOU WANT TO BLAME ME, FINE. HERE I AM. NOW STOP THIS--
DUDE! SERIOUSLY!
IT'S GREAT YOU'RE TRYING TO BE A HERO HERE...
...BUT HOW ABOUT *I* GIVE IT A GO FIRST?
THE FOREMAN'S SAFE. BUT THAT THING JUST TOOK OUT A CHUNK OF A BUILDING!

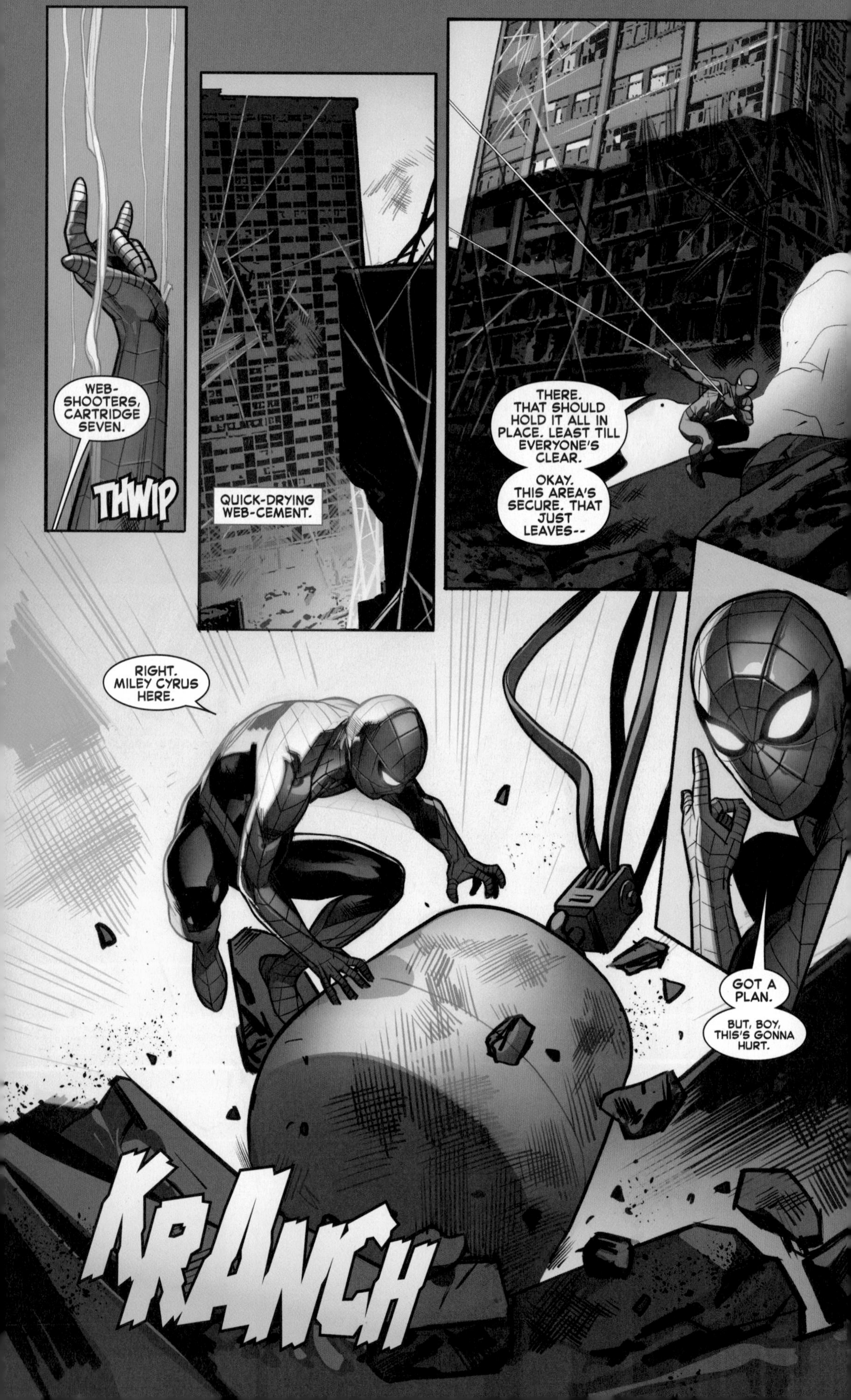
WEB-SHOOTERS, CARTRIDGE SEVEN.
THWIP
QUICK-DRYING WEB-CEMENT.
THERE. THAT SHOULD HOLD IT ALL IN PLACE. LEAST TILL EVERYONE'S CLEAR.
OKAY. THIS AREA'S SECURE. THAT JUST LEAVES--
RIGHT. MILEY CYRUS HERE.
GOT A PLAN.
BUT, BOY, THIS'S GONNA HURT.
KRANCH

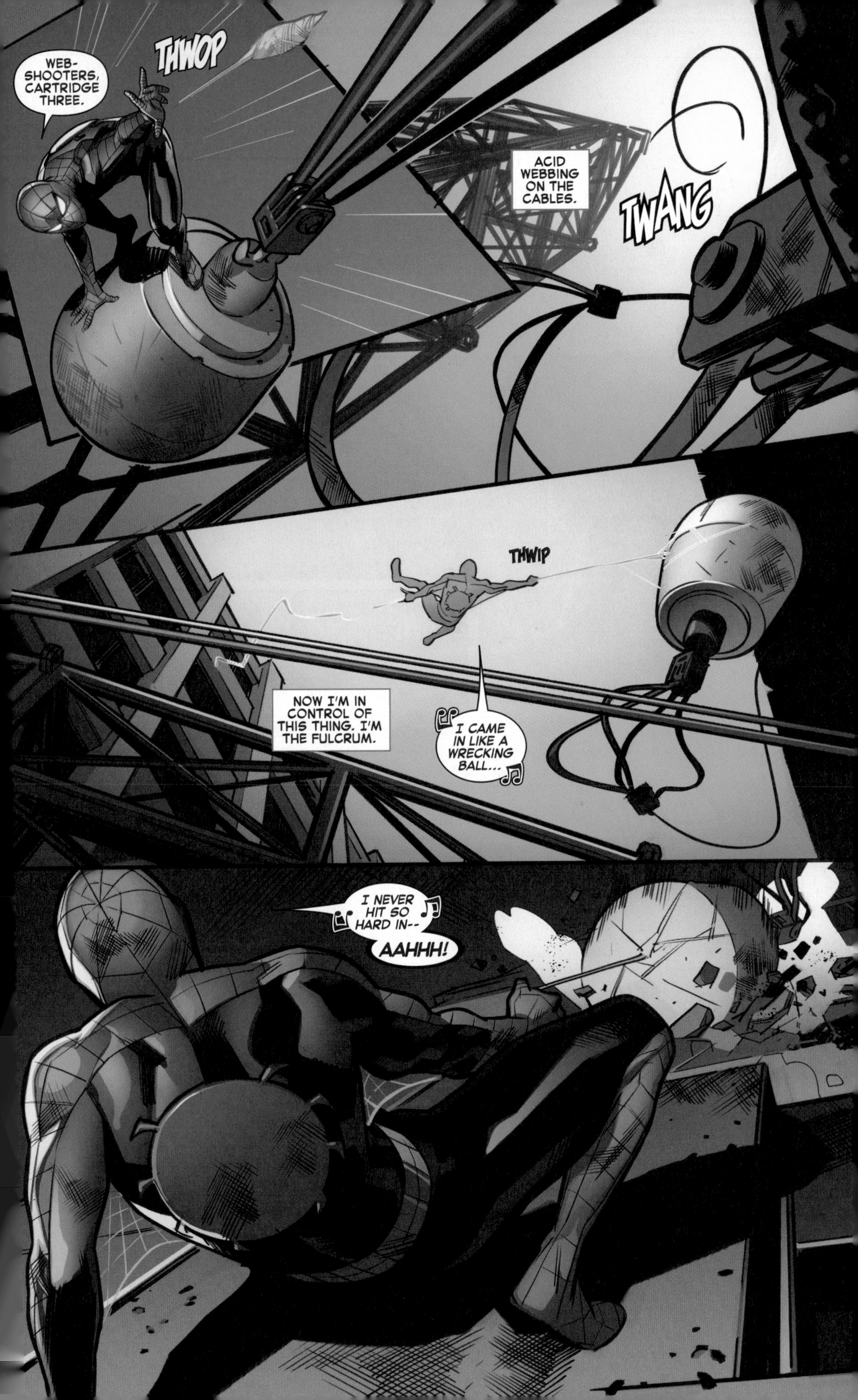
WEB-SHOOTERS, CARTRIDGE THREE.
THWOP
ACID WEBBING ON THE CABLES.
TWANG
THWIP
NOW I'M IN CONTROL OF THIS THING. I'M THE FULCRUM.
I CAME IN LIKE A WRECKING BALL...
I NEVER HIT SO HARD IN--
AAHHH!

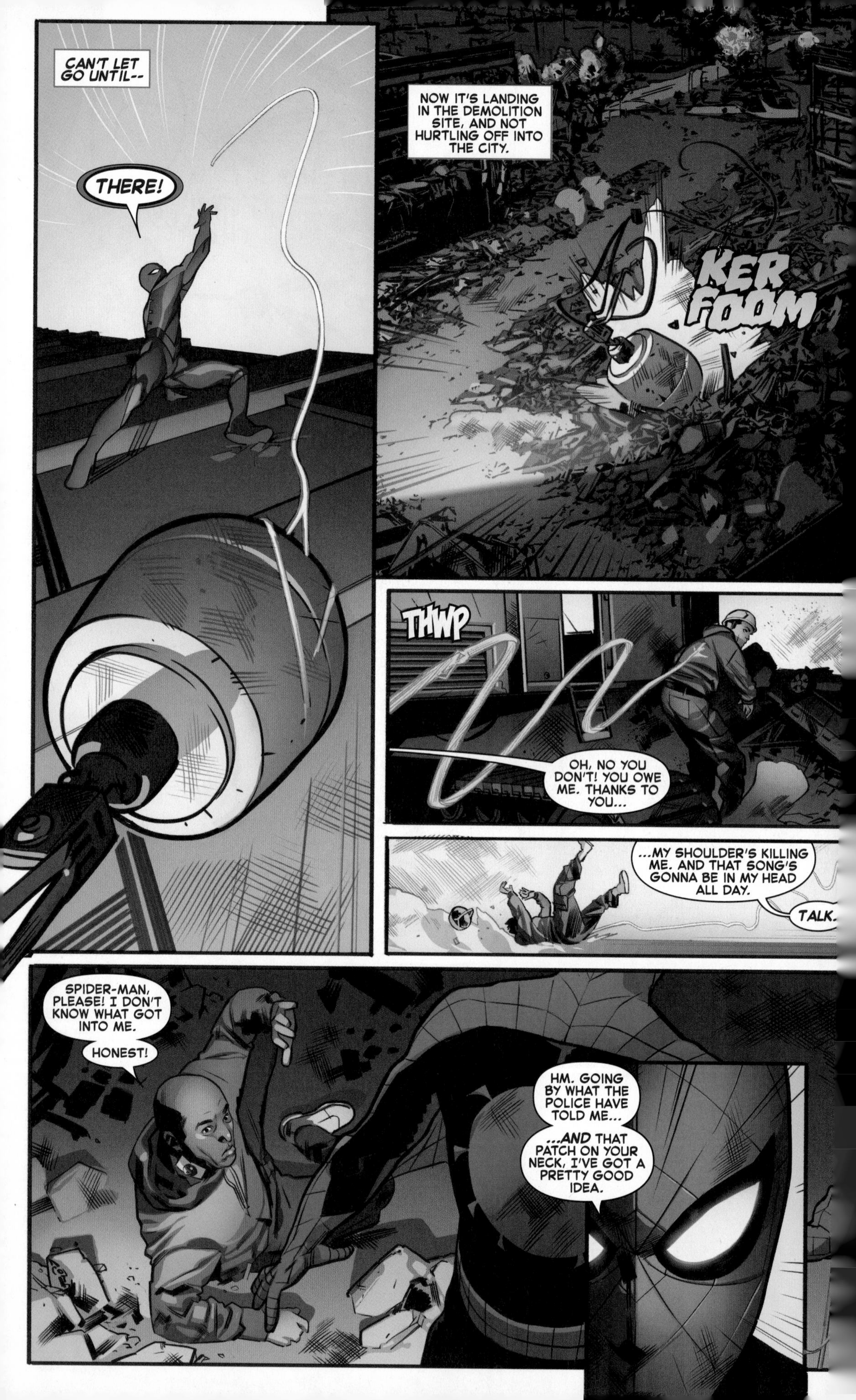
CAN'T LET GO UNTIL--
THERE!
NOW IT'S LANDING IN THE DEMOLITION SITE, AND NOT HURTLING OFF INTO THE CITY.
KER FOOM
THWP
OH, NO YOU DON'T! YOU OWE ME. THANKS TO YOU...
...MY SHOULDER'S KILLING ME. AND THAT SONG'S GONNA BE IN MY HEAD ALL DAY.
TALK.
SPIDER-MAN, PLEASE! I DON'T KNOW WHAT GOT INTO ME.
HONEST!
HM. GOING BY WHAT THE POLICE HAVE TOLD ME...
...AND THAT PATCH ON YOUR NECK, I'VE GOT A PRETTY GOOD IDEA.

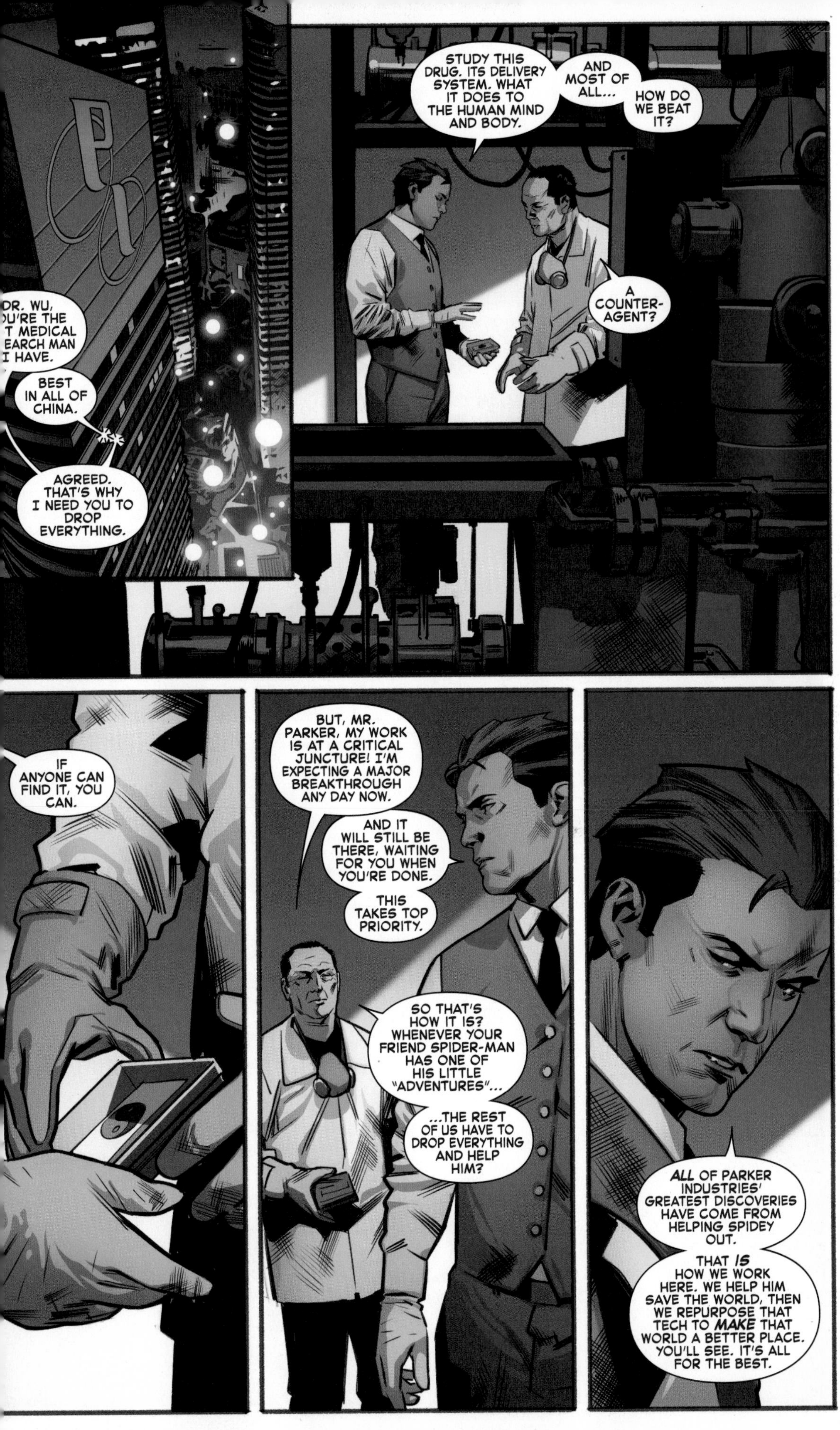
DR. WU, YOU'RE THE BEST MEDICAL RESEARCH MAN I HAVE.
BEST IN ALL OF CHINA.
AGREED. THAT'S WHY I NEED YOU TO DROP EVERYTHING.
STUDY THIS DRUG. ITS DELIVERY SYSTEM. WHAT IT DOES TO THE HUMAN MIND AND BODY.
AND MOST OF ALL...
HOW DO WE BEAT IT?
A COUNTER-AGENT?
IF ANYONE CAN FIND IT, YOU CAN.
BUT, MR. PARKER, MY WORK IS AT A CRITICAL JUNCTURE! I'M EXPECTING A MAJOR BREAKTHROUGH ANY DAY NOW.
AND IT WILL STILL BE THERE, WAITING FOR YOU WHEN YOU'RE DONE.
THIS TAKES TOP PRIORITY.
SO THAT'S HOW IT IS? WHENEVER YOUR FRIEND SPIDER-MAN HAS ONE OF HIS LITTLE "ADVENTURES"...
...THE REST OF US HAVE TO DROP EVERYTHING AND HELP HIM?
ALL OF PARKER INDUSTRIES' GREATEST DISCOVERIES HAVE COME FROM HELPING SPIDEY OUT.
THAT *IS* HOW WE WORK HERE. WE HELP HIM SAVE THE WORLD, THEN WE REPURPOSE THAT TECH TO *MAKE* THAT WORLD A BETTER PLACE. YOU'LL SEE. IT'S ALL FOR THE BEST.

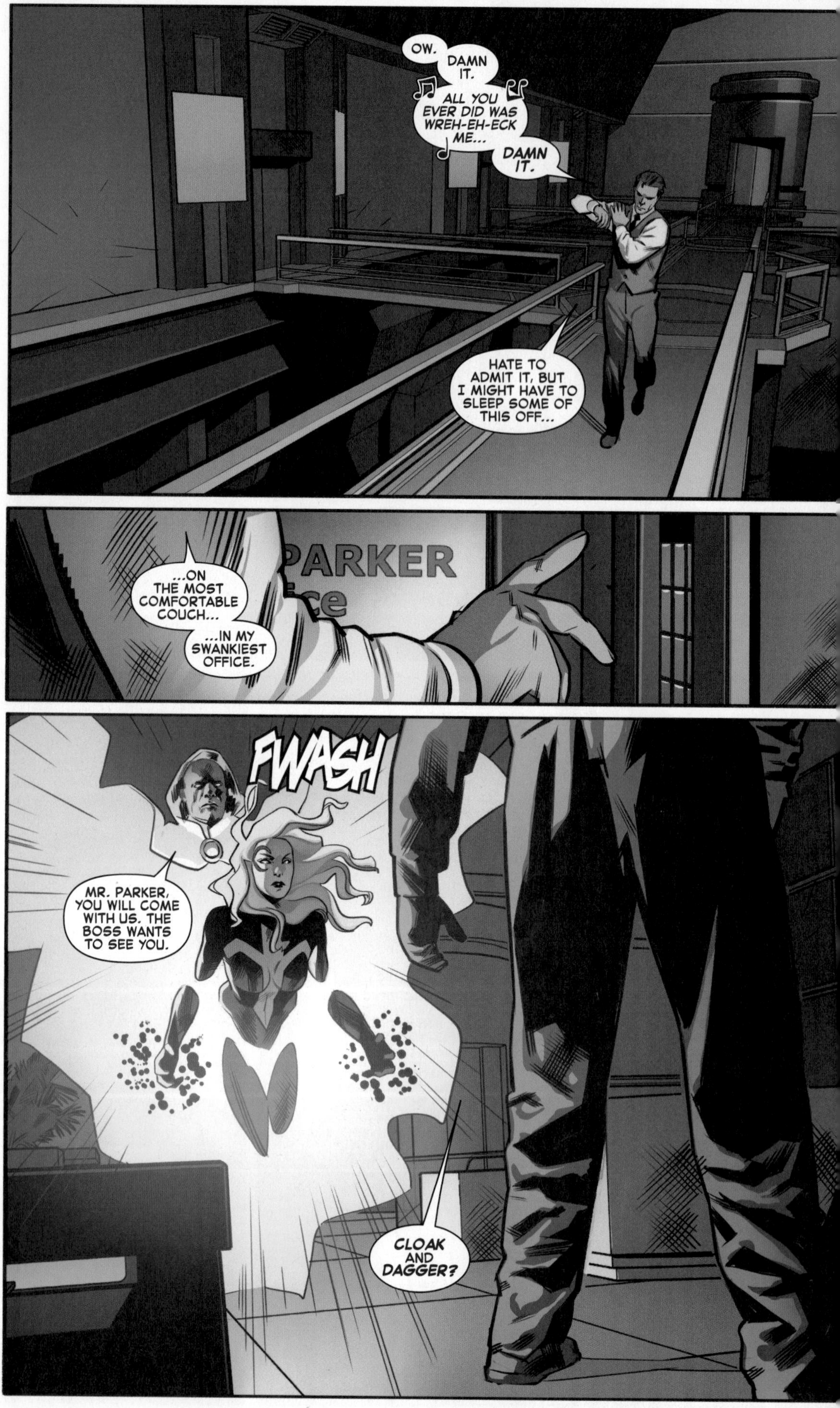
OW.
DAMN IT.
ALL YOU EVER DID WAS WREH-EH-ECK ME...
DAMN IT.
HATE TO ADMIT IT, BUT I MIGHT HAVE TO SLEEP SOME OF THIS OFF...
...ON THE MOST COMFORTABLE COUCH...
...IN MY SWANKIEST OFFICE.
PARKER
FWASH
MR. PARKER, YOU WILL COME WITH US. THE BOSS WANTS TO SEE YOU.
CLOAK AND DAGGER?

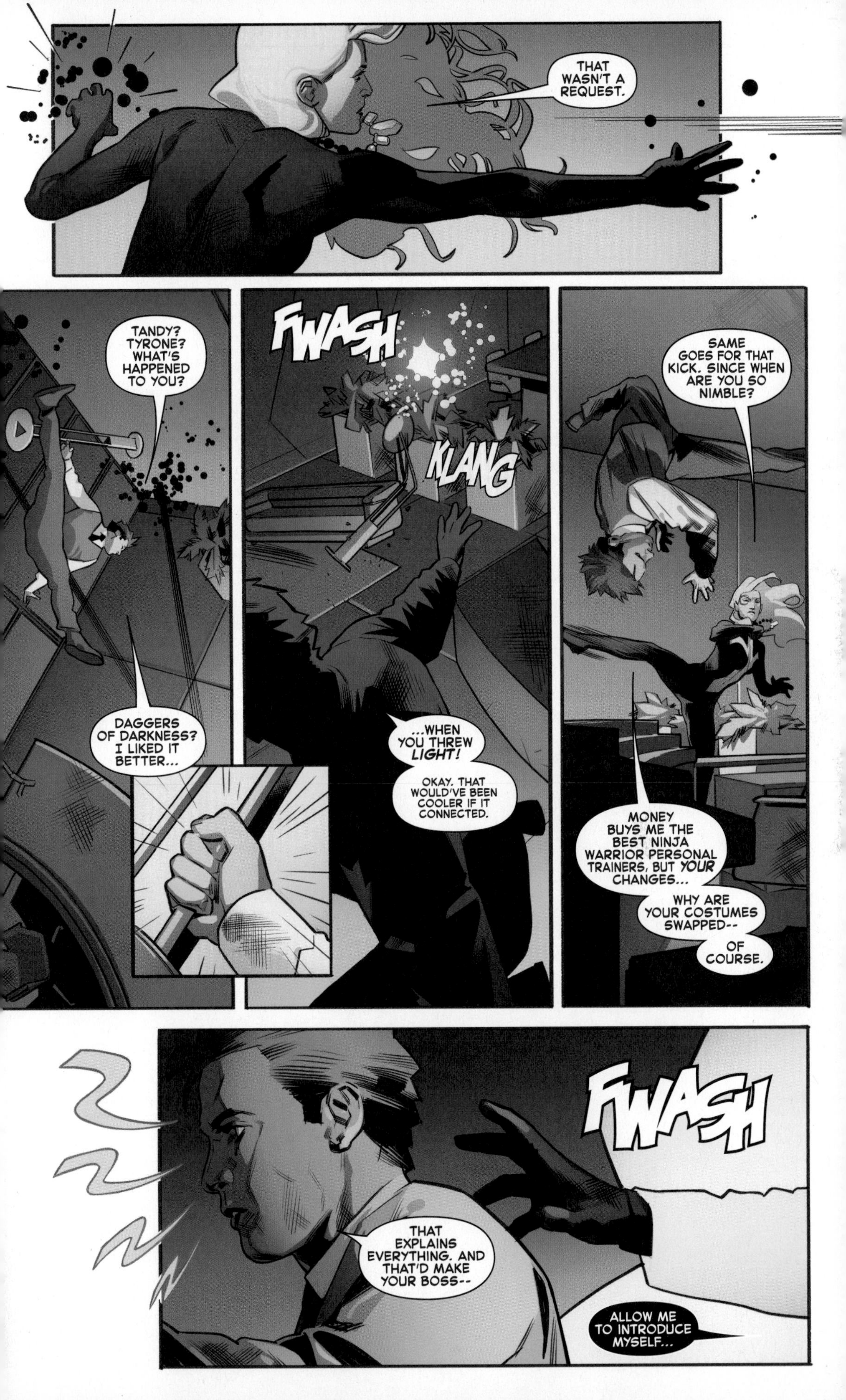
THAT WASN'T A REQUEST.
TANDY? TYRONE? WHAT'S HAPPENED TO YOU?
DAGGERS OF DARKNESS? I LIKED IT BETTER...
FWASH
KLANG
...WHEN YOU THREW LIGHT!
OKAY. THAT WOULD'VE BEEN COOLER IF IT CONNECTED.
SAME GOES FOR THAT KICK. SINCE WHEN ARE YOU SO NIMBLE?
MONEY BUYS ME THE BEST NINJA WARRIOR PERSONAL TRAINERS, BUT YOUR CHANGES...
WHY ARE YOUR COSTUMES SWAPPED--
OF COURSE.
FWASH
THAT EXPLAINS EVERYTHING. AND THAT'D MAKE YOUR BOSS--
ALLOW ME TO INTRODUCE MYSELF...

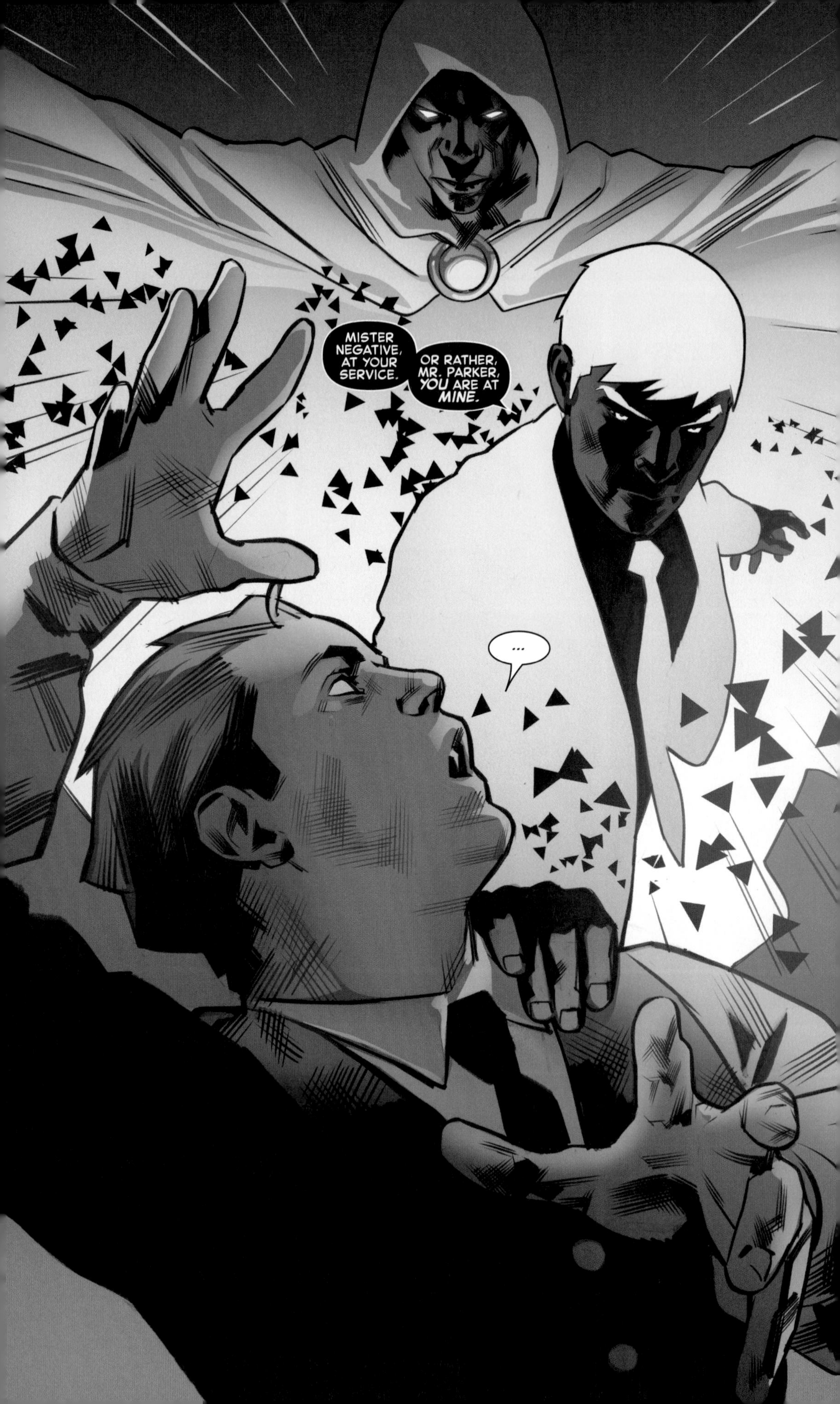
MISTER NEGATIVE, AT YOUR SERVICE.
OR RATHER, MR. PARKER, YOU ARE AT MINE.
...

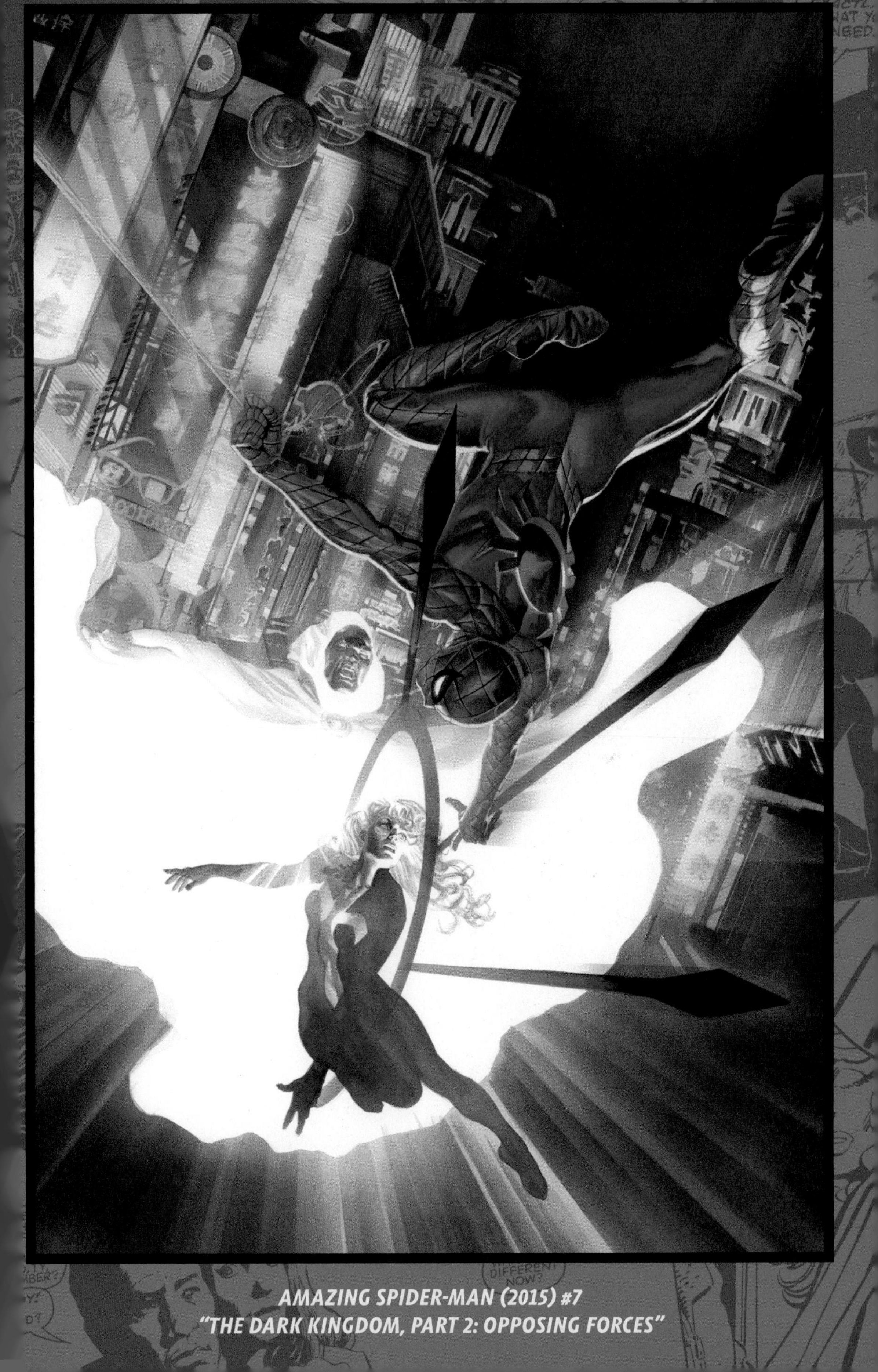

AMAZING SPIDER-MAN (2015) #7
"THE DARK KINGDOM, PART 2: OPPOSING FORCES"

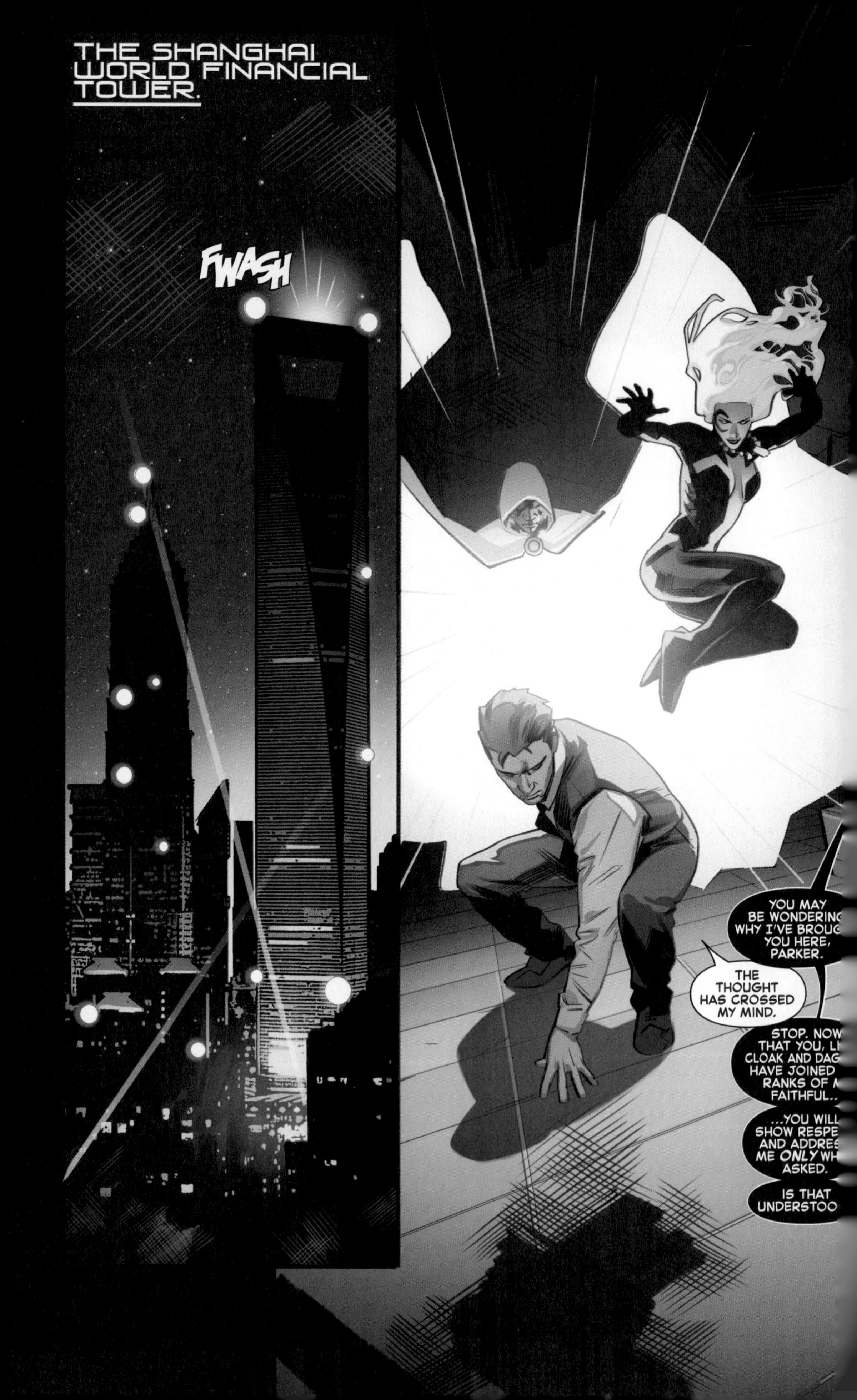
THE SHANGHAI WORLD FINANCIAL TOWER.
FWASH
YOU MAY BE WONDERING WHY I'VE BROUG YOU HERE, PARKER.
THE THOUGHT HAS CROSSED MY MIND.
STOP. NOW THAT YOU, LI CLOAK AND DAG HAVE JOINED RANKS OF M FAITHFUL..
...YOU WILL SHOW RESPE AND ADDRES ME ONLY WH ASKED.
IS THAT UNDERSTOO

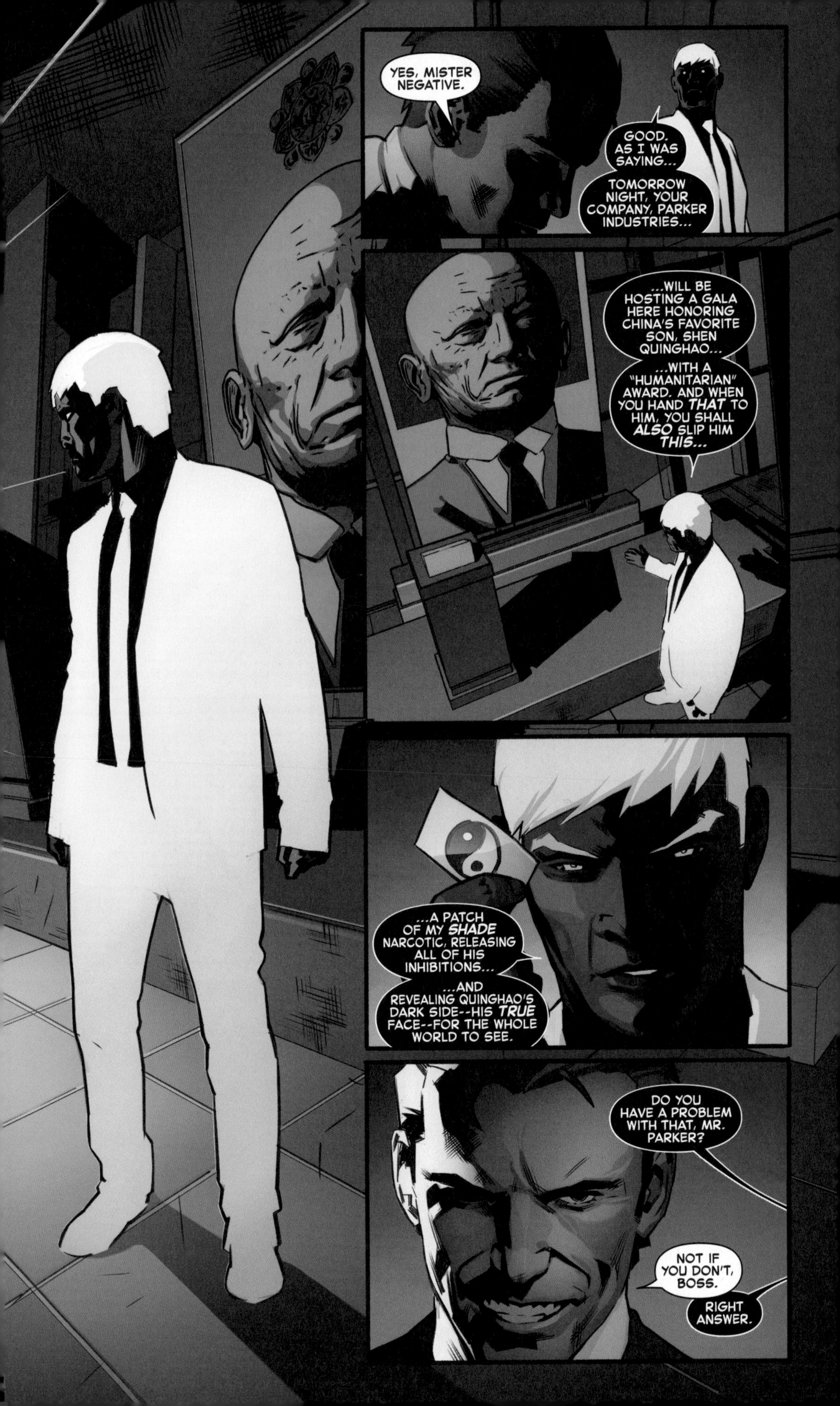
YES, MISTER NEGATIVE.
GOOD. AS I WAS SAYING...
TOMORROW NIGHT, YOUR COMPANY, PARKER INDUSTRIES...
...WILL BE HOSTING A GALA HERE HONORING CHINA'S FAVORITE SON, SHEN QUINGHAO...
...WITH A "HUMANITARIAN" AWARD. AND WHEN YOU HAND *THAT* TO HIM, YOU SHALL *ALSO* SLIP HIM *THIS...*
...A PATCH OF MY *SHADE* NARCOTIC, RELEASING ALL OF HIS INHIBITIONS...
...AND REVEALING QUINGHAO'S DARK SIDE--HIS *TRUE* FACE--FOR THE WHOLE WORLD TO SEE.
DO YOU HAVE A PROBLEM WITH THAT, MR. PARKER?
NOT IF YOU DON'T, BOSS.
RIGHT ANSWER.

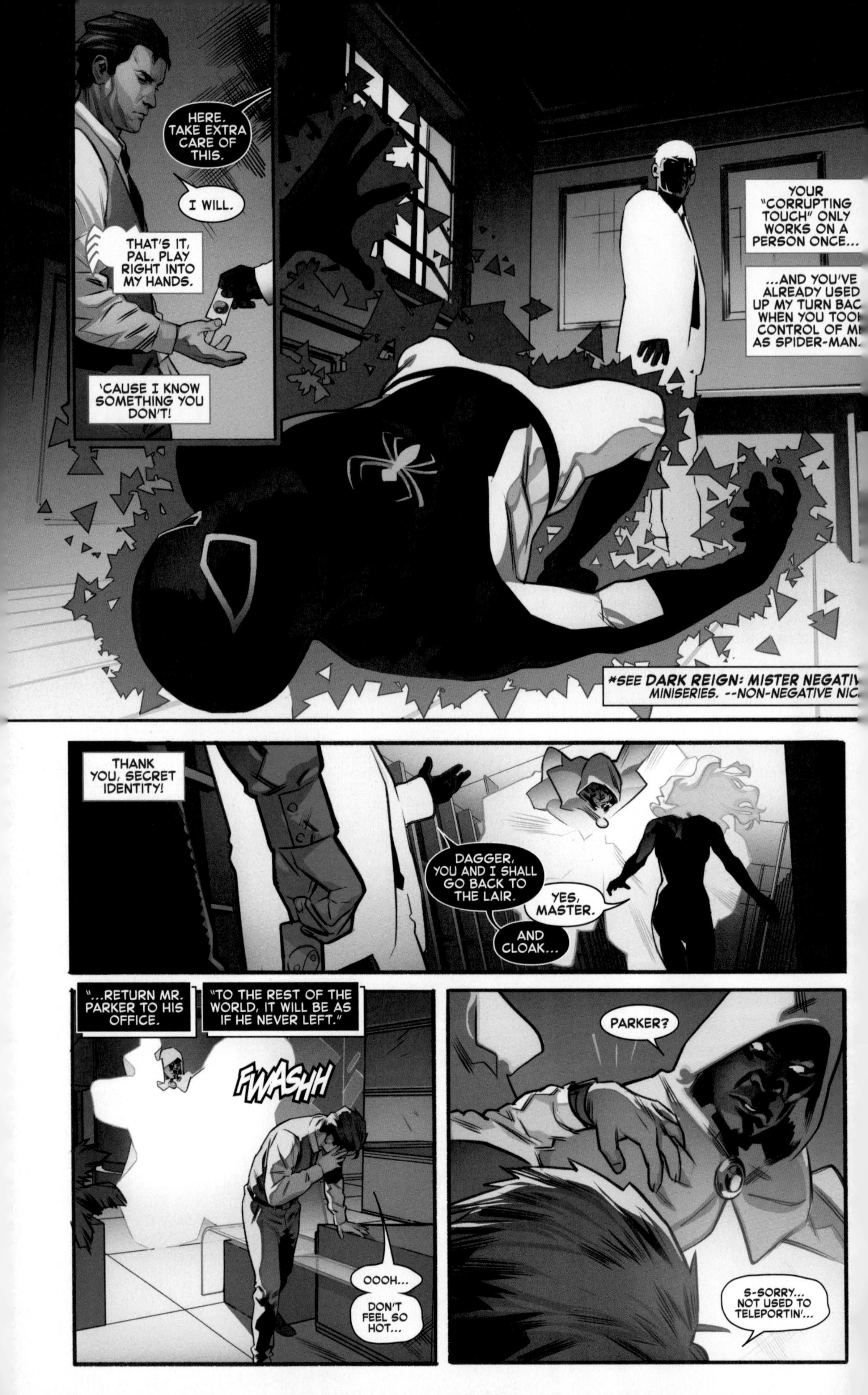
HERE. TAKE EXTRA CARE OF THIS.
I WILL.
THAT'S IT, PAL. PLAY RIGHT INTO MY HANDS.
'CAUSE I KNOW SOMETHING YOU DON'T!
YOUR "CORRUPTING TOUCH" ONLY WORKS ON A PERSON ONCE...
...AND YOU'VE ALREADY USED UP MY TURN BAC WHEN YOU TOOI CONTROL OF MI AS SPIDER-MAN.
*SEE DARK REIGN: MISTER NEGATIV MINISERIES. --NON-NEGATIVE NIC
THANK YOU, SECRET IDENTITY!
DAGGER, YOU AND I SHALL GO BACK TO THE LAIR.
YES, MASTER.
AND CLOAK...
"...RETURN MR. PARKER TO HIS OFFICE.
"TO THE REST OF THE WORLD, IT WILL BE AS IF HE NEVER LEFT."
FWASHH
OOOH...
DON'T FEEL SO HOT...
PARKER?
S-SORRY... NOT USED TO TELEPORTIN'...

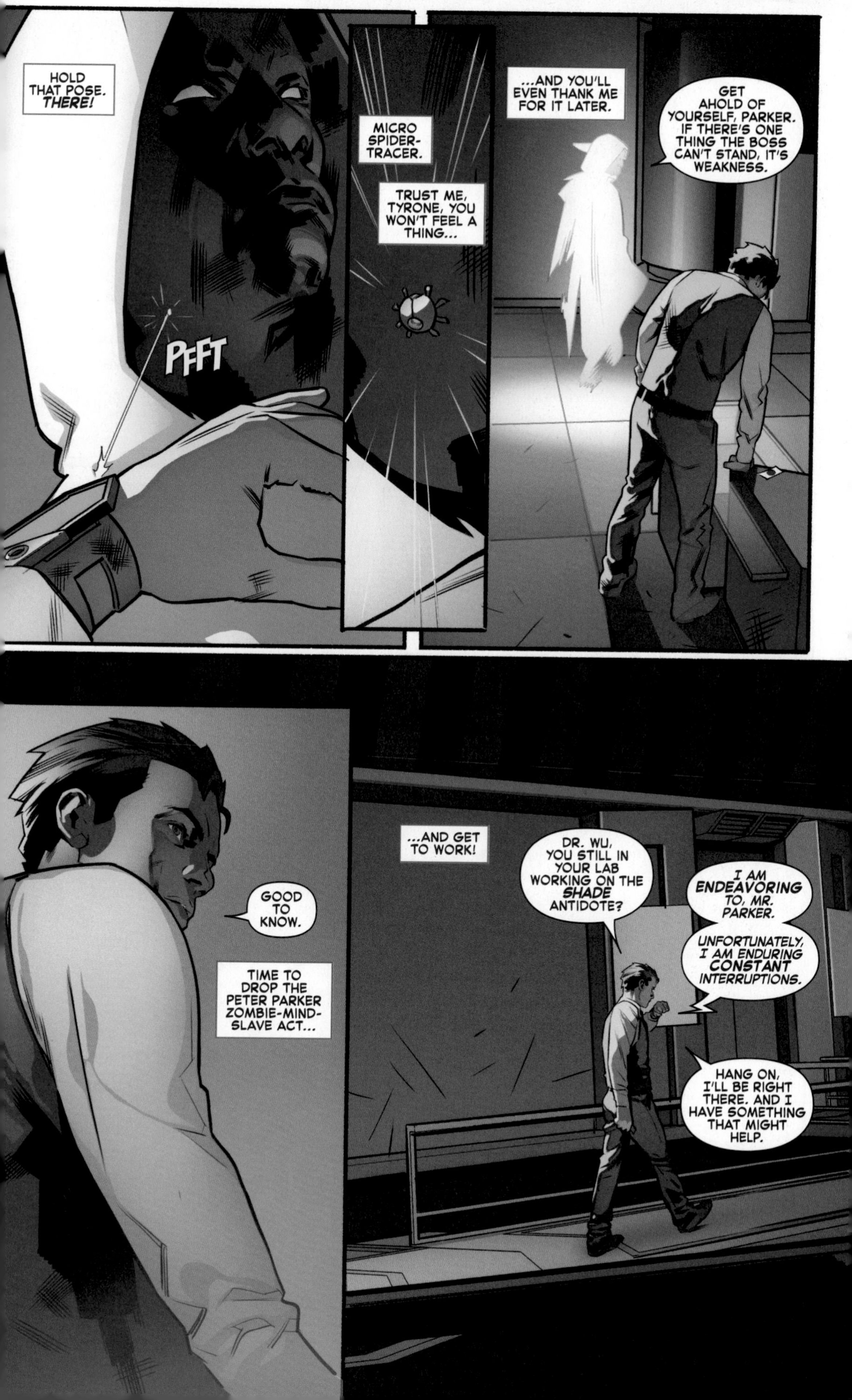
HOLD THAT POSE. THERE!
PFFT
MICRO SPIDER-TRACER.
TRUST ME, TYRONE, YOU WON'T FEEL A THING...
...AND YOU'LL EVEN THANK ME FOR IT LATER.
GET AHOLD OF YOURSELF, PARKER. IF THERE'S ONE THING THE BOSS CAN'T STAND, IT'S WEAKNESS.
GOOD TO KNOW.
TIME TO DROP THE PETER PARKER ZOMBIE-MIND-SLAVE ACT...
...AND GET TO WORK!
DR. WU, YOU STILL IN YOUR LAB WORKING ON THE SHADE ANTIDOTE?
I AM ENDEAVORING TO, MR. PARKER.
UNFORTUNATELY, I AM ENDURING CONSTANT INTERRUPTIONS.
HANG ON, I'LL BE RIGHT THERE. AND I HAVE SOMETHING THAT MIGHT HELP.

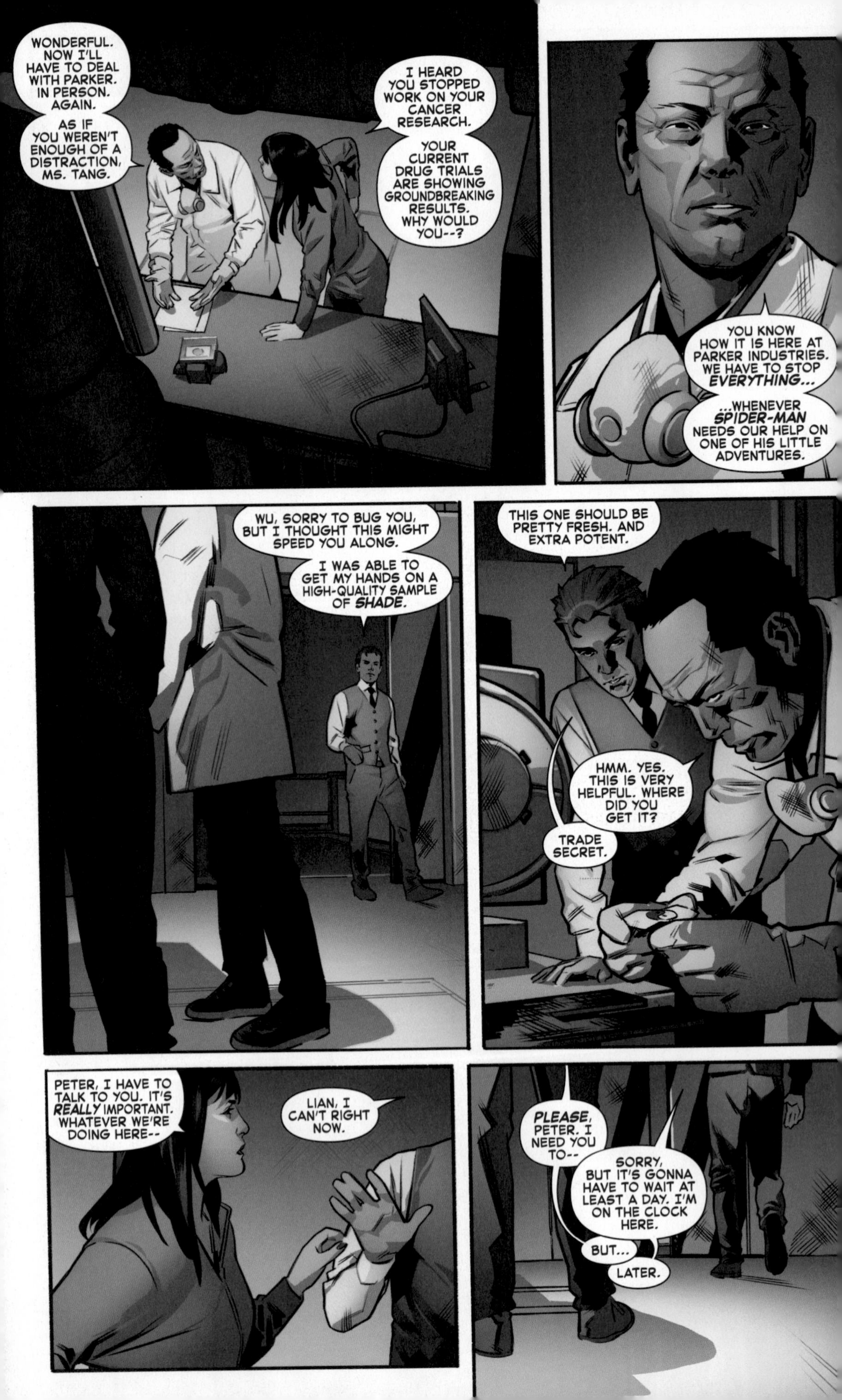
WONDERFUL. NOW I'LL HAVE TO DEAL WITH PARKER. IN PERSON. AGAIN.
AS IF YOU WEREN'T ENOUGH OF A DISTRACTION, MS. TANG.
I HEARD YOU STOPPED WORK ON YOUR CANCER RESEARCH.
YOUR CURRENT DRUG TRIALS ARE SHOWING GROUNDBREAKING RESULTS. WHY WOULD YOU--?
YOU KNOW HOW IT IS HERE AT PARKER INDUSTRIES. WE HAVE TO STOP *EVERYTHING...*
...WHENEVER *SPIDER-MAN* NEEDS OUR HELP ON ONE OF HIS LITTLE ADVENTURES.
WU, SORRY TO BUG YOU, BUT I THOUGHT THIS MIGHT SPEED YOU ALONG.
I WAS ABLE TO GET MY HANDS ON A HIGH-QUALITY SAMPLE OF *SHADE.*
THIS ONE SHOULD BE PRETTY FRESH. AND EXTRA POTENT.
HMM. YES. THIS IS VERY HELPFUL. WHERE DID YOU GET IT?
TRADE SECRET.
PETER, I HAVE TO TALK TO YOU. IT'S *REALLY* IMPORTANT. WHATEVER WE'RE DOING HERE--
LIAN, I CAN'T RIGHT NOW.
PLEASE, PETER. I NEED YOU TO--
SORRY, BUT IT'S GONNA HAVE TO WAIT AT LEAST A DAY. I'M ON THE CLOCK HERE.
BUT...
LATER.

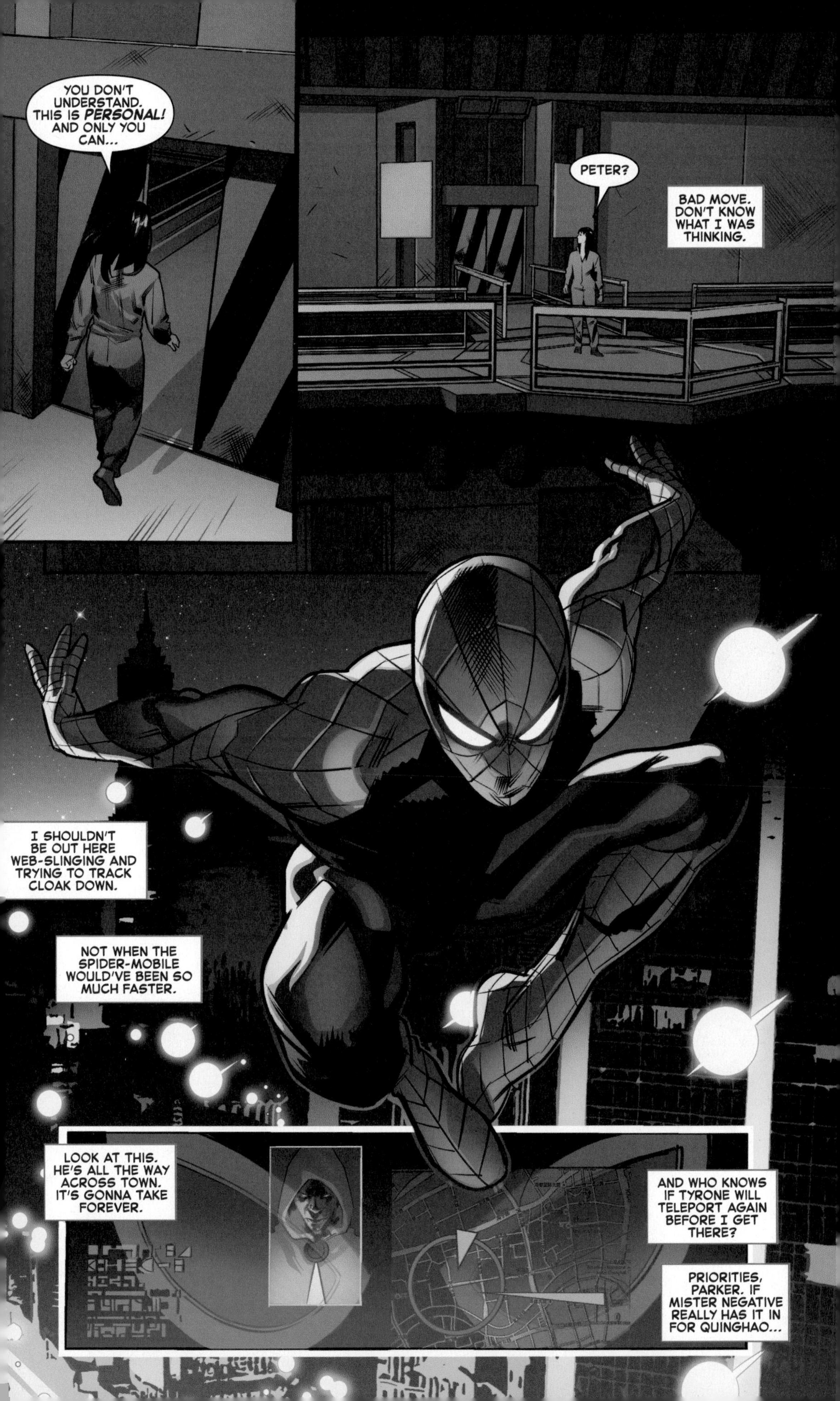

YOU DON'T UNDERSTAND. THIS IS *PERSONAL!* AND ONLY YOU CAN...
PETER?
BAD MOVE. DON'T KNOW WHAT I WAS THINKING.
I SHOULDN'T BE OUT HERE WEB-SLINGING AND TRYING TO TRACK CLOAK DOWN.
NOT WHEN THE SPIDER-MOBILE WOULD'VE BEEN SO MUCH FASTER.
LOOK AT THIS. HE'S ALL THE WAY ACROSS TOWN. IT'S GONNA TAKE FOREVER.
AND WHO KNOWS IF TYRONE WILL TELEPORT AGAIN BEFORE I GET THERE?
PRIORITIES, PARKER. IF MISTER NEGATIVE REALLY HAS IT IN FOR QUINGHAO...

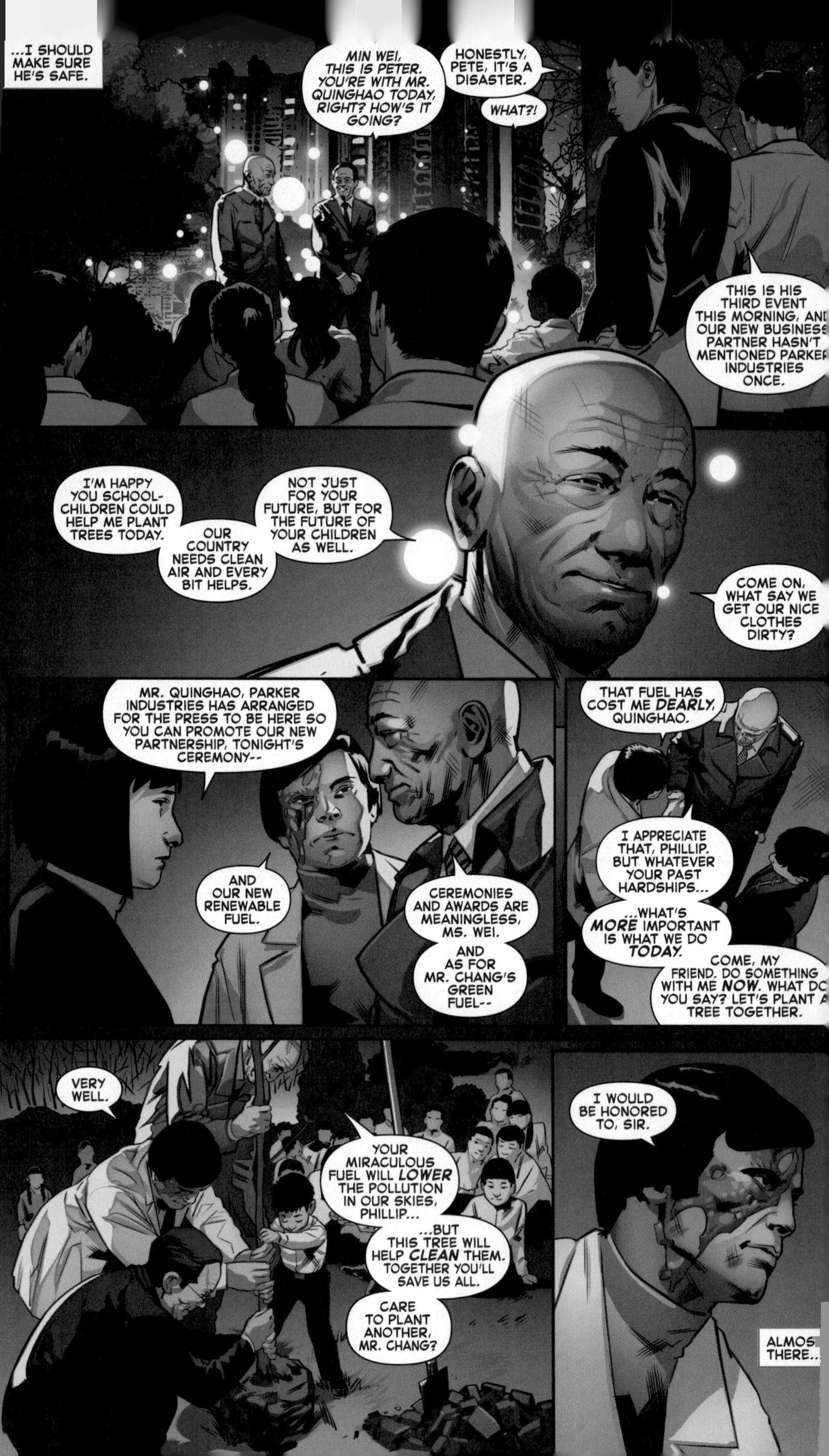
...I SHOULD MAKE SURE HE'S SAFE.
MIN WEI, THIS IS PETER. YOU'RE WITH MR. QUINGHAO TODAY, RIGHT? HOW'S IT GOING?
HONESTLY, PETE, IT'S A DISASTER.
WHAT?!
THIS IS HIS THIRD EVENT THIS MORNING, AND OUR NEW BUSINESS PARTNER HASN'T MENTIONED PARKER INDUSTRIES ONCE.
I'M HAPPY YOU SCHOOL-CHILDREN COULD HELP ME PLANT TREES TODAY.
OUR COUNTRY NEEDS CLEAN AIR AND EVERY BIT HELPS.
NOT JUST FOR YOUR FUTURE, BUT FOR THE FUTURE OF YOUR CHILDREN AS WELL.
COME ON, WHAT SAY WE GET OUR NICE CLOTHES DIRTY?
MR. QUINGHAO, PARKER INDUSTRIES HAS ARRANGED FOR THE PRESS TO BE HERE SO YOU CAN PROMOTE OUR NEW PARTNERSHIP, TONIGHT'S CEREMONY--
AND OUR NEW RENEWABLE FUEL.
CEREMONIES AND AWARDS ARE MEANINGLESS, MS. WEI.
AND AS FOR MR. CHANG'S GREEN FUEL--
THAT FUEL HAS COST ME DEARLY, QUINGHAO.
I APPRECIATE THAT, PHILLIP. BUT WHATEVER YOUR PAST HARDSHIPS...
...WHAT'S MORE IMPORTANT IS WHAT WE DO TODAY.
COME, MY FRIEND. DO SOMETHING WITH ME NOW. WHAT DO YOU SAY? LET'S PLANT A TREE TOGETHER.
VERY WELL.
YOUR MIRACULOUS FUEL WILL LOWER THE POLLUTION IN OUR SKIES, PHILLIP...
...BUT THIS TREE WILL HELP CLEAN THEM. TOGETHER YOU'LL SAVE US ALL.
CARE TO PLANT ANOTHER, MR. CHANG?
I WOULD BE HONORED TO, SIR.
ALMOST THERE...

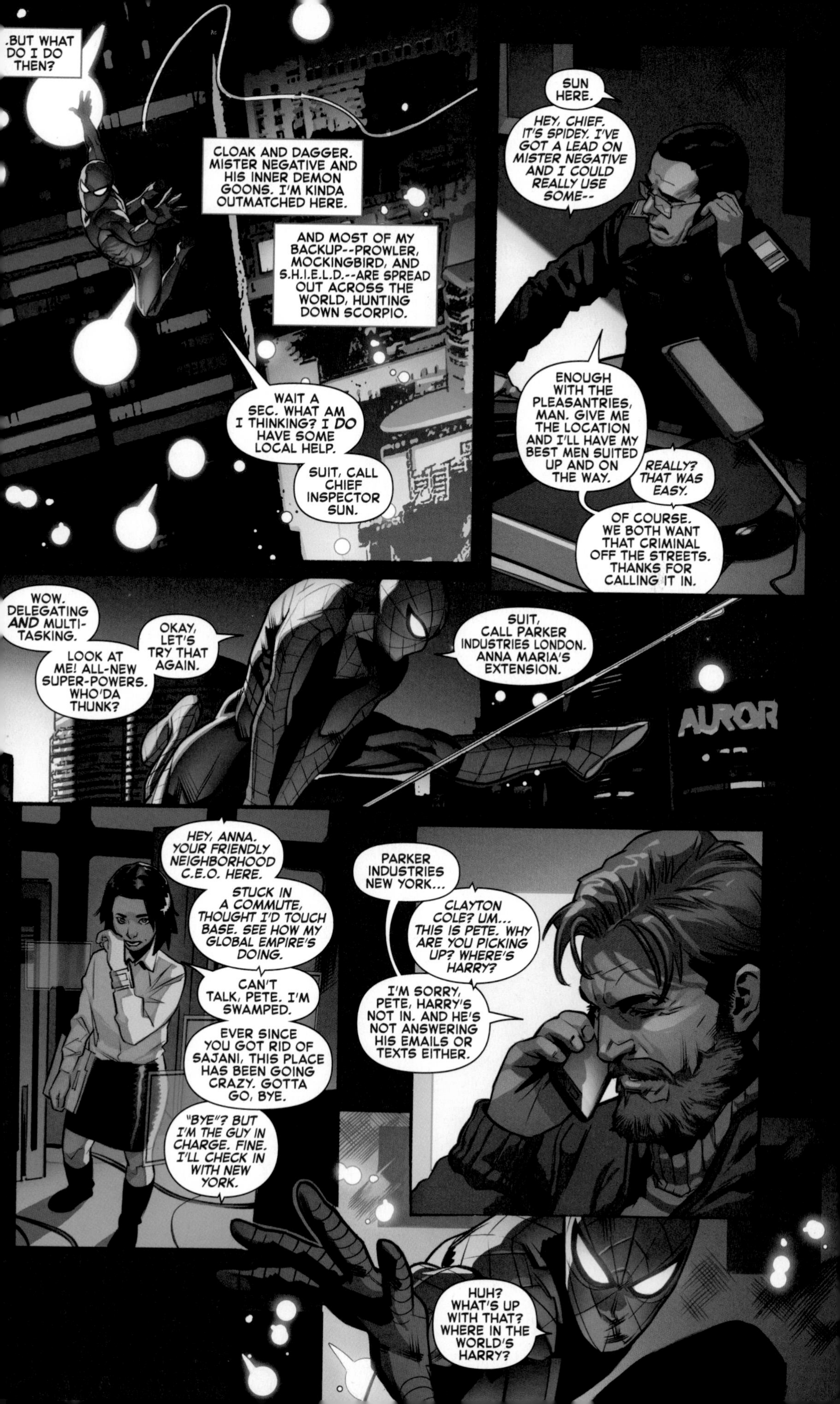

...BUT WHAT DO I DO THEN?
CLOAK AND DAGGER. MISTER NEGATIVE AND HIS INNER DEMON GOONS. I'M KINDA OUTMATCHED HERE.
AND MOST OF MY BACKUP--PROWLER, MOCKINGBIRD, AND S.H.I.E.L.D.--ARE SPREAD OUT ACROSS THE WORLD, HUNTING DOWN SCORPIO.
WAIT A SEC. WHAT AM I THINKING? I DO HAVE SOME LOCAL HELP.
SUIT, CALL CHIEF INSPECTOR SUN.
SUN HERE.
HEY, CHIEF. IT'S SPIDEY. I'VE GOT A LEAD ON MISTER NEGATIVE AND I COULD REALLY USE SOME--
ENOUGH WITH THE PLEASANTRIES, MAN. GIVE ME THE LOCATION AND I'LL HAVE MY BEST MEN SUITED UP AND ON THE WAY.
REALLY? THAT WAS EASY.
OF COURSE. WE BOTH WANT THAT CRIMINAL OFF THE STREETS. THANKS FOR CALLING IT IN.
WOW. DELEGATING AND MULTI-TASKING.
LOOK AT ME! ALL-NEW SUPER-POWERS. WHO'DA THUNK?
OKAY, LET'S TRY THAT AGAIN.
SUIT, CALL PARKER INDUSTRIES LONDON. ANNA MARIA'S EXTENSION.
AUROR
HEY, ANNA. YOUR FRIENDLY NEIGHBORHOOD C.E.O. HERE.
STUCK IN A COMMUTE, THOUGHT I'D TOUCH BASE. SEE HOW MY GLOBAL EMPIRE'S DOING.
CAN'T TALK, PETE. I'M SWAMPED.
EVER SINCE YOU GOT RID OF SAJANI, THIS PLACE HAS BEEN GOING CRAZY. GOTTA GO, BYE.
"BYE"? BUT I'M THE GUY IN CHARGE. FINE. I'LL CHECK IN WITH NEW YORK.
PARKER INDUSTRIES NEW YORK...
CLAYTON COLE? UM... THIS IS PETE. WHY ARE YOU PICKING UP? WHERE'S HARRY?
I'M SORRY, PETE, HARRY'S NOT IN. AND HE'S NOT ANSWERING HIS EMAILS OR TEXTS EITHER.
HUH? WHAT'S UP WITH THAT? WHERE IN THE WORLD'S HARRY?

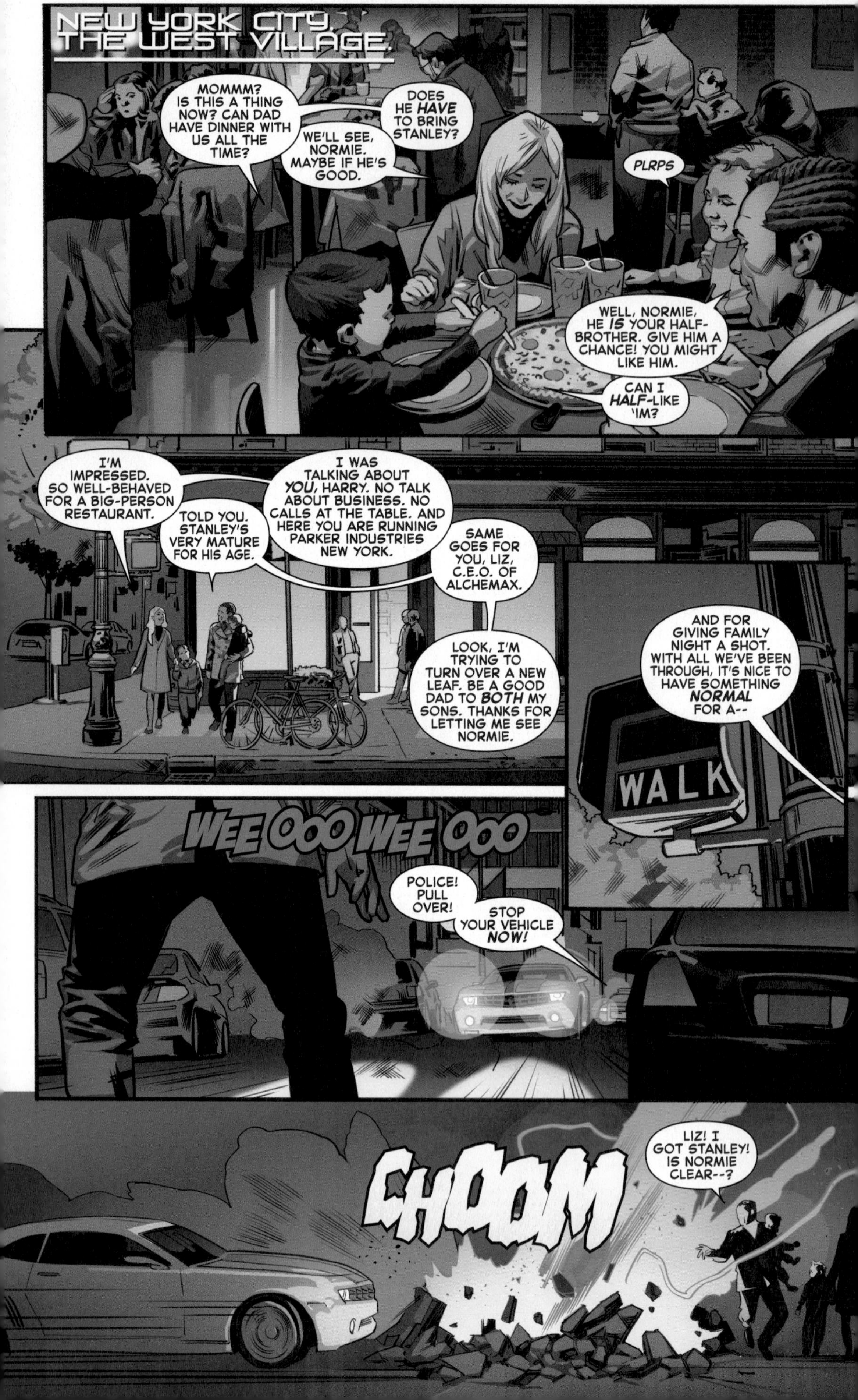
NEW YORK CITY. THE WEST VILLAGE.
MOMMM? IS THIS A THING NOW? CAN DAD HAVE DINNER WITH US ALL THE TIME?
DOES HE HAVE TO BRING STANLEY?
WE'LL SEE, NORMIE. MAYBE IF HE'S GOOD.
PLRPS
WELL, NORMIE, HE IS YOUR HALF-BROTHER. GIVE HIM A CHANCE! YOU MIGHT LIKE HIM.
CAN I HALF-LIKE 'IM?
I'M IMPRESSED. SO WELL-BEHAVED FOR A BIG-PERSON RESTAURANT.
TOLD YOU. STANLEY'S VERY MATURE FOR HIS AGE.
I WAS TALKING ABOUT YOU, HARRY. NO TALK ABOUT BUSINESS. NO CALLS AT THE TABLE. AND HERE YOU ARE RUNNING PARKER INDUSTRIES NEW YORK.
SAME GOES FOR YOU, LIZ, C.E.O. OF ALCHEMAX.
LOOK, I'M TRYING TO TURN OVER A NEW LEAF. BE A GOOD DAD TO BOTH MY SONS. THANKS FOR LETTING ME SEE NORMIE.
AND FOR GIVING FAMILY NIGHT A SHOT. WITH ALL WE'VE BEEN THROUGH, IT'S NICE TO HAVE SOMETHING NORMAL FOR A--
WALK
WEE OOO WEE OOO
POLICE! PULL OVER!
STOP YOUR VEHICLE NOW!
CHOOM
LIZ! I GOT STANLEY! IS NORMIE CLEAR--?

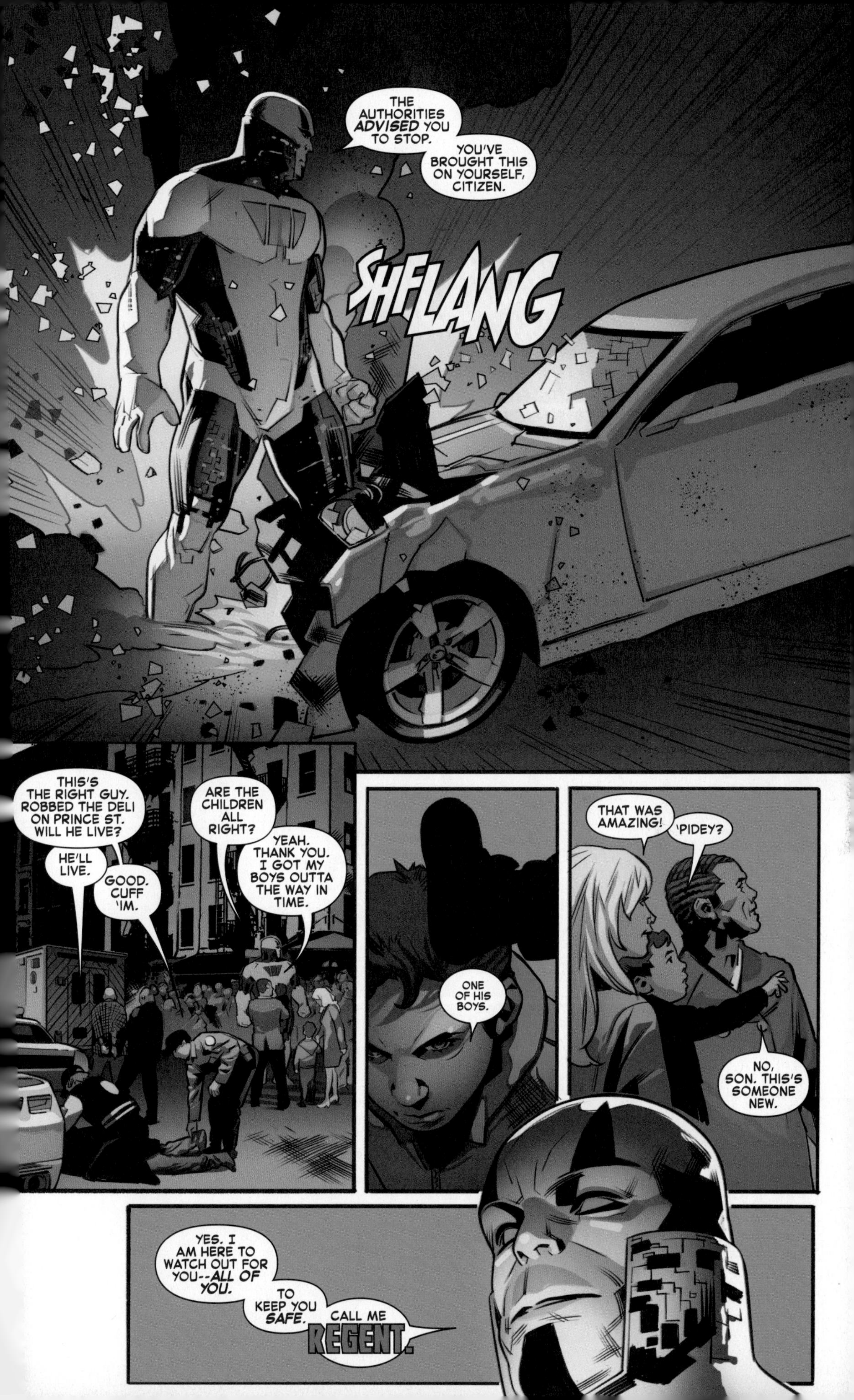
THE AUTHORITIES *ADVISED* YOU TO STOP.
YOU'VE BROUGHT THIS ON YOURSELF, CITIZEN.
SHFLANG
THIS'S THE RIGHT GUY. ROBBED THE DELI ON PRINCE ST. WILL HE LIVE?
HE'LL LIVE.
GOOD. CUFF 'IM.
ARE THE CHILDREN ALL RIGHT?
YEAH. THANK YOU. I GOT MY BOYS OUTTA THE WAY IN TIME.
ONE OF HIS BOYS.
THAT WAS AMAZING!
'PIDEY?
NO, SON. THIS'S SOMEONE NEW.
YES. I AM HERE TO WATCH OUT FOR YOU--*ALL OF YOU.*
TO KEEP YOU *SAFE.*
CALL ME
REGENT.

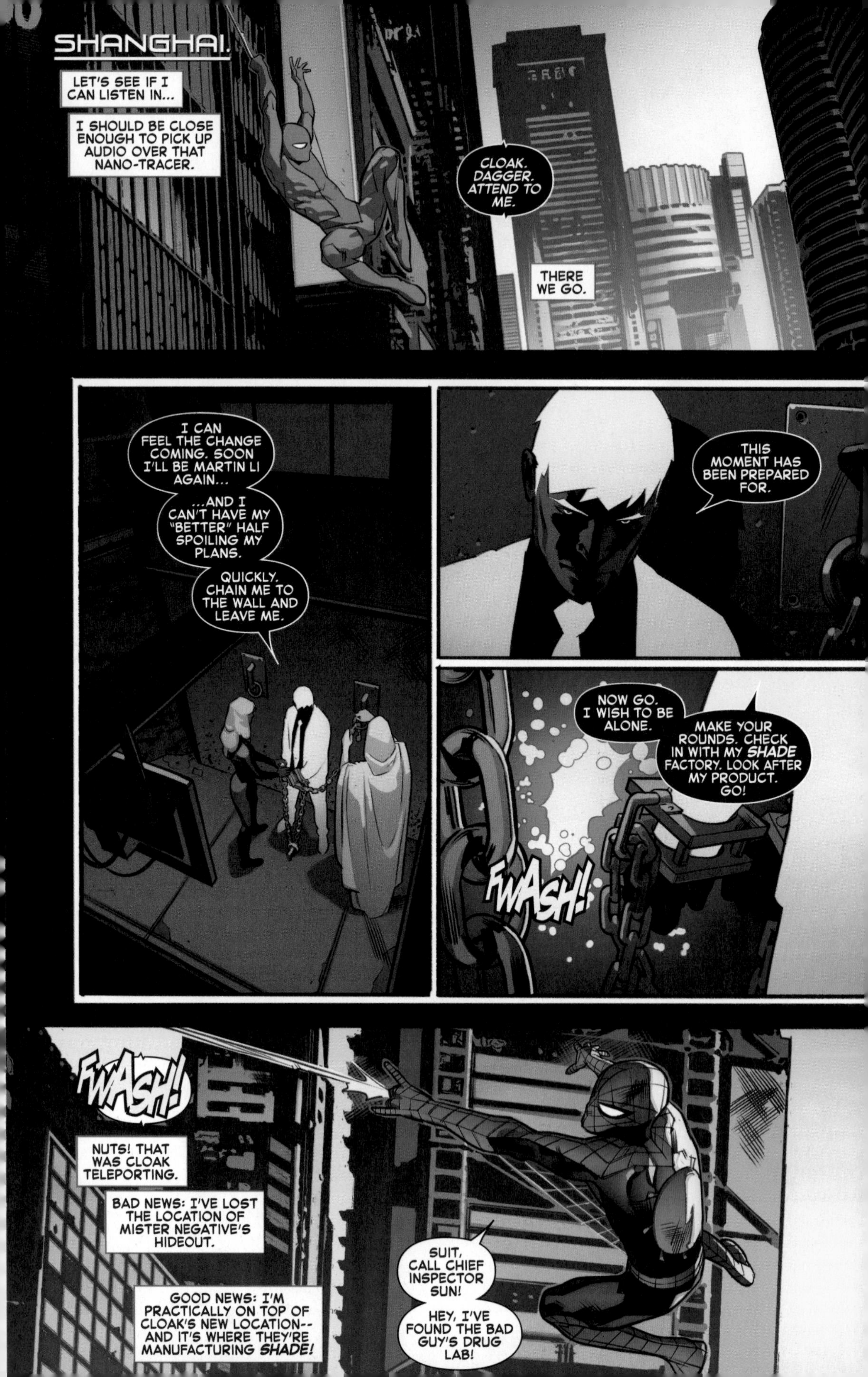
SHANGHAI.
LET'S SEE IF I CAN LISTEN IN...
I SHOULD BE CLOSE ENOUGH TO PICK UP AUDIO OVER THAT NANO-TRACER.
CLOAK. DAGGER. ATTEND TO ME.
THERE WE GO.
I CAN FEEL THE CHANGE COMING. SOON I'LL BE MARTIN LI AGAIN...
...AND I CAN'T HAVE MY "BETTER" HALF SPOILING MY PLANS.
QUICKLY. CHAIN ME TO THE WALL AND LEAVE ME.
THIS MOMENT HAS BEEN PREPARED FOR.
NOW GO. I WISH TO BE ALONE.
MAKE YOUR ROUNDS. CHECK IN WITH MY *SHADE* FACTORY. LOOK AFTER MY PRODUCT. GO!
FWASH!!
FWASH!!
NUTS! THAT WAS CLOAK TELEPORTING.
BAD NEWS: I'VE LOST THE LOCATION OF MISTER NEGATIVE'S HIDEOUT.
GOOD NEWS: I'M PRACTICALLY ON TOP OF CLOAK'S NEW LOCATION-- AND IT'S WHERE THEY'RE MANUFACTURING *SHADE!*
SUIT, CALL CHIEF INSPECTOR SUN!
HEY, I'VE FOUND THE BAD GUY'S DRUG LAB!

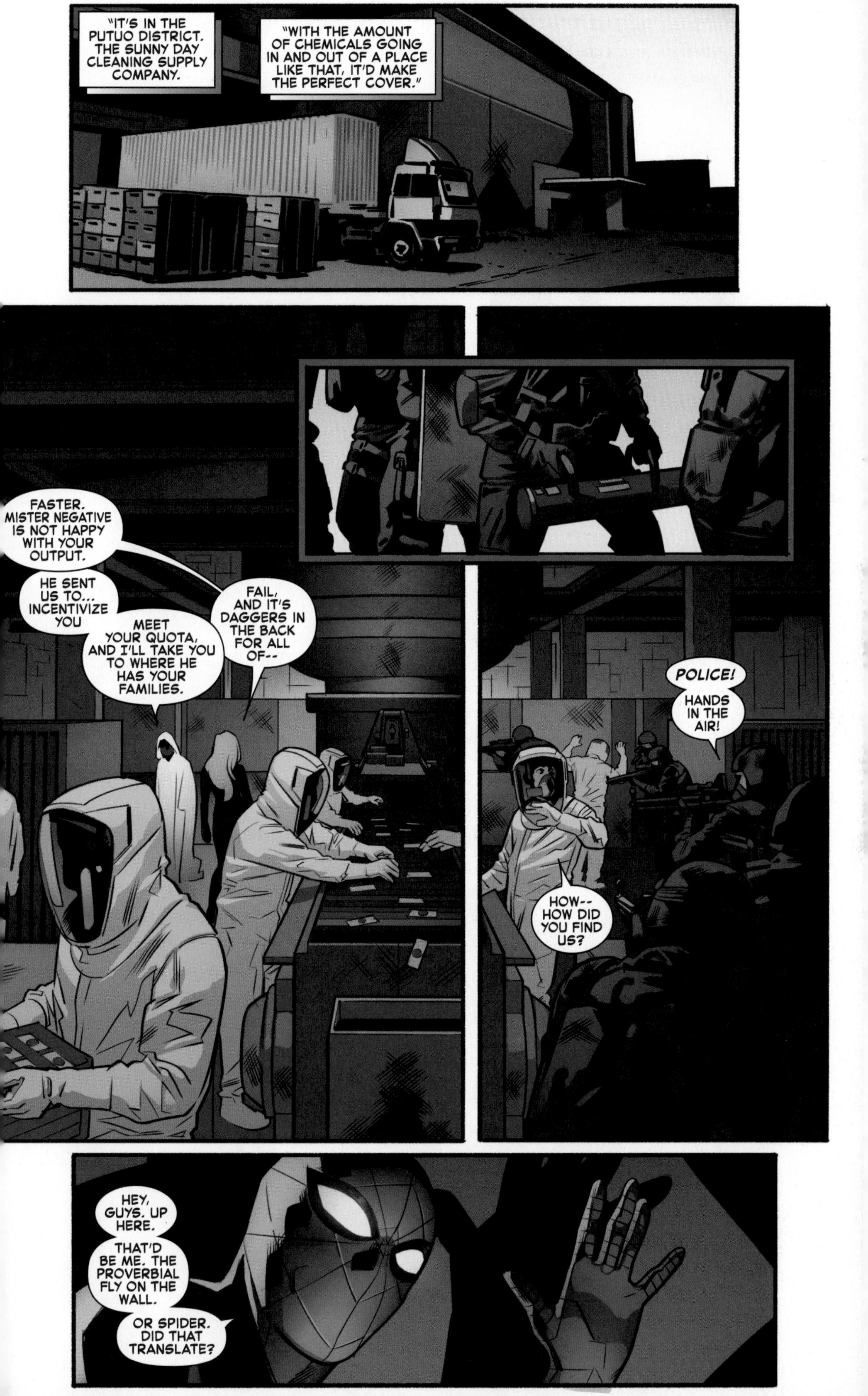

"IT'S IN THE PUTUO DISTRICT. THE SUNNY DAY CLEANING SUPPLY COMPANY.
"WITH THE AMOUNT OF CHEMICALS GOING IN AND OUT OF A PLACE LIKE THAT, IT'D MAKE THE PERFECT COVER."
FASTER. MISTER NEGATIVE IS NOT HAPPY WITH YOUR OUTPUT.
HE SENT US TO... INCENTIVIZE YOU
MEET YOUR QUOTA, AND I'LL TAKE YOU TO WHERE HE HAS YOUR FAMILIES.
FAIL, AND IT'S DAGGERS IN THE BACK FOR ALL OF--
POLICE!
HANDS IN THE AIR!
HOW-- HOW DID YOU FIND US?
HEY, GUYS. UP HERE.
THAT'D BE ME. THE PROVERBIAL FLY ON THE WALL.
OR SPIDER. DID THAT TRANSLATE?

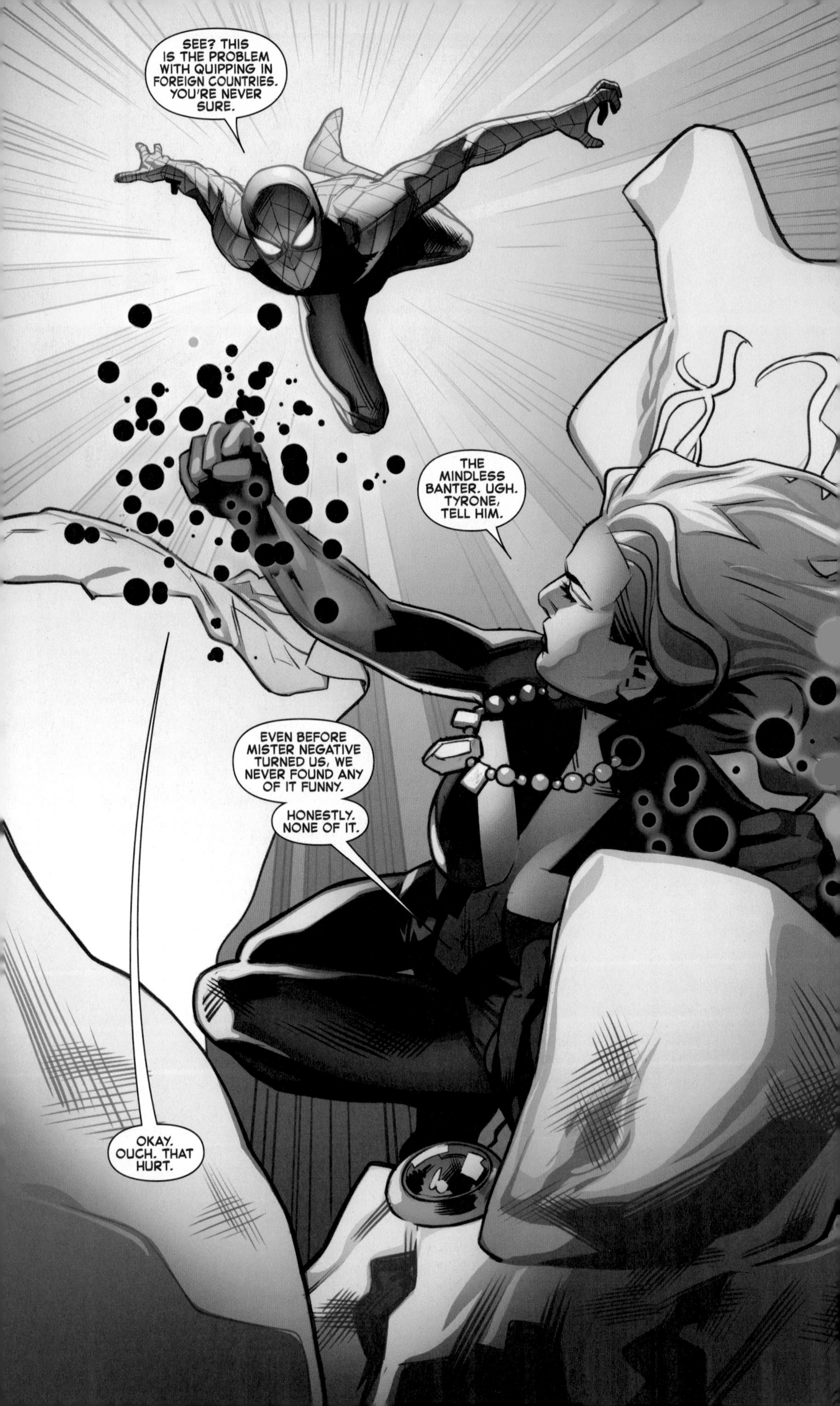
SEE? THIS IS THE PROBLEM WITH QUIPPING IN FOREIGN COUNTRIES. YOU'RE NEVER SURE.
THE MINDLESS BANTER. UGH. TYRONE, TELL HIM.
EVEN BEFORE MISTER NEGATIVE TURNED US, WE NEVER FOUND ANY OF IT FUNNY.
HONESTLY. NONE OF IT.
OKAY. OUCH. THAT HURT.

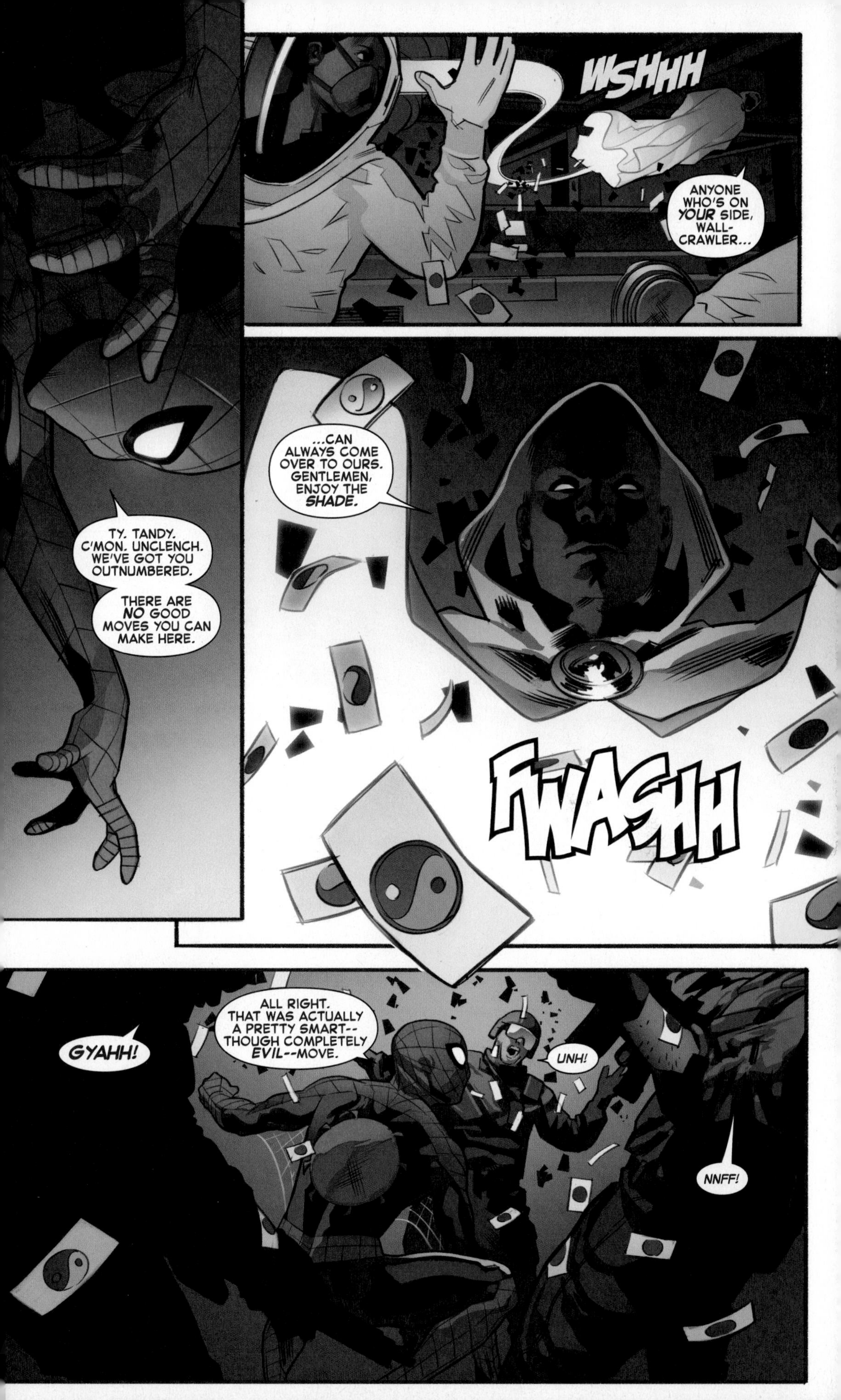
TY. TANDY. C'MON. UNCLENCH. WE'VE GOT YOU OUTNUMBERED.
THERE ARE NO GOOD MOVES YOU CAN MAKE HERE.
WSHHH
ANYONE WHO'S ON YOUR SIDE, WALL-CRAWLER...
...CAN ALWAYS COME OVER TO OURS. GENTLEMEN, ENJOY THE SHADE.
FWASHH
GYAHH!
ALL RIGHT. THAT WAS ACTUALLY A PRETTY SMART--THOUGH COMPLETELY EVIL--MOVE.
UNH!
NNFF!

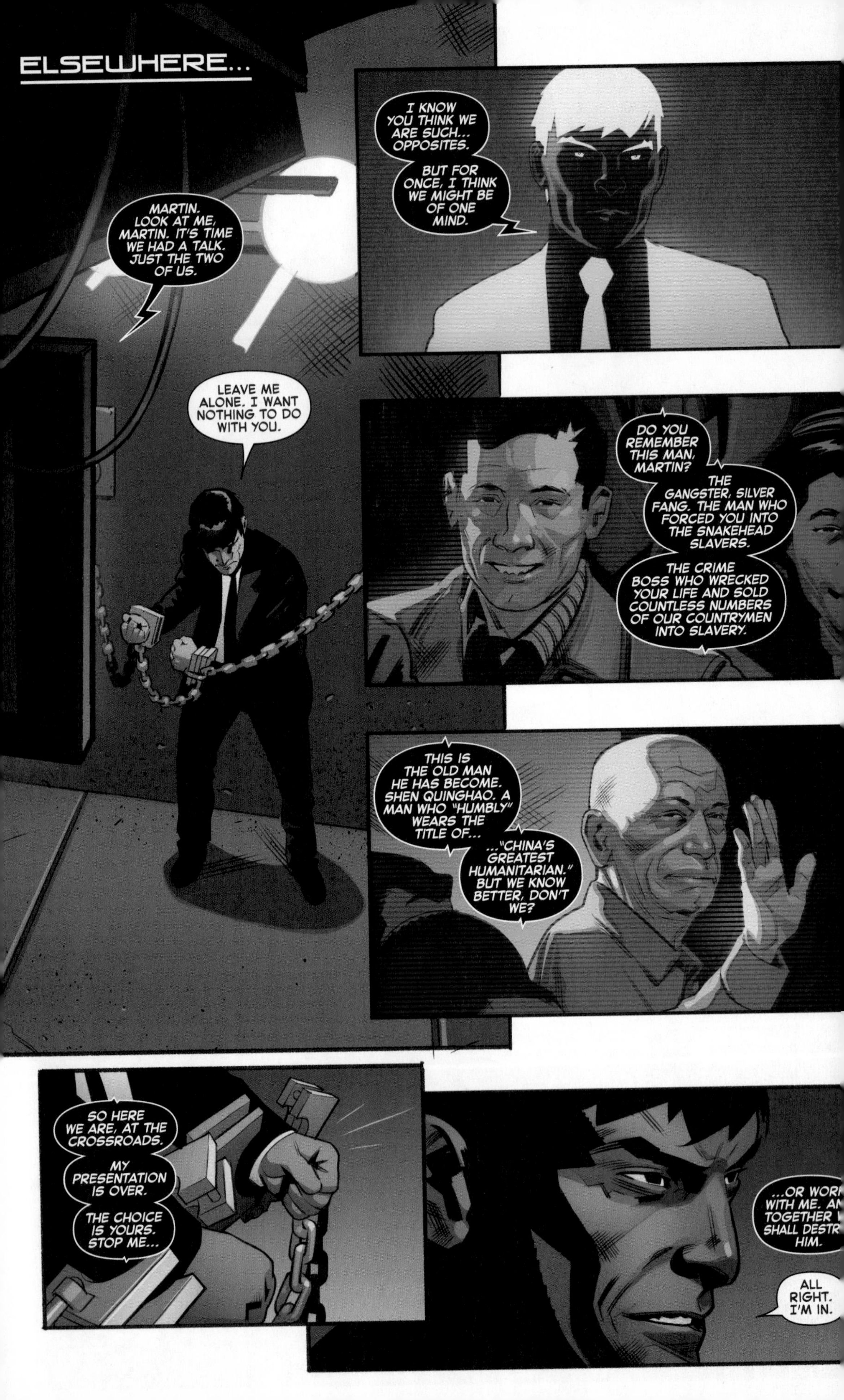
ELSEWHERE...
MARTIN. LOOK AT ME, MARTIN. IT'S TIME WE HAD A TALK. JUST THE TWO OF US.
I KNOW YOU THINK WE ARE SUCH... OPPOSITES.
BUT FOR ONCE, I THINK WE MIGHT BE OF ONE MIND.
LEAVE ME ALONE. I WANT NOTHING TO DO WITH YOU.
DO YOU REMEMBER THIS MAN, MARTIN?
THE GANGSTER, SILVER FANG. THE MAN WHO FORCED YOU INTO THE SNAKEHEAD SLAVERS.
THE CRIME BOSS WHO WRECKED YOUR LIFE AND SOLD COUNTLESS NUMBERS OF OUR COUNTRYMEN INTO SLAVERY.
THIS IS THE OLD MAN HE HAS BECOME. SHEN QUINGHAO. A MAN WHO "HUMBLY" WEARS THE TITLE OF...
..."CHINA'S GREATEST HUMANITARIAN." BUT WE KNOW BETTER, DON'T WE?
SO HERE WE ARE, AT THE CROSSROADS.
MY PRESENTATION IS OVER.
THE CHOICE IS YOURS. STOP ME...
ALL RIGHT. I'M IN.

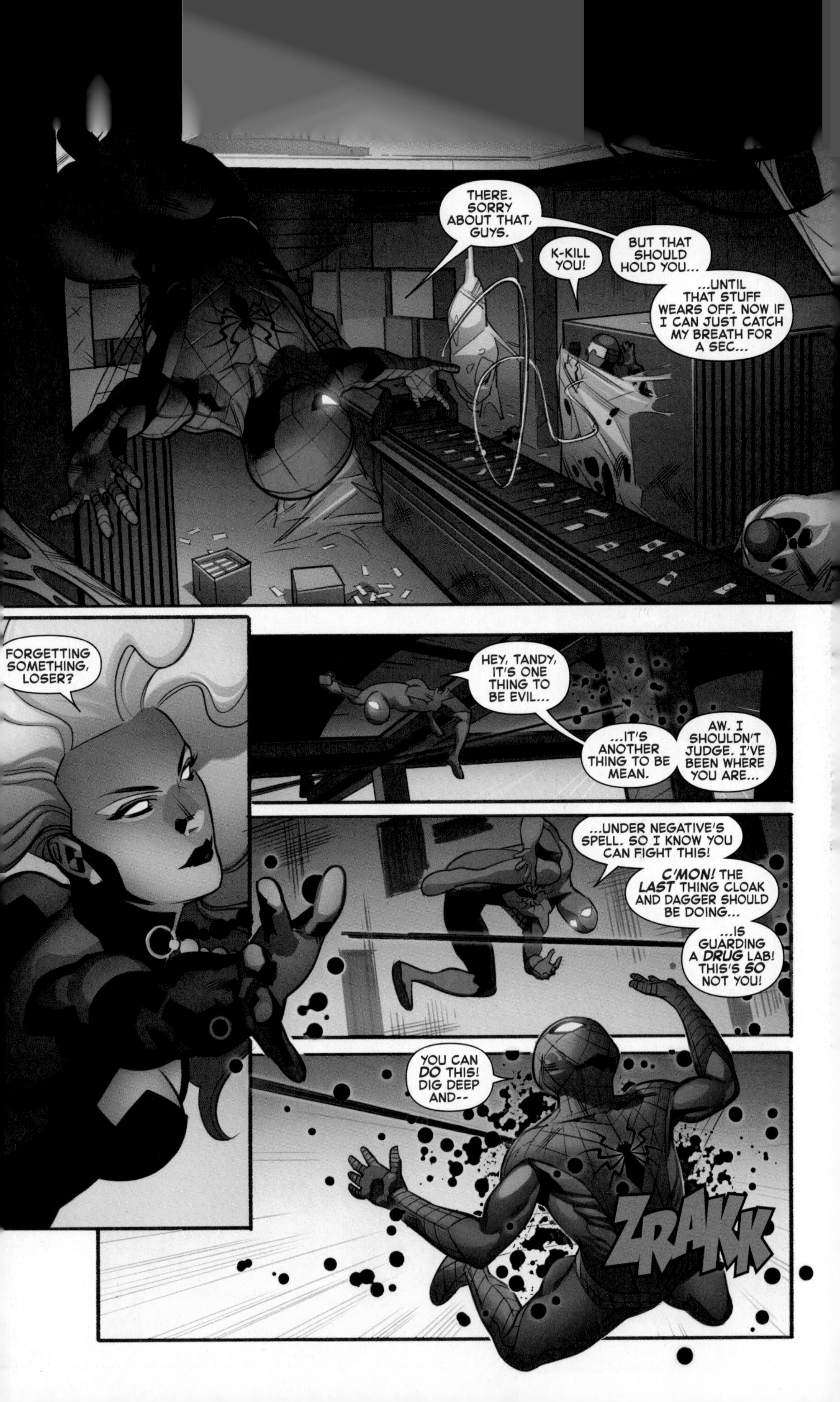
THERE. SORRY ABOUT THAT, GUYS.
K-KILL YOU!
BUT THAT SHOULD HOLD YOU...
...UNTIL THAT STUFF WEARS OFF. NOW IF I CAN JUST CATCH MY BREATH FOR A SEC...
FORGETTING SOMETHING, LOSER?
HEY, TANDY, IT'S ONE THING TO BE EVIL...
...IT'S ANOTHER THING TO BE MEAN.
AW. I SHOULDN'T JUDGE. I'VE BEEN WHERE YOU ARE...
...UNDER NEGATIVE'S SPELL. SO I KNOW YOU CAN FIGHT THIS!
C'MON! THE LAST THING CLOAK AND DAGGER SHOULD BE DOING...
...IS GUARDING A DRUG LAB! THIS'S SO NOT YOU!
YOU CAN DO THIS! DIG DEEP AND--
ZRAKKK

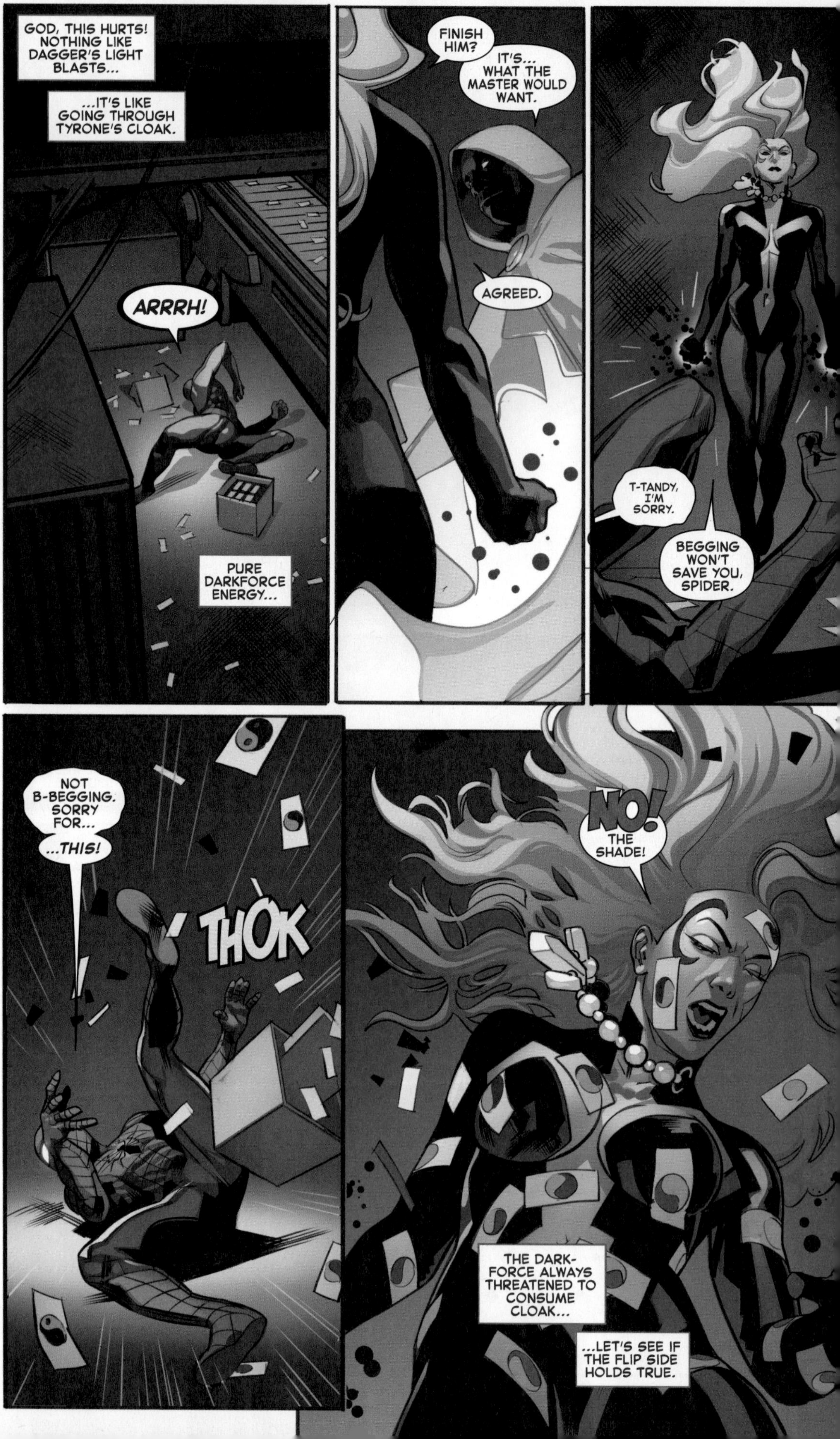
GOD, THIS HURTS! NOTHING LIKE DAGGER'S LIGHT BLASTS...
...IT'S LIKE GOING THROUGH TYRONE'S CLOAK.
ARRRH!
PURE DARKFORCE ENERGY...
FINISH HIM?
IT'S... WHAT THE MASTER WOULD WANT.
AGREED.
T-TANDY, I'M SORRY.
BEGGING WON'T SAVE YOU, SPIDER.
NOT B-BEGGING. SORRY FOR...
...THIS!
THOK
NO! THE SHADE!
THE DARK-FORCE ALWAYS THREATENED TO CONSUME CLOAK...
...LET'S SEE IF THE FLIP SIDE HOLDS TRUE.

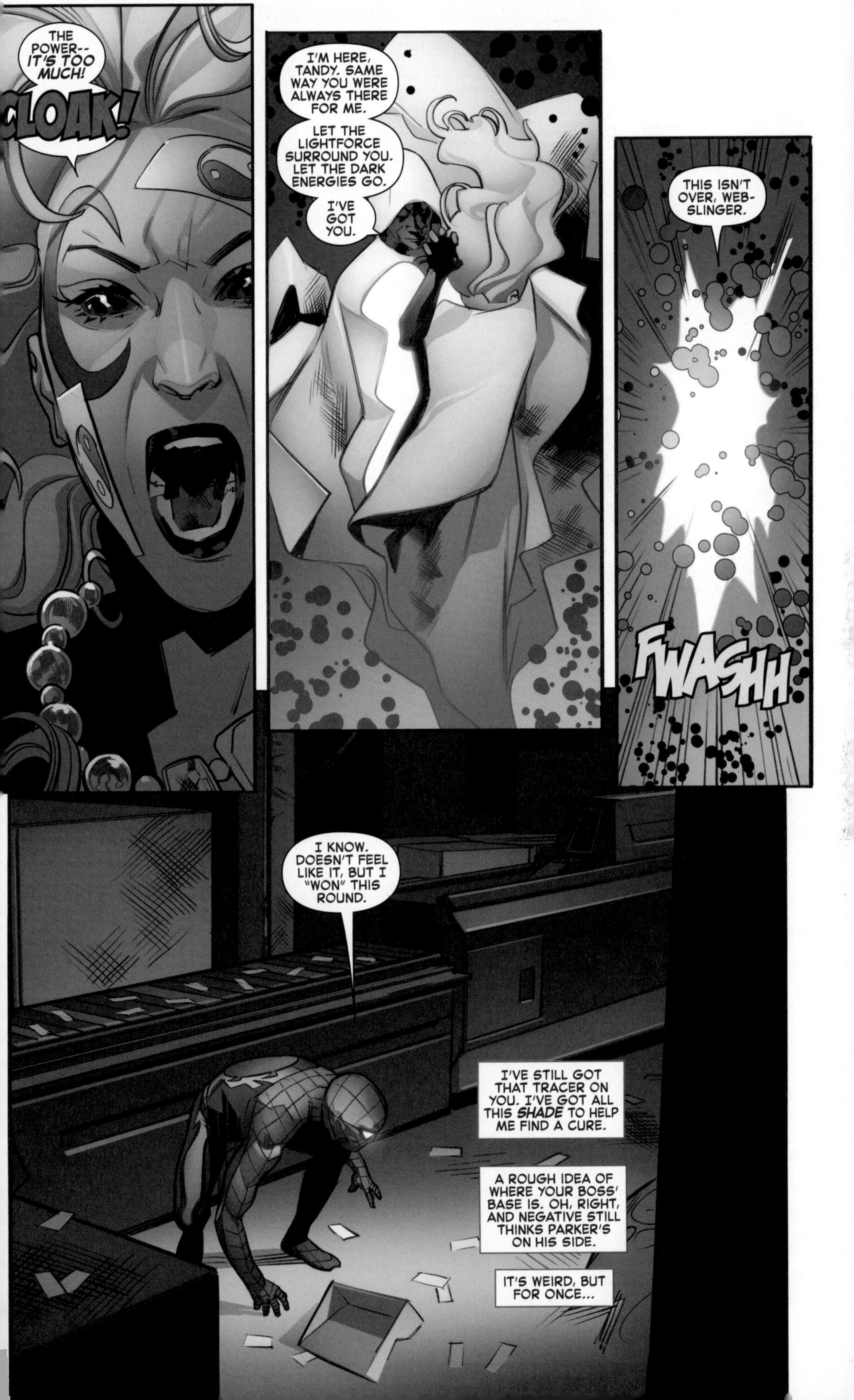
THE POWER-- IT'S TOO MUCH!
CLOAK!
I'M HERE, TANDY. SAME WAY YOU WERE ALWAYS THERE FOR ME.
LET THE LIGHTFORCE SURROUND YOU. LET THE DARK ENERGIES GO.
I'VE GOT YOU.
THIS ISN'T OVER, WEB-SLINGER.
FWASHH
I KNOW. DOESN'T FEEL LIKE IT, BUT I "WON" THIS ROUND.
I'VE STILL GOT THAT TRACER ON YOU. I'VE GOT ALL THIS SHADE TO HELP ME FIND A CURE.
A ROUGH IDEA OF WHERE YOUR BOSS' BASE IS. OH, RIGHT, AND NEGATIVE STILL THINKS PARKER'S ON HIS SIDE.
IT'S WEIRD, BUT FOR ONCE...

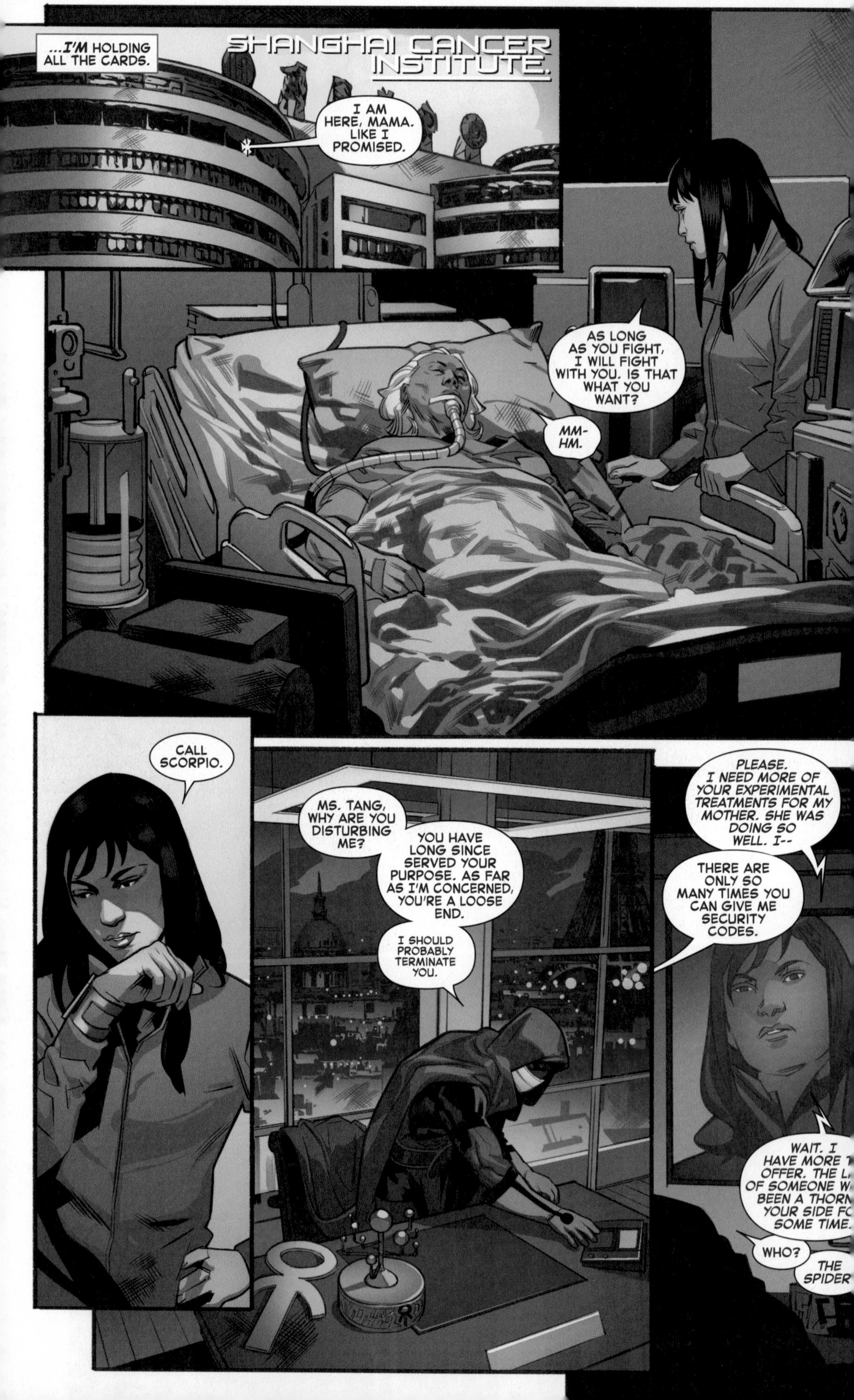

...*I'M* HOLDING ALL THE CARDS.
SHANGHAI CANCER INSTITUTE.
I AM HERE, MAMA. LIKE I PROMISED.
AS LONG AS YOU FIGHT, I WILL FIGHT WITH YOU. IS THAT WHAT YOU WANT?
MM-HM.
CALL SCORPIO.
MS. TANG, WHY ARE YOU DISTURBING ME?
YOU HAVE LONG SINCE SERVED YOUR PURPOSE. AS FAR AS I'M CONCERNED, YOU'RE A LOOSE END.
I SHOULD PROBABLY TERMINATE YOU.
PLEASE. I NEED MORE OF YOUR EXPERIMENTAL TREATMENTS FOR MY MOTHER. SHE WAS DOING SO WELL. I--
THERE ARE ONLY SO MANY TIMES YOU CAN GIVE ME SECURITY CODES.
WAIT. I HAVE MORE T OFFER. THE L OF SOMEONE W BEEN A THORN YOUR SIDE FO SOME TIME.
WHO?
THE SPIDER

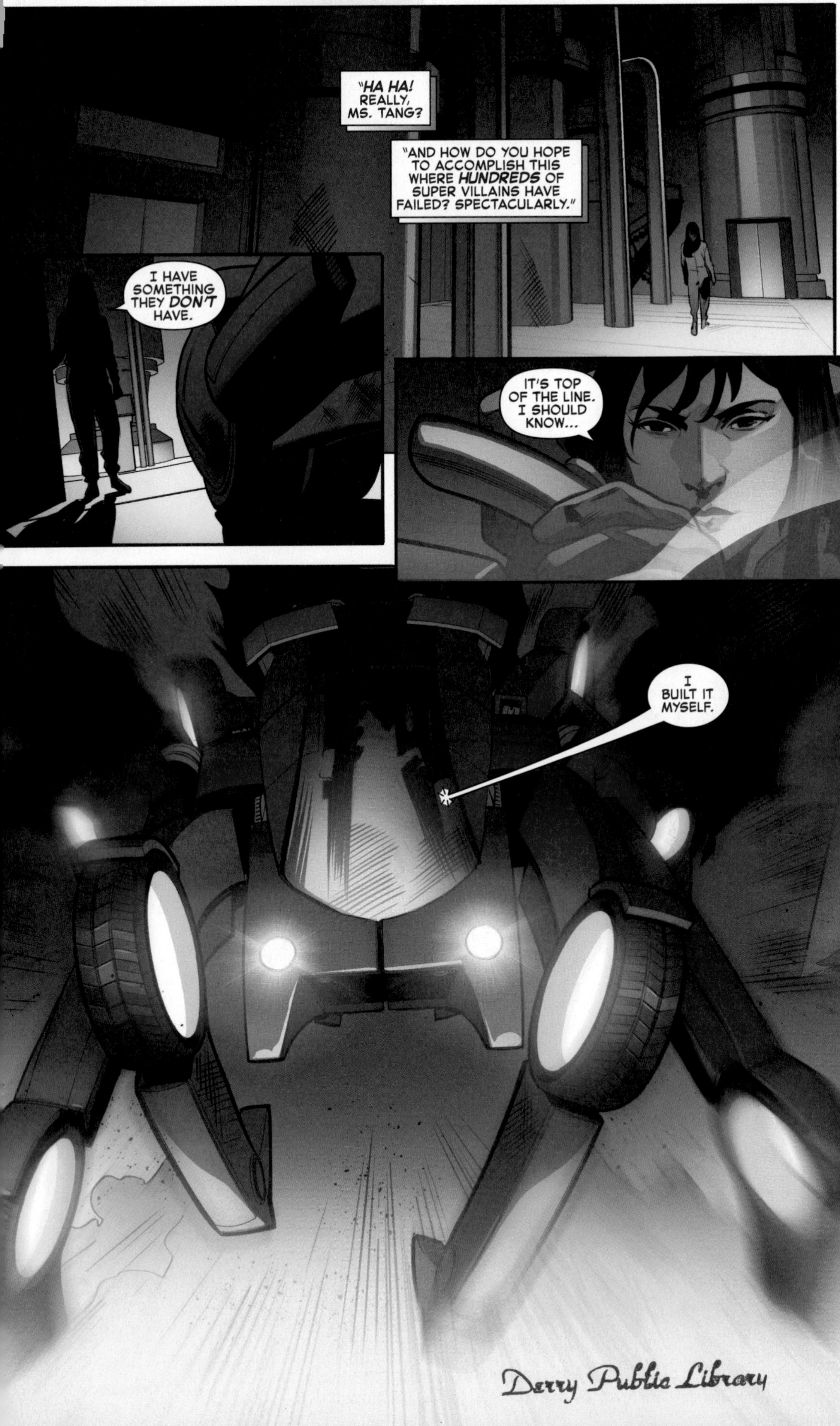
"HA HA! REALLY, MS. TANG?
"AND HOW DO YOU HOPE TO ACCOMPLISH THIS WHERE HUNDREDS OF SUPER VILLAINS HAVE FAILED? SPECTACULARLY."
I HAVE SOMETHING THEY DON'T HAVE.
IT'S TOP OF THE LINE. I SHOULD KNOW...
I BUILT IT MYSELF.

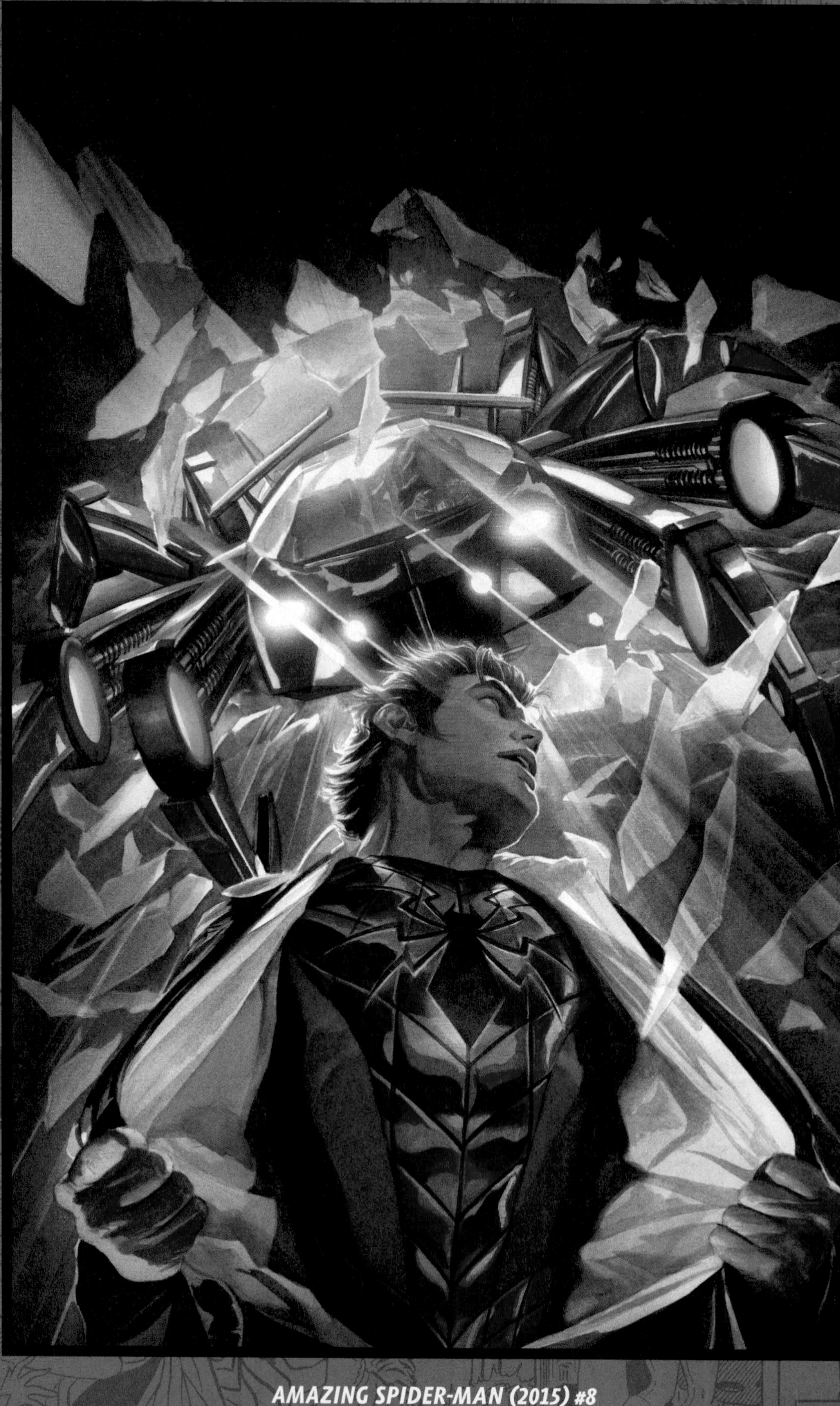

AMAZING SPIDER-MAN (2015) #8
"THE DARK KINGDOM, PART 3: BLACK & WHITE"

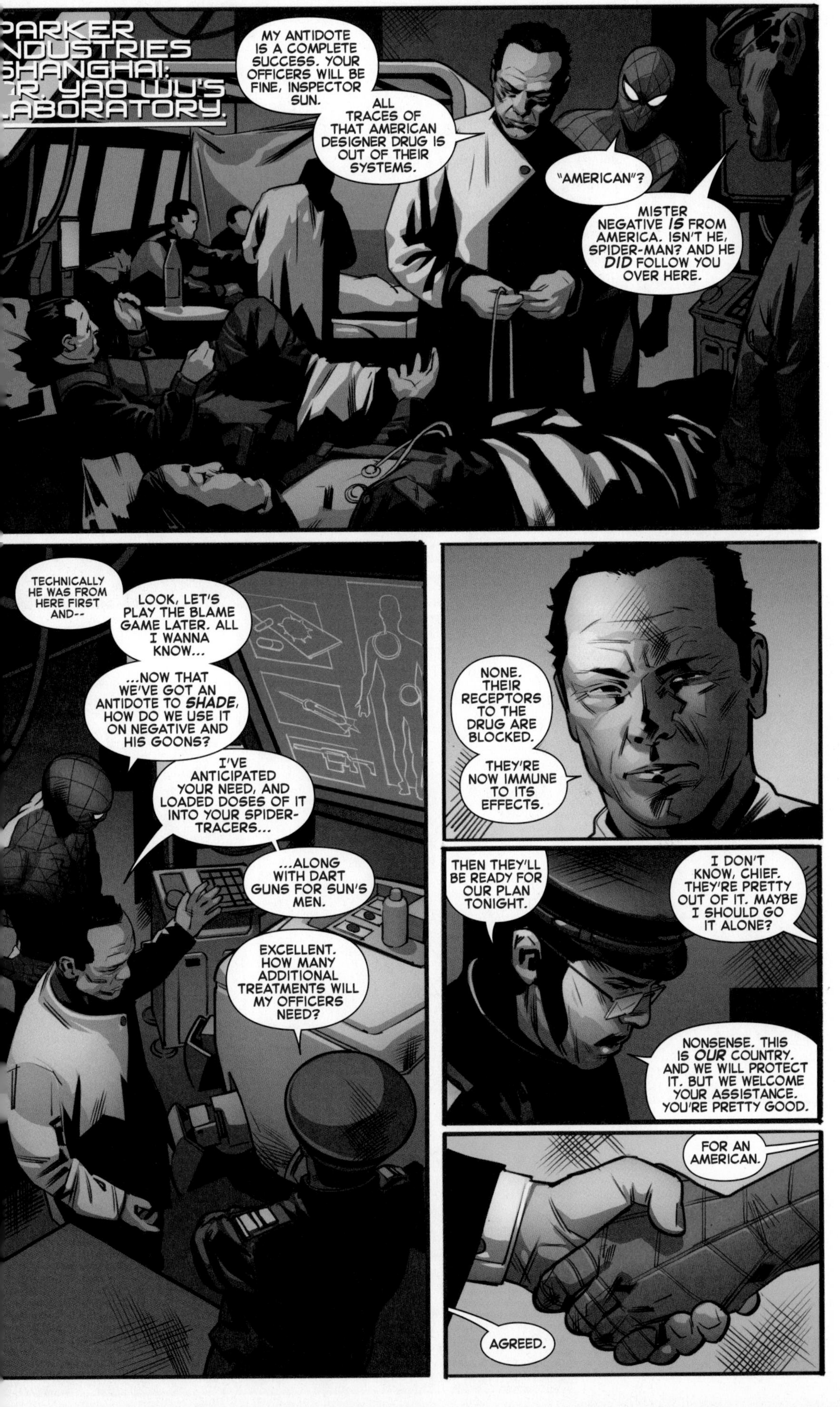
PARKER NDUSTRIES SHANGHAI: R. YAO WU'S LABORATORY.
MY ANTIDOTE IS A COMPLETE SUCCESS. YOUR OFFICERS WILL BE FINE, INSPECTOR SUN.
ALL TRACES OF THAT AMERICAN DESIGNER DRUG IS OUT OF THEIR SYSTEMS.
"AMERICAN"?
MISTER NEGATIVE *IS* FROM AMERICA. ISN'T HE, SPIDER-MAN? AND HE *DID* FOLLOW YOU OVER HERE.
TECHNICALLY HE WAS FROM HERE FIRST AND--
LOOK, LET'S PLAY THE BLAME GAME LATER. ALL I WANNA KNOW...
...NOW THAT WE'VE GOT AN ANTIDOTE TO *SHADE*, HOW DO WE USE IT ON NEGATIVE AND HIS GOONS?
I'VE ANTICIPATED YOUR NEED, AND LOADED DOSES OF IT INTO YOUR SPIDER-TRACERS...
...ALONG WITH DART GUNS FOR SUN'S MEN.
EXCELLENT. HOW MANY ADDITIONAL TREATMENTS WILL MY OFFICERS NEED?
NONE. THEIR RECEPTORS TO THE DRUG ARE BLOCKED.
THEY'RE NOW IMMUNE TO ITS EFFECTS.
THEN THEY'LL BE READY FOR OUR PLAN TONIGHT.
I DON'T KNOW, CHIEF. THEY'RE PRETTY OUT OF IT. MAYBE I SHOULD GO IT ALONE?
NONSENSE. THIS IS *OUR* COUNTRY. AND WE WILL PROTECT IT. BUT WE WELCOME YOUR ASSISTANCE. YOU'RE PRETTY GOOD.
FOR AN AMERICAN.
AGREED.

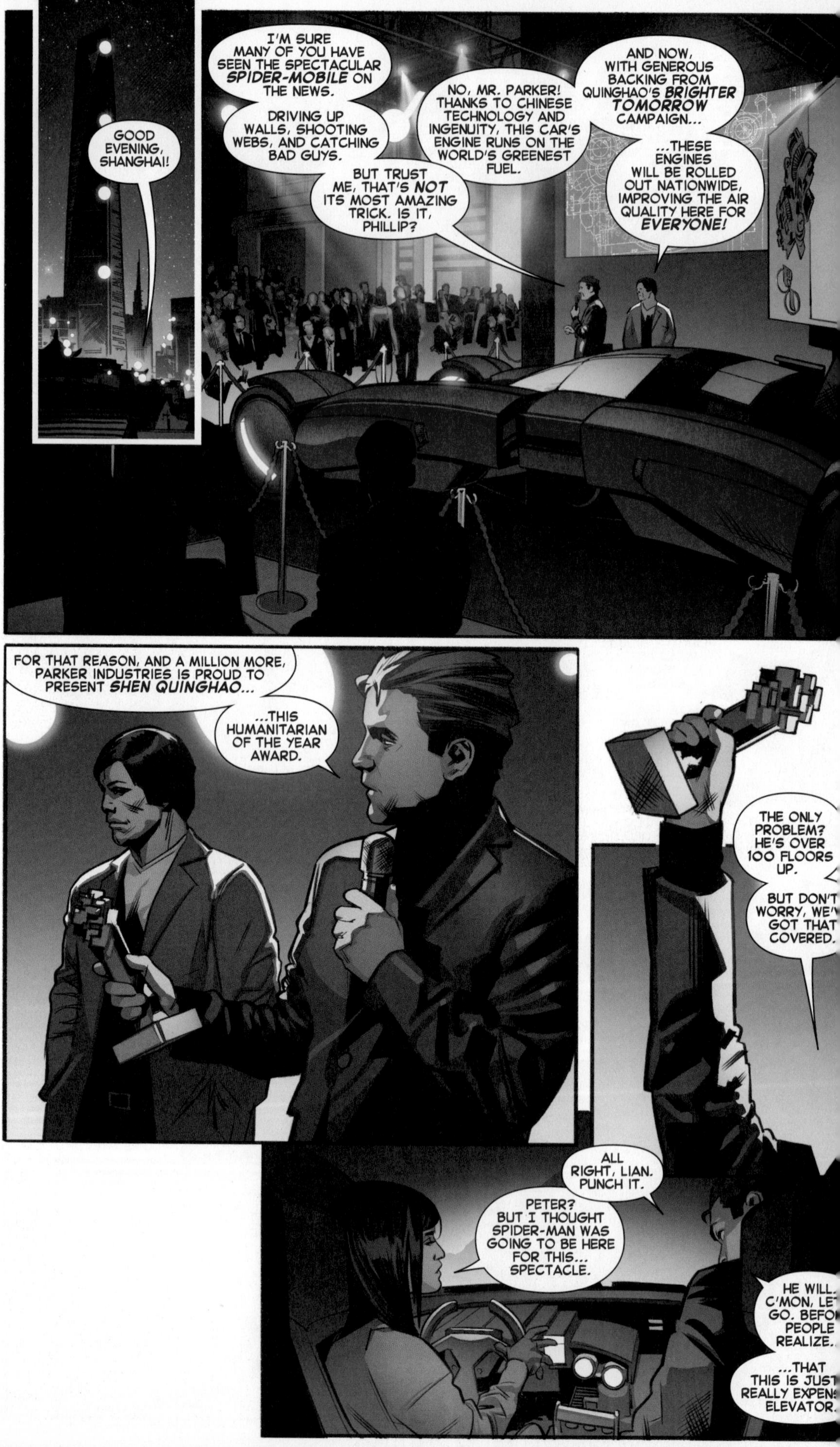
GOOD EVENING, SHANGHAI!
I'M SURE MANY OF YOU HAVE SEEN THE SPECTACULAR SPIDER-MOBILE ON THE NEWS.
DRIVING UP WALLS, SHOOTING WEBS, AND CATCHING BAD GUYS.
BUT TRUST ME, THAT'S NOT ITS MOST AMAZING TRICK. IS IT, PHILLIP?
NO, MR. PARKER! THANKS TO CHINESE TECHNOLOGY AND INGENUITY, THIS CAR'S ENGINE RUNS ON THE WORLD'S GREENEST FUEL.
AND NOW, WITH GENEROUS BACKING FROM QUINGHAO'S BRIGHTER TOMORROW CAMPAIGN...
...THESE ENGINES WILL BE ROLLED OUT NATIONWIDE, IMPROVING THE AIR QUALITY HERE FOR EVERYONE!
FOR THAT REASON, AND A MILLION MORE, PARKER INDUSTRIES IS PROUD TO PRESENT SHEN QUINGHAO...
...THIS HUMANITARIAN OF THE YEAR AWARD.
THE ONLY PROBLEM? HE'S OVER 100 FLOORS UP.
ALL RIGHT, LIAN. PUNCH IT.
PETER? BUT I THOUGHT SPIDER-MAN WAS GOING TO BE HERE FOR THIS... SPECTACLE.

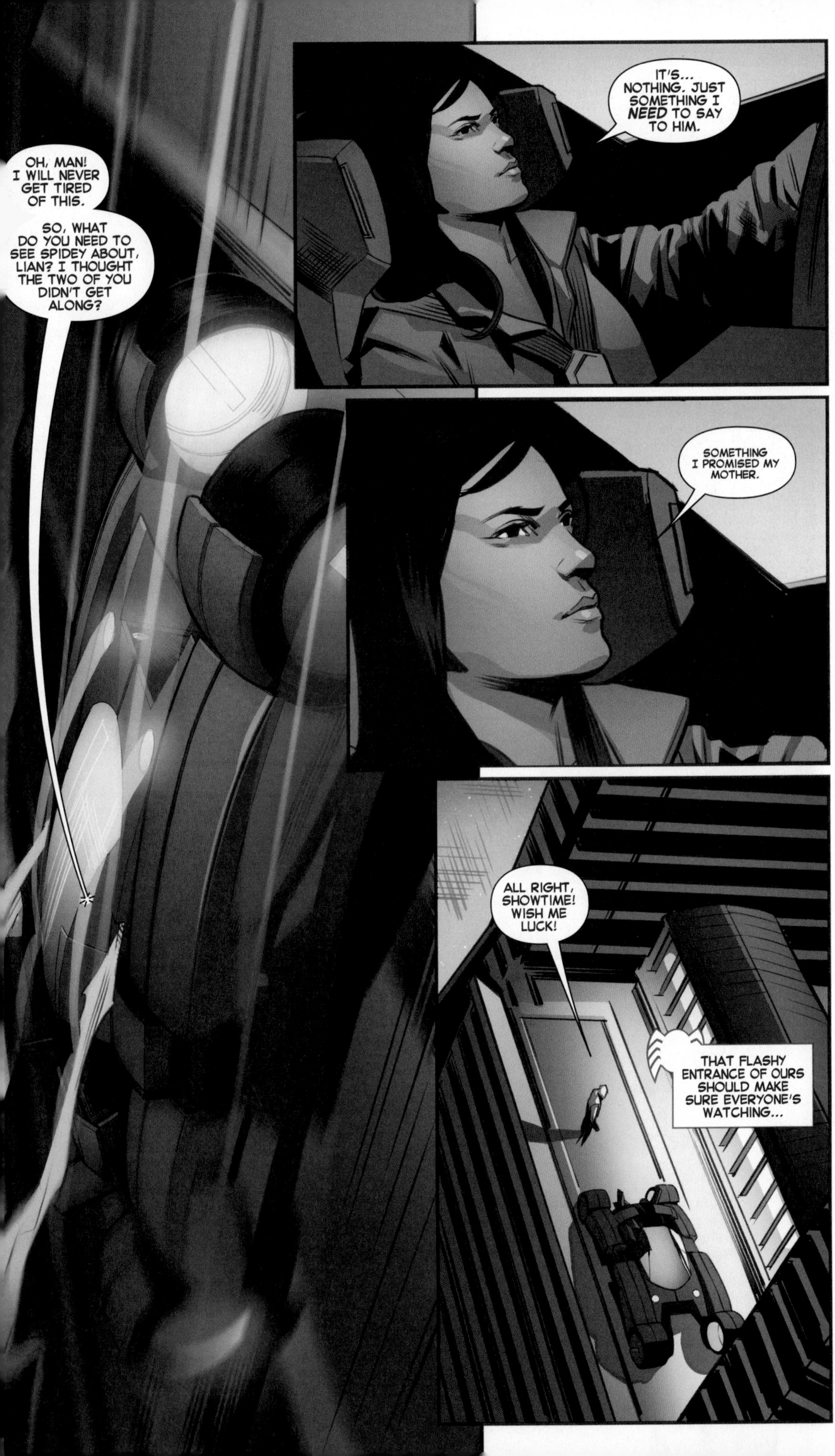
OH, MAN! I WILL NEVER GET TIRED OF THIS.
SO, WHAT DO YOU NEED TO SEE SPIDEY ABOUT, LIAN? I THOUGHT THE TWO OF YOU DIDN'T GET ALONG?
IT'S... NOTHING. JUST SOMETHING I NEED TO SAY TO HIM.
SOMETHING I PROMISED MY MOTHER.
ALL RIGHT, SHOWTIME! WISH ME LUCK!
THAT FLASHY ENTRANCE OF OURS SHOULD MAKE SURE EVERYONE'S WATCHING...

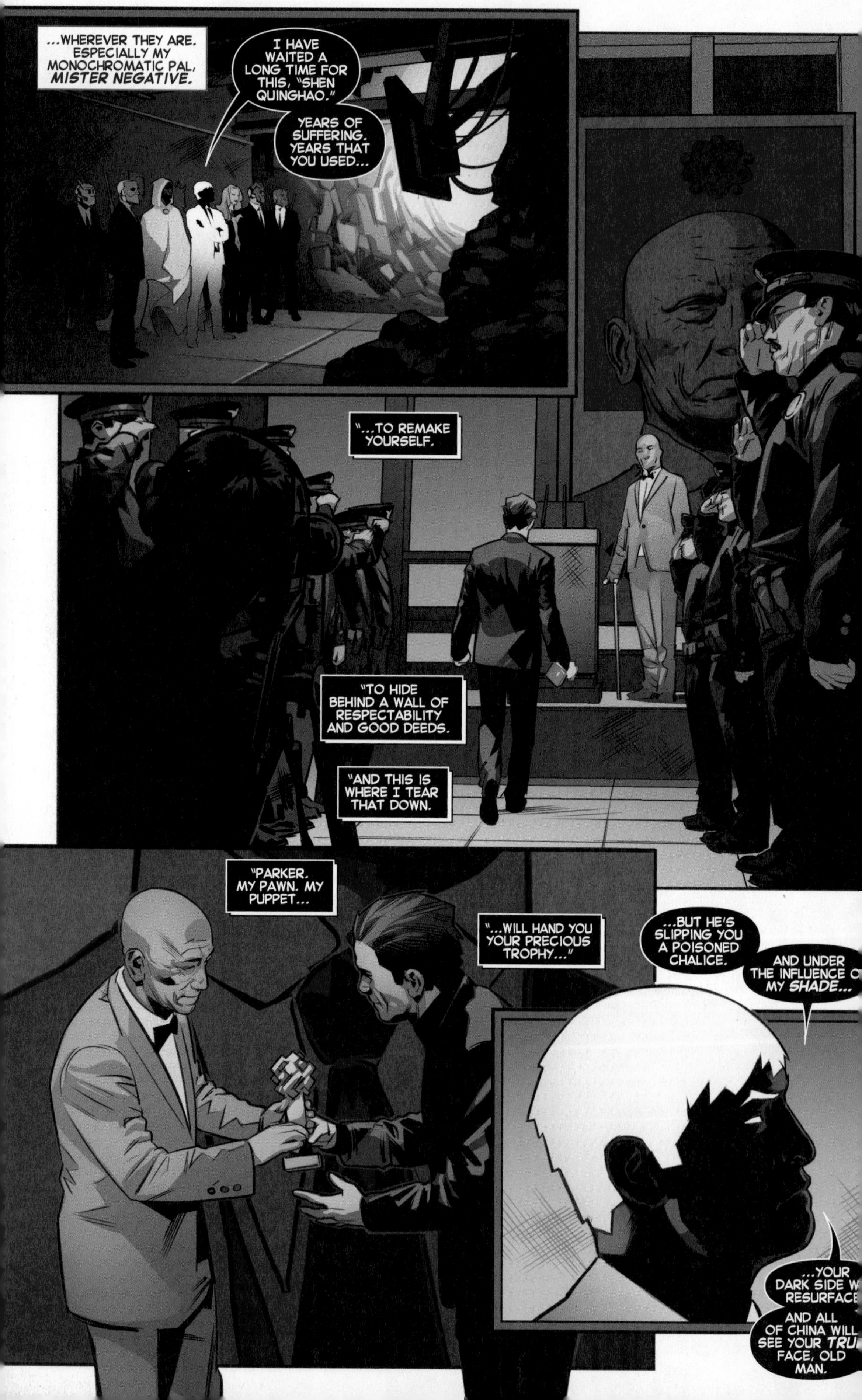
...WHEREVER THEY ARE. ESPECIALLY MY MONOCHROMATIC PAL, *MISTER NEGATIVE.*
I HAVE WAITED A LONG TIME FOR THIS, "SHEN QUINGHAO."
YEARS OF SUFFERING. YEARS THAT YOU USED...
"...TO REMAKE YOURSELF.
"TO HIDE BEHIND A WALL OF RESPECTABILITY AND GOOD DEEDS.
"AND THIS IS WHERE I TEAR THAT DOWN.
"PARKER. MY PAWN. MY PUPPET...
"...WILL HAND YOU YOUR PRECIOUS TROPHY..."
...BUT HE'S SLIPPING YOU A POISONED CHALICE.
AND UNDER THE INFLUENCE O MY *SHADE...*
...YOUR DARK SIDE W RESURFACE
AND ALL OF CHINA WILL SEE YOUR *TRU* FACE, OLD MAN.

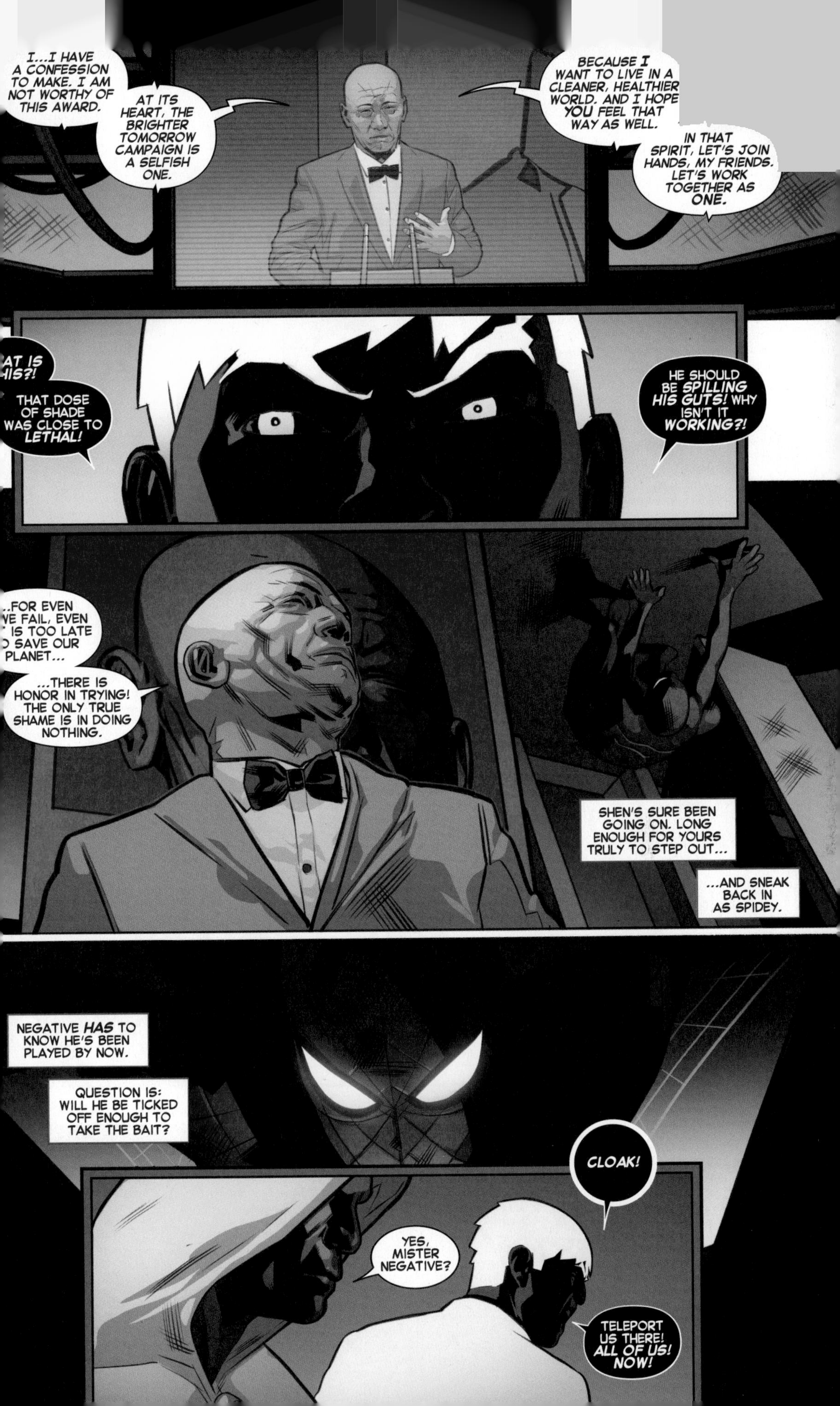
I...I HAVE A CONFESSION TO MAKE. I AM NOT WORTHY OF THIS AWARD.
AT ITS HEART, THE BRIGHTER TOMORROW CAMPAIGN IS A SELFISH ONE.
BECAUSE I WANT TO LIVE IN A CLEANER, HEALTHIER WORLD. AND I HOPE YOU FEEL THAT WAY AS WELL.
IN THAT SPIRIT, LET'S JOIN HANDS, MY FRIENDS. LET'S WORK TOGETHER AS ONE.
AT IS HIS?!
THAT DOSE OF SHADE WAS CLOSE TO LETHAL!
HE SHOULD BE SPILLING HIS GUTS! WHY ISN'T IT WORKING?!
..FOR EVEN VE FAIL, EVEN IS TOO LATE SAVE OUR PLANET...
...THERE IS HONOR IN TRYING! THE ONLY TRUE SHAME IS IN DOING NOTHING.
SHEN'S SURE BEEN GOING ON. LONG ENOUGH FOR YOURS TRULY TO STEP OUT...
...AND SNEAK BACK IN AS SPIDEY.
NEGATIVE HAS TO KNOW HE'S BEEN PLAYED BY NOW.
QUESTION IS: WILL HE BE TICKED OFF ENOUGH TO TAKE THE BAIT?
CLOAK!
YES, MISTER NEGATIVE?
TELEPORT US THERE! ALL OF US! NOW!

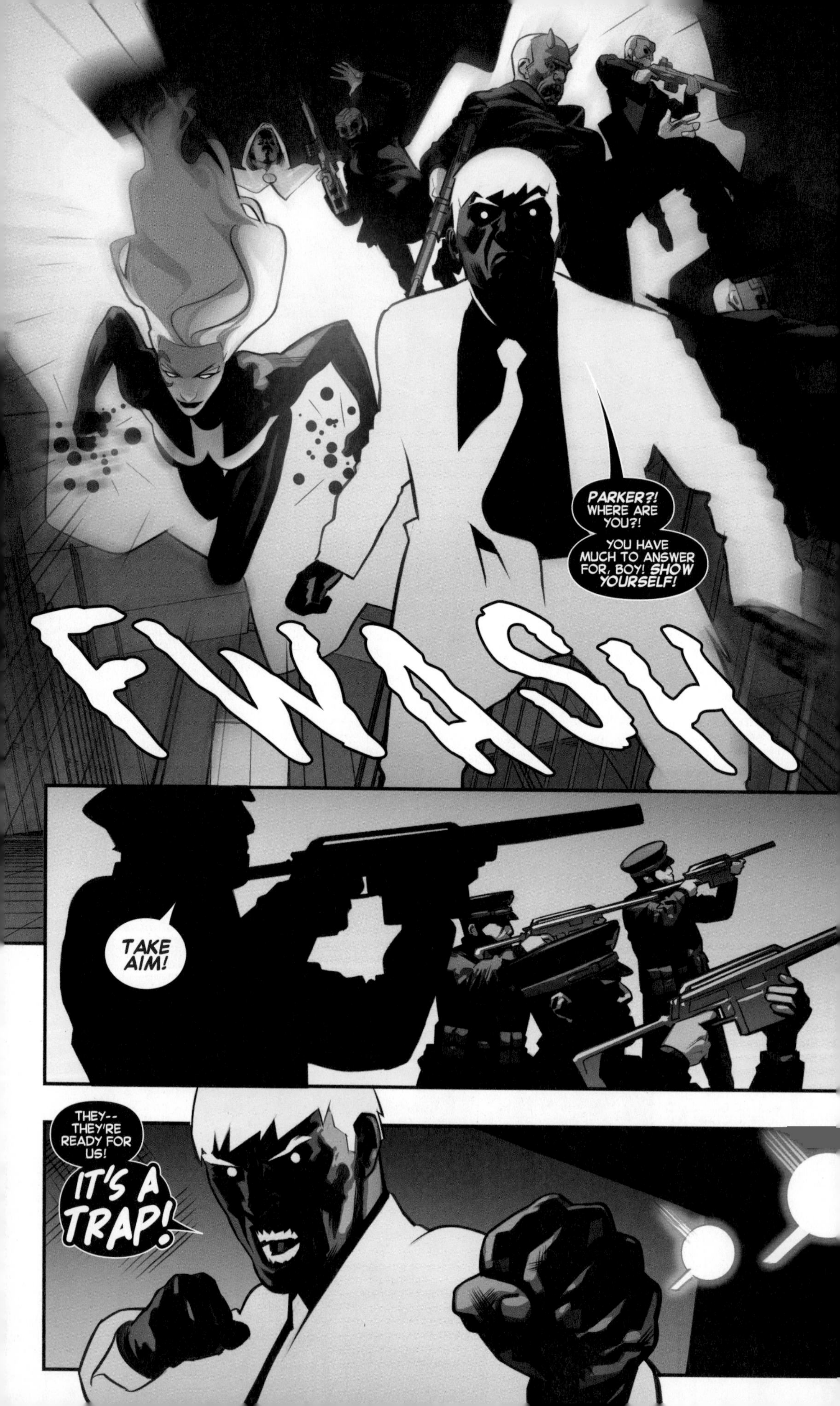
PARKER?! WHERE ARE YOU?!
YOU HAVE MUCH TO ANSWER FOR, BOY! SHOW YOURSELF!
FWASH
TAKE AIM!
THEY-- THEY'RE READY FOR US!
IT'S A TRAP!

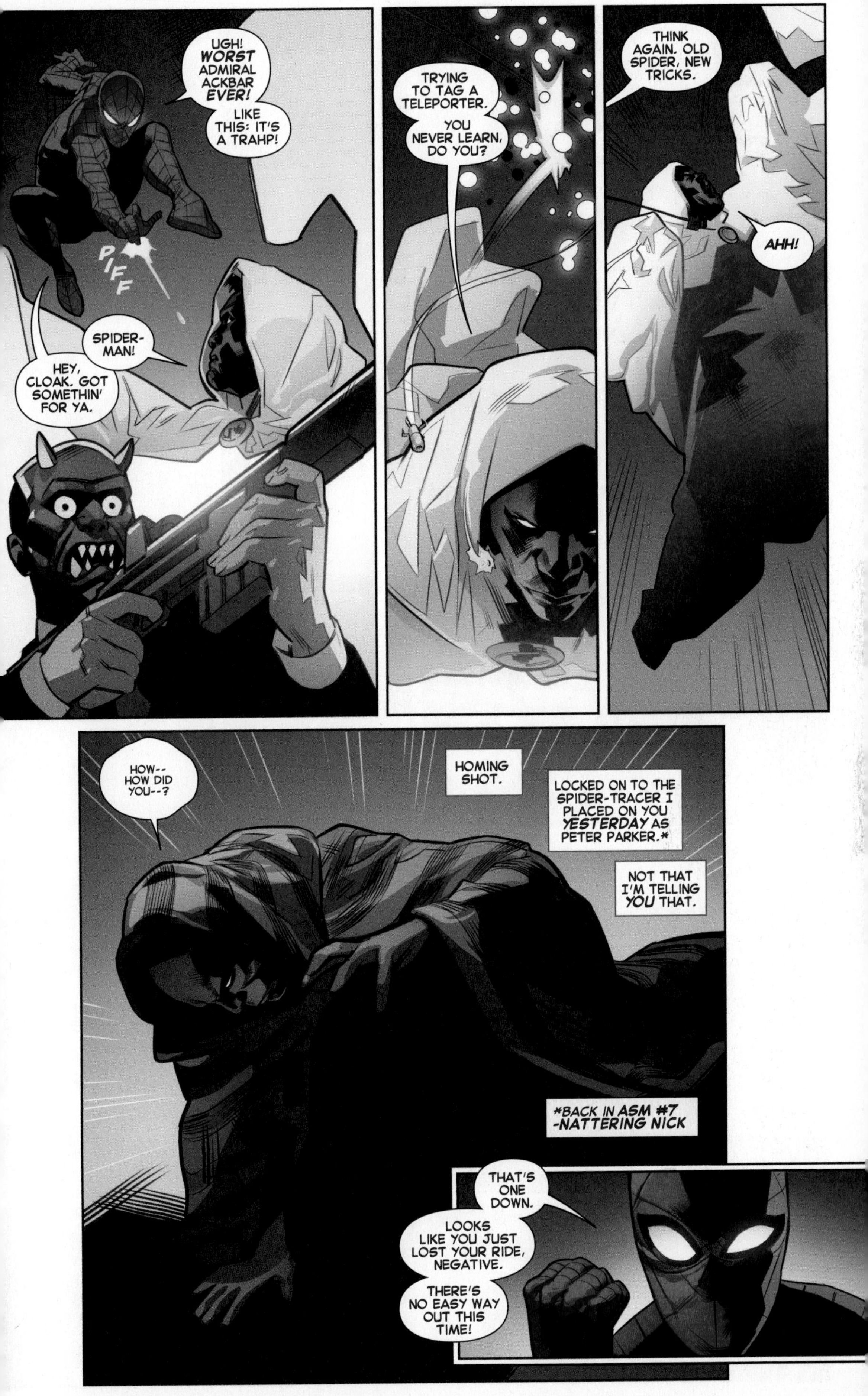
UGH! WORST ADMIRAL ACKBAR EVER!
LIKE THIS: IT'S A TRAHP!
PIFF
SPIDER-MAN!
HEY, CLOAK. GOT SOMETHIN' FOR YA.
TRYING TO TAG A TELEPORTER.
YOU NEVER LEARN, DO YOU?
THINK AGAIN. OLD SPIDER, NEW TRICKS.
AHH!
HOW-- HOW DID YOU--?
HOMING SHOT.
LOCKED ON TO THE SPIDER-TRACER I PLACED ON YOU YESTERDAY AS PETER PARKER.*
NOT THAT I'M TELLING YOU THAT.
*BACK IN ASM #7 -NATTERING NICK
THAT'S ONE DOWN.
LOOKS LIKE YOU JUST LOST YOUR RIDE, NEGATIVE.
THERE'S NO EASY WAY OUT THIS TIME!

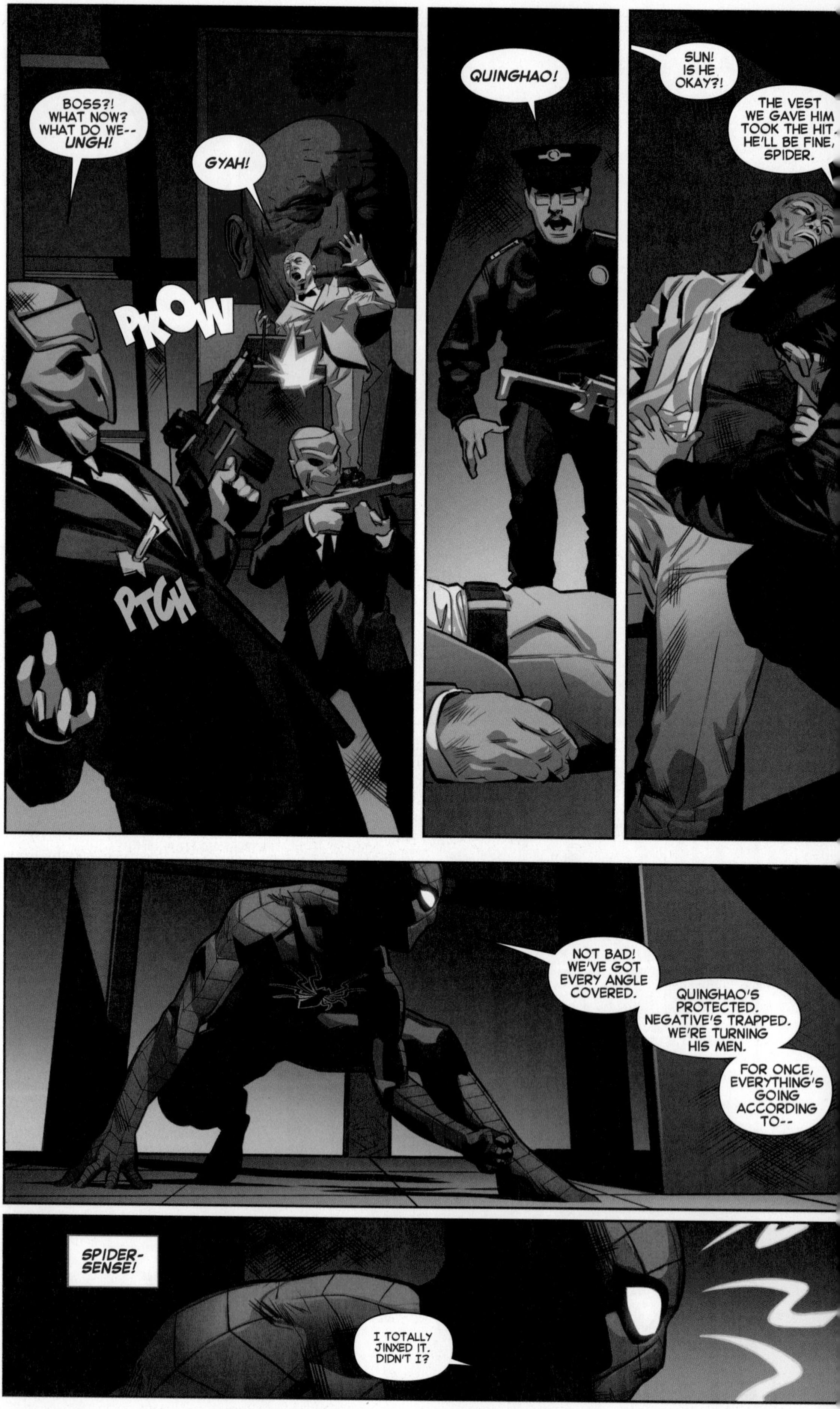
BOSS?! WHAT NOW? WHAT DO WE-- *UNGH!*
GYAH!
PKOW
PTCH
QUINGHAO!
SUN! IS HE OKAY?!
THE VEST WE GAVE HIM TOOK THE HIT. HE'LL BE FINE, SPIDER.
NOT BAD! WE'VE GOT EVERY ANGLE COVERED.
QUINGHAO'S PROTECTED. NEGATIVE'S TRAPPED. WE'RE TURNING HIS MEN.
FOR ONCE, EVERYTHING'S GOING ACCORDING TO--
SPIDER-SENSE!
I TOTALLY JINXED IT. DIDN'T I?

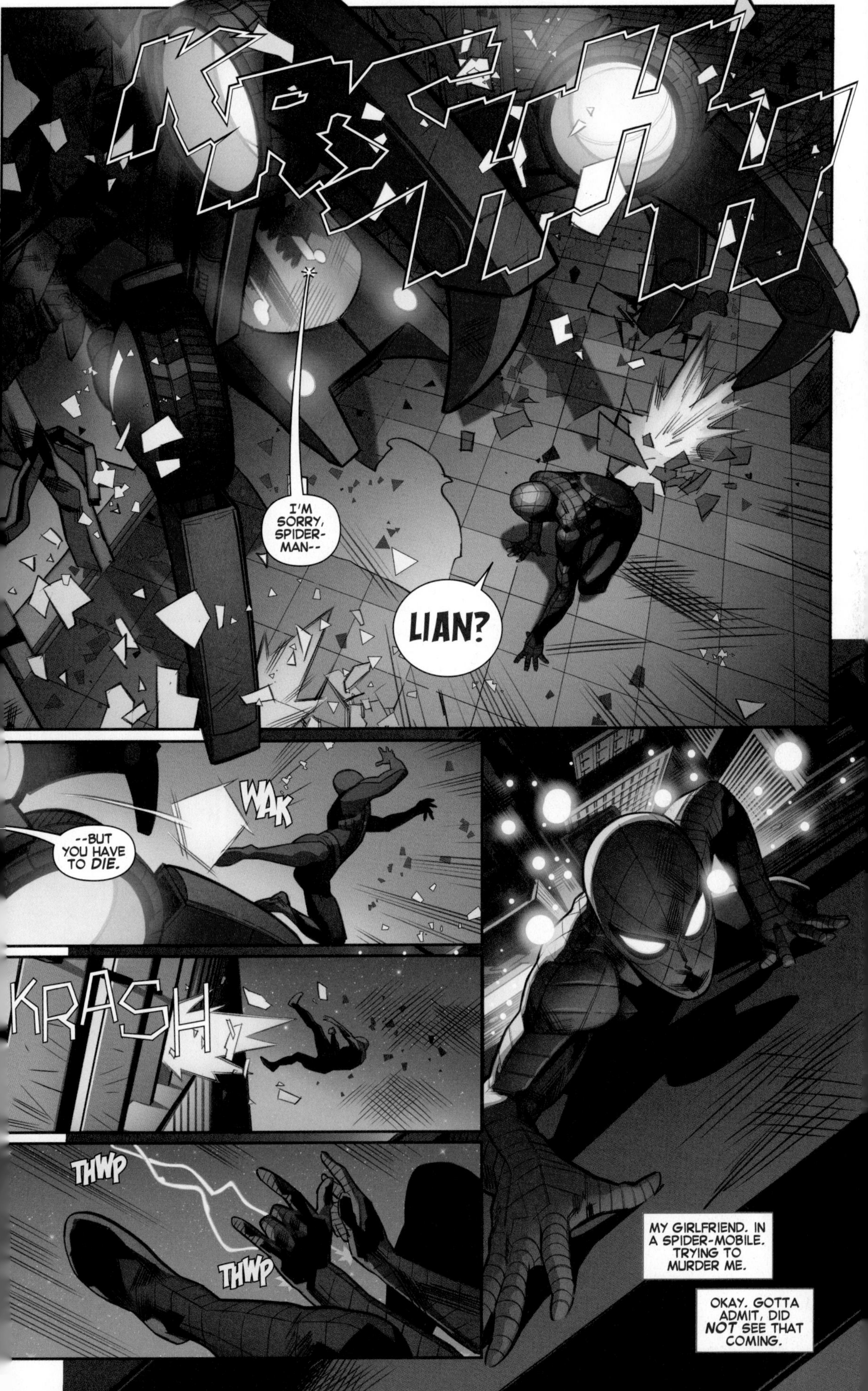
I'M SORRY, SPIDER-MAN--
LIAN?
--BUT YOU HAVE TO *DIE.*
WAK
KRASH
THWP
THWP
MY GIRLFRIEND. IN A SPIDER-MOBILE. TRYING TO MURDER ME.
OKAY. GOTTA ADMIT, DID ***NOT*** SEE THAT COMING.

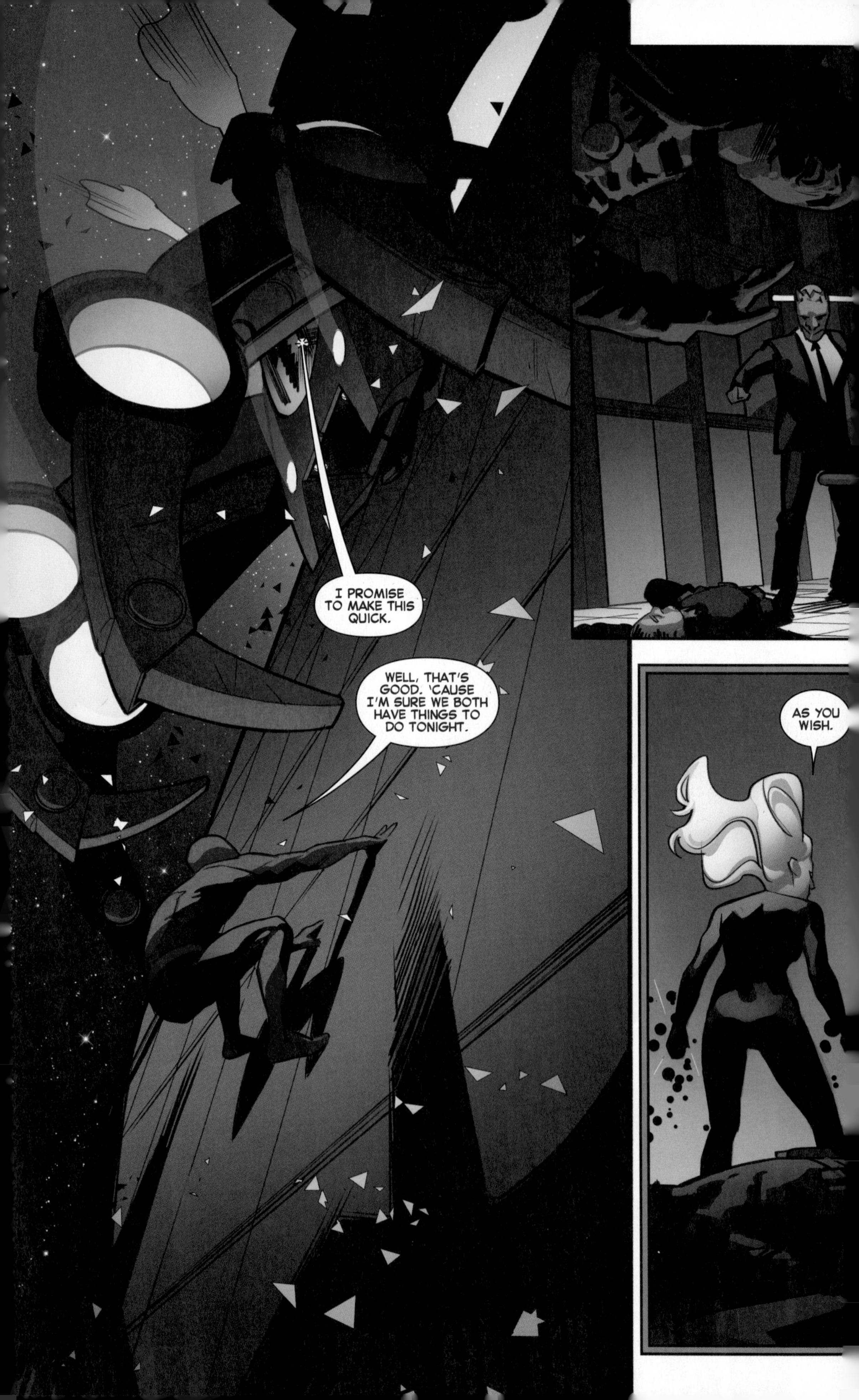
I PROMISE TO MAKE THIS QUICK.
WELL, THAT'S GOOD. 'CAUSE I'M SURE WE BOTH HAVE THINGS TO DO TONIGHT.
AS YOU WISH.

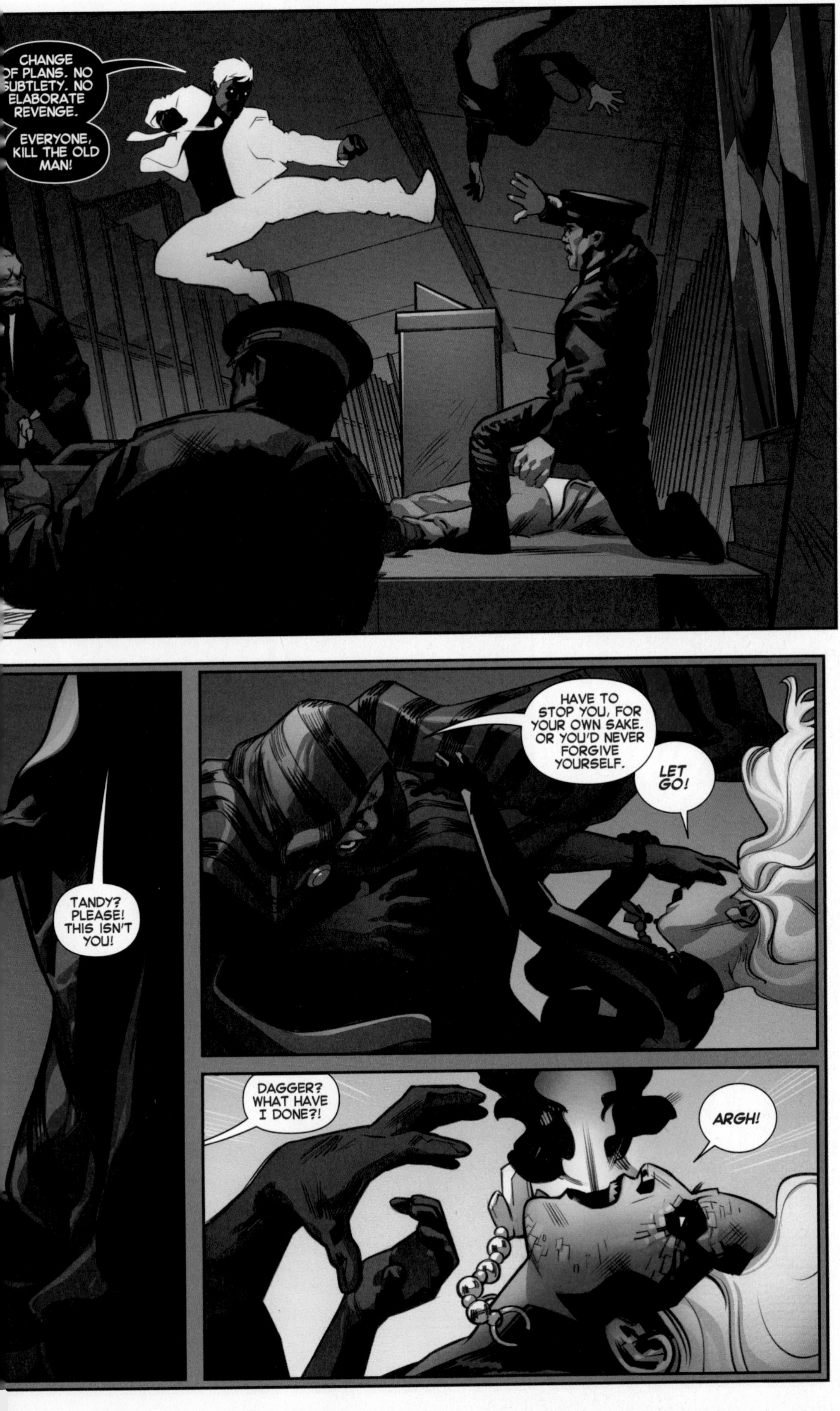
CHANGE OF PLANS. NO SUBTLETY. NO ELABORATE REVENGE.
EVERYONE, KILL THE OLD MAN!
TANDY? PLEASE! THIS ISN'T YOU!
HAVE TO STOP YOU, FOR YOUR OWN SAKE. OR YOU'D NEVER FORGIVE YOURSELF.
LET GO!
DAGGER? WHAT HAVE I DONE?!
ARGH!

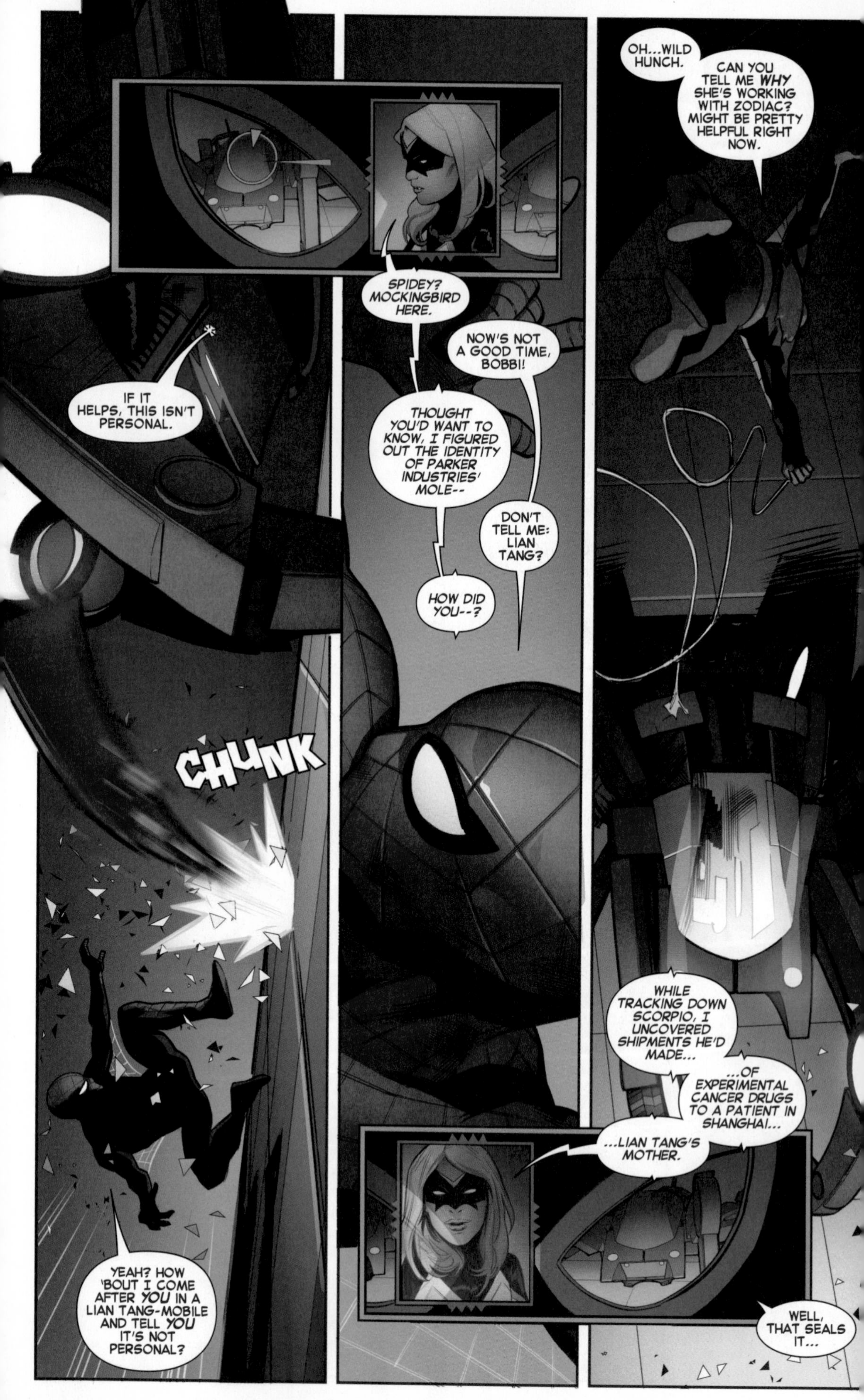

IF IT HELPS, THIS ISN'T PERSONAL.
CHUNK
YEAH? HOW 'BOUT I COME AFTER *YOU* IN A LIAN TANG-MOBILE AND TELL *YOU* IT'S NOT PERSONAL?
SPIDEY? MOCKINGBIRD HERE.
NOW'S NOT A GOOD TIME, BOBBI!
THOUGHT YOU'D WANT TO KNOW, I FIGURED OUT THE IDENTITY OF PARKER INDUSTRIES' MOLE--
DON'T TELL ME: LIAN TANG?
HOW DID YOU--?
OH...WILD HUNCH.
CAN YOU TELL ME *WHY* SHE'S WORKING WITH ZODIAC? MIGHT BE PRETTY HELPFUL RIGHT NOW.
WHILE TRACKING DOWN SCORPIO, I UNCOVERED SHIPMENTS HE'D MADE...
...OF EXPERIMENTAL CANCER DRUGS TO A PATIENT IN SHANGHAI...
...LIAN TANG'S MOTHER.
WELL, THAT SEALS IT...

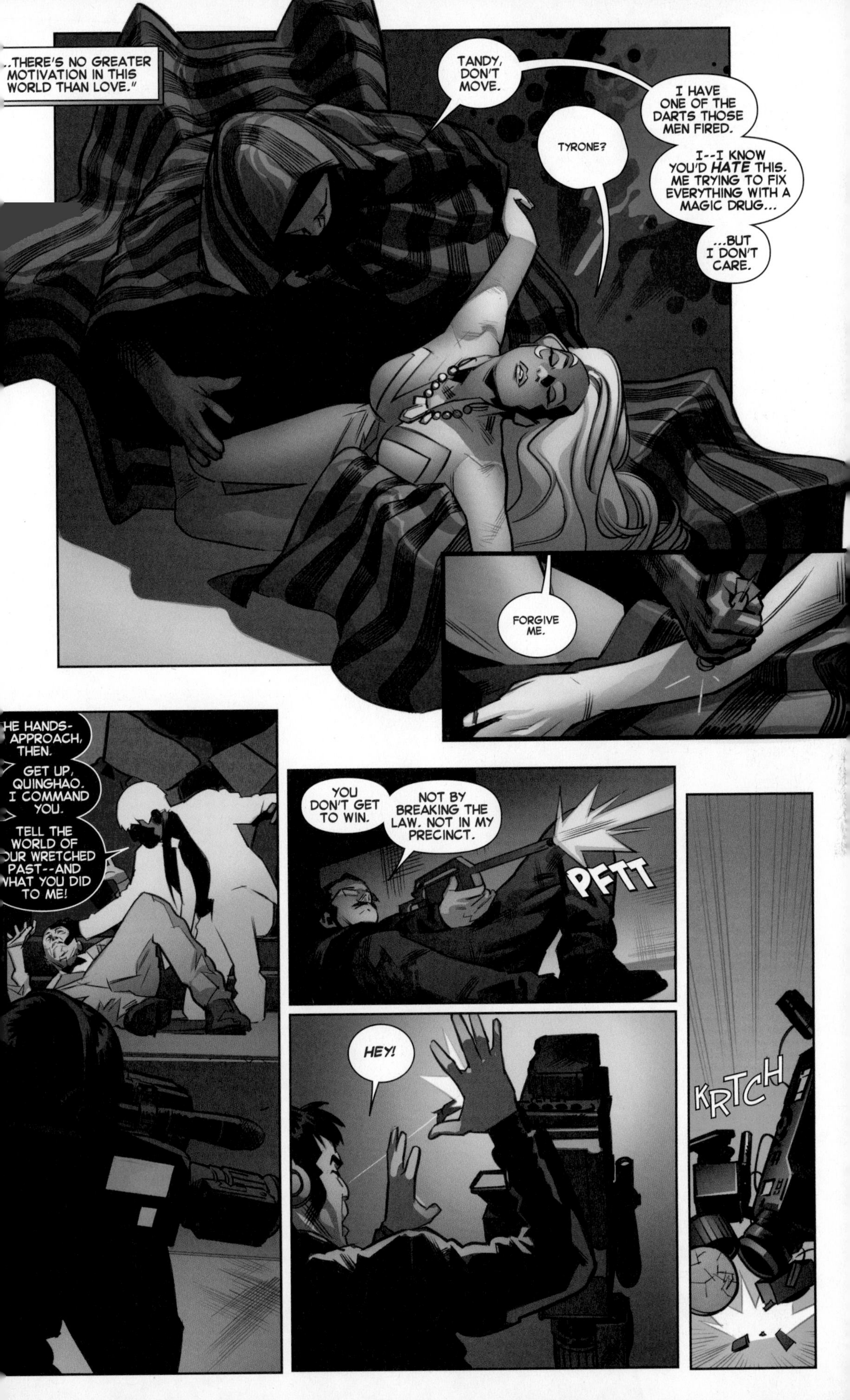
..THERE'S NO GREATER MOTIVATION IN THIS WORLD THAN LOVE."
TANDY, DON'T MOVE.
I HAVE ONE OF THE DARTS THOSE MEN FIRED.
TYRONE?
I--I KNOW YOU'D HATE THIS. ME TRYING TO FIX EVERYTHING WITH A MAGIC DRUG...
...BUT I DON'T CARE.
FORGIVE ME.
HE HANDS- APPROACH, THEN.
GET UP, QUINGHAO. I COMMAND YOU.
TELL THE WORLD OF UR WRETCHED PAST--AND VHAT YOU DID TO ME!
YOU DON'T GET TO WIN.
NOT BY BREAKING THE LAW. NOT IN MY PRECINCT.
PFTT
HEY!
KRTCH

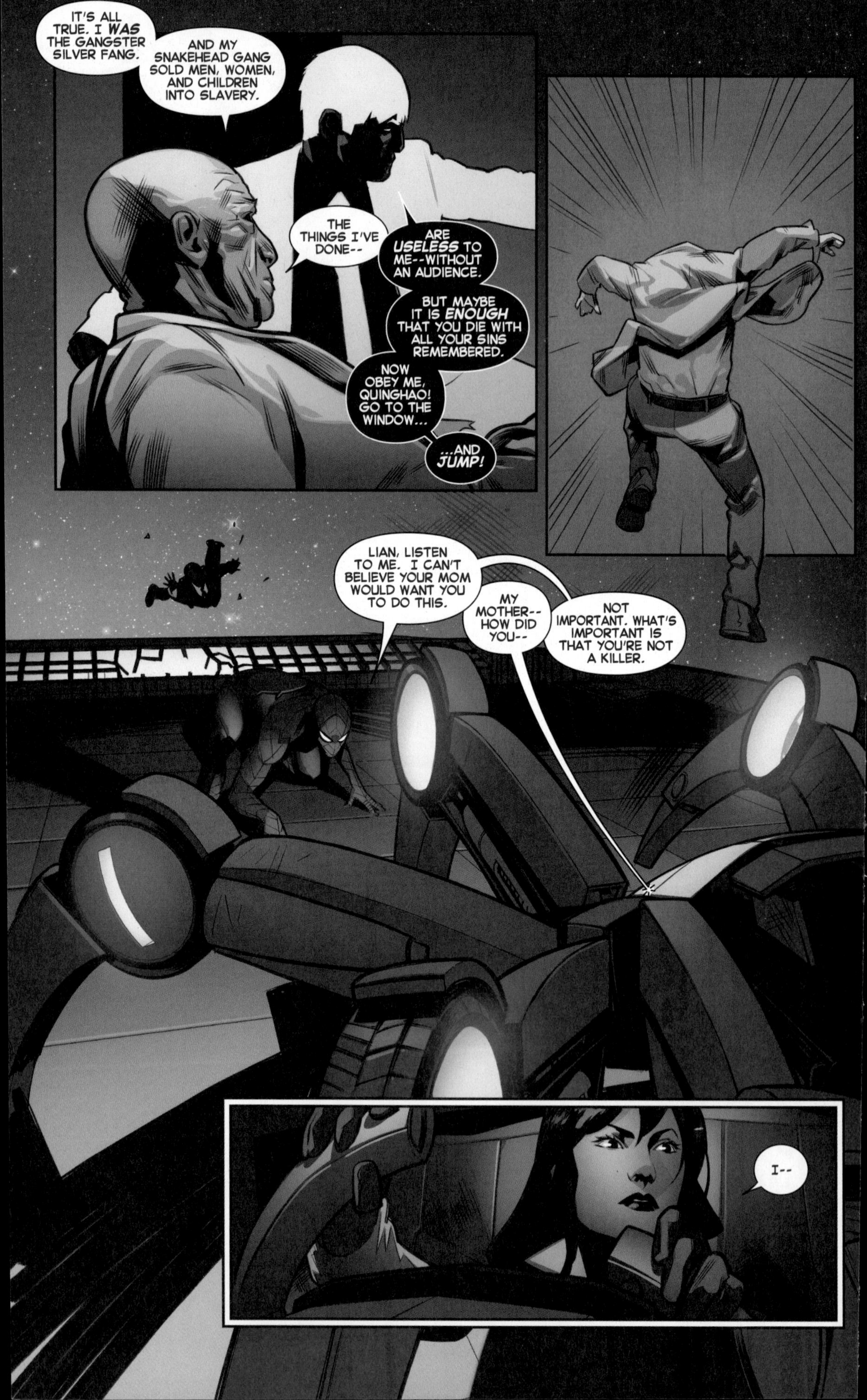
IT'S ALL TRUE. I WAS THE GANGSTER SILVER FANG.
AND MY SNAKEHEAD GANG SOLD MEN, WOMEN, AND CHILDREN INTO SLAVERY.
THE THINGS I'VE DONE--
ARE USELESS TO ME--WITHOUT AN AUDIENCE.
BUT MAYBE IT IS ENOUGH THAT YOU DIE WITH ALL YOUR SINS REMEMBERED.
NOW OBEY ME, QUINGHAO! GO TO THE WINDOW...
...AND JUMP!
LIAN, LISTEN TO ME. I CAN'T BELIEVE YOUR MOM WOULD WANT YOU TO DO THIS.
MY MOTHER--HOW DID YOU--
NOT IMPORTANT. WHAT'S IMPORTANT IS THAT YOU'RE NOT A KILLER.
I--

WHAT ARE YOU--?

QUINGHAO! SHE CAUGHT HIM!

BUT SHE HAD TO REACH OUT, AND AT *THAT* ANGLE--

I'VE GOT YOU!

HANG ON!

THWIP

KRKSHH

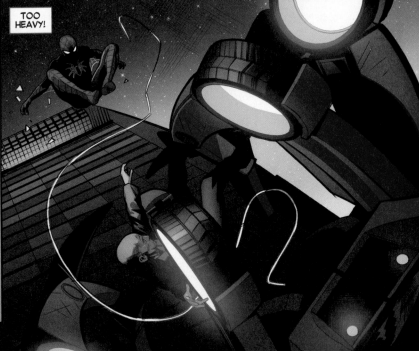

TOO HEAVY!

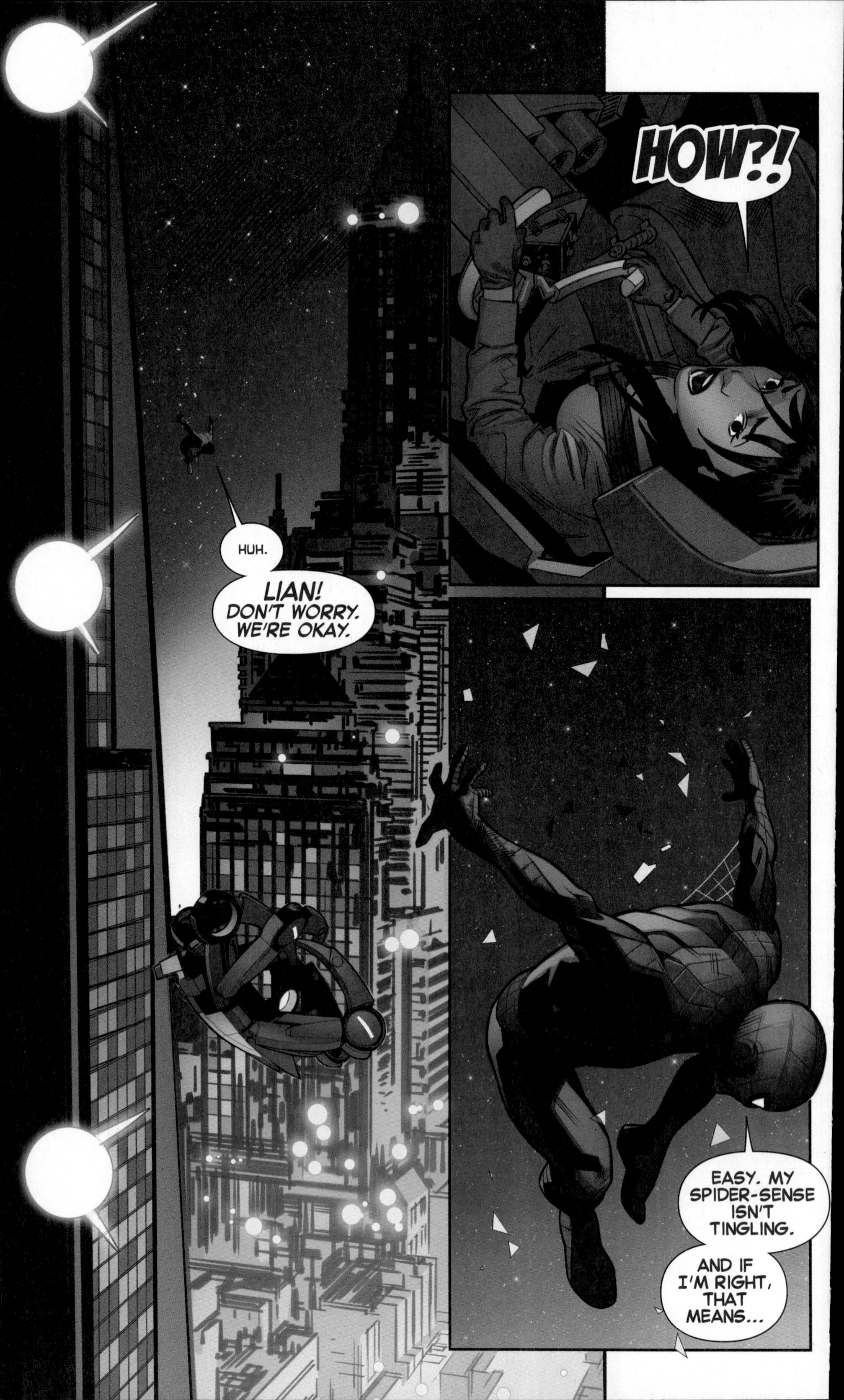
HUH.
LIAN! DON'T WORRY. WE'RE OKAY.
HOW?!
EASY. MY SPIDER-SENSE ISN'T TINGLING.
AND IF I'M RIGHT, THAT MEANS...

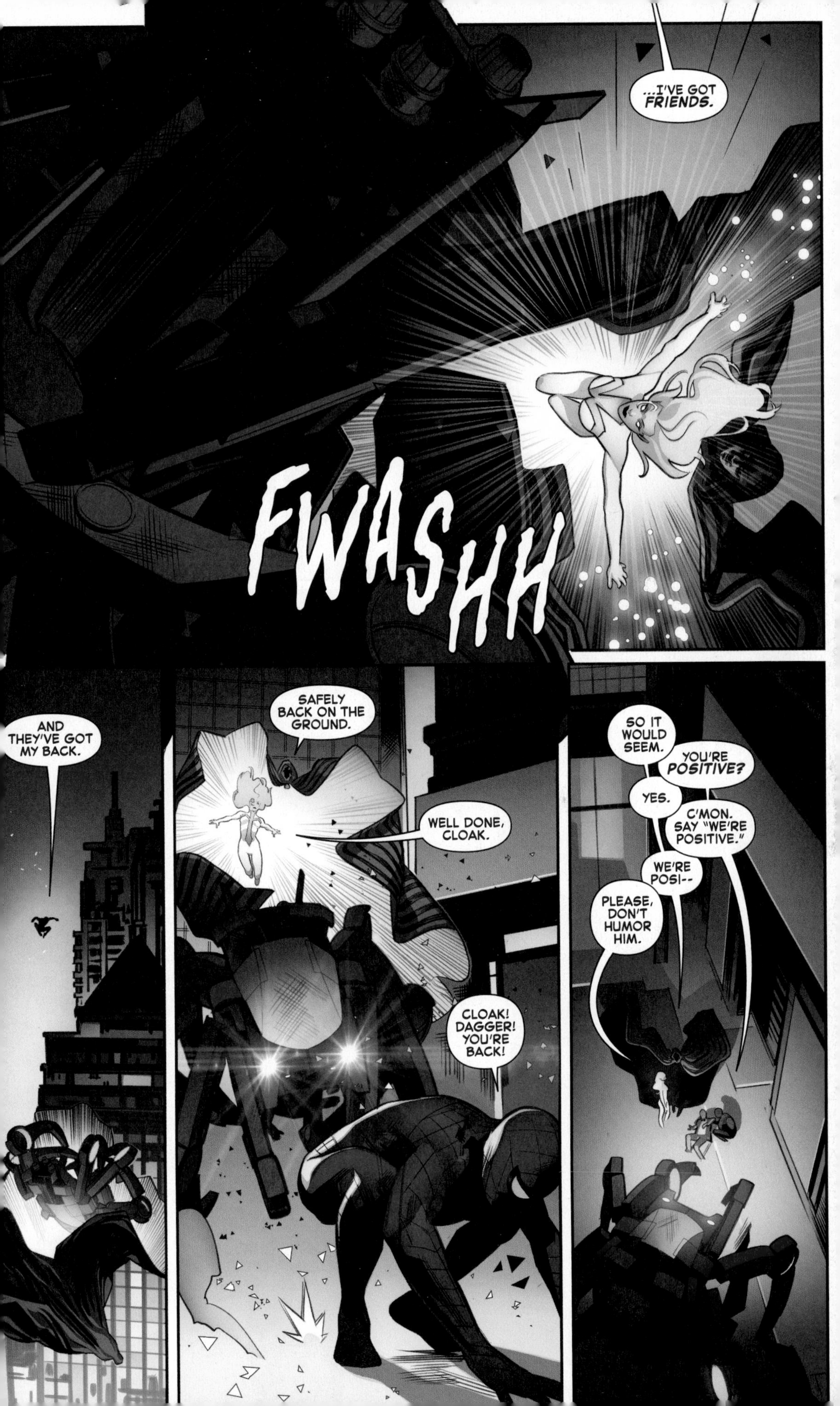

...I'VE GOT FRIENDS.
FWASHH
AND THEY'VE GOT MY BACK.
SAFELY BACK ON THE GROUND.
WELL DONE, CLOAK.
CLOAK! DAGGER! YOU'RE BACK!
SO IT WOULD SEEM.
YOU'RE POSITIVE?
YES.
C'MON. SAY "WE'RE POSITIVE."
WE'RE POSI--
PLEASE, DON'T HUMOR HIM.

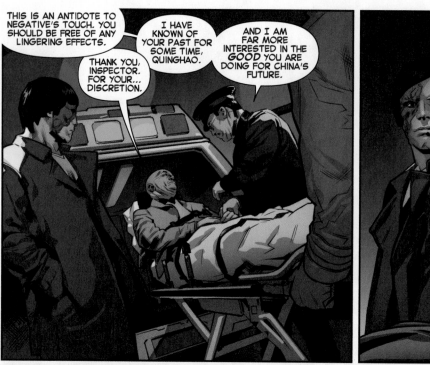

THIS IS AN ANTIDOTE TO NEGATIVE'S TOUCH. YOU SHOULD BE FREE OF ANY LINGERING EFFECTS.

THANK YOU, INSPECTOR. FOR YOUR... DISCRETION.

I HAVE KNOWN OF YOUR PAST FOR SOME TIME, QUINGHAO.

AND I AM FAR MORE INTERESTED IN THE *GOOD* YOU ARE DOING FOR CHINA'S FUTURE.

YOU ARE A LUCKY MAN, QUINGHAO. SOME OF US CARRY OUR MISTAKES WITH US FOR ALL TO SEE. MAYBE THAT'S HOW IT SHOULD BE.

I WON'T BE SHARING MY HARD WORK WITH A MAN LIKE YOU.

GOODBYE, SHEN.

WHAT HAPPENS TO ME NOW?

I'M FIRED? GOING TO JAIL? WHAT? JUST TELL ME MOTHER WILL BE--

LIAN, STOP...

I GAVE ZODIAC OUR SECURITY CODES. I TRIED TO *KILL* YOU. I--

I UNDERSTAND.

I KNOW WHAT IT MEANS TO RISK EVERYTHING TO HELP FAMILY. SO DOES PETER.

WE'D BE HYPOCRITES IF WE DIDN'T GIVE YOU A CHANCE...

...TO *WORK* WITH US. WE'RE GOING TO HELP YOUR MOM. AND YOU'RE GOING TO HELP US TAKE DOWN ZODIAC.

I WAS ONLY THEIR MOLE.

FINE. LET'S SEE WHAT YOU CAN "DIG UP" FOR THE GOOD GUYS.

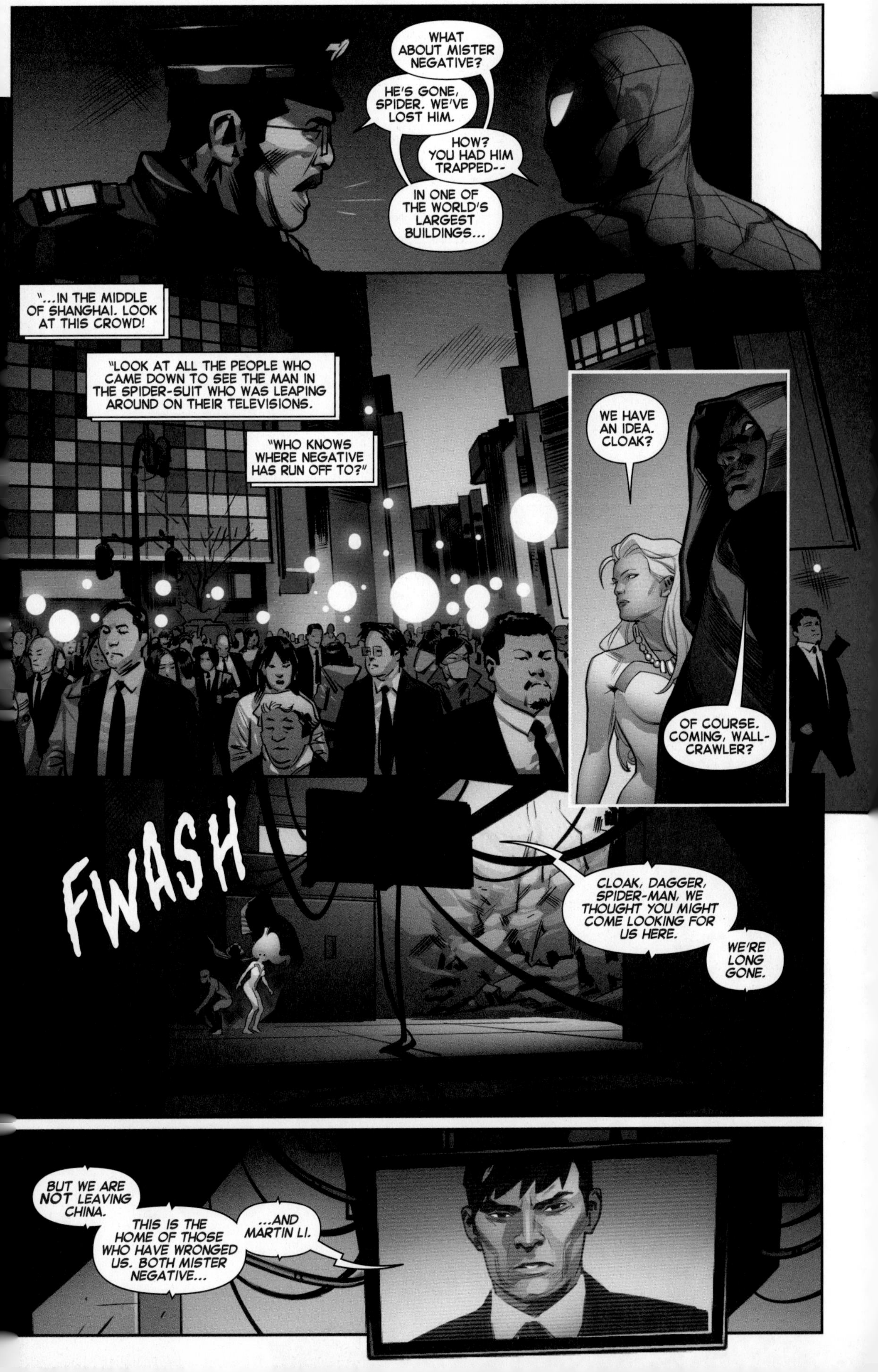

WHAT ABOUT MISTER NEGATIVE?
HE'S GONE, SPIDER. WE'VE LOST HIM.
HOW? YOU HAD HIM TRAPPED--
IN ONE OF THE WORLD'S LARGEST BUILDINGS...
"...IN THE MIDDLE OF SHANGHAI. LOOK AT THIS CROWD!
"LOOK AT ALL THE PEOPLE WHO CAME DOWN TO SEE THE MAN IN THE SPIDER-SUIT WHO WAS LEAPING AROUND ON THEIR TELEVISIONS.
"WHO KNOWS WHERE NEGATIVE HAS RUN OFF TO?"
WE HAVE AN IDEA. CLOAK?
OF COURSE. COMING, WALL-CRAWLER?
FWASH
CLOAK, DAGGER, SPIDER-MAN, WE THOUGHT YOU MIGHT COME LOOKING FOR US HERE.
WE'RE LONG GONE.
BUT WE ARE NOT LEAVING CHINA.
THIS IS THE HOME OF THOSE WHO HAVE WRONGED US. BOTH MISTER NEGATIVE...
...AND MARTIN LI.

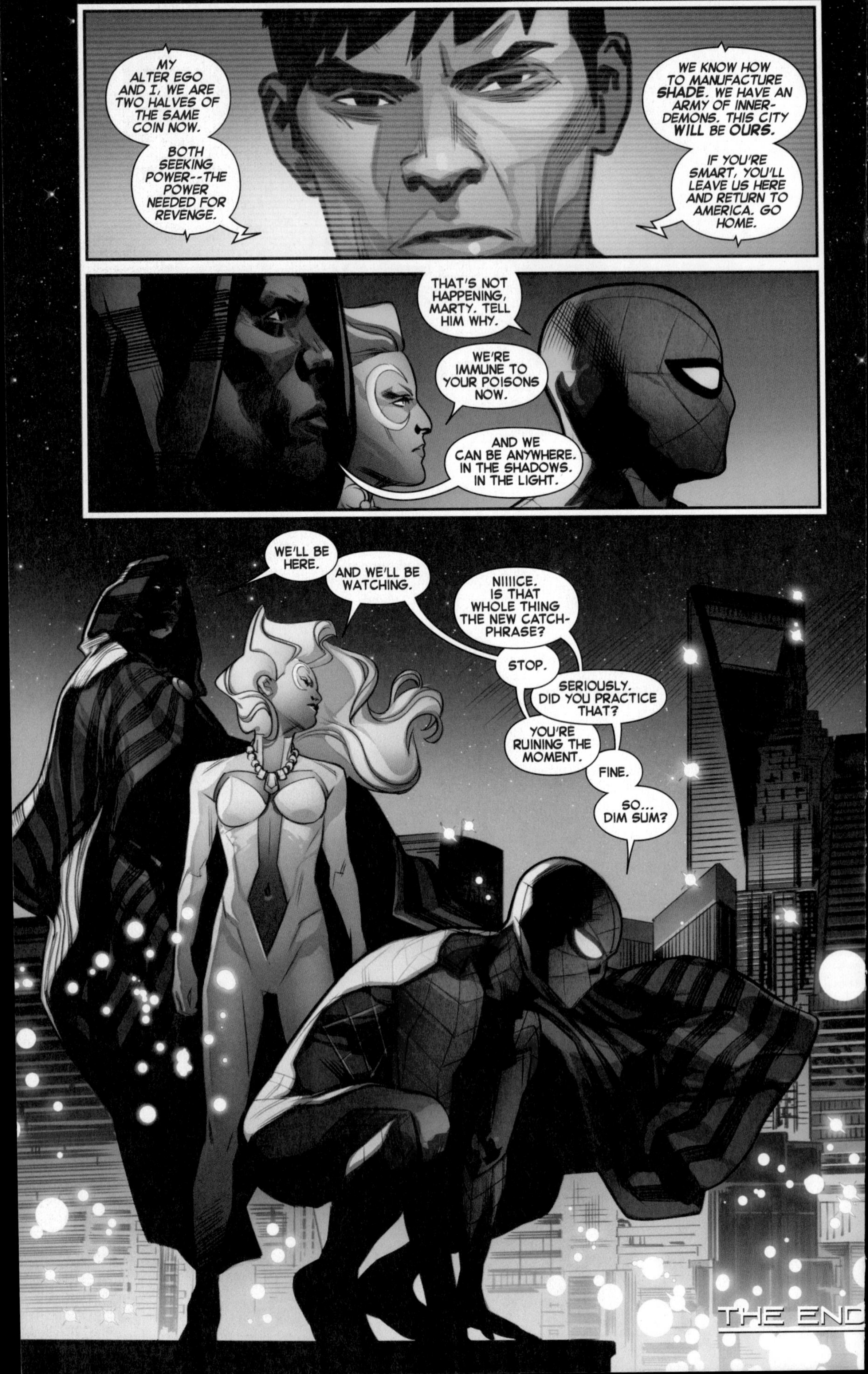

MY ALTER EGO AND I, WE ARE TWO HALVES OF THE SAME COIN NOW.
BOTH SEEKING POWER--THE POWER NEEDED FOR REVENGE.
WE KNOW HOW TO MANUFACTURE SHADE. WE HAVE AN ARMY OF INNER-DEMONS. THIS CITY WILL BE OURS.
IF YOU'RE SMART, YOU'LL LEAVE US HERE AND RETURN TO AMERICA. GO HOME.
THAT'S NOT HAPPENING, MARTY. TELL HIM WHY.
WE'RE IMMUNE TO YOUR POISONS NOW.
AND WE CAN BE ANYWHERE. IN THE SHADOWS. IN THE LIGHT.
WE'LL BE HERE.
AND WE'LL BE WATCHING.
NIIIICE. IS THAT WHOLE THING THE NEW CATCH-PHRASE?
STOP.
SERIOUSLY. DID YOU PRACTICE THAT?
YOU'RE RUINING THE MOMENT.
FINE.
SO... DIM SUM?
THE END

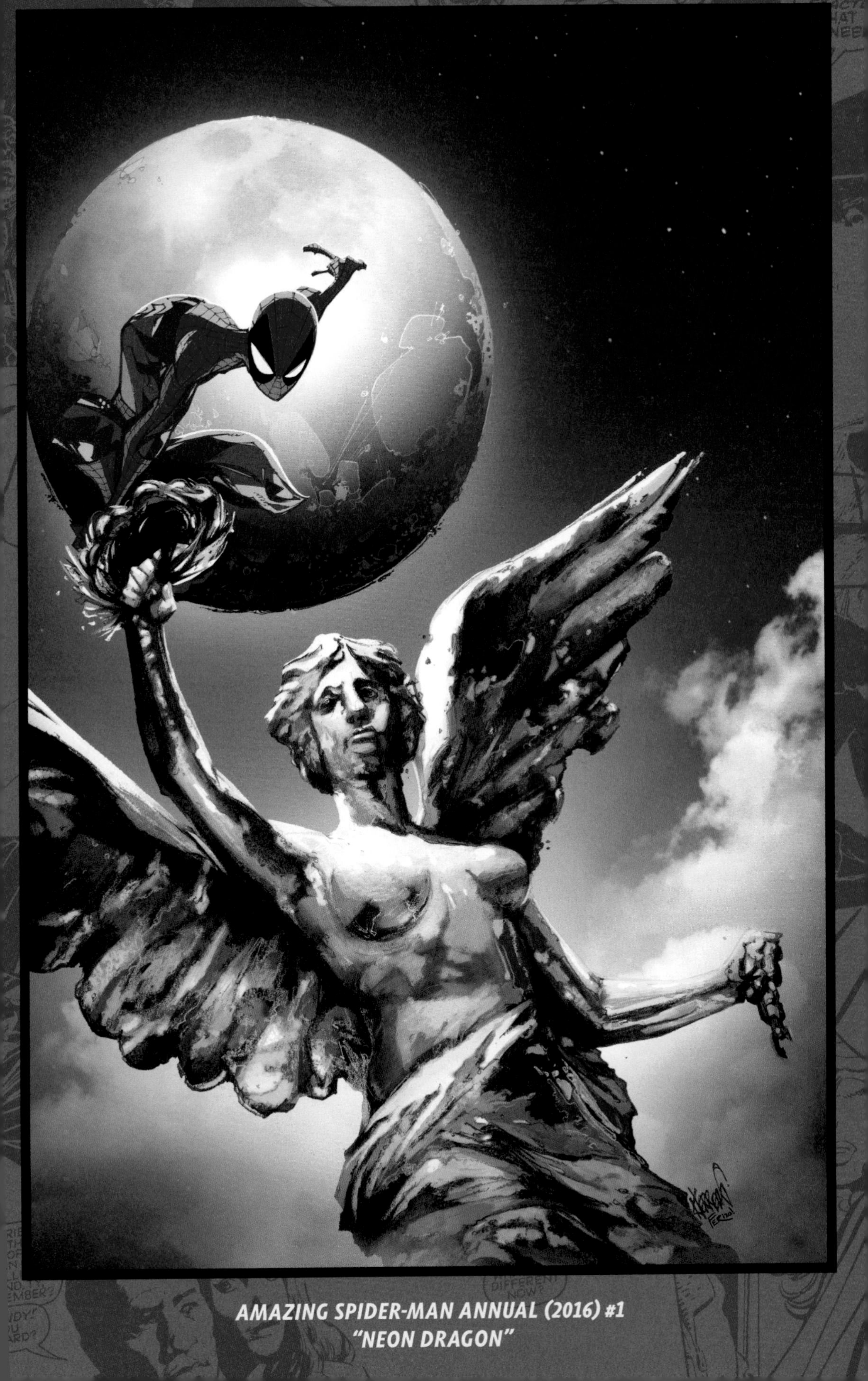

AMAZING SPIDER-MAN ANNUAL (2016) #1
"NEON DRAGON"

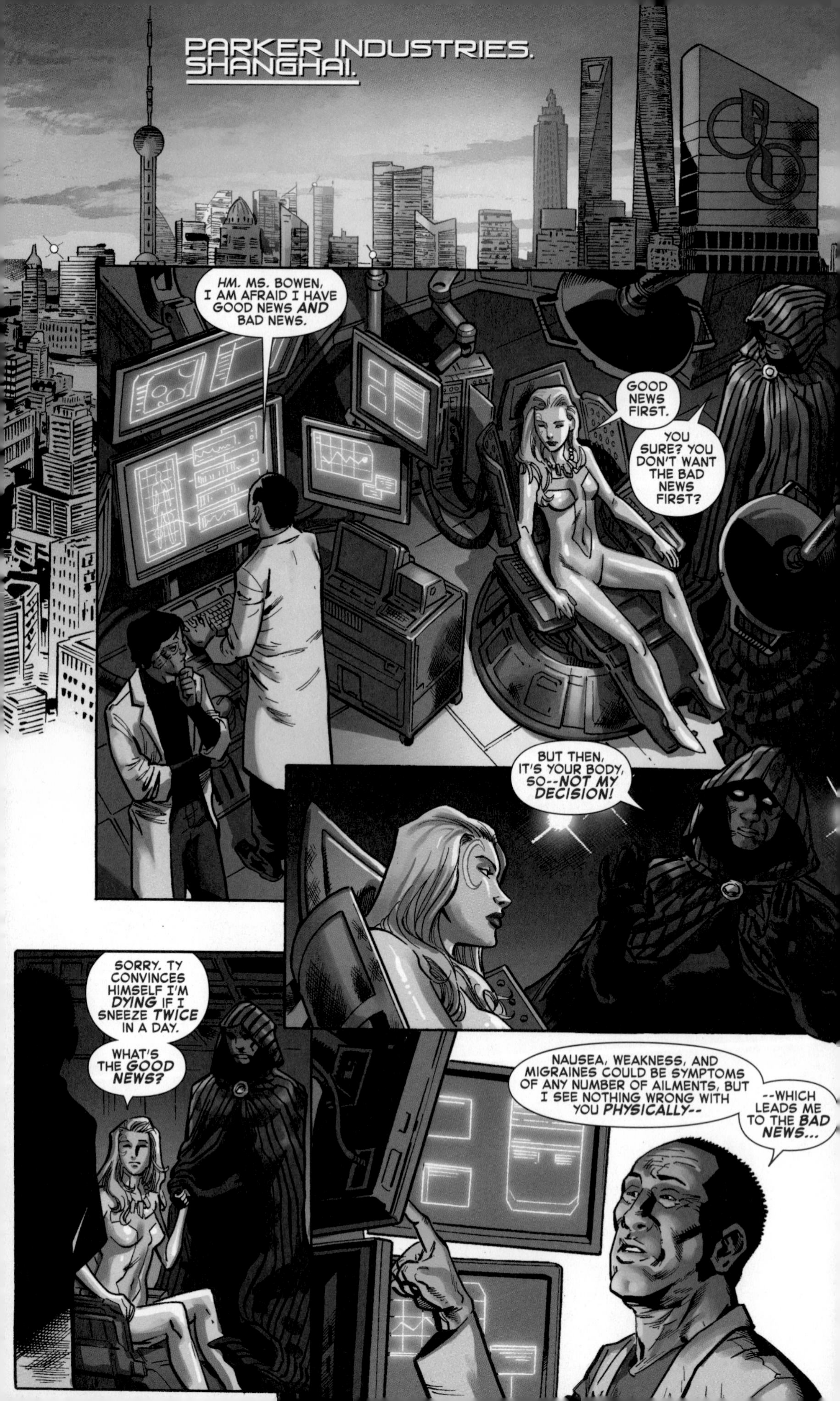
PARKER INDUSTRIES. SHANGHAI.
HM. MS. BOWEN, I AM AFRAID I HAVE GOOD NEWS AND BAD NEWS.
GOOD NEWS FIRST.
YOU SURE? YOU DON'T WANT THE BAD NEWS FIRST?
BUT THEN, IT'S YOUR BODY, SO--NOT MY DECISION!
SORRY. TY CONVINCES HIMSELF I'M DYING IF I SNEEZE TWICE IN A DAY.
WHAT'S THE GOOD NEWS?
NAUSEA, WEAKNESS, AND MIGRAINES COULD BE SYMPTOMS OF ANY NUMBER OF AILMENTS, BUT I SEE NOTHING WRONG WITH YOU PHYSICALLY--
--WHICH LEADS ME TO THE BAD NEWS...

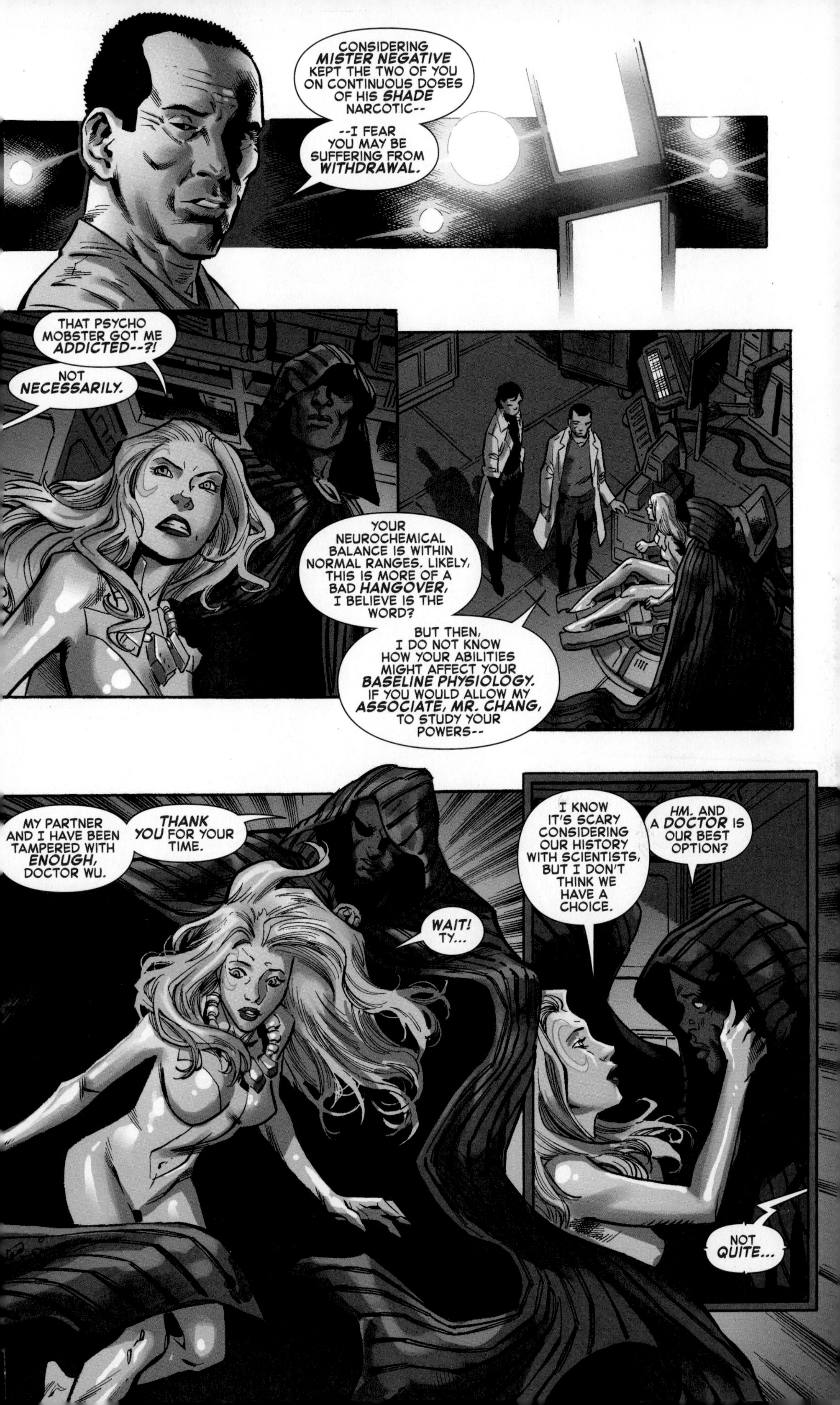
CONSIDERING MISTER NEGATIVE KEPT THE TWO OF YOU ON CONTINUOUS DOSES OF HIS SHADE NARCOTIC--
--I FEAR YOU MAY BE SUFFERING FROM WITHDRAWAL.
THAT PSYCHO MOBSTER GOT ME ADDICTED--?!
NOT NECESSARILY.
YOUR NEUROCHEMICAL BALANCE IS WITHIN NORMAL RANGES. LIKELY, THIS IS MORE OF A BAD HANGOVER, I BELIEVE IS THE WORD?
BUT THEN, I DO NOT KNOW HOW YOUR ABILITIES MIGHT AFFECT YOUR BASELINE PHYSIOLOGY. IF YOU WOULD ALLOW MY ASSOCIATE, MR. CHANG, TO STUDY YOUR POWERS--
MY PARTNER AND I HAVE BEEN TAMPERED WITH ENOUGH, DOCTOR WU.
THANK YOU FOR YOUR TIME.
WAIT! TY...
I KNOW IT'S SCARY CONSIDERING OUR HISTORY WITH SCIENTISTS, BUT I DON'T THINK WE HAVE A CHOICE.
HM. AND A DOCTOR IS OUR BEST OPTION?
NOT QUITE...

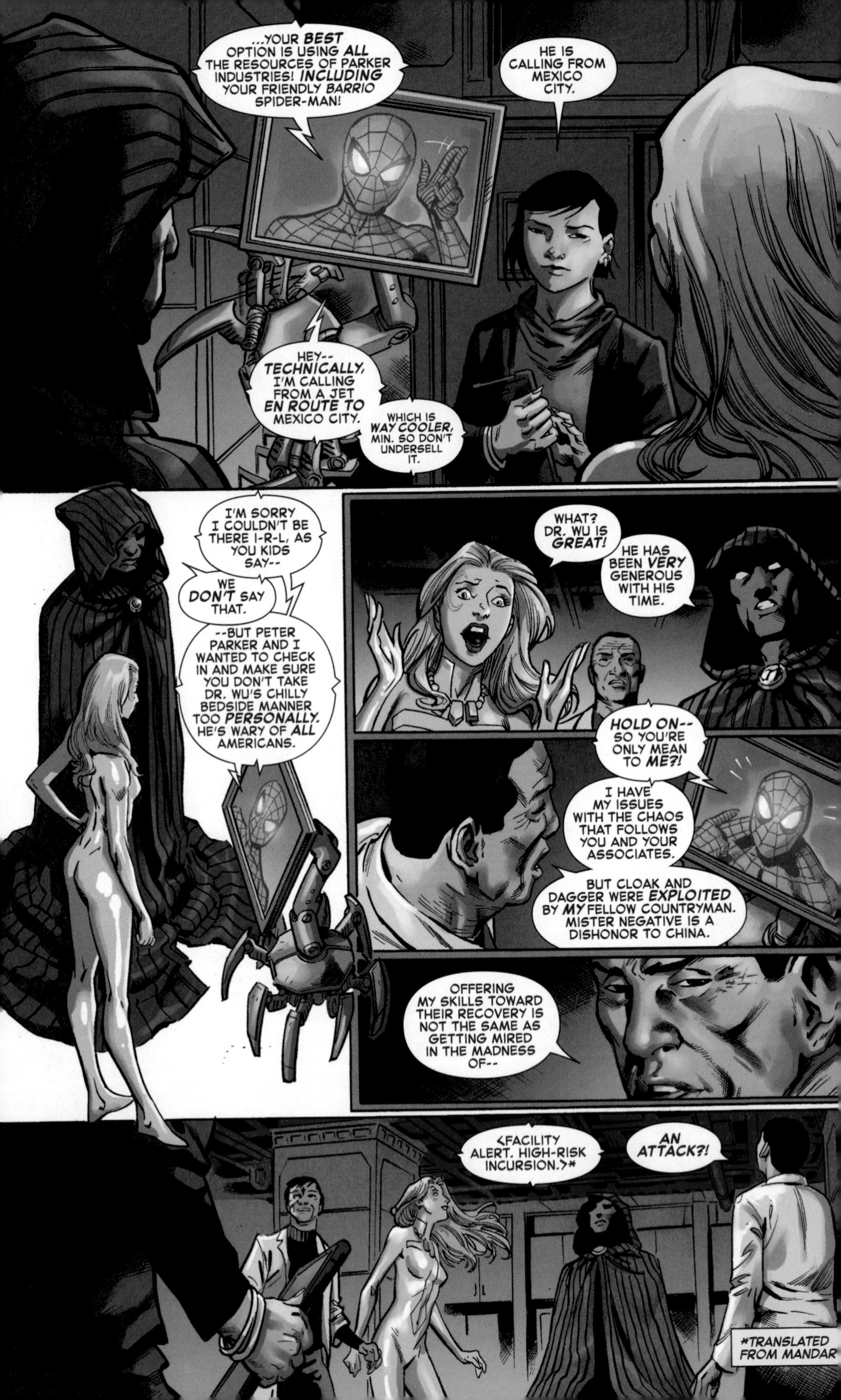
...YOUR BEST OPTION IS USING ALL THE RESOURCES OF PARKER INDUSTRIES! INCLUDING YOUR FRIENDLY BARRIO SPIDER-MAN!
HE IS CALLING FROM MEXICO CITY.
HEY-- TECHNICALLY, I'M CALLING FROM A JET EN ROUTE TO MEXICO CITY.
WHICH IS WAY COOLER, MIN. SO DON'T UNDERSELL IT.
I'M SORRY I COULDN'T BE THERE I-R-L, AS YOU KIDS SAY--
WE DON'T SAY THAT.
--BUT PETER PARKER AND I WANTED TO CHECK IN AND MAKE SURE YOU DON'T TAKE DR. WU'S CHILLY BEDSIDE MANNER TOO PERSONALLY. HE'S WARY OF ALL AMERICANS.
WHAT? DR. WU IS GREAT!
HE HAS BEEN VERY GENEROUS WITH HIS TIME.
HOLD ON-- SO YOU'RE ONLY MEAN TO ME?!
I HAVE MY ISSUES WITH THE CHAOS THAT FOLLOWS YOU AND YOUR ASSOCIATES.
BUT CLOAK AND DAGGER WERE EXPLOITED BY MY FELLOW COUNTRYMAN. MISTER NEGATIVE IS A DISHONOR TO CHINA.
OFFERING MY SKILLS TOWARD THEIR RECOVERY IS NOT THE SAME AS GETTING MIRED IN THE MADNESS OF--
<FACILITY ALERT. HIGH-RISK INCURSION.>*
AN ATTACK?!
*TRANSLATED FROM MANDAR

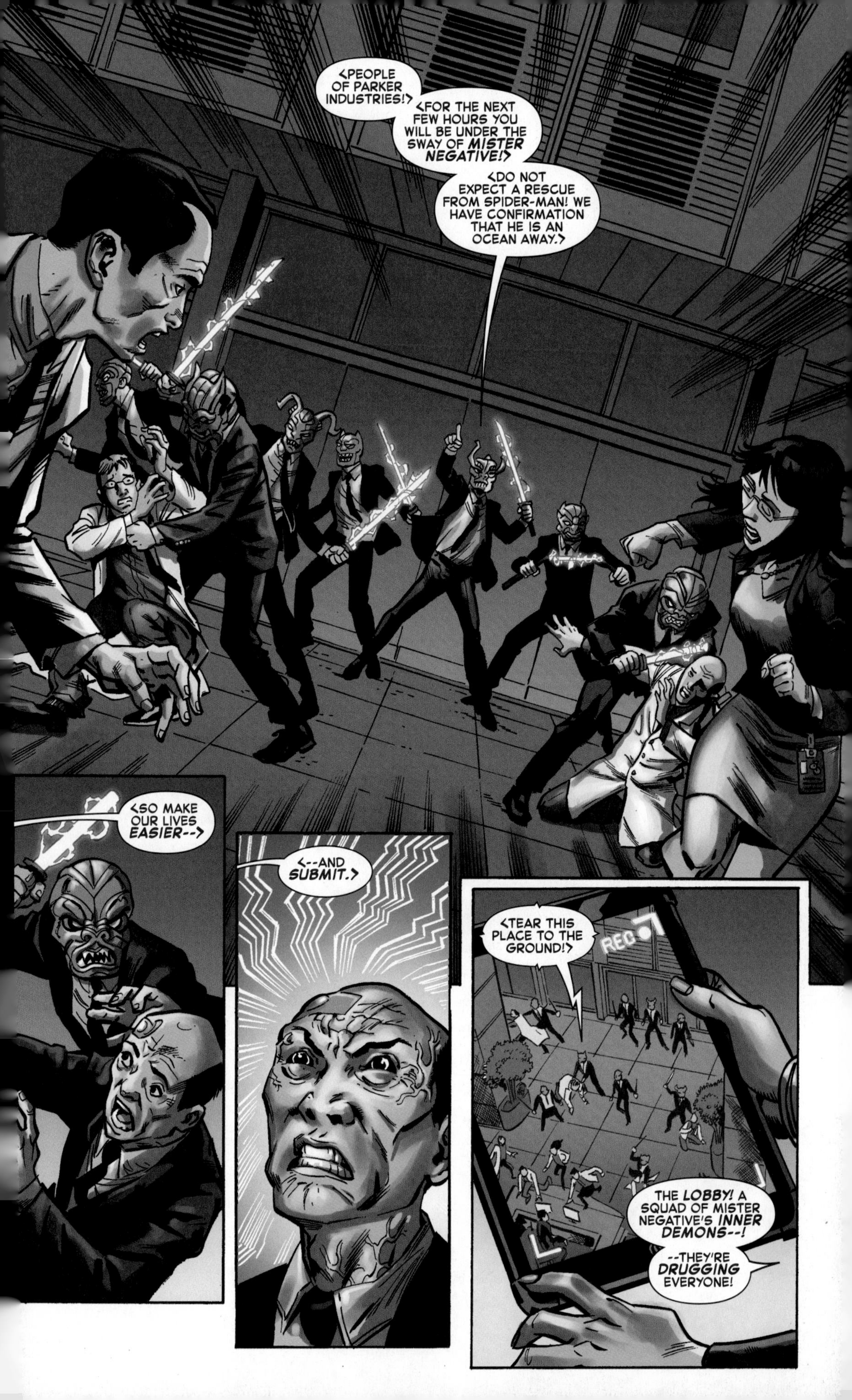

<PEOPLE OF PARKER INDUSTRIES!>
<FOR THE NEXT FEW HOURS YOU WILL BE UNDER THE SWAY OF *MISTER NEGATIVE!*>
<DO NOT EXPECT A RESCUE FROM SPIDER-MAN! WE HAVE CONFIRMATION THAT HE IS AN OCEAN AWAY.>
<SO MAKE OUR LIVES *EASIER*-->
<--AND *SUBMIT.*>
<TEAR THIS PLACE TO THE GROUND!>
REC
THE *LOBBY!* A SQUAD OF MISTER NEGATIVE'S *INNER DEMONS*--!
--THEY'RE *DRUGGING* EVERYONE!

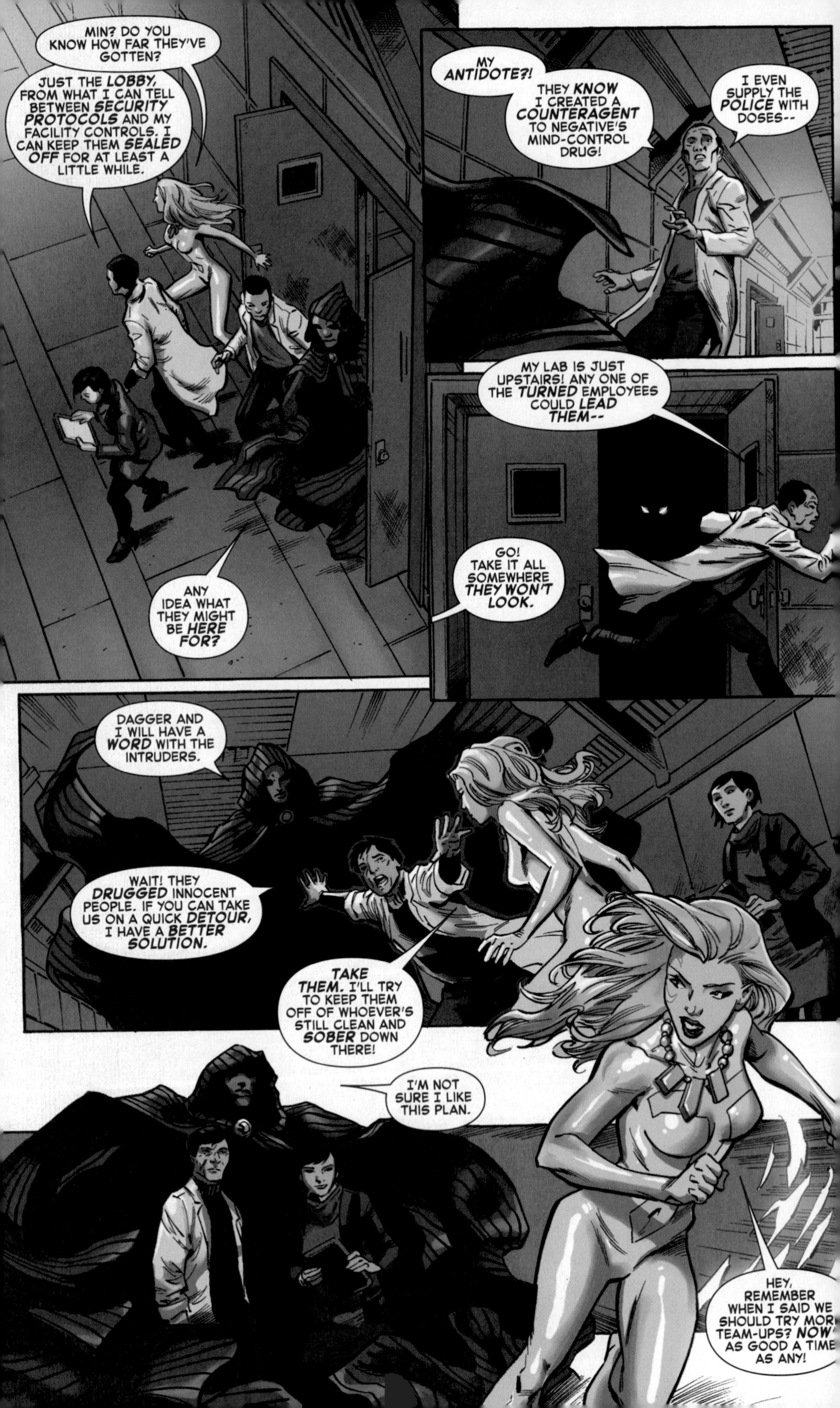

MIN? DO YOU KNOW HOW FAR THEY'VE GOTTEN?
JUST THE LOBBY, FROM WHAT I CAN TELL BETWEEN SECURITY PROTOCOLS AND MY FACILITY CONTROLS. I CAN KEEP THEM SEALED OFF FOR AT LEAST A LITTLE WHILE.
ANY IDEA WHAT THEY MIGHT BE HERE FOR?
MY ANTIDOTE?!
THEY KNOW I CREATED A COUNTERAGENT TO NEGATIVE'S MIND-CONTROL DRUG!
I EVEN SUPPLY THE POLICE WITH DOSES--
MY LAB IS JUST UPSTAIRS! ANY ONE OF THE TURNED EMPLOYEES COULD LEAD THEM--
GO! TAKE IT ALL SOMEWHERE THEY WON'T LOOK.
DAGGER AND I WILL HAVE A WORD WITH THE INTRUDERS.
WAIT! THEY DRUGGED INNOCENT PEOPLE. IF YOU CAN TAKE US ON A QUICK DETOUR, I HAVE A BETTER SOLUTION.
TAKE THEM. I'LL TRY TO KEEP THEM OFF OF WHOEVER'S STILL CLEAN AND SOBER DOWN THERE!
I'M NOT SURE I LIKE THIS PLAN.
HEY, REMEMBER WHEN I SAID WE SHOULD TRY MOR TEAM-UPS? NOW AS GOOD A TIME AS ANY!

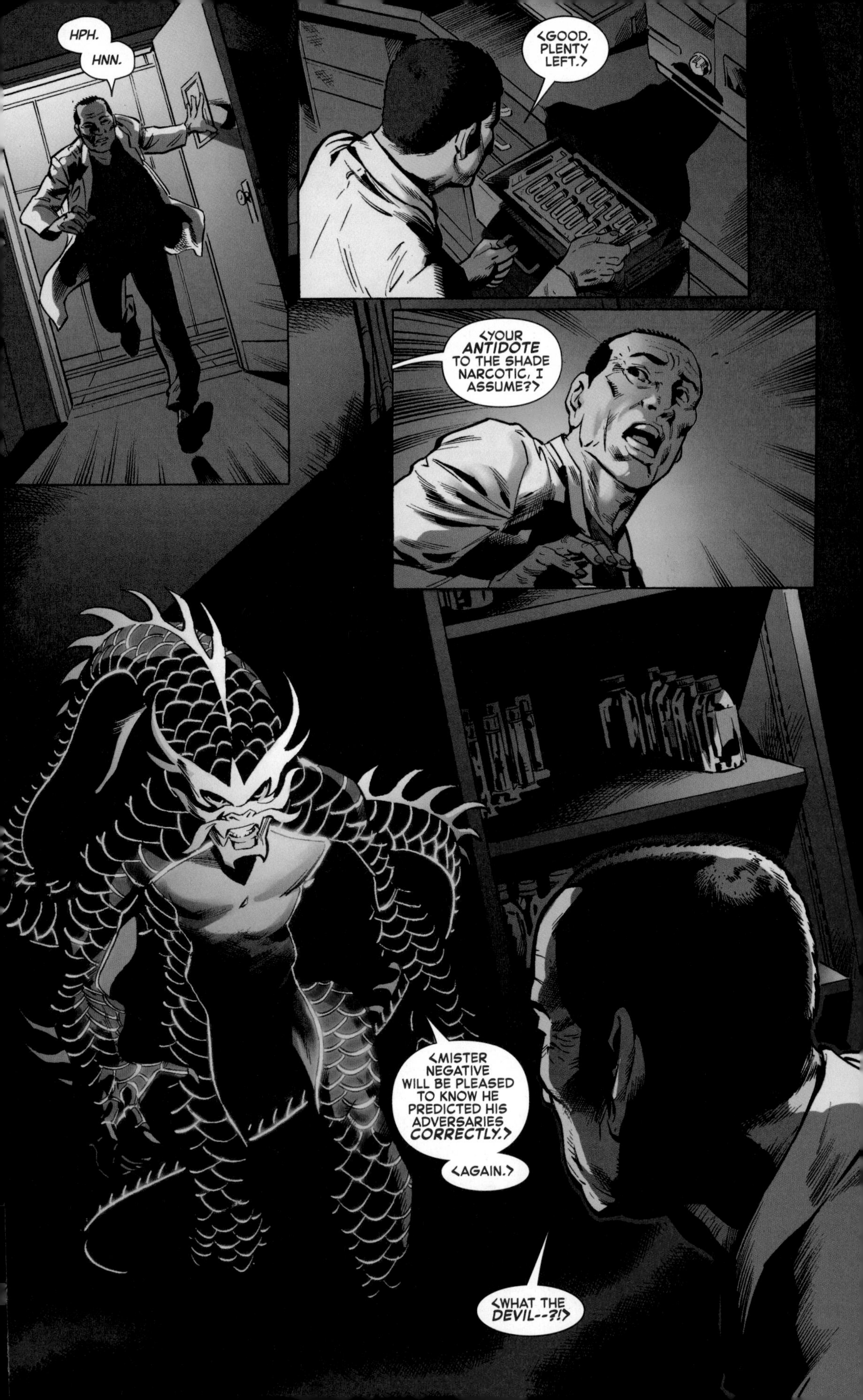
HPH.
HNN.
<GOOD. PLENTY LEFT.>
<YOUR ANTIDOTE TO THE SHADE NARCOTIC, I ASSUME?>
<MISTER NEGATIVE WILL BE PLEASED TO KNOW HE PREDICTED HIS ADVERSARIES CORRECTLY.>
<AGAIN.>
<WHAT THE DEVIL--?!>

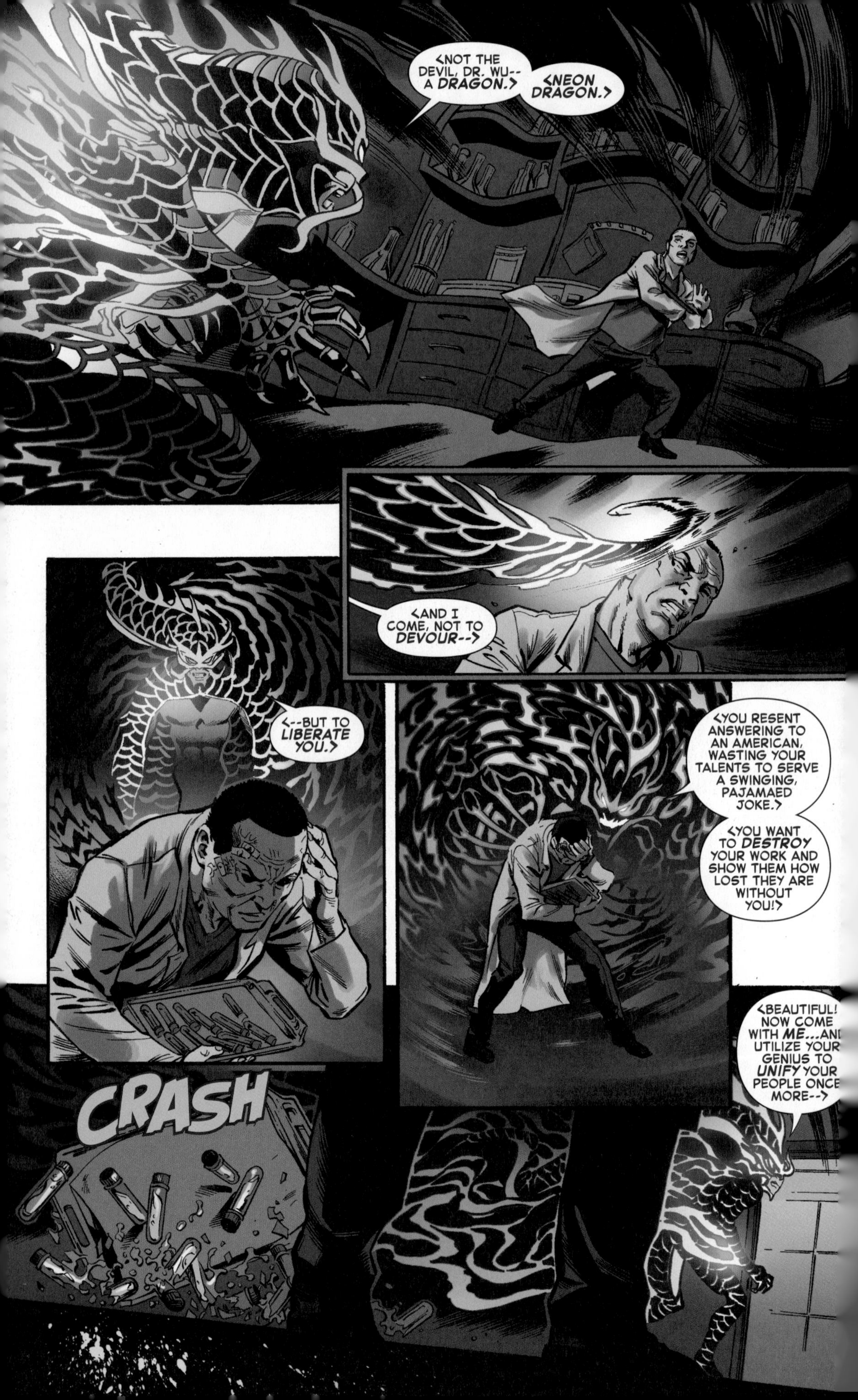
<NOT THE DEVIL, DR. WU-- A DRAGON.>
<NEON DRAGON.>
<AND I COME, NOT TO DEVOUR-->
<--BUT TO LIBERATE YOU.>
<YOU RESENT ANSWERING TO AN AMERICAN, WASTING YOUR TALENTS TO SERVE A SWINGING, PAJAMAED JOKE.>
<YOU WANT TO DESTROY YOUR WORK AND SHOW THEM HOW LOST THEY ARE WITHOUT YOU!>
CRASH
<BEAUTIFUL! NOW COME WITH ME...AND UTILIZE YOUR GENIUS TO UNIFY YOUR PEOPLE ONCE MORE-->

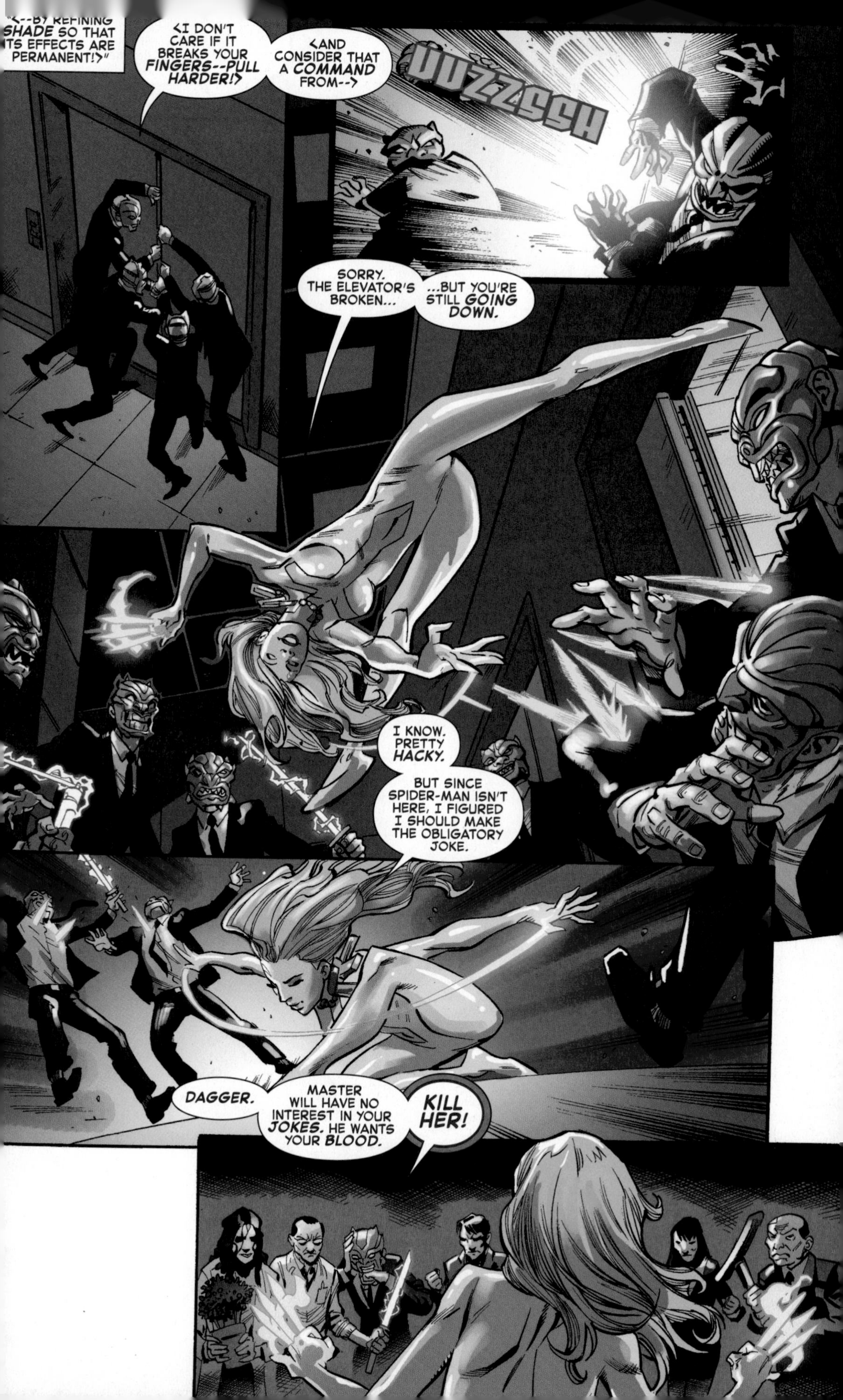
<--BY REFINING SHADE SO THAT TS EFFECTS ARE PERMANENT!>"
<I DON'T CARE IF IT BREAKS YOUR FINGERS--PULL HARDER!>
<AND CONSIDER THAT A COMMAND FROM-->
SORRY. THE ELEVATOR'S BROKEN...
...BUT YOU'RE STILL GOING DOWN.
I KNOW. PRETTY HACKY.
BUT SINCE SPIDER-MAN ISN'T HERE, I FIGURED I SHOULD MAKE THE OBLIGATORY JOKE.
DAGGER.
MASTER WILL HAVE NO INTEREST IN YOUR JOKES. HE WANTS YOUR BLOOD.
KILL HER!

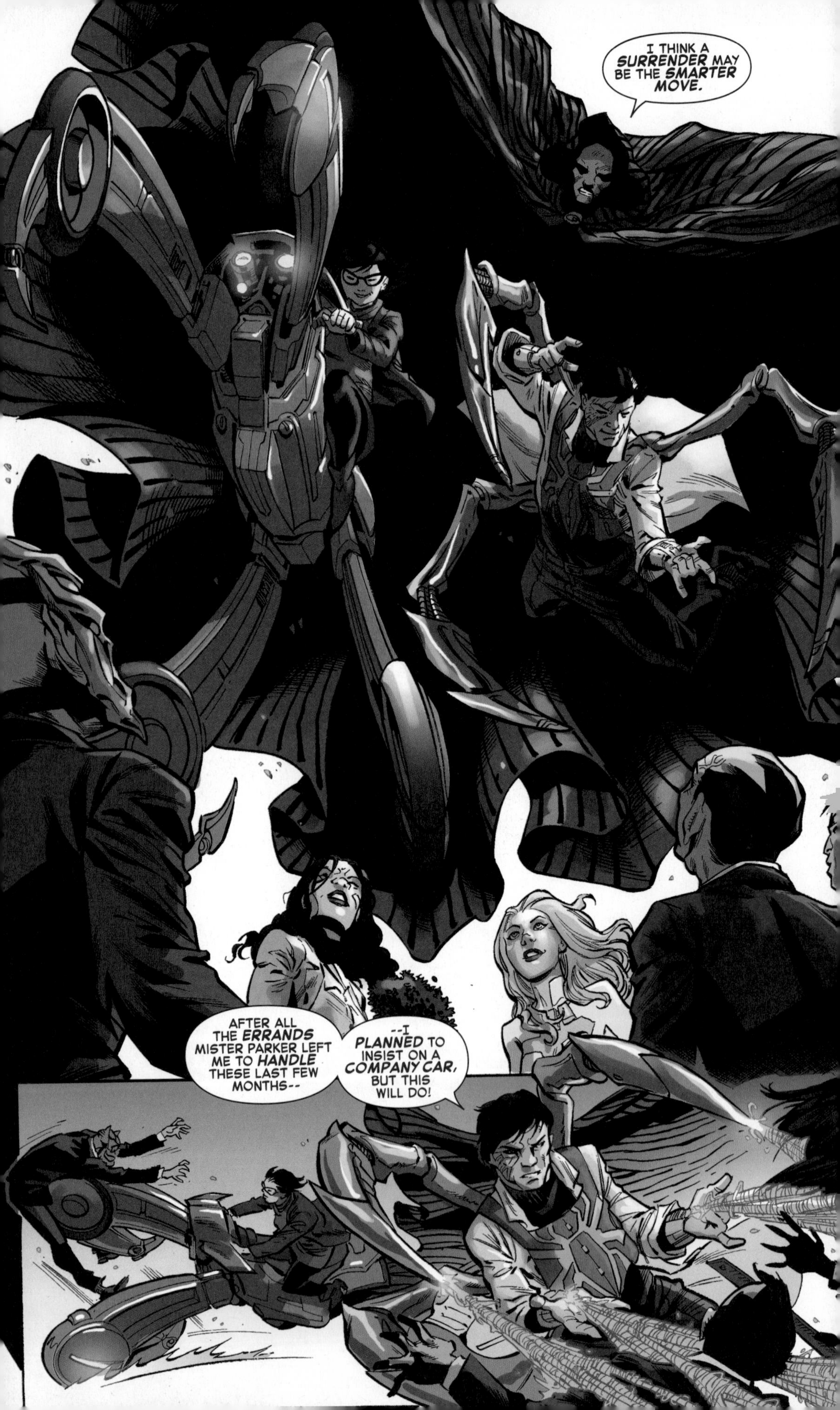
I THINK A SURRENDER MAY BE THE SMARTER MOVE.
AFTER ALL THE ERRANDS MISTER PARKER LEFT ME TO HANDLE THESE LAST FEW MONTHS--
--I PLANNED TO INSIST ON A COMPANY CAR, BUT THIS WILL DO!

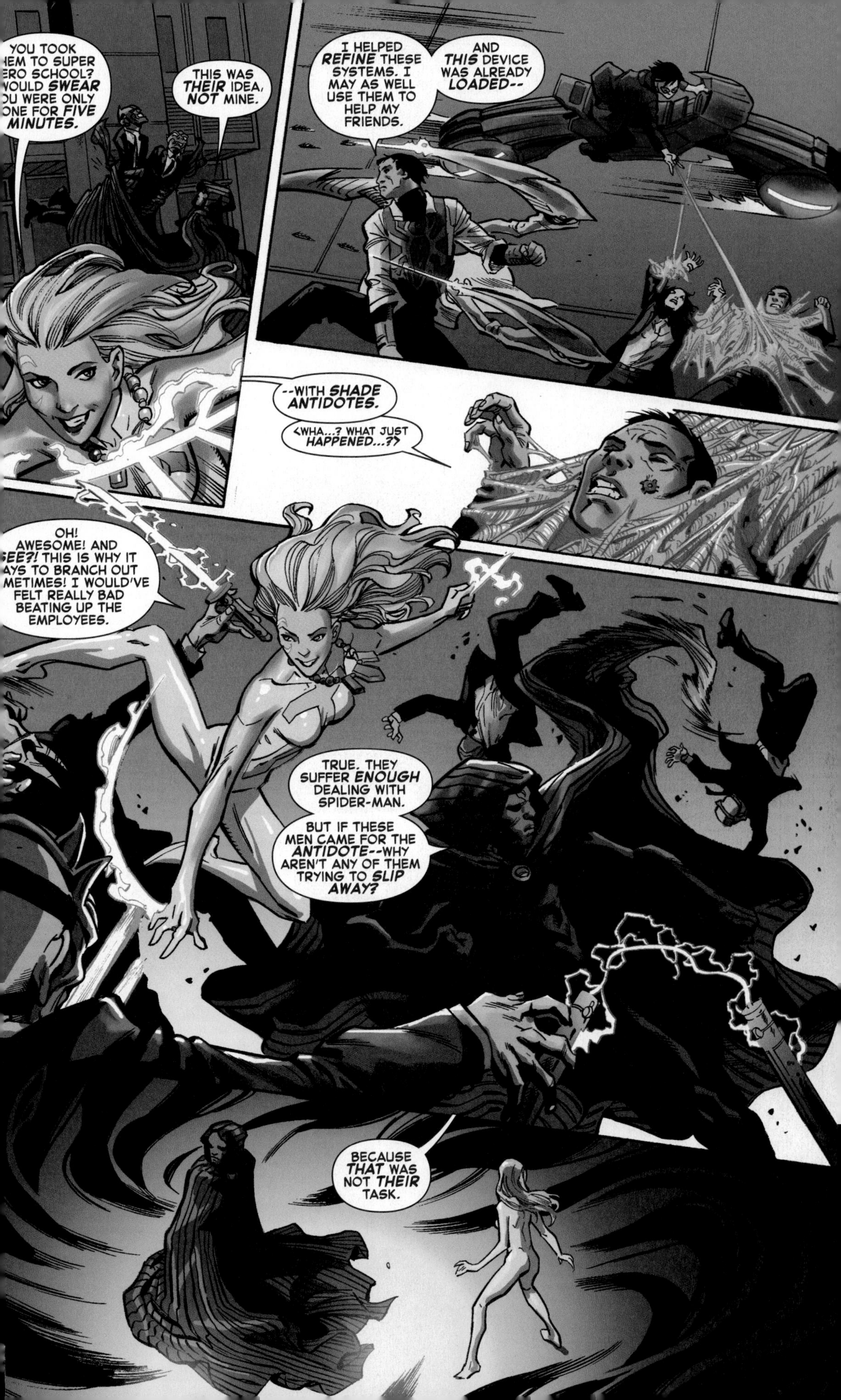
YOU TOOK HEM TO SUPER ERO SCHOOL? WOULD SWEAR OU WERE ONLY ONE FOR FIVE MINUTES.
THIS WAS THEIR IDEA, NOT MINE.
I HELPED REFINE THESE SYSTEMS. I MAY AS WELL USE THEM TO HELP MY FRIENDS.
AND THIS DEVICE WAS ALREADY LOADED--
--WITH SHADE ANTIDOTES.
<WHA...? WHAT JUST HAPPENED...?>
OH! AWESOME! AND SEE?! THIS IS WHY IT AYS TO BRANCH OUT METIMES! I WOULD'VE FELT REALLY BAD BEATING UP THE EMPLOYEES.
TRUE. THEY SUFFER ENOUGH DEALING WITH SPIDER-MAN.
BUT IF THESE MEN CAME FOR THE ANTIDOTE--WHY AREN'T ANY OF THEM TRYING TO SLIP AWAY?
BECAUSE THAT WAS NOT THEIR TASK.

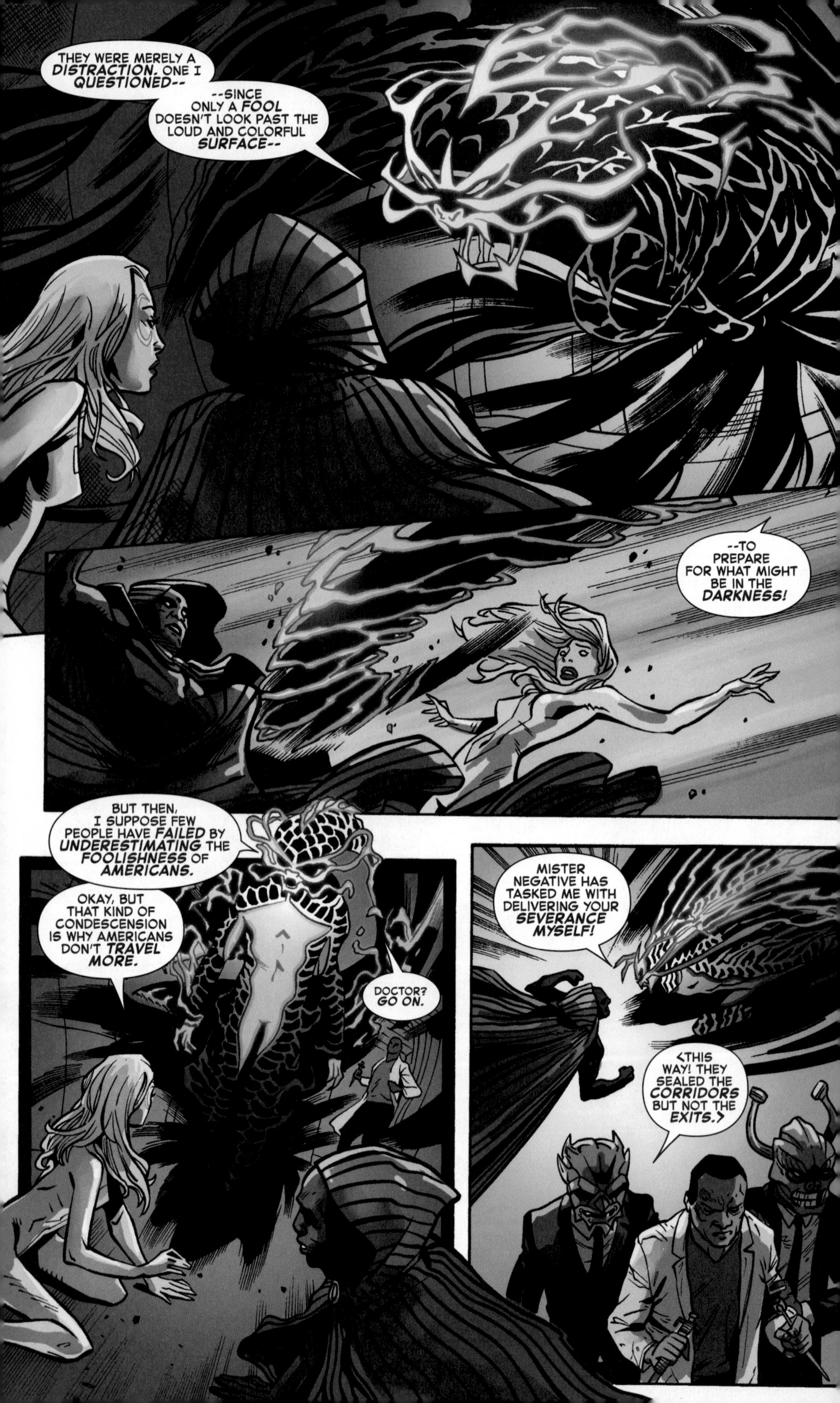

THEY WERE MERELY A DISTRACTION. ONE I QUESTIONED--
--SINCE ONLY A FOOL DOESN'T LOOK PAST THE LOUD AND COLORFUL SURFACE--
--TO PREPARE FOR WHAT MIGHT BE IN THE DARKNESS!
BUT THEN, I SUPPOSE FEW PEOPLE HAVE FAILED BY UNDERESTIMATING THE FOOLISHNESS OF AMERICANS.
OKAY, BUT THAT KIND OF CONDESCENSION IS WHY AMERICANS DON'T TRAVEL MORE.
DOCTOR? GO ON.
MISTER NEGATIVE HAS TASKED ME WITH DELIVERING YOUR SEVERANCE MYSELF!
<THIS WAY! THEY SEALED THE CORRIDORS BUT NOT THE EXITS.>

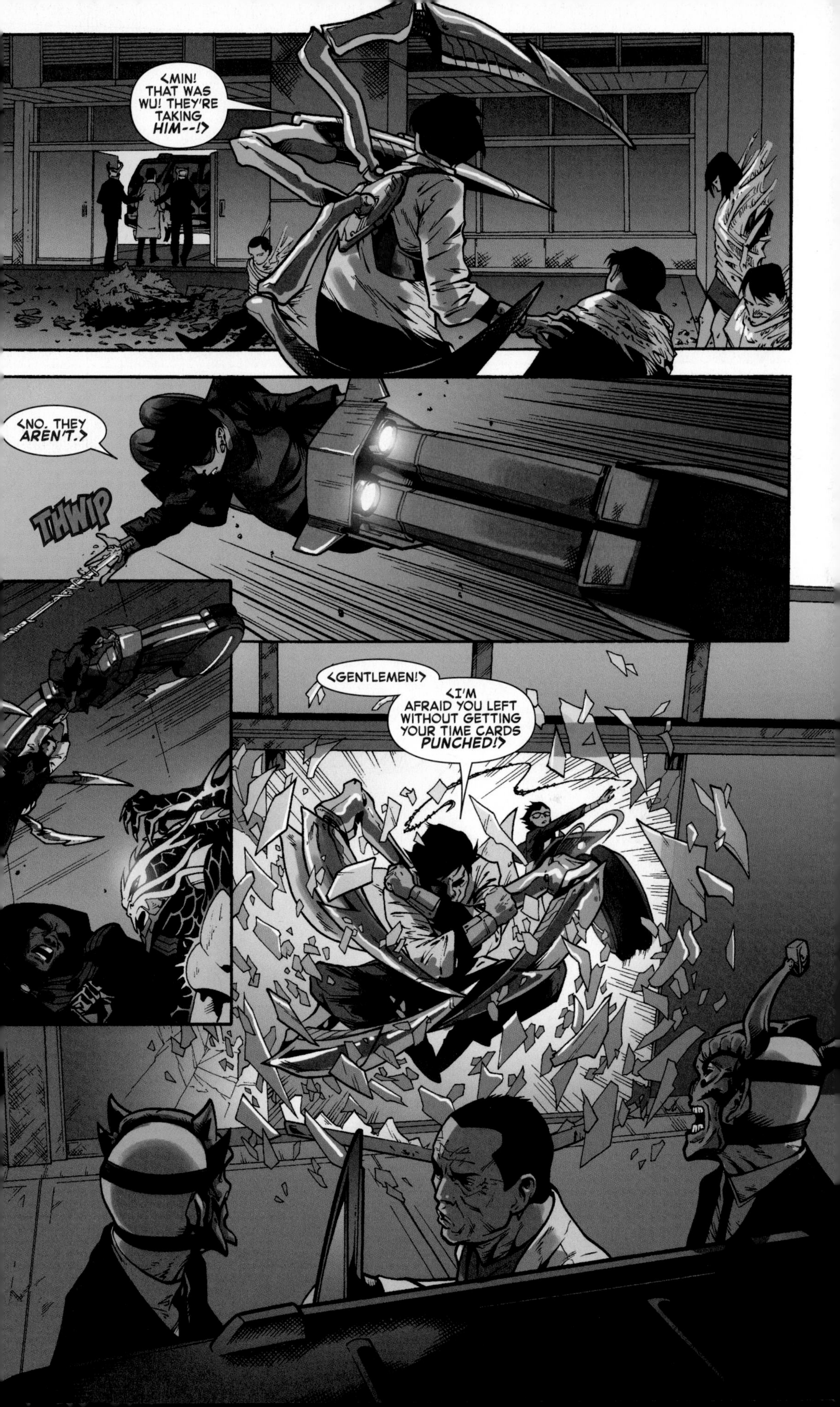
<MIN! THAT WAS WU! THEY'RE TAKING HIM--!>
<NO. THEY AREN'T.>
THWIP
<GENTLEMEN!>
<I'M AFRAID YOU LEFT WITHOUT GETTING YOUR TIME CARDS PUNCHED!>

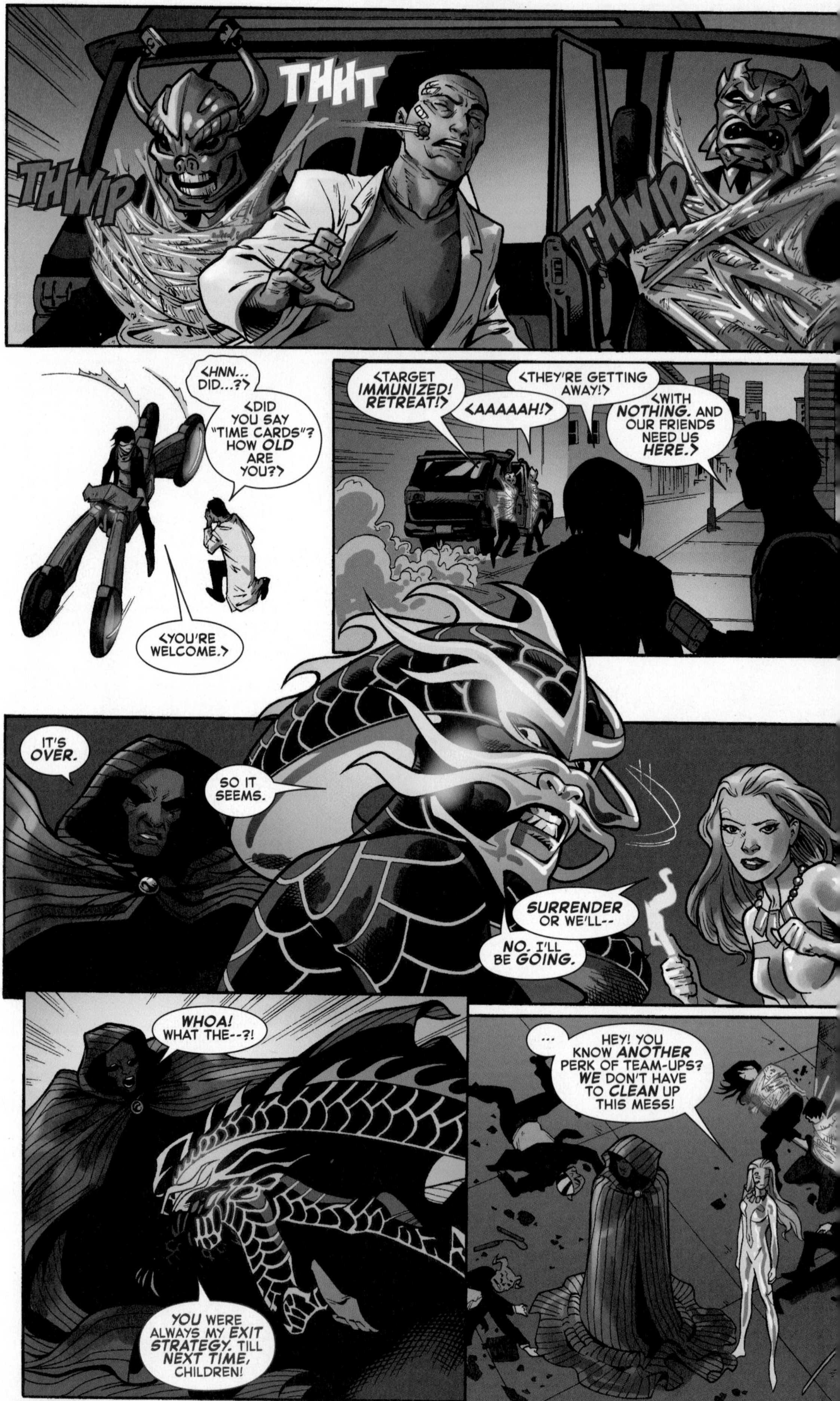
THHT
THWIP
THWIP
<HNN... DID...?>
<DID YOU SAY "TIME CARDS"? HOW OLD ARE YOU?>
<YOU'RE WELCOME.>
<TARGET IMMUNIZED! RETREAT!>
<THEY'RE GETTING AWAY!>
<AAAAAH!>
<WITH NOTHING. AND OUR FRIENDS NEED US HERE.>
IT'S OVER.
SO IT SEEMS.
SURRENDER OR WE'LL--
NO. I'LL BE GOING.
WHOA! WHAT THE--?!
YOU WERE ALWAYS MY EXIT STRATEGY. TILL NEXT TIME, CHILDREN!
...
HEY! YOU KNOW ANOTHER PERK OF TEAM-UPS? WE DON'T HAVE TO CLEAN UP THIS MESS!

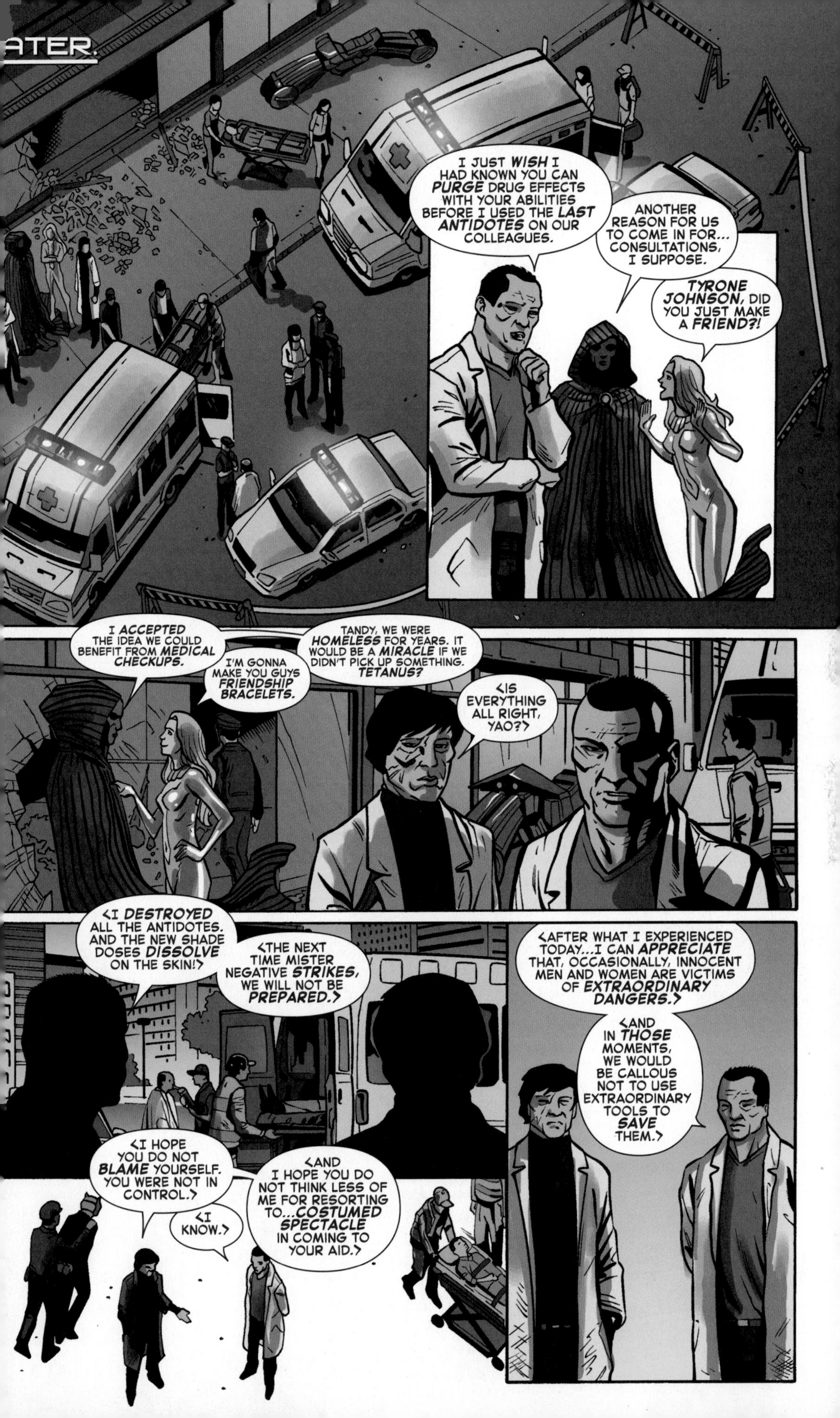
ATER.
I JUST WISH I HAD KNOWN YOU CAN PURGE DRUG EFFECTS WITH YOUR ABILITIES BEFORE I USED THE LAST ANTIDOTES ON OUR COLLEAGUES.
ANOTHER REASON FOR US TO COME IN FOR... CONSULTATIONS, I SUPPOSE.
TYRONE JOHNSON, DID YOU JUST MAKE A FRIEND?!
I ACCEPTED THE IDEA WE COULD BENEFIT FROM MEDICAL CHECKUPS.
I'M GONNA MAKE YOU GUYS FRIENDSHIP BRACELETS.
TANDY, WE WERE HOMELESS FOR YEARS. IT WOULD BE A MIRACLE IF WE DIDN'T PICK UP SOMETHING. TETANUS?
<IS EVERYTHING ALL RIGHT, YAO?>
<I DESTROYED ALL THE ANTIDOTES. AND THE NEW SHADE DOSES DISSOLVE ON THE SKIN!>
<THE NEXT TIME MISTER NEGATIVE STRIKES, WE WILL NOT BE PREPARED.>
<I HOPE YOU DO NOT BLAME YOURSELF. YOU WERE NOT IN CONTROL.>
<I KNOW.>
<AND I HOPE YOU DO NOT THINK LESS OF ME FOR RESORTING TO...COSTUMED SPECTACLE IN COMING TO YOUR AID.>
<AFTER WHAT I EXPERIENCED TODAY...I CAN APPRECIATE THAT, OCCASIONALLY, INNOCENT MEN AND WOMEN ARE VICTIMS OF EXTRAORDINARY DANGERS.>
<AND IN THOSE MOMENTS, WE WOULD BE CALLOUS NOT TO USE EXTRAORDINARY TOOLS TO SAVE THEM.>

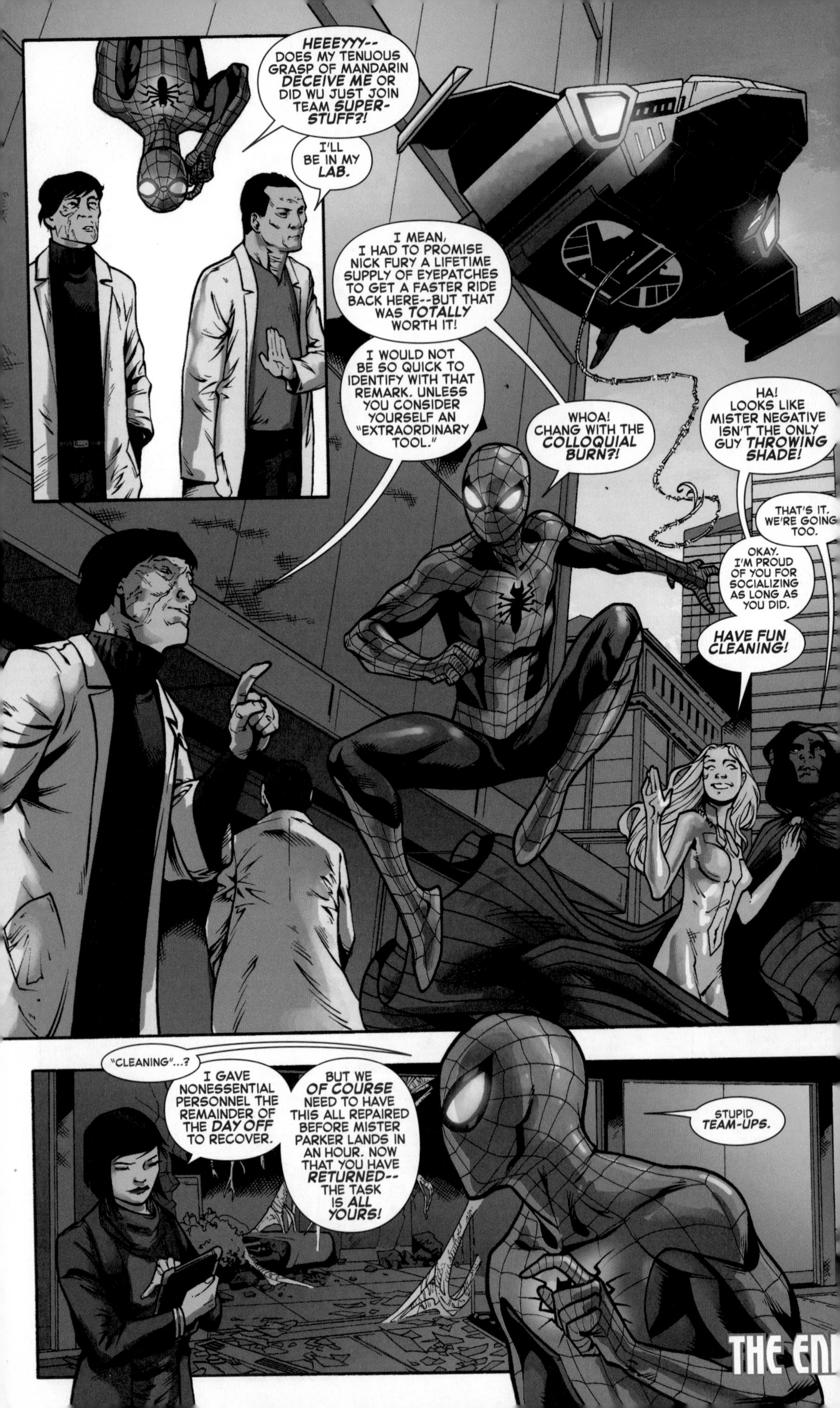

HEEEYYY-- DOES MY TENUOUS GRASP OF MANDARIN DECEIVE ME OR DID WU JUST JOIN TEAM SUPER-STUFF?!
I'LL BE IN MY LAB.
I MEAN, I HAD TO PROMISE NICK FURY A LIFETIME SUPPLY OF EYEPATCHES TO GET A FASTER RIDE BACK HERE--BUT THAT WAS TOTALLY WORTH IT!
I WOULD NOT BE SO QUICK TO IDENTIFY WITH THAT REMARK. UNLESS YOU CONSIDER YOURSELF AN "EXTRAORDINARY TOOL."
WHOA! CHANG WITH THE COLLOQUIAL BURN?!
HA! LOOKS LIKE MISTER NEGATIVE ISN'T THE ONLY GUY THROWING SHADE!
THAT'S IT. WE'RE GOING TOO.
OKAY. I'M PROUD OF YOU FOR SOCIALIZING AS LONG AS YOU DID.
HAVE FUN CLEANING!
"CLEANING"...?
I GAVE NONESSENTIAL PERSONNEL THE REMAINDER OF THE DAY OFF TO RECOVER.
BUT WE OF COURSE NEED TO HAVE THIS ALL REPAIRED BEFORE MISTER PARKER LANDS IN AN HOUR. NOW THAT YOU HAVE RETURNED-- THE TASK IS ALL YOURS!
STUPID TEAM-UPS.
THE END

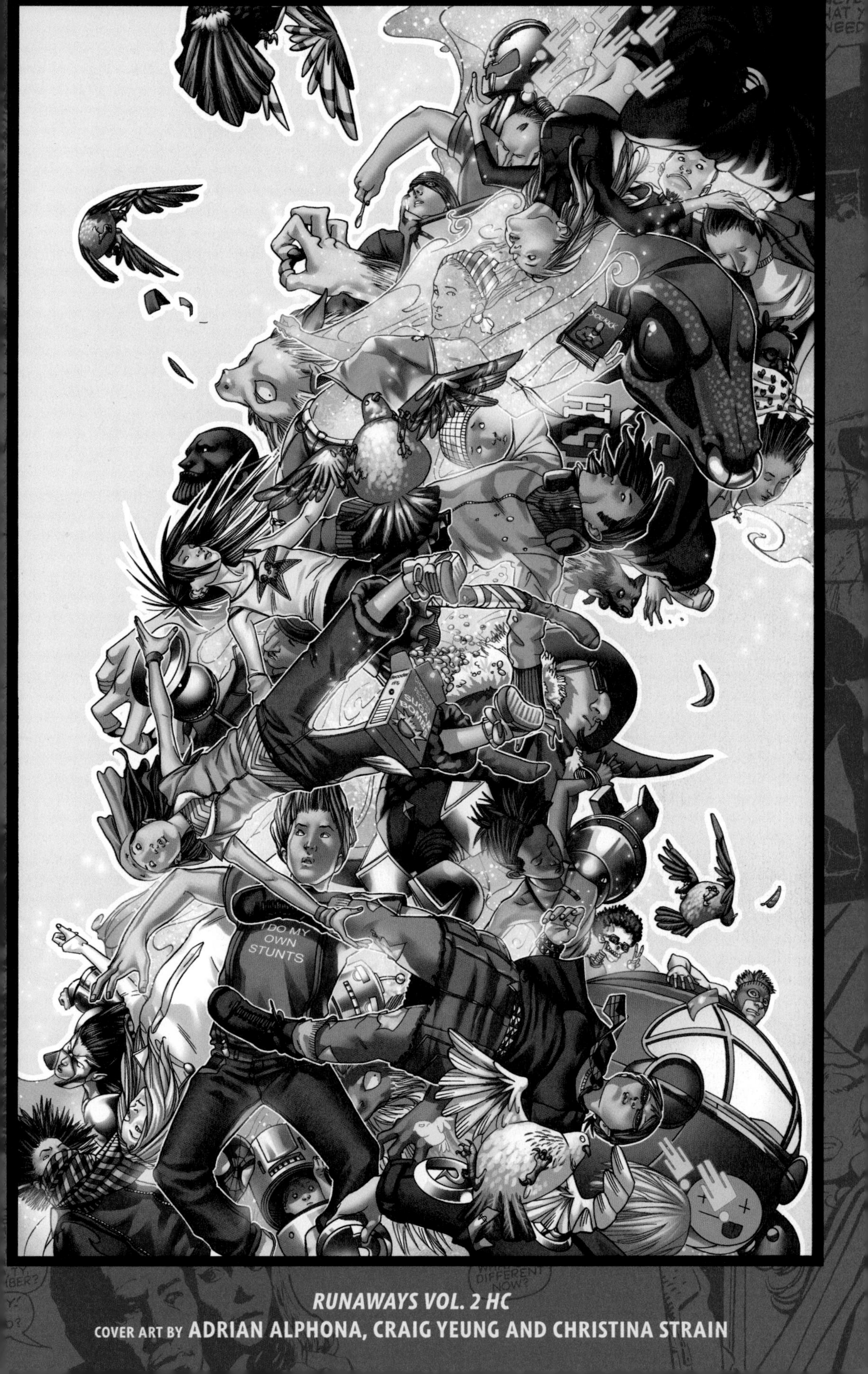
SIDEKICK
SUGAR BOMB
I DO MY OWN STUNTS

RUNAWAYS VOL. 2 HC

COVER ART BY ADRIAN ALPHONA, CRAIG YEUNG AND CHRISTINA STRAIN

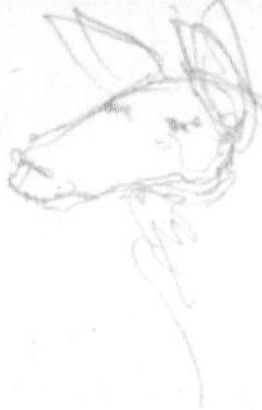

Page Sixteen

Page Sixteen, SPLASH

Pull out to this SPLASH for a big group shot of Cloak and all of our Runaways, as FOUR LITTLE WINGED GOBLINS suddenly appear in midair bursts of smoke! Everyone looks freaked out, except for Victor, who smiles as he continues to charge up his glowing hands with electricity. Cloak takes a step back here, Adrian, deciding to *observe* the Runaways rather than fight.

Security Daemon

1) Victor: More fun than Monopoly, I hope.

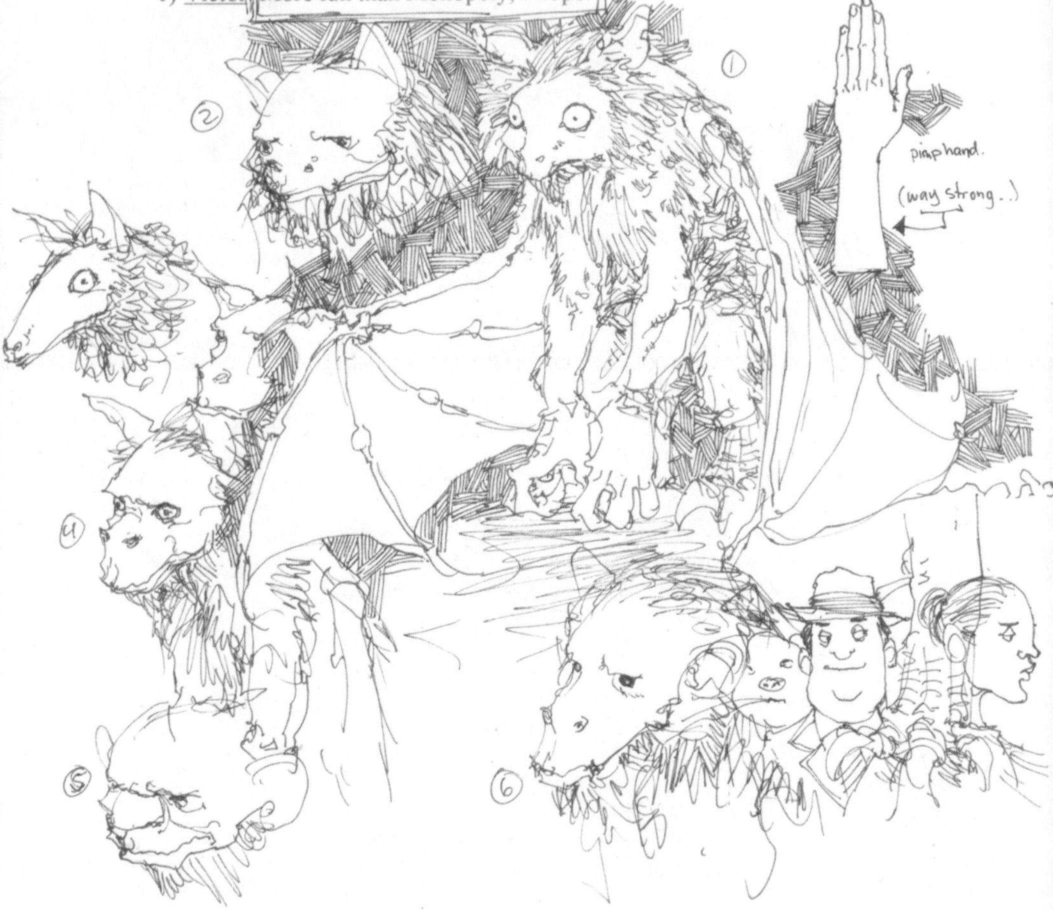

1
2
pimp hand.
(way strong..)
4
5
6

RUNAWAYS (2005) #9 SCRIPT EXCERPT BY **BRIAN K. VAUGHAN**, WITH SKETCHES BY **ADRIAN ALPHONA**

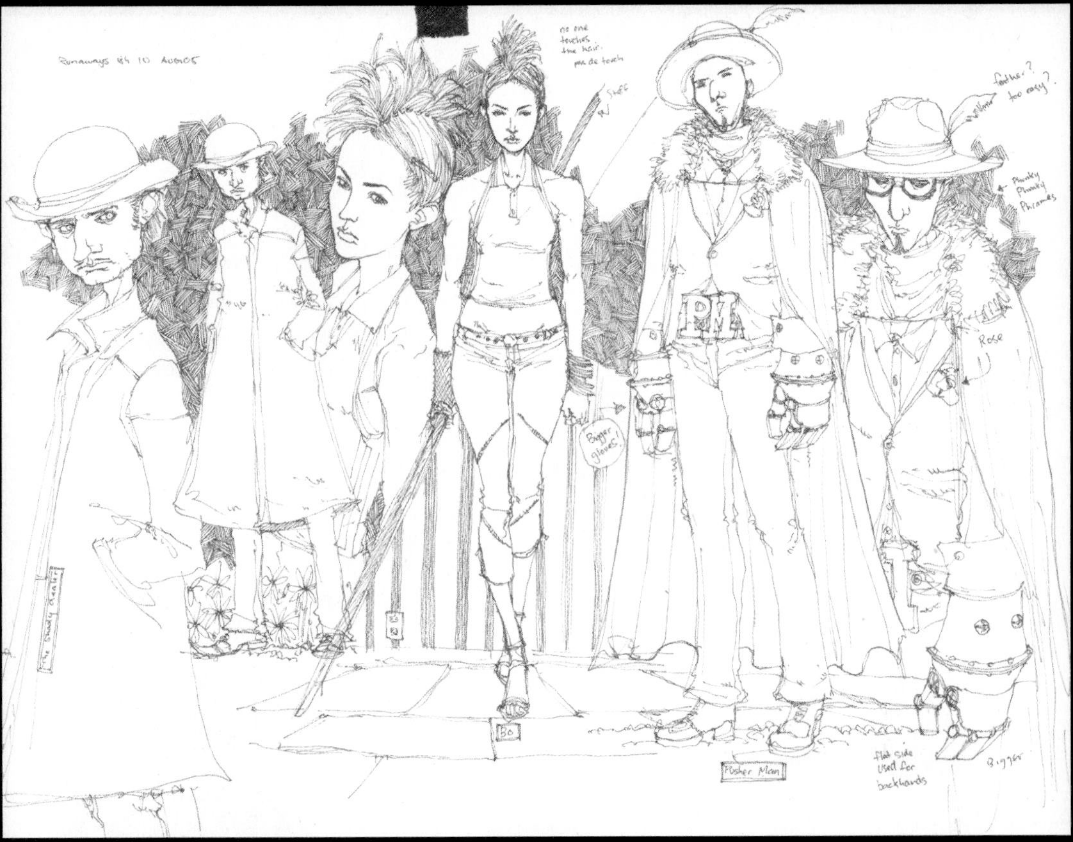
Runaways 84 10 AUG05
no one
touches
the hair.
pas de touch
Staff
feather?
too easy?
Phunky
Phunky
Phrames
PM
Rose
Bigger gloves!
Bo
Fisher Man
flat side
used for
backhands

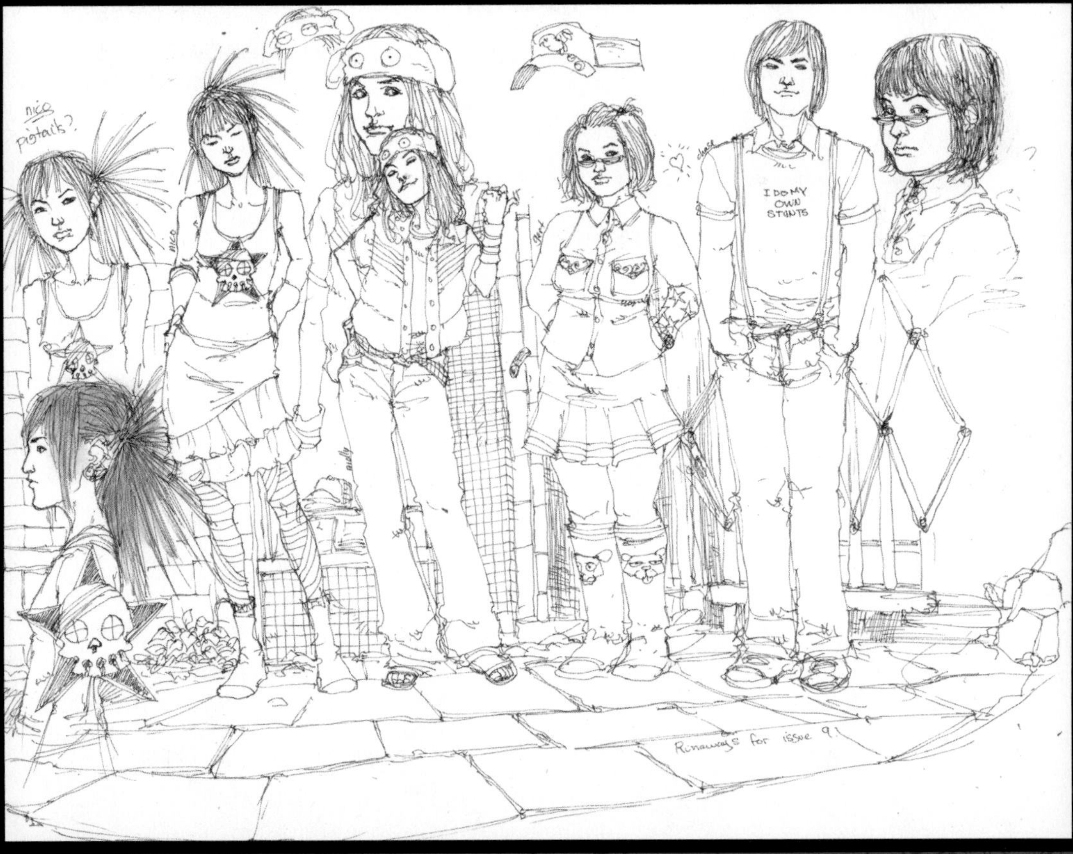
nico
pigtails?
I DO MY
OWN
STUNTS
Runaways for issue 9.

RUNAWAYS CHARACTER SKETCHES BY ADRIAN ALPHONA

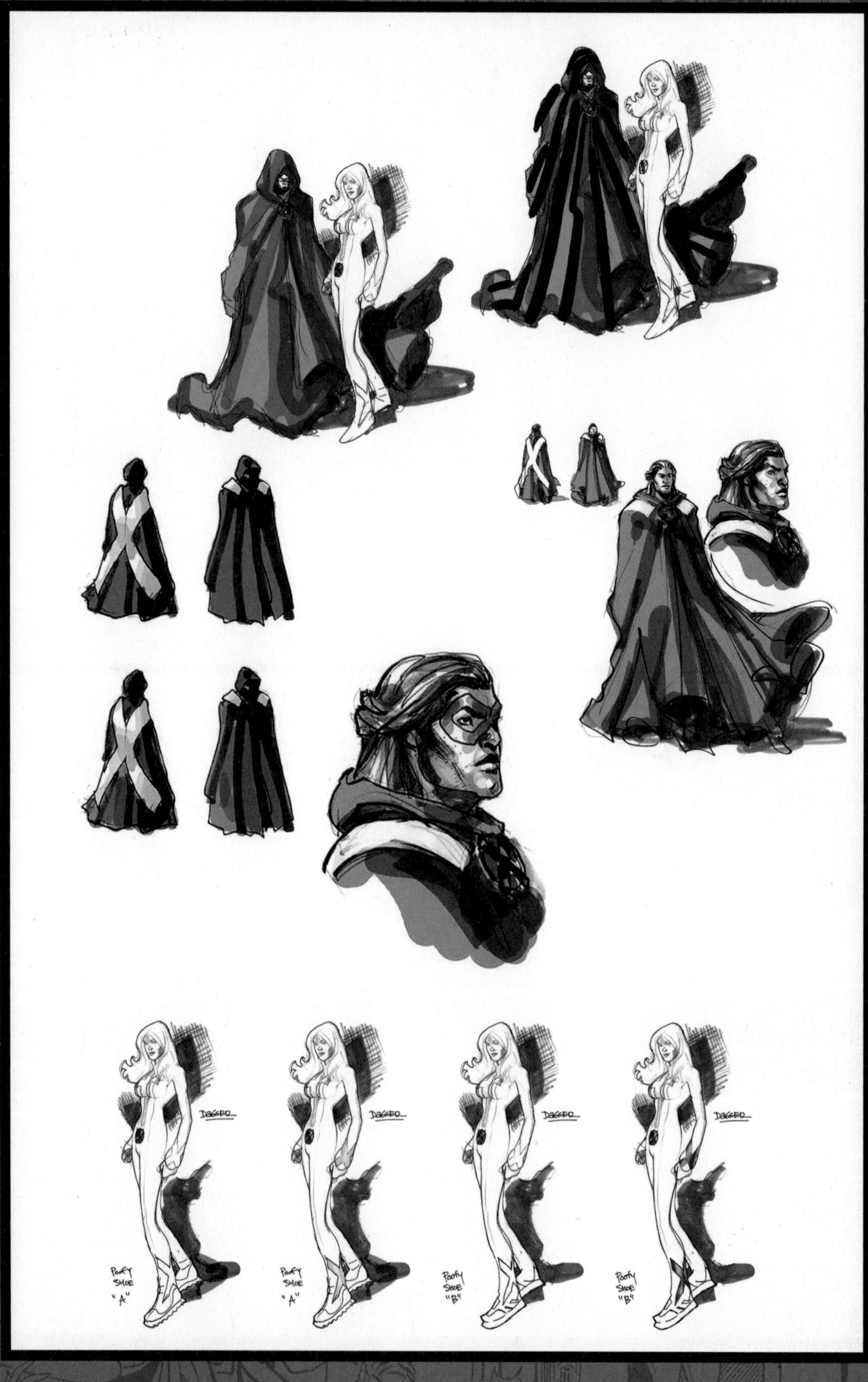
DAGGER
DAGGER
DAGGER
DAGGER
Poofy Shoe "A"
Poofy Shoe "A"
Poofy Shoe "B"
Poofy Shoe "B"

CLOAK & DAGGER "DARK X-MEN" COSTUME DESIGNS BY **TERRY DODSON**